The
ORIGIN
BISHC

The

ORIGINAL
BISHOPS

OFFICE AND ORDER *in the*
FIRST CHRISTIAN COMMUNITIES

Alistair C. Stewart

B
Baker Academic
a division of Baker Publishing Group
Grand Rapids, Michigan

© 2014 by Alistair C. Stewart

Published by Baker Academic
a division of Baker Publishing Group
P.O. Box 6287, Grand Rapids, MI 49516-6287
www.bakeracademic.com

Printed in the United States of America

Library of Congress Cataloging-in-Publication Data is on file at the Library of Congress in Washington, DC.

All translations of Scripture and other ancient writings are the author's own unless otherwise indicated.

14   15   16   17   18   19   20   7   6   5   4   3   2   1

For the churchwardens and parishioners
of The Bridge Parishes
who were not deceived
who refreshed me often

Contents

Preface

What follows is an account of the rise of the monepiscopate. As a historian, I seek simply to present the evidence on the basis of which a story may be told, from which readers may draw their own conclusions. I may clarify now, however, that throughout the work "monepiscopate" is defined not as a system of ecclesiastical governance in which there is one *episkopos*, but as a system in which an *episkopos* has responsibility for more than one congregation and has subordinate ministers in those congregations. The reason for the distinction will become clear as the argument unfolds.

I was not always so modest as simply to present a narrative. The origins of this book are to be found in the mid 1990s when, as an angry young Anglo-Catholic *Neutestamentler*, I was asked to contribute an essay on ministry in the New Testament to a collection marking the 250th anniversary of Codrington College in Barbados. A trawl of the library shelves turned up Käsemann and Schillebeeckx, and newly published was Bartlett. My contribution, titled "Class, Charisma and the Canon," was an attack on their theological, as well as their historical, work that suggested they had failed not only to take the canon seriously but also to observe the role of social class in the supposedly charismatic and office-free assemblies of the earliest Christian centuries. Episcopacy, I argued, was essential for the church because it protected the socially inferior from the worst impact of the class system, as even within the canonical literature we see the inversion of prevailing social norms, the pseudo-Pauline Pastoral Epistles offering a corrective to Paul by adding criteria for competence to the requirement to act as patron. Elements from that *juvénile* may have survived the redactional process and may be found below, for even if no longer young, I am still angry! The allusion to Trotsky in the postscript is no more accidental than that to Ussher in the title.

Although I continued to be fascinated by the topic of office and order in early Christian communities, it was a further ten years before I returned to the subject as the result of an invitation to contribute to a volume of essays. In "Prophecy and Patronage" I revisited my earlier essay and set out the agenda that I intended to follow when I found time to write the book that is now presented. Largely as a result of the research undertaken, these agenda are confined to the final chapter, as I came to realize that much preliminary ground needed to be cleared; in particular I found that one cornerstone of the consensus—namely, the collective leadership of early Christian communities—is seriously defective. I had always felt that it was suspect, but I could not substantiate my doubts.

I made several false starts on the book, but finally the work got underway when, in 2009, I was able to spend a term away from parochial duties. In the event, though I had no idea at the time that this would be the case, I never returned to my parishes, except to keep a final Holy Week. As a result, I was able to continue to work at the book even after my sabbatical, though only after I had spent thirty months working with a fair degree of constancy at the manuscript was the work of Jochen Wagner published. Through Wagner I learned of the work of Roger Gehring. The extent to which the narrative that I essay conforms to theirs, though formed entirely independently, encourages me to think that the work is a step at least in the right direction and may lead to the establishment of a new, and better-founded, consensus.

In the light of events, I can no longer thank Alexander the coppersmith, who first suggested the sabbatical. The Lord will reward him. Nonetheless, I may acknowledge the gracious hospitality of St. Stephen's House and of Codrington College granted during that period. Everyone at both institutions made me welcome, but I have to single out Ian Boxall at St. Stephen's House as a most patient dialogue partner. It was also a blessing to meet Brian Capper during that sabbatical, as a result of which I came to a deeper understanding of the Essenes. Since the somewhat extended sabbatical concluded, I have incurred further debts of gratitude. In particular I must acknowledge Eric Woods and Jim Richardson at Sherborne Abbey, both of whom have been immensely supportive at difficult times, as well as anonymous benefactors at the abbey whose kindness has been overwhelming. I have enjoyed presenting aspects of this work to interested, though occasionally baffled, parishioners, and I thank Jon Riding for his suggestion, provided in one of these groups, that the Bar Kokhba revolt might provide a context for Ignatius's journey westward. I also extend particular thanks to Frances Young, who took time to revisit the past by reading her sometime student's manuscript and pinpointing confusions in the argument. Father Allen Brent likewise read the manuscript, finally putting me right on the subject of Ignatius as *episkopos*. I am also very grateful to James Ernest at Baker Academic; I know that he has labored hard to win acceptance for this work.

It is about twelve years ago that I accepted the incumbency of the parishes that would become The Bridge Parishes. As I prepare to leave the villages for the last time, I dedicate this work to those who labored with me and who stood by me in my trials.

Sturminster Marshall
On the feast of St. Clement of Rome 2012

Abbreviations

General

cf.	compare	ibid.	in the same source
chap(s).	chapter(s)	i.e.	that is
col(s).	column(s)	n(n).	note(s)
e.g.	for example	repr.	reprint
esp.	especially		

Ancient Texts, Text Types, and Versions

LXX	Septuagint

Apocrypha

4 Macc.	4 Maccabees

Old Testament Pseudepigrapha

1 En.	1 Enoch (Ethiopic Apocalypse)	Let. Aris.	Letter of Aristeas

Dead Sea Scrolls and Related Texts

CD-A	Damascus Document[a]	1QS	1Q Rule of the Community

Philo

Contempl.	De vita contemplativa (On the Contemplative Life)	Ios.	De Iosepho (On the Life of Joseph)
Legat.	Legatio ad Gaium (On the Embassy to Gaius)	Spec.	De specialibus legibus (On the Special Laws)
Flacc.	In Flaccum (Against Flaccus)		

Josephus

C. Ap.	Contra Apionem (Against Apion)	B.J.	Bellum judaicum (Jewish War)
		Vita	Vita (The Life)
A.J.	Antiquitates judaicae (Jewish Antiquities)		

Mishnah, Talmud, and Related Literature

b.	Babylonian Talmud	*Ketub.*	*Ketubbot*
m.	Mishnah	*Meg.*	*Megillah*
t.	Tosefta	*Roš. Haš.*	*Roš Haššanah*
y.	Jerusalem Talmud	*Šabb.*	*Šabbat*
		Soṭah	*Soṭah*
'Abod. Zar.	*'Abodah Zarah*	*Sukkah*	*Sukkah*
B. Bat.	*Baba Batra*	*Ta'an.*	*Ta'anit*
'Erub.	*'Erubin*	*Yoma*	*Yoma*
Giṭ.	*Giṭṭin*		

Apostolic Fathers

Barn.	*Barnabas*	Ign. *Pol.*	Ignatius, *To Polycarp*
1–2 Clem.	*1–2 Clement*	Ign. *Rom.*	Ignatius, *To the Romans*
Did.	*Didache*	Ign. *Smyrn.*	Ignatius, *To the Smyrnaeans*
Herm.	*Shepherd of Hermas*	Ign. *Trall.*	Ignatius, *To the Trallians*
Ign. *Eph.*	Ignatius, *To the Ephesians*	*Mart. Pol.*	*Martyrdom of Polycarp*
Ign. *Magn.*	Ignatius, *To the Magnesians*	Pol. *Phil.*	Polycarp, *To the Philippians*
Ign. *Phld.*	Ignatius, *To the Philadelphians*		

New Testament Apocrypha and Pseudepigrapha

Acts John	*Acts of John*	*Hom.*	*Homiliae (Homilies)*
Acts Pet.	*Acts of Peter*	*Rec.*	*Recognitiones (Recognitions)*
Acts Phil.	*Acts of Philip*		
Ep. Clem.	*Epistula Clementis (Letter of Clement to James)*		

Papyri

P.Berl.Leihg.	*Berliner Leihgabe griechischer Papyri.* Edited by T. Kalén et al.	P.Mich.	Michigan Papyri
P.Egerton	Egerton Papyri	P.Mil.	*Papiri della R. Università di Milano.* Edited by A. Vogliano
P.Flind.Petrie	*The Flinders Petrie Papyri.* Edited by J. Mahaffy	P.Monac.	*Byzantinische Papyri in der königlichen Hof- und Staatsbibliothek zu München.* Edited by A. Heisenberg and L. Wenger
P.Gr.Vind.	Fayyum Fragment		
P.Lond.	Greek Papyri in the British Museum		
P.Mas.	*Masada II: The Yigael Yadin Excavations 1963–1965, Final Reports; The Latin and Greek Documents.* Edited by H. M. Cotton and J. Geiger	P.Oxy.	Oxyrhynchus Papyri
		P.Rylands	Rylands Papyri
		P.Tebt.	Tebtunis Papyri

Other Ancient Texts

Can. eccl. ap.	*Canones ecclesiastici apostolorum*	*Test. Dom.*	*Testamentum Domini*
Can. Hipp.	*Canones Hippolyti*	*Trad. ap.*	*Traditio apostolica*
Did. ap.	*Didascalia apostolorum*	*Vit. Pol.*	*Vita Polycarpi (Life of Polycarp)*

Greek and Latin Authors

Aelius Aristides

Pan.   *Panathenaikos*

Rom.   *Ad Romam*

Ambrosiaster

Quaest.   *Quaestiones Veteris et Novi Testamenti*

Appian

Bell. mith.   *Bella mithridatica (The Mithridatic Wars)*

Apuleius

Metam.   *Metamorphoses (The Golden Ass)*

Aristides

Apol.   *Apologia*

Aristotle

Pol.   *Politica (Politics)*

Arrian

Ind.   *Indica*

Athanasius

Apol. sec.   *Apologia secunda (= Apologia contra Arianos) (Defense against the Arians)*

Athenaeus

Deipn.   *Deipnosophistae*

Charisius

Dig.   *Digesta*

Cicero

Off.   *De officiis*

Clement of Alexandria

Paed.   *Paedagogus (Christ the Educator)*

Strom.   *Stromata (Miscellanies)*

Cyprian

Ep.   *Epistulae*

Dio Chrysostom

Conc. Apam.   *De concordia cum Apamensibus (Or. 40) (On Concord with Apamea)*

In. cont.   *In contione (Or. 48) (Political Address in the Assembly)*

Nicaeen.   *Ad Nicaeenses (Or. 39) (To the Nicaeans)*

Sec.   *De secessu (Or. 20) (Retirement)*

2 Tars.   *Tarsica altera (Or. 34) (Second Tarsic Discourse)*

Tumult.   *De tumultu (Or. 46) (Protest against Mistreatment)*

Ven.   *Venator (Or. 7) (The Hunter [Eubeoan Discourse])*

Diodorus Siculus

Bib. hist.   *Bibliotheca historica (Library of History)*

Diogenes Laertius

Vit.   *Vitae philosophorum (Lives of Eminent Philosophers)*

Epictetus

Diss.   *Dissertationes (Diatribai)*

Epiphanius

Pan.   *Panarion (Adversus haereses) (Refutation of All Heresies)*

Eusebius

Hist. eccl.   *Historia ecclesiastica (Ecclesiastical History)*

Eutychius

Ann.   *Annales*

Hippolytus

Haer.   *Refutatio omnium haeresium (Refutation of All Heresies)*

Noet.   *Contra Noetum (Against Noetus)*

Trad. ap.   *Traditio apostolica (The Apostolic Tradition)*

Horace

Sat.   *Satirae (Satires)*

Irenaeus

Epid.   *Epideixis tou apostolikou kērygmatos (Demonstration of the Apostolic Preaching)*

Haer.   *Adversus haereses (Against Heresies)*

Jerome

Ep.	Epistulae
Vir. ill.	De viris illustribus (On Illustrious Men)

(John) Chrysostom

Adv. Jud.	Adversus Judaeos (Discourses against Judaizing Christians)
Hom. Phil.	Homiliae in epistulam ad Philippenses

Justin

1 Apol.	Apologia i (First Apology)
Dial.	Dialogus cum Tryphone (Dialogue with Trypho)

Juvenal

Sat.	Satirae (Satires)

Libanius

Ep.	Epistulae

Liberatus

Brev.	Breviarium

Leo

Serm.	Sermones

Martial

Epig.	Epigrammata (Epigrams)

Onasander

Imp. off.	De imperatoris officio (On the Duty of a General)

Origen

Cels.	Contra Celsum (Against Celsus)
Hom. Lev.	Homiliae in Leviticum

Palladius

Vit. Joh.	De vita S. Johannis Chrysostomi dialogus (Dialogue on the Life of St. John Chrysostom)

Pausanius

Descr.	Graeciae descriptio (Description of Greece)

Petronius

Sat.	Satyricon

Philostratus

Vit. soph.	Vitae sophistarum

Plato

Resp.	Respublica (Republic)

Pliny the Younger

Ep.	Epistulae

Plutarch

An seni	An seni res publica gerenda sit
Num.	Numa
Quaest. conv.	Quaestiones conviviales

Seneca

Brev. vit.	De brevitate vitae (On the Shortness of Life)

Severus ibn al-Mukaffa

Hist. patr.	Historia patriarchum

Socrates of Constantinople

Hist. eccl.	Historia ecclesiastica (Ecclesiastical History)

Sozomen

Hist. eccl.	Historia ecclesiastica (Ecclesiastical History)

Strabo

Geogr.	Geographica (Geography)

Suetonius

Claud.	Divus Claudius

Synesius

Ep.	Epistulae

Tacitus

Ann.	Annales

Tertullian

Apol.	Apologeticus (Apology)
Bapt.	De baptismo (Baptism)
Cor.	De corona militis (The Crown)
Exh. cast.	De exhortatione castitatis (Exhortation to Chastity)
Jejun.	De jejunio adversus psychichos (On Fasting, against the Psychics)
Marc.	Adversus Marcionem (Against Marcion)
Praescr.	De praescriptione haereticorum (Prescription against Heretics)

Xenophon

Oec.	Oeconomicus

Secondary Sources

AB	Anchor Bible	CPJ	*Corpus papyorum judaicarum.*
AGJU	Arbeiten zur Geschichte des		Edited by V. Tcherikover. 3
	antiken Judentums und des		vols. Cambridge, 1957–1964
	Urchristentums	CPPC	Collana patristica e del pen-
AJA	*American Journal of*		siero cristiano
	Archaeology	*CR*	*Classical Review*
AnBib	Analecta biblica	CSHJ	Chicago Studies in the History
ANES	*Ancient Near Eastern Studies*		of Judaism
APT	Acta philosophica et	DK	Dialog der Kirchen
	theologica	DMAHA	Dutch Monographs on Ancient
ASMA	Aarhus Studies in Mediterra-		History and Archaeology
	nean Antiquity	EB	Études bibliques
Aug	*Augustinianum*	ECS	Early Christian Studies
AUSS	*Andrews University Seminary*	EKKNT	Evangelisch-katholischer Kom-
	Studies		mentar zum Neuen Testament
BAFS	The Book of Acts in Its First-	*EMC*	*Echos du monde classique*
	Century Setting	*EstEcl*	*Estudios eclesiásticos*
BE	Bibliotheca ekmaniana	*ExpTim*	*Expository Times*
BEFAR	Bibliothèque des écoles fran-	FB	Forschung zur Bibel
	çaises d'Athènes et de Rome	FRLANT	Forschungen zur Religion und
BEL	Bibliotheca "Ephemerides		Literatur des Alten und Neuen
	liturgicae"		Testaments
BETL	Bibliotheca ephemeridum	GDECS	Gorgias Dissertations: Early
	theologicarum lovaniensium		Christian Studies
BH	Biblische Handbibliothek	*GIBM*	*The Collection of Ancient*
BIS	Biblical Interpretation Series		*Greek Inscriptions in the*
BNTC	Black's New Testament		*British Museum.* Edited by
	Commentaries		C. Newton
BSGRT	Bibliotheca scriptorum	GNT	Grundrisse zum Neuen
	graecorum et romanorum		Testament
	teubneriana	*GTJ*	*Grace Theological Journal*
BSIH	Brill Studies in Intellectual	HNT	Handbuch zum Neuen
	History		Testament
BSS	Black Seas Studies	HS	Humanitas Supplementum
BTB	*Biblical Theology Bulletin*	*HTR*	*Harvard Theological Review*
CA	Christianismes anciens	HTS	Harvard Theological Studies
CBQ	*Catholic Biblical Quarterly*	*HvTSt*	*Hervormde teologiese studies*
CCWJCW	Cambridge Commentary on	IC	*Inscriptiones Creticae.* Edited
	Writings of the Jewish and		by Margherita Guarducci
	Christian World	ICC	International Critical
CH	*Church History*		Commentary
CIG	*Corpus inscriptionum grae-*	*ID*	*Inscriptions de Délos*
	carum. Edited by A. Boeckh. 4	*IEph.*	*Die Inschriften von Ephesos.*
	vols. Berlin, 1828–1877		Edited by H. Wankel
CIJ	*Corpus inscriptionum*	*IG*	*Inscriptiones graecae.* Editio
	judaicarum		minor
CIL	*Corpus inscriptionum*	*IGBulg*	*Inscriptiones graecae in Bul-*
	latinarum		*garia repertae.* Edited by G.
CIRB	*Corpus inscriptionum regni*		Mihailov
	Bosporani		

IGLS	Inscriptions grecques et latines de la Syrie. Edited by L. Jalabert et al.	KBANT	Kommentare und Beiträge zum Alten und Neuen Testament
IGRR	Inscriptiones graecae ad res romanas pertinentes. Edited by R. Cagnat	LBW	Le Bas, P., and W. H. Waddington. *Voyage archéologique en Grèce et en Asie Mineure.* Vol. 3, *Inscriptions grecques et latines recueillies en Grèce et en Asie Mineure.* Paris, 1870
IGUR	Inscriptiones graecae urbis Romae. Edited by L. Moretti		
IIasos	Die Inschriften von Iasos. Edited by W. Blümel	LD	Lectio divina
ILeuk.	Inscriptions du sanctuaire de la Mère des Dieux autochthone de Leukopétra (Macédoine). Edited by P. M. Petsas et al.	Lindos	C. Blinkenberg. *Lindos: Fouilles et recherches, 1902– 1914.* 2 vols. Berlin, 1941
		LNSAS	Leicester-Nottingham Studies in Ancient Society
ILS	Inscriptiones latinae selectae. Edited by H. Dessau	LNTS	Library of New Testament Studies
IMagn.	Die Inschriften von Magnesia am Maeander. Edited by O. Kern	MAIGL	Catalogue général des antiquités egyptiennes du Musée d'Alexandrie: Iscrizioni greche e latine. Edited by E. Breccia
IMT	Inschriften Mysia und Troas. Edited by M. Barth and J. Stauber	MAMA	Monumenta Asiae Minoris Antiqua. Manchester and London, 1928–1993
IPriene	Inschriften von Priene. Edited by F. H. von Gaertringen	MDAI(A)	Mitteilungen des deutschen archäologischen Instituts, athenische Abteilung
IScM	Inscriptiones Scythiae Minoris graecae et latinae	MH	Museum helveticum
JAC	Jahrbuch für Antike und Christentum	NewDocs	New Documents Illustrating Early Christianity. Edited by G. H. R. Horsley and S. Llewelyn. North Ryde, New South Wales, 1981–
JBL	Journal of Biblical Literature		
JECS	Journal of Early Christian Studies		
JEH	Journal of Ecclesiastical History	NHS	New History of the Sermon
JES	Journal of Ecumenical Studies	NIBC	New International Biblical Commentary
JETS	Journal of the Evangelical Theological Society	NIGTC	New International Greek Testament Commentary
JHS	Journal of Hellenic Studies		
JÖAI	Jahreshefte des Österreichischen archäologischen Instituts	NovT	Novum Testamentum
		NovTSup	Novum Testamentum Supplements
JR	Journal of Religion	NTAF	The New Testament and the Apostolic Fathers
JRH	Journal of Religious History		
JRS	Journal of Roman Studies	NTC	The New Testament in Context
JSNT	Journal for the Study of the New Testament		
JSNTSup	Journal for the Study of the New Testament: Supplement Series	NTD	Das Neue Testament Deutsch
		NTOA	Novum Testamentum et Orbis Antiquus
		NTS	New Testament Studies
JTS	Journal of Theological Studies	NTT	New Testament Theology
KAV	Kommentar zu den Apostolischen Vätern	OCA	Orientalia christiana analecta
		OECS	Oxford Early Christian Studies

OGIS	*Orientis graeci inscriptiones selectae*. Edited by W. Dittenberger	SEA	*Studia ephemeridis Augustinianum*
PG	Patrologia graeca [= Patrologiae cursus completus: Series graeca]. Edited by J.-P. Migne. 162 vols. Paris, 1857–1886	SecCent	*Second Century*
		SEG	*Supplementum epigraphicum graecum*
		SIG	*Sylloge inscriptionum graecarum*. Edited by W. Dittenberger. 3rd ed.
PGM	*Papyri graecae magicae: Die griechischen Zauberpapyri*. Edited by K. Preisendanz. Berlin, 1928	SJLA	Studies in Judaism in Late Antiquity
PRSt	*Perspectives in Religious Studies*	SNTSMS	Society for New Testament Studies Monograph Series
PRStSS	Perspectives in Religious Studies: Special Studies	SNTW	Studies of the New Testament and Its World
QD	Quaestiones disputatae	SocRel	*Sociology of Religion*
QL	*Questions liturgiques*	SPA	Studien der patristischen Arbeitsgemeinschaft
RAr	*Revue archéologique*	ST	*Studia theologica*
RB	*Revue biblique*	STAC	Studien und Texte zu Antike und Christentum
RDC	*Revue de droit canonique*		
REG	*Revue des études grecques*	STDJ	Studies on the Texts of the Desert of Judah
ResQ	*Restoration Quarterly*		
RevScRel	*Revue des sciences religieuses*	StLit	*Studia liturgica*
RIChrM	*Recueil des inscriptions chrétiennes de Macédoine du IIIe au VIe siècle*. Edited by D. Feissel	StPatr	Studia patristica
		STT	Studia traditionis theologiae
		SU	Schriften des Urchristentums
RIDA	*Revue internationale des droits de l'antiquité*	SVTQ	*St. Vladimir's Theological Quarterly*
ROC	*Revue de l'orient Chrétien*	TAM	*Tituli asiae minoris*. Vienna, 1901–
RSR	*Recherches de science religieuse*		
		TANZ	Texte und Arbeiten zum neutestamentlichen Zeitalter
SAC	Studies in Antiquity and Christianity	TET	Textes et études théologiques
SANT	Studien zum Alten und Neuen Testament	TF	Theologische Forschung
		ThA	Theologische Arbeiten
SB	Sources bibliques	T.Mom.Louvre	*Catalogue des étiquettes de momies du Musée du Louvre*. Edited by F. Baratte and B. Boyaval
SBAZ	Studien zur biblischen Archäologie und Zeitgeschichte		
SBEC	Studies in the Bible and Early Christianity	TQ	*Theologische Quartalschrift*
		TS	*Theological Studies*
SBL	Studies in Biblical Literature	TSAJ	Texte und Studien zum antiken Judentum
SBLDS	Society of Biblical Literature Dissertation Series	TUGAL	Texte und Untersuchungen zur Geschichte der Altchristlichen Literatur
SBLSBS	Society of Biblical Literature Sources for Biblical Study		
SBLSymS	Society of Biblical Literature Symposium Series	TZ	*Theologische Zeitschrift*
		VC	*Vigiliae christianae*
SBS	Stuttgarter Bibelstudien	VCSup	Vigiliae christianae Supplements
SC	Sources chrétiennes		
ScEs	*Science et esprit*	VetChr	*Vetera christianorum*

VIEGM	Veröffentlichungen des Instituts für Europäische Geschichte Mainz	*ZAC*	*Zeitschrift für antikes Christentum*
WBC	Word Biblical Commentary	*ZNW*	*Zeitschrift für die neutestamentliche Wissenschaft und die Kunde der älteren Kirche*
WGW	Wissenskultur und gesellschaftlicher Wandel		
WMANT	Wissenschaftliche Monographien zum Alten und Neuen Testament	*ZPE*	*Zeitschrift für Papyrologie und Epigraphik*
		ZpraktTh	*Zeitschrift für praktische Theologie*
WUNT	Wissenschaftliche Untersuchungen zum Neuen Testament	*ZRGG*	*Zeitschrift für Religions- und Geistesgeschichte*
		ZTK	*Zeitschrift für Theologie und Kirche*

Introduction

Defining the Field of Inquiry and the Terminology Employed

In the aftermath of the American War of Independence, in 1784, an aged John Wesley appointed Thomas Coke as "superintendent" of Methodist societies in the newly independent colonies. In a letter to the societies that he charged Coke to print and circulate, by which he sought to justify his action in what might be understood as the ordination of a bishop, he stated, "Lord King's account of the primitive church convinced me many years ago, that Bishops and Presbyters are the same order."[1] King's opinion, however, is not simply that the terms "bishop" and "presbyter" were synonymous, but rather that presbyters, while holding the same order as bishops, discharged a distinct office, subordinate to that of the bishop.[2] Wesley thus rather misrepresents King's position. Nonetheless, his action, on the basis of a historical understanding of the relationship between bishop (better, *episkopos*) and presbyter in the earliest Christian communities, finally severed the remaining bonds between Methodism and Anglicanism, as Anglicans perceived that the historic line of episcopal succession had been breached, while Methodists considered that it had been sustained.

Whereas Wesley mentions King in his letter to the American Methodists, it would seem that a greater influence was exercised by Edward Stillingfleet.[3]

---

1. Cited from Samuel Drew, *The Life of the Reverend Thomas Coke LLD* (London: [Wesleyan Methodist] Conference, 1817), 67. The work to which he refers is *An Enquiry into the Constitution, Discipline, Unity and Worship of the Primitive Church* (London: J. Wyat and R. Robinson, 1691), published anonymously but known to be the work of Peter King, later Lord King.

2. King, *Enquiry*, 52–78.

3. Edward Stillingfleet, *Irenicum: A Weapon-Salve for the Churches Wounds* (London: Henry Mortlock, 1662). Wesley had read this work; it is mentioned in a letter to his brother dated July

1

This is interesting because, as will be argued below, Stillingfleet, in the seventeenth century, is one of the forgotten founders of a consensus regarding the origins of office in Christian communities that is still current and that the present work seeks finally to demolish. We leave this momentarily, however, to return to King.

More interesting in King's argument than his explanation of the relationship between bishop and presbyter in the first centuries is his suggestion that bishops were the original officers in the church, and yet that their responsibilities extended only to individual congregations. In what follows I argue the same. In time, however, the responsibility of these bishops (better, *episkopoi*) extended beyond single congregations to groups of congregations within a defined area.

The extension of episcopal responsibilities to more than one congregation or Christian community and the corresponding appointment of subordinate officers is, I suggest, a development that emerges near the turn of the third century.[4] It is in the last decade of the second century that Demetrius emerges in Alexandria as sole bishop taking control of independent schools,[5] and probably in the first decade of the third that we find Serapion of Antioch engaging with the church at Rhossos regarding the *Gospel of Peter*.[6] By the middle of the third century we find Cyprian in Africa convening councils of bishops from across the province to determine questions of discipline,[7] and, perhaps most significant of all, we may observe the report of the Liberian catalog that Pontianus, the bishop of Rome, "and the presbyter Hippolytus [*Pontianus episcopus et Yppolitus presbyter*] were deported to Sardinia on the island of Vocina" in 235.[8] At this point, on the basis of the joint mention of Pontianus as bishop and Hippolytus as presbyter, and given that a precise date is then given for the ordination of Pontianus's successor, we can say that Rome had a sole bishop recognized by the self-defining catholic congregations of the city, and under whom presbyters served in the individual churches.[9] Thus, the

---

16, 1755. For further discussion of this point, see Adrian Burdon, *Authority and Order: John Wesley and His Preachers* (Aldershot: Ashgate, 2005), esp. 36–42.

4. Interestingly, King gives no account of this development, considering it to have taken place at an even later date, in contrast to the overwhelming consensus that places this development early in the second century.

5. See Alistair Stewart(-Sykes), "Origen, Demetrius and the Alexandrian Presbyters," *SVTQ* 48 (2004): 415–29, with references.

6. Eusebius, *Hist. eccl.* 6.12.3–6.

7. Thus, J. B. Rives (*Religion and Authority in Roman Carthage from Augustus to Constantine* [Oxford: Clarendon, 1995], 290–94) suggests that Cyprian as bishop acts much like a Roman provincial governor.

8. Within the *Chronography of 354*.

9. Allen Brent, *Hippolytus and the Roman Church in the Third Century: Communities in Tension before the Emergence of a Monarch-Bishop*, VCSup 31 (Leiden: Brill, 1995), 453–57, in

same phenomenon of a sole bishop within a city of multiple congregations, assisted by subordinate officers, is to be found in multiple locations in this period, whereas, as will be observed below, evidence earlier than that is entirely lacking and evidence, at least for Rome, that this was not the case is strong. This system of sole bishops heading multiple congregations may properly be called "monepiscopacy," for each bishop is a sole bishop set over congregations in a defined area with subservient ministers (presbyters and deacons). The purpose of this book is to trace the history by which this system and its prevalence came about; if this is a development, we must of necessity discuss earlier systems of church order from which this system emerged.

Even before the discussion begins, however, some clarification of terminology may prove helpful. I have already offered a definition of "monepiscopacy," but I may reiterate that the term *monepiskopos* is used in this book to indicate not a single *episkopos* (as opposed to multiple *episkopoi*) holding office in a single Christian community,[10] which will be seen to be a tautological usage, but rather an *episkopos* exercising leadership over several Christian communities with subordinate ministers in those communities.[11] This has, in the past, also been described as a "monarchical bishop." This latter term is avoided

---

conclusion. It might be argued that monepiscopacy had actually emerged at the time of Victor, some forty or so years previously, and that the Hippolytean community, which did not recognize Victor's monepiscopate, was simply a small and insignificant grouping within the larger body of Roman Christianity (so Manlio Simonetti, "Roma cristiana tra vescovi e presbiteri," *VetChr* 43 [2006]: 5–17). However, even if this is so, monepiscopacy is established by the time of the episcopate of Pontian. We may also note the report found in Eusebius, *Hist. eccl.* 5.28.10–12, of Natalius, bishop of an independent Christian school in Rome, petitioning for communion not simply before Zephyrinus the bishop but also to the clergy and laity.

10. As by, e.g., Kenneth A. Strand, "The Rise of the Monarchical Episcopate," *AUSS* 4 (1966): 65–88.

11. This is in direct contradiction to the terminology employed by, e.g., Hamilton Hess, *The Early Development of Canon Law and the Council of Serdica*, OECS (Oxford: Oxford University Press, 2002), 18–19n11; Jochen Wagner, *Die Anfänge des Amtes in der Kirche: Presbyter und Episkopen in der frühchristlichen Literatur*, TANZ 53 (Tübingen: Francke, 2011), 20; both following Georg Schöllgen, "Monepiskopat und monarchischer Episkopat: Eine Bemerkung zur Terminologie," *ZNW* 77 (1986): 146–51, in defining *monepiskopos* as a sole bishop exercising leadership in a single congregation (he uses Ignatius as an example) as opposed to "monarchical episcopate," which implies that such an *episkopos* governs without the necessity of consultation or the consent of others to his actions. Thus he suggests that the term should not apply to Ignatius, for whom the *episkopos* was meant to govern in harmony with the presbytery and was unable to make certain decisions without consultation. In this light, he notes the manner in which Ignatius suggests that a meeting be called by Onesimus at Ephesus to determine if the *diakonos* Burrhus might travel with him (Ign. *Eph.* 2:1). For Schöllgen, *Didascalia apostolorum* provides the first example of a monarchical *episkopos*. However, I am not sure that the bishop of the *Didascalia* is even a *monepiskopos* in the sense in which the term is employed here, let alone a monarchical *episkopos*. The bishop of the *Didascalia* is discussed in chap. 3, under the heading "The Syrian *Didascalia Apostolorum*."

because of the negative connotation that it has come to attract. In the same way, I avoid the term "presbyter-bishop" to describe an *episkopos* in a single household for the simple reason that it seems to presuppose a degree of synonymy between the terms that, as will be suggested, did not exist.

The full rationale for the approach taken here will emerge as the argument of the book unfolds. Nonetheless, it will be seen that terminological confusion masks a confusion over the nature of *episkopoi*, who are assumed to have wider responsibility than a single congregation or household, a confusion that results in part from the failure to distinguish office held in a congregation from office held in a wider context, such as a diocese or district. This goes back to the time of Chrysostom, who argues for synonymy between *episkopos* and *presbyteros* in reading Philippians 1:1 on the grounds that a single city would not have more than one *episkopos*;[12] the term must therefore, he suggests, include *presbyteroi*. More recent studies of the formation of early Christianity recognize that there may be multiple and independent Christian communities within a single city.[13] On this basis, it is suggested here, there may likewise be multiple *episkopoi* in a single city, each holding office in his own congregation. Hence the importance of the distinction that needs to be made between office in a single congregation (*Gemeindeamt*) and office in a wider body consisting of multiple congregations (*Kirchenamt*), and the point at which multiple and independent congregations form a single church in fact as well as in theory needs to be clearly stated. Baur saw the significance of the distinction in the discussion of church order,[14] but since then it seems to have been forgotten. So Kertelge recognizes that the term *ekklēsia* might connote either a single congregation (*Einzelkirche*) or the church overall (*Gesamtkirche*) and notes the evidence for communication between churches,[15] but he does not consider the possibility that there might be something in between, namely, an *Ortskirche*, a diocese. Similarly Rohde, in speaking of "monarchical episcopacy" in the context of the Pastoral Epistles, asks whether this refers to leadership of a single congregation or something like metropolitan responsibility,[16] without

12. Chrysostom, *Hom. Phil.* 2, 195A–C.

13. Thus, for Rome in particular, which has been the subject of intense study, note the seminal work by Peter Lampe, *Die stadtrömischen Christen in den ersten beiden Jahrhunderten*, WUNT 18/2 (Tübingen: Mohr Siebeck, 1987).

14. F. C. Baur, *Das Christenthum und die christliche Kirche der drei ersten Jahrhunderte*, 2nd ed. (Tübingen: Fues, 1860), 270–71.

15. Karl Kertelge, *Gemeinde und Amt im neuen Testament*, BH 10 (Munich: Kösel, 1972), 73–76.

16. Joachim Rohde, *Urchristliche und frühkatholische Ämter: Eine Untersuchung zur frühchristlichen Amtsentwicklung im Neuen Testament und bei den apostolischen Vätern*, ThA 33 (Berlin: Evangelische Verlagsanstalt, 1976), 83. Although it is not spelled out, he evidently

seeing the significance of the question that he raises. More recently there has been some discussion of the relationship of the house-church and the church found in a given area,[17] but the implications of such a discussion for church order do not seem to have been observed.

The question as to whether an *episkopos* in a city who does not exercise control over all Christian congregations in that place might properly be termed a *monepiskopos* may also be anticipated here. Thus in the argument over the establishment of monepiscopacy at Rome, considered here in chapter 1, the significance of the separation of the Asian communities from the control of the *episkopos* is disputed. It might be possible to see them as dissident groups separate from the *episkopos*[18] or alternatively to state that, given that the Asian groups are still separate, monepiscopacy is not yet established,[19] a question that also raises the difficulty of defining the boundaries of Christianity in the earliest period. For the sake of clarity, I restate that the term *monepiskopos* is employed here simply to mean an *episkopos* with responsibility for more than one Christian congregation who has subordinate ministers in the individual congregations.

With terminology clarified, the object of the work is also clarified: my intention is to trace the means by which Christian leadership in local settings came to be in the hands of individuals with responsibility for multiple congregations and subordinate officers by about the turn of the third century.

Of course, mine is far from being the first effort to explore this field. I have mentioned Stillingfleet and King, and so already in 1932 a critical review of recent research suggested that the literature was already too vast to enable a complete account to be given, and thus the author would restrict himself to the prior fifty years.[20] A relatively recent book on the subject begins with a review of the manner in which, during the nineteenth century, a consensus position on the emergence of monepiscopacy and the establishment of other orders was established, and of the manner in which the consensus was both maintained and questioned in various ways through the twentieth century, a review that runs to 240 closely argued pages.[21] What is particularly interesting is that this

---

assumes that leadership heretofore had been collective, as otherwise this collective leadership might not form into the leadership of an individual.

17. See esp. Roger W. Gehring, *House Church and Mission: The Importance of Household Structures in Early Christianity* (Peabody, MA: Hendrickson, 2004), 155–59, and references.

18. So Simonetti, "Roma cristiana."

19. So Brent, *Hippolytus*.

20. Olof Linton, *Das Problem der Urkirche in der neueren Forschung: Eine kritische Darstellung* (Uppsala: Almqvist & Wiksell, 1932), 3.

21. James Tunstead Burtchaell, *From Synagogue to Church: Public Services and Offices in the Earliest Christian Communities* (Cambridge: Cambridge University Press, 1992).

account begins with Rothe, who was actually seeking to adjust aspects of a consensus that already existed. Thus, given the vast literature, and given that the same arguments are constantly repeated, I will eschew repeating such a review. Many works, moreover, repeat the same "facts" or elaborate slightly upon them. I refer here to the synonymy of *episkopos* and *presbyteroi*, the emergence of a *monepiskopos* from a collective presbyterate, and the origin of *presbyteroi* in the synagogues. These assertions will be familiar enough to anyone acquainted with the discussion; so often are they made that to cite each occasion on which they are made would unnecessarily swell the footnotes and bibliography with otiose citation. All are shown to be baseless, not facts at all but rather scholarly fictions originating in the learned polemics of the seventeenth century; indeed, all are found in Stillingfleet's work.

However, in the light of attention lavished on this field of inquiry in the past, some justification is required for another addition to the corpus; a reviewer of one relatively recent work on the subject remarks that the debate over early Christian office has the inevitability of death and taxes.[22] My claim is to have shaken the kaleidoscope of evidence to see what is, I think, a new picture.[23] It is a picture with some similarity to those recently produced,[24] yet it is, I think, sufficiently distinct.

The foundation of the consensus is that *episkopoi* and *presbyteroi* were the earliest offices in the church. The terms, however, according to the consensus, were synonymous and interchangeable because every local church was originally under the direction of a group of persons, a collegial leadership deriving from the synagogue (from which the title "presbyters" derived). From this group there grew an individual leader. Although frequently manifested in the nineteenth and twentieth centuries, this picture seems to have originated in the seventeenth century and subsequently to have become the fundamental assumption from which further explorations departed; Baur describes it as the conventional hypothesis as early as 1835.[25] Although various aspects of

22. J. H. Elliott, "Elders as Honored Household Heads and Not Holders of 'Office' in Earliest Christianity," *BTB* 33 (2003): 77–82.

23. I have the image of the sources for church order as a kaleidoscope, which gives a different picture each time it is shaken, from Loofs, cited by Hans Lietzmann, "Zur altchristlichen Verfassungsgeschichte," in *Kleine Schriften I*, ed. Kurt Aland, TUGAL 67 (Berlin: Akademie-Verlag, 1958), 141.

24. In particular, Wagner's *Die Anfänge des Amtes in der Kirche*, which appeared even as I thought that I was completing this work. Indeed, in view of the similarities in the picture, as well as our mutual dependence on Campbell's exegesis of Titus 1:5, it may not be premature to suggest that the foundations of a new consensus may be being laid.

25. F. C. Baur, *Die sogenannten Pastoralbriefe des Apostels Paulus aufs neue kritisch untersucht* (Stuttgart and Tübingen: J. G. Cotta, 1835), 80.

the consensus have been questioned, especially since the latter part of the nineteenth century, this picture has never completely or satisfactorily been overturned. As will be observed throughout this work, even attempts radically to question the consensus stumble over the question of the relationship between the terms *episkopos* and *presbyteros*.

Chapter 1 seeks to offer a clear explanation of the relationship of the terms, suggesting that they are not synonymous. Rather, I argue that the apparent synonymy between *presbyteros* and *episkopos* comes about because Christian leaders, gathering from across a city, might collectively be termed "presbyters." The fundamental unit of the church was, however, the single congregation, and each of these congregations was led by a single *episkopos*. This is not, however, simply an argument over words, even though this clarification is helpful, as the chapter clarifies that there was no such collegial leadership in individual communities,[26] and that this is the significance behind the lack of synonymy between *episkopos* and *presbyteros*. Collegiality occurred at the level of a city, and I suggest that it is from the gathering of presbyters (who may well have been *episkopoi* in their own congregations) across a city that monepiscopacy emerges. The existence of such a gathering and the emergence of monepiscopacy from this group have already been suggested with regard to Rome. In chapter 1 I show that there are many other cities where the same thing appears to have taken place.

Thus, whereas the notion of collegial leadership has been the universal starting point, the history presented here is inevitably a different history due to its distinct starting point. I suggest that church order was episcopal from the beginning, even though the *episkopoi* are simply single domestic leaders in single churches.

It is on the basis of recognizing that there was no original collegial leadership that it is possible to reach a new understanding of the duties of these leaders as, in chapter 2, I seek to revive Hatch's hypothesis that the original *episkopoi* were economic officers and to provide new evidence to support the argument. The same is shown to be true of *diakonoi*. It is the very nature of the economic office undertaken by the *episkopoi*, in particular their direction of the meals of the community, that necessitates their being single leaders.

It is also on the basis of this insight that in chapter 3 I examine the role of presbyters and present a new hypothesis regarding their origin. I demonstrate that there is no evidence for the much-asserted origin of presbyters in Judaism.

---

26. Recently, Hermann J. Vogt ("Frühkirche und Amt: Neu in der Diskussion," *ZAC* 8 [2003]: 462–84) has recently suggested the same, but his treatment is marred, as argued below, by an identification of appointees (the officers, who are individuals) with those who appoint them (who indeed may be a collective body).

There is, however, much evidence pointing to the use of *presbyteroi* to denote senior members of guilds and associations in the Hellenistic cities. This explains the employment of the term to denote the gathering of leaders from across a city. However, it is also shown that individual churches might have presbyters, and that these were simply senior men within the community who offered patronage. Again, this is not a new theory, but it is proposed with new evidence to support it and is freed from objections that might have been leveled at it in the past. These presbyters, however, seem to have been a phenomenon restricted to the churches of Asia or of Asian cultural background, as other churches, while having patronal groups alongside an *episkopos* and deacons, did not identify their patrons as presbyters.

On the basis of the argument of the first three chapters, chapter 4 examines all the remaining evidence for Christian leadership prior to the emergence of monepiscopacy. On this basis, the hypothesis proposed in chapter 1, that monepiscopacy emerged from the gatherings of citywide presbyters, is tested with regard to every Christian community for which there is sufficient evidence to mount an investigation. It is possible to demonstrate that federation, the basis on which monepiscopacy was able to emerge, existed in a great many communities, even if the actual process of emergence is less certain. A great deal of chapter 4 is concerned with Ignatius of Antioch, who often is held to have been the first *monepiskopos*. I suggest that he was no such thing, in that there was never more than one *episkopos* in a congregation in any event. More to the point, he is simply an *episkopos* in a congregation, and the *episkopoi* whom he addresses are likewise congregational leaders, which means in turn that we know even less about ministry at the time of Ignatius than previously thought.

Chapter 5 attempts to explain the development of monepiscopacy out of federation; although it is possible to characterize the process as one of centralization, employing a political analogy, it is not possible to explain it or to describe the process in detail. Nonetheless, although chapter 5 ends with a confession of ignorance, at least we are more aware of the contours of our ignorance.

The relationship of elders to bishops—the fundamental matter of this book—is, as Campbell points out, a matter largely discussed by Anglophone scholars. German scholarship, he suggests, has been dominated by the question of the relationship of charisma and office,[27] a subject about which a consensus

---

27. R. Alastair Campbell, *The Elders: Seniority within Earliest Christianity*, SNTW (Edinburgh: T&T Clark, 1994), 2. It may simply be, however, that the German tradition considers the discussion of the relationship of *episkopoi* and *presbyteroi* closed.

has also been built up that has recently been questioned; this too is addressed in the final chapter. The consensus notes that ministries are described by Paul but officers are not; rather, in the earliest Pauline communities the stress is on function, and the impression is given that these functions might be performed by any member of the congregation. By the time of the Pastoral Epistles, however, such charismatic freedom is gone, and the idea of a contribution inspired by the Spirit has given way to investment in offices, as local officers take over from the charismatic individuals. This narrative is told, often with the implicit—and in the older literature, explicit—statement that the narrative is one of decline, and that the movement from Spirit-inspired freedom to bureaucratic officers is a move toward the moribund. Whereas this view has been questioned, even those who question it have stumbled over the relationship between *presbyteroi* and *episkopoi*. Thus, it is only in the final chapter that this decline narrative is finally refuted.

This history is of obvious theological and ecclesial interest. This work, however, is simply a history, and so questions of theology, ecumenism, and ecclesiology are addressed only in a postscript and there only allusively. I, like King, have sought to undertake this work with an "impartial hand,"[28] mindful that dogmatic positions have in the past skewed the reading of the evidence. It is for the Wesleys of the present to use, abuse, or ignore it.

28. King, *Enquiry*, title page.

On *Episkopoi* and *Presbyteroi*

I t is a fact now generally recognised by theologians of all shades of opinion, that in the language of the New Testament the same officer in the Church is called indifferently 'bishop' (*episkopos*) and 'elder' or 'presbyter' (*presbyteros*)." So wrote Lightfoot in 1868.[1] That this should be a "fact" in the middle of the nineteenth century indicates that the hypothesis that the two terms are synonymous was already well established and entrenched. As Campbell comments, "Facts of that kind have proved to be in short supply in the century since Lightfoot wrote."[2]

The Alleged Synonymy of *Episkopos* and *Presbyteros*

It is hard to say where exactly such a "fact" originated. According to Linton, this position has its roots in the seventeenth century,[3] and we find synonymy argued by Salmasius in 1641, as by Stillingfleet in 1662, though it was hardly

---

1. J. B. Lightfoot, *Saint Paul's Epistle to the Philippians*, 4th ed. (London: Macmillan, 1878), 95.
2. R. Alastair Campbell, *The Elders: Seniority within Earliest Christianity*, SNTW (Edinburgh: T&T Clark, 1994), 183.
3. Olof Linton, *Das Problem der Urkirche in der neueren Forschung: Eine kritische Darstellung* (Uppsala: Almqvist & Wiksell, 1932), 3–5.

an undisputed position then.[4] Here is certainly the foundation of the wider narrative that concluded that the episcopate was not a continuation of the apostolate, but that the "monarchical episcopate" had derived from the original order of undifferentiated and collectively governing presbyters and *episkopoi*, a narrative that seems to have attained a status approaching fact by the earlier part of the nineteenth century; in 1835 Baur describes this hypothesis as the usual one (*gewöhnlich*) and cites Neander as holding this common opinion.[5] Baur himself was yet to be convinced,[6] yet when Seyerlin, in 1887, set out what was by then the common ground for Protestant historical analysis (which he contrasted to dogmatic Roman Catholic attempts to derive the church order of the Roman church from apostolic precedent), this much was considered concluded.[7] It is a consensus that, in spite of numerous attempts to overturn it, is alive and well.[8]

However, Lightfoot himself no doubt had some role in establishing the "fact" in the Anglophone world, not the least in that he was an Anglican and in time would become a bishop himself. In the history of the study of church order one constantly finds explicit or implicit statements of the writer's own fundamental convictions and of the direct ecclesial interest motivating the work. Thus Lightfoot's Anglicanism was significant because he was the first

4. Salmasius (Claude de Saumaise), *Walonis Messalini de episcopis et presbyteris contra D. Petauium* (Leiden: Johannis Maire, 1641), 3–82; Edward Stillingfleet, *Irenicum: A Weapon-Salve for the Churches Wounds* (London: Henry Mortlock, 1662), 264–94.

5. F. C. Baur, *Die sogenannten Pastoralbriefe des Apostels Paulus aufs neue kritisch untersucht* (Stuttgart and Tübingen: J. G. Cotta, 1835), 80. I have not found the edition employed by Baur, but this opinion is set out in a revised (1847) edition: August Neander, *Geschichte der Pflanzung und Leitung der christlichen Kirche durch die Apostel*, 4th ed. (Hamburg: Friedrich Berthes, 1847), 249–51.

6. So *Pastoralbriefe*, 80–85. Richard Rothe (*Die Anfänge der christlichen Kirche und ihrer Verfassung: Ein geschichtlicher Versuch* [Wittenberg: Zimmermann, 1837], 180), in opposing Baur, notes the coincidence of the view of Baur with that of Hammond, citing J. Clerici, ed., *Annotationes in NT* (Amsterdam: 1699). I have not been able to find that particular version of Hammond's work, but his view may be established from the fifth edition, in which it is clear that although he believed that the terms were synonymous, he is also clear that both terms mean (*mon*) *episkopos*. So he writes, "Although this title of πρεσβύτεροι *Elders* have [*sic*] been also extended to a second order in the church . . . in the Scripture-times it belonged principally, if not alone, to Bishops" (*A Paraphrase and Annotations upon All the Books of the New Testament*, 5th ed. [London: J. Macock and M. Flesher, for Richard Royston, 1681], 380). In this light, he takes references to elders and their ordination throughout the New Testament as references to bishops.

7. R. Seyerlin, "Die Entstehung des Episcopats in der christlichen Kirche mit besondere Beziehung auf die Hatch-Harnack'sche Hypothese," *ZpraktTh* 9 (1887), cited by Linton, *Problem*, 3. This article was not available to me. Nonetheless, I may suggest that, given Calvin's conviction that the two terms were synonymous and monepiscopacy was the result of "corruption," the Protestant position is equally a dogmatic one.

8. So, very recently, Otfried Hofius, "Die Ordination zum Amt der Kirche und die apostolische Sukzession nach dem Zeugnis der Pastoralbriefe," *ZTK* 107 (2010): 265–66.

leading scholar from a communion claiming catholicity and retaining a historic episcopate to express what had, in Protestant circles, long been a prevailing orthodoxy.

However, although the identity of *episkopoi* and *presbyteroi* was an established part of the consensus established in the nineteenth century (and originating in the seventeenth) regarding the first emergence of office within the church, the explanation of the identity varied. For Lightfoot, the identity came about because the term *episkopos* derived from Gentile congregations and *presbyteros* from Jewish; but although of distinct origin, these institutions, episcopate and presbyterate, were nonetheless the same thing, precisely as Neander had argued. Although it has been questioned, and although the very rough division between Hellenistic and Jewish forms of Christianity would never be asserted today, this equation has never been satisfactorily overturned. It is the argument of this opening chapter that the terms were never synonymous. This provides the first step in dismantling the larger consensus and, by way of explaining many of the texts that allegedly demonstrate synonymy, the first step in constructing a new picture.

However, before discussing the texts, I must define "synonym." The term here is employed to indicate two words that mean precisely and only the same thing and are therefore completely interchangeable. Whereas this may seem a statement of the obvious, we read in Ysebaert an argument that *episkopos* and *presbyteros* are synonyms but then meet the conclusion that they are "partial synonyms."[9] A partial synonym is not a synonym. We may term a partial synonym a "perionym," a term coined to denote two words in unspecified relationship that inhabit the same semantic domain but are not synonyms. I will not deny that there is some overlap of meaning between the terms, but overlap is not the same as identity. Thus, in English an example of synonyms is "rubbish" and "garbage." However, it is unlikely that the same person would use the two words, since one reflects British usage, the other American. An example of a pair of perionyms is "college" and "university" in British English. "College" is a term often used to refer to a university in general parlance ("I met my wife at college," "My son is going to college"), but there are colleges that are not universities at all, and colleges that are constituent parts of universities. Thus, if one is speaking generally, "college" may refer to university, but "university" would not be used of a college that is not a university. One cannot correctly say, "My university is Anytown Technical

9. Joseph Ysebaert, *Die Amtsterminologie im neuen Testament und in der alten Kirche: Eine lexikographische Untersuchung* (Breda: Eureia, 1994), initially at 60, and after a confident statement of synonymy, the term "partiell" is introduced at 123.

College." *Presbyteros* and *episkopos*, I will suggest, are perionyms but not synonyms. The relationship between the terms can be established only on the basis of close examination of their use in context. It is on the basis of such an examination of the texts employed to support synonymy that I will argue for a more complex relationship between the terms.

The idea that the terms *presbyteros* and *episkopos* are directly synonymous is still widely held. Thus we may observe (to take a random selection) recent assertions by Trebilco,[10] by Knight (who refers to Lightfoot in support of his argument),[11] and by Hawthorne (who also refers to Lightfoot),[12] Jay's summary of the position,[13] and Merkle's recent defense.[14] As Merkle himself notes, as often as not, these assertions are not so much argued as taken for granted.[15] It is also noteworthy that Lightfoot, rather than, say, Ritschl, should be counted the authority by these conservative scholars. However, in view of the status granted him, I may begin my own examination of the interrelationship of the two terms by noting that of Lightfoot. He bases his argument on a number of texts from the New Testament and one from *1 Clement*. In doing so, he employs the same texts as did Neander, Rothe, and Ritschl before him,[16] as indeed those employed by Salmasius, and the same as those many since who have followed the consensus of synonymy. In examining these texts, we will find that in all but two of the instances cited by Lightfoot the synonymy of *episkopos* and *presbyteros* is patently not the only possible interpretation of the texts, and that the explanation of these texts as indicating synonymy has been questioned in these cases. In the two cases where the equation does seem to be the most obvious explanation at first sight, a new alternative explanation is proffered here. It is with these two texts, Acts 20:17–18, 28 and Titus 1:5–8, which were central

10. Paul Trebilco, *The Early Christians in Ephesus: From Paul to Ignatius* (Grand Rapids: Eerdmans, 2007), 187–88.

11. George W. Knight III, *The Pastoral Epistles: A Commentary on the Greek Text*, NIGTC (Grand Rapids: Eerdmans; Carlisle: Paternoster, 1992), 155, 175–77.

12. Gerald F. Hawthorne, *Philippians*, WBC 43 (Waco: Word, 1983), 10.

13. Eric G. Jay, "From Presbyter-Bishops to Bishops and Presbyters," *SecCent* 1 (1981): 125–62.

14. Benjamin L. Merkle, *The Elder and Overseer: One Office in the Early Church* (Frankfurt: Peter Lang, 2003). The power of the consensus is such that both David L. Bartlett (*Ministry in the New Testament* [Minneapolis: Fortress, 1993], 167–68) and James Tunstead Burtchaell (*From Synagogue to Church: Public Services and Offices in the Earliest Christian Communities* [Cambridge: Cambridge University Press, 1992], 297), in spite of their otherwise diametrically opposed views, are in thrall to it.

15. Merkle, *Elder and Overseer*, 2.

16. Neander, *Geschichte*, 249–51; Rothe, *Anfänge*, 173–93; Albrecht Ritschl, *Die Entstehung der altkatholischen Kirche: Eine kirchen- und dogmengeschichtliche Monographie*, 2nd ed. (Bonn: Adolph Marcus, 1857), 399–415.

to Salmasius's argument and therefore are the crown witnesses in this trial, that the examination begins.

On Acts 20, Lightfoot writes, "St Paul is represented as summoning to Miletus the 'elders' or 'presbyters' of the Church of Ephesus. Yet in addressing them immediately after he appeals to them as 'bishops' or 'overseers' of the church."[17] On Titus 1, Lightfoot writes, "the same identification appears still more plainly. . . . 'That thou shouldest set in order the things that are wanting and ordain *elders* in every city, as I appointed thee; if any one be *blameless*, the husband of one wife, having believing children who are not charged with riotousness or unruly; for a *bishop* must be *blameless* etc.'"[18] In other words, having directed Titus to appoint presbyters, the author gives the qualifications that are given elsewhere for *episkopoi* and then justifies his argument by stating that these are episcopal qualifications.

That there is a prima facie case to answer for those wishing to argue against synonymy at these points at least is unquestionable. However, there is a distinct possible explanation of the phenomenon that must be explored. Rather than starting with documenting the uses of the terms—a method that, after over three hundred years, appears to have achieved no unanimity beyond the vague notion of "partial synonymy"—I begin with an account of the development of church order in one city and then examine the manner in which the terms are used there. In that case, it is the history that leads us to comprehend the terminology rather than the other way around. On the understanding of the terminology thus supplied, I may then seek to determine whether other histories may be illuminated.

The Evidence for Synonymy Explained in Terms of Federation

Whereas the texts mentioned above tend to imply synonymy, in that the terms *episkopos* and *presbyteroi* are mentioned apparently in the same breath and referring to the same people, the apparent synonymy may be explained by suggesting that the scattered Christian communities of the first centuries might have operated some form of loose federation by which individual Christian officers from different communities in a city or area might meet together to deal with issues of common concern, and that the references to presbyters in the two instances that are fundamental to the consensus are references to gatherings of these leaders. However they may have been designated in their individual communities, I suggest that they were known as presbyters in their

17. Lightfoot, *Philippians*, 97.
18. Ibid.

common gathering, and that references to presbyters in the texts adduced for synonymy are references to these people in that capacity. If this is the case, then the terms are not synonymous but overlapping; *presbyteroi* would be a collective term that might well include *episkopoi*.

There have been, however, other ways of attempting to explain the relationship without admitting complete synonymy but admitting a degree of relationship between the terms. These positions will be discussed more extensively in the course of the argument across the chapters, but it may briefly be summarized here to demonstrate the rationale for seeking a further explanation, namely, that no suggestion to date is entirely satisfactory. In laying out the positions, I follow the classification proposed by Merkle.[19] It should be noted, however, that this discussion largely takes place in the context of interpreting the Pastoral Epistles. However, solutions that make sense in one context need to be transferable.

In the first instance it may be argued that the term *presbyteros* never denotes an office but refers simply to an older man.[20] This argument, which is presented primarily in the context of the Pastoral Epistles, will be discussed in detail below; in particular it will be argued that this is the use intended in 1 Timothy. However, it is hard to reconcile this understanding of the term with the use of Acts 20, for we are hardly meant to understand that Paul is summoning all the elderly males of Ephesus. There is a degree of special pleading evident when Harvey, for instance, reads the appointment of elders at Acts 14:23 to mean that those who were already elders were appointed to bear particular responsibilities in the church.[21]

The same objection may be made to the position that *episkopoi* are *presbyteroi* who perform particular functions (i.e., that the terms are "partial synonyms"). Again, this may be an adequate position to cover the use of the terms in 1 Timothy, but it does not account for the use in Acts 20. *Presbyteroi* are summoned, and *episkopoi* are addressed, but one would not expect a group (*presbyteroi*) to be summoned and only a subgroup (the *episkopoi* among them) to be addressed.

A variation of this position is the hypothesis that the *episkopos* is a *presbyteros* with functions of leadership (i.e., the *episkopos* is a senior among

---

19. Merkle, *Elder and Overseer*, 4–19.

20. Typically by Joachim Jeremias, *Die Briefe an Timotheus und Titus; Der Brief an die Hebräer*, 11th ed., NTD 9 (Göttingen: Vandenhoeck & Ruprecht, 1975), 31, 36. Note, however, that his argument is concerned with the use of the term in the Pastoral Epistles, not in the New Testament as a whole. A wider survey of literature is essayed in Campbell, *Elders*, though again there is a concentration in Campbell's work on the Pastoral Epistles.

21. A. E. Harvey, "Elders," *JTS* 25 (1974): 331.

the elders),[22] but again the same objection may be raised. Why should only a subgroup in the audience be addressed?

Finally, it might be suggested that the two are entirely distinct, that the *episkopos* of 1 Timothy is a *monepiskopos*.[23] However, the fact that in Acts 20 *presbyteroi* are summoned and *episkopoi* addressed indicates that there must be some kind of relationship between the two terms. It may be argued that the *monepiskopos* of 1 Timothy has developed from the situation envisaged by Acts 20, but in that instance some rationale has to be provided as to why multiple *episkopoi* who are *presbyteroi* become single *episkopoi* who are not.

Indeed, I will argue below that there is a strong distinction between the two terms, but some relationship between them must be maintained: the terms are perionymous, and the term *presbyteroi* here denotes a gathering of Christian leaders who individually in their own communities are known as *episkopoi*. It is because the terminology is confusing that the terms are explained on the basis of history rather than the other way around. The reason for suggesting that *presbyteroi* is a collective term for gathered church leaders is not simply because it solves the exegetical problems, but rather because this is a well-attested organizational model in early Christianity. In maintaining this position, I am proposing nothing new, as precisely this explanation of the terms was proposed by Baur,[24] though one may refer to more recent literature (and avoid Baur's position that the Pastoral Epistles are a work deriving from the latter part of the second century) in order to establish the point. In particular, in order to establish the position just described I discuss examples of federation within early Christianity. I begin this study with Rome because there has been extensive and relatively recent work that allows us to see the manner in which the monepiscopacy formed and demonstrates the existence of federation between leaders of the individual churches at a citywide level.

Roman Christianity as Federation

Although to turn to second-century Rome may seem to be a digression, here the question of the relationship between *episkopoi* and *presbyteroi* is capable of a clear answer that overturns the consensus as far as Rome is concerned. On that basis, I may go on to ask whether the same situation may apply to other communities. In particular, I may suggest, the federation in Rome provides an

---

22. So, e.g., Ceslas Spicq, *Saint Paul: Les Épitres pastorales*, EB (Paris: Gabalda, 1947), xlvi–xlvii.

23. So, e.g., Ernst Käsemann, "Ministry and Community in the New Testament," in *Essays on New Testament Themes*, trans. W. J. Montague (London: SCM, 1964), 87.

24. Baur, *Pastoralbriefe*, 80–86.

explanation of the apparent synonymy in Acts 20 and offers an interpretation of Titus 1:5 that is more coherent than any offered to date.

Recent studies, in particular those of Lampe and Brent, have led to a picture of Roman Christianity as made up of fractionalized communities that gradually cohere to find themselves under a monepiscopate in the third century.[25] The conception of fractionalized house-churches is derived from a number of sources. Thus, Romans 16:3–16 contains greetings to a variety of households, each of which, we may surmise, is an independent household church.[26] Justin similarly indicates that there are churches throughout the city, while claiming no knowledge of any but his own, which meets on private premises;[27] his community, therefore, is entirely independent. Hermas's references to household leadership allow us to deduce, moreover, that he is a sole leader among other householders.[28] Subsequently we hear of Polycarp's visit to Rome, when he celebrated Pascha with the Asian communities in the capital and received hospitality from Soter, even though the two had different liturgical practices of such diversity that they could be contained only in a very loose network indeed.[29] Thus, it is only at the time of Victor that the network begins to tighten, as Asian paschal practice at Rome is called into question.[30] Finally, we may observe that such a pattern would be entirely in keeping with the organization of Judaism within the city, which consisted of a diversity of synagogues based on racial and social lines.[31]

This picture of Roman Christianity has been questioned by Caragounis;[32] however, his critique is based largely on just one argument of Lampe, in which he notes that Romans is addressed not to a church but simply to Christians.

25. Note in particular Peter Lampe, *Die stadtrömischen Christen in den ersten beiden Jahrhunderten*, WUNT 18/2 (Tübingen: Mohr Siebeck, 1987); Allen Brent, *Hippolytus and the Roman Church in the Third Century: Communities in Tension before the Emergence of a Monarch-Bishop*, VCSup 31 (Leiden: Brill, 1995).

26. So Lampe, *Stadtrömischen Christen*, 135–53. Similarly in Peter Lampe, "The Roman Christians of Romans 16," in *The Romans Debate*, ed. K. P. Donfried (Peabody, MA: Hendrickson, 1991), 216–30. Note also William L. Lane, "Social Perspectives on Roman Christianity in the Formative Years from Nero to Nerva," in *Judaism and Christianity in First-Century Rome*, ed. K. P. Donfried and P. Richardson (Grand Rapids: Eerdmans, 1998), 196–214.

27. *Acta Justini* 3.

28. See, with references, Alistair Stewart(-Sykes), *From Prophecy to Preaching: A Search for the Origins of the Christian Homily*, VCSup 59 (Leiden: Brill, 2001), 106.

29. Eusebius, *Hist. eccl.* 5.24.

30. Eusebius, *Hist. eccl.* 5.23.

31. For discussion of the decentralized nature of synagogal communities at Rome see chap. 3, under the heading "Presbyters in the Synagogues of Rome."

32. C. C. Caragounis, "From Obscurity to Prominence: The Development of the Roman Church between Romans and *1 Clement*," in Donfried and Richardson, *Judaism and Christianity*, 245–79.

Caragounis replies that there is no consistency in Paul's addresses, in that he employs this address to the Thessalonians and Corinthians, but not to the Philippians. Is it not possible, however, that as in Rome, there is likewise no single church in Philippi, which is why there is also a plural address to *episkopoi* and *diakonoi*?[33] Second, Caragounis denies any connection with the synagogue. Whereas his denial seems to be based more on theological than historical grounds (he sees the Jerusalem church, which was obedient to the law, as "sub-Christian"),[34] the point is that the diverse synagogues of Rome provide the model for diverse house-churches within the city rather than their direct genesis. Instead of scattered house-churches Caragounis sees a central place of worship. How would this occur, one may ask, when the number of Christians is relatively small, when there is no public transport across a large city? Even if the picture of scattered house-churches is, ultimately, hypothetical, it is a far better hypothesis than that of a central Christian community.

Turning to *1 Clement*, Caragounis notes that even if there had been fractionalized Christian communities at the time of Romans, the manner in which *1 Clement* speaks on behalf of the entire Roman church indicates that by now the church has been united, even though no evidence is left in the record.[35] Lane also recognizes a certain centralization and formalization of leadership structures in the Roman church at the time of *1 Clement*, but he continues to maintain, largely on the basis of the contemporaneous evidence of Hermas, that the individual house-churches with their leaders also continued.[36] In order to give an adequate answer to Caragounis's point that the church is here acting in concert, we must explain how both can be true. Doing so must involve examining the significance of the titles of the leaders.

Lampe points to some degree of centralization in the Roman community, in particular regarding relief for the poor.[37] Brent takes this picture further and finds evidence of gatherings of the leaders of the churches to discuss particular issues;[38] it is from this gathering that *1 Clement* is written, from this gathering that relief for the poor comes to be organized centrally, in this gathering that Hermas's visions are discussed, and in this gathering that particular doctrinal differences between the communities that effectively threaten the identity of

---

33. This question is discussed below, under the heading "Philippians as Further Evidence of Federation (and Not Synonymy)."

34. Caragounis, "From Obscurity to Prominence," 255n48.

35. Ibid., 271.

36. Lane, "Social Perspectives," 226–42.

37. Lampe, *Stadtrömischen Christen*, 333–45. Lane ("Social Perspectives," 236, 241) also notes that some centralization has taken place by the time of *1 Clement* and recognizes that this has an effect on the titles of the officers of the church, but he is not clear precisely how this operates.

38. Brent, *Hippolytus*, 433–36.

forming catholic Christianity are discussed. Thus it is possible to read the condemnation of Marcion by Roman presbyters as a withdrawal of their recognition of him as a presbyter and a withdrawal of their recognition of his school[39] and similarly to see the plea of Natalius to be received back into the church made before Zephyrinus, as before "clergy and laity,"[40] as the act of an *episkopos* of a community not recognized by the federation coming to a gathering of the federated leaders. This unity between the diverse communities is given liturgical expression through the exchange of the *fermentum*.[41] It is in this context, Brent suggests, that the leaders are collectively known as presbyters.

In view of the importance of this designation, and that of the individual leaders, Brent's argument must be examined closely. He starts by noting, as I have, the original diversity and plurality of Christian meeting places in Rome. He questions the extent to which all might be considered households and suggests that philosophical schools might also be adequate characterizations of some of these communities (a point to which I refer in the final chapter) and further suggests that the later Roman *tituli* might be a relic of this earlier form of loose organization. He then asks the critical questions: "i) Were [*sic*] each group independent, with their own presbyters, or was there any attempt at mutual recognition as a common *ekklēsia*? and ii) was the term *presbyteros* completely synonymous with *episkopos* or was it possible that they were two groups, who[se] membership possibly overlapped, with different functions?"[42]

Following Lampe, Brent answers the first question by suggesting that there is evidence of letters being passed around congregations, such as that of Paul, or that of Ignatius, and that of Dionysius of Corinth to Soter.[43] These letters, he suggests, were passed around by means of a common meeting of presbyters, to which reference is made by Hermas, as Hermas is instructed to read his book within the city "together with the presbyters who preside over the church."[44] Beyond this, Hermas is directed to send a copy of his book of visions to Clement, who is to send the work on to cities outside Rome, in accordance with his commission. Clement is thus identified as one who would communicate with churches beyond the city, so explaining his role in the production of *1 Clement* and his identification as the author of an anonymous letter sent in the name of the Roman church.

39. Reported by Epiphanius, *Pan.* 42.2.1–5.
40. Reported by Eusebius, *Hist. eccl.* 5.28.10–12.
41. *Fermentum* is the fragment of Eucharistic bread exchanged between Christian congregations as a sign of their unity.
42. Brent, *Hippolytus*, 410.
43. Eusebius, *Hist. eccl.* 4.23.10.
44. *Herm.* 8:2–3: μετὰ τῶν πρεσβυτέρων τῶν προϊσταμένων τῆς ἐκκλησίας.

In support of this characterization of independent communities in com-munication (having discussed Victor's involvement in the paschal controversy, and suggesting that this was a local issue), Brent notes the exchange of the *fermentum* in a later period and suggests, with reference to Irenaeus's obser-vation that those before Victor had sent the eucharist to other parishes, that this was the means by which, at an earlier period, distinct communities had demonstrated their mutual recognition. He characterizes the dispute between the schools of Callistus and "Hippolytus" as a dispute between two such distinct communities that had broken off relations with each other. On this basis he sees the assertion that Callistus had insulted "Hippolytus" publicly (*dēmosia*) as a further reference to the central gathering of Christian leaders.[45]

The condemnation of Marcion is seen as yet further evidence for such a gathering, here determining the boundaries of orthodoxy (likewise the oc-casion for the debate described in Hippolytus, *Haer.* 9.12, we may surmise), and, less certainly, suggests that the condemnation of Noetus by presbyters in Smyrna is a fictionalized account of a Roman council transferred to Smyr-na.[46] Primary, moreover, is Hermas's reference to the preeminent presbyters.[47] There is ample evidence to envisage the gathering of individual leaders from different Christian communities on a citywide basis—*kata polin*, we might say.[48]

As to the designation of these leaders, Brent turns, fundamentally, again to *Shepherd of Hermas* 8:3, where the term "presbyters" designates those who are in the council. He defends the idea that each community had an individual leader, however, often termed *episkopos*, with reference to Natalius, who is the *episkopos* of the Theodotians,[49] and noting *Shepherd of Hermas* 43 (a depic-tion of a prophet) and the single president (*proestōs*) to whom Justin refers[50] as indicating that individual communities knew individual leaders. We may add to this the usage of Irenaeus, where Victor's predecessors are referred to

45. Hippolytus, *Haer.* 9.12.15–16: διὰ τὸ δημοσίᾳ ἡμῖν ὀνειδίζοντα εἰπεῖν· δίθεοί ἐστε.

46. Brent, *Hippolytus*, 429. Here we part company. Brent states here that Smyrna is by now under monepiscopacy, and this is the reason for his supposition that this is a transferred account. We are less sure, however, of the date of the advent of monepiscopacy to Smyrna (see chap. 4 below, under the heading "Smyrna").

47. *Herm.* 8:3.

48. The rationale for employing a Greek term will be discovered below. Compare to this ac-count, however, Manlio Simonetti, "Roma cristiana tra vescovi e presbiteri," *VetChr* 43 (2006): 5–17, esp. 11–12. Simonetti suggests that there is no evidence of such a gathering; I have presented sufficient evidence, however. Simonetti struggles with the evidence of different designations for leaders of the Roman churches and suggests that unification under a monepiscopate comes about with Victor, but he gives no account of the process or any rationale for its occurrence.

49. Eusebius, *Hist. eccl.* 5.28.12.

50. Justin, *1 Apol.* 67.

as *presbyteroi*,[51] whereas there is no doubt that Victor was an *episkopos* (even if not, as assumed by Eusebius, a *monepiskopos*).

There is no question that Hermas's use of *presbyteroi* here is both a collective term and one that has a degree of specificity, for elsewhere he refers more generally to leaders of the church rather than terming them "presbyters";[52] likewise there is no question that he is aware of *episkopoi*, a term used when their duties are in question.[53] The hypothesis of federation, and the terming of the federated leaders as *presbyteroi*, clarifies this otherwise confusing usage. In other words, far from Rome being under presbyteral leadership,[54] and far from the presbyters being those from whom *episkopoi* are recruited,[55] the *episkopoi* were the individual congregational leaders from whom came the *presbyteroi*, those leaders who met as a council and so formed the federation.

We may test this hypothesis, moreover, by examining the use of the terms in *1 Clement*. We see that perfect sense is made of each passage if it is hypothesized that "presbyters" is a collective designation of individual leaders otherwise known as *episkopoi*. The book of *1 Clement* is significant here not least because passages from this letter have been used in support of synonymy.[56]

The key passages are *1 Clement* 42:4–5; 44:1–4; 57:1. The first passage describes the apostles' appointment of *episkopoi* and *diakonoi*: "I shall appoint their bishops [*episkopous*] in righteousness and their deacons [*diakonous*] in faith," a development justified through a citation of LXX Isaiah 60:17. As Clement turns to the matter of strife, he states that the apostles knew that strife would occur over the "name" of *episkopos*, and for this reason they appointed a provision by which others should succeed those *episkopoi* and *diakonoi* whom they had appointed. In reference to what is happening he then states, "How blessed are the presbyters."[57] From this, Lightfoot deduces synonymy, whereas I may state that the passage may equally be understood by seeing "presbyters" as a collective noun, in the manner in which Clement would be familiar from Roman usage. Similarly, Lona rather strangely deduces from this that the constitution of the Corinthian church was basically

51. Quoted in Eusebius, *Hist. eccl.* 5.24.14.
52. *Herm.* 6:6; 17:7.
53. *Herm.* 13:1; 104.
54. So Jay, "Presbyter-Bishops," 162.
55. So Norbert Brox, *Der Hirt des Hermas*, KAV 7 (Göttingen: Vandenhoeck & Ruprecht, 1991), 534–35.
56. By Lightfoot, *Philippians*, 97–98. Note also Joachim Rohde, *Urchristliche und frühkatholische Ämter: Eine Untersuchung zur frühchristlichen Amtsentwicklung im Neuen Testament und bei den apostolischen Vätern*, ThA 33 (Berlin: Evangelische Verlagsanstalt, 1976), 105.
57. *1 Clem.* 44:5.

presbyteral;[58] he justifies this rather strained conclusion in view of the earlier mention of *episkopoi* and *diakonoi*, referring back to the citation of Isaiah and implying that the terms must be synonymous. But were *episkopoi* and *diakonoi* unknown, Clement would hardly have employed the passage or claimed that the apostles would have appointed officers so designated. Again it is better to see the term "presbyters" as a collective, and so, when he speaks in *1 Clement* 57:1 of submission to the presbyters on the part of the whole Corinthian church, we may suspect that he is envisaging an acceptance of the overall authority of the collective group just as, in *1 Clement* 47:6, the "sedition against its presbyters" of the Corinthian church likewise refers to a collective gathering.

Alternatively, one would have to suppose that the terms were completely synonymous, in which case we would be referring to a single community with collective leadership exercising office.[59] Although that is a logical possibility, we will see below that there is no reason to suppose that any such community ever existed. Such a reading of *1 Clement* does not, therefore, prove the hypothesis of federation, although it tends to support it, and in no way does it militate against it.[60] We should also note the explanation essayed by Barlea, from without the consensus, that the Corinthian Christian community had originally been governed by *episkopoi* and *diakonoi*, but that presbyters, a novel introduction, have caused the stress to which the Roman letter is addressed.[61] This is just a possible reading, but it depends on seeing episcopal and presbyteral systems as two distinct strands of Christian leadership that conflict and coalesce. This hypothesis, which is found in various versions of which Barlea's is but one, is criticized below. For the moment, however, it may be suggested that if Barlea's explanation is correct, then Clement's reference to the appointment of *episkopoi* and *diakonoi* by the apostles is a somewhat clumsy way of defending the presbyters against such *episkopoi*.

Thus the system of elders in Rome came about through federation of diverse Christian households. Of these households it is possible that some may have been under single householders, like that of Hermas himself, whereas others, formed out of more than one household, may have had more complex organizational structures; some may have been termed *episkopoi*, others not.

58. Horacio E. Lona, *Der erste Clemensbrief*, KAV 2 (Göttingen: Vandenhoeck & Ruprecht, 1998), 468.

59. The reading apparently adopted by Jay, "Presbyter-Bishops," 135–36.

60. Hermann J. Vogt ("Frühkirche und Amt: Neu in der Diskussion," ZAC 8 [2003]: 465) also has harsh words for those who attempt to derive presbyteral and collective leadership from the statements of *1 Clement*.

61. Octavian Barlea, *Die Weihe der Bischöfe, Presbyter und Diakone in vornicänischer Zeit*, APT 3 (Munich: Societas Academica Dacoromana, 1969), 92, 99.

Justin, as we have seen, refers to the "president" (*proestōs*), a term that, as Brent points out, is employed by Diogenes Laertius to refer to the founders of philosophical schools,[62] though this term may be used as an explanatory term, given the apologetic context. However, what is critical to note is that the interchangeability of terms operates only at a citywide level; therefore, this does not mean that the terms or function of *episkopoi* and *presbyteroi* are interchangeable at the level of the single Christian household. Thus, when Lampe asks whether all presbyters (he is working on the assumption that presbyters were the fundamental form of governance in the Roman church) are also bishops,[63] we may respond by asking instead whether all bishops are also presbyters.

The problem with the hypothesis of collective leadership is that it fails to take account of the domestic origins of Christian communities, a failure due, I suggest, to the conviction buried deep in the history of the theory that the synagogue provided the model for Christian organization. However, if a Christian community had grown out of a household, then it would by default have a single leader by virtue of its reflection of a single household, unless by some process of negotiation other householders had agreed to be subordinated to a single householder. Possibly, these individuals were known as *episkopoi*, and perhaps they were assisted, as I will suggest, by *diakonoi* from the beginning; it is also possible that the other patron householders took some title, especially if households united to form a single domestic congregation. I will explore this in detail below. For the moment, all that I need to state is that it is too simplistic to assert, as does Jay, that "for about a century and a half the church's ministry was basically presbyteral."[64] The situation is more complex; in speaking, moreover, of presbyteries, we need to distinguish between presbyteries within individual communities and those that in some sense had oversight of distinct communities in one location, like the Roman presbyters to whom Hermas, Epiphanius's source, and Clement refer. In Baur's language, we need to distinguish between *Gemeindeamt* and *Kirchenamt*—that is, between office in a single congregation and church office in a wider context.

We may note that it is a result of the consensus of synonymy, and of the further underlying consensus that early Christian leadership was invariably plural (an issue to which I will turn in due course), that Lampe was unable to distinguish between an *episkopos* within a single Christian community and an *episkopos* set over more than one Christian community, which leads him to

---

62. Allen Brent, "Diogenes Laertius and the Apostolic Succession," *JEH* 44 (1993): 370–71, with reference to Diogenes Laertius, *Vit.* proem. 19.

63. Lampe, *Stadtrömischen Christen*, 337.

64. Jay, "Presbyter-Bishops," 162.

the assumption that any single leader in any Christian household must have been known as a *presbyteros*, and never as an *episkopos*. This assumption, in turn, leads him to suggest that an *episkopos* is a *presbyteros* with a particular function, namely, the relief of the poor. This is the second point with which I must take issue, for although this fits in with the evidence on the origin of the *episkopos* that indicated that the distribution of goods was his primary duty (an argument discussed in the next chapter), this in turn leads him to trace the origins of the monepiscopate to the centralization of this duty. I have argued, with Brent, against this elsewhere, suggesting instead that the monepiscopate derived from the function of corresponding with churches outside Rome.[65] This is not the point at which to pursue that particular argument, however. What I may state as established is that independent Christian communities within the city had a meeting point. Representatives of congregations might gather and be collectively known as *presbyteroi*. Such a gathering communicated with other churches (so through *1 Clement*), circulated literature (such as the visions of Hermas or, indeed, possibly Paul's letter to the Romans, since there is more than one house-church named therein), and determined the extent to which doctrinal diversity might be tolerated within the federation (thus withdrawing recognition from Marcion). And from this gathering monepiscopacy eventually emerged.

Significant, however, is the absence of evidence for the coordination of relief for the poor. I will suggest below that this is a primary function of the *episkopos* within early Christian communities, but the absence of evidence indicates that it was performed at the level of the single household. In time, certainly, there was a citywide system, but that system came about only after a significant number of Roman churches had united under a sole bishop, about the time of Victor. Thus, it is under Zephyrinus that the first Christian cemetery is found, under the management of Callistus.

I have suggested that individual Roman household churches might have a relationship at a citywide level, and that the representatives of the individual churches might collectively be known as presbyters. In other words, the Roman Christian communities had formed a federation, and such references to presbyters as are found in the literature of Rome prior to the final establishment of monepiscopacy are references to the leaders of the individual communities in their federal aspect. If this is the case, then we may inquire if the same is true elsewhere; in particular, if this was the case at Ephesus, then this provides an alternative explanation for the terminology both of Acts 20 and of Titus 1:5–9, the main supports for the hypothesis of synonymy.

---

65. Brent, *Hippolytus*, 411–12.

Federation at Corinth

Before turning to Ephesus, however, I may give brief attention to Corinth. Although there is no direct evidence for church order in the city between the time of Paul and the correspondence of Dionysius of Corinth approximately a century later, indirect evidence is supplied by *1 Clement*. Insofar as we can reconstruct the situation addressed from Rome, we may glean something of the stage of ecclesial development here.

In an earlier work I have discussed the occasion of the letter of the Roman communities to Corinth, and I suggested that the strife is within households, and that the cause of the strife is not ecclesiastical office as such but rather an attempt by teachers operating within households to gain authority over the householders who had exercised leadership hitherto.[66] The only point that might add to that consideration is the possibility that these teachers are not native to Corinth but are visitors.[67] However, at that point I discussed neither the terminology employed for officers nor the relationship between the individual households and the Corinthian church overall.

All that is said directly of this by Clement is that certain presbyters had been deposed; the leaders are at all points described as *presbyteroi*.[68] Thus governance of the church by a board of presbyters has been suggested here, with the rider, derived from Clement's language regarding oversight (*episkopē*), that these presbyters are synonymous with *episkopoi*.[69] If, however, I were to assume for the present that the order of Corinth is the same as that of Rome, I might well suggest that these presbyters are not named as such within their own communities but are presbyters *kata polin*; for this reason the audience, whom I may suggest are these same presbyters *kata polin*, understand the references to *episkopoi* as referring to the leadership of individual households. I suggest further that this is the audience because otherwise it is hard to see how the letter might be addressed to the entire Corinthian church rather than to the individual households making up the federated institution.

---

66. Alistair Stewart(-Sykes), "Prophecy and Patronage: The Relationship between Charismatic Functionaries and Household Officers in Early Christianity," in *Trajectories through the New Testament and the Apostolic Fathers*, ed. A. F. Gregory and C. M. Tuckett, NTAF (Oxford: Oxford University Press, 2005), 184–88.

67. So Rudolf Knopf, *Die Lehre der zwölf Apostel; Die zwei Clemensbriefe*, HNT (Tübingen: Mohr Siebeck, 1920), 130–31.

68. *1 Clem.* 44:5; 47:6; 54:2; 57:1.

69. So, e.g., Patrick Burke, "The Monarchical Episcopate at the End of the First Century," *JES* 7 (1970): 510–11; Barbara E. Bowe, *A Church in Crisis: Ecclesiology and Paraenesis in Clement of Rome* (Minneapolis: Fortress, 1988), 149.

Apart from making sense of the language of *1 Clement* without resort to a hypothesis of synonymy (which would beg the question why a single nomenclature is not employed throughout) and allowing us to posit a situation in which there is an imaginable audience that would understand what was written to them, this picture of a federated set of individual Christian communities would cohere with what is known from Paul's letters: there are a number of individual Christian households that may be of independent origin or of differing theological outlook, or both,[70] but that are in contact with one another (for were they not, then there would be no basis for conflict among them). Thus, alongside references to house-churches in Corinth, Paul mentions the whole church (*hē ekklēsia holē*) in 1 Corinthians 14:23, implying that individual house-churches (or perhaps their representatives) might gather in a common location. To turn forward, this would then allow us to see Dionysius of Corinth in the middle of the second century possibly as an emerging *monepiskopos* within the federation, or otherwise as the *episkopos* among the gathered presbyters entrusted with the responsibility of corresponding with other churches, but in either event mirroring the same line of development as that seen in Rome.[71]

Federation at Ephesus

Going beyond Rome, and evidence derived from Rome, and supplied with the possibility that the relationship between *episkopoi* and *presbyteroi* is other than as Lightfoot envisaged it—namely, that *presbyteroi* might be a corporate term for leaders of individual Christian communities from across a city meeting together, as it was at Rome—we may inquire whether the same might be true elsewhere. In particular we may ask whether the Christian communities of Ephesus likewise knew federation. If this is the case, then it may explain why, in Acts 20, the presbyters who are gathered may be described as *episkopoi*. It is notable that at Ephesus, in which Pauline congregations, the Johannine school, and the community addressed by the seer of Revelation may all be found, there is as great a diversity as that known in Rome, but the question of whether there might have been any federation between them or even among congregations of the same school lies open.

70. Jochen Wagner (*Die Anfänge des Amtes in der Kirche: Presbyter und Episkopen in der frühchristlichen Literatur*, TANZ 53 [Tübingen: Francke, 2011], 43) suggests as many as six persons who might credibly be considered to have been householders and household-church leaders.
71. If *2 Clement* is Corinthian, which is far from certain, then the reference to the audience being exhorted by the presbyters at 17:3 may continue to indicate that federation is functioning, though uncertainty over both date and provenance limits the value of this evidence.

THE JOHANNINE SCHOOL AT EPHESUS

First, we may note the possibility that the Johannine school in Ephesus was itself a federation of distinct communities around Ephesus. A possible scenario may be mapped out on the basis of 3 John, centering on the figure of Diotrephes. According to 3 John, Diotrephes had refused hospitality to certain of the envoys of the presbyter who wrote the letter and was expelling his supporters from the congregation. It is difficult to be certain of the precise nature of the dispute between Diotrephes and the presbyter. Smalley sums up the possible causes of dispute as polity, according to which Diotrephes is seen either as a monarchical bishop, aggregating authority to himself, or as a representative of a charismatic type of leadership that is being threatened by the presbyter. Alternatively, Smalley suggests, the dispute is doctrinal, either Diotrephes or the presbyter being perceived as a proto-gnostic.[72]

To take the second group of arguments first, there is nothing said in the letter that pertains to doctrine. Smalley uses this argument from silence as sufficient, thinking that if doctrine were at issue John would say so. Although on the basis of the silence we cannot rule out doctrinal differences absolutely, even less can we assert them on the same basis. As Malherbe puts it, "The most that can be claimed for any of these theories . . . is that they may be probable."[73]

It is therefore more probable that the argument is about church organization, especially since a coherent situation can be outlined on the basis of the evidence that takes into account all the phenomena met in the letter. Diotrephes is clearly in a position of authority, as he is able to refuse hospitality and to exclude those who offer hospitality to the envoys of the presbyter. The emphasis on hospitality indicates that this community is at least half a day's travel from Ephesus, which means that hospitality is necessary for the envoys and also indicates that the church is meeting in a domestic setting, a context that, as I will observe below, is critical for the development of offices in the church. The letter makes the matter of hospitality explicit, whereas nothing is said regarding doctrinal difference.

Diotrephes, on the basis that he is able to extend or to refuse hospitality, is to be seen as a householder functioning as a leader within his own household. As such, he is no kind of "monarchical bishop," as his position as householder is sufficient for him to hold authority.[74] Donfried similarly perceives of the differ-

---

72. Stephen S. Smalley, *1, 2, 3 John*, WBC 51 (Waco: Word, 1984), 354–57, with references.

73. Abraham J. Malherbe, "The Inhospitality of Diotrephes," in *God's Christ and His People: Studies in Honour of Nils Alstrup Dahl*, ed. Jacob Jervell and Wayne A. Meeks (Oslo: Universitetsforlaget, 1978), 223.

74. So, likewise, Harry O. Maier, *The Social Setting of the Ministry as Reflected in the Writings of Hermas, Clement and Ignatius* (Waterloo, ON: Wilfrid Laurier University Press, 1991),

ence between the presbyter and Diotrephes running along lines of hierarchical authority,[75] and Malherbe also notes the social significance of Diotrephes's position as a householder.[76] However, although Diotrephes may be acting as a householder, he does not exercise any authority outside his own house, and the presbyter's somewhat gentle approach indicates that he has no such authority either, except a degree of moral authority.[77] Diotrephes and John may be seen as *presbyteroi*, equal through their federation; the author of the letter introduces himself as "the presbyter" in order to remind Diotrephes of the responsibilities of federation. Although Smalley denies that there would be any social advantage in Diotrephes's actions,[78] if Diotrephes is leader by virtue of house ownership, then there is the question of continuing social status that might be maintained by his actions, and that would be threatened were another to assume some authority over him. Diotrephes and the elder are in federation, but each is straining the limits of the federation. If this is recognized, then I may suggest that Gaius, the addressee of the letter, was likewise a presbyter in federation and may indeed inquire whether "the presbyters who gathered in Asia with John, the disciple of the Lord"[79] are more than tradents of Irenaean memory,[80] but are indeed presbyters in a Johannine federation. I will observe below that one of the primary functions of the presbyters as gathered leaders was the policing of the boundaries of a relatively diffuse church, and so it may well be that Irenaeus is referring precisely to presbyters in federation, and that

---

149–50. The idea that he represents charismatic authority is based on a widespread fiction of charismatic opposition to office. Thus, typical is Hans von Campenhausen (*Ecclesiastical Authority and Spiritual Power in the Church of the First Three Centuries*, trans. J. A. Baker [London: A&C Black, 1969], 122), who contrasts Diotrephes, whom he calls a monarchical bishop, with the "man of the Spirit." See the comments on this general approach to church order in chap. 5 below, under the heading "Institutionalization as an Explanation of Monepiscopacy," as well as those in Stewart(-Sykes), "Prophecy and Patronage."

75. K. P. Donfried, "Ecclesiastical Authority in 2–3 John," in *L'Évangile de Jean: Sources, rédaction, theologie*, ed. Marinus de Jonge, BETL 44 (Gembloux: Duculot, 1977), 325–33.

76. Abraham J. Malherbe, *Social Aspects of Early Christianity*, 2nd ed. (Philadelphia: Fortress, 1983), 103–10.

77. So C. C. Black, "The Johannine Epistles and the Question of Early Catholicism," *NovT* 28 (1986): 143.

78. Smalley, *1, 2, 3 John*, 356.

79. Irenaeus, *Haer.* 2.22.5; cited in Greek by Eusebius, *Hist. eccl.* 3.23.3.

80. As they would be characterized by W. C. van Unnik, "The Authority of the Presbyters in Irenaeus' Works," in Jervell and Meeks, eds., *God's Christ and His People*, 248–60. There is no doubt that in earlier usage the term might connote tradents of collective memory, as is suggested by Frances M. Young, *The Theology of the Pastoral Letters*, NTT (Cambridge: Cambridge University Press, 1994), 107, with reference to Papias's usage quoted in Eusebius, *Hist. eccl.* 3.39, but I may suggest that this function has, by the time of Irenaeus, become specifically that of those who are identified as presbyters by virtue of their episcopal office.

the term is used for bearers of tradition in view of their role of policing the boundaries of orthodoxy and of propagating literature.

For the moment, however, it is sufficient to note that the communication within the Johannine school, taking in the elder who writes, Gaius, and Diotrephes, indicates a degree of federation of distinct Johannine communities within and around the city of Ephesus.

THE JOHANNINE SCHOOL AND OTHERS IN EPHESIAN FEDERATION

Going beyond the possibility of federation within the Johannine school, we may inquire whether the diverse Christian groups within the city, in particular communities of Pauline foundation represented by the Pastoral Epistles, might have federated in some way with communities of other origin, such as the Johannine school. Such a possibility has been put forward recently by Trebilco.[81] He suggests three possible relationships between the various Christian groups within the city: first, they are ignorant of one another's existence; second, they are hostile to one another; and third, there is a degree of "non-hostile interaction." It is for this third option that he argues.[82]

First, he suggests that it is most improbable that the communities were ignorant of one another's existence on the basis of the picture of Christianity as a network of distinct but related communities drawn by Bauckham and Thompson.[83]

Outright hostility he excludes because, although both the Pastoral Epistles and the Johannine Epistles have opponents in mind, the positions of the opponents cannot be identified with the different communities. Thus, 1 John is hostile toward docetism, of which there is no trace in the Pastoral Epistles, whereas the Pastoral Epistles are hostile toward ascetic groups drawing on the Jewish law, a position of which there is no trace in the Johannine Epistles.[84]

Thus, it is possible that the communities interact. There is, Trebilco suggests, some congruence of vocabulary and tradition that makes interaction probable. For instance, 1 Timothy 6:13–14 makes reference to the good

---

81. Trebilco, *Early Christians in Ephesus*, 588–627.

82. There is also the possibility that they were united at an early stage. Thus Robert Lee Williams (*Bishop Lists: Formation of Apostolic Succession of Bishops in Ecclesiastical Crises*, GDECS 3 [Piscataway, NJ: Gorgias, 2005], 84–85) suggests that the churches of Pauline foundation subordinated themselves to the authority of the Johannine elder. This is hard to believe. Williams's evidence is the manner in which Paul as apostle claimed authority as apostle over local leaders; there is no basis, however, to believe that the same respect would be shown by churches of Pauline foundation to the Johannine elder.

83. Trebilco, *Early Christians in Ephesus*, 591–93, with reference to contributions in *The Gospels for All Christians: Rethinking the Gospel Audiences*, ed. Richard J. Bauckham (Grand Rapids: Eerdmans, 1998).

84. Trebilco, *Early Christians in Ephesus*, 593.

confession of Jesus before Pilate, a confession that is most complete in the Gospel of John and to which it is most likely that reference is made here; and in 2 Timothy 3:14, the statement that the hearers should abide in (*menein en*) the tradition is close to the statement of John 8:31 that the hearers should abide in (*meinēte en*) the word of the Johannine Christ. We may therefore agree with Trebilco that there was non-hostile interaction between the Pauline and the Johannine communities in Ephesus. This was not necessarily an interaction without problems; it is possible that the overrealized eschatology of the opponents of "Paul" at 2 Timothy 2:18 is derived from a misunderstanding not of Pauline theology but rather of the equally realized eschatology of the Johannine school.[85] Such evidence, however, does not constitute evidence of federation such as that found at Rome. Nonetheless, if we were to hypothesize such federation, then we may find that this would be more than adequate to explain the apparent synonymy of presbyter and *episkopos* at Acts 20, as may now be observed.

ACTS 20 AS EVIDENCE FOR FEDERATION AT EPHESUS

Although Acts is hardly the most reliable basis on which to construct history, Acts 20 is one of the fundamental texts on which the consensus of synonymy is built. As we have seen, at Acts 20:17 Paul summons the elders of the Ephesian church (*presbyterous tēs ekklēsias*) to Miletus and addresses them, reminding them to shepherd the flock "in which the Holy Spirit has set you as overseers [*episkopous*]."[86] The basis for alleging synonymy is clear; thus not only Lightfoot, but virtually every commentator, has assumed that this refers to a single group of people known by two alternate titles[87] or else has denied that *episkopos* here is a title.[88] However, the text may also indicate that federation is meant. By this understanding, in referring to the group, Luke refers to them as *presbyteroi*, whereas when Luke's Paul, in his speech, refers to them in their individual settings, he refers to them as *episkopoi*. Thus, if the possibility of federation among Christian communities across traditions and within theological traditions has been established, then we may explain

85. See P. H. Towner, "Gnosis and Realized Eschatology in Ephesus (of the Pastoral Epistles) and the Corinthian Enthusiasm," *JSNT* 31 (1987): 95–124.

86. Acts 20:28.

87. Well expressed by C. K. Barrett: "It is evident that the words were in Luke's time more or less equivalent; had it not been so Luke could hardly have written as he did" ("Paul's Address to the Ephesian Elders," in Jervell and Meeks, eds., *God's Christ and His People*, 113).

88. Thus Rudolf Schnackenberg, "Episkopos und Hirtenamt: Zu Apg 20,28," in *Schriften zum Neuen Testament: Exegese in Fortschritt und Wandel* (Munich: Kösel, 1971), 247–66; Evald Lövestam, "Paul's Address at Miletus," *ST* 41 (1987): 7–8; Bartlett, *Ministry in the New Testament*, 132.

the apparent synonymy of terms within Acts 20 on that basis. However, even if these are simply the leaders of the Pauline churches, it is entirely possible that they have the collective designation of presbyters.

There are, however, other possible interpretations.

First, we may note the suggestion of Schnackenberg that the term *episkopoi* here is not a title at all, but rather is bound up to the shepherd imagery employed at this point, as the gathered presbyters are said to be *episkopoi* to shepherd the church of God.[89] On this understanding there would be a single class of leaders called, individually and collectively, "presbyters"; this understanding of the evidence of Acts 20 would be entirely consistent and would conform, moreover, with the evidence of Acts 14:28 noted below. Although Schnackenberg seems fundamentally to follow the consensus in his comments overall on the formation of Christian office, his argument is interesting in that he points out that the term *episkeptesthai* is employed in the Septuagint in the context of discussing the duties of (metaphorical) shepherds. Thus, in Jeremiah 23:2 the shepherds of Israel who have scattered the flock are said not to have looked out for them (*ouk epeskepsasthe auta*), and God himself, in Ezekiel 34:11, states that he will seek out the sheep and will oversee them (*episkepsomai auta*). Lövestam similarly suggests that the imagery of the shepherd, derived from Ezekiel 34, stands behind the latter part of the speech; the charge to the hearers not to profit from the flock but to protect it is implicitly contrasted with the behavior of the false shepherds arraigned by Ezekiel.[90]

Prast and Schürmann likewise suggest that *episkopos* is a functional description of the duties of the presbyters,[91] and Trebilco comes close to this position: "*Episkopos* is not used here as an official title, but rather indicates the function of the presbyters. Thus all the elders perform the function of overseeing." However, such is the power of the consensus and the confusion over what synonymy actually means that Trebilco then contradicts his previous statement: "Probably both terms were used in Luke's time for leaders."[92]

89. Schnackenberg, "Episkopos und Hirtenamt." He is followed by Dietrich-Alex Koch, "Die Entwicklung der Ämter in frühchristlichen Gemeinden Kleinasiens," in *Neutestamentliche Ämtermodelle im Kontext*, ed. Thomas Schmeller, Martin Ebner, and Rudolf Hoppe, QD 239 (Freiburg: Herder, 2010), 182.

90. Lövestam, "Paul's Address," 7–8.

91. Franz Prast, *Presbyter und Evangelium in nachapostolischer Zeit: Die Abschiedsrede des Paulus in Milet (Apg 20,17–38) im Rahmen der lukanischen Konzeption der Evangeliumsverkündigung*, FB 29 (Stuttgart: Katholisches Bibelwerk, 1979), 358; Heinz Schürmann, "Das Testament des Paulus für die Kirche," in *Traditionsgeschichtliche Untersuchungen zu den synoptischen Evangelien: Beiträge*, KBANT (Düsseldorf: Patmos, 1968), 332. Schürmann several times writes of "episcopal presbyters."

92. Trebilco, *Early Christians in Ephesus*, 187–88.

However, either the leaders were called *presbyteroi*, if the reference to *episkopoi* is purely functional, or they were called *episkopoi*.

An interesting variation on the functional hypothesis is provided by Bobertz, who suggests that one of the presbyters might be designated the *episkopos* on occasion and act as the "president" when the eucharistic meal was celebrated.[93] However, although this may make sense of the variation in terms in Titus, in that those who are to be appointed as presbyters are to have the qualities attached to an *episkopos* (because they may have to act as such on occasion), it makes no sense of the language of Acts 20, in that there is no reason why those presbyters should be described as *episkopoi* if they are to act as such only on occasion, nor does it make sense of an address to *episkopoi* as opposed to *presbyteroi* (which would be the obvious collective designation).

The reason for rejecting Schnackenberg's suggestion is simply that the appearance of the term *episkopos* for a leader in an individual church, both at a time prior to Luke's writing and in a period probably roughly contemporary, supports the probability that the term is a fixed term to refer to leaders and therefore is not here simply a reference to the function of people called "presbyters." Perhaps the septuagintal language of "shepherds" and "watchers" provoked the use of the term here, but, more to the point, the employment of the term implies that the hearers would have understood that it applied to themselves, since it was a recognized title. It perhaps is possible that the existence of the title provokes the shepherd imagery rather than the other way around. I will suggest an alternative derivation of the term in the next chapter, one that gains better support by virtue of its wider attestation.

Other suggestions that may be noted are those of Budesheim, who suggests that the speech, including the reference to *episkopoi*, was found by Luke in a source, whereas the reference to *presbyteroi* at Acts 20:17 is the result of Luke's composition and is a redactional transition,[94] and of Blasi, for whom it is the mention of *presbyteroi* that is in the source and of *episkopoi* that is redactional.[95] In either event, the implication is that for Luke, at any rate, the terms had a degree of overlap.

Nonetheless, the point is made that this statement in Acts 20 is not as straightforward as it seems at first; *presbyteros* and *episkopos* are not simply

93. Charles A. Bobertz, "The Development of Episcopal Order," in *Eusebius, Christianity, and Judaism* ed. Harold W. Attridge and Gohei Hata (Detroit: Wayne State University Press, 1992), 187.

94. Thomas L. Budesheim, "Paul's Abschiedsrede in the Acts of the Apostles," *HTR* 69 (1976): 24.

95. Anthony J. Blasi, "Office Charisma in Early Christian Ephesus?" *SocRel* 56 (1995): 248–49. Blasi's argument is that Luke is attempting to forge an identification of the two groups. On this, see my comments in chap. 5 below, under the heading "*Verschmelzung* as an Explanation of Monepiscopacy."

synonyms. Moreover, we may note that in Acts 20:17 the elders are qualified as presbyters "of the church" (*tēs ekklēsias*). Whereas this use of the singular might imply that all the elders are found within a single Christian community, it is clear enough that elders from a number of Christian communities are intended; we are hardly meant to imagine that there is a single Ephesian Christian community. Similarly, at Acts 20:28 there is a singular use of the word when those who are made *episkopoi* are told to shepherd "the church" (*tēn ekklēsian*) of God. The plurality of *episkopoi* indicates once again that a plurality of Christian communities is intended, but that collectively they form a single church, even as they federate. We may note the same usage in Paul's writing, as he addresses the "church of God . . . in Corinth."[96] In Corinth there certainly are individual households that collectively make up the church; although at this time they might not properly be identified as a federation, the conditions are in place by which such a federation might come about and, as is suggested below, federate rapidly.

There is more here than an address to Ephesian elders, for when Paul discusses his ministry, it does not have reference simply to the report of the Ephesian ministry described in the previous chapter; there is nothing in the speech of Paul's tears, nor clear reference to the persecution at Ephesus, but there is reference to speaking from house to house, which did not occur in Ephesus. Lambrecht thus suggests that this is a retrospective of Paul's entire missionary activity in that part of Asia;[97] as such, we may imagine a wider gathering of elders from the Christian communities. In particular it would be surprising if there were no Christian presence in Miletus itself, given that Luke has stated that the whole of Asia had heard the word of God. Indeed, in the light of the programmatic role of this speech in Acts overall, Dibelius suggests that the historical context is left behind as Luke, through Paul, addresses the whole of the church in what is effectively his will and testament, appealing constantly to his own example as a means for directing the future conduct of the church's leaders.[98] Although certainly the concerns addressed go far beyond those of any single Christian community, we may best see this in the light of the idea of federated local communities proposed here rather

---

96. 1 Cor. 1:2: τῇ ἐκκλησίᾳ τοῦ θεοῦ . . . ἐν Κορίνθῳ.

97. J. Lambrecht, "Paul's Farewell-Address at Miletus (Acts 20,17–38)," in *Les Actes des Apôtres: Traditions, rédaction, théologie*, ed. J. Kremer, BETL 48 (Gembloux: Ducolot, 1979), 335.

98. Martin Dibelius, "The Speeches in Acts and Ancient Historiography," in *Studies in the Acts of the Apostles*, ed. Heinrich Greeven, trans. Mary Ling (London: SCM, 1956), 155–58. Lövestam ("Paul's Address," 1) similarly suggests that the character of the speech is such that it is addressed to all those with responsibility for leadership in Pauline congregations.

than an abstract church. A federated group of local Christian communities collectively makes up the Asian church.[99]

If each is, in his (or her) own congregation, an *episkopos*, this would explain the employment of the term here. Collectively, however, in their gathering at Miletus they may be considered the presbyters of the church, and this designation is employed to refer to their summons to Miletus.[100] Lightfoot's explanation of the variation in terms is thus not the only possible explanation of the vocabulary employed. This alternative explanation is itself based on a hypothesis, but it has at least as much right of consideration as the standard reading, especially in the light of other evidence of federations. I am not concerned at this point with the content of Paul's speech; for the moment I am solely concerned with the issue of whether "presbyter" and *episkopos* are synonymous terms here, and whether I may claim to have propounded an explanation for the flexibility in terminology within the speech alternative to synonymy.

In its setting in the narrative of Acts, Lambrecht points out, Paul's speech is a hinge between the Asian ministry and his arrest in Jerusalem. As such, it is addressed from the (idealized) time of Paul to the realities of the contemporary readers in contemporary Asia.[101] This raises the question of whether it casts any light on issue of the designation of leaders in Ephesus itself, albeit at the time of Luke rather than of Paul. This is hard to say. The speech certainly is a Lukan construction,[102] and although Trebilco argues that the speech records some Ephesian tradition,[103] it would be unwise to build history on such a foundation. Lambrecht and Barrett similarly suggest that there may be some tradition behind the narrative of Paul's leave-taking at Miletus,[104] but that does not mean that the speech attributed to Paul would in all its details be an accurate account, and we may recall that our concern here is with a very small detail within the speech.[105] However, even if the Pauline farewell constructed

---

99. Pius-Roman Tragan ("Les 'destinateurs' du discours de Milet: Une approche du cadre communautaire d'Ac 20,18–35," in *À cause de l'évangile: Études sur les Synoptiques et les Actes offertes au P. Jacques Dupont à l'occasion de son 70e anniversaire*, LD 123 [Paris: Cerf, 1985], 780) similarly sees the whole leadership of the Asian church implied in the content of Paul's address.

100. So, similarly, Wagner (*Anfänge*, 118) sees the term as indicating an "örtliches Gremium."

101. Lambrecht, "Paul's Farewell-Address," 333.

102. So Prast, *Presbyter und Evangelium*, 28–38, giving ample argument.

103. Trebilco, *Early Christians in Ephesus*, 176–83.

104. Lambrecht, "Paul's Farewell-Address," 321; Barrett "Paul's Address," 108–9.

105. There was, of course, no stenographic account of Paul's speech; we may, moreover, note with Dibelius ("Speeches in Acts," 139) the manner in which contemporary writers felt free to recast speeches by examining the speeches of biblical characters in Josephus, comparing *B.J.* 1.19.4 with *A.J.* 15.5.3, and the two versions of Claudius's speech conferring the *ius honorum* on the people of Gaul at *CIL* 13.1668 and Tacitus, *Ann.* 11.24. Lambrecht ("Paul's Farewell-Address") suggests, interestingly, that the term *episkopos* may be intended as a recollection of

in this speech is fictive, it represents the reality of the time of Luke for some Christian communities in major urban centers at least. There are individual leaders in churches, collectively and federally known as the presbyters, known individually as *episkopoi*.

This account may be compared to that of Trebilco, who argues for communication between and among Ephesian churches: "Luke envisaged a joint leadership structure in the Ephesian community."[106] If by this he means federated leadership, I would agree; but it seems that he means that the community, including all the individual Christian gatherings and households, was governed by a single board of directors. Of this there is no evidence. Trebilco summons up the idea of joint leadership on the basis that no individual leader is named. However, this illustrates a fundamental confusion in the consensus, namely, the inability to distinguish between an *episkopos* in a single community (an *Einzelgemeinde*) and a *monepiskopos* (set over an *Ortskirche*), which comes about through the assumption that leadership was originally collective. I will return to that point, but for the present it is sufficient to suggest that the picture of individual household churches in Rome enables us to see Ephesus likewise as a series of individual churches with their own leaders, contributing to a federation, and that this, rather than synonymy, provides an adequate explanation of the terminology employed when referring to these leaders in Acts 20.

THE QUESTION OF *PRESBYTEROI* AT ACTS 14:23

Whereas the possibility of a reference to *episkopoi* meeting in federation at Ephesus might supply a rationale for the description of these *episkopoi* as presbyters, we must wrestle with the uncertainty as to whether Luke has any actual knowledge of Ephesus. The speech is redactional and thus, it might be argued, has no relevance for Ephesus but rather for the place of composition. Such an argument might then develop the statement in Acts 14:23 that Paul and Barnabas appointed (*cheirotonēsantes*) presbyters for the church (*kat' ekklēsian*). This, it might be argued, is a redactional statement, as this concludes a journey that brings the apostles back to Antioch, from which they went forth at Acts 13:1,[107] or else, even if not a purely redactional construction, it is told in Luke's language and thus reveals more of Luke than it does of the

---

Pauline ecclesiology, with reference to Phil. 1:1. However, he states, "In his [Luke's] own days, on the other hand, the authority in the churches of Asia Minor was probably in the hands of the πρεσβύτεροι." The latter assertion remains to be tested. I may already, at this stage of the inquiry, however, suggest that this takeover of episcopal authority by presbyters, only for it in time to be returned to the hands of *episkopoi*, would be a strange proceeding.

106. Trebilco, *Early Christians in Ephesus*, 188.

107. So Gerd Lüdemann, *Early Christianity according to the Traditions in Acts: A Commentary*, trans. John Bowden (London: SCM, 1989), 163–64.

historical situation that it reports.[108] Thus, it might be argued, Luke knows simply presbyteral order, and this presbyteral order is that to which reference is made in his redactional construction of Paul's speech.

Some attention, however, needs to be paid to the statement that the presbyters were appointed "for the church" (*kat' ekklēsian*). This might be taken to mean that a plurality of presbyters was appointed in each church, taking the *kata* as distributive.[109] Alternatively, however, given that the plurality of churches in and around Ephesus is described as a single *ekklēsia*, it may be that the plurality of leaders is intended for a plurality of churches. As such, *kat' ekklēsian* is seen to qualify not the verb but the noun, "presbyters," and the *kata* is simply used as a genitive. The presbyters are specifically described as being presbyters of the church, just as we read of the presbyters of the church at Acts 20:17, and as such, this may, once again, be a collective designation.

Even if the account is taken at face value, as it is by Nellessen, who argues that there is little redactional language in this verse, and that the scenario is entirely historically comprehensible,[110] this interpretation may still hold good. Paul and Barnabas are appointing leaders for the church, the passage states. The leaders are not individually termed, but rather are termed by a collective title.[111]

Whereas nothing explicitly is said regarding the function of the presbyters, their appointment by the apostles in the context of the apostles' departure may be taken to indicate that they are to continue in their own churches the apostles' functions, described in Acts 14:22 as "strengthening" (*epistērizontes*) and "exhorting" (*parakalountes*).[112] The same, indeed, may be seen as the function of the speech at Miletus.[113] Beyond the text, however, I may suggest that the federation of presbyters is the means by which the congregations may remain in contact with one another, once the apostle who goes from one to the other has ceased to be present with them.

108. So Prast, *Presbyter und Evangelium*; Koch "Entwicklung," 167–68. The possibilities with regard to redactional construction or reported tradition are laid out by E. Nellessen, "Die Presbyter der Gemeinden in Lykaonien und Pisidien (Apg 14,23)," in Kremer, *Les Actes des Apôtres*, 493–95.

109. So, apparently, C. K. Barrett, *A Critical and Exegetical Commentary on the Acts of the Apostles*, 2 vols., ICC (Edinburgh: T&T Clark, 1994), 1:687–88; Nellessen, "Presbyter der Gemeinden," 493; Prast, *Presbyter und Evangelium*, 212. Prast claims the support of Henry Cadbury in seeing this *kata* as distributive, claiming it as typically Lukan style. However, Cadbury (*The Style and Literary Method of Luke*, HTS 6 [Cambridge, MA: Harvard University Press, 1920], 117) simply states that it is a grammatical peculiarity of Luke in temporal phrases.

110. Nellessen, "Presbyter der Gemeinden."

111. So also Wagner, *Anfänge*, 118–19.

112. So Prast, *Presbyter und Evangelium*, 216.

113. As is argued by Schürmann, "Testament des Paulus." See the discussion on pp. 329–30 below regarding the question of succession.

Titus as Evidence for Federation at Ephesus

If Acts is a poor basis on which to construct history, Titus is even less secure.[114] Nonetheless, the fact that presbyters are mentioned in Titus 1:5, and that subsequently the qualifications for *episkopoi* are given, means it is possible that the terms are being used here synonymously. Once again, it is suggested, the phenomenon may be explained by postulating a federation of Christian communities at Ephesus; the fictive Paul is, I may suggest, instructing the fictive Titus to establish the same system in (fictive) Crete. I may also note the possibility that Acts 20 and the Pastoral Epistles lie along a common trajectory, with a common view of ecclesiastical leadership.[115]

At this point I must note that only Titus is under consideration. I will discuss 1 Timothy in due course. The letters to Timothy assume the existence of presbyters, whereas Titus seems to be introducing them. This, plus the different fictive settings of the letter, is sufficient to allow me for the moment at least to discuss the letters without reference to each other. This is not to deny the extent of common ground between them, not the least that both are addressed to apostolic delegates for their direction. These delegates have a specific role, and they are not local officers as such. Fiore compares these letters to the appointment charter for an *oikonomos*, P.Tebt. 703, which sets out specific duties and concludes by stating the general qualities of the officer.[116] As such, the note does not simply convey instructions regarding duties but conveys the legitimating power of the superior.[117] Wolter points out that the same is the case with imperial officers, noting in particular the example of Pliny, who is in Bithynia to represent Trajan and to act on his behalf.[118] Likewise, Titus and Timothy's activity is legitimated by Paul. However, by virtue

---

114. The pseudonymy and the relative lateness of the Pastoral Epistles are assumed, rather than argued, throughout. However, even if the Pastoral Epistles are authentic and not interpolated, this barely affects the arguments presented, although we would have to imagine that the direction of these apostolic delegates regarding the appointment and arrangement of officers is taking place slightly earlier than we would otherwise anticipate. I am increasingly inclining to the view that, whereas 1 Timothy certainly is pseudonymous, 2 Timothy may be authentic.

115. So Bartlett, *Ministry in the New Testament*, 153–54. For a summary of linkage between the Pastoral Epistles and Luke-Acts and literature, see Jerome D. Quinn, "The Last Volume of Luke: The Relation of Luke-Acts to the Pastoral Epistles," in *Perspectives on Luke-Acts*, ed. C. H. Talbert, PRStSS 5 (Edinburgh: T&T Clark, 1978), 62–75.

116. On *oikonomoi* more generally, see chap. 2 below, under the heading "*Episkopoi* in Households and Associations."

117. Benjamin Fiore, *The Function of Personal Example in the Socratic and Pastoral Epistles*, AnBib 105 (Rome: Biblical Institute Press, 1986), 79–84.

118. Michael Wolter, *Die Pastoralbriefe als Paulustradition*, FRLANT 146 (Göttingen: Vandenhoeck & Ruprecht, 1988), 167. He also points out Domitian's *Mandata* to Claudius Athenodorus (*IGLS* 5.1998).

of the apostolic nature of their delegation, the setting of the letter would seem to imply that they are present with the congregations in order simply to perform the instructions given, to set right what is amiss; thus, the powers of the apostolic delegates are to pass to the local officers. The addressees are both temporary delegates and mirror the relations that are to be obtained between the officers and the congregations.[119] For this reason, the instructions given to Timothy reflect those that in turn are to qualify the officers. Moreover, much of the material relating to these officers, as to groups within the congregation, is traditional; as such, the implication is that this charge in turn is to be passed on. However, although the two letters form a collection, I consider the presbyters of Titus separately from those of 1 Timothy because I intend to argue that the presbyters of Titus 1:5 are, like those of Rome, persons who, whatever their status and title in their individual congregations, are to hold office as presbyters on a citywide basis.

Titus is told to appoint *kata polin presbyterous*.[120] According to Quinn, the introduction of presbyters is precisely the purpose of this passage. With reference to Titus 1:5, he notes that "Paul" begins by stating that presbyters should be appointed in every town and gives some qualification for such presbyters. Then he goes on to state that an *episkopos* must be blameless and proceeds with a further list of qualifications. The shift from the plural to the singular is odd, so Quinn suggests that the term (*episkopos*) belongs with the subsequent list of qualifications, which is derived from a different Jewish background, namely, an Essene background (he believes that the *episkopos* here is derived from the *mebaqqer*, a point about which discussion must also be postponed), and has been left in place by the redactor to assure the hearers of the fundamental compatibility of the presbyters, who are now being appointed, and the *episkopos*, who is a known quantity.[121] The terms, for Quinn, are intended to be "nearly" synonymous, but he is not clear exactly what the extent of their similarity and distinction actually is. Meier similarly equates presbyter and *episkopos* and likewise recognizes that the qualifications are traditional, and that *episkopos* was the word that stood in this qualification list. He smoothes over the transition by reading the singular as generic.[122] But if the passage is really about appointing presbyters, why should the term *episkopos* then be introduced?

119. Thus Hermann von Lips, *Glaube, Gemeinde, Amt: Zum Verständnis der Ordination in den Pastoralbriefen*, FRLANT 122 (Göttingen: Vandenhoeck & Ruprecht, 1979), 108.

120. Titus 1:5.

121. Jerome D. Quinn, *The Letter to Titus: A New Translation with Notes and Commentary and an Introduction to Titus, I and II Timothy, the Pastoral Epistles*, AB 35 (New York: Doubleday, 1990), 88.

122. John P. Meier, "Presbyteros in the Pastoral Epistles," *CBQ* 33 (1973): 337–39.

I must agree that the qualifications for these presbyters are the same as those for *episkopoi*, and I note that the introduction is an introduction of presbyters. I may also agree that the qualification list is traditional and is intended to qualify *episkopoi*. However, if the terms are synonymous, then there are three possible explanations of "Paul's" agenda here: (1) officers are being introduced for the first time; (2) an existing officer known to the Cretans, the *episkopos*, is being renamed as a *presbyteros*; (3) no new kind of officer is being introduced to the Cretan church.

The second possibility would be an exercise in pointlessness, especially given that the term *episkopos* is known in Ephesus, to the polity of which Crete is being conformed.

However, the first possibility, which is actually the situation largely assumed, on the basis that the church order of Crete is undeveloped, is equally problematic. For this to succeed, it must be assumed that the fictive community where Titus finds himself had previously had no officer at all. Were it further assumed that the island had been evangelized by a Pauline mission and that this mission, like Paul, was uninterested in the establishment of office, and if it were further assumed that the letter is to be dated to a period not long after the departure of the evangelizing apostle(s), this would be possible, but these are large assumptions.[123] What is more telling is that, as we have already seen, having instructed the appointment of *presbyterous*, Titus 1:7 uses the term *episkopos* in what is likely to be a traditional list. It would seem impossibly confusing for a community without church order (as this construction would have it) to be told to appoint officers called *presbyteroi* and then to be presented with a traditional list of qualifications for an *episkopos* without yet knowing what either of these creatures actually was.

If no new officer, however, is being introduced, that too would seem odd. Why, in this event, is the subject addressed? A distinct solution is not hard to find. Whereas there is something new being introduced, the introduction is not of officers *tout court*—for the Cretan community, I may suggest, is familiar with *episkopoi* and would recognize the qualification list—nor is any particular kind of officer being introduced, but rather the existing officers are being appointed to distinct and new responsibilities. The introduction is an introduction of presbyters. These presbyters must be distinct from *episkopoi* (for otherwise there would be no point introducing them), but there must be a relationship with the *episkopoi* because their qualifications are the same as episcopal qualifications, and the episcopal qualifications are introduced with a resumptive *gar*. The key lies in observing that presbyters whom Titus is to appoint are presbyters *kata polin*.

123. It is, nonetheless, a set of assumptions made by Merkle, *Elder and Overseer*, 142–48.

Generally, *kata polin* is rendered as a distributive "in every town" and beyond that is allowed to pass without comment.[124] However, the history of exegesis raises a number of significant questions. In particular, it is entirely possible that this construction is simply used as a genitive, as Baur suggests. As such, it would mean that presbyters are to be appointed not "in every town" but "for each town."[125] In spite of the denial by Rothe, who cites Salmasius, this is grammatically possible;[126] Rothe is led to his reading not simply by the grammar of the text but also due to his conviction that the synagogues were under corporate leadership. The reading proposed here is also derived less from grammar than from an attempt to see the text in a historical context. The question that follows from this is whether, given that more than one town is concerned, there is a single presbyter being appointed to each town or multiple presbyters for each town. Whereas Hammond had sought to suggest the former,[127] a view that might be sustainable if the *kata* is read as distributive, this is rather difficult if the clause is read adjectivally.

We may next inquire whether *kata polin* qualifies the verb *katastēsēs* (in which case it might be argued that one presbyter per town is appointed) or the noun *presbyterous*. The question is barely asked, although discussion of the passage seems to assume that the clause is governed by the verb, whereas I suggest that *kata polin* qualifies *presbyterous* and explains the nature of the presbyters who are to be appointed.[128] They are presbyters holding office on a citywide basis. This interpretation does not appear to have been suggested

---

124. So, e.g., Knight, *Pastoral Epistles*, 288; I. Howard Marshall, *A Critical and Exegetical Commentary on the Pastoral Epistles*, ICC (Edinburgh: T&T Clark, 1999), 152; William Mounce, *Pastoral Epistles*, WBC 46 (Nashville: Nelson, 2000), 387, without discussion; also, David C. Verner, *The Household of God: The Social World of the Pastoral Epistles*, SBLDS 71 (Chico, CA: Scholars Press, 1981), 156, deducing thereby that the city (rather than the individual household) is the primary element in the author's understanding of Christian groups. Certainly this reading goes back to Rothe, *Anfänge*, 183–84.

125. So Baur, *Pastoralbriefe*, 81. According to Rothe (*Anfänge*, 184), Baur has overlooked the distributive meaning of κατά. Rather, I may respond on Baur's behalf as on my own, it is not overlooked, but a different understanding is preferred.

126. Rothe (*Anfänge*, 182–83) cites Salmasius, *Walonis Messalini de episcopis et presbyteris*, 91. However, Salmasius (92) admits that this is a possible reading.

127. Hammond (*Paraphrase and Annotations*, 715), who refers to his reading of κατά as "church by church" (394) and here, as there, suggests that one elder (= bishop) should be appointed to each town. It is difficult, though not impossible, to sustain the distributive sense of κατά and yet suggest a distribution of single *presbyteroi*, as Hammond does. This is actually the reading opposed by Salmasius, who writes, "Non igitur Paulus Tito mandavit, ut plures sic in tota insula constitueret Episcopos, quo singulae civitates unum ac suum haberent sed ut καταστήσῃς κατὰ πόλιν πρεσβυτέρους, id est per singulas civitates Cretae insulae plures designaret Presbyteros eosdem Episcopos" (*Walonis Messalini de episcopis et presbyteris*, 92).

128. So Campbell, *Elders*, 197–98. However, as will be observed below, Campbell fails to exploit the insight that his exegesis gains and confuses the matter again.

before Campbell, though Baur comes close, but is, I maintain, critical for the interpretation of the passage. It is entirely possible that *kata* with the accusative might qualify a noun, as it is used as such within this letter at Titus 1:4, where Titus is described as Paul's child "in a common faith" (*kata koinēn pistin*).

If we allow that the expression *kata polin* qualifies the noun "presbyters" rather than the verb "appoint" (*katastēsēs*), then the instruction is not simply to appoint presbyters but specifically to appoint town-presbyters. Titus, according to this understanding, is being instructed to appoint not officers for individual churches, but rather officers who will act *kata polin* in the manner that already occurs in Ephesus, from which the letter is being sent (and as at Rome). Although this is not stated, it would be reasonable to suppose that these *presbyteroi* are to be appointed from the already existing *episkopoi*. If this hypothesis may be allowed to stand for a moment, then in this light the following list of qualifications for *episkopoi* makes complete sense. The qualifications that apply to *episkopoi* thus apply, *a minore ad maius*, to *kata polin presbyteroi*. The switch from plural to singular is also readily explainable, for although there was a plurality of *episkopoi* across Crete, the singular is used in the traditional list on the basis that it applied to a single household, and that this is taken and used as a generic singular. The *presbyteroi kata polin* are, however, by their very nature to be plural.

While I acknowledge a major debt to Campbell in this argument, it seems strange that he then goes on to identify these presbyters *kata polin* with *monepiskopoi*; this confusion, which is hard to explain, rather vitiates his argument. But if we accept his insight that *kata polin* qualifies *presbyterous*, then we may readily see these presbyters in the light of federated presbyters elsewhere. A similar confusion emerges in the work of Wagner, who accepts on the basis of Campbell's work that the presbyters are city-elders;[129] he explains the shift to *episkopoi* by arguing that the city-presbyters are the pool from whom the *episkopos* is to be elected. This certainly makes sense of the progress of thought, but once again this assumes that monepiscopacy has already emerged. I must return to this point below, but for the moment let us accept that Titus is referring to city-presbyters, who may also be *episkopoi*, and not simply using two synonymous terms to describe one office.

Greater clarity yet may be found by engaging at this point with the arguments put by Merkle against Campbell.[130] Merkle is arguing for complete synonymy here; he is at least clear about what he means.

---

129. Wagner, *Anfänge*, 161.
130. Merkle, *Elder and Overseer*, 142–48.

First, he suggests that the connective *gar* in Titus 1:7 ties the two sections together, implying that the same office is meant. But the *gar* works in the same way for the suggestion that they are the same people, though not the same office; that is to say, the *episkopoi* who already exist are the candidates to be *presbyteroi*.

Second, he presents a group of arguments relating to the switch from plural *presbyteroi* to the singular *episkopos*. There is little here with which to disagree, but also nothing that necessitates a view that the two offices are identical.

Third, he points out that *kathistēmi*, used to refer to the appointment of somebody to an office, requires an accusative, and that the only accusative here is *presbyterous*. *Presbyterous* must therefore connote an office. Again I agree, except to say that the office is not the office of presbyter but specifically presbyter *kata polin*.

Fourth, he points out the possibility that the singular *episkopos* with the definite article may be the result of employing a preformed unit of tradition. Again, I may agree, but without reaching the same conclusions that he draws from that insight, namely, that the offices are identical. With him we may indeed compare the qualification list at 1 Timothy 3:2 and also note the absence of the qualification "not a new convert"[131] from the list in Titus. Merkle explains the absence by suggesting that the Cretan church is a new church, and thus all the converts would be new. I may rejoin by suggesting that since these *episkopoi* have already been appointed, the qualification is not relevant; what is relevant is that these *episkopoi* are qualified to go to the next stage of responsibility, one that takes them beyond their own household.

Finally, he suggests that given that the church in Crete was a new foundation, it would not know the "developed concept of a monarchical bishop." I may point out that, yet again, he confuses a single *episkopos* holding responsibility in a single Christian community and a *monepiskopos*.

To read Titus 1:5–8 as making provision for the appointment of *presbyteroi kata polin* from those who were already *episkopoi* (*kat' oikon*) not only solves all the exegetical problems associated with the passage but also coheres with what is known of practice elsewhere. Because the phrase has since Rothe, as far as I can see, universally been taken to mean "in every town," the (plural) presbyters of Titus are discussed in the light of the presbyters of 1 Timothy. If, however, *kata polin* qualifies the *presbyterous* rather than the verb, then the discussion must be different. The presbyters of 1 Timothy are not the same as the presbyters *kata polin* of Titus because they are not

---

131. 1 Tim. 3:6: μὴ νεόφυτον.

defined according to their jurisdiction,[132] and so one usage cannot be brought to bear upon the other.

I will return to the Pastoral Epistles below, and so I do not discuss the presbyters of 1 Timothy here, though it may be seen already that if the terms are used in distinct senses in the two letters (the term is not qualified in this way in 1 Timothy), then a great deal of confusion may be avoided. If, however, the presbyters of Titus are specifically *kata polin*, we may ask why such an institution was deemed necessary for Crete, beyond the fact that it was already found in Ephesus. I have already noted that the functions of federation in Rome were fundamentally communication with outside churches, the delineation of orthodoxy, and the transmission of writings. Principal among the concerns of the Pastoral Epistles is the growth of what might somewhat anachronistically be called "heresy." Thus I may suggest that the rationale behind introducing this institution to Crete is that the presbyters *kata polin* were to be the means by which the boundaries of doctrine were to be policed. Additionally, since the fictive setting is a piece of writing, I may suggest further that this writing was to be distributed through the means of the network of presbyters to the churches across the cities. Thus, the functions of transmitting writings and communicating beyond the city are being performed, as they were at Rome, by presbyters gathering *kata polin*.

The terms *episkopos* and *presbyteros* here, as in Acts 20, are not synonymous. There is a degree of overlap, but that is something distinct. The term *presbyteroi*, in both instances, denotes a gathering of those who act in their own communities as *episkopoi*; that is made clear in this instance by the attachment of a qualification list for *episkopoi*, with the implication that the presbyters *kata polin* are to be drawn from that group. In both instances, as in those instances drawn from the Roman evidence, *presbyteroi* is a collective term.

LATER EVIDENCE OF FEDERATION AT EPHESUS

In an attempt to deal with the issues raised at Rome due to the practice of Christians of Asian descent fasting on Sunday in preparation for the celebration of Pascha on 14 Nisan, Victor, acting, I have already suggested, principally as correspondent on behalf of the presbyters at Rome, wrote, according to Eusebius, to all the churches. Extant is a reply from Polycrates at Ephesus.[133] In this letter, defending Quartodeciman practice—the observance of the Pascha as an annual event on 14 Nisan—he states that he is an *episkopos*, as were seven of his kin. It is possible that, by now, the monepiscopate is established

132. The nature of the *presbyteroi* of 1 Timothy is discussed in chap. 3, under the heading "*Episkopos* and Presbyters in 1 Timothy."
133. Eusebius, *Hist. eccl.* 5.23–24.

in Ephesus. It is also possible that he is continuing to write as an *episkopos* of a single Christian community, and it is in this sense that he refers to himself. However, the fact that he apparently is writing on behalf of the Ephesian church would imply that if he is *episkopos* of a single household, he is nonetheless the correspondent on behalf of the gathered Ephesian churches.

It is impossible to be certain whether he writes as *monepiskopos* or as representative, or indeed whether he writes solely on behalf of the Johannine churches in Ephesus. The fact that no other letter from any other Ephesian group exists in the archive indicates, however, that he writes on behalf of the Ephesian congregations, either as *monepiskopos* or as representative. If the latter is the case, then this provides evidence for continued federation; if the former is the case, however, as is more probable, then this does not necessitate a denial that federation might have once existed in Ephesus, but rather implies that this federation has now brought about the monepiscopate as it would at Rome, and that the Pauline congregations have been brought into a single church with those of Johannine heritage.[134]

CONCLUSION ON FEDERATION AT EPHESUS

It is noteworthy that in going from Paul to Polycrates, I have leaped over Ignatius. Nonetheless, I have presented an argument to the effect that leaders of Christian communities in Ephesus were in contact with one another, that they met regarding matters of common concern, and that if we suppose, along Roman lines, that their collective designation was "presbyters," while *episkopos* was a designation that might be employed for them within their individual Christian communities, then the language is readily explainable in each context in which it is met.

Philippians as Further Evidence of Federation (and Not Synonymy)

This chapter started by examining the instances that have been adduced for the synonymy of the terms *episkopos* and *presbyteros*. I have concentrated on two particular texts that indicate synonymy, Acts 20 and Titus 1:5–8. I have argued that, just as in Rome, so in Ephesus leaders of individual Christian churches enjoyed some form of federation, and that *qua* federation, however they may have been designated within their own communities, they were known collectively as presbyters. For this reason there is fluidity in the address at Acts 20:17, and for this reason the qualifications of those who are to act in this way are the same as those given for individual *episkopoi* within

---

134. It is also noteworthy, if Polycrates is indeed *monepiskopos*, that Christians of Jewish descent (like Polycrates himself) are now in communion with non-law-observant Pauline Christians.

individual congregations. I further suggested that the Paul of Titus is urging
that this Ephesian institution be extended to Crete. In this light, I turn to other
evidence of federation that in turn may support the hypothesis developed thus
far, that "presbyter" might be a term denoting representatives of individual
congregations as part of a gathering from a larger area. In doing so, I may
have reference to another of the texts adduced by Lightfoot that is the basis
for the consensus.

One of the puzzles of Philippians is the opening address to the *episkopoi*
and *diakonoi* of the Philippian church,[135] puzzling because it provides the
only instance of any mention of these officers in a Pauline letter. I return to
the rationale for this address below, but even at this point I may suggest that
the letter provides evidence for a degree of federation among the churches
of Philippi. In doing so, I may note the suggestion of Campbell, followed by
Gehring, that there would have been more than one household church in any
given city. Thus, in Philippians Campbell explains the address to *episkopoi*
and *diakonoi* as implying an address to the leaders of the congregations in
Philippi collectively, suggesting in turn that the individuals addressed later in
the letter are the leaders of the individual household congregations.[136] Gehring
goes further and notes that the evidence of Acts, in reporting the foundation of two distinct house-churches, is an indication that there were multiple
congregations in the city.[137] If we accept that the individuals mentioned are
household leaders, we may recognize the significance of the plural address
to *episkopoi* as indicating that distinct congregations are being addressed
in a common letter that might be circulated around the churches in the city.[138]
For this to occur, there must be some loose relationship among the churches;
thus, the house-churches are characterized as a single *ekklēsia*.[139] In observing
this move toward federation, we once again see that one of the purposes of
federation was the transmission of literature. The federated leaders are not,
however, addressed as *presbyteroi*, which may be counted as an argument
against the reconstruction of early Christian community organization so far
essayed. I may respond, however, by pointing out that the Philippian letter is
somewhat earlier than any of the other evidence surveyed here. It is possible
that although communication is taking place between leaders of the churches,

135. Phil. 1:1.
136. Campbell, *Elders*, 123–25.
137. Roger W. Gehring, *House Church and Mission: The Importance of Household Structures in Early Christianity* (Peabody, MA: Hendrickson, 2004), 131–32.
138. So Ernst Dassmann, "Hausgemeinde und Bischofsamt," in *Vivarium: Festschrift Theodor Klauser zum 90. Geburtstag*, JAC 11 (Münster: Aschendorff, 1984), 89.
139. Phil. 4:15. On this, see Malherbe, *Social Aspects*, 70, 100–101.

it is not yet formalized, and the leaders of the individual churches have yet to adopt a formal corporate identity.

This account, moreover, may be contrasted to that of Lightfoot, who, noting the address solely to *episkopoi* and *diakonoi*, states, "It is incredible that he should recognise only the first and third order and pass over the second, though the second was absolutely essential to the existence of a church and formed the staple of its ministry."[140] One does not need to be a logician to see that this is a basically fallacious argument. Indeed, were it not for the influence that Lightfoot subsequently exercised, one would hardly be moved to bother to engage with such arguments.

Ysebaert does not use Lightfoot's argument, offering instead different arguments to sustain the thesis of the synonymy of *episkopos* and *presbyteros* based on Philippians 1:1. First, he notes that Paul is said in Acts 14:23 to have appointed *presbyteroi*, and yet the address here is to *episkopoi* and *diakonoi*. Further, he notes, Polycarp writes to the Philippians and mentions the presbyters, among them Valens.[141] I will return to the case of Valens below; there I will argue that the address to presbyters is an indication that the federation among Philippian communities is such that the institution of presbyters *kata polin* has come about by the time of that correspondence. Valens as a presbyter may well also be an *episkopos*; however, that is evidence not of the synonymy of the terms but rather of perionymy. As to Acts 14:23, which has already been discussed, I may respond that this is hardly reliable historical evidence for Philippi, not the least because first, Philippi is not mentioned in this account; second, as will be argued more extensively below, it seems that the Philippian church is not of Pauline foundation; and third, as pointed out above, the terminology, like that in Acts 20, might include reference to *episkopoi*.

Therefore, the address to the Philippian *episkopoi* and *diakonoi* provides no evidence for synonymy. What it does provide is evidence that the diverse Christian households of Philippi sustained communication with one another, and that the agents of communication were the appointed officers of the churches.

Conclusion

The federation of individual Christian households at a citywide level has been demonstrated with varying degrees of certitude in Ephesus, Corinth, Philippi, and Rome. The least certain of these is Ephesus, given that the two main sources, Titus and Acts 20, are not necessarily direct sources for the city.

140. Lightfoot, *Philippians*, 96–97.
141. Ysebaert, *Amtsterminologie*, 62–67.

However, in each instance the relationship between the words *presbyteros* and *episkopos* is readily explained by taking *presbyteroi* as a collective term for individual *episkopoi* gathered together.

We may see the process of federation as almost a natural development; even if not formalized, as soon as there is more than one Christian congregation in a city or town, the question of how the congregations are to relate to one another is raised. It is natural for such contact to be undertaken by the individual leaders of the houses.[142] This realization, while not entirely new,[143] enables us to escape from confusion over terminology, and in particular it enables us to clarify the relationship between the terms *presbyteroi* and *episkopoi*, a clarification that in turn opens up new possibilities in the search for the origins of monepiscopacy.

The principal aim of this chapter has been to examine the foundation of the consensus that the terms *presbyteros* and *episkopos* were synonymous, a consensus for which Lightfoot was taken as spokesperson. He discussed six texts that, he suggested, indicated that the two terms were synonymous. Two of these texts, Titus 1:5 and Acts 20, at first glance indicate synonymy. In response to this I have hypothesized a distinct picture of the formation of Christian office that offers an alternative understanding of the texts; synonymy is thus not proved. I may admit that the alternative proposed is likewise not proved, but as an alternative reading it is at least as credible.

Lightfoot's other texts were Philippians 1:1; 1 Peter 5:1–2; *1 Clement* 42; 44, and a group of texts from 1 Timothy. In the course of this discussion not only have the most compelling texts been addressed, but all the others, except those of 1 Timothy and 1 Peter, also have been treated. At this point, therefore, I may give brief attention to the text from 1 Peter, reserving a more detailed discussion for a later point and putting 1 Timothy aside altogether for the present. For the moment, all that is needed is to show that 1 Peter is a poor basis for arguing synonymy. Lightfoot writes, "St Peter, appealing to the 'presbyters' of the churches addressed by him, in the same breath urges them to 'fulfil the office of bishops' (*episkopountes*) with disinterested zeal (1 Pet. 5:1, 2)."[144] Whereas this stops short of asserting absolute synonymy, it might seem that there is a case to answer, given that the terms appear in such proximity, and given that the author addresses himself to the presbyters as a fellow presbyter (*sympresbyteros*). The text, however, is uncertain because

142. So Dassmann, "Hausgemeinde," 89.
143. In particular some form of federation is suggested by Rohde, *Urchristliche und früh-katholische Ämter*, 45. Here, however, the treatment is once again vitiated by a failure to appreciate the possibility that a single household might have a single *episkopos*.
144. Lightfoot, *Philippians*, 97.

the participle, *episkopountes*, is not secure in the manuscript tradition. The editors of the United Bible Societies' *Greek New Testament* were unable to determine the correct text,[145] and so there is little on which to base an assumption of synonymy. All the other texts may be read as indicating not that the terms were directly synonymous, but nonetheless that they were related, and that the relationship between them might readily be explained by postulating federation among individual Christian communities.

The idea of federation does not mean that the terms are not overlapping terms; indeed, my opening discussion allowed for a degree of relationship between the terms, but overlap is not the same as synonymy.

One implication of abandoning synonymy is the disappearance of the idea of multiple bishops in single communities. The idea of synonymy meant that when there was reference to multiple presbyters, this was taken as being the same as multiple *episkopoi*, and when multiple *episkopoi* are mentioned in a context, there was no inquiry made as to whether these were in a single community or multiple communities. The question was not asked because the distinction was not significant. However, if the hypothesis of federation has any validity, it requires us to distinguish between a local congregation and a gathering of congregational leaders. Hence, the term *monepiskopos*, or "monarchical *episkopos*," was conventionally used to describe a situation in which there was one bishop only, on the assumption that there had once been more than one. However, we may now ask whether Christian communities that knew the office of *episkopos* ever had more than one at a time. If they only ever had one, then the term *monepiskopos*, referring to a sole bishop in a community, would be simply a tautology. Further argument will be supplied below, but at this point I may suggest that there was never more than one *episkopos* in any given Christian congregation, though there might be multiple *episkopoi* across a town. A very clear statement of the idea of multiple *episkopoi* is presented by Zahn, which, in view of its clarity, may be allowed to stand for the consensus of collective leadership of which he is one representative:

> If we had only I Tim, we might infer from iii.1–13 that the officers of the Church were simply one *episkopos* and a number of *diakonoi*. The error of this conception we should immediately discover, however, from the fact that in both apostolic and post-apostolic times, whenever these two titles are used comprehensively to denote the officers of the local Church, several *episkopoi* as well as several *diakonoi* are mentioned. A form of government in which all the official service

145. Bruce M. Metzger, *A Textual Commentary on the Greek New Testament: A Companion Volume to the United Bible Societies' Greek New Testament* (London: United Bible Societies, 1971), 695–96.

.in the local Church was performed by one bishop and a number of deacons never existed.[146]

As evidence for this assertion he cites Philippians 1:1 as making reference to a "single church."[147] We do not know, however, that it was of a single church, and not of a number of Philippian churches, or rather a series of independent congregations that saw themselves as making up a single church.[148] As already suggested, the addresses to individuals may well be addresses to individual house-church leaders. Zahn continues by noting *1 Clement* 42:4, as well as *Shepherd of Hermas* 13:1 and the mention of plural *episkopoi* in the ninth *Similitude* (*Herm.* 104:2). Again, I have demonstrated in each instance that there is reference here to distinct churches. He goes on to say, "The single *proestōs* over against the plurality of *diakonoi* in Just *Apol.* 1.65, 67, can prove nothing to the contrary; for the *proestōs* is here viewed as the leader of the worship, and such leading can hardly be performed by more than one at a time."[149]

Here Zahn has a point; this statement does not prove that there was only a single *episkopos* in existence, but it does imply this, as will be noted below. For the moment it is sufficient to assert that there is no evidence to gainsay such an assertion and none to assert collegial leadership.[150]

There are further instances of reference to multiple *episkopoi*—again we may observe Acts 20—but in all these cases multiple Christian communities are being addressed, and so there is nothing here to suggest that there was necessarily more than one *episkopos* in each of these communities. In the following chapter I will present evidence of single leaders within single communities. Here is the significant point. The alleged synonymy of *episkopos* and *presbyteros* is essential if the hypothesis of multiple leaders in single Christian communities is to be sustained; the discussion of the relationship between these terms is thus not simply an argument over designation, but an argument over whether early Christian leadership was individualistic or collective. In the history of scholarship it is not clear whether the theory of synonymy gave rise to the idea of multiple leaders or whether the theory of multiple leaders led to an assumption of synonymy. To some extent this does

146. Theodor Zahn, *Introduction to the New Testament*, trans. John Moore Trout et al., 3 vols. (Edinburgh: T&T Clark, 1909), 2:91.

147. Ibid., 2:123.

148. Note the understanding of Malherbe (*Social Aspects*, 70, 101) of the manner in which independent churches might understand themselves as parts of a whole, noting that a letter to one house-church might serve as a letter to all, considered as a single entity.

149. Zahn, *Introduction to the New Testament*, 2:123.

150. The fact that the evidence for colleges of elders is thin to the point of being nonexistent is pointed out by Vogt, "Frühkirche und Amt," 469–70.

not matter; what does matter is that without synonymy there is no support for the theory of multiple leaders in single communities. There is, as already suggested, a fundamental confusion between *Gemeindeamt* and *Kirchenamt* (here using the terms in the sense in which Baur used them, to distinguish between office in a single congregation and office in a wider community);[151] so, in each instance when we meet an *episkopos*, we need to establish whether his office is a *Gemeindeamt* or a *Kirchenamt*—an office serving a congregation or an office serving a wider constituency—and when we cannot be sure about this, we at least must admit as much and refrain from drawing any further conclusion from uncertain evidence. That there might be multiple independent *episkopoi* is a consequence of recognizing that a town or city might have multiple independent Christian communities.

It is this inability, moreover, to distinguish congregational authority from federal authority that runs as a fault line through the work of Wagner, who, writing after Campbell, recognizes the possibility that there might be presbyters who hold office *kata polin*, and that individual house-churches might be in the hands of individual leaders.[152] However, when speaking of the Roman leadership at the time of *1 Clement*, Wagner states simply that leadership is collegial.[153] Certainly we may agree that the leadership of the Roman congregations overall is collegial, but the extent of the power and authority of this collegial gathering is, I may suggest, somewhat limited; and what is significant at this stage is the episcopate exercised in the individual congregations. His comments on Rome, based on the evidence provided by Hermas, suffer from the same problem, namely, that because there is no Roman episcopate, he suggests that the individual household congregations had collective leadership, and the terms "presbyter" and *episkopos* function as synonyms.[154] However, the households as such, I may suggest, had no collective leadership of themselves; rather, leadership, including liturgical leadership, was found solely within the individual churches, whereas the role of the federation was not that of leadership but, as has already been suggested, a policing of the boundaries of orthodoxy, the transmission of literature, and the conduct of relations with churches beyond the city.

Proof of the essentially episcopal nature of early Christian ministry is found in the survival in rural areas of single *episkopoi* in single communities, *episkopoi* who are not *monepiskopoi*, not because they are not single, but

151. Compare the use by Adolf von Harnack, who employed the terms to distinguish local officers from charismatic ministers whose ministry might extend to any congregation.

152. E.g., Wagner, *Anfänge*, 69, 118, 161.

153. Ibid., 234–35.

154. Ibid., 289–92.

because they have no subordinate ministers and hold responsibility in a single community. Thus, in an anonymous second-century anti-Montanist source, we meet Zotikos, a bishop from a village, Cumana.[155] Bishops from villages are encountered among the signatories of the Councils of Ancyra, Neocaesarea, and Nicaea,[156] and Sozomen reports even in the fifth century that "there are . . . many cities in Scythia, and yet they all have but one bishop; whereas, in other nations bishops serve as priests (*episkopoi hierountai*) even in villages, as I have myself observed in Arabia, and in Cyprus, and among the Novatians and Montanists of Phrygia."[157] I may suggest that these non-monepiscopal single *episkopoi* are a survival of an older system of single communities headed by *episkopoi*; they have survived either because of the remote nature of their villages—since within isolated villages there were neither other Christian communities with whom to federate[158] nor was there any advantage or reason formally to associate with other Christian communities—or, in the case of the Novatian and Montanist communities, who by virtue of their division from the wider church do not develop in the same manner and have retained an undeveloped ecclesiology, because of ecclesiastical isolation. A similar explanation may be applied to the reports of rural bishops among Quartodeciman communities in the fifth century.[159] If the hypothesis of multiple leadership had any validity, one would expect to find councils of presbyters in these rural situations.

In the process of showing that the hypothesis of synonymy stands on shaky ground, I have formulated a hypothesis regarding the original question, namely, the manner in which the monepiscopate emerged. I have argued that the sole bishop with subservient ministers (a *monepiskopos*) emerged from leadership

155. Quoted in Eusebius, *Hist. eccl.* 5.16.17.

156. Franz Gillmann, *Das Institut der Chorbischöfe im Orient: Historisch-kanonistische Studie* (Munich: Lentner, 1903), 33–4.

157. Sozomen, *Hist. eccl.* 7.19.

158. On the evangelization of the countryside and evidence for rural Christians in the first three centuries, see Gillmann, *Institut*, 16–26. The remote nature of the villages in Cappadocia is the reason adduced by C. H. Turner ("Ancient and Modern Church Organization," in *Studies in Early Church History* [Oxford: Clarendon, 1912], 31–70, 64–66) for the continuing prominence of *chorepiskopoi* in that region. However, he suggests that they were a creation of that period resulting from the peculiarities of the organization in that province. Similarly, J. Parisot ("Les chorévêques," *ROC* 6 [1901]: 157–61) suggests that they are an institution of the earlier part of the fourth century brought about in order to assist bishops of large areas. This might be arguable were it not for the earlier evidence of village *episkopoi*. Rather, I may suggest, the old institution is being reorganized and redefined, and the contemporary conciliar legislation is an indication of this rather than of the introduction of the office. The point is that, even taking account of the scanty evidence for rural Christianity in the early centuries, only *episkopoi* are found, except in Egypt, and not councils of presbyters.

159. On which, see Gillmann, *Institut*, 37.

of a federation of otherwise independent churches. I have discussed this process at Rome in some detail, have indicated that a similar process may have happened at Ephesus, and have moreover indicated that the conditions were set for this to happen elsewhere. Further examination will determine whether the same process did indeed occur elsewhere.

Before broaching that question, however, other issues must be discussed. Although I have shown that *presbyteros* and *episkopos* certainly are not synonyms, and I have shown that in many of the passages adduced in support of synonymy the term *presbyteroi* is a collective one, referring to a gathering of church leaders, this does not exhaust the discussion of presbyters. I will argue below that beyond the gathering of presbyters *kata polin*, some individual Christian communities had presbyters, though these were clearly distinguished from *episkopoi*. Before undertaking that discussion, however, I must inquire further into the duties of the *episkopos* before returning to the matter of presbyters in chapter 3.

The Economic Functions
of *Episkopoi* and *Diakonoi*

Just as my first chapter took off from a critical review of the findings of a nineteenth-century Anglican scholar, so does the second. In the second of his Bampton lectures on the organization of the Christian churches, given in 1880, Edwin Hatch argued that the origin of the Christian *episkopos* lay in the financial officers of pagan *collegia*.[1] In this chapter I intend to offer broad support to this view of the origin of the episcopate, beginning by following Hatch's argument and adding further argument, as well as noting criticisms of Hatch's view. This chapter will also assess the proposed alternative to Hatch's view, which is that the office of *episkopos* follows a Jewish model, before proceeding with the argument for an economic origin also for *diakonoi*.

The Economic Functions of *Episkopoi*

Hatch was not alone in propounding his view, as a similar position had already been taken by Heinrici;[2] Harnack, moreover, took up Hatch's work, but there

---

1. Published as *The Organization of the Early Christian Churches* (London: Longmans, 1881), 26–55.
2. John S. Kloppenborg ("Edwin Hatch, Churches and Collegia," in *Origins and Method: Towards a New Understanding of Judaism and Christianity; Essays in Honour of John C. Hurd,*

was a swift negative reaction.[3] The motivations for objection to Hatch's work were largely theological and ecclesial rather than historical.[4] Nevertheless, his work was forgotten as the debate moved into new areas. It is only in the relatively recent past that the model of *collegia* has been employed once again to understand the formation of Christian churches.

The attempt to trace the origin of Christian offices to corresponding offices outside the church from which they might have developed has been described by Hanson as "futile."[5] Among the futile attempts that he lists is that of Hatch; his grounds for such a characterization is the variety of understandings of office that is exhibited. It might also be suggested that the variety that one might anticipate in congregational organization, which would mirror the variety of theological understandings and liturgical practices in early Christianity, would preclude such an approach. However, an examination of Hatch's thesis and the evidence exhibits a surprising uniformity. This is not to say that there were no other possible means of community organization, but the weight of evidence that supports Hatch's thesis is impressive, especially since there is now evidence not known to Hatch that sustains his suggestion.

The Argument That the Office of Episkopos Was Originally Economic

There are two parts to Hatch's argument: first, the churches imitated voluntary associations in their organization; second, in doing so they borrowed the term *episkopos* for one who performed similar economic and administrative functions in the churches. The two parts of the argument, however, may be read independently, since it is entirely possible for an organization not based on a *collegium* nonetheless to borrow a term for one who performed a corresponding office.

Collegia, or associations, were common throughout the Roman Empire. They performed a number of functions and might be based on a common trade,[6] on

---

ed. Bradley H. McLean, JSNTSup 86 [Sheffield: JSOT Press, 1993], 215n12) suggests that Hatch was unaware of Heinrici's work.

3. For a balanced review of the reactions to Hatch's lectures, see Norman F. Josaitis, *Edwin Hatch and Early Church Order* (Gembloux: Duculot, 1971), 73–121. For a review of scholarship around the time of Hatch as of reactions to Hatch's work, see Kloppenborg, "Edwin Hatch."

4. As Josaitis (*Edwin Hatch*, 112–21) makes clear, Hatch was not a disinterested historian but likewise a controversialist.

5. R. P. C. Hanson, "Office and Concept of Office in the Early Church," in *Studies in Christian Antiquity* (Edinburgh: T&T Clark, 1985), 120–21.

6. J. P. Waltzing (*Étude historique sur les corporations professionelles chez les Romains depuis les origines jusqu'à la chute de l'Empire d'Occident*, vol. 4 [Louvain: Peeters, 1900], 4) lists 167 known associations formed of people in a common trade from Rome and Ostia alone.

a household, or on a religious or philosophical faith.[7] They might be concerned with social support in times of need, with the burial of their members and dependents, simply with convivial gathering, or with some combination of these purposes. One may readily see that such an organization might provide a model for the forming Christian church.

There is likewise no question that the term *episkopos* was widely used in Hellenistic associations and in civic government. Thus Hatch notes that in Rhodes a list of civic officials refers to *episkopoi* among the functionaries of the state;[8] that Mithridates appoints Philopoimen as *episkopos* of Ephesus (here some kind of city governor);[9] that *episkopoi* report to the Indian kings on all matters relating to the kingdom;[10] and that, according to the jurist Charisius, *episcopi* are held responsible for food supply in some civic settings.[11] Whereas Lietzmann suggests that some of these earlier uses relating to government are not relevant to the inquiry because their time scale lies outside that of the formation of the Christian church,[12] nonetheless the term continues to be employed in governance into the early centuries of the Common Era; thus, Lietzmann notes that the head of the Ephesian mint is known as *episkopos*.[13]

Religious societies likewise might have *episkopoi* whose functions were the care of the building or of the financial assets of the organization. A list of officials responsible for the maintenance of a temple for Apollo at Rhodes refers to, among others, *episkopoi*.[14] Plutarch refers to the *pontifex maximus* as "the overseer of the sacred virgins";[15] although the *pontifex* was a cultic official, the function described here is clearly not cultic but rather a matter of guardianship, just as the aforementioned Rhodian inscription distinguishes between *episkopoi* and *hieropoioi*. Other associations likewise might refer to their financial officers as *episkopoi*. At Thera an association charges the

---

A useful list of professional associations in Roman Asia is found in Philip A. Harland, *Associations, Synagogues, and Congregations: Claiming a Place in Ancient Mediterranean Society* (Minneapolis: Fortress, 2003), 39–40.

7. Examples of associations that are both domestic and cultic are those of Dionysius under Agripinilla (*IGUR* 160) and of Zeus and Agdistis at Philadelphia (*SIG* 985).

8. *IG* 12.1 49.

9. Appian, *Bell. mith.* 48.

10. Arrian, *Ind.* 12.5.

11. Charisius, *Dig.* 50.4.18.

12. Hans Lietzmann, "Zur altchristlichen Verfassungsgeschichte," in *Kleine Schriften I*, ed. Kurt Aland, TUGAL 67 (Berlin: Akademie-Verlag, 1958), 144.

13. Ibid., 147.

14. *IG* 12.1 731. The *episkopoi* are distinct from the ἱεροποιοί.

15. Plutarch, *Num.* 9.5: τῶν ἱερῶν παρθένων ἐπίσκοπος. He is also *episkopos* over sacrifices, ensuring that they are properly carried out.

episkopoi Dion and Meleippus to receive and invest funds.[16] Similarly, in Syria *episkopoi* are often mentioned in building inscriptions with the implication that they are to oversee the building and, in some cases, are responsible for employing the funds of others not only in overseeing the construction, but also in determining that the building should be commenced.[17] Hatch argues that this use of the term in associations and government was the basis for the origin of its Christian use, and that, like their civic counterparts and the *episkopoi* of other associations, their chief duties were not liturgical but charitable and administrative.

Below I will have cause to dispute the distinction between charitable and liturgical roles, but for the present I may add to the evidence adduced by Hatch indicating that the role of an *episkopos* was economic.

In the first instance we may note further evidence of the existence of *episkopoi* within civic administration. A stele dating from a period after the Peloponnesian War relates the tribute to be paid to Athens. "The *boulē*, the governors [*archontes*] in the cities, and the *episkopoi* shall see to it that the tribute payments be collected each year and brought to Athens." Thus, *episkopoi* are linked with archons as responsible for ensuring that the complete payment is made.[18] From Rhodes we have two lists of city officers, including some called *episkopoi*,[19] though there is nothing here that illuminates their function. Finally, we may note an honorific list from Lindos that mentions *episkopoi* among many other civic officers.[20]

Beyond the cities of the Hellenistic world, moreover, we may note the language of the Septuagint. Thus, Bobertz suggests that *episkopos* might designate a priest within the Septuagint,[21] and that the term is adopted to denote the priestly role of the *episkopos* in the eucharistic celebration. The texts that he cites, however, denote nothing of the kind. Thus, whereas Numbers (LXX)

16. *IG* 12.3 329. See, with brief discussion, C. Wescher, "Note sur une inscription de l'île de Théra," *RAr* 13 (1866): 245–49.

17. *OGIS* 611 (Hauran) refers to *episkopoi* of all the works. P. Le Bas and W. H. Waddington (*Voyage archéologique en Grèce et en Asie Mineure*, vol. 3, *Inscriptions grecques et latines recueillies en Grèce et en Asie Mineure* [Paris: Didot, 1870]) list a number of significant inscriptions. Notably, LBW 2308 and LBW 2309 refer to overseeing furnishings and buildings; LBW 2412 and LBW 1990 imply that the *episkopoi* have undertaken this work out of funds. All of these inscriptions are from the second century CE, with the exception of LBW 1990, which is from the third century, and all are from Syria.

18. *IG* 1³ 34.

19. *IG* 12.1 49; *IG* 12.1 50. This second may be dated to the first century CE.

20. *Lindos* 2.378.

21. Charles A. Bobertz, "The Development of Episcopal Order," in *Eusebius, Christianity, and Judaism*, ed. Harold W. Attridge and Gohei Hata (Detroit: Wayne State University Press, 1992), 185.

refers to Eleazar as a priest, when the text refers to him as an *episkopos*, the reference is not to his priestly capacity but because of his responsibility for the materiel of sacrifice: "Eleazar the son of Aaron the priest is supervisor [*episkopos*] for the oil of the lamp, and the incense of agreement, and the daily offering, and the oil for anointing, the supervision [*episkopē*] of the entire tabernacle and everything in it in the holy place, in all the works."[22] It is likewise in the context of economic supervision that 2 Chronicles 34:12 and 34:17 employ the term. First, the responsibility for building works on the temple is mentioned: "And over them [the workers] were supervisors [*episkopoi*] Jeth and Abdias, Levites of the sons of Merari, and Zacharias and Mosollam, of the sons of Caath, who supervised [*episkopein*]."[23] Subsequently, Josiah is told that the funds found in the temple have been delivered to the supervisors (*epi cheira tōn episkopōn*) and to those who undertook the work.[24]

Similarly, we may note a number of uses of the term to refer to officers in cultic associations. At Lindos a list of cult officials includes five *episkopoi*, listed after the priest. They have their own clerk.[25] Likewise, we may note a decree passed by a Dionysiac association on Delos honoring a donor in which the *episkopos* has charge of the arrangements, including financial arrangements;[26] the *episkopos* here could well have been the executive officer of the association. To conclude, we may note the memorial at Nice to C. Mimmius Macrinus, whose honors are given as prefect, *agonothete*, and *episcopus*.[27] Once again there is no clear indication of the function that he performed as *episcopus*, or even for whom he performed it.

Nonetheless, there is ample evidence for the appearance of *episkopoi* as officers in associations, in cults, and in civic governance; the review here is by no means exhaustive. The function of these *episkopoi* is not always clear, but when it does emerge, their function is chiefly concerned with the finance and the provision of goods within the community. Therefore we have grounds to take Hatch's argument seriously. However, to sustain the argument requires the ability to demonstrate a continuity of function, as well as title, between the Christian *episkopoi* and the *episkopoi* of the Hellenistic world.

This was not overlooked by Hatch. For him, the essence of the church was charity, and he was able to point to the great emphasis laid upon almsgiving

22. LXX Num. 4:16: ἐπίσκοπος Ελεαζαρ υἱὸς Ααρων τοῦ ἱερέως . . . ἡ ἐπισκοπὴ ὅλης τῆς σκηνῆς.
23. 2 Chron. 34:12.
24. 2 Chron. 34:17.
25. *Lindos* 1.278. Christian Blinkenberg (*Lindos: Fouilles et recherches, 1902–1914*, vol. 1, *Inscriptions, Nos. 1–281* [Berlin: de Gruyter, 1941]) comments here that their function is totally unknown, while observing the appearance of *episkopoi* elsewhere.
26. *ID* 1522.
27. *CIL* 5.7914.

and support for orphans and widows in early Christianity. But even if the term *episkopos* is generally financial in significance, and even if there is a system of relief for the poor in the churches, it does not necessarily follow that this was the bishop's role. However, Hatch does present some evidence for the bishop functioning in a financial role. He points in particular to the evidence of Justin by which the offerings of the Christians, publicly made, were placed in the hands of the president of the assembly in order to be distributed,[28] and to the manner in which Polycarp refers to widows, being recipients of charity, as the altar of the church.[29] He suggests that bishops showed hospitality,[30] refers to Cyprian's charity, and to the manner in which later legislation laid emphasis on discipline for the bishop in the administration of funds,[31] and finally notes that in later times eulogies on bishops emphasize the charitable activities of the bishops, ending this passage of argument by quoting Jerome: "The glory of a bishop is to relieve the poverty of the poor."[32] Although some of this evidence is from a later period, in view of which one might argue that this charitable and economic activity was a development that took place after the rise of the monepiscopate and is not germane to the original functions of a bishop, we certainly have sufficient grounds here to take Hatch's arguments seriously.

New Arguments for Episkopoi as Economic Officers

In particular, in pursuing the suggestion that the fundamental duty of the earliest Christian *episkopoi* was economic, we should note the evidence that was not available to Hatch, as well as that which he overlooked, all of which seems to offer ample attestation that the fundamental function of *episkopoi* in early Christian circles was comparable to that of the *episkopoi* in civil society and in associations.

THE ECONOMIC FUNCTION OF EPISKOPOI IN THE DIDACHE

In examining evidence unknown to Hatch or overlooked by him, we may turn in the first instance to the *Didache* and to the qualifications laid down for *episkopoi* (and *diakonoi*). Those to be appointed, states the Didachist, are to be gentle, not money-loving, honest, and tested.[33] Whereas these might be considered qualifications for any office, the emphasis on honesty and on a disregard for money indicates that care for finance is a primary responsibility.

28. Hatch, *Organization*, 40, with reference to Justin, *1 Apol.* 67.
29. Ibid., 41, with reference to Pol. *Phil.* 4.
30. Ibid., 45, with reference to *Herm.* 104.
31. Ibid., 47.
32. Ibid., 47–48, quoting Jerome, *Ep.* 52.6.
33. *Did.* 15:1.

Moreover, as De Halleux observes, meekness is linked in *Didache* 5:2 to a proper concern for the poor.[34] It is close in significance to the concern that the bishop and the deacon be free of avarice; this too indicates that the function for which qualification is being sought is the handling of money. A similar concern for an absence of avarice is exhibited in Onasander's treatise on the general.[35] Here the rationale is given that a general should not be corrupt in management. The qualifications given are those of an economic administrator. This much becomes clear as the duties of the officers are described: "For they themselves liturgize for you the liturgy of the prophets and teachers."[36]

I may suggest that the *leitourgia* of the bishops and deacons was a public office undertaken at one's own expense; thus, the term "liturgize" is here likewise used in its ancient sense: the bishops provide financial support for the teachers and prophets and enable them to carry out their ministry. The term in this sense and the institution of *leitourgiai* were still very much current in the first centuries of the Common Era. This may be illustrated both from literature and from papyri. Thus, P.Oxy. 1119 is concerned with the *leitourgia* of tax collection, P.Oxy 1412 uses the term *leitourgēmata* for public responsibilities, P.Oxy. 82 concerns a fair and even distribution of public works, termed "liturgies," and P.Gr.Vind. 25824 is a journal discussing the dealings of prefects under Trajan with those in Egypt whose liturgy particularly involved the supply of grain.[37] In the second century Dio Chrysostom frequently refers to *leitourgiai* as the responsibility of wealthy citizens,[38] and Strabo, in describing the system of relief for the poor at Rhodes, states that the provision of food for the poor was considered a *leitourgia*.[39]

Just as the requirement for meekness and the concern for lack of avarice indicate that the concern of the bishop and the deacon is financial, so the reason for these qualifications is explained by explaining their function, which is to support those who exercise a ministry in the assembly. The liturgizing of the liturgy of the prophets and teachers is not the performance of the office of prophets and teachers, as is generally assumed,[40] but rather is social and economic support for those who do exercise this office.

34. A. De Halleux, "Ministers in the *Didache*," in *The* Didache *in Modern Research*, ed. Jonathan A. Draper, AGJU 37 (Leiden: Brill, 1996), 313.

35. Onasander, *Imp. off.* 1.1, 8. See B. S. Easton, "New Testament Ethical Lists," *JBL* 51 (1932): 10–11.

36. *Did.* 15:1: ὑμῖν γὰρ λειτουργοῦσι καὶ αὐτοὶ τὴν λειτουργίαν.

37. For some discussion of this, see Hubert Metzger, "Zur Stellung der liturgischen Beamten Ägyptens in frührömischer Zeit," *MH* 2 (1945): 54–62.

38. Dio Chrysostom, *Ven.* 26.2–4; *Sec.* 2.2; *2 Tars.* 1.4; *Tumult.* 6; 14.

39. Strabo, *Geogr.* 14.2.5.

40. Initially suggested by Adolf von Harnack, *Die Lehre der zwölf Apostel: Nebst Untersuchungen zur ältesten Geschichte der Kirchenverfassung und des Kirchenrechts*, TUGAL

THE ECONOMIC FUNCTION OF *EPISKOPOI* IN *1 CLEMENT*

A similar point may be gathered from *1 Clement* 40:2, where it is stated that God commanded the offering of donations and public services (*prosphoras kai leitourgias*); this is part of an argument for good order, based on the careful ordering of the cult, and is subsequently picked up at *1 Clement* 44:4, where it is stated that it would be sinful to remove from *episkopē* those who have "blamelessly and in a holy manner offered the gifts" (*prosenenkontas ta dōra*). On this, Campenhausen writes, "In what the essential work of the bishops consists is made clear in *1 Clement*; like the priests of the old covenant they 'present the gifts,' that is to say, they are the leaders of worship, and at the celebration of the eucharist they offer prayer on behalf of the congregation."[41] In response to such assertions, Bowe suggests that we should not overemphasize "the cultic aspects of . . . *leitourgia*."[42] She notes Lightfoot's suggestion that the offerings were as much alms and offerings for the *agapē* as prayers or thanksgivings.[43] Moreover, Bowe notes that the adverbs used of the service of the presbyters in offering, "blamelessly" and "in a holy manner" (*amemptōs* and *hosiōs*), are part of the vocabulary of moral conduct rather than of ritual purity, and finally that in *1 Clement* 44:6 the presbyters are said to have given good service (*kalōs politeumenous*), which is, she notes, language used not of cultic officials but of public servants. I may thus suggest that Clement's *leitourgia* is a public office, and that the offering of gifts to which he refers in the same context is a sacrifice only insofar as the gifts are offered, but that the primary reference is to the gifts that are offered as a *leitourgia*.[44] As I will note in more detail below, the distinction between the cultic and the economic does not apply in the formative period of Christianity, because the liturgy is a point at which economic goods are delivered, but Bowe's point is valid nonetheless. The "essential work" of an *episkopos* is the work of providing gifts for the

2/1–2 (Leipzig: Hinrichs, 1886), 140–41, and subsequently followed by, among others, Kurt Niederwimmer, *The Didache: A Commentary*, trans. Linda M. Maloney, ed. Harold W. Attridge (Minneapolis: Fortress, 1998), 201; Willy Rordorf and André Tuilier, *La doctrine des douze apôtres (Didachè)*, SC 248 (Paris: Cerf, 1998), 73. Harnack believed that the passage related to the replacement of wandering charismatics by localized ministers.

41. Hans von Campenhausen, *Ecclesiastical Authority and Spiritual Power in the Church of the First Three Centuries*, trans. J. A. Baker (London: A&C Black, 1969), 85.

42. Barbara E. Bowe, *A Church in Crisis: Ecclesiology and Paraenesis in Clement of Rome* (Minneapolis: Fortress, 1988), 150–52.

43. J. B. Lightfoot, *The Apostolic Fathers*, 5 vols. (1890; repr., Peabody, MA: Hendrickson, 1989), 1.2:135n.

44. Thus Ulrich Volp ("Liturgical Authority Reconsidered: Remarks on the Bishop's Role in Pre-Constantinian Worship," in *Prayer and Spirituality in the Early Church*, vol. 3, *Liturgy and Life*, ed. Bronwen Neil, Geoffrey D. Dunn, and Lawrence Cross [Strathfield, New South Wales: St Paul's, 2003], 195) notes this possible understanding of Clement's words here.

poor and lending economic support in general to the church. In the light of this understanding of *leitourgia* as a means by which concrete gifts are given in a eucharistic context, we should likewise not go to the other extreme, namely, to see the language of offering as entirely symbolic and representative of a good ministry, and solely called forth by the usage of the Old Testament.[45]

THE ECONOMIC FUNCTION OF *EPISKOPOI* IN THE DIRECTIONS OF IGNATIUS TO POLYCARP

Ignatius's direction of duties addressed to Polycarp is also noteworthy; it is the most comprehensive list of the duties of a bishop within the earliest period. Apart from refuting heresy with individuals,[46] Polycarp is to care for widows,[47] ensure that slaves do not purchase manumission from the funds of the church,[48] and oversee the marriage of individuals.[49] His principal concern is therefore, once again, with the financial management of the church, for although this last duty, overseeing marriage, might not appear at first sight to be related to the funds and finance of the church, this inevitably would be bound up to the question of a dowry and the disposition of funds;[50] the desire (*epithymia*) that Ignatius states might otherwise motivate the marriage would thus be desire after money.

THE ECONOMIC FUNCTION OF *EPISKOPOI* IN THE CHURCH ORDER LITERATURE

It is at the risk of becoming tedious that I next turn to *Didascalia apostolorum*, which, though dating perhaps from the fourth century, certainly contains material from an earlier period among its sources.[51] This source speaks extensively of the bishop's duties with regard to offerings; it is the

---

45. So, e.g., Horacio E. Lona, *Der erste Clemensbrief*, KAV 2 (Göttingen: Vandenhoeck & Ruprecht, 1998), 463–64.

46. Ign. *Pol.* 2:1–3.

47. Ign. *Pol.* 4:1.

48. Ign. *Pol.* 4:3.

49. Ign. *Pol.* 5:2.

50. See Margaret Y. MacDonald, "The Ideal of the Christian Couple: Ign. *Pol.* 5.1–2 Looking Back to Paul," *NTS* 40 (1994): 105–25; Alfred Niebergall ("Zur Entstehungsgeschichte der christlichen Eheschliessung," in *Glaube, Geist, Geschichte: Festschrift für Ernst Benz zum 60. Geburtstag am 17. November 1967*, ed. Gerhard Müller and Winfried Zeller [Leiden: Brill, 1967], 107–24) seems to think that some liturgical action is intended. William R. Schoedel ("Ignatius and the Reception of Matthew in Antioch," in *Social History of the Matthean Community: Cross-Disciplinary Approaches*, ed. David L. Balch [Minneapolis: Fortress, 1991], 149) suggests that the concern is group endogamy as a means of maintaining the tight boundaries of the sect.

51. See the discussion of the redactional history of this document in the introduction to Alistair Stewart(-Sykes), *The Didascalia Apostolorum: An English Version*, STT 1 (Turnhout: Brepols, 2009).

bishop's responsibility to ensure that they are collected and to distribute them among the poor.

> Therefore just as it was not allowed to a stranger, that is to anyone who was not a Levite, to go up to the altar, or to make any offering without the high priest, so you likewise should do nothing without the bishop. If anyone does anything without the bishop he does it in vain, and his good work will not be put to his account, because it is improper that anything should be done without the high priest. Therefore you should make your offerings to the high priest, doing so yourself or through the deacons. He will share what he has received with each as each deserves.[52]

Such passages may be multiplied; the whole tenor of the chapters regarding widows in this church order is an insistence that charity shown to widows should be directed through the bishop. The fact that this church order insists on this episcopal role is not an indication that this was not something central to the episcopate; rather, as I argue elsewhere, it is a sign of conflict between the bishop and private individuals as a result of the social advantage that might come about through the exercise of charity.[53]

THE ECONOMIC FUNCTION OF THE *EPISKOPOI* OF PHILIPPIANS 1:1

As has already been noted, Philippians is unique in the Pauline literature for mentioning officers; the reason for joining the *episkopoi* and *diakonoi* to the greetings to the saints has puzzled commentators, though since Chrysostom the case has been made that the bishops and deacons are responsible for sending the gift that occasions the letter.[54] The fundamental problem with such a reading is that these officers are not mentioned on the occasion when thanks are particularly given for the gift at Philippians 4:10.[55] Even if there has been no editorial interference, we should note that the gift is that of the congregation and thanks are therefore given to all, whereas, I may suggest, the *episkopoi* and the *diakonoi* are the agents by whom the collection was organized and transmitted. One may refine this further with reference to the

52. *Did. ap.* 2.27.1–3.
53. Stewart(-Sykes), *Didascalia Apostolorum*, 56–69.
54. Chrysostom, *Hom. Phil.* 2 195D. Among modern commentators note Helmut Merkel, *Die Pastoralbriefe*, 13th ed., NTD 9/1 (Göttingen: Vandenhoeck & Ruprecht, 1991), 91; Eduard Lohse, "Die Entstehung des Bischofsamtes in der frühen Christenheit," *ZNW* 71 (1980): 63–64. Martin Dibelius (*An die Thessalonicher I, II; An die Philipper*, 3rd ed., HNT 11 [Tübingen: Mohr Siebeck, 1937], 60–62) suggests that these officers are the agents of the collection, but that this does not mean that they had any leadership role.
55. Pointed out by, e.g., Richard S. Ascough, *Paul's Macedonian Associations: The Social Context of Philippians and 1 Thessalonians*, WUNT 2/161 (Tübingen: Mohr Siebeck, 2003), 82.

suggestion of Best that the greeting as employed by Paul, "to all the saints which are in Philippi with the *episkopoi* and *diakonoi*," was that used by the Philippian congregations in their letter to him. The greeting is thus repeated, but the offices are not brought to the fore when the contribution of the Philippians is discussed.[56] In other words, the Philippian congregations had ordered themselves along associational lines and adopted these titles in imitation of other Philippian associations.[57]

Whereas Philippians of itself offers no guidance as to the function of these officers, the economic activity of *episkopoi* elsewhere in early Christianity seems to indicate that this is the rationale behind their mention here. In the light of the corroborating evidence from elsewhere, other suggestions, such as the idea that these are the evangelists of the community,[58] or that they were actually absent from the community, seem weak indeed.

An interesting suggestion is made by Campbell: the Philippian churches, based on individual households, had gathered in council from across the city, and the *episkopoi* and *diakonoi* were those who met and represented the congregations, like the *presbyteroi kata polin* (discussed above in chap. 1).[59] This is attractive, but it is odd that they should not be termed *presbyteroi* as elsewhere. Certainly it would appear that a degree of federation is occurring, but quite possibly it is a new phenomenon, that the churches have gathered solely for the purpose of channeling gifts to Paul, and for this reason they are represented by the *episkopoi* and the *diakonoi* of the congregations. However, the suggestion that there was communication between diverse Philippian congregations is nonetheless noteworthy, not least because this explains the plurality of *episkopoi* in the address by recognizing that the letter is addressed not to a single congregation but to several; thus, rather than envisaging a single congregation with a number of *episkopoi*, we may envisage a number of congregations, each one with an *episkopos*.

This text is also noteworthy because of the failure to mention presbyters. As we have seen, this led Lightfoot to take it as evidence for the synonymy of presbyters and *episkopoi*. His reasoning, as already suggested, is fallacious,

56. Ernest Best, "Bishops and Deacons: Philippians 1,1," in *Studia Evangelica 4: Papers Presented at the Third International Congress on New Testament Studies Held at Christ Church, Oxford, 1965*, ed. F. L. Cross, TUGAL 102 (Berlin: Akademie-Verlag, 1968), 371–76.

57. So Peter Pilhofer, *Philippi*, vol. 1, *Die erste christliche Gemeinde Europas*, WUNT 87 (Tübingen: Mohr Siebeck, 1995), 140–47.

58. Dieter Georgi, *The Opponents of Paul in Second Corinthians*, SNTW (Edinburgh: T&T Clark, 1987), 29–30. For a critique of Georgi's thesis, see below under the heading "*Diakonoi* in Other Hellenistic Contexts."

59. R. Alastair Campbell, *The Elders: Seniority within Earliest Christianity*, SNTW (Edinburgh: T&T Clark, 1994), 130–31.

not the least because it depends on the rather large assumption that presbyters are indeed essential to the existence of a church. *Didascalia apostolorum* was little known at the time at which Lightfoot wrote, and the *Didache* lay undiscovered.[60] However, the *Didache* makes no mention of the institution of presbyters, and although they receive mention in *Didascalia apostolorum*, they are entirely tangential, and in some cases their appearance appears to be the result of redactional interference. I will return to the question of the presbyters in the *Didache* and in *Didascalia apostolorum* below, but here at least I may suggest that, quite apart from the elementary logical error in Lightfoot's reasoning, presbyters are not mentioned because their role is not in question. There is absolutely no evidence here for synonymy; indeed, quite the opposite is the case. If the Philippian congregations had presbyters, then their role would not be that of *episkopoi*; that is to say, they would not be economic administrators. The text is significant not for indicating synonymy, but rather because it indicates association between the Philippian congregations for an economic purpose.

The Economic Function of *Episkopoi* in Acts 20

We have seen that in departing Asia, Paul, as constructed by Luke, addresses himself to the group of *episkopoi*, collectively termed *presbyteroi*. Two warnings are given; these certainly are *vaticinia ex eventu*, mirroring the ecclesiastical situation of Luke's day. In the first instance a warning is given about false teaching. In the second instance the *episkopoi* are exhorted to protect the weak, and they are given the example of Paul's support of himself by his own labor.[61] Lambrecht suggests that "shortcomings with regard to the efficacious assistance of the poor existed" and goes on to ask, "Could it even be suggested that Luke is reacting here against abuses on the part of the leaders who were taking their being supported by the community too much for granted?"[62]

It is, however, because of the economic role of *episkopoi* that this issue is mentioned. That is to say, support of the weak and supply of the needs of the Christian community are primary responsibilities of the *episkopoi*. It is unlikely that these *episkopoi* are supported by their community, as Lambrecht seems to suggest, because, as I will argue below, these *episkopoi* either are wealthy householders or hold a position in a household. Rather, what is being suggested is a want of generosity on the part of these *episkopoi* and

---

60. We charitably take the publication date as 1868, although the work was subsequently issued with corrections (that which I am using is dated 1898).

61. Acts 20:29–36.

62. J. Lambrecht, "Paul's Farewell-Address at Miletus (Acts 20,17–38)," in *Les Actes des Apôtres: Traditions, rédaction, théologie*, ed. J. Kremer, BETL 48 (Gembloux: Ducolot, 1979), 336.

householders; it is for this purpose that Paul draws attention to the manner in which he was self-supporting, namely, to give an example of generosity. Once again, there is indication that the office of *episkopos* was an economic office.

THE ECONOMIC FUNCTION OF *EPISKOPOI* IN THE CANONS OF THE COUNCIL OF NEOCAESAREA

I have already noted the survival of *episkopoi* in small villages; in the fourth century these become the subject of legislation, in particular because they are something of an anachronism. One of these councils, that of Neocaesarea, betrays the fact that not only are they anachronistic by being rural *episkopoi*, but also that their understanding of their office is somewhat anachronistic. Thus, the fourteenth canon states that "the *chorepiskopoi*, however, are indeed after the pattern of the seventy; and as fellow-servants, on account of their devotion to the poor, they have the honor of making the oblation." That is to say, the offering is still an offering by the *episkopos* of the village in support of the poor.

CONCLUSION

The evidence presented by Hatch for the economic role of the *episkopos* in early Christian congregations was relatively thin. However, there is much material not available to Hatch indicating that his fundamental insight was correct. Moreover, once this is adopted as a working hypothesis, texts such as Philippians 1:1, which of themselves do not clearly or explicitly state that these are the functions of the *episkopos*, may readily be understood in this light because they are not seen in isolation.

Objections to the Hypothesis That Episkopoi Were Economic Officers

Numerous objections were raised to Hatch at the time he delivered and published his lectures; although these tended to be raised on theological rather than historical grounds, there are a number of possible pertinent objections to Hatch's hypothesis that need to be noted.

THE NONECONOMIC FUNCTIONS OF *EPISKOPOI* IN CHRISTIAN CHURCHES

The fundamental argument leveled against Hatch is that put by Burtchaell: "The borrowing by Christians of the title *episkopos* . . . leads him too easily to assume that it must then denote a financial officer, without checking to see whether that was in fact his [the bishop's] primary function (it was not)."[63] At

---

63. James Tunstead Burtchaell, *From Synagogue to Church: Public Services and Offices in the Earliest Christian Communities* (Cambridge: Cambridge University Press, 1992), 81–82n33.

this point I have already reviewed enough evidence to observe not only that Hatch did indeed present evidence that the *episkopos* was a financial officer, but also that there is additional ample evidence that points in that direction.

THE STATUS OF AN *EPISKOPOS*

The main problem with Hatch's argument is that the function of the *episkopos*, as distinct from the various other officers mentioned in these inscriptions, is sometimes unclear, and in no case is the *episkopos* the chief of the officials. Even the *episkopos* who governs Ephesus reports to the king,[64] and the *episkopoi* reported by Arrian (who seems to be describing the caste system) are second in rank,[65] below those who may form members of the governing councils and from whom chief officers are appointed.

This is not necessarily a fatal objection. If the model of civic governance and associations is to be taken seriously, then we need not assume that the *episkopos* of Christian groups was necessarily the head of the organization. At this point in the work I have yet to explore the role of presbyters, other than those who held office in a federation like that of Rome, but I may suggest now the possibility that the *episkopos* was appointed by presbyters (as I will argue was the case in the Asian communities, which therefore exhibited a strained balance of power). We must also recall that for a Christian group, the true head of the organization is Christ, and so although an officer may have day-to-day charge of a Christian group, that does not make him the true head. Again, the significance of this comment will emerge below when the position of broker is discussed.

It is also to be observed that these *episkopoi*, even in religious settings, do not have duties that are specifically religious; that is, they do not teach, prophesy, or offer sacrifices. Again I postpone discussion of this point. Nevertheless it is an important point that must be observed and answered if the connection is to be sustained. I may, however, point out even at this stage that because a ritual meal was the center of Christian religious practice, whereas sacrifice was seen to be abolished, those with responsibility regarding the meal and its provision would naturally come to prominence in the cult.

THE LATER EMERGENCE OF *EPISKOPOI* WITH ECONOMIC FUNCTIONS?

A final objection to Hatch is that of Brent, who, interestingly, alleges that the economic role of the *episkopos* is one that emerges only in the mid-second century. Thus, he allows that the *episkopoi* described by Hermas are economic

64. Appian, *Bell. mith.* 48.
65. Arrian, *Ind.* 12.5.

functionaries (dating Hermas to the middle of the century, which may be some-what late) but suggests that this is not true in the earliest period.[66] Whereas much of this argument depends on dating works of very uncertain date, such as the *Didache* and the *Shepherd of Hermas*, which may well predate or be roughly contemporary with Ignatius (whose date likewise is uncertain),[67] I may still point to Philippians 1:1 and most especially to the *Didache*. *Episkopoi* and *diakonoi* here are, I have already suggested, economic officers. Note that the mention of their appointment within the text is made immediately after a discussion of meals within the community and the necessity for reconciliation before eating together.[68] The chapters are linked with *oun*; thus, I may suggest that the appointment of *episkopoi* and *diakonoi* is discussed in the light of the foregoing material. They are to supply the meal, liturgizing the prophets and teachers through the provision of food.

In general we must not overlook the fact that the ritual meal of the church was a *Sättigungsmahl* (full meal); there is, moreover, evidence for a much greater variety of eucharistic foods than those that would be known in later centuries.[69] As such, although the situation of the first centuries was unlike the situation described in *Didascalia apostolorum* in that there the offerings received at the eucharist are administered separately, this nonetheless is an occasion on which food was shared. By the time of *Didascalia apostolorum*, the administration of charity has become separated from the ritual meal, and so admittedly there has been some development by the third century; however, this development was not ex nihilo but rather, I suggest, arose from a situation much like that of the first century. The ritual meal of the first century was not only a ritual meal but also a meal that extended charity, both in granting a meal to those who might not otherwise eat[70] and, possibly, through the grant of *aphoreta* in common with wider Roman dining practices.[71] It is from this that the social support system of *Didascalia apostolorum* has developed. I may suggest that as the eucharistic meal was transferred to a morning and the

66. Allen Brent, "The Ignatian Epistles and the Threefold Ecclesiastical Order," *JRH* 17 (1992): 26.

67. On the dating of Ignatius see pp. 239–40.

68. *Did.* 15:1.

69. For an overall discussion of the foodstuffs employed in early Christian ritual meals, see Andrew B. McGowan, *Ascetic Eucharists: Food and Drink in Early Christian Ritual Meals*, OECS (Oxford: Oxford University Press, 1999).

70. Thus, in a satyric context, Martial (*Epig.* 3.60) is dependent on dinner invitations in order to eat.

71. An *apophoretum* was a gift given at the end of a dinner. For pagan practice, see the satyric version of patronage dispensed by Trimalchio (Petronius, *Sat.* 56–57). For Christian adoption, see Hippolytus, *Trad. ap.* 28.

nature of the meal consequentially altered, with the result that only the ritual foods were given, so the locus of charity had to change. Different communities responded in different ways; it is in this period that we find meals given out of charity (the *agapē*), whereas the response of the Didascalist community was to set up a support system through the *episkopos*,[72] and that of the community of *Apostolic Church Order* (*Canones ecclesiastici apostolorum*) was to give *apophoreta* at the eucharist.[73]

The Church as Not Necessarily Associational

As we have seen, Hatch suggested that the church in the Hellenistic world, at least, was modeled on the association. In more recent years the associational model for early Christian groups has been revived,[74] though it is more common for the household to be seen as the basis for understanding the organization of early Christian groups.[75] Although revived, the associational model for understanding early Christianity has not gone unchallenged. In particular, the household is upheld as an alternative model for the formation of the Christian church that is seen as excluding associational behavior.

There is no doubt that the household was a significant model for the organization of some Christian churches.

In the Pauline churches, in the first instance, there is ample evidence of domestic organization. In 1 Corinthians 16:19 greetings are conveyed from the church that met in the house of Prisca and Aquila. However, this simply implies that the church met in domestic premises. The terms *oikos* and *oikia* might imply simply a domestic building, but they might also term the members of a household, which might in turn be an extensive group in the ancient world, going beyond the extended family to include slaves, freedmen, and clients.[76] Thus, a domestic setting in a Pauline context need not mean that the entire household was Christian, nor that some worshipers in a house might not be members of the household. We may observe the Epistle to Philemon, where Philemon himself is clearly a host of a domestically based church, but one

---

72. Such is the process legislated at *Did. ap.* 2.27.1–3, discussed above.

73. So note *Can. eccl. ap.* 18.3: "The presbyters on the right are to assist those who oversee the altar, so that they may distribute the gifts of honor and receive them as necessary."

74. See the essays in John S. Kloppenborg and Stephen G. Wilson, eds., *Voluntary Associations in the Graeco-Roman World* (London: Routledge, 1996).

75. On the household, see Roger W. Gehring, *House Church and Mission: The Importance of Household Structures in Early Christianity* (Peabody, MA: Hendrickson, 2004), especially the review of prior discussion at 1–16.

76. For discussion of the relationship between the terms, in which it is argued that there is an intersection between the terms, which are, however, not quite synonymous, see Hans-Josef Klauck, *Hausgemeinde und Hauskirche im frühen Christentum*, SBS 103 (Stuttgart: Katholisches Bibelwerk, 1981), 15–20; see also the comments on Klauck's work by Gehring, *House Church*, 8–9.

of his slaves, Onesiphorus, is not a Christian. Similarly, we may observe that in his discussion of the Christian lifestyle Aristides suggests that Christians persuade their slaves within their households to adopt Christianity and then call them "brothers" without distinction,[77] which implies that there might be pressure to convert but that such conversion was not required. These churches met in houses but were not necessarily household congregations. Nonetheless, the very domestic basis of the setting would lead inevitably to leadership falling upon the head of the household, just as in the cult of Zeus and the other gods, Dionysius, the householder, acts as priest.[78] Earlier we have observed, within the Johannine tradition, that Diotrephes, who refuses the delegates of the elder in 3 John, may best be understood as a householder, exercising power over whom he might allow into his house; at that point I suggested that he, although not an officer, did not need an office because his authority derived from his position within the household. Household conversions are also found within Acts,[79] as are domestic meeting places;[80] we may note, moreover, that domestic meeting places continue to be found into the second century,[81] and that the beginnings of Christian architecture come about due to the adaptation of domestic premises for Christian gatherings.

It is on the basis of this evidence of household organization that Meeks launches his major critique of the associational model, suggesting in turn that the basis for the church was domestic *tout court*.[82] He begins by observing certain similarities between the association and the church but, while admitting certain similarities, also suggests that there are a number of fundamental social differences between the Pauline churches and associations. He suggests that membership of the church was both more socially diverse and more ideationally restricted; there was a clear distinction between those who were baptized and those who were not that undercut any other distinction—for instance, a distinction based on class. There is, however, some indication in the Corinthian correspondence that such boundaries were not being strictly observed and, indeed that, even though theoretically the church was free of divisions based on social status, the members of lower social status were

77. Aristides, *Apol.* 15.6.

78. This association is recorded at *SIG* 985; it is founded in response to a night vision had by Dionysius, its founder.

79. E.g., Acts 16:15 (Lydia and her household).

80. Thus, bread is broken *kat' oikon* in Acts 2:46. For more on this, see chap. 4 below, under the heading "Philippi."

81. Thus, note the diversity of households at Smyrna greeted by Ignatius (Ign. *Smyrn.* 13:1–2; Ign. *Pol.* 8:2). On Smyrna, see chap. 4 below, under the heading "Smyrna."

82. Wayne E. Meeks, *The First Urban Christians: The Social World of the Apostle Paul* (New Haven: Yale University Press, 1983), 75–84.

repressed within the activities of the church. Theoretically, the dissolution of vertical societal shifts would represent a real difference between the church and the associations, but relative social homogeneity and relative fluidity of boundaries are not part of an association's fundamental self-understanding and therefore do not affect an associational model in any way. Moreover, whereas many associations, particularly those based on trades, may well have been socially homogeneous,[83] those based on a household, as Harland points out, would include all those within the household,[84] thus necessarily embracing social diversity. Some, indeed, are consciously socially diverse.[85] Moreover, within the associations the use of titles and honors indicates that members did not see themselves as socially homogenous; that is to say, whatever the social status of the association's members within wider society, within the subgroup of the association there was definite social stratification mirroring the wider society, with *ordines* and *plebs*.[86] Similarly, associations might court the powerful, again indicating that social homogeneity was not necessary to an association's self-understanding.[87] Paul may oppose the manner in which the Corinthian church fails to dissolve social stratification, but the reality is that, like an association, the social norms of wider society are found likewise within the church.

Ideational exclusivity might theoretically undercut social division, but it does not appear to have done so. Likewise, whereas some associations might be relatively easy to join,[88] others might have strict rules regarding membership and the conditions of membership.[89] However, the church is distinct from

83. Though even here we have to be careful. Harland (*Associations*, 43) points to the stele left by an association of Ephesian fishermen and fish merchants (*IEph.* 20 [see also *NewDocs* 5:95–114]) recording highly disparate amounts given by members toward a new fishery toll office. The disparate amounts indicate a high degree of social and economic diversity among members.

84. Harland, *Associations*, 30.

85. Notably the association recorded at *SIG* 985. As S. C. Barton and G. H. R. Horsley ("A Hellenistic Cult Group and the New Testament Churches," *JAC* 24 [1981]: 16–17) point out, the inscription repeats the provision that "men and women, slave and free" are welcome to the association, thus underscoring that point.

86. So many associations have a decurionate; see, e.g., *CIL* 5.2850, recording a decurion and quaestor of the *collegium fabrum* at Padua, and decurion of the *collegium fabrum* at Cetium (*CIL* 3.5659). Slaves might be decurions, as at the collegium at Luna recorded (*CIL* 11.1356).

87. See the Pompeiian graffiti, indicating support by associations for powerful individuals (e.g., *CIL* 4.206, 113, 710, 960). Among monuments and honors for patrons, note, e.g., *CIL* 6.29702 (patrons receiving *sportulae*), *CIL* 6.29700 (a patron being honored by position within the association), *CIL* 9.5439 (a statue erected in honor of a patron's father), and *CIL* 5.865 (a statue erected to a patron).

88. *CIL* 14.2112 refers simply to the payment of monthly dues as a condition of membership.

89. Principally, of course, membership of professional or veterans' associations was restricted to members of that profession or to veterans. Note, however, the ethical conditions imposed upon and the vow that must be sworn by those entering the *oikos* of Dionysius to participate in

other associations, unless synagogues are counted as associations likewise, in the extent to which they claim exclusivity.[90]

Similarly, Meeks points out that there is no evidence that the Pauline communities kept a common chest of money. Here the activity of the Philippian community may provide evidence to the contrary, though otherwise Meeks is right in this respect. We need, however, to be aware of the possibility of distinction between the churches of Pauline foundation and those that were founded independently of him, with which he might come into contact, and in particular not to make the Pauline model the normative model for all first-century Christian communities.

Meeks next points to the absence of titles and honors for leaders within Pauline churches as compared to the multiplicity of officers, their designations, and the honors given them within the associations. Kloppenborg finds this argument forced because the letter to the Philippians does refer to *episkopoi* and, moreover, both refers to the Philippian Christians as Paul's crown (*stephanos*), which is, as Kloppenborg notes, the language of honorific designation, and speaks of the service (*leitourgia*) offered by the Philippians.[91] However, it is to be noted that all this evidence refers to one Pauline letter, and so again this may be the exception among the churches known to Paul, and in particular it might not be of Pauline foundation. Of the evangelization of Philippi we know nothing, however, unless the account of Acts 16:12 is taken at face value. However, Paul neither indicates nor implies that he had any founding role in the Philippian church, a silence that is significant, given that he claims this role in writing to the Corinthians, the Galatians, and the Thessalonians. It is possible that these congregations, with their offices and their associational self-understanding, had formed independently of his influence.

Nonetheless, there is a challenge here to the associational model in that households generally do not have named officers. Paul, we may deduce, anticipated the household as the basic model, and for this reason he does not refer

---

the cultus of the gods in the association recorded in *SIG* 985, as well as the close examination of entrants to an association of *eranistoi* by all the officers of the association recorded in their rules in *IG* 2² 1369.

90. Harland (*Associations*, 71) suggests that associations might be similarly exclusive, citing *SEG* 29.1205 regarding "worshipers (*therapeutae*) of Zeus at Sardis" who were "not to participate in the mysteries of Sabazaios." However, this makes reference not to ordinary worshipers but specifically to *neokoroi*. Moreover, although this inscription comes from the first or second century CE, this is actually a regulation dating from some five hundred years earlier, from the Persian period. We know that the exclusion was maintained, but I may note that this was countercultural, in that the rationale for the copying of the regulation is that a particular *neokoros* is instructed to obey this regulation. The very fact that the regulation had to be repeated is an indication that it was in danger of not being kept.

91. Kloppenborg, "Edwin Hatch," 238, with reference to Phil. 2:17; 4:1.

to titles and officers within the household. Consequently the householders exercised patronage and, as a result, power. Thus, the disputes within the domestic congregations of Corinth are best understood as emerging from the household setting in which they found themselves. In the later development of the Pauline churches, as manifested in the Pastoral Epistles, household imagery is prominent. But this applies to the Pauline churches only; in the case of the Philippian church, which is not, I suggest, of Pauline foundation, there is much more evidence of economic activity like that of the association. Thus, although the Pauline churches manifest little associational behavior, this need not be true of other Christian groups.

There is yet more to say. For even the Philippian church, with its offices and associational behavior, may well have met in domestic premises.[92] The distinction between a household and an association is not clear-cut in that it was entirely possible for an association to have a domestic or familial basis,[93] and it is therefore possible that associational Christian groups might emerge from domestic groups and continue to meet in domestic premises. The household may affect the church in a number of ways, but it does not prevent it being understood either by its own members, or by outsiders, as an association. Household and association are not mutually exclusive categories.

However, McCready suggests that there are four distinct differences between churches and associations, such that the comparison should be questioned. Two of his distinctions are essentially those suggested by Meeks, though two are different.

First, McCready notes that Christian communities prepared their members for entrance through instruction and continued to give them direction and instruction. He contrasts this to the "predominantly social dimensions of voluntary associations."[94] Once again we struggle with generalizations. *IG* 2² 1368 records the activities of the Iobacchi at Athens, including a priest's speaking of God (*theologia*) and limiting the right of entry. We may be mindful of the extent to which scholastic activity marked Christian activity in some communities, but we should not make this critical for noting a distinction between churches and associations.

---

92. So John Reumann, "Church Office in Paul, Especially in Philippians," in McLean, *Origins and Method*, 82–91, 90, suggests that the Philippian churches are both households and associations.

93. E.g., the Dionysiac association of Agripinilla (*IGUR* 160) (on which, see Bradley H. McLean, "The Agripinilla Inscription: Religious Associations and Early Church Formation," in McLean, *Origins and Method*, 239–70), the *Collegium quod est in domu Sergiae Paullinae* (*CIL* 6.9148), and, once again, *SIG* 985, whose shrine was within Dionysius's house.

94. Wayne O. McCready, "*Ekklēsia* and Voluntary Associations," in Kloppenborg and Wilson, *Voluntary Associations*, 64.

There is, however, one fundamental distinction between churches and associations noted by McCready that is significant: churches are both localized and translocal.[95] As we have already seen, local churches within cities fostered contacts with one another and shared literature. In the earliest stages of development, the apostle, one charged with carrying messages around the churches, might be the basis for this translocal consciousness, and in a later period the representative presbyters seem to have taken on this role. We also see Christians traveling and, in doing so, finding bonds of fellowship in other Christian churches. And so the Philippian Christian communities, those among the Pauline churches showing the highest degree of associational behavior, are in communication with one another to the extent that they have organized a collection for Paul.

This aspect of distinction has, however, been disputed. Ascough argues that national associations might keep contact with their native land and that members of cultic associations might go to other associations elsewhere attached to the same cult and find membership.[96] This much is true, but the extent to which Christian communities intentionally formed networks is distinct both within and beyond their immediate locality. Thus Ascough cites the example of an association of Tyrian merchants at Puteoli who were unable to pay their rent. They wrote to Tyre, who in turn contacted a Tyrian association in Rome, to assist those at Puteoli.[97] What is to be noticed is that the request was channeled through Tyre, and there was no direct contact between the two Tyrian associations. However, to use a comparable example, when Polycarp came to Rome, he had contact with the Asian Christian communities but also with non-Asian.[98] When Quartodeciman practice becomes an issue in Rome at the end of the second century, there is contact between the non-Asian and the Asian communities in Rome (had there been none, there would not have been a problem) and also between Victor (on behalf of the Roman presbyters) and Polycrates.[99]

Whereas locality might not be part of an associational belief system, it is a recognizable phenomenon in the light of the translocal nature of churches, for which fellowship with Christians beyond the local fellowship was fundamental. Beyond this, however, we must pose the question of whether, in the

95. Ibid., citing an unpublished paper by Thomas A. Robinson. Robinson's views on this matter are expressed in his *Ignatius of Antioch and the Parting of the Ways: Early Jewish-Christian Relations* (Peabody, MA: Hendrickson, 2009), 87.

96. Richard S. Ascough, "Translocal Relationships among Voluntary Associations and Early Christianity," *JECS* 5 (1997): 223–41.

97. *CIG* 5853.

98. So Irenaeus, in Eusebius, *Hist. eccl.* 5.24.16.

99. Eusebius, *Hist. eccl.* 5.24.1.

earliest stages, there was anything between the immediate congregation and the worldwide fellowship of Christians; as I have already begun to argue, it is the formation of a view of church that is beyond the individual congregation but is more localized than simply a metaphysical view of a church as a communion that is central to the emergence of monepiscopacy and, thus, central to the change in the nature of episcopate as well as to a church that is less recognizable as an association and more recognizable to us as a church.

The purpose of this section was to take issue with those who argue against Hatch's fundamental argument that the duties of the *episkopos* are economic on the grounds that the churches were not associations. However, we have seen that the associational model is not necessary to sustain Hatch's insight into the origin of *episkopoi*. Even so, some churches, we have seen, manifest associational behavior. Of others we are less sure. What is perhaps most significant is that the church among those addressed by Paul that manifests associational behavior to the greatest extent is the one in Philippi; of all these churches, this is the one that manifests the existence in its organization of *episkopoi*.

The associational model is a ready model by which the episcopal office, understood as basically sumptuary or financial, might enter the church. However, it is to be noted that principally *episkopos* was a title derived from governmental activity, and I may suggest that it entered the associations through that route. There is a rationale for this: associations mirrored governments, a role that was of particular significance in a setting of social destabilization, as veterans were settled in *coloniae* and slaves were transferred from owner to owner.[100] The association supplied the opportunity for a *cursus honorum* in which the qualifications were somewhat different from those in an average town,[101] and so slaves and freedmen, who could not participate in civic government, might find a place of honor in an association.[102] In the same way, I may suggest, churches provided the basis by which persons of relatively low social status might achieve some degree of compensatory status.

However, households similarly might mirror government. According to Pliny, the household is a state, as far as slaves within the household are concerned.[103] Associations and households alike, despite Paul's rhetoric of equality, manifested the same stratified understanding of society and honor found throughout the classical world.

100. So John S. Kloppenborg, "Collegia and *Thiasoi*: Issues in Function, Taxonomy and Membership," in Kloppenborg and Wilson, *Voluntary Associations*, 17–18.

101. Ibid., 18.

102. Thus, *CIL* 14.2874 lists the names of two freedmen who were *magistri* of the association and two slaves who held the position of *ministri*, whereas *CIL* 14.2875 names four slave *magistri*.

103. Pliny, *Ep.* 8.16.

Ultimately, the problem with the associational model is that it is too broad to be useful. Whereas associations might meet in domestic premises, others owned their own dedicated meeting places. Some were relatively open, others closed on the basis of professional or confessional boundaries. Thus, if we were to compare a church to an association, we might say that it was an association based on religious belief, usually meeting in domestic premises and performing religious functions, but in doing so we would hardly be advancing our understanding of the church. Indeed, although Meeks denies strong influence from the associations on the formation of Christianity, he nonetheless admits certain similarities. Both were small and tightly knit groups, he suggests, and both were the result of a free decision to join.[104] Even here we may suggest that such generalization is unsafe; some associations were large, and one wonders about the extent to which the slaves of Agripinilla,[105] those of Dionysius,[106] or indeed those of the household of Stephanas in Corinth exercised free choice about joining the community.

Conclusions on the Economic Role of Episkopoi and the Associational Model of Church

Even if there is absolutely no influence from the association on the formation of Christian groups, which is unlikely, this does not altogether invalidate Hatch's argument. The term *episkopos* is a widely employed one for an economic functionary, and it may have come into Christian usage solely on the basis of its common use. If the church is modeled on an association, then the link is more probable; but it is possible that the term, having found its way into associations from civic government, might find its way to Christian groups in the same manner. In addition, the manner in which the term has echoes of the shepherd imagery of the Septuagint would commend it to Christian use.[107] The presence of the term in Scripture might not of itself be

104. Meeks, *First Urban Christians*, 78.
105. *IGUR* 160.
106. This Dionysius is recorded in *SIG* 985, having had a vision regarding his household cult. See, for discussion, Stanley K. Stowers, "A Cult from Philadelphia: *Oikos* Religion or Cultic Association?" in *The Early Church in Its Context: Essays in Honor of Everett Ferguson*, ed. Abraham J. Malherbe, Frederick W. Norris, and James W. Thompson, NovTSup 90 (Leiden: Brill, 1998), 287–301. While I appreciate his point that there was little in terms of freedom of membership (301) and his emphasis on the domestic basis of this religious practice, I wonder whether his title assumes a false dichotomy.
107. Note the discussion of the contributions of Rudolf Schnackenberg, "Episkopos und Hirtenamt: Zu Apg 20,28," in *Schriften zum Neuen Testament: Exegese in Fortschritt und Wandel* (Munich: Kösel, 1971), 247–66; Evald Lövestam, "Paul's Address at Miletus," *ST* 41 (1987): 1–10, considered in chap. 1 above, under the heading "Acts 20 as Evidence for Federation at Ephesus."

a sufficient rationale for its adoption, but the echo of Scripture might make this title, rather than other comparable official titles on offer, more attractive. The term "shepherd" (*poimēn*) is employed once in the New Testament to describe church leaders,[108] but in other instances where the same function is described, in 1 Peter 5:1–4 and Acts 20:28, it appears in a context where *episkopos* is also employed. In the church order literature likewise the term "shepherd" is a virtual synonym for *episkopos*,[109] and so the possibility cannot be excluded that the term was in use but was, if so used, an alternative designation for the *episkopos*.[110]

Beyond the matter of designation, however, the point to observe above all is that there is ample evidence of *episkopoi*, both Christian and otherwise, exercising an economic ministry; it is in this light that we may see the use of the term as entirely appropriate.

Thus, whereas Hatch's conclusions on the associational model of the church have been found, ultimately, of limited heuristic value, one point overall is of lasting significance: he argued that the role of the early Christian *episkopos* was fundamentally financial. Whereas much of the evidence that he cited might be used to suggest that the role of the *episkopos became* financial, further discoveries and new understanding of some of the earliest Christian literature has shown him to be correct on this fundamental point.

Next we may note that amid all the difficulties and uncertainties of classifying associations, and amid all the qualifications that must be placed upon any general statement regarding them, there is one aspect of associational behavior that, if not central, is at least widespread and is fundamental to the church: participation in ritual meals. This is not a matter of borrowing from associations, however, as the ritual meal is essential to the church's activity, but it is an activity that nonetheless would be recognized by Greco-Roman observers as associational.

Members of associations ate together; in particular, associations with a strong religious dimension sacrificed and engaged in ritual meals. *CIL* 14.2112, from early in the second century CE, sets out the feast days of the association of Diana and Antinoos. Similarly, we may observe the rules of the College of Aesculapius and Hygia from Rome at about the same time.[111] *CPJ* 139 is a list of contributors to a dining club in Egypt in the first century BCE, and from a similar time P.Lond. 2710 makes provision for a guild of Zeus to eat

108. Eph. 4:11.
109. *Can. eccl. ap.* 18.2; *Did. ap.* 2.1.
110. In agreement with Helmut Merklein, *Das kirchliche Amt nach dem Epheserbrief*, SANT 33 (Munich: Kösel, 1973), 368.
111. *CIL* 6.10234.

together on a monthly basis.[112] *IGBulg.* 3.2 1626 refers to an association called the "diners of the God Asclepius" (*synposiastai theou Asklēpiou*), whose name is fairly self-explanatory. *ID* 1520 is an honorific inscription from a guild dedicated to Poseidon on behalf of a patron and describes the sacrifice of a bull and the accompanying banquet. I will note other examples below of gymnastic associations sacrificing and eating together. It is important to observe that these associations combine both a social and a ritual element in eating and drinking together, for, as Harland rightly reminds us, religious life was not distinct from the social life of the polis.[113]

Likewise, members of the church ate together. This statement at least needs no justification, but surprisingly it seems overlooked in discussions of the formation of church order. Just as non-Christian associations and Christian gatherings each ate together, so both groups needed to ensure that food was available. Associations made provision for the supply of food from patrons, from officers, or from a common chest. We can assume that the church did likewise. The role of an officer within the church must therefore be intimately related to the need to ensure a supply of food.

It is this fact that leads me to seek to uphold Hatch's fundamental insight into the charitable role of the *episkopos*. Josaitis, otherwise a sympathetic critic of Hatch, states, "We may only turn to the Acts to see that the principal ministerial works consisted in preaching, teaching, baptizing, breaking bread, imparting the gift of the Holy Spirit."[114] In response, I may observe in the first instance that Acts tells us little of the work of *episkopoi* unless, as will be discussed below, James is to be considered one; the functions described here are those of apostles. The information regarding *episkopoi* in Acts is to be gotten from the exhortation to the gathering at Miletus, and, as already noted, this exhortation indicates that at least part of the role of these leaders is that they be mindful of the weak and supply the church's physical needs.

Most significantly, we must not forget that the eucharist, over which the *episkopos*, I will argue, presided, was in the earliest period a *Sättigungsmahl*, and that a considerable variety of foods were consumed in the context of sacred meals. Next, we should recall that in a society in which food supply was unreliable, the grant of a meal, in churches as in civic sacrifices and associational meals, was in and of itself a means of extending charity. Thus, whatever else the *episkopos* did, he dispensed food. Finger therefore rightly reminds us that ritual meals and charitable activity are not necessarily separate

112. For the text with some commentary, see C. H. Roberts, T. C. Skeat, and A. D. Nock, "The Gild of Zeus Hypsistos," *HTR* 29 (1936): 39–88.
113. Harland, *Associations*, 108–12.
114. Josaitis, *Edwin Hatch*, 128.

and distinct activities in early Christianity.[115] It is at the meal that the poor may be fed. The same, it may be suggested, is the case in associations and in civic sacrifices. Here too was the opportunity for people to obtain a meal in a society in which the food supply was not guaranteed. If there is a difference, it lies in the scope of inclusion rather than in the activity itself.

This, in turn, is the basis on which to claim *episkopoi* as fundamentally financial officers, in that the liturgy is the point at which, at least initially, charity is offered. There is no contradiction in seeing the *episkopos* as both liturgical president and financial agent.[116] Therefore, whereas Brent is right to distinguish the activity of a first-century *episkopos* from that of the *episkopos* of *Didascalia apostolorum* on the grounds that the *episkopos* of the latter administers charity outside the liturgy, I may suggest that the charitable activity of the bishop in the Didascalist community is a derivation from that of his first-century predecessor, as it remains the case that the liturgy is the point at which the offerings of the people for the relief of the poor are collected, the difference being that they are not distributed at that point.

The gathering for a meal was a critical point at which the Christian association offered charity. There was, moreover, a second point at which something of this nature might be in the realm of an *episkopos*: hospitality might be a means of extending charity. We have already noted that the issue in 3 John between the *presbyteros* and Diotrephes was Diotrephes's refusal of hospitality to envoys of the *presbyteros*. It was argued that Diotrephes was a householder and in a position to make such a refusal. As a householder, we may now see, he is not an *episkopos*, even less a *monepiskopos*;[117] however, he effectively functions as such in that he is the head of his own household and exercises authority within it.[118]

In time, moreover, we read of hospitality as a duty of *episkopoi*;[119] although there are fewer apostles with the passing of time, as the federated presbyters take over the function of communication within cities, nonetheless communication

---

115. Reta Halteman Finger, *Of Widows and Meals: Communal Meals in the Book of Acts* (Grand Rapids: Eerdmans, 2007), 49.

116. Note Volp: "The New Testament texts seem to have administrative and management matters in mind rather than liturgical functions" ("Liturgical Authority," 194).

117. See Theodor Zahn, *Introduction to the New Testament*, trans. John Moore Trout et al., 3 vols. (Edinburgh: T&T Clark, 1909), 3:375–76. See also my discussion in chap. 1 above, under the heading "The Johannine School at Ephesus."

118. Compare Abraham J. Malherbe: "We have found no evidence that to have a church meet in one's home bestowed any authority on the host" ("The Inhospitality of Diotrephes," in Jervell and Meeks, eds., *God's Christ and His People*, 229). The point, however, is that the host has power *ab initio* and does not need ecclesiastical authority.

119. Titus 1:7–8.

by letter continues between representatives of federations. As literature is disseminated among congregations (note Polycarp's correspondence with the Philippians regarding, at least in part, Ignatius's correspondence; Clement's writing on behalf of the Roman church to the Corinthians; and subsequently Victor's correspondence with Polycrates and others), these letters have to be carried, requiring hospitality for the letter carrier both en route and on arrival. Beyond this, hospitality is still required for traveling Christians in a world in which inns generally were to be avoided and it was preferable to find hospitality with "kin," a term that, in Christian circles, might extend to any other Christian.[120] Showing hospitality, it seems, came to fall to *episkopoi* rather than to individual householders, although I may suggest, in view of the appearance of the quality of hospitality in *Haustafeln*, that this was a secondary development and that it came to be an episcopal duty only after the office was established. In particular this may have been the case because the exercise of hospitality might be the means of obtaining *honor*. D'Arms points out that the prestige of hosting a Roman dignitary might be sufficient reciprocation in return for the hospitality extended.[121] However, I may suggest that this was a secondary development, and that primary in the establishment of this office was the fundamental Christian act of worshiping together at table.

The Implications of the Economic Role of the Episkopos

If the *episkopos* is a financial officer, then a significant set of issues derives from that fact. These, first, regard the relationship between a financial officer and the practice of patronage, and, second, oblige us to examine the conflicting models of household and association as means of understanding the formation of early Christian groupings in a new way. This examination in

120. So Horace and Maecenas, traveling to Brindisium (Horace, *Sat.* 1.5), stay variously at inns (which involve Horace apparently being poisoned by water) but also with relatives and acquaintances. In the Christian literature we may recollect *Acts John* 60–61, with its report of bed bugs, and *Vit. Pol.* 27, in which Polycarp and Camerios stay in an inn (which falls down during the night!) because there are no Christians in the vicinity. Even later, monks are directed to use inns only as a last resort, if there is no hospitality available either from Christian people or in a church building (Pseudo-Athanasius, *Syntagma doctrinae* 8). On the subject in general, see Tönnes Kleberg, *Hôtels, restaurants et cabarets dans l'antiquité romaine: Études historiques et philologiques*, BE 61 (Uppsala: Almqvist & Wiksell, 1957). Note also Michael B. Thompson, "The Holy Internet: Communication between Churches in the First Christian Generation," in *The Gospels for All Christians: Rethinking the Gospel Audiences*, ed. Richard J. Bauckham (Grand Rapids: Eerdmans, 1998), 49–70; on the remarkable amount of traveling undertaken by early Christians and on traveling conditions in general, see Caroline A. J. Skeel, *Travel in the First Century: With Special Reference to Asia Minor* (Cambridge: Cambridge University Press, 1901).

121. John H. d'Arms, "Control, Companionship and *clientela*: Some Social Functions of the Roman Communal Meal," *EMC* 3 (1984): 333–34.

turn brings questions of its own regarding the relationship between economic officers and the patrons themselves.

The *Episkopos* and the Exercise of Patronage

Here patronage is defined, following Saller, to be a reciprocal exchange of goods and services between two parties in an asymmetrical relationship over a period of time.[122] It is thus distinguished from both a purchase in a market (which is not a relationship of duration) and the exchange of gifts between equals (a horizontal relationship, though this is often hard to define). Such relationships were widespread in the ancient world. A similar definition is offered by Garnsey and Woolf: patronage is "an enduring bond between two persons of unequal social and economic status which is implied and is maintained by periodic exchanges of goods and services, and also has social and affective dimensions."[123] The counterpart to the patron is the client, the inferior party in the relationship. Patrons controlled resources, such as land, food, jobs, and government favor, and so needed to be cultivated. The return need not be financial, but honorific. To be seen as powerful is as important as being powerful, and so powerful patrons might build up a retinue of supporters, who call on them in the morning *salutatio* and accompany them as they walk around the city. Epictetus calls a judge to account, asking how he obtained his post, suggesting that it was obtained through flattery, through sleeping in doorways of the powerful so that he could greet them in the morning, and through sending gifts;[124] Juvenal describes a client following his patron and filling his ears with flattery throughout the day in the hope of obtaining a dinner invitation.[125] Even allowing for satyric and comic exaggeration in both examples, there is more than a grain of truth in these pictures. Thus, Seneca claims that those who seek office in this way are obtaining it at the price of life.[126]

Beyond *honor*, loyalty (*fides*) was a significant part of the relationship of *clientela*. Freed slaves, for instance, became on manumission clients of their former masters; in turn, a high degree of loyalty was expected and was shown. This might be in small matters. In the opening scene of the *Andria*, for example, a patron asks his freedman for an expression of his *fides*, namely, his support

---

122. Richard P. Saller, *Personal Patronage under the Early Empire* (Cambridge: Cambridge University Press, 1982), 1.

123. Peter Garnsey and Greg Woolf, "Patronage of the Rural Poor in the Roman World," in *Patronage in Ancient Society*, ed. Andrew Wallace-Hadrill, LNSAS 1 (London: Routledge, 1989), 154.

124. Epictetus, *Diss.* 3.7.29–33.

125. Juvenal, *Sat.* 1.132–33.

126. Seneca, *Brev. vit.* 19.3–20.1.

in entrapping his son through a subterfuge.[127] However, a freedman's *fides* was meant to be absolute; thus the Lex Aelia Sentia of 4 CE (Augustus) refers to punishment for disloyal freedmen, and Claudius directs that freedmen who failed to demonstrate *fides* or gratitude were to be reenslaved.[128]

This will prove significant when we come to consider the manner in which there might be competition within Christian communities for positions of leadership. We have already noted Ignatius's instruction to Polycarp not to allow church funds to be employed for the manumission of slaves.[129] If church funds or private funds were employed for that purpose, this would create a situation in which the freedman would owe primary *fides* toward the manumitting individual, who in turn might use this loyalty to threaten the position of the *episkopos*. Cicero states that the greatest degree of *fides* derives from patronage of the poor,[130] and so we may similarly see the way in which *Didascalia apostolorum* restricts the patronage of poor widows to bishops, and excludes private patrons, as a means by which there is no conflict of *fides* within the church.

Beyond personal patronage, however, it is to be noted that individuals might act as patrons to groups, in particular to associations, including religious associations broadly defined, and including Christian churches. We have already noted associations courting the powerful, receiving funding or premises from them, and giving in return honorific designations, voting them statues and granting them votes. It is possible, therefore, that the Christian church might likewise receive patronage; indeed, the entire structure of domestic Christianity implies that those who acted as hosts were perceived as patrons. To achieve a position of status within a Greco-Roman city required significant wealth. Pliny's Comum required one hundred thousand sesterces of a councilor (the price of a small farm), and, as Bekker-Nielsen points out, similar sums are possessed by the two councilors from Prusa whose financial situations are known.[131] However, patronage within a church might be a means by which persons of more moderate means could receive *honor*. Greater persons might act as patrons to towns, providing public feasts to persons capable of offering adequate reciprocity;[132] we may thus see the high social status of Christian leaders such as Stephanas and Alce as relative only.

127. *Andria* 1.1.
128. Suetonius, *Claud.* 25.
129. Ign. *Pol.* 4:3.
130. Cicero, *Off.* 2.62–71.
131. Tønnes Bekker-Nielsen, *Urban Life and Local Politics in Roman Bithynia: The Small World of Dion Chrysostomos*, BSS 7 (Aarhus: Aarhus University Press, 2008), 67.
132. So *TAM* 2.578 (from Lycia); *SEG* 1.276 (from Macedonia).

Having already pointed out that a meal was a context in which charity might be given, I may now point out that it is, by virtue of this act, an event that might be the locus at which patronage is both offered and manifested. We may note the comic descriptions by Juvenal and Martial regarding the manner in which inferior food is offered to clients, as the patron demonstrates to other members of the patronal classes his prominence in having a *clientela* and reenforces his superior status with regard to his *clientela*.[133] Despite the comic exaggeration (we are not meant really to believe that fish from the sewers were served up), Pliny reassures us that this was not an invention.[134] In the same way, great concern was shown regarding the order of seating at a meal, because the manner in which seating was arranged both manifested and reinforced social structures.[135] This same social stratification was manifested and reinforced at public banquets, as well as private occasions, and through similar means.[136]

These realities illuminate certain aspects of ritual meals in Christian circles. That the distinction in food would seem to have taken place at the ritual meals of the Corinthian community is deduced by Theissen from a number of comments addressed by Paul to the Corinthians.[137] Moreover, Stephanas is, by virtue of his status as a householder, host and thus patron to the Corinthian Christians. Thus, if the central locus of early Christian gathering is a meal, and an *episkopos* is an officer with an economic role within the Christian gathering, then it is possible for an *episkopos* to act patronally. Just as the supply of food might constitute a patronal act for the church, so the seating arrangements of the officers would make a statement regarding the proper hierarchy. For this reason, we must see the activity of Christian leaders at ritual meals in the light of the manner in which patrons throughout Roman society demonstrated benevolence as a means to obtain recognition.

As I have noted that hospitality becomes a function of *episkopoi* as both the church and the office develop into the second century, so I may suggest that hospitality also became a means of exercising patronage. I have suggested

133. E.g., Juvenal, *Sat.* 5.12–19; Martial *Epig.* 3.60; 4.68.

134. Pliny, *Ep.* 2.6, describing Pliny's attendance at a dinner in which different food and wine were served to guests of different status.

135. "The *cena* . . . implicated diners in a hierarchical and competitive environment" (Keith Bradley, "The Roman Family at Dinner," in *Meals in a Social Context: Aspects of the Communal Meal in the Hellenistic and Roman World*, ed. Inge Nielsen and Hanne Sigismund Nielsen, ASMA 1 (Aarhus: Aarhus University Press, 1998), 26–55, 39. Plutarch, *Quaest. conv.* 1.2–3 (615D–619) is an extended discussion of the need to ensure proper order in the seating of guests.

136. So Onno M. van Nijf, *The Civic World of Professional Associations in the Roman East*, DMAHA 17 (Amsterdam: J. C. Gieben, 1997), 149–88.

137. Gerd Theissen, *The Social Setting of Pauline Christianity: Essays on Corinth*, trans. and ed. John H. Schütz (Philadelphia: Fortress, 1982), 155–63.

that the *leitourgia* of the *episkopoi* and *diakonoi* of the *Didache* consisted of the economic support of prophets and teachers, and I may go on from there to suggest that this economic support consisted primarily of hospitality. A picture of such patronal hospitality may be obtained from Lucian's *De mercede conductis potentium familiaribus*; the manner in which his changing status is illustrated by his changing place at table is an indication of the manner in which hospitality is bound up to, not distinct from, the exercise of patronage relationships. Hospitality need not consist of the exercise of uneven relationships, but if a relationship between the persons who are host and guest is already uneven, then this is reflected in the actions of host and guest.[138] Thus Diotrephes's refusal of hospitality is a refusal of patronage of those who are already a *clientela* of the elder and whose *fides*, therefore, would not be his.

It need not have been the case, however, that the householder or *episkopos* became the patron. Early Christian documents show a variety of attitudes toward patronage; in particular, to pick up a point made earlier, if God is truly the head of the church, then God is truly the patron, and so the *episkopos* or the householder need not be the patron. Stoops shows that *Acts of Peter*, while depicting household gatherings of Christians and extensive benefactions by wealthy individuals, explicitly demonstrates, both in its narrative and in editorial comment, that the householders and benefactors should not become leaders in the Christian community by virtue of their benefaction.[139] However, in doing so it seems to be running against the Pauline model, by which household leaders become ecclesiastical leaders by default.

Even if not a patron, however, an *episkopos* may occupy the position of power known as the broker. The broker is the agent by which access to a yet more powerful patron might be obtained, thereby becoming a patron not through the direct supply of goods but through being the conduit. Thus Pliny writes to Trajan requesting senatorial rank for Voconius Romanus, thereby becoming patron to Voconius by being the means by which Voconius might access the emperor.[140] The patron-broker system might set up complex networks of mutual loyalty and indebtedness. For example, Pliny agrees to represent a town, Firmium, on the approach of Statius Sabinus, who was patron of the town.[141] Consequently the town gained representation through its patron

---

138. See Igor Lorencin, "Hospitality versus Patronage: An Investigation of Social Dynamics in the Third Epistle of John," *AUSS* 46 (2008): 165–74. Lorencin contrasts patronage and hospitality but in doing so assumes that relationships are equal from the start. The contrast is thus based purely on its (flawed) premises.

139. Robert F. Stoops Jr., "Patronage in the Acts of Peter," in *The Apocryphal Acts of Apostles*, ed. Dennis R. MacDonald, Semeia 38 (Decatur, GA: Scholars Press, 1986), 91–100.

140. Pliny, *Ep.* 10.3.

141. Pliny, *Ep.* 6.18.

acting as broker. In response, Pliny uses the language of horizontal relationships, *amicitia*, but this may be seen as a subtle means of putting himself into a relationship of patronage toward Sabinus.

It is as brokers that Estrada characterizes the role of the apostles in the opening chapters of the book of Acts. Estrada suggests that the apostles are not "hierarchical" leaders but rather brokers between God (the patron) and the people (the clients).[142] This actually is hierarchical, but the point is nonetheless made that the patron is God, not the apostles themselves. As the apex of the human leadership, it is significant that the apostles have an echelon of influence above them. As such, they have taken over from Jesus, who, in Luke, acts as broker for the patronage of God.[143] This was the point of observing above, when it was suggested that *episkopoi* were never the leaders in associations, that God was always the true head of the church. Nonetheless, if the *episkopos* oversees a meal, then, even if he is a broker under God, he is in a position of patronage toward those being fed.

Episkopoi in Households and Associations

I have already discussed the extent to which churches are based on households. Although some churches manifest associational behavior, and although it is possible that Jewish models provided the basis for the formation of offices in some Christian communities, these insights do not contradict any conception of the church as based on a household, because associations might be formed on a household basis and synagogues might meet within a domestic setting.[144]

The issue with the household model is that households generally do not generate offices, except insofar as they reflect wider society. If the householder is simply the leader of his house, there is no reason for him to receive any title. For this reason I may agree with the many studies that have pointed out that there are no clear indications of titles or offices in the Pauline churches. But while agreeing that this is the case, I do not need to follow any romanticizing notion that this is because there was order based solely on the Spirit.[145] Rather,

---

142. Nelson P. Estrada, *From Followers to Leaders: The Apostles in the Ritual of Status Transformation in Acts 1–2*, JSNTSup 255 (London: T&T Clark, 2004), 52–62.

143. So Halvor Moxnes, "Patron-Client Relations and the New Community in Luke-Acts," in *The Social World of Luke-Acts: Models for Interpretation*, ed. Jerome H. Neyrey (Peabody, MA: Hendrickson, 1991), 241–68.

144. On synagogues adapted in stages from domestic buildings, see the examples from Priene and Delos discussed by Peter Richardson, "Building 'An Association (*synodos*) . . . and a Place of Their Own,'" in *Community Formation in the Early Church and in the Church Today*, ed. Richard N. Longenecker (Peabody, MA: Hendrickson, 2002), 36–56.

145. Such ideas and contributions are discussed at length in chap. 5 below, under the heading "Institutionalization as an Explanation of Monepiscopacy."

if a household simply became a Christian household, there was no need to designate leadership by titles, as leadership simply rested in the leadership of the household. I have already noted the role of Stephanas at Corinth; moving beyond the Pauline churches, I may note Hermas as an example of an individual householder exercising leadership by virtue of his status. Finally, I may observe that the Agripinilla inscription, in spite of the vast number of titles given to contributors, gives none to the patroness. Thus, to return to Acts 14:23, I may note that this passage is taken as historically impossible by Campenhausen,[146] who observes that Paul does not appoint specific leaders in the church and is defended by Nellesen, who argues that a Jerusalem-Jewish model of presbyteral leadership is being installed at the behest of Barnabas.[147] I have already argued that the leaders are not individually identified; thus, there is no reason why the passage should be historically impossible (which is not the same as saying that it is historical fact), as Paul effectively installs householders as leaders of churches. He does not appoint leaders by title but leaders by effect.

Single-household churches, therefore, did not necessarily have titled officers. We may recollect the uncertainty at Acts 20:28 as to whether the statements regarding *episkopoi* related to function or to office; the same issue will be confronted when 1 Peter comes under consideration below. While that matter is not being discussed here, I may note that householders might function in the same way as officers of the congregation without actually bearing any title, as in the case of Diotrephes, owner of a house and thus in a position to refuse hospitality to envoys of the elder. Even if these presbyters *kata polin* are not titled *episkopoi*, they function as such within their own households. Thus, if we are to account for the manifestation of officers in some household churches, such as in Philippi, some hypothesis is required. I may suggest that even if the church was a domestic church, if it had officers such as *episkopoi*, then it was not simply a household but rather a gathering of different persons, including other householders, in a single house. In this instance it becomes more properly understood as a domestically based association rather than simply a household, and in that instance it might be necessary to appoint an officer to manage the funds provided by the various patrons and to ensure that the ritual meals might take place with sufficient food. Leaders of individual households, taking leadership by virtue of their position, were not necessarily termed *episkopoi*.

146. Campenhausen, *Ecclesiastical Authority*, 77.
147. E. Nellessen, "Die Presbyter der Gemeinden in Lykaonien und Pisidien (Apg 14,23)," in Kremer, *Les Actes des Apôtres*, 493–98.

Episkopoi, however, do come to appear in household churches. A clue to the reason for this may be gleaned from another title employed for the *episkopos* of Titus, namely, God's "steward" (*oikonomos*).[148] The *oikonomos* was an officer whom one might expect to find in an organization in which money and goods such as food are handled, whether the household model is more prominent in the organization's self-understanding or whether the self-understanding of the society and the titles employed for its officers are derived from government.

The *oikonomos* was a financial officer, whether major or minor, of a large household, estate, or city. In Xenophon's dialogue on estate management, the function of an *oikonomos* is initially defined as being the good management of his own or another's estate.[149] Beyond the private realm, we find *oikonomoi* in civic and in national government; thus *IG* 12 suppl. 644 is an inscription from Macedonia regarding the role of a royal *oikonomos*. Found in an underground chamber, which may well have been a storeroom, the decree sets out the responsibilities of *oikonomoi* for ensuring that there is a constant supply of the fundamental military materiel, grain, wine, and wood.[150] The term may be used for an imperial procurator,[151] for a city official,[152] for the manager of an imperial estate,[153] or indeed, perhaps significantly for our purpose, for an officer in a religious cult association.[154]

Although often a member of the slave class, or a freedman,[155] it is notable that in the *Deipnosophistae* the *oikonomos* has overall charge of the banquet.[156] Thus, when we read in Titus that the *episkopos* is the *oikonomos* of God, we would not perhaps be far wrong in seeing this *oikonomos* as likewise in charge of the Christian gathering at table as an extension of the role of an *oikonomos* in the provision of food. That the office of *episkopos* was, in the community circulating the Pastoral Epistles as elsewhere, fundamentally economic is indicated not simply in the qualification lists given, which may be

148. Titus 1:7.
149. Xenophon, *Oec.* 1.2.
150. For some discussion, see C. Bradford Welles, "New Texts from the Chancery of Philip V of Macedonia and the Problem of the 'Diagramma,'" *AJA* 42 (1938): 245–60.
151. P.Tebt. 2.296.12.
152. *ILeuk.* 78; *TAM* 2.1151; *SEG* 39.1316 record *oikonomoi* τῆς πόλεως.
153. See the inscription recorded by J. G. C. Anderson, "An Imperial Estate in Galatia," *JRS* 27 (1931): 18–21.
154. *SEG* 4.509 (regarding a Serapaeum in Magnesia). The *oikonomoi* are to make arrangement and provision for the sacrifices.
155. A point emphasized in Dale B. Martin, *Slavery as Salvation: The Metaphor of Slavery in Pauline Christianity* (New Haven: Yale University Press, 1990), 15–22. As an example, we may note Gaius from Bithynia, who is an *oikonomos*, apparently of the city, who is manumitted by his masters, the citizens (*CIG* 3777).
156. Athenaeus, *Deipn.* 1B.

simply traditional,[157] but in one particular instruction given to the *episkopos*. Without yet entering into the issue of the identity or function of presbyters in 1 Timothy, I may note the direction that they are to be given a double portion of food at the meals of the community. I may also note that the fictive addressee is Timothy, whose duties are to be taken on by *episkopoi* and who, as Roloff suggests, is the model *episkopos*.[158] From this I may deduce in turn that it was the responsibility of the *oikonomos*—that is to say, of the *episkopos*—to ensure that this double portion was assigned. In other words, the qualification list, the terminology employed of the *episkopos*, and the particular duty that is outlined indicate that he had primary responsibility for the management of the church's household.

Once again, this domestic model does not exclude insights from voluntary associations or government. Not only does Pliny argue that the household is a ministate, Philo several times makes the same point.[159] We have already noted that households and cities alike have *oikonomoi*; moreover, *oikonomoi* might well function within associations and cults. At Magnesia the *oikonomoi* of the city are responsible for sacrificing three victims as well as for sharing out the portions in the cult of Zeus Sosipolis[160] as for Sarapis,[161] here presumably functioning in their civic capacity, whereas, in Egypt, *oikonomoi* are responsible for the supply of bread to the priestesses of the Serapeion at Memphis.[162]

157. So Hans-Werner Bartsch, *Die Anfänge urchristlicher Rechtsbildung*, TF 34 (Hamburg: Herbert Reich, 1965). Bartsch suggests that lying behind much material in the Pastoral Epistles is a traditional church order, found elsewhere in the church order tradition.

158. Jürgen Roloff, *Der erste Brief an Timotheus*, EKKNT 15 (Zürich: Benziger; Neukirchen-Vluyn: Neukirchener Verlag, 1988), 170.

159. "There are two kinds of states, the greater and the smaller. And the larger ones are called really cities; but the smaller ones are called houses. And the superintendence and management of these is allotted to the two sexes separately; the men having the government of the greater, which government is called a polity; and the women that of the smaller, which is called economy" (Philo, *Spec.* 3.170). "Accordingly, in consequence of this opinion of his purchaser, he was appointed superintendent of his house, apparently indeed by his master, but, in fact and reality, by nature herself, which procured for him the government of a mighty city, and nation, and country. For it was necessary that one who was destined to be a statesman should be previously practiced and trained in the management of a single household; for a household is a city on a small and contracted scale, and the management of a household is a contracted kind of polity; so that a city may be called a large house, and the government of a city a widely spread economy. And from these considerations we may see that the manager of a household and the governor of a state are identical, though the multitude and magnitude of the things committed to their charge may be different" (Philo, *Joseph*, 38–39).

160. *IMagn.* 98.

161. *IMagn.* 99.

162. John Reumann, "'Stewards of God': Pre-Christian Religious Application of *oikonomos* in Greek," *JBL* 77 (1958): 345. Reumann cites a number of similar examples.

In conclusion, whether a Christian community based itself on a domestic, an associational, or a civic model, there would be the occasion for somebody to perform the role of an *oikonomos*, for central to the ritual of the group was the sharing of a meal. In view of the economic function of the early *episkopoi*, we may readily see the office of *episkopos* being equivalent to that of *oikonomos*.[163] Thus, I may say that the term *episkopos* may have been brought into Christian use as a term commonly employed throughout the empire, both in governance and in free associations, to refer to somebody with practical responsibilities within the organization, and that such a title might come about when the group begins to handle food or finance without the family. Once this has occurred, then in turn it becomes possible for a transition from traditionally legitimated leaders (householders) to bureaucratically legitimated leaders (*episkopoi*) to take place, even though their roles remain the same. The household, in many instances, may have been the origin of Christian meeting, but households begin to multiply from early on. Thus, whether households combine or individual Christian households relate to others within the city, the original household is overtaken and office begins to form, even as households become domestically based associations.

EPISKOPOI, OIKONOMOI, AND PATRONS

In chapter 1 I suggested that *episkopoi* and *presbyteroi* were not synonymous. We have now seen what the function of an *episkopos* was; although I have yet to explore the role of presbyters (apart from those standing as representatives of individual communities in federations), it seems less likely that, as a multiple group, they would have the same responsibility.

Beyond this, in what follows I must be careful to determine whether the *episkopos* is acting in an economic role by virtue of employment or by virtue of offering a *leitourgia*. We have already noted that in the *Didache* the *episkopos* is explicitly said to be offering a liturgy, and that the same is the case in *1 Clement*. Although this should not be made determinative of every appearance of the *episkopos* in his economic capacity (for *oikonomoi*, we have seen, may be slaves who are employed for the task), it does seem that the task was taken on as an honor. Such is the craving for honor in the society in which Christianity grew up that occasionally there is a blurring of the distinction between *leitourgiai* and *archai*. Quass cites the case of Zosimos,

---

163. See Hermann von Lips, *Glaube, Gemeinde, Amt: Zum Verständnis der Ordination in den Pastoralbriefen*, FRLANT 122 (Göttingen: Vandenhoeck & Ruprecht, 1979), 147–50. Von Lips, failing to appreciate the economic role of an *episkopos*, takes the image simply as referring to the relationship obtaining between God and the *episkopos* and sees the *episkopos* principally in didactic terms.

a "scribe of the council and the people" at Priene, who subsidized the city by providing his own materials, thus combining *archē* with *leitourgia* and being duly honored.[164] However, I may observe, as I did in discussing brokers, that the *episkopos* identified in this manner is effectively being subordinated, for in identifying the *episkopos* as an *oikonomos*, "Paul" is making it clear that the *episkopos* is subject to God, who is the proper householder.[165]

This set of questions in turn raises questions about the payment of officials. Clearly, patrons do not receive payment, except insofar as they may receive food in proportion to their generosity, which, given that a patron does not need food in the way that the poor do, is a manifestation not of financial support but of *honor*. It is possible that *episkopoi* might receive payment if they are employed, but even here the evidence is opposed. The first evidence of a paid *episkopos* comes from the late second century and from a separated group in Rome,[166] and that individual's actions are attributed to covetousness, whereas at a similar time the Montanist practice of paying ministers receives negative comment.[167] I have already noted Lambrecht's suggestion that the Paul of Acts 20 is indicating that leaders may be taking advantage of their support, and I stated there that such a view is unlikely. Barrett similarly deduces from Paul's emphasis in this speech on working with his hands that Luke is opposed to a paid or maintained ministry: "I Peter 5:2 clearly implies that there were money-grubbing pastors."[168] There is, however, no evidence of *episkopoi* receiving payment in this period; as I have already argued, the point of Paul's emphasis on the manner in which he was self-supporting is to encourage generosity on the part of these *episkopoi*. I must reiterate that there is no evidence for persons taking on *episkopē* except as an *honor*; it is more likely that the problem lay in *episkopoi* seeking the office in order to obtain such *honor*, and this may be the reason why Paul warns of those who distort the truth in order to draw people after them. As such, I may suggest that alternative teaching might be a means of luring away a *clientela*. It is true that among *episkopoi* there might,

164. Friedmann Quass, *Die Honoratiorenschicht in den Städten des griechischen Ostens: Untersuchungen zur politischen und sozialen Entwicklung in hellenistischer und römischer Zeit* (Stuttgart: Franz Steiner, 1993), 297–98, with reference to *IPriene* 112, 113, 114: γραμματεὺς τῆς βουλῆς καὶ τοῦ δήμου.

165. So von Lips, *Glaube*, 147–48.

166. Eusebius, *Hist. eccl.* 5.28.10–12.

167. Apollonius, quoted in Eusebius, *Hist. eccl.* 5.18.2.

168. C. K. Barrett, "Paul's Address to the Ephesian Elders," in Jervell and Meeks, eds., *God's Christ and His People*, 118. Barrett states that a "part-time and unpaid" ministry was likely to be joined to a charismatic view of authority. It is hard to know where to start criticizing that statement, but I may begin by noting that the prophets of the *Didache* might demand payment, whereas the local officers, the *episkopoi* and *diakonoi*, subsidized the activities of the charismatics.

in view of their economic task, be the opportunity for embezzlement, but this is a different matter altogether.

The treatment of the term by Williams raises some particularly interesting points regarding the social status of the *oikonomos* and the position of the *oikonomos* in the exercise of patronage.[169] She cites Diodorus's implied criticism of the Egyptian king Remphis, who amassed a large amount of wealth through management of the revenues but did not spend on sacrifices to the gods or to benefactions to the populace. Thus, "he was not so much a King as an efficient *oikonomos*."[170] In other words, Williams notes, he did not behave in a manner befitting a king. However, in this context the king was collecting and hoarding a limited amount of wealth; we likewise see *oikonomoi* distributing wealth, such as those supplying the bull for sacrifice,[171] or crowns for funerals,[172] either as a *leitourgia* or as an office (recalling that the distinction may be blurred),[173] but in either event playing a central role in the civic cult. Here we may see the manner in which the early Christian economic *episkopoi* exercised their office.

Finally, in the light of the discussion here, we may return to the question of whether there were multiple or single *episkopoi* in any given Christian community. I have observed already that the Pastoral Epistles employ domestic language to relate to the duties of the *episkopos* and assume that this person is a householder. Indeed, he is to watch over the household of the church as though it were his own. Thus it is rather less likely that there is more than one, as we may struggle to find multiple *oikonomoi* in households. As Merkel puts it, "Where the household with its hierarchical structure serves as an analogy for the congregation, then there can only be one householder ('bishop')."[174] The same, moreover, would be true if the *episkopos* is functioning by virtue of his status as a householder, for, as Aristotle makes clear, the householder exercises a single rule (*monarchia*) over the members of his household.[175] The idea of multiple *episkopoi* derives in the first instance from the hypothesis of the synonymy of *presbyteros* and *episkopos*; the fact that presbyters are found in the plural indicates, it is argued, that *episkopoi*

169. Ritva H. Williams, *Stewards, Prophets, Keepers of the Word: Leadership in the Early Church* (Peabody, MA: Hendrickson, 2006), 57–63.

170. Diodorus Siculus, *Bib. hist.* 1.62.5–6, cited by Williams, *Stewards*, 57.

171. As in the festival of Zeus Sosipolis at Magnesia (*IMagn.* 98).

172. E.g., *IPriene* 83, 109.

173. Thus, these gifts might be provided from city funds (so *IMagn.* 98) or from the *oikonomos*'s own (so in Priene [*SIG* 1003 = *IPriene* 174]).

174. "Wo das Haus mit seinem Ordnungsgefüge als Analogie zur Gemeinde dient, kann es nur einen Hausverwalter ('Bischof') geben" (Merkel, *Die Pastoralbriefe*, 90).

175. Aristotle, *Pol.* 1255B.

must likewise be plural. From there, and on the assumption, to be examined below, that presbyters are derived from the synagogue and that Christian churches are imitating synagogal patterns of leadership, the idea of collective leadership in each Christian community is read into the evidence. Thus the plural *presbyteroi*, for instance, in Acts 14:23 is taken to mean that a group of elders is appointed to each church,[176] whereas, as I have argued above, the plural *presbyteroi* are being appointed to plural Christian communities. If the understanding of the formation of the church in domestic premises has any relevance whatsoever, it implies that leadership devolved upon an individual, and, on this basis alone, the idea of collective leadership that underlies the consensus is untenable from the start.

However, although *presbyteroi* may in some instances be a collective title for gathered leaders of Christian communities, I will observe below that there are *presbyteroi* who are not *episkopoi* and who are entirely distinct from the presbyters *kata polin* identified in chapter 1, and who will be qualified as "congregational presbyters." I may also preempt the argument below by noting that this, like the appearance of the *episkopos* with defined economic function, comes about once the church has outgrown the single household and has become more deliberately associational. In this instance the *episkopos* would not be the single householder, and therefore he may indeed be not a patron offering a *leitourgia* but rather an officer functioning as an *oikonomos*; this leads in turn to the question of who actually did provide the necessary patronage. I will suggest below that this was the role of the congregational presbyters. Before discussing these *presbyteroi*, however, or indeed the *diakonoi* who are found so often in the company of *episkopoi*, I must note a further challenge to the theory outlined here.

Alternative Jewish Sources for the Office of *Episkopos*

When Hatch first propounded his suggestion, the countervailing suggestion was that the *episkopos* had derived not from pagan institutions but from the synagogue. Although this latter suggestion may contain a degree of apologetic motivation, I may nonetheless discuss the possibility that the office had emerged from Jewish institutions, a discussion that may take place in the light of the recognition that the role of the *episkopos* was financial.

There are two versions of the suggestion that episcopal office derived from Jewish circles: (1) the office was derived from that of the *archisynagōgos* (a

---

176. So, e.g., C. K. Barrett, *A Critical and Exegetical Commentary on the Acts of the Apostles*, 2 vols., ICC (Edinburgh: T&T Clark, 1994), 1:688.

position whose most prominent modern proponent is Burtchaell); (2) the more proximate model was the *mebaqqer* of Essene communities.

Episkopos *as* Archisynagōgos[177]

When Crispus, an *archisynagōgos* at Corinth, follows Paul, it causes great consternation;[178] similarly, when a Jewish delegation is turned away by the proconsul, the *archisynagōgos* Sosthenes is beaten.[179] As Burtchaell notes, "The two men were of strategic importance to the communities they served."[180]

The appearance of the term in the *Historia Augusta* also points to the central role of the *archisynagōgos* in Jewish society, as it is recorded that Alexander Severus was insulted by "the people of Antioch, of Egypt and of Alexandria," who called him a "Syrian *archisynagogus* and high-priest,"[181] whereas subsequently it is said of Egypt that there is no *archisynagōgos*, no Samaritan, and no Christian presbyter who is not an astrologer or a soothsayer.[182] Patristic authors also refer to the *archisynagōgos*; Epiphanius includes it in a list of Jewish titles,[183] and Palladius notes a rumor that the patriarch took payment either annually or biennially for the replacement of *archisynagōgoi*.[184] This may be a garbled version of the role of *archisynagōgoi* in collecting money for the patriarchate, which is said to be a responsibility of *archisynagōgoi* in *Codex Theodosianus* 16.8.14. However, the relatively late date of all this non-Jewish evidence should be observed.

The central role of the *archisynagōgos* in some Jewish societies is borne out to an extent by the inscriptional evidence. However, by the very nature of inscriptional evidence a different emphasis emerges. From this evidence two things about the office of *archisynagōgos* emerge clearly: first, the office might be hereditary;[185] second, the title frequently appears in connection with

177. Beyond literature cited here, note the discussion by Lee I. Levine, *The Ancient Synagogue: The First Thousand Years*, 2nd ed. (New Haven: Yale University Press, 2005), 415–27.

178. Acts 18:8.

179. Acts 18:12–17.

180. Burtchaell, *From Synagogue to Church*, 243.

181. "Syrum archisynagogum eum uocantes et archiereum" (*Historia Augusta, Alexander Severus* 28.7).

182. *Historia Augusta, Quadriga tyrannorum* 8.3.

183. Epiphanius, *Pan.* 30.11.1. We may note that this list includes presbyters.

184. Palladius, *Vit. Joh.* 15.

185. Note esp. *CIJ* 1404: "Theodotus, son of Vettenus and synagogue-ruler, son of a synagogue-ruler and grandson of a synagogue-ruler, built the synagogue for the reading of the law and instruction in the commandments; also the strangers' lodgings and the dining rooms and water facilities and hostel for the use of those from foreign lands. The foundation of this his fathers and the elders [*presbyteroi*] and Simonides laid." This inscription is discussed in chap. 3

the provision of goods or buildings.[186] Both imply a patronal role for the *archisynagōgos*, as the hereditary office would imply that the office was held by somebody of wealth, and wealth is passed on through families and found in a relatively restricted number of families. We may also infer that the office was honorary, and that its function was principally concerned with the social and economic support of the Jewish community.

In Acts we meet the *archisynagōgos* directing proceedings within the synagogue.[187] This led to the characterization of the *archisynagōgos* as a liturgical officer. However, there is nothing to prevent a person prominent in society being given a minor liturgical role. In the Church of England it was custom until recently for the mayor of a town or city to read a lesson in church annually. Thus, rabbinic literature points to a liturgical role, for although the account of the *rosh ha-knesset* (*archisynagōgos*) in the Mishnah handing on the scroll of the law from the attendant and onward—which would indicate a similar role in handing on the scroll of the law[188]—is clearly legendary in its setting, we need to ask whether there is some historical kernel that brings about the construction of the legend. We may note in this respect the provision of the Tosefta that the *rosh ha-knesset* should read in the absence of any other qualified person.[189] When Rajak and Noy discount such a liturgical role as not borne out by the epigraphic evidence, they have, I think, slightly overstated their case,[190] as epigraphy does not tell the whole story. There is no reason simply to discount evidence such as Acts 13:15, for even if this is a fictive setting, one would expect a fictive setting to have verisimilitude. The liturgical role of the *archisynagōgos* appears, however, to have been somewhat limited, a kind of master of ceremonies at the reading of the law.

The evidence cited here is from a wide geographical spread and from an extended period. Rajak and Noy rightly criticize assumptions based on the static nature of Judaism, and so, given that this is an inquiry into the formation of Christianity, I must be careful in my use of this evidence. The fundamental change in Jewish life and liturgy after the first century CE (the majority of the inscriptional evidence being after the parting of the ways) was the rise of the

below, under the heading "Presbyters in the Jewish Communities of Jerusalem." Note also *CIJ* 584: "The tomb of Joseph, a synagogue ruler, son of Joseph, a synagogue-ruler."

186. *CIJ* 548, 722, 744, 766, 803, 1531, and 1404 above, conveniently collected by Tessa Rajak and David Noy, "*Archisynagogoi*: Office, Title and Social Status in the Greco-Jewish Synagogue" *JRS* 83 (1993): 90–91.

187. Acts 13:15.

188. *m. Yoma* 7.1; *m. Soṭah* 7.7–8.

189. *t. Meg.* 4.21. A similar provision is made in *b. Giṭ.* 59b–60a, where the employment of the *rosh ha-knesset* to read is seen as something of a last resort.

190. Rajak and Noy, "*Archisynagogoi*," 82.

rabbinate. If this is the case, then it is possible that the synagogal role of the *archisynagōgos* might gradually be reduced and ultimately disappear as it was supplanted by the new class of rabbis, whereas the honorific and patronal role continued. Thus, it is in the later period that we find a child *archisynagōgos*.[191]

However, it is likely, given the position in the community of the two Corinthian *archisynagōgoi*, that alongside minor liturgical functions and alongside a role in the representation of the community, the *archisynagōgos* was expected to act as patron of the community. Like the officers of the *polis*, they were expected to shoulder part of the financial burden of their office. Thus, if the role of the early Christian *episkopos* was fundamentally financial and administrative and a means to act as a patron to the community through the offering of a *leitourgia*, then the suggestion that the office originated in that of the *archisynagōgos* is reasonable;[192] it is not, however, proved on that basis. It simply means that church and synagogue shared the same social structures derived from wider society. Moreover, insofar as the Christian *episkopos* offered patronage fundamentally in a liturgical (in the modern sense of the word) setting, we may observe a distinct difference between this figure and the *archisynagōgos*. Principally the *archisynagōgos* had a role in worship; it was relatively minor and honorific, a reward for patronage supplied outside the liturgy. The *episkopos* stands in the center of worshiping activity of Christians, exercising patronage in that setting.

The Episkopos *as* Mebaqqer

The suggestion that the office and title of *episkopos* derived from that of the Essene *mebaqqer* is more recent.[193] The comparison is slightly difficult, for the duties of *mebaqqer* are distinct in the *Community Rule* and the *Damascus Document*. Indeed, the difference between the Essenism of the *Community*

---

191. So, in the fifth century, we find a three-year-old *archisynagōgos* (*CIJ* 587).

192. See Walter Ameling, "Die jüdischen Gemeinden im antiken Kleinasien," in *Jüdische Gemeinden und Organisationsformen von der Antike bis zur Gegenwart*, ed. Robert Jütte and Abraham P. Kustermann, Aschkenas 3 (Vienna: Böhlau, 1996), 39. For Ameling, this patronal function is a major point of distinction between an *archisynagōgos* and an *episkopos*.

193. For the proposal, see Joachim Jeremias, *Die Briefe an Timotheus und Titus; Der Brief an die Hebräer*, 11th ed., NTD 9 (Göttingen: Vandenhoeck & Ruprecht, 1975), 23; idem, *Jerusalem in the Time of Jesus: An Investigation into Economic and Social Conditions during the New Testament*, trans. F. H. Cave and C. H. Cave, 3rd ed. (London: SCM, 1969), 261; B. E. Thiering, "*Mebaqqer* and *episkopos* in the Light of the Temple Scroll," *JBL* 100 (1981): 59–74; Jerome D. Quinn, *The Letter to Titus: A New Translation with Notes and Commentary and an Introduction to Titus, I and II Timothy, the Pastoral Epistles,* AB 35 (New York: Doubleday, 1990), 88. For further bibliography, see Campbell, *Elders*, 155–59; Thiering, "*Mebaqqer* and *episkopos*," 69–70n25.

Rule and that of the *Damascus Document*—the one regulating the affairs of
an enclosed community, the other dealing with Essenes living in the world; the
one practicing complete community of goods, the other practicing charity—is
the chief difficulty in using the term; either may be used as a base of comparison with forming Christianity, but not both. If the office of *episkopos* is
to be derived from that of the *mebaqqer*, we need to ask from which kind of
mebaqqer the *episkopos* is being alleged to derive. In the *Community Rule* the
mebaqqer chairs the council of the many[194] and has administrative functions
relating to the pooling of the wealth of individuals joining the community.[195]
Similarly, in the *Damascus Document* he chairs the council and collects and
administers alms,[196] though his functions here are more widespread, ensuring
that none is harassed or oppressed[197] (perhaps a reference to the social role of
the *mebaqqer* in the charitable works of the community), giving instruction,[198]
and regulating entry to the community.[199] The fundamental argument in favor
of equating *episkopos* and *mebaqqer* would be the linguistic argument of
Milik that the Hebrew *bqr* is often rendered as *episkeptein* in the Septuagint.[200]
Beyond this any argument must hinge on similarity of function. Here, perhaps,
the argument is at its strongest. The administration of goods is fundamental
to *mebaqqer* and *episkopos* alike. Even though there are distinctions between
the duties of the *mebaqqer* of the *Damascus Document* and of the *Community Rule*, each has a significant role in the management of the association's
property. We may also note that just as *episkopoi* are described as shepherds
in early Christian literature, so is the *mebaqqer*.[201]

However, it is on the grounds of function that Leaney denies any connection between the *mebaqqer* and the *episkopos*.[202] He argues, first, that the
mebaqqer is an administrator, whereas the *episkopos* has pastoral functions,
and, second, that the *episkopos* had developed from the presbyters and therefore
could not have originated in any other office. However, these arguments are
based on the very assumptions that the present work is intended to overthrow:
the equivalence of presbyter and *episkopos* and the statement that the duties

194. 1QS VI, 12, 14.
195. 1QS VI, 20.
196. CD-A XIV, 12–16.
197. CD-A XIII, 10.
198. CD-A XIII, 8.
199. CD-A XIII, 11–13.
200. J. T. Milik, *Ten Years of Discovery in the Wilderness of Judaea*, trans. J. Strugnell
(London: SCM, 1959), 100.
201. At CD-A XIII, 9.
202. A. R. C. Leaney, *The Rule of Qumran and Its Meaning: Introduction, Translation and
Commentary* (London: SCM, 1966), 189.

of the *episkopos* were not fundamentally economic. There are grounds for tracing the origin of the episcopate to the *mebaqqer* of Essene communities. Both officers are fundamentally concerned with the distribution of the goods of the community. Moreover, given that the *mebaqqer* has a privileged role in the discussions of the community but thereby is not under obligation to speak, we may perhaps compare his role to that of the bishop in the conversations of the household church: he is one given particular authority to speak but is not under actual obligation so to do.[203]

Moreover, the designation of the *archisynagōgos* as *rosh ha-knesset* in the Mishnah[204] puts one in mind of the function of the *mebaqqer* alongside the "council of the many," which is generally agreed to have been a council not of selected individuals (akin to the presbytery) but of all members.[205] It may be that the *mebaqqer* is the Essene equivalent of the *archisynagōgos*, and so, if an origin to the episcopate is being sought within Judaism, part of the question that needs to be determined is the relationship between any Christian community and Essene Judaism. In the case of the *Didache* a link with Essene Judaism is possible,[206] so the derivation of the Didachist *episkopos* from this origin is likewise conceivable, but this need not mean that the same is true elsewhere. Much depends on the relationship between any given Christian community and the forming Jewish community from which it may have emerged or to which it may relate; thus, I am forced to agree with Merklein that the *episkopoi* mentioned in Philippians 1:1 had no relationship with the Essene office, as it is most improbable that this Gentile and European community would have had any Essene contact.[207] I will argue below that there was a Christian community in Jerusalem that had grown from an Essene community and was organized on

203. Thus, see the provisions of *Trad. ap.* 28 and the discussion of a silent bishop in Ephesus in chap. 4 below, p. 277.

204. *m. Yoma* 7.1; *m. Soṭah* 7.7–8.

205. So also Campbell, *Elders*, 62; M. A. Knibb, *The Qumran Community*, CCWJCW 2 (Cambridge: Cambridge University Press, 1987), 129; Sarianna Metso, *The Textual Development of the Qumran Community Rule*, STDJ 21 (Leiden: Brill, 1997), 121, 134. Metso's work is particularly significant because she traces the manner in which the Cave 1 *Rule of the Community* has been built up of redactional layers, reminding us therefore that this rule applies to those actually at Qumran, whereas celibate Essene communities outside might be organized distinctly again. This creates yet further complication for an attempt to derive the Christian *episkopos* from the Essene official.

206. Classically, J.-P. Audet, "Affinités littéraires at doctrinales du 'Manuel de discipline,'" *RB* 59 (1952): 219–38; more recently, C. N. Jefford, "Conflict at Antioch: Ignatius and the *Didache* at Odds," in *Papers Presented at the Thirteenth International Conference on Patristic Studies Held in Oxford 1999: Critica et Philogica, Nachleben, Tertullian to Arnobius, Egypt before Nicea, Athanasius and His Opponents*, ed. M. F. Wiles and E. J. Yarnold, StPatr 36 (Louvain: Peeters, 2001), 262–69.

207. Merklein, *Kirchliche Amt*, 374.

Essene lines, but also that this community had not influenced the organization of other Christian communities and thus is a dead end in the narrative.

Thus, whereas we cannot absolutely rule out any influence from Essene community formation on early Christianity, further argument beyond that already supplied by the proponents of such a process is needed.

Caveats Regarding Proposed Jewish Models for Episkopoi

There are grounds, particularly in the economic and patronal role of the *episkopos*, for tracing the origin of the office to Jewish communities. However, apart from the problem posed by the very imprecision of the term "Jewish communities," there is a further, truly fundamental issue. The *archisynagōgos* had limited liturgical functions, but the *episkopos* is fundamental to the proceedings of most Christian communities. Of the liturgical role of the *mebaqqer* we know nothing, which indicates that if he had one, it was somewhat restricted. If any relationship is to be sustained, this objection must be met.

A second point to be noted, in view of the discussion of associations above, is that the synagogues, and indeed Essene communities,[208] might themselves be understood as associations. Thus, when *collegia* were banned, there was a specific exemption for synagogues, which were seen, at least by Roman legislators, as associations.[209] Josephus uses the language of associations when referring to the Jewish community of Sardis,[210] and the Jewish community of Miletus imitated the behavior of associations by reserving seats in the theater.[211]

There is more than simply functional similarity. Weinfeld points to the similarity of the Essene hierarchy of priest, *mebaqqer*, and council to the organization of the Iobacchi, who likewise have a priest and a steward, as to the similarity in admission procedures between the two groups.[212] Likewise, he points out the manner in which similar demands are made of members with regard to the treatment of fellow members, relating both to behavior in speech and to seating arrangements, having reference among other associations to the Iobacchi again, to the guild of Zeus Hypsistos,[213] and to a private

208. So, particularly, B. W. Dombrowski, "*HaYahad* in 1QS and τὸ κοινόν: An Instance of Early Greek and Jewish Synthesis," *HTR* 59 (1966): 293–307.

209. On the subject overall, see Peter Richardson, "Early Synagogues as Collegia in the Diaspora and Palestine," in Kloppenborg and Wilson, *Voluntary Associations*, 90–109.

210. Josephus, *A.J.* 14.235.

211. See the picture in Harland, *Associations*, 110.

212. Moshe Weinfeld, *The Organizational Pattern and the Penal Code of the Qumran Sect: A Comparison with Guilds and Religious Associations of the Hellenistic-Roman Period*, NTOA 2 (Göttingen: Vandenhoeck & Ruprecht, 1986), 20–23.

213. P.Lond. 2710.

association in Egypt known to us from P.Mich. 243.[214] He does not deny that there are distinctions, which derive from the particularity of Essene Judaism, between the Essene groups and associations, but this does not affect the fact that they are one kind of voluntary association. Although theologically distinct from other voluntary associations, simply through Jewish practice they may organizationally be the same.

Here two warnings may be sounded. In the first instance these similarities apply to the Essenes of the *Community Rule*, but not to those of the *Damascus Document*. Second, by classifying Jewish communities as associations, we are in danger of running into the problem of generalization once again; anything that can be said of all Jewish communities and all associations is likely to be so general as to be uninformative.[215] However, the associational nature of the *Community Rule* may be borne in mind as the inquiry continues and as we turn from the general to the specific. In particular, we may, in the light of the prior part of the chapter, recall that these Essenes ate together. If there is a relationship between the *mebaqqer* of Essene communities and the economic *episkopos* of Christian communities, it relates to their economic role in the ritual meals of the community.

The Economic Functions of *Diakonoi*

Above I concluded that Hatch was right in pointing to the economic activity of the *episkopoi* of associations as the means by which the term *episkopos* entered Christian discourse. In particular, the office was fundamentally concerned with the distribution of food. Insights based on the domestic origin of Christianity and the basically cultic function of *episkopoi* do not contradict this overall thesis, as the household might be the locus of association, and the fundamental ritual of the household church was the sharing of food. However, it appears that the church outgrows its domestic origin; it is at that stage that the *episkopos* can no longer simply be identified with the householder and becomes more clearly a defined office.

In exercising this office, *episkopoi* were joined, I may now point out, by *diakonoi*, a title that appears with equal frequency, notably in a number of the instances observed above of episcopal economic activity.[216] Although the

214. Weinfeld, *Organizational Pattern*, 23–28.
215. So, similarly, Sandra Walker-Ramisch, "Graeco-Roman Voluntary Associations and the Damascus Document: A Sociological Analysis," in Kloppenborg and Wilson, *Voluntary Associations*, 128–45.
216. Thus Phil. 1:1; *Did.* 15:1; *Did. ap.* 2.27.3; 2.28.6; 3.12.1. Although not discussed above, I may also note 1 Tim. 3:1–19 as an instance of the appearance of *diakonoi* alongside *episkopoi*.

focus of this study is the episcopate and its genesis, a brief study of the role and origin of the *diakonos* will bring further support to the argument of this chapter. My inquiry will demonstrate a close relationship between *episkopoi* and *diakonoi*, which will bear out the hypothesis of the economic and associational origins of *episkopoi*. The close connection between the offices of *diakonoi* and *episkopoi*, which will be shown, should in turn make us suspect, when we meet *diakonoi* with *presbyteroi* but without an *episkopos*, that these presbyters are presbyters *kata polin*.[217]

Here again I follow the lead of Hatch, whose second Bampton lecture discusses the origins of the diaconate. Hatch starts by suggesting that there was originally a single class of minister, the *episkopos*, but that rapidly "a division of labour became imperative."[218] He points to the institution of the seven in Acts 6:1–6, while noting that they are not titled as *diakonoi*. Nonetheless, he notes that the order of deacons was established as such by the time of the Pastoral Epistles; yet, given that the qualifications of the *episkopos* and the *diakonos* were so similar, he suggests that even then the *diakonoi* were not clearly distinguished from the *episkopoi*. This lack of distinction was due, he argues, to the fact that the office and ministry of the deacon was closely bound up to that of the (economic) *episkopos*, being likewise economic and charitable.

As the basis for this argument, he observes that the gifts are distributed by deacons in the report of Justin Martyr[219] and that whereas, within the *Pseudo-Clementine* literature, the *episkopos* holds the monies, it is the role of the *diakonoi* to seek out the distressed and to relieve them.[220] He goes on to suggest, therefore, that this title is derived from that of those who distributed the portions from sacrifice in the Greco-Roman world. Thus both the ministry and the name were derived from the general practice of Hellenistic society. As evidence for this last assertion he cites *CIG* 1793 b add. (= *IG* 9.1² 2.247), a list of cultic personnel including a sacrificial slaughterer (*hierothytēs*), a butcher (*mageiros*), a *diakonos*, and a chief wine steward (*archoinochous*), from which it is possible to deduce that the *diakonos* had some kind of role in distributing the sacrifice. He also cites *CIG* 3037 (= *IEph.* 3418), a list of priests and *diakonoi* of the twelve gods.

Hatch's evidence for the deacon's economic role within the Christian church, as for the deacon's role in associational life, is thus somewhat limited, though he goes on to point out the close relationship between bishop and deacon in a later period and also to argue that the deacon joined with the bishop in

217. Thus, note the discussion of Smyrna and Philippi below in chap. 4, pp. 207–18.
218. Hatch, *Organization*, 49.
219. Justin, *1 Apol.* 65.5.
220. Hatch, *Organization*, 50, with reference to *Pseudo-Clementines, Ep. Clem.* 5; *Hom.* 3:67.

discipline.[221] Again, however, the evidence that Hatch presents may be supplemented through new discovery and insight. First, however, I may refer yet again to the fundamental point made above: the eucharistic assembly is the locus for charity, and the eucharist was, in the first generation at least, a *Sättingungsmahl*. Thus, the manner in which the deacons in Justin's account take the gifts to those not present is indicative that they might likewise carry the charitable goods of the church. It is noteworthy in this respect that Hermas observes that the *diakonoi* might enrich themselves on the basis of the church's gifts;[222] to do so, they must have access to them.

To supplement Hatch's evidence, we may first observe a number of inscriptions discovered since the time of Hatch that indicate that a *diakonos* might be a member of cultic personnel; though just a selection, this is sufficient to make the case.[223] *IEph.* 3415, *IEph.* 3417, *IEph.* 3416 and 3416A, *IG* 4 824 are lists of cultic personnel including *diakonoi*. Their function, however, is clear in none of these. In the same way, mention is made of *diakonoi*, apparently in a cultic context, in *SEG* 35.714, whereas *IMagn.* 217 is a list of persons dedicating a herm, namely, *komaktores*, heralds (*kērykes*), and *diakonoi*. Again, there is no indication of their function, nor indeed is it certain what *komaktores* were.[224] *IG* 9.1² 2.250 and 2.251, *IMagn.* 109, *IG* 4.774 and 4.824, additional lists of cult personnel, include a *diakonos* after a butcher. In the first instance the *diakonos* is followed by a sacrificial slaughterer, and in *IG* 9.1² 2.252 there is a *diakonos* who precedes the butcher. Similarly, *IMT* 2019 is a thanksgiving inscription dedicated by a cavalry officer (*hipparchos*), a comptroller (*dioikētēs*), a scribe, five *diakonoi*, and a wine steward (*oinophylax*). These thus have an obvious similarity to the inscriptions known to and cited by Hatch; on this basis we may agree, on a wider base of evidence than was available to him, that one possible understanding of the word was an assistant at the sacrificial cult, especially given the connection between *diakonoi* and butchers, sacrificial slaughterers, or wine stewards, although the precise nature of this assistance is often less than clear. It is possible that they distributed or assisted in distributing the sacrifice, an interpretation that might gain support from Josephus's description of the priests under Josiah's reforms distributing (*diakonoumenōn*) the meat from the sacrifices to the crowd,[225] although, as

221. Ibid., 51–54.
222. *Herm.* 103.2.
223. Beyond these, note may be taken of the numerous inscriptions noted by Manuel Guerra Gómez, "Diáconos helénicos y biblicos," *Burgense* 4 (1963): 51–56.
224. John N. Collins (*Diakonia: Re-interpreting the Ancient Sources* [New York: Oxford University Press, 1990], 167) suggests *coactores*.
225. Josephus, *A.J.* 10.72.

Collins points out, there may be a more generalized meaning of exercising a role within a sacred setting.[226]

Hatch does not make explicit this link between the *diakonoi* of the sacrificial cults and those of Christian communities, but he suggests that the cultic use in antiquity derived from a more common use of the term *diakonos*, referring to someone who waits on tables.[227] However, this is problematic. For although this is frequently asserted as the fundamental meaning of the term, classically by Beyer,[228] it is hard to find an occasion where the term is used in this sense without some cultic overtone. Thus, as examples of the word's use as "waiter," Beyer quotes Xenophon, *Hiero* 4.2, which refers to despots having their *diakonoi* taste food lest it be poisoned; but here we may note that Xenophon states that the wine is tasted by the *diakonos* before being offered to the gods, providing therefore perhaps a hint of some ritual role. Next he cites Demosthenes, *In Neaeram* 59.33, which refers to *diakonoi* setting tables at a feast, though Beyer does not note that the location of this feast is the temple of Athena in Kolion. Finally, he cites Herodotus *Historiae* 4.71.1–5, which refers to Scythian burial customs in which, when a king dies, a *diakonos* is killed and buried with the king, alongside his cupbearer and other servants. Here, unfortunately, it is impossible to tell what role the *diakonos* played in the king's household; being singled out for such treatment, he would not seem simply to be a waiter. Collins, moreover, points out that places in which one might expect to find the term do not actually supply it. Thus in Athenaeus's *Deipnosophistae*, *diakonoi* prepare a "Spartan" dinner.[229] However, this is not at a dinner in the present, but is a historical anecdote; these *diakonoi*, moreover, are not simply waiters but cooks as well, we may presume, and are found in a military setting. Similarly, Athenaeus discusses a particular kind of dinner found among Doric Greeks; here, he states, the *diakonos* accompanies the person distributing the meat (who properly might be termed a waiter) and calls out the name of the donor. Again, this implies something of a ritual context.[230] In a Jewish context we may note the manner in which the young associates of the Therapeutae who wait at table are described as *diakonoi*;[231] but again, we note, the whole context is cultic.

226. Collins, *Diakonia*, 164.
227. Hatch, *Organization*, 50.
228. H. W. Beyer, "διακονέω," in *Theological Dictionary of the New Testament*, vol. 2, ed. G. Kittel and G. Friedrich, trans. G. W. Bromiley (Grand Rapids: Eerdmans, 1964), 81–93.
229. Athenaeus, *Deipn.* 4.138c.
230. Athenaeus, *Deipn.* 139c. As Collins points out, "The almost rubrical quality attaching this usage is discernible" (*Diakonia*, 159).
231. Philo, *Contempl.* 75.

One may continue thus. There is little enough evidence of the use of the term to signify a waiter, except in particular contexts that involve attendance at a meal of ritual import. Even less is there evidence for a signification of humility or lowliness in the choice of the term (the denial of which assertion is one of the fundamental purposes of Collins's work). A *diakonos* might be a servant, but as a servant he is not a slave, and in a domestic context he appears to be a servant with a certain degree of proximity to his master. Even so, Collins has demonstrated that there is a vast range of meaning in the term and argues on the basis of the usages of the term that what is central to its significance is the idea of agency.

There is little point in repeating Collins's extensive argument regarding the range of meaning of the term and its cognates in the Greek of the period prior to the formation of the church's office; I may agree that agency is basic to its meaning. I may ask, however, how this relates to the ministry of the *diakonos* in Christian communities. Ultimately, the meaning of a term with such a range of signification can be determined only on the basis of its use. I may begin by noting the manner in which the term is used in the texts that indicated that the bishop had an economic role, for in many of the texts cited above with regard to *episkopoi*, *diakonoi* appear as well.

Thus, even if Hatch's suggestion that the role of *diakonoi* derived ultimately from the use of the term as "waiter" is wanting, we may nonetheless observe, on the basis of a wider range of literature than was available to him, that the role of the *diakonos*, like that of the *episkopos*, related to the economic and charitable functions of the church.

The Economic Role of Diakonoi in the Didache

In directing *episkopoi* to liturgize (i.e., financially underwrite) the *leitourgia* of prophets and teachers, the *Didache* likewise states that *diakonoi* are to be appointed.[232] Clearly, then, their office is economic; the qualifications for being a *diakonos* are, moreover, no different from those of an *episkopos*.[233] We may, however, note again that this statement of economic duties is slightly different than that made elsewhere regarding *episkopoi* in that the *episkopoi* are clearly the patrons rather than agents of the patrons. If the *episkopoi* are the patrons, as are the *diakonoi*, how do the terms differ? If the *leitourgia*

---

232. *Did.* 15:1–2: Χειροτονήσατε οὖν ἑαυτοῖς ἐπισκόπους καὶ διακόνους ἀξίους τοῦ κυρίου, ἄνδρας πραεῖς καὶ ἀφιλαργύρους καὶ ἀληθεῖς καὶ δεδοκιμασμένους· ὑμῖν γὰρ λειτουργοῦσι καὶ αὐτοὶ τὴν λειτουργίαν τῶν προφητῶν καὶ διδασκάλων. Μὴ οὖν ὑπερίδητε αὐτούς· αὐτοὶ γάρ εἰσιν οἱ τετιμημένοι ὑμῶν μετὰ τῶν προφητῶν καὶ διδασκάλων.
233. The observation of Harnack, *Lehre*, 142–43.

is taken to mean simply their function at the ritual meal of the community, then there is no question that the *diakonoi* are the assistants of the *episkopoi*, but if the terms are describing the same activity—economic support—then a distinction is hard to see. It is possible, indeed, that the *kai* here is epexegetic, and that the *episkopoi* and *diakonoi* are the same people. Such a proposal has indeed also been offered with regard to Philippians 1:1 by both Collange and Hawthorne, although in that instance it is motivated by an assumption that there was a single, presbyteral order within the church.[234] In Philippians it is an unnecessary hypothesis, whereas here the distinction is genuinely unclear.

As a result of the common misunderstanding of the term *leitourgousi* in *Didache* 15:2, Collins considers that these *diakonoi* assist at the eucharistic table.[235] His argument is based on the obvious relationship with the *episkopoi*; the basis for seeing the *episkopoi* in the Didachistic community as supervisors of the eucharistic assembly, as Collins suggests they are, is, however, less than secure. The *Didache* says nothing about eucharistic supervision,[236] so we cannot be certain, even though both the ritual role of *diakonoi* in the practice of sacrifice and Collins's own observation that *diakonos*, though used to refer to a "waiter," is not without religious overtones would point in the direction of this argument. It is possible, given that *Didache* 14, in regulating community meals, refers to them as offerings, that the direction to appoint *episkopoi* and *diakonoi* is placed immediately after because these are the officials who are to supply these offerings on behalf of the community. But the distinction remains unclear.

The role of *episkopos* and *diakonos* in the eucharist of the Didachistic community, and indeed the relationship between them, is uncertain. All that can be said is what the text says: they underwrite the ministry of prophets and teachers. This is sufficient, however, to anchor the fundamental point that their office is economic.

The Economic Role of Diakonoi *in* 1 Clement

Clement gives an account of the origin of ministry, in which the apostles appoint their firstfruits as *episkopoi* and *diakonoi*.[237] It is perhaps redundant

234. Jean François Collange, *The Epistle of Saint Paul to the Philippians*, trans. A. W. Heathcote (London: Epworth, 1978), 38–39; Gerald F. Hawthorne, *Philippians*, WBC 43 (Waco: Word, 1983), 7–8.

235. Collins, *Diakonia*, 238.

236. See comments in Alistair Stewart(-Sykes), "Prophecy and Patronage: The Relationship between Charismatic Functionaries and Household Officers in Early Christianity," in *Trajectories through the New Testament and the Apostolic Fathers*, ed. A. F. Gregory and C. M. Tuckett, NTAF (Oxford: Oxford University Press, 2005), 165–89.

237. *1 Clem.* 42:4.

by now to observe the absence of presbyters as an appointed order. However, after turning to a discussion of the manner in which Moses solved the
strife and faction within Israel regarding the priesthood, the subject overall of the letter, Clement goes on to discuss the strife in Corinth over the
episcopate.

At this point, therefore, Collins suggests that the *diakonoi* are left behind
almost as soon as they are mentioned. He suggests that they do not come
into the discussion over *episkopē* but had been mentioned alongside bishops
earlier solely because they provided the full complement of cultic personnel.[238]
We cannot be so sure on either point. We have already seen that the discussion of *leitourgia* in *1 Clement* 44 is less a discussion of cult as a discussion
of charity and may therefore, on the basis of the *Didache* alone, anticipate
seeing *diakonoi* joining in this *leitourgia*. Clement refers to the "aforementioned" persons, which might be taken to include *diakonoi*, except that he
goes on to mention presbyters. This is what leads Collins to suppose that the
deacons have been left behind, as he cannot see that the deacons might also
be presbyters. However, as I have already argued, this mention of presbyters
does not relate in any way to the office of presbyter, but rather the term is
employed as a collective noun. It would be reasonable to suggest that the
diakonoi are still in purview in this chapter and participate in some way in
the bishop's *leitourgia*.

Collins suggests that the deacons here are the "nonpresbyteral liturgical assistants of presbyters in the presbyters' capacity of bishop."[239] I may respond to
this that they are simply the liturgical assistants of bishops. Collins continues,
"Because the liturgy included a sacred meal, the deacons presumably acted as
ritual waiters, but they would have done this not on a title of being waiters for
the assembly but in their capacity as attendants to those responsible for the
conduct of the service. Their role would also have included functions associated
with other aspects of this service like readings and offerings."[240] However, we
know little of readings or readers in the early assemblies and nothing to associate *diakonoi* with reading, whereas I may suggest that the offerings were
those *of* the *diakonoi* and *episkopoi*. It is indeed possible that the *diakonoi*
assisted at the table, but whether they did so as agents of the *episkopoi* or in
some other capacity is not so clear. Nonetheless, Collins's recognition of the
centrality of the meal rite to the liturgy is welcome, and I may agree with the
vision of *diakonoi* assisting at the tables.

238. Collins, *Diakonia*, 238–39.
239. Ibid., 239.
240. Ibid.

The Economic Role of Diakonoi *in the Church Order Literature*

In turning to the church order literature, unknown to Hatch, I may note the manner in which the deacons' role with regard to the offerings reported by Justin appears to have been known in Syrian communities likewise. Thus, *Testamentum Domini*, in describing the manner in which the church should be built, demands a house of offerings, where the "the priest should be seated and the chief of the deacons, together with the readers so that the names of those who offer offerings, or those on whose account they are offering, may be written down"; similarly, "the deacons' house should be on the right of the entrance on the right so that they may observe the eucharists, and the offerings which are offered."[241]

There is also ample evidence in *Didascalia apostolorum* for deacons' activities in the relief of need (they are described as "fellow-workers in almsgiving"),[242] as well as the manner in which their ministry is tied closely to that of the *episkopos*.[243] Similarly, *Apostolic Church Order* directs that the deacon should principally be active in obtaining money from wealthier Christians and redistributing it to the poor.[244] It is particularly noteworthy that these duties are ascribed to deacons in chapters belonging to two distinct redactional levels; the fundamental duties of deacons in this community, a community into the church order of which, I have argued elsewhere, the diaconate is an intrusion,[245] remain as they were in such communities in which the diaconate was a native institution. Finally, I may note what *Canones Hippolyti* says of the deacon, in supplementing the directions of *Traditio apostolica*: "He informs the bishop, so that he may pray over them or give them what they need, but also to people whose poverty is not apparent but who are in need. They are to serve also those who have the alms of the bishops, and they are able to give to widows, to orphans, and to the poor."[246]

The Economic Role of Diakonoi *in Philippians*

We may observe again that *diakonoi* are mentioned alongside *episkopoi* at Philippians 1:1. If, as I have argued above, the reason for the mention of these

---

241. *Test. Dom.* 1.19.
242. *Did. ap.* 3.12.1; 3.13.7; 4.5.1
243. *Did. ap.* 2.10.3; 2.17.3; 2.44.1.
244. *Can. eccl. ap.* 21; 22.
245. Alistair Stewart(-Sykes), "Deacons in the Syrian Church Order Tradition: A Search for Origins," in *Diakonia, diaconiae, diaconato: Semantica e storia nei Padri della Chiesa; XXXVIII Incontro di studiosi dell'antichità cristiana, Roma, 7–9 maggio 2009*, ed. V. Grossi et al., SEA 117 (Rome: Institutum patristicum Augustinianum, 2010), 111–20.
246. *Can. Hipp.* 5.

officers in this instance is that they had identified themselves as such when they transmitted the gift to Paul, and that the reason for their doing so was that the transmission of the gift was part of their economic office, then what is true of *episkopoi* should be seen as true of *diakonoi*: their function lay in the care and transmission of the gifts of the community. The precise distinction between them here is not clear, but, in distinction to the *Didache*, there is no reason at all to press the suggestion that a single class of people is meant. Collins indeed argues strongly against such a suggestion on the grounds that if the *diakonos* is an agent, then there must be an element of subordination to the person for whom the agent acts. He is unsure about the possibility that the title indicates an economic office relating to the collection, as argued above, and indeed suggests that the term is introduced by Paul himself.[247] I may refer to the argument above regarding the rationale for the introduction of the greeting, as well as the observable fact that Paul tends not to use titles (given that he assumes a household model), as seeing this as an unlikely suggestion; however, I may agree nonetheless with Collins's overall conclusion that the *diakonoi* are distinct from the *episkopoi* but that their roles are closely related. Their role, moreover, is economic.

Preliminary Conclusion on the Economic Role of Diakonoi

There is reason to understand the functions of *diakonoi* as assistants to the *episkopoi* in their charitable work, as Hatch suggested. There are also reasons, however, to be cautious, as it is difficult to see why Christians should derive the term from the cultic assistants of sacrifice in antiquity. In early Christianity there is a clear suspicion in regard to sacrifice, for which reason, we may presume, words relating to a sacrificing (or butchering) priesthood are avoided, together with any term related to the apparatus of sacrifice. The argument does not apply to *episkopoi* in the same way because, as was noted above, the *episkopoi* seem not to have been closely involved in the cultic aspects of the associations. We may also note, with Collins, the relative scarcity of the term *diakonos* in cultic and sacrificial settings within the inscriptional evidence.[248]

It is thus, in accordance with his insight that agency is central to the word *diakonos*, that Collins argues that its use comes about because the *diakonos* is at each point the agent of the *episkopos*.

If the word signifies the bishop's functionary, the reason it was selected for this signification will not lie in the nature of any particular task undertaken

247. Collins, *Diakonia*, 236–37.
248. Ibid., 167.

for the bishop whether that be in the distribution of bread and wine, the handling of his financial affairs, the care of his destitute or the preaching of his word. Of these activities only the first and last have any real place in the field of meaning covered by the word *diakonos* and of these the preaching of the word has no place in the history of the diaconate as preserved in the earliest documents.[249]

This conclusion, though significant, I may note again, suffers once again from an artificial distinction between cult and charity. Collins suggests that the Christians would not have chosen the word *diakonos* because of its use in associations for ritual waiters, even though he recognizes, on the basis of the evidence that he gathers, that there is a cultic overtone to the use of the term. He concludes rather that the *diakonos* is the agent of the *episkopos* in the realm of cultic activity and that there is no relevance to the work of administration.[250] The work of charity and administration, however, is, I stress again, work undertaken within the cult. The use of the term in associational, and civic sacrifice, if not the immediate route by which the word enters Christian usage, seems to be sharing a semantic field with the Christian usage.

The Diakonos *as Economic Agent in Further Early Christian Contexts*

Thus far I have examined the literature employed above in the initial survey of episcopal ministry; Hatch's conclusion regarding the origin of the term *diakonos* has not been shown altogether to convince, although, once again, his fundamental insight—*diakonoi* were associated with *episkopoi* in their economic office—appears to hold good. To seek further to test that hypothesis, I may extend the field slightly further to observe the use of the term elsewhere, namely, in the Pastoral Epistles, in the letters of Ignatius, and in the letter of Polycarp to the Philippians.

THE *DIAKONOS* OF THE PASTORAL EPISTLES

One relatively short section of 1 Timothy is devoted to the qualifications of the *diakonos*,[251] although nothing is actually said about this person's duties or, indeed, about the relationship between this office and that of the *episkopos*. Nonetheless, the qualification list is revealing in that it fits well with the supposition of an economic role: deacons are to be honest, to be sober, and to have no love of money. The manner in which the statements of qualification move,

249. Ibid., 244.
250. Ibid.
251. 1 Tim. 3:8–13.

moreover, from those of the *episkopos* to those of the *diakonos*, indicates a close relationship between the two.

THE IGNATIAN *DIAKONOS*

Turning to Ignatius, we may first note the appointment of deacons as messengers.[252] This is entirely in keeping with how the term is occasionally used to signify a messenger.[253] However, the majority of appearances of the *diakonoi* in Ignatius's writings relate to his constant refrain that persons should be subject to the three orders of *episkopos*, *presbyteros*, and *diakonos*, or that those serving in such orders should be respected.[254]

Nevertheless, despite his insistence on the presence of the *diakonoi*, Ignatius is not clear what the function of the deacon is. From his statement that the deacon is the type of Christ, whereas the bishop is the type of God the Father, we may perhaps deduce that as the bishop is in the central seat at the eucharistic meal, ensuring that people are fed, so the deacons ensure that the bishop's will is done. Thus, when Ignatius denies, in writing to the Trallians, that the *diakonoi* are ministers of food and drink,[255] we may deduce that they are precisely that, namely, that they assist with the distribution of the eucharistic gifts.[256] We may compare their activity here to that of the *diakonoi* in Justin's report of Christian worship, and below I will suggest a reason for Ignatius's denial (or rather redefinition) of the deacon's task at table.

Deacons are said to be charged with the *diakonia* of Jesus Christ in *Magnesians* 6:1, which Collins suggests should be interpreted as meaning that they have a commission like that of Christ, namely, that they should do the bishop's will as Christ did that of the Father.[257] This close relationship to the *episkopos*, Collins suggests, is the rationale for Ignatius's reference to the *diakonoi* as his "fellow-slaves." All this we may accept, and, in view of the close relationship of this ministry with that of the *episkopos*, we may deduce that there was likewise an economic aspect to their service.

Finally, as Powell notes, certain aspects of Ignatius's typological language indicate a close relationship between the *episkopos* and the *diakonoi* by which we may reason that insofar as the ministry of an *episkopos* is economic, so is that of a *diakonos*. Thus, he points out, whereas the *diakonos*

---

252. Ign. *Phld.* 10:1.
253. So of Hermes in *SEG* 30.326. See also Rom. 16:1–2.
254. Ign. *Trall.* 3:1; 7:2; Ign. *Phld.* 7:1; Ign. *Smyrn.* 8:1; Ign. *Pol.* 6:1.
255. Ign. *Trall.* 2:3.
256. So also Lietzmann, "Zur altchristlichen Verfassungsgeschichte," 176. On this passage see chap. 4 below, p. 289.
257. Collins, *Diakonia*, 240.

is generally considered the type of Christ,[258] in *Trallians* 2:1 the *episkopos* is to be obeyed as Jesus Christ; and whereas in *Smyrnaeans* 8:1 the *diakonoi* are to be reverenced as the command of God (*theou entolē*), in *Trallians* 13:2 the term *entolē* ("command") is applied to the *episkopos*, to whom submission is due.[259]

THE *DIAKONOS* IN POLYCARP'S WRITINGS

Diakonoi make a brief appearance in Polycarp's letter to the Philippians in the context of what is effectively a *Haustafel*.[260] Nothing is said of their duties directly, but a general exhortation is given that is effectively a qualification list: deacons are to be blameless (*amemptoi*), as they are *diakonoi* of God and of Christ rather than of people. They are not to be insincere or slanderous, not to be lovers of money, but to be self-restrained in all things, compassionate, attentive, and proceeding on the way of the Lord's truth.

The first point to be noticed in what is at first sight an unremarkable list of qualities is the distinction in many ways from that of 1 Timothy. It seems highly probable that Polycarp had access to 1 Timothy, and so a close verbal comparison may be undertaken. Whereas Lightfoot asserts that the passage is derived from 1 Timothy,[261] the only direct verbal correspondence noted is the statement that *diakonoi* should not be insincere (*mē dilogous*).[262] Berding, however, notes other parallels; he compares "not slanderous" (*mē diaboloi*) to 1 Timothy 3:11 (*mē diabolous*), "not lovers of money" (*aphilargyroi*) to 1 Timothy 3:3 (*aphilargyron*), and "attentive" (*epimeleis*) to 1 Timothy 3:5, which asks how somebody unable to care for his own household is able to take care of (*epimelēsetai*) the church of God.[263] Of these parallels, however, one occurs in the passage of 1 Timothy relating to women and the other two in that relating to *episkopoi*.

The options are that Polycarp's writing stands in a common milieu, into consideration of which other *Haustafeln* should be brought, without being closely related to them,[264] or that Polycarp has reworked 1 Timothy. If the

258. E.g., Ign. *Magn.* 3:1; Ign. *Trall.* 3:1.
259. Douglas Powell, "Ordo presbyterii," *JTS* 26 (1975): 307.
260. Pol. *Phil.* 5:2.
261. Lightfoot, *Apostolic Fathers*, 2.3:330–31.
262. 1 Tim. 3:8.
263. Kenneth Berding, *Polycarp and Paul: An Analysis of Their Literary and Theological Relationship in Light of Polycarp's Use of Biblical and Extra-Biblical Literature*, VCSup 62 (Leiden: Brill, 2002), 74–75.
264. The conclusion of Michael W. Holmes, "Polycarp's *Letter to the Philippians* and the Writings That Later Formed the New Testament," in *The Reception of the New Testament in the Apostolic Fathers*, ed. Andrew F. Gregory and C. M. Tuckett (Oxford: Oxford University Press, 2005), 217.

latter is the case, then it is significant that two terms relating to *episkopoi* have been brought into the discussion of *diakonoi*; in particular, these terms relate to the financial aspect of ministry and indicate once again the proximity of diaconal roles to those of the *episkopos*. If the writing stands in a common milieu, I may suggest that the same conclusion is brought about: beyond a deacon's general character, the requirement that the *diakonos* be free of avarice indicates that this is a *leitourgia* relating to the economic life of the Christian community.

Conclusions on the Economic Role of Diakonoi

A sampling of a wider range of early Christian literature once again indicates that the duties of the *diakonoi*, in coordination with those of the *episkopos*, were fundamentally economic. The term *diakonos* probably derived from a background similar to that of associational and civic sacrifice, though it is possible that, as Collins argues, it came more generally from the signification of the term to refer to an agent, and that the role of the *diakonos* in distribution is simply that of being the agent of the *episkopos*. In either event, I conclude that the ministry was economic and was closely tied to that of an *episkopos*. Given that the cult was the primary locus of such economic activity, Hatch's concentration on the ritual aspect of the ministry of the *diakonos* proves to be correct, even though it is not a diminution in the role.

Challenges to the View of Diakonoi as Economic Officers

Although I have found much to support Hatch's view that the office of the *diakonos*, like that of the *episkopos*, was economic and originated in civic discourse, being passed thence to the associations, this is challenged by those who view this office, like that of the *episkopos*, as deriving from the synagogue, and by those who seek some other origin for the Christian use of the term in other uses of the term in Hellenistic society. I may thus examine their arguments.

THE CHALLENGE OF THE SYNAGOGAL PATTERN, AGAIN

In keeping with his overall theory of synagogal origins, Burtchaell identifies the synagogal *hazzan* as the forerunner of the *diakonos*. These synagogal functionaries are termed by Philo and Josephus alike as *neōkoroi*.[265] As such, I may suggest that they are coming into existence in the first century, the time at which synagogal buildings begin to be found. Later sources record the

265. Philo, *Spec.* 1.156; Josephus, *B.J.* 1.153.

hazzan performing liturgical duties within the temple relating to the reading of the Torah, as well as having general duties of care for the priests and for the premises.[266] Whereas these sources are later, Levine suggests that there is no reason why they should not be considered accurate on these points, as there is no particular reason why they should be constructed in a later period. However, given that the *hazzan* had a role within the liturgy of the synagogue relating to the reading of the Torah,[267] it is possible that these functions have been retrojected, in particular, as suggested above, in handing on the scrolls of the law in *m. Yoma* 7.1 and *m. Soṭah* 7.7–8, given that the *archisynagōgos* also makes an appearance here. Nonetheless, the role of the *hazzan* is a role established in some synagogues at least by the time of any parting of ways, assuming that the attendant (*hyperetēs*) mentioned at Luke 4:20 is to be identified with the *hazzan*. Other minor liturgical roles indicated in the rabbinic literature are those of informing the priest when to begin the blessing,[268] announcing to the priests the time at which they should sound the shofar when assembling for prayers in time of drought,[269] and, in the great Alexandrian synagogue, signaling to the congregation the point at which they were to respond to the Torah benedictions.[270]

Burtchaell may be going slightly beyond the evidence (or drawing in evidence from various different periods) when he speaks of a "choir director, sacristan, master of ceremonies, janitor, Hebrew teacher, hostel manager, bailiff, caterer, plumber,"[271] but not wildly so. Levine notes that often a room was set aside within a synagogue building for use by the *hazzan* and suggests that this indicates that the *hazzan* was likely to spend a lot of time there.[272] It was indeed a multifaceted role.

However, once again, it must be asked to what extent this role accords to that of the *diakonos*. On the basis of my initial discussion of the *diakonos*'s role at least, it does not. As we have seen, the role of the *diakonos* was one of assisting at the ritual meals of the Christian community, by which in turn the charity of the church was extended to those in need. This role is never that of the *hazzan*, nor is the setting. Rather, in later rabbinic writings, at least, we read of those who are appointed to collect and distribute charity in a synagogal setting, but these are not *hazzanim*.[273] Moreover, in the Ignatian

---

266. Levine, *Ancient Synagogue*, 438.
267. *t. Meg.* 3.21.
268. *Sifre* Numbers 39; *t. Meg.* 3.21 indicate that the *hazzan* faced Jerusalem with the people.
269. *t. Ta'an.* 1.13.
270. *t. Sukkah* 4.6.
271. Burtchaell, *From Synagogue to Church*, 248–49.
272. Levine, *Ancient Synagogue*, 436, referring to *b. 'Erub.* 55b; 74b.
273. *b. Meg.* 27a; *b. B. Bat.* 8a–b; *b. Roš. Haš.* 4a–5b; *b. Ta'an.* 24a; *b. Šabb.* 118b.

correspondence we may deduce the activity of several deacons at the gathering of the church, whereas there was only ever one *hazzan*.[274]

Thus, although the term *hazzan* is made equivalent to *diakonos* in one inscription,[275] and *diakonos* is used by Philo as equivalent to *hypēretēs*,[276] a term commonly used of the *hazzan*, this is insufficient to secure the point that the Christian *diakonos* was derived from the synagogal *hazzan*, but simply indicates that their roles might be broadly analogous, given the very different organizations in which they served. Indeed, the use of the term by Philo tells us nothing of the *hazzan*, but it does communicate to us something of the role of the *diakonos* in the Christian assembly.

In Philo's discussion Joseph is discussing his role in Egypt as the means by which the gifts of God might be made available. It is in this context, that of administering the gifts of God to his brothers, that he describes himself as a *hypēretēs* and a *diakonos*. Thus this usage points to that argued above: if the *diakonos* originated alongside the *episkopos*, and the role of the *episkopos* was, in origin at least, the financial support of the church, then we may see the *diakonos* as one who is, as it were, broker of the gifts of the *episkopos*, originally, at least, within a ritual context.

The fundamental rationale that might motivate a search for the origin of Christian offices in the synagogue is the plain fact that the first of those who worshiped Jesus were Jewish. Therefore, one might reasonably suppose, when they organized their own communities on departure from the synagogue, they would imitate the common pattern.

If this is the underlying assumption, it is easy to see how an error might occur, for there is no evidence that those who first worshiped Jesus left the synagogue. Rather, as is indicated by the fact that the specific act of Christian worship, the ritual meal, took place as the sabbath concluded, the functioning of the Jesus movement was an addition to, not a replacement of, the synagogue.

As I have argued elsewhere, it is not long before Christians begin to observe some synagogal functions within their own assemblies. However, this does not occur in the first generation, and, I may suggest, the fundamental activity of the Christian movement, the ritual meal, and therefore the offices required for the ritual meal to take place—either a householder acting as host or, in the case of a congregation gathered from several houses, officers to preside over

---

274. So Brian Capper, "Order and Ministry in the Social Pattern of the New Testament Church," in *Order and Ministry*, ed. Christine Hall and Brian Hannaford (Leominster, UK: Gracewing, 1996), 73.

275. Nemias is recorded as ἀζζανα καὶ . . . διάκονος in *CIJ* 805 (*IGLS* 4.1321).

276. Philo, *Joseph* 241.

the meal and assist at it—would already be in place at the time that synagogal functions begin to be practiced.

Consistently in examining the suggestion that Jewish offices might have given rise to Christian offices, I have observed that the liturgical functions of the Jewish officers were not comparable to those of the Christians. Herein lies the reason for that.

DIAKONOI IN OTHER HELLENISTIC CONTEXTS

At 2 Corinthians 11:23 the opponents of Paul characterize themselves as *diakonoi* of Christ (*diakonoi Christou*). As such, Georgi suggests, they are referring to their missionary activity.[277] To support this contention he notes that *diakonos* might refer to an envoy, and he pays particular attention to several passages in Epictetus describing the missionary activity of the cynic as the work of a *diakonos*, such as the characterization of Diogenes as the *diakonos* of Zeus,[278] and the description of the service of God (*diakonia tou theou*) as performing the task of a messenger, a lookout and a herald.[279] Thus he points to 1 Thessalonians 3:2, in which Timothy is described as a *diakonos* of God in his missionary activity, and 1 Corinthians 3:5, in which Paul himself and Apollos are described as *diakonoi*.

There is no question that this is one possible meaning of the term. But that does not mean that it is the only meaning. The *diakonoi* of the cult, already observed in the inscriptional evidence, certainly are not missionaries. Georgi takes the argument a step too far in suggesting that the use of the term in Philippians 1:1 is likewise a characterization of missionaries. The arguments that he employs to deny that the *episkopoi* and *diakonoi* of Philippi are economic officers are those we have already seen and countered, namely, that little is said about them in the course of the letter and a denial that Pauline communities had officers as such. Moreover, when he comes to the Pastoral Epistles and the work of Ignatius, Georgi has to suggest that there is a gap between the reality of the situation, in which the *diakonoi* are missionaries, and the ideal of the writers, which is to see *diakonoi* as subordinate cultic officers. If this is the case, however, we have to ask where Ignatius and "Paul" got their idea of *diakonoi* in the role assigned to them if the word was clearly established as simply meaning a "missionary" at the time.

Whether Georgi is correct or not in suggesting that "envoy" is a meaning of *diakonos* in Stoic and Cynic discourse,[280] the point is that this is not the

---

277. Georgi, *Opponents of Paul*, 27–32.
278. Epictetus, *Diss*. 3.24.64
279. Epictetus, *Diss*. 3.22.69: ἄγγελον καὶ κατάσκοπον καὶ κήρυκα τῶν θεῶν.
280. Collins (*Diakonia*, 170–76) suggests that Georgi has overstated the evidence.

only meaning in current Greek usage. We have to ask which meaning of the term best fits each context. In settings describing the activities of the church in cult and charity, the nearest usage of the term is that which refers to persons identified as *diakonoi* performing analogous functions in analogous settings. The role of *diakonoi* in *1 Clement*, the Pastoral Epistles, and the *Didache* is clearly cultic and economic. In the writings of Ignatius the term may be employed to signify an envoy, as it is of those who are to go to Antioch, but otherwise it refers to a liturgical role. In Philippians the meaning is not self-evident, but in the light of the occasion of the letter, namely, the communities' gifts to Paul, the associational language used elsewhere in the letter, and the association of these *diakonoi* with *episkopoi*, it is the liturgical meaning of the term that is the most likely.

The Origin of Diakonoi

Although *diakonoi* are mentioned in Philippians and in 1 Timothy, the New Testament documents do not explicitly illuminate their role. However, in both instances they appear alongside *episkopoi*. Beyond the canonical documents, the same phenomenon may be observed, particularly in the *Didache* and in *Didascalia apostolorum*, in one of which presbyters make no appearance, and in the other of which they are marginal. I may suggest that it is because of their close association with *episkopoi* that *diakonoi* do not clearly emerge elsewhere in the New Testament. Just as Hatch suggests that Christian leaders came to be called *episkopos* because of their responsibility in handling the offerings received at the church,[281] so I may note in turn that, by the third century, these offerings were received by the bishop at the hands of the deacons and see this as further support for a relative lack of differentiation between the roles of *episkopos* and *diakonos*. That the offerings, both eucharistic and charitable, were distributed by *diakonoi*[282] does not necessarily mean that the term was derived from the function of *diakonoi* at religious festivals, though this is possible. It is also possible that the term is developed solely by virtue of the relationship of the *diakonos* to that of the *episkopos* in the financial administration of the church, but in either event their economic function in the distribution of goods is established.

The problem lies in finding the actual distinction between *episkopoi* and *diakonoi* at the point of origin. In the cult, we may imagine, the *diakonoi* served from side tables, whereas the *episkopos* acted as *oikonomos*. But on

281. Hatch, *Organization*, 40.
282. Justin, *1 Apol.* 55; 57; *Pseudo-Clementines, Ep. Clem.* 5; *Hom.* 3.67.

what basis were the roles assigned? Both offices are undertaken as *leitourgiai*, as in the associations. In the qualification lists in the Pastoral Epistles, *diakonoi* and *episkopoi* alike are expected to be householders,[283] and the qualification lists continue to have a great deal in common. In the *Didache* the two stand together in offering financial support to the prophets and teachers, and the same would appear to be true in the Philippian community. The best that can be offered is a tentative suggestion: by whatever means the officers were appointed, whether by popular election or by choice of the patrons, it was simply a matter of appointment, and the same people might be eligible for appointment as *episkopos* or *diakonos*; they had distinct cultic roles, as already suggested, and the matter of who was appointed to which office was simply a matter of the choice of those with the responsibility to appoint.

Conclusion

It is at this point that I may return to Rome, finally, to illustrate the argument of the chapter that the principal function of early Christian *episkopoi* and *diakonoi* was economic. In chapter 1 I sketched out a picture of leadership in Rome by which individual churches had individual leaders, but I suggested that the leaders gathered, and that whereas the persons who gathered were collectively known as presbyters, the probability was that in their own communities they were known as *episkopoi*. I may now test this hypothesis through a close examination of what Hermas says about leadership. As already noted, he himself is a household leader.[284] However, he is told to share his revelations with churches overseas by means of Clement, with widows and orphans through Grapte, apparently a female teacher of these groups, and "within this city with the presbyters who support [*proistamenōn*] the church."[285] From this, one might think that leadership in Rome was presbyteral, but Hermas is a householder, and so there is no room for collective presbyteral office in a household.[286] This is the evidence on which the hypothesis of presbyters on a citywide basis within Rome is based. Additionally, I may note that certain leaders (*proēgoumenoi*) are upbraided for not being united in their thinking (*ou thelete . . . sunkerasai hymōn tēn phronēsin epi to auto*).[287] This too may be a reference to gatherings of leaders in which some do not participate.

283. 1 Tim. 3:12 directs that the *diakonos* should keep his household well.
284. *Herm.* 3; 46; 66.
285. *Herm.* 8:2–3.
286. So Campbell, *Elders*, 130, with reference to Pauline households.
287. *Herm.* 17:7–10.

There are, moreover, references to *episkopoi* and *diakonoi* within Hermas's work. One reference to *episkopoi* is simply a passing reference to heroic figures from the past. The other, however, is significant: a reference to *episkopoi* who support the needy and the widow and who offer hospitality.[288] If, as we may now see, *episkopoi* are the economic officers, rather than simply the leaders, of the community, we may see that here likewise there is reference to economic activity. Moreover, *diakonoi* are likewise economic officers, as they are accused (in some cases) of enriching themselves on the offerings of the church, which implies that they had part of the care of the church's finances in their hands and thus were in a position to enrich themselves.[289]

In a later period the function of deacons is clearly the relief of the poor and the management of the church's goods, as the *oikonomos* of the bishop's household.[290] It is for this reason that I may assert, against Lampe, that it was the communication of the leading *episkopos* of Rome with other churches, rather than his role in the centralization of poor relief, that led to his emergence as *monepiskopos*. This of course indicates that the role of an *episkopos* was no longer economic, but there is evidence that the role of the *diakonos* at Rome continued to be so into the third century.[291]

Episkopoi and *diakonoi* therefore had well-defined economic functions within the church. Although the terms themselves are neutral, their common usage within civic society, shared with associations more generally, provides a means by which we may see their use within the associations that made up early Christianity. Ultimately, it is the overlap in purpose between the *episkopoi* and *diakonoi* of associations, rather than the common use of the words, or even the common extent of aims and functions between the churches and associations, that is the clue to the derivation. It is this common function, combined with the common use of the words, and the fact that *episkopoi* are found accompanied by *diakonoi*, which leads me finally to reject hypotheses that derive the term from Septuagintal usage,[292] even though, I may repeat, the presence of the word *episkopos* in the Scriptures might further commend the adoption and usage of this common term.

The function of *presbyteroi* is, however, less well-defined, which is further indication of the lack of any real synonymy. This is the subject for the next

288. *Herm.* 104.

289. *Herm.* 103:2.

290. Noted also by Hatch, *Organization*, 50. However, Hatch fails to exploit the insight that this gives.

291. Thus, note the comments of Leo in *Serm.* 85.2 on the role of Laurence in the maintenance of the poor.

292. Such as that of Schnackenberg, "Episkopos und Hirtenamt." Note also Bobertz, "Episcopal Order," 185–87.

chapter, for, as noted at the end of chapter 1, whereas it had been shown that *presbyteroi* might be a collective noun for the gathering of Christian leaders within a city, not all evidence has been considered, and so it cannot be said that this is the only meaning of the term.

Fundamental to the ritual of Christianity was the gathering to eat. This meal is the focus for the church's activity in worship, but also in socialization, as patronage and leadership may be exercised and charity offered through the provision of food. It is by virtue of this liturgical context, therefore, that economic officers and patrons come to exercise leadership in worship and leadership in Christian communities overall.

Presbyters in Early Christian
Communities

In chapter 1 the relationship of the terms *presbyteros* and *episkopos* was discussed. There I concluded that, in some communities at least, a gathering of *episkopoi* from across the congregations might be termed "presbyters." However, I noted there, as at the end of chapter 2, that this does not exhaust the possible meanings of the term *presbyteros*. In this chapter I will suggest that within some individual congregations there were persons identified as presbyters. I will argue that they were not *episkopoi* and are carefully to be distinguished from the presbyters who held office *kata polin*. Indeed, I will suggest that they did not hold office at all. If the idea of synonymy and of presbyteral leadership, particularly at Rome, originated in confusion between presbyters in a single congregation and presbyters *kata polin*, we should be careful not to make the opposite error by denying the existence of congregational presbyters altogether. An exploration of the role of these presbyters is the substance of the second part of the chapter. The first part is devoted to an exploration of the origins of the term in order to clarify the function of those who bore the title.

The usual explanation of the use of the title "presbyter" is that the term is borrowed from the synagogue. Thus, I begin this chapter not with a distinguished nineteenth-century Anglican, but with an Anglican figure of the seventeenth century, as I note the origins of this consensus, which is bound up to that of the synonymy of *episkopos* and *presbyteros*. Stillingfleet sets out, at some length, the hypothesis of collegial leadership in early Christian communities and traces this to the synagogue:

> The other thing remaining to be spoken to, as to the correspondence of the Church with the Synagogue in its constitution, is, what order the Apostles did settle in the several Churches of their plantation for the ruling and ordering the affairs of them. Before I come to speak so much to it as will be pertinent to our present purpose and design, we may take notice of the same name for Church rulers under the Gospel, which there was under the Synagogue, *viz.* that of *Presbyters*.[1]

The idea that the church derived its organizational patterns from the synagogue, and that the synagogue in turn was under the management of boards of presbyters, derives in turn from the widely held assumption that presbyters held office and leads to the identification of these presbyters with *episkopoi*. Thus, all these parts of the consensus are bound up to one another. However, the examination of the evidence for presbyters in synagogues will show that such evidence is altogether wanting, and so a different route for the entry of the term into Christian discourse is proposed, which shows the evidence for Christian presbyters in a new light. While the conclusion of the chapter, that there were elders within Christian communities who were honored persons, is not new, it is put onto a surer evidential footing.

The Hypothesis of the Jewish Origin of Presbyters

I have already discussed the idea that early Christian leadership was collective, and although I have not dismissed outright the possibility of collegial leadership of individual (as opposed to federated) Christian communities, I have noted the absence of any secure evidence for this, the wealth of evidence that points away from it, and the inherent improbability that a household, which was governed by a single person, would give rise to a collective form of leadership in any community based on a household model. Given that all the evidence is capable of multiple interpretations, almost any reconstruction is bound to be hypothetical to an extent, including that offered thus far, namely, the federation of individual Christian leaders known as *episkopoi* leading to

1. Edward Stillingfleet, *Irenicum: A Weapon-Salve for the Churches Wounds* (London: Henry Mortlock, 1662), 285. This is part of an extended argument (230–345).

the emergence of monepiscopacy. However, as has been noted already, the consensus of collective leadership itself was based on a presupposition: the Jewish origin of such collective groups of leaders. If, however, it can be shown that such a group of elders in the synagogue did not exist, then the other parts of the consensus—collective leadership of congregations and the identity of *episkopoi* and presbyters—lose their last remaining support.

It seems likely that the origin of the hypothesis of the synagogal origin of presbyters originated with Stillingfleet, though Vitringa is more often given the dubious credit of originating the hypothesis.[2] The point of Stillingfleet's, as of Vitringa's, work was to propose an origin for ecclesial organization overall within the synagogue; it is not a coincidence, I may suggest, that Vitringa was a Protestant, or that Stillingfleet was arguing for the reconciliation of the Church of England with Puritan separatists in the period of the restoration and so found in the synagogal presbyters and the synonymy of presbyter and *episkopos* the basis on which to defend the validity of presbyteral ordination, while arguing on practical grounds for the acceptance of episcopate. Whatever its origin, by the nineteenth century the hypothesis of the synagogal origin of presbyters had, together with the synonymy of *episkopos* and *presbyteros* and the originally collective nature of Christian leadership, attained the status of a "fact" on both sides of the North Sea, and it is treated as such by Rothe, as well as Lightfoot.[3]

Whether theories of the origin of Christian ministry assume a growth of the episcopate from the presbyterate, or whether the two systems are seen as having two distinct origins, the institution of presbyters seen as emerging from the synagogue, thus representing a Jewish strand in the formation of Christian ministries, is a central plank. It is best represented in recent scholarship in the work of Burtchaell,[4] for whom the whole apparatus of Christian ministry

2. Campegius Vitringa, *De synagogo vetere libri tres* (Frankeren: Johan Gyzelaar, 1696), 609–20. The origin of the hypothesis is attributed to Vitringa by Paul F. Bradshaw, *The Search for the Origins of Christian Worship: Sources and Methods for the Study of Early Liturgy*, 2nd ed. (London: SPCK, 2002), 193.

3. "Wies nun aber wieder die Verfassung der jüdischen Synagoge unmittelbar den Weg. Sie hatte ja einen Vorstand, dem eine ganz ähnliche Aufgabe gestellt war, das Collegium der Gemeindeältesten. . . . Nach der Analogie dieses Synagogenvorstandes wurde nun auch wirklich frühzeitig, unstreitig auf die Veranstaltung der Apostel hin, in den christlichen Gemeinden ein eigentlicher Gemeindevorstand eingeführt, das Collegium der Presbyteren oder der Bischöfe" (Richard Rothe, *Die Anfänge der christlichen Kirche und ihrer Verfassung: Ein geschichtlicher Versuch* [Wittenberg: Zimmermann, 1837], 172–73). "Over every Jewish synagogue, whether at home or abroad, a council of 'elders' presided" (J. B. Lightfoot, *Saint Paul's Epistle to the Philippians*, 4th ed. [London: Macmillan, 1878], 96). See also Edwin Hatch, *The Organization of the Early Christian Churches* (London: Longmans, 1881), 59. Hatch, however, introduces some twists of his own, as is observed below.

4. James Tunstead Burtchaell, *From Synagogue to Church: Public Services and Offices in the Earliest Christian Communities* (Cambridge: Cambridge University Press, 1992), 228–33.

(and not just the presbyterate), alongside much else, is derived from forming Judaism, though the assertion is made so frequently in modern literature without examination that it may be found in almost any discussion of the subject, even though its origins in the ecclesiastical politics of the seventeenth century are forgotten.[5]

Whereas there is the important distinction between Burtchaell and those who preceded him, in that he derives the whole threefold order, rather than the presbyterate alone, from Jewish models, nonetheless he may represent the most recent thorough statement of that position. The contrary position in recent scholarship is put forth by Campbell, for whom the elders were in no sense officeholders but rather honored persons in the community by virtue of age and experience.[6]

The problem with both positions is that they assume a monolithic development of Christian ministry. It is hypothetically possible that there were such offices in some synagogues in some communities, and that they in turn influenced the development of Christian office. Such a picture, however, is localized, and the evidence for synagogue organization in the formative period of Christianity is slight. In particular we may note that the synagogue itself was a forming institution, and thus it is difficult to say to what extent Christianity formed itself on synagogal models when the synagogal models themselves might not have been fully established.[7] However, there is some evidence of Jewish community organization in a number of centers that became Christian centers. Within these we may inquire as to the possibility of influence, and the possible existence of presbyters within these Jewish communities.

Evidence for Presbyters in Synagogues within Centers of Christianity

My concern in this section is not to give an overall description of community organization in forming Jewish communities, but solely to determine whether the term "presbyters" was used among them to designate leaders.

5. E.g., J. N. D. Kelly, *A Commentary on the Pastoral Epistles: I Timothy, II Timothy, Titus*, BNTC (London: Black, 1963), 15; C. K. Barrett, *A Critical and Exegetical Commentary on the Acts of the Apostles*, 2 vols., ICC (Edinburgh: T&T Clark, 1994), 1:566; Theodor Schneider, "Das Amt in der frühen Kirche: Versuch einer Zusammenschau," in *Das kirchliche Amt in apostolischer Nachfolge*, vol. 2, *Ursprünge und Wandlungen*, ed. Gunther Wenz, Wolfgang Beinert, and Dorothea Sattler, DK 13 (Freiburg: Herder, 2006), 11–38, 24–25.

6. R. Alastair Campbell, *The Elders: Seniority within Earliest Christianity*, SNTW (Edinburgh: T&T Clark, 1994).

7. Wayne O. McCready, "*Ekklēsia* and Voluntary Associations," in *Voluntary Associations in the Graeco-Roman World*, ed. John S. Kloppenborg and Stephen G. Wilson (London: Routledge, 1996), 63.

PRESBYTERS IN THE JEWISH COMMUNITIES OF ALEXANDRIA[8]

When Philo accuses Aulus Avilius Flaccus, sometime governor of Egypt, of various crimes against the Jews, he refers to the *gerousia* within Alexandria that had charge (*epimelēsomenēn*) of Jewish affairs in the city, of which Flaccus had arrested thirty-eight members.[9] In light of this, I may readily agree that there was a council of elders set over the (fairly substantial)[10] Jewish community of Alexandria and may indeed see it functioning similarly to the Christian presbyters whose existence at Rome I have deduced. This council had authority on inner-Jewish matters, particularly relating to the maintenance of Jewish law and custom, such rights being confirmed under Claudius after a period of tension within the city.[11] I will examine Alexandrian Christianity in due course, but here I may note the possibility that Jewish community organization contributed to that of Christianity in the city.

Whether each synagogue similarly was under the management of benches of elders is less certain. In *t. Sukkah* 4.6 and *b. Sukkah* 51b we find reference to the seventy-one thrones of the elders of Alexandria set in the great synagogue; this implies that these elders were part of a single gathering, whereas there were a number of synagogues in the city.[12] Thus, when Burtchaell states that "each of the synagogues in Alexandria . . . surely had its own bench of elders,"[13] he is going beyond the evidence presented by Philo. Within the synagogue Philo refers to "one of the elders" interpreting the Scriptures,[14] but this does not necessarily refer to one of the elders within the synagogue and may refer to one from within the wider Jewish community, and, in any event, the word *presbyteros* is not employed here.

Outside Alexandria, but within Egypt, there is reference to "the presbyters of the Jews in Tebtenu" in P.Monac. 3.49, although *archontes*, a much

---

8. This section concerns itself solely with the issue of the governance of Jewish institutions in Alexandria. For a more general treatment of Alexandrian Jews in the period, see Esther Starobinski-Safran, "La communauté juive d'Alexandrie a l'époque de Philon," in *Alexandrina: Hellénisme, judaïsme et christianisme à Alexandrie; Mélanges offerts au P. Claude Mondésert* (Patrimoines; Paris: Cerf, 1987), 45–75.

9. Philo, *Flacc.* 74. Here I do not enter into the question of whether the reference to presbyters in *Let. Aris.* 310, which refers to an acclamation of the LXX translation by, among others, the πρεσβύτεροι τῶν ἑρμενέων, refers to the translators themselves (so Campbell, *Elders*, 39–40) or to some other group. It is sufficient for my purposes to demonstrate the existence of a *gerousia* in Alexandria.

10. It is not possible to give a precise number. However, Philo reports that the city was divided into five *quartiers* and that two of them were substantially Jewish (*Flacc.* 55). Strabo (cited by Josephus, *A.J.* 14.117) states that a substantial part of the city was allocated to Jews.

11. Josephus, *A.J.* 19.280; P.Lond. 1912.

12. Philo, *Legat.* 132.

13. Burtchaell, *From Synagogue to Church*, 230n20.

14. Philo *Hypothetica* 7.13; τῶν ἱερέων δέ τις ὁ παρὼν ἢ τῶν γερόντων εἷς.

more common term, also appears in the document. The relationship between presbyters and *archontes* is unclear due to the mutilated state of the papyrus, but it is possible that the *archontes* form an umbrella body, whereas the presbyters in the village of Tebetnu are the local managers.[15] If the latter is the case, then this is in keeping with Kasher's interpretation of *CPJ* 432, a report of income and expenditure relating to the city of Arsinoe. Among debtors are mentioned two synagogues, one described as a *proseuchē* and the other as a *eucheion*, the first of which, described as being of the Thebans, has designated *archontes*. Kasher deduces from this that the *archontes* are an umbrella body, responsible for the payment, in this instance, on behalf of the two synagogues.[16]

Beyond this, there is no evidence. It is possible that elders held some form of office in the Egyptian synagogue outside Alexandria, but no more than possible. If they did hold office, then it is more probable, given the honorific content of the term, that they did so by virtue of age and status within the community, and that they exercised not liturgical, but broadly managerial, functions.

Presbyters in the Jewish Communities of Jerusalem

In pursuing evidence for presbyters within Judaism, Burtchaell notes evidence of the existence of a sanhedrin of seventy, plus the high priest, in Jerusalem.[17] In addition, he notes that both Luke and Josephus make reference to such a *synedrion*. Although neither of these two authors is exactly a disinterested reporter, the existence of this body may be considered reasonably likely.[18] It is clear, however, from all the references made to this sanhedrin, whether in Josephus, Luke, or the rabbinic literature, that it is a juridical (and perhaps political) body set over Jewish affairs throughout the city. This tells us nothing of the organization of local synagogues.[19] Although Luke refers to this gathering as a "presbytery" (*presbyterion*) on occasion,[20] there is no reference to its members as "presbyters," whereas Josephus simply refers to

---

15. So S. R. Llewelyn, *NewDocs* 9:70–72.

16. Aryeh Kasher, *The Jews in Hellenistic and Roman Egypt: The Struggle for Equal Rights*, TSAJ 7 (Tübingen: Mohr Siebeck, 1985), 140–41.

17. Burtchaell, *From Synagogue to Church*, 230, with reference to *1 En.* 90:20–27; Josephus, *B.J.* 4.336.

18. Although for a dissenting opinion, note E. P. Sanders, *Judaism: Practice and Belief* (London: SCM, 1992), 472–90.

19. We do not know how many synagogues there were in first-century Jerusalem, or how many of these gatherings had dedicated buildings; *y. Meg.* 3.1.73d records 480; *b. Ketub.* 105a records 394. These figures almost certainly are exaggerated, assuming that the synagogue had a greater centrality in Jewish life in Jerusalem than was the case.

20. Luke 22:66; Acts 22:5.

the *synedrion*,[21] to the council (*boulē*),[22] and on one occasion to "the corporation of the Jerusalemites."[23]

In regard to the organization of local Jerusalem synagogues in the first century CE we depend on a single inscription, which makes reference to presbyters alongside an *archisynagōgos*; although the dating of the inscription is disputed, the majority of commentators continue to date it prior to 70 CE.[24]

> Theodotus, son of Vettenus and synagogue-ruler [*archisynagōgos*], son of a synagogue-ruler and grandson of a synagogue-ruler, built the synagogue for the reading of the law and instruction in the commandments; also the strangers' lodgings and the dining rooms and water facilities and hostel for the use of those from foreign lands. The foundation of this his fathers and the *presbyteroi* and Simonides laid.[25]

The appearance of an *archisynagōgos* here indicates that this individual synagogue at least was under local management, even though Theodotus is more probably commemorated as a donor rather than as an active official, given that the purpose of the inscription was to commemorate his funding of building improvement. This fits with the argument, presented above, that *archisynagōgoi* were fundamentally patrons of their communities rather than liturgical leaders.

The inscription makes reference to pilgrims. Similarly, we may note reference to a synagogue of the Alexandrians in the Tosefta (*t. Meg.* 2.17) and the Babylonian Talmud (*b. Meg.* 26a) and may also note Acts 6:9, which refers to at least one Hellenophone synagogue in Jerusalem,[26] although we should always be alert to the possibility that a gathering, rather than a building, is intended. However, the evidence of expatriate gatherings in Jerusalem tends to imply that the synagogue of the Theodotus inscription might be completely detached from the resident sanhedrin and, like other synagogues in the city, might be concerned to serve pilgrims and expatriates. Thus, we should observe, with Martin, the fact that Theodotus's name is Greek, and that his father's

21. E.g., Josephus, *A.J.* 14.91, 168; 16.337.

22. Josephus, *B.J.* 2.331, 336.

23. Josephus, *Vita* 190: τὸ κοινὸν τῶν Ἱεροσολυμιτῶν.

24. For a summary of the debate with bibliography and a defense of the first-century dating of this inscription, see Stephen K. Catto, *Reconstructing the First-Century Synagogue: A Critical Analysis of Current Research*, LNTS 363 (London: T&T Clark, 2007), 83–85.

25. *CIJ* 1404.

26. Or possibly as many as five. So David A. Fiensy, "The Composition of the Jerusalem Church," in *The Book of Acts in Its Palestinian Setting*, ed. Richard J. Bauckham, BAFS 4 (Grand Rapids: Eerdmans, 1995), 233.

name is Latin, and indeed that the inscription itself is written in Greek.²⁷ All this points to synagogues in Jerusalem serving an expatriate or transitory community. In addition, there is the possibility that different groupings within forming Judaism might have their own gatherings.²⁸

The appearance of the term "presbyters" in this inscription tells us nothing of "normal" synagogue organization in Jerusalem. Indeed, the probability is that it does not speak of office in any way. The inscription states that the synagogue had been founded by "his [presumably, Theodotus's] ancestors and by the *presbyteroi* and by Simonides." In the context of a reference to Theodotus's ancestors the *presbyteroi* are similarly likely to be people in the past. This section of the inscription may thus be translated as "which his ancestors, and people of old, and Simonides founded."

There is no evidence at all for the use of the term "presbyters" in first-century CE Palestine to refer to people holding office in any synagogue.

PRESBYTERS IN THE SYNAGOGUES OF ROME

Certainly a substantial Jewish population lived in Rome at the time of the formation of Christianity, and there is evidence for a number of synagogues there.²⁹ In contrast to Alexandria, however, this population was not, at the time of the formation of Christianity, an inculturated and localized population, but rather was made up of immigrant communities, some of which had come to the city relatively recently.

"In Rome," Burtchaell states, "while many burial inscriptions identify the incumbent as a notable, only a single stone honors an elder, despite the fact that we know the synagogues there had colleges of elders."³⁰ In view of Burtchaell's statement that "we know" that Roman synagogues had colleges of elders, it may be asked how we know this. The probability, given that the synagogues of Rome appear to have been organized at least on occasion on ethnic grounds, may well indicate that there was no common organizational basis whatsoever.³¹ This question has already been examined in detail by Frey, who in the

27. Matthew J. Martin, "Interpreting the Theodotus Inscription: Some Reflections on a First-Century Jerusalem Synagogue Inscription and E. P. Sanders' 'Common Judaism,'" *ANES* 39 (2002): 164–65.
28. On the possibility of an Essene synagogue in Jerusalem, see Rainer Riesner, "Synagogues in Jerusalem," in Bauckham, *Book of Acts,* 190–91.
29. For a discussion of numbers and of the synagogues, see Harry J. Leon, *The Jews of Ancient Rome* (Philadelphia: Jewish Publication Society, 1960), 135–66.
30. Burtchaell, *From Synagogue to Church,* 235. Here he refers to *CIJ* 1.378: "Here lies Metrodorus an elder" ([Μ]ητρό[δ]ωρος [πρεσβ]ύτερος [ἐνθάδε κ]ῖτε).
31. So Margaret H. Williams, "The Structure of Roman Jewry Reconsidered: Were the Synagogues of Ancient Rome Entirely Homogeneous?" *ZPE* 104 (1994): 129–41.

first instance concludes that there was no overarching *gerousia* in Rome.[32] He does believe, however, that individual synagogues might have had benches of elders, as there are inscriptions from different synagogues recording the office of *gerousiarch*.[33] We may concede the possibility that these synagogues were under collective leadership; however, the body of which this person was head was not designated collectively as presbyters. We may also observe that *CIJ* 504 likewise makes reference to an *archisynagōgos*. Whereas Leon suggests that the title "presbyter" might have been used for members of individual synagogues' *gerousiai*, he also points out that evidence for the use of the title outside Rome derives from the fourth century or later.[34]

Frey further confronts the issue of the relative rarity of the term, concluding that presbyters in the Jewish community did not have a function as such, but that the term was simply honorific. For this reason, those who did have functions are more likely to be commemorated with reference to the functions that they actually performed,[35] and given that the designation is collective, an individual is unlikely to be commemorated using this term. These conclusions have subsequently been endorsed by Leon.[36] My own discussion may be brief because, whatever the means of the internal organization(s) of Roman Jews, there were no presbyters among them. I must agree with Frey that the Roman synagogue had no influence on Christian office in the city: "The members of the ecclesiastical hierarchy . . . have no parallel within the Jewish communities."[37]

I have already given an account of the formation of the episcopate in Rome, and I have seen no reason to refer to any kind of relationship with the synagogue in the city. The apparent absence of office-holding presbyters in the Roman synagogue, as well as the apparent continuing independence of individual synagogues within the city, with no overarching central body, makes this all the more compelling.

PRESBYTERS IN THE SYNAGOGUES OF ANTIOCH

Although Antioch had a long-standing and substantial Jewish population,[38] we know virtually nothing of its internal organization. Josephus refers to the

32. Jean Baptiste Frey, *Corpus of Jewish Inscriptions: Jewish Inscriptions from the Third Century B.C. to the Seventh Century A.D.* (New York: Ktav, 1975), 237.

33. *CIJ* 425, 504, 533.

34. Leon, *Jews*, 181.

35. Jean Baptiste Frey, "Les communautés juives à Rome aux premiers temps de l'église," *RSR* 21 (1931): 138–39; also Campbell, *Elders*, 53.

36. Leon, *Jews*, 168–70.

37. "Les membres de la hiérarchie ecclésiastique . . . n'ont aucun parallèle dans les communautés juives" (Frey, "Communautés," 159).

38. Josephus implies that Jews first came to Antioch early in the Seleucid period (*C. Ap.* 2.39; *A.J.* 12.119). The precise size of the population can only be estimated. C. H. Kraeling ("The Jewish Community at Antioch," *JBL* 51 [1932]: 136) suggests forty-five thousand in the first

archōn of the Antiochene Jews,[39] and, centuries later, Libanius to the "ruler of those who rule among them";[40] both statements imply that there was a senior *archōn* with overall charge of Jewish affairs in the city. There is also a tomb of a "gerousiarch of Antioch" in Beth She'arim in Galilee.[41] This evidence may point to an active *gerousia*, or simply an executive of archons, or both. It does not indicate the employment of the term *presbyteroi*,[42] but it does imply some degree of central organization in Antiochene Judaism. To this evidence, cited by Kraeling and by Meeks and Wilken, I may add a slightly opaque statement in the *Codex Justinianus* 1.9.1, dating from the third century, referring to the union of the Jews (*universitati Iudaeorum*) established in Antioch. Again this would point to the existence of a central organization overseeing Jewish affairs in the city.

Some confusion has been caused by Josephus's statement in *Contra Apionem* 2.39: "Those of us [Jews] who dwell at Antioch are called Antiochenes; for the founder Seleucus gave them citizenship [*politeian*]," which may be read as suggesting that all Antiochene Jews were citizens. However, the probability is that the statement is to be interpreted, as both Kasher and Zetterholm suggest, as meaning that, like the Alexandrian Jews, they constituted a *politeuma*.[43] I may suggest that this is what Chrysostom means when he refers to the Jewish *politeia* in Antioch.[44] Again, this would imply some degree of central organization. As to the organization of individual synagogues, however, we know nothing; it would be unwise to extrapolate from the *politeuma* to individual synagogue communities. We cannot have Binder's confidence that the synagogues knew a council of presbyters.[45]

Thus, once again, evidence that might provide a basis for seeing presbyters as a synagogal institution is wanting, although, once again, a degree of central organization is exhibited.

---

century CE; Wayne Meeks and Robert Wilken (*Jews and Christians in Antioch in the First Four Centuries of the Common Era*, SBLSBS 13 [Missoula, MT: Scholars Press, 1978], 8) suggest twenty-two thousand. It is, in any event, a substantial population.

39. Josephus, *B.J.* 7.47.

40. Libanius, *Ep.* 1251: ἀρχόντων τῶν παρ' αὐτοῖς ἄρχοντα. This letter is translated in Meeks and Wilken, *Jews and Christians*, 60.

41. Published in ibid., 54.

42. Although the term is found in a dedication of a building in Apamea in the late fourth century. See ibid., 53.

43. Kasher, *Jews*, 305; Magnus Zetterholm, *The Formation of Christianity in Antioch: A Social-Scientific Approach to the Separation between Judaism and Christianity* (London: Routledge, 2003), 32–37.

44. Chrysostom, *Adv. Jud.* 1.3.

45. Donald D. Binder, *Into the Temple Courts: The Place of the Synagogues in the Second Temple Period*, SBLDS 169 (Atlanta: Society of Biblical Literature, 1999), 371.

Presbyters in the Ephesian Synagogues

The Ephesian Jews seem likewise to have enjoyed a strong central organization. There was sufficient organization for them to have petitioned as a group for various rights and privileges, such as exemption from military service and the observation of the sabbath,[46] and a second-century inscription charges the Jews of Ephesus with care of a tomb.[47] Evidence for presbyters, however, is limited to a single inscription of uncertain date, referring to the *archsynagōgoi* and the elders.[48] Whereas this may indicate that the representatives of the various synagogues were known as presbyters, it may equally apply to individual synagogues; nothing, moreover, may be inferred about their function. A single inscription is insufficient grounds for any conclusion.

Preliminary Conclusions

Although Jewish communities in some cities had a strong central organization, along the model exhibited in Roman and Ephesian Christianity, there is little evidence for any designation of presbyters, and such evidence that may be found is remarkably uninformative. Certainly there are no grounds to share the confidence of earlier generations of scholars that the presbyters of the synagogue provide a ready model for collective leadership in Christian communities.

"Elder" as a Term of Honor Rather Than Office in Synagogues

As has already been noted, a contrary position is put forth by Campbell, for whom "elder" does not denote an office but is simply a generalized term of honor awarded on the basis of age. Campbell studies the use of the term in the literature of forming Judaism and in the New Testament and concludes, "Eldership was not an office among the Jews of this period, but was rather a collective term for leaders of whatever kind, and is usually found accompanying other more precise terms. . . . It is evidence of a way of thinking about society, but is not the title of an office within it."[49] Thus, when he turns to the synagogue, he points out that there is no evidence of presbyters running the synagogue as such, none for presbyters having a liturgical role or a role of individual management. Rather, the evidence points to an understanding of presbyters simply as senior persons in the community, with responsibility for

---

46. Josephus, *A.J.* 14.223–230, 262–264; 16.167–168.
47. *IEph.* 1677.6–7.
48. τῶν ἀρχι<σ>υναγωγῶν καὶ τῶν πρεσβ(υτέρων) πολλὰ τὰ {τὰ} ἔ[τη] (*IEph.* 1251).
49. Campbell, *Elders*, 44.

the synagogue as for other aspects of the community, who may, by virtue of seniority, have a place on a council, but who are not officers.

I cannot help but concur. The silence in the sources regarding the office of presbyter in the synagogues is deafening.

Conclusions on Jewish Presbyters

There is no question that some Jewish communities had representative councils. Thus, as Burtchaell notes, the Mishnah provides that twenty-three members might form a sanhedrin for a town of 120 Jewish persons.[50] Although one may be skeptical of the evidence of the Mishnah as respecting the first century CE, there is ample evidence that local councils within Jewish communities exercised legal and political functions. All this simply demonstrates that the ancient Israelite tradition of a gathering of elders continued to be upheld into the first century CE. It does not demonstrate that all individual synagogues were under the management of boards of elders. One should also note at this point that the duties of these elders seem primarily to be not religious but political, and finally, and critically for the question at hand, that they are referred to not as *presbyteroi* but as *gerontes*, or more often as *archontes*, and collectively as a *gerousia* or a *synedrion*. The link with the elders of Israel is made by the Mishnah simply to justify the number of seventy on the Greater Sanhedrin with reference to Numbers 11:16.

We should not be too troubled at the apparently civil aspect of many of these functions, since, as Burtchaell rightly points out, there is no easy bisection of religions and civil duties,[51] but the cohesion of civic and religious duties is less obvious within Christianity, which does not relate to an established and identifiable *politeuma*; this in turn makes the derivation of Christian presbyters from these Jewish elders rather less certain.

Finally, if Christian presbyters were universally a derivation from synagogue organization, then one would expect to find the term commonly used in Jewish communities, given the centrality of the function that would be inferred, but it is found fairly infrequently. Much more widely attested is the title *archōn*. Burtchaell and Frey see these *archontes* as some kind of executive group drawn from the wider council of elders,[52] and Kasher argues the same with respect to those of Arsinoe.[53] The question of the precise function of *archontes* and their relationship to presbyters in Jewish community life is beyond this work,

50. *m. Sanh.* 1.1, 6.
51. Burtchaell, *From Synagogue to Church*, 243.
52. Frey, *Jewish Inscriptions*, lxxxvii.
53. Kasher, *Jews*, 140–41.

however, although the suggestion that they are the executive would be borne out by the fact that *archontes* in many cities were the executive of the city, answerable to the *boulē*. However, it is sufficient to note here that designated presbyters in synagogues were far from a universal phenomenon, and presbyters with specific responsibilities even more rare. It is in the light of such thin evidence that Banks writes, "In view of the suggestions that the notion of eldership was drawn from the synagogue, it should be noted that there is no evidence whatever for the synagogue having such positions."[54]

Again, I am forced to agree, at least as far as the period of formative Christianity is concerned. Levine puts forth the opposite case: "There is no question that the presbyter was an integral part of the synagogue officialdom in many locales";[55] although he counts thirty inscriptions, none are of a date that would be likely to affect forming Christianity, and likewise they seem not to be found in the centers where Christianity formed. It is possible that presbyters were an institution in some synagogues in the Common Era, but not in a way, at a time, or in a location whereby they might influence the formation of Christian presbyters. However, since there is no question that presbyters are found with some frequency in early Christian literature, and that, without prejudice to the argument below, it is possible that some at least held some form of office, the question is raised as to how the term entered Christian discourse as used for those with liturgical and managerial functions.

There is the possibility that the term derives from Jewish usage, but not the usage of the contemporary synagogue. Such is a passing suggestion from Lietzmann, who suggests that *presbyteroi* had a biblical echo that *gerontes* did not, and that these officers were so named after the analogy of the naming of the gathering as *ekklēsia* rather than *synagogē*.[56] I have already countenanced the possibility that *episkopoi* entered Christian usage by a similar route, and I may well accept that such biblical usage might color Christian understanding of such a term, but it does not of itself explain why the term should be extracted from the scriptural narrative as a term for office unless it was already current in the linguistic realm. The nascent Christian communities, we may surmise, did not sit down with a *tabula rasa* in some kind of modernized (or quasi-Rothean) version of the apostolic fiction in order to invent offices;

---

54. Robert Banks, *Paul's Idea of Community: The Early House Churches in Their Cultural Setting* (Peabody, MA: Hendrickson, 1994), 149. Similarly A. E. Harvey ("Elders," *JTS* 25 [1974]: 318–31) describes the existence of synagogue elders as "suppositious."

55. Lee I. Levine, *The Ancient Synagogue: The First Thousand Years*, 2nd ed. (New Haven: Yale University Press, 2005), 432.

56. Hans Lietzmann, "Zur altchristlichen Verfassungsgeschichte," in *Kleine Schriften I*, ed. Kurt Aland, TUGAL 67 (Berlin: Akademie-Verlag, 1958), 156.

rather, institutions formed by default and would seek language from the surrounding society. Similar societal institutions, such as synagogues and other associations, would be the primary source of language, whereas scriptural usage and familiarity would be a secondary filter only.

One critical matter, however, does emerge from even this cursory examination. The scattered and diverse synagogues of Rome had no central body, but those of Alexandria and of Egypt beyond, of Antioch, of Ephesus (probably), and to an extent of Jerusalem had a central council, a basis for federation, unparalleled, as noted above, by other associations. Thus, whereas the Jewish origin of Christian presbyters in individual churches would appear a scholarly myth, the means by which individual ministers of diverse Christian communities might meet in federation would, at the time of their formation, readily be modeled on the practice of existing Jewish communities.

A Non-Jewish Origin for Christian Presbyters

If the evidence for an established and identifiable group of presbyters in forming Jewish communities at the time of the formation of Christianity is so thin, it may be worth reopening the question from the beginning and seeking an origin in wider Hellenistic and non-Jewish circles. The conception of the Jewish origin of the designation has been so common and extensive for so long that, apart from that of Hatch, no inquiry in this direction appears to have been made.[57]

Given that some Christian communities behaved in an associational manner, and given that associational titles often reflected those of civic government, a first point of inquiry must be the presence of defined presbyters in civic governance and associations as a means by which the designation might enter early Christian usage.

I may clarify here that I am speaking of persons specifically identified as *presbyteroi* and not of a *gerousia*. Although associations might mirror civic government and have *gerousiai*,[58] and although civic *gerousiai* existed, they

---

57. Hatch (*Organization*, 62–67), while accepting the synagogal institution of presbyters, and suggesting that the organization of Jewish Christian communities had derived the institution from that root, nonetheless suggested that presbyters in Gentile churches were an independent and spontaneous development, arguing in particular for a renewed role for the *gerousia* in the cities of Asia in the early empire. Whereas much of the detail in his argument is questionable, and whereas the division between Jewish and Gentile churches is also problematic, credit must be given for this insight; it is strange that this part of his work should be forgotten, when his work on *episkopoi* in associations is widely recollected.

58. For instance, the sodality described at *IC* 3.3.7.

had by the first century CE long ceased to exercise real power. I may quote Bekkers-Nielsen, noting that this rather mirrors the situation that we have met in seeking to identify synagogal *presbyteroi*:

> The *gerousia* crops up from time to time in the epigraphic record for Bithynia. . . . When the achievements of a Bithynian politician are recorded . . . membership of the *gerousia* is never mentioned and offices within a *gerousia* only rarely. Either *gerousia* membership was rarely combined with an urban political career or it was considered too insignificant to include in the overview of a person's *cursus*.[59]

The *gerousia* as a political institution was thus barely functional.

Associations defined as consisting of *presbyteroi*, however, or divided into age groups among which *presbyteroi* figure, are widely attested. Here I quote Rhodes and Lewis:

> In the hellenistic and Roman periods we find in many places, particularly in Asia Minor, corporations of "young men," *neoi*, and of "elders," *presbyteroi*. . . . These bodies were commonly associated with a gymnasium; they could also have religious interests; though it is possible in principle, it is not easy in practice to draw a line between *gerousiai* of a primarily religious and those of primarily social kind. Like any body within the state, these corporations could pass decrees dealing with their own affairs or honouring their members and benefactors, but occasionally honours awarded by the young men, and more often honours awarded by the elders are recorded in a way which seems to place them on a level with honours awarded by the council and the people.[60]

I illustrate this with a few examples, out of a great many, that bear out Rhodes and Lewis's assertions.

At Iasos, Sopatros dedicates a stoa, and he is described as "the gymnasiarch of the younger and the older men."[61] The gymnasium of the elders at Iasos is also mentioned in an inscription honoring its founder,[62] as is reference to a gymnasiarch of the *presbyteroi*.[63] Reinach suggests that these gymnasia are

---

59. Tønnes Bekker-Nielsen, *Urban Life and Local Politics in Roman Bithynia: The Small World of Dion Chrysostomos*, BSS 7 (Aarhus: Aarhus University Press, 2008), 79.

60. P. J. Rhodes and David M. Lewis, *The Decrees of the Greek States* (Oxford: Clarendon, 1997), 539.

61. *Ilasos* 250: τῶν τε νέων καὶ τῶν πρεσβυτέρων (originally published by Théodore Reinach, "Inscriptions d'Iasos," *REG* 6 [1893]: 187).

62. *Ilasos* 93; see Reinach, "Inscriptions d'Iasos," 169–70.

63. *Ilasos* 87.

based on age divisions.[64] These presbyters are recorded, moreover, as being authorized by the assembly to collect funds.[65] Beyond Iasos, *SEG* 43.371, likewise honoring a gymnasiarch, makes mention of the presbyters, alongside the *neoi*, as do (here from Troas) *MDAI(A)* 32 (1907) 273,10 and, in a long honorific inscription, *SEG* 29:1244, which refers to dinners for the two groups.[66] Similarly, at Cos we hear of a gymnasiarch of the presbyters.[67]

Thracian references to older men who sing hymns (*hymnōdoi presbyteroi*), such as *IScM* 1.100 and *IGBulg.* 2 666, may appear to indicate a different use, but even here the primary reference is gymnastic; the first of these inscriptions is a commemoration of victory at a contest, and, moreover, *IGBulg.* 1² 17 refers to younger men who sing hymns (*hymnōdoi neōteroi*).

Going beyond the gymnasium, we may note defined groups of *presbyteroi* in wider society. *IEph.* 803 is an inscription from the beginning of the first century CE in which the *presbyteroi* state that they are honoring Epaphras, priest of the divine Augustus. Here the nature of their designation is not clear, but nonetheless they are clearly a defined group. Similarly, we may observe, also from Ephesus, a dedicatory inscription to "Artemis, Caesar and the presbyters."[68] Though the context is not clear, we may again note that the presbyters are a defined group within Ephesian society and are in a position of honor. The term is not vague, as the *presbyteroi* are members of a clearly defined group. The same is true at Chios, where the elders honor Megakles for his piety toward the gods and his munificence toward themselves.[69]

Such usage certainly entered associational life. In Paphos, somewhere between 50 and 100 BCE, an engineer (whose name is lost) in charge of the catapults was honored by the state; in his memory the corps of senior artillerymen (*to tagma tōn presbyterōn aphetōn*) was to sacrifice to Aphrodite, and that of the junior artillerymen (*to tōn neōterōn*) to Leto.[70] Whereas these titles may be merely descriptive, the fact that they are organized according to *tagma* implies an organization within the association corresponding to that of gymnasia. That this association is related to the military may mean that it is closer than other associations to gymnastic organization due to the close relationship

64. Reinach, "Inscriptions d'Iasos," 163–64. For an attempt to categorize these age divisions more precisely, see Martin P. Nilsson, *Die hellenistische Schule* (Munich: Beck, 1955), 34–42. Nilsson, however, concentrates on the younger age divisions.
65. *IIasos* 23. See Reinach, "Inscriptions d'Iasos," 166–68.
66. The editors suggest, again, that this relates to the gymnasium.
67. γυμνασιαρχήσαντα τῶν πρεσβυτέρων (*CIG* 2508).
68. *IEph.* 711.
69. *SEG* 26.1021.
70. Published by W. M. Calder, "Documents from Phrygia and Cyprus," *JHS* 55 (1935): 75–78.

between gymnasia and the military.[71] Nonetheless, we may note a *systema* of presbyters at Magnesia who make a grant of oil toward the city[72] and, in Delos, an association of senior warehousemen from Alexandria who honor Krokos with a statue on account of his goodwill toward them and other foreigners.[73]

The fact that the traders in this latter instance are Alexandrian is not insignificant, as a number of professional associations in Alexandria use the title. Thus, we may note the millers of Alexandria who had presbyters and a priest,[74] the senior builders (*tektones presbyteroi*) from Ptolemais,[75] and, in a religious context, the senior shrine-carriers (*presb[yterōn] pastophorōn*) of an Arsinoe serapeum.[76] The continued strength of elders within the villages of Egypt may be the reason for the presence of the title in this context.[77] The Egyptian context may also be the reason for the sole appearance of the term in relation to the synagogue, that at Tebtenu,[78] their position comparable to those elders of the priests of Kronos in Tebtenu who receive a petition to release a tenant from a lease of temple land.[79]

Specifically religious associations knew the term. I may point to a series of inscriptions from a guild of Zeus Hypsistos listing adopted brethren (possibly an inner group of the association), in some instances heading up the list of names with persons identified as *presbyteros*.[80]

Finally, we find the term *presbyteros* used on its own honorifically, for instance at *IEph*. 707C, in which the council and the people honor Leucus Pomp(us), a presbyter. In this light, we may observe *CIJ* 2.931: "Here lies Isaac, an elder of the Cappadocians, a flax-merchant from Tarsus." Whereas Isaac probably is Jewish, by virtue of his name, the designation as presbyter is as

71. One of the original purposes of gymnasia was military training, and a relationship continued in the Hellenistic period. On the subject of the relationship of gymnasia and the military in general, see Marcel Launey, *Recherches sur les armées Hellénistiques*, vol. 2, BEFAR 169 (repr., Paris: de Boccard, 1987), 813–74. Launey (830–34) specifically notes training in the use of catapults in gymnasia.

72. *IMagn*. 116.

73. *ID* 1528: (σύνοδος τῶν ἐν᾽ Ἀλεξανδρείᾳ πρεσβυτέρων ἐγδοχέων).

74. *MAIGL* 23. On this, see Max L. Strack, "Die Müllerinnung in Alexandrien," *ZNW* 4 (1903): 213–34.

75. *IGRR* 1.1155, from the first century BCE.

76. P.Lond. 2.345.

77. So Pierre Benoit, "Les origines apostoliques de l'épiscopat selon le Nouveau Testament," in *L'évêque dans l'église du Christ*, ed. H. Bouëssé and A. Mandouze, TET (Bruges: Desclée de Brouwer, 1963), 28.

78. Found in P.Monac. 3.49, discussed above under the heading "Presbyters in the Jewish Communities of Alexandria."

79. P.Tebt. 309, addressed to τ]οῖς δέκα πρεσβυτέροις [ἱερεῦσι ἀπὸ τ]οῦ ὄντος ἐν κώμῃ [Τεβτύνι ἱεροῦ] θεοῦ μεγάλου Κρόνου, in 116/7 CE.

80. *CIRB* 1278–1286.

likely to refer to his position in the community rather than to any position in the synagogue.[81] The point to notice is that the term is sufficiently defined as to allow its honorific use.

We might multiply such examples, but the point is already made that the designation of a group of persons as *presbyteroi* in associations, and most particularly in the gymnasium, is widely attested. The possibility that Christian groups borrowed terminology from defined groups within the gymnasium is strong because of the powerful influence exercised by these gymnasial presbyters in the civic life of the first century CE, particularly in western Asia Minor. Strack, however, discounts the uses of *presbyteroi* bound up with *neoi* or *neōteroi* as irrelevant, as he is intent on reading *presbyteroi* as an office.[82] However, as I shall note, the terms appear together in Christian settings as well. Christian presbyters may be, as in wider society, a defined group who do not actually exercise an office but nonetheless are honored and influential persons within the subsociety.

It is significant, moreover, that the term used in this manner is found across the eastern Mediterranean world. This means that, in whatever geographical setting it was first used in Christian discourse, as Christians across the empire communicated with one another, they readily understood the import of an address to or from *presbyteroi*. My suggestion is that it was by virtue of the associational modeling of early Christian communities, and in particular their reliance on groups of patrons, that these Christian communities come to designate the leading males among them as presbyters. The patronal activity of the presbyters already noted is significant, as is their participation as a group in the practice of granting *honor*.

It is indeed surprising that this evidence from the Hellenistic world is relatively unnoticed; possibly that is because so much is inscriptional, whereas it has left little impact on literary sources. The only recent scholars to have observed it at all seem to be Harvey and Karrer. Harvey suggests, however, that these *presbyteroi* were associations on their own rather than recognizing that they were a rank within the associations, and in particular within the gymnasia.[83] Karrer, conversely, suggests that this Hellenistic use solely provides a context for Christian acceptance, rather than the adoption, of the term "presbyter,"

81. *CIJ* 2.931: ἐνθάδε κῖτε Ἰσάκις πρεσβύτερος τῆς Καππαδόκων Τάρσου λινοπώλου. The same may well be true of Eirenopoios in Smyrna, whose title is given as πρ(εσβύτερος) κὲ πατὴρ τοῦ στέματος (*CIJ* 739). This inscription is not discussed as evidence for Jewish presbyters at Smyrna because it dates from the fourth century.

82. Strack, "Müllerinnung," 233. Strack is not alone in noticing the parallel, but when noticed, its significance seems to have escaped commentators. Strack at least is clear in his reason for discounting this evidence.

83. Harvey, "Elders," 320.

a term that he suggests has originated as an official designation within the Christianity of Jerusalem and has been carried on from there.[84] I will assess the status of presbyters in the Christianity of Jerusalem below, but even without that discussion I may ask whether it is prima facie more probable that the use of one Christian group with little association with other Christian groups, by virtue of a particular view of law observance, would successfully export a designation or whether Christian groups would adopt a term from the surrounding milieu in order to designate a group of people holding an identical status and performing a comparable role within their community. It begs the question, moreover, of where the Jerusalem Christians might have derived the title given that, as we have already seen, it was not a current synagogal office.

A connection was made in 1887 by Hicks on the basis of the very limited epigraphic evidence available to him, though he seems to think (he is not altogether clear on this point) that the term was received within Judaism from the Hellenistic world and passed into Christianity through a Jewish medium.[85] It would be simpler, however, to suggest that the same Hellenistic environment brought about Christian usage.

The evidence cited thus far indicates the strong presence of a defined group of *presbyteroi* within wider Hellenistic society. We must, however, ask whether in any sense this group might hold office. Campbell argued that in Jewish circles the term was purely honorific, and that the boundaries of such a group were porous; the boundaries of the *presbyteroi* in associations do not, however, appear to be porous in the same way. Thus, although I have agreed with Campbell that *presbyteroi* generally did not hold office or anything resembling office in synagogues, I must ask whether the same is true of the *presbyteroi* of associations, since it is clear that here we are engaged with a different field of usage. The question is particularly put in view of the assertions of Merkle that *presbyteroi* do indeed hold office in the Hellenistic world, and that the designation in Christian circles might readily imply an office, equivalent, he would argue, to *episkopos*.[86]

Many of Merkle's examples refer to ancient Sparta, in which there was an active and powerful *gerousia* but which was already ancient history by the turn of the Common Era. However, particularly in Egypt there is, as already noted,

84. Martin Karrer, "Das urchristliche Ältestenamt," *NovT* 32 (1990): 182–84.

85. "All these terms [γερουσία, πρεσβύτεροι, συνέδριον] so familiar to us first in their Jewish, and afterwards in their Christian usage, had been commonly employed before, in a precisely analogous sense, in Graeco-Roman civic life" (E. L. Hicks, "On Some Political Terms in the New Testament," *CR* 1 [1887]: 44).

86. Benjamin L. Merkle, *The Elder and Overseer: One Office in the Early Church*, SBL (Frankfurt: Peter Lang, 2003), 23–53.

a continuing strong presence of functioning elders in the villages. Thus, one list of village officers is headed by *presbyteroi*.[87] Individually, moreover, people identify themselves, or are identified, as a *presbyteros*,[88] which is in turn an indication that this is not an undefined and porous group. However, although the group is defined, this does not mean that it is an office. The functions of these *presbyteroi* are not designated; a possible exception is provided by a letter to Kleon, an architect, from one Demetrius, who had been hustled by a mob, until the intervention of certain *presbyteroi*, who dispersed them.[89] Whereas Merkle seems to think that this is a police force (giving a technical meaning to the phrase *hoi presbyteroi hoi parestēkotes*),[90] Mahaffy's interpretation, that these were certain elder men who were standing by, would seem just as likely.[91] Given the absence of any definition of function attached to these Egyptian village elders, whereas many functions are indeed designated, I may suggest that these presbyters come close to holding office, but that there is a general duty of oversight rather than a specific office as such. Beyond Egypt, the prominent role of *presbyteroi* in proposing honors fits with the statement of Plutarch that older men are called on first to speak in the assemblies.[92] Again this implies a recognized designation and something more than a purely honorific designation, but not an office as such, but rather a designation of rank, based on age (though given that the gymnasia were the preserve of the free male, I suggest that such rank was based not on age alone but also social status). Presbyters, I may suggest, provide leadership and are a defined group but do not hold office as such. The distinction between leadership and office is one that seems to be little observed in discourse on the subject but is nonetheless vital.

As a final example of this associational usage, but one from beyond the world of Hellenistic cities, we may observe the presence of *zeqenim* in the association represented by the *Community Rule* of the Essenes. The rule states that when the council of the many assembles, the elders are seated after the priests.[93] Campbell denies that this is an identifiable group, suggesting that the word here has been substituted for "Levites" on the basis that elsewhere, where there are lists, Levites are listed after the priests. [94] However, the only

87. P.Oxy. 2121.
88. E.g., Kronion in P.Mil. 222; Apugcheus at P.Berl.Leihg. 16.
89. P.Flind.Petrie 4.6.
90. Merkle, *Elder and Overseer*, 41.
91. John P. Mahaffy, ed., *The Flinders Petrie Papyri: With Transcriptions, Commentaries, and Index*, vol. 2, *Autotypes I. to XVIII; Appendix: Autotypes I. to III* (Dublin: Academy House, 1893), 10.
92. Plutarch, *An seni* 784D.
93. 1QS VI, 8–9.
94. Campbell, *Elders*, 60–61.

other relevant passage (I put the Essenism of the *Damascus Document*, like that described by Josephus, to one side) where there is such a list is 1QS II, 19–23. Levites follow priests there, and are followed by the people, but the context is liturgical. Second, he points out the rarity of the term in the *Community Rule* and in other scrolls as opposed to officers such as the priests and the *mebaqqer*; however, I may respond that these are officers, and that the regulation of the community was in their hands. I may thus agree with Merkle that the title "refers to a specific group of leaders in the community,"[95] but this does not make eldership an office. Rather, it is yet another example of associational usage extending beyond the Hellenistic *polis*.

The consensus held that presbyters were officers in synagogues, and that the Christian use of the term derived from this usage. A brief examination has shown that the term is little used. It is principally a term of honor applied to older men in the community; some Jewish communities were under an umbrella of management, and some individual synagogue communities might have benches of elders, but the evidence does not support the consensus that the synagogue is the route by which the term entered Christian discourse and does not support the idea that presbyters were managers.

A hypothesis with far better support has proved to be the origin of the term within Greek discourse, particularly associational discourse relating to the gymnasium but also closely tied up with civic governance, a route from which it might enter the discourse of other associations, among which some early Christian communities may be numbered. As we have noted, these elders did not hold office as such, but nonetheless they were a clearly defined group and exercised a degree of authority.

Two objections to such a view of the formation of presbyters may be raised. First, presbyters in this Hellenistic context are often found in the company of *neoi*, whereas, it may be alleged, in Christian circles we find *presbyteroi* on their own. However, in Polycarp's letter to the Philippians,[96] in the Pastoral Epistles,[97] and in 1 Peter[98] we do find discourse concerning presbyters accompanied by discourse concerning *neōteroi*. Similarly, in Acts 5:6 the body of Ananias is carried off by the *neōteroi*. Just as Grapte gives instruction to particular groups, so I may suggest that instruction was given to other groups within early Christian circles, and that particular groups had standing within the community. Because *presbyteroi* have so often been thought to be a group of office-holding functionaries, attempts have been made to assign office and

---

95. Merkle, *Elder and Overseer*, 37.
96. Pol. *Phil.* 5:3.
97. 1 Tim. 5:1; Titus 2:6.
98. 1 Pet. 5:5.

function to the *neōteroi* as well, such as identifying them with *diakonoi* or seeing them as the laity as opposed to the clergy.[99] If the *presbyteroi* of the church
are a group within the association like *presbyteroi* elsewhere, then we may see
that the *neoi* or *neōteroi* are likewise a group, and that some churches at least
had imitated the gymnasium in dividing congregations into specific groups.

Second, one may object that the gymnasium is hardly a model likely to be
adopted by the church. In response to this I must point out the central role
of the *gymnasion* in Hellenistic political life. According to Pausanias, a *polis*
should have an agora, a theater, a gymnasium, and several temples,[100] and
similarly, Aelius Aristides, in his encomia of Rome and of Athens, mentions
gymnasia alongside temples, schools, and libraries as indications of civiliza-
tion.[101] Gymnasia were places of intellectual as well as physical training; they
might include libraries within their complex of buildings[102] (an aspect considered of particular importance by Rostovtzeff, as it was a means by which a
Hellenized elite within eastern cities might keep company with other members
and transmit Hellenistic values to the young),[103] and likewise they were eating
places and were bound up to the offering of sacrifice.[104] As such, insofar that
religion was ever distinguishable from public life, they were religious institutions
likewise, principally dedicated to heroic cults and to Hermes (on the grounds
of their educational function), but dedicated to other deities as well and, like
associations, often also attaching to their functions a funerary element,[105] or
honorary recollection of their founders and benefactors.[106] Moreover, like the

99. For references to these positions, see Ceslas Spicq, "La place ou le rôle des jeunes dans
certaines communautés néotestamentaires," *RB* 76 (1969): 518.

100. Pausanius, *Descr.* 10.1.

101. Aelius Aristides, *Pan.* 246; *Rom.* 97.

102. For evidence and discussion, see Peter Scholz, "Elementarunterricht und intellektuelle
Bildung im hellenistischen Gymnasion," in *Das hellenistische Gymnasion*, ed. Daniel Kah and
Peter Scholz, WGW 8 (Berlin: Akademie-Verlag, 2004), 103–28.

103. M. Rostovtzeff, *The Social and Economic History of the Hellenistic World* (Oxford:
Clarendon, 1941), 1058–60.

104. Note the examples set out by Elena Mango, "Bankette im hellenistischen Gymnasion,"
in Kah and Scholz, *Hellenistische Gymnasion*, 293–96. Among these examples we may note
IG 12.7 390 (a gymnasiarch establishes the offering of a sacrifice to Hermes and Herakles,
together with a dinner that took place in the gymnasium) and, most significantly for the present purposes, an honorific inscription, published by Franz Cumont ("Ein neues Psephisma aus
Amphipolis," *JÖAI* 1 [1898]: 180–84 [= *SEG* 30.546]), in which the *presbyteroi* specifically are
invited to dine in the gymnasium.

105. See the discussion of this point with the evidence presented by Jean Delorme, *Gymnasion:
Étude sur les monuments consacrés a l'éducation en Grèce (des origines à l'Empire Romain)*,
BEFAR 196 (Paris: de Boccard, 1960), 453–55.

106. Beyond the literature and evidence cited here, see Sophia Aneziri and Dimitris Damaskos,
"Städische Kulte im hellenistischen Gymnasion," in Kah and Scholz, *Hellenistische Gymnasion*,
248–71.

household and like many other associations, the gymnasia, in their internal organization, imitated the structures of the *polis*,[107] while the office of gymnasiarch was a recognized *leitourgia*. Given the elite status of the *presbyteroi* of the gymnasium, we can come to understand how they came to supplant the older *gerousiai* in the cities and likewise may see that such a structure might readily transmit itself into Christianity once Christian gatherings extend beyond individual households but continued to eat in a hierarchical manner.

An Interim Conclusion

Whereas there is no evidence to support the oft-repeated assertion that presbyters are found within the synagogue, and so none to support the position that Christian churches were managed by presbyters along a synagogal model, there is ample evidence from Hellenistic associational usage that a defined group of older men might have a particular place within the association. This is a usage that would readily commend itself to Christian adoption. These Hellenistic presbyters were not, however, officers.

However, we have already seen the term *presbyteroi* functioning as a collective noun to denote the individual leaders of Christian communities gathering from across a defined urban area, those characterized in Titus 1:5 as presbyters who have a representative role on a citywide basis (*kata polin presbyteroi*). When meeting the term in Christian discourse prior to the emergence of monepiscopacy, we may ask whether this is the only meaning, whether all references to presbyters are references to this group.

The title might be chosen for the gathering of leaders on the basis of its honorific and status-conferring value, but the model from the Hellenistic world would lead us to expect that *honor* and status might be bestowed within individual Christian congregations. Here I must anticipate some conclusions from the following investigation that will show that there were indeed honored individuals within Christian congregations who were identified as presbyters. However, it will be shown that although they were an honored group, they were not officers. This is close to the position taken by Campbell. However, Campbell does not examine the evidence of the use of the term in Hellenistic discourse. Whereas he is right to note that the term is often used somewhat fuzzily, particularly in Jewish discourse regarding elders, the evidence of the wider Hellenistic milieu indicates that the groups of presbyters who, as he suggests, are basically honored persons are nonetheless clearly designated and

107. Thus, see *SEG* 8.641, a decree of former gymnasiarchs honoring Sarapion.

readily identifiable. Moreover, although not holding office as such, they may well exercise leadership and hold authority in the community.

That "presbyter" might mean one of two things is confusing. Moreover, at this point a further terminological confusion may be noted as in a later period, after the establishment of monepiscopacy, a presbyter was an officer subordinate to a *monepiskopos* and holding a position of leadership within an individual congregation. This is, I suggest, a derivation from the term "presbyter" employed *kata polin*, since the congregational leaders already held this title as a group. These various meanings, to an extent, meld into each other; the title referring to representatives is a term of honor rather than of office as such, though the probability is that these presbyters also hold office within their individual congregations. Conversely, those who are simply presbyters on the basis of age, while not necessarily a functioning executive, may exercise authority within the *ekklēsia* precisely as the presbyters exercised authority within the civic *ekklēsiai*. Finally, the ordained presbyters who held office under a *monepiskopos* held that title because they had previously been members of a citywide council and, to an extent, as will be seen below, continued to do so. Nonetheless, we must be aware that, ultimately, these are different things, and, when meeting the term in the literature, we must ask at each point which is meant.

Presbyters and *Episkopoi* in Early Christian Communities

I am now at the point at which I may begin to investigate the formation of the threefold order in early Christianity, equipped to do so in a new way by having dismissed various presuppositions that have dogged previous attempts.

In the first instance, the present investigation does not labor under the presupposition that presbyter and *episkopos* are necessarily directly equivalent terms. Chapter 1 set out an alternative hypothesis and, in doing so, gave an account of the emergence of the monepiscopate in some Christian communities; chapter 2, in arguing that *episkopoi* and *diakonoi* originally were economic offices, enabled us to see that these were offices with specific duties as opposed to general oversight.

Chapter 3 has thus far disposed of the view that the institution of presbyters derived from the synagogue and demonstrated an alternative source for the designation: the civic world, the gymnasia and the associations of the cities of the eastern Roman Empire. It is also worth observing that fundamental to many of the early statements of synonymy was the idea that *episkopoi* and *presbyteroi* were the same thing but that one terminology was Gentile

Hellenistic and the other Jewish. The absence of any evidence to sustain a Jewish origin to the Christian presbyterate and the positive evidence of a possible origin within (Gentile) Hellenistic society means that there is no basis on which to sustain such an understanding. The theory of federation put forward in chapter 1 remains a hypothesis still, but now it is the only hypothesis holding the field.

Finally, I may recollect the point made at the conclusion of chapter 1 and reiterated in chapter 2: we are not to expect to find collective leadership within early Christian groups. Prior to the complete investigation that follows, I cannot exclude such a possibility, but thus far I have found all evidence presented to be inconclusive at best. If there are no presbyters in charge of synagogues, then such a picture of Christian leadership looks even less likely.

In chapter 1 I argued for a particular narrative of the emergence of leadership in Rome and Ephesus. Further reference to this narrative was made in chapter 2. Therefore, in the remainder of this chapter I revisit that narrative in an attempt to see whether the hypothesis of presbyters as derived from the presbyters of the Hellenistic world conforms to the narrative laid out so far. In particular, I will concentrate on two communities: the Ephesian congregation constructed by 1 Timothy and the Roman congregation behind *Traditio apostolica*.

In the earlier examination 1 Timothy was not mentioned; the overall point of the argument at that point was to explore the relationship between the terms "presbyter" and *episkopos* in order to show that they were not synonymous, and to suggest that when the terms appear to be synonymous in early Christian literature, there is reference to a gathering of congregational *episkopoi* who were collectively known as presbyters. I did not discuss 1 Timothy because there is no apparent use of the terms as synonyms but because, as will be argued, it provides evidence of presbyters quite apart from those who hold office *kata polin*—that is, presbyters within individual Christian communities, the term denoting persons holding position within individual Christian communities who were not *episkopoi* but honored older men. It is now possible to argue for this position, having clarified the possible origin of the term within associations, as this is precisely the role of associational presbyters. This usage of the term is perhaps the earlier use, one that was extended subsequently to those holding office on a citywide basis. However, this in itself is a demonstration of the potential confusion caused by terminology and hence the necessity of examining the organization of each Christian community individually and without presupposition as to the meaning of the terms employed by them. For the same reason, there was no detailed examination of the evidence provided by *Traditio apostolica*. It is argued below that the Hippolytean community that this document represents had, at least prior to the emergence of mon-episcopacy, likewise known presbyters within the congregation.

The discussion of *episkopos* and presbyters at Ephesus and Rome is also significant because it has already been established that monepiscopacy in these cities grew out of federation. In what follows I attempt to demonstrate that this had not occurred at the time of 1 Timothy, and that *Traditio apostolica* retains traces of the time at which it had not occurred at Rome. The problem that I will have to confront is the possibility that the term "presbyter" might mean one of two things: a member of a citywide council or a person honored in his own congregation. Thus, whenever the term is met, I need to establish its meaning. However, for the present I must argue for the existence of these congregational presbyters.

Episkopos *and Presbyters in 1 Timothy*

Broadly speaking, there have been five attempts to explain the relationship between presbyters and the *episkopos* in 1 Timothy. First, it has been recently suggested that the presbyters are presbyters *kata polin* gathered with a *mon-episkopos*. Second, the idea of synonymy has been called into play, such that the presbyters *are episkopoi*; in particular, this solution is intended to reconcile the statements of 1 Timothy to Titus 1:5, which is unnecessary if the presby-ters of Titus 1:5 are distinct from those of 1 Timothy 5, as is argued below. Third, it is suggested that the *episkopos* is a *monepiskopos*, though the latter term is often used to mean simply a sole bishop in a congregation, due to the confusion that has plagued discussion of church order from the beginning. Fourth, it is suggested that 1 Timothy represents a combination of systems, presbyteral and episcopal, a hypothesis that, I suggest, is unnecessary because there is no evidence of any purely presbyteral system. Fifth, it is suggested that the presbyters are simply older men. It is this final hypothesis for which I argue below. Although this is not the first time it has been suggested, it is supported with new evidence.

Preliminary Considerations

Having argued above that the evidence of Acts 20 pointed to a gathering of Christian leaders individually known as *episkopoi* and collectively as *presby-teroi*, I turn to other evidence of leadership at Ephesus in order to see whether such a picture may be sustained or needs in some way to be modified. In par-ticular, I have suggested that cities such as Ephesus were the original location in which the designation of Christian leaders as presbyters might originate. I must therefore pay particular attention to evidence for presbyters from this location.

Although the primary purpose of this discussion is to test the theory regarding the origin of presbyters proposed earlier in the chapter, it is necessary to discuss the wider question of church order in the Pastoral Epistles. This task is made more complex because of confusion resulting from the theory of synonymy (or versions of it, such as "partial synonymy") and also, I may suggest, because of confusion between monepiscopacy (understood as government by a sole bishop over a defined area with subservient ministers) and episcopacy (understood as government by a sole bishop within a single Christian household). This in turn derived from the presumption that there were once multiple leaders in a single community, an assumption found wanting.

The particular problem that dogs the discussion is the perceived need to reconcile statements in 1 Timothy and Titus. I have already discussed the relationship between *presbyteroi* and *episkopoi* in Titus. There, I suggested, the presbyters whose appointment is proposed at Titus 1:5 were specifically qualified as presbyters *kata polin*, and these presbyters, therefore, were the same people as the *episkopoi* mentioned slightly later in the same letter, though performing a distinct function. Appointments were to be made from the *episkopoi* of persons who would have a representative role on a citywide basis, and these persons would, in their representative citywide function, be known as *presbyteroi*. However, since the conventional reading of this verse is that presbyters are being appointed, this has to be reconciled with statements regarding presbyters in 1 Timothy, and it is therefore assumed that the presbyters in 1 Timothy must likewise hold an office, even though there is no statement that they are appointed and no qualification list. Alternatively, suggestions that elders do not hold office, a belief derived from the absence of any statement of appointment or qualification in 1 Timothy, have to explain the apparent appointment of presbyters in Titus.[108] If, however, *kata polin* is taken, as proposed above, as a qualification of *presbyteros*, we may see that the presbyters *kata polin* of Titus are distinct from the presbyters of 1 Timothy 5:17–19 and, indeed, of Titus 2:2, and so the complications disappear. If 1 Timothy were read without reference to Titus or to other contemporary documents, nobody would suppose that presbyters held office, as these persons appear but twice: once when it is stated that Timothy should not speak harshly to a *presbyteros*,[109] and once when it is directed that *presbyteroi* who are generous in their support (*kalōs proestōtes*, the translation of which offered here will

108. So, typically, and in the context of a critical discussion of earlier attempts to explain the church order of the Pastoral Epistles, Frances M. Young, *The Theology of the Pastoral Letters*, NTT (Cambridge: Cambridge University Press, 1994), 104–5.
109. 1 Tim. 5:1.

be justified below) should be duly rewarded through honor.[110] Significantly, presbyters do not appear in the discussion of officers in the third chapter. The usage in 1 Timothy 5:1 clearly indicates an older man, as similar directions are given at that point regarding younger men, and older and younger women; thus, a reader without knowledge of Titus would naturally take the latter reference likewise to denote older men.

Moreover, it is important, I suggest, to take the fictive destinations of the letters into account. First Timothy is addressed to Timothy at Ephesus, whereas Titus is addressed to the situation in Crete. Whereas, no doubt, there is an underlying unity, the fictive situations addressed must differ, and this must be the reason for the differing addressees and destinations. The letters construct a situation, and we must note that each constructs a different situation. Thus, the letters to Timothy assume the existence of presbyters and *episkopoi*, whereas that to Titus assumes the existence of *episkopoi* but is introducing a distinct office, that of presbyters *kata polin*; in that sense, the incomplete business to which Titus 1:3 refers is being made complete.[111]

The relationship between *episkopoi* and *presbyteroi kata polin* in Titus is clear enough if the findings of the first chapter are accepted, namely, that they are the same people, acting as *episkopoi* in their own individual congregations, who are called on to act on a different basis and to form a federation. If the relationship between *episkopoi* and presbyters, here not qualified as *kata polin*, is distinct in 1 Timothy, then that too may be a relationship relatively easy to explain, as it is explained on its own terms rather than in an attempt to reconcile the situation to that of Titus. I will thus set out my own hypothesis about the relationship between *episkopos* and elders in 1 Timothy (given that Titus has already been discussed) and then canvass other possibilities, following prior discussion. I will conclude by showing that a coherent shape emerges if *presbyteroi* are understood as a group of honored older men within the group, along the model of the associational presbyters already met, and are entirely distinguished from the *presbyteroi kata polin* of Titus. The *episkopos* of 1 Timothy is likewise a congregational *episkopos* and is the chief officer of the congregation, assisted by *diakonoi*, whereas the presbyters are not officers at all.

---

110. 1 Tim. 5:17.

111. André Cousineau ("Le sens de ‹presbuteros› dans les Pastorales," *ScEs* 28 [1976]: 147–62) does note the possibility that the fictive destinations are constructing different situations. However, in keeping with the fundamental notion drawn from the consensus that the *presbyteroi* are necessarily officeholders, he concludes that they are being appointed for the first time in Crete (as "presbyter-bishops"), whereas the more developed situation of Ephesus means that such a collegium of office-holding presbyters already exists.

Presbyters in 1 Timothy

On the basis of the associational parallel, which later I will prove by closer exegesis, I suggest that the Paul of 1 Timothy knows a group of patrons whose collective title is *presbyteroi* and also knows an officer known as the *episkopos* (who is assisted by *diakonoi*). The church order redacted into 1 Timothy sets out responsibilities for officers (in chap. 3) and then goes on to discuss the duties of the *episkopos* toward other members of the community, including those patrons who are identified as presbyters (in chap. 5); as such, the presbyters are an ecclesiastical class (*kirchlicher Stand*) but do not perform any ecclesial office (*kirchliches Amt*),[112] and they are comparable to the widows, directions concerning whom are also given in the same context in 1 Timothy 5. Thus, this is a radically naive reading, undertaken without reference to material from outside 1 Timothy, not seeking to reconcile these statements with those regarding presbyters in Titus on the grounds that the discussion in Titus is distinct, but simply understanding the statements made in 1 Timothy on their own terms. Nonetheless, I may note even now that the same situation existed in the Hippolytean community in Rome at the time of the first redaction of *Traditio apostolica* (around the end of the second century): there were officeholders called *episkopos* and *diakonoi*, and patron elders within the community.

As already noted, previous solutions to the problem caused by the apparently confusing terminology fall broadly into five groups, although there are many minor variations between them.

The first solution to be considered is a relatively new one in the discussion, and it emerges from the work of Campbell, in particular from his identification of a group of elders who exercise authority *kata polin*. If the presbyters of Titus are to hold office *kata polin*, then we must inquire whether the same is true of the presbyters mentioned in 1 Timothy. In that case it might be possible to read the discussion of presbyters in 1 Timothy 5 as a collective noun for *episkopoi* gathered from across a city, whereas the discussion of the appointment of an *episkopos* in 1 Timothy 3 relates to a single household. Although he does not identify the townwide remit of the presbyters of Titus 1, Marshall nonetheless suggests something similar to this, only to reject it.[113] He suggests that the elders who are appointed singly to towns in Titus 1:5 are presented as gathered in 1 Timothy 5. However, he suggests that the directions in 1 Timothy

---

112. A distinction derived from Karl Kertelge (*Gemeinde und Amt im neuen Testament*, BH 10 [Munich: Kösel, 1972], 141), who applies this to the widows.

113. I. Howard Marshall, *A Critical and Exegetical Commentary on the Pastoral Epistles*, ICC (Edinburgh: T&T Clark, 1999), 178.

5:17 make sense only if this chapter regards a single congregation, and that a wider gathering is not intended in this instance. Here he is right.

Without accepting Marshall's exegesis of Titus 1:5, it might be possible that Timothy is speaking of the gathering of elders across a town, on the assumption that they would eat together. Nonetheless, this is stretching the evidence somewhat. There are, moreover, further objections to this view in that the chapter directs that those presbyters who offer patronage with particular generosity (the manner in which *kalōs proestōtes* in 1 Tim. 5:17 is to be read, as will be argued below) should be given a double portion, and especially that such honor should be given to those who labor in preaching and teaching, in that, if these presbyters are *episkopoi*, it is hard to imagine that there were any who did not so labor, and so the statement is entirely redundant.[114] Moreover, in view of the issue regarding commensality between law-observant Christians and non-law-observant Christians, I may also suggest that a gathering of elders from across a city (assuming that the two groups had any sort of communication with each other, an issue discussed above in chap. 1) in order to eat together would be an occasion beset with difficulty. As such, I must conclude, with Marshall, that presbyters within a single congregation are intended in 1 Timothy 5 and thus desist from any attempt at identifying them with the presbyters of Titus 1.

Nonetheless, something similar is essayed by Wagner[115] on the basis of his suggestion that the city presbyters of Titus are the constituency from whom the *episkopos* is elected. Thus, at any Christian gathering, he suggests, there would be city-presbyters present, and he suggests that these presbyters are referred to here. If his argument regarding the relationship of city presbyters to *episkopoi* were to be sustained, this would be entirely feasible. His suggestion is that the presbyters were those who, for whatever reason, had a particular place in the *Ortsgemeinde*, the district congregation. But if this is the case, then there must likewise be an *Ortsepiskopos*, in other words a *monepiskopos*, beyond the individual *episkopoi* in the individual households, and a district congregation distinct from the individual congregations within the district. Whereas none of this is totally impossible, the argument depends on monepiscopacy being established in the community of the Pastoral Epistles, brings about the problem of two distinct levels of episcopacy—episcopacy *kat' oikon* and episcopacy *kata polin*—and presupposes a district congregation of the existence of which there is no evidence and that is inherently unlikely.

114. An argument employed by Jochen Wagner, *Die Anfänge des Amtes in der Kirche: Presbyter und Episkopen in der frühchristlichen Literatur*, TANZ 53 (Tübingen: Francke, 2011), 165.
115. Wagner, *Anfänge*, 164–65.

As already suggested, the confusion comes about because of the inability to distinguish the single congregation (*Einzelgemeinde*) from the church in a locality (*Ortskirche*), and in the case of Wagner's arguments in particular the attribution to the presbyters of the *Ortskirche* a greater degree of power than they seem to have exercised, at least on the basis of the Roman evidence. The Roman evidence suggests that the greater likelihood is that there never was an *Ortsgemeinde* with a structure of leadership but simply individual congregations whose leaders met to consider issues of mutual concern.

The second explanation of those previously offered takes off from the hypothesis of identity between *episkopoi* and *presbyteroi* and the synonymy of the terms.[116] That Titus 1:5 is a *locus classicus* for the argument for identity has already been observed. However, this argument has numerous problems.

First, we may note the objection that the *episkopos* in the Pastoral Epistles always appears in the singular, and the elders (apart from 1 Tim. 5:19, where the discipline of an individual elder is the issue) in the plural. In order to sustain synonymy, therefore, the singular throughout has to be seen as generic.[117] I have already suggested that this is the case at Titus 1:7, but this represents a special case, in that the redactor is here citing a tradition, and given that it has already been made clear (through the direction to appoint *presbyteroi kata polin*) that the persons concerned are plural. They are plural there, moreover, because, I may suggest, they are in more than one church or congregation. It should also be noted that whereas the reference at 1 Timothy 3:1–2 is to a singular *episkopos*, reference is made in 1 Timothy 3:8 to plural *diakonoi*: "deacons likewise should be settled, not double-tongued."

If, however, the terms really are synonymous (as opposed to perionymous), it might be argued that an audience would automatically recognize the shifts between singular and plural. Thus it would be possible to suggest, on the basis of synonymy, that if the terms are interchangeable, when 1 Timothy 5 speaks of presbyters, the audience would know that the same people are intended as the *episkopoi* of 1 Timothy 3. The argument makes sense only if strict synonymy is maintained. However, commentators are often imprecise in their use of the term. Thus, Kelly states at one point that the two offices are synonymous, and later that they overlap;[118] we find out what he means when he suggests that

116. So, e.g., George W. Knight III, *The Pastoral Epistles: A Commentary on the Greek Text*, NIGTC (Grand Rapids: Eerdmans; Carlisle: Paternoster, 1992), 175–77. See also the literature cited by Hermann von Lips, *Glaube, Gemeinde, Amt: Zum Verständnis der Ordination in den Pastoralbriefen*, FRLANT 122 (Göttingen: Vandenhoeck & Ruprecht, 1979), 112–13.

117. This, at least, is the usual position of advocates of synonymy. This is taken to an extreme by Allen Brent ("The Enigma of Ignatius of Antioch," *JEH* 57 [2006]: 433), who suggests that there must be a plurality of *episkopoi because* the singular is generic.

118. Kelly, *Pastoral Epistles*, 13.

the church is "feeling its way towards a clear distinction between the board of elders charged with general supervision and the executive officials of the community."[119] Here he has reference to 1 Timothy 5:17, referring to *kalōs proestōtes presbyteroi*. However, the "board of elders" are not charged with supervision; *proestōtes*, the term employed here, does not mean that the elders supervise, but rather that the elders are patrons, as will be observed further below. More to the point, if the church is seeking to distinguish the *episkopos*, as an executive official, from the supervising presbyters, then the terms are not synonyms at all. A similar view to that of Kelly is proposed by Cousineau, who suggests that the elders (who are officers) are beginning to specialize; those elders who are designated *episkopoi* teach,[120] though this is not a necessary function of *presbyteroi*. In order to sustain this, however, he has to accept that *presbyteroi* has two different meanings in 1 Timothy 5 (first meaning "older men" and then referring to officeholders), reading back the directions regarding the double reward (*diplē timē*) to 1 Timothy 3; the reality is that either the *episkopos* or the *presbyteroi* might teach.[121] A further problem is that many of the qualifications presented as appropriate to the *episkopos* in 1 Timothy 3 are not really relevant to a teaching office at all, and so an *episkopos* can hardly be described as a teaching *presbyteros*. It is suggested below that teaching was not an original function of either group, for which reason the (traditionally based) qualification list does not really embrace this criterion.

In favor of a solution based on strict synonymy is that it does at least make coherent sense of both documents. Titus is told to appoint presbyters, who turn out to be *episkopoi*, and Timothy is advised about the appointment of *episkopoi* who are meant when the discussion turns to *presbyteroi*. We must wonder, however, if the title is precisely interchangeable, why the author is at least not consistent in his use. As already noted, "garbage" and "rubbish" are synonyms but are rarely found employed by the same person, even less by the same person in the same sentence; even if they are so used, there is only one meaning for each English word, and the meaning is clearly identical. *Episkopos* and *presbyteros*, even if potentially synonymous, are not obvious synonyms, as each term has a variety of meaning. Thus, as already pointed out in the discussion of Titus, such a solution presupposes immense exegetical

119. Ibid., 15–16. A similar view is held by Joachim Rohde, *Urchristliche und frühkatholische Ämter: Eine Untersuchung zur frühchristlichen Amtsentwicklung im Neuen Testament und bei den apostolischen Vätern*, ThA 33 (Berlin: Evangelische Verlagsanstalt, 1976), 83–88. Rohde holds that there is movement toward what he terms monarchical episcopate, but that for the present an *episkopos* is a *presbyteros* with particular functions.

120. Cousineau, "Sens de 'presbuteros.'"

121. A common function employed by von Lips (*Glaube*, 115) to argue for a close association between presbyter and *episkopos*.

sophistication on the part of the original readers of Titus if the situation being addressed, whether fictive or real, is taken seriously: a community that had no leaders is told first to appoint leaders called *presbyteroi*, then to appoint leaders called *episkopoi*, and is meant to know that they are the same thing.

A final problem with synonymy is that it fails to explain how a situation might emerge in which the terms are not synonymous, namely, the distinction toward which, according to Kelly, the church is feeling its way. Why should the leading *presbyteros* be called an *episkopos* if the term means the same thing?

I thus accept that it is possible that the Pastoral Epistles refer to the two offices with complete identity; however, this is not a solution that solves all the problems, and it raises problems of its own. If one were trying to reconcile the statements of 1 Timothy and Titus on the assumption that the *presbyteroi* are identical in both letters, then there would be some reason to reach for such a hypothesis and to try to account for its difficulties. If the two are to be read independently, then this hypothesis lends nothing but confusion to the discussion. Moreover, it would mean that there is no relationship at all between these documents and others deriving from the early Christian milieu in terms of structures of leadership, as no other early Christian document knows of ministry by committee. Thus, especially given that I have been able to give a good account of what Titus means, this hypothesis should be abandoned unless nothing better can be found.

The third group of explanations of the church order of the Pastoral Epistles clusters around the idea that the *monepiskopos* has emerged, or is emerging and is being legitimated or directed.[122] It should be clarified that here *episkopos* means *monepiskopos* throughout, and *presbyteroi* are always subordinate ministers.

One of the problems, as always with such a discussion, is what is intended by *monepiskopos*, whether this is a sole bishop in a single Christian community or a sole bishop set over a number of Christian communities (as the term is used here). I will assume the latter here; it goes without saying, at this stage in the argument, that there would be only one *episkopos* in a congregation. However, as already noted, earlier treatments might not have such clarity. Thus, when Prast speaks of a movement toward monepiscopacy, he means a movement away from multiple *episkopoi* in a single church toward a single *episkopos* within it;[123] such a discussion is predicated on the assumption that

122. Classically by A. T. Hanson, *The Pastoral Epistles*, New Cambridge Bible Commentary (London: Marshall, Morgan & Scott, 1982), 31–38.

123. Franz Prast, *Presbyter und Evangelium in nachapostolischer Zeit: Die Abschiedsrede des Paulus in Milet (Apg 20,17–38) im Rahmen der lukanischen Konzeption der Evangeliums-verkündigung*, FB 29 (Stuttgart: Katholisches Bibelwerk, 1979), 405–8.

there were multiple *episkopoi* at one time, something that has yet to be proved and, I may now state, is entirely without basis.

We may take as typical of the views of those proposing the emergence of monepiscopacy in the Pastoral Epistles the argument of Hanson. He claims that there is a deliberate confusion over the respective roles of elders and *episkopoi* because the author, conscious that there were no *episkopoi* in the Pauline church, wishes to smooth over the introduction.[124] The whole purpose of the letter, according to this view, is to instruct the (new) *monepiskopos*, who has emerged from the *episkopos*-presbyters under the guise of Timothy.[125] Of course, this assumes that this is the means by which monepiscopacy came about. If this was the process, and so far no evidence has been cited that suggests that it was, then one is hard put to see why the office would need literary justification, given that the elders among whom the office emerged presumably would have supported the development (which without their support would not have taken place).

The *episkopos* of the Pastoral Epistles is probably not a *monepiskopos* in the sense in which the term is used here, as there is no indication that there are subservient ministers in other churches and none that he is a source of ordination for other ministers. As we have seen, those appointed *kata polin* are presbyters, collectively. Thus, if the argument above regarding the interpretation of Titus 1:5 is accepted, we may already see that monepiscopacy is virtually excluded because were there a monepiscopate, then there would be no basis to appoint *presbyteroi kata polin*, even less to appoint them from among those who were already *episkopoi*. As to monepiscopacy in the more common sense—the single leader of a single congregation—I may agree that

---

124. Hanson, *Pastoral Epistles*, 33. Hanson comments that "there does not seem to be any difference between the functions of the bishop and of the presbyter" (34). One wonders whether the deliberate confusion that he attributes to the author is his own confusion.

125. I may nonetheless agree that Timothy is a cipher for the functions of the *episkopos* (so Roloff, *Erst Brief*, 169–79) with the understanding that the *episkopos* would take over from the apostolic delegate, just as those of Acts 20 took over from Paul. It is the presence of an apostolic delegate that causes Kelly (*Pastoral Epistles*, 14) to suggest that the *episkopos* of the Pastoral Epistles is nothing like the Ignatian *episkopos* (whom he describes as "monarchical bishop" without further defining the term) as there would be no room under these arrangements for an apostolic delegate. However, Kelly himself observes that the nature of the delegate's brief is that it is temporary. Key to that matter is succession. As suggested above, the responsibilities of Timothy reflect those of the *episkopos*, and the nature of the fictive situation is that the delegate is to establish the officers of the churches in their duties, as the task is then handed on to local officers (so also Prast, *Presbyter und Evangelium*, 393). Hans von Campenhausen (*Ecclesiastical Authority and Spiritual Power in the Church of the First Three Centuries*, trans. J. A. Baker [London: A&C Black, 1969], 107) similarly argues that the *episkopos* of the Pastoral Epistles is a *monepiskopos* (though he may simply mean a sole bishop in a congregation) on the grounds that the letters are addressed to individuals rather than to whole communities.

the *episkopos* of 1 Timothy is *monepiskopos* in this sense simply because there was, as already argued, never more than one *episkopos* in a congregation anyway.

Here I may deal with the argument of Campbell, who claims to propose a new hypothesis, though in reality it is simply another version of the monepiscopacy theory.[126] At heart is a fundamental confusion; given that I have already adopted his reading of Titus 1:5, I may deal with his treatment in some detail.

Campbell's first point is that the church of the Pastoral Epistles is founded on a domestic basis. Here we are in agreement. Campbell, however, then goes on to say, "The most significant development in the ordering of these churches in the period after the death of Paul is the emergence of a single *episkopos* over the church at a certain place."[127] I may agree with this too, as monepiscopacy develops and is clearly visible by the third century. However, Campbell appears to be thinking of a period rather closer to Paul's death. He states that Ignatius assumes monepiscopacy in Asia Minor, and that this means that monepiscopacy is established in Antioch. For Campbell, the Pastoral Epistles are a witness to this occurring in Ephesus likewise. He suggests that since the founding apostles are absent from their churches, a need arises for leadership along apostolic lines, and thus that a leader arises from "among the overseers of the various house-churches (*or elders*)."[128] The Pastoral Epistles are written to legitimate the authority of the new overseer: "to enable them [the local churches] to adopt a single shepherd, with the title of *episkopos*, as leader of those who as *episkopoi* in their own households were already known as the elders in relation to the local church as a whole."[129]

Campbell supports this hypothesis first in his reading of the instruction to appoint presbyters *kata polin* in Titus. I have already followed him here. However, he then turns to the statement at 1 Timothy 3:1 that whoever wishes to be an *episkopos* desires a noble task. He states, however, that the "first bearers of the title *episkopos* will hardly have been candidates for a position that came to them by virtue of being 'first fruits' and household leaders . . . but one can see why a person might need encouragement to stand out from among the other household leaders and elders of the church to assume the role of city *episkopos*."[130] We have already heard that *episkopoi* are to be appointed as *presbyteroi kata polin*, but here the talk is of an *episkopos*.

---

126. Campbell is followed by Robert Lee Williams, *Bishop Lists: Formation of Apostolic Succession of Bishops in Ecclesiastical Crises*, GDECS 3 (Piscataway, NJ: Gorgias, 2005), 47–53.
127. Campbell, *Elders*, 195.
128. Ibid., 196, italics mine.
129. Ibid.
130. Ibid., 198.

For Campbell, this means precisely a city *episkopos* rather than simply a domestic leader of a household congregation. But there is nothing in the Pastoral Epistles about a city *episkopos*; only presbyters hold office *kata polin*. Campbell apparently is suggesting that these presbyters then assume the title of *episkopos*. Why? Even if we accept that the terms are completely synonymous, this is confusing. And no account is given as to why the writer should suddenly shift terminology.

According to Campbell, the point of the household imagery in 1 Timothy 3 is to apply a traditional list to a citywide appointment. If this is so, why is nothing said either here or in Titus about it being citywide? The single *episkopos* of 1 Timothy gives every appearance of referring to a single household, whereas the reference to the plural presbyters of Titus is to the gathering of the domestic *episkopoi* on a citywide basis, as at Rome. Thus Titus points us to a presbytery along Roman lines. But 1 Timothy does not point to a citywide episcopate. Campbell writes of the "new post of *episkopos kata polin*,"[131] but this is nowhere to be found in the text. Titus speaks of *presbyteroi kata polin*. The confusion, I may suggest, is due to the continued hold of the consensus regarding synonymy, despite Campbell's attempt to free himself from it, and to a failure to recognize that there is a stage of development between leadership of individual household churches and monepiscopacy, namely, federation; thus, elders *kata polin* are read as being the same thing as *episkopoi kata polin*, whereas there is no reason why they should be the same thing at all and ample reason why they should not. If the elders *kata polin* are not *episkopoi kata polin*, then the *episkopos* of 1 Timothy is not to be seen as holding office *kata polin* but simply in a household, unless evidence to the contrary may be adduced. Indeed, the very fact that "Paul" is proposing federation without monepiscopacy in writing to "Titus" militates against any reading of the episcopate of 1 Timothy as monepiscopal.

Campbell's overall theory of development is sound. He suggests that there is progression from a situation where there are individual leaders (*episkopoi*) in households to one where a single individual (an *episkopos*) takes control over these churches (hence being a *monepiskopos*), whereas those collectively known as presbyters continue to be known as such individually.[132] However, this has not happened in Ephesus at the time of the Pastoral Epistles. That it may have happened in Ignatius's Antioch (as Campbell claims, though this will be disputed below) is simply not relevant.

131. Ibid., 201.
132. Campbell describes these as "stage one" (a single *episkopos* in a single house-church with no presbyters), "stage two" (multiple households with multiple *episkopoi* known as presbyters), and "stage three" (monepiscopate). See his diagram at ibid., 205.

Though claiming to offer a critique of Campbell, Gehring proposes a similar process. In doing so he is less confused than Campbell in regard to terminology, and his work has the merit of distinguishing carefully between the local church, by which he means the sum of house-churches in a given locality, and the individual house-church. Gehring simply argues that, from the gathered presbyters *kata polin*, a single *episkopos* for the city had emerged: "The legitimization, new formation, and expansion of the office of overseer would have emerged out of an already existing presbyteral organization of the church at the citywide level, on the one hand, and out of an already existing episcopal-patriarchal structure at the house-church level, on the other hand."[133]

Although this is precisely the narrative that was presented above with regard to Rome and Ephesus, and that, as will be suggested, was also the course of events that took place elsewhere, I need to ask whether indeed this had taken place at the time of 1 Timothy.

There are a number of debatable points in Gehring's reconstruction, but there is one point that counts significantly against his narrative, and that is the direction in 1 Timothy 5:17 regarding the elders who are to be given double *honor*. If we accept that the *episkopoi* of the individual household congregations had formed a presbytery, then there would still be one presbyter in each congregation, the original householder, with a coordinating *episkopos* over all. If that is the case, then the task of teaching must likewise fall to these single elders in each congregation. However, the whole implication of rewarding particularly those elders who teach is that there are elders who do not do so. Thus, we are expected to see individual leaders who play no role in teaching and who receive *honor*, but who would of necessity bestow this *honor* upon themselves. Gehring seems to suggest that there are multiple presbyters, however, which would obviate this objection; but this, I suggest, is where the confusion comes about. "There are a multiple number of elders in the congregation," he states,[134] but in support of this cites Titus 1:5, which concerns not individual congregations but the city as a whole. Seeing the presbyters *kata polin* as forming some kind of office, as Gehring suggests,[135] is entirely reasonable, but this assumes that the presbyters of 1 Timothy 5 are the same presbyters *kata polin*, whereas, I suggest, this was not an office that was borne at the level of the individual congregation. As already suggested, this chapter describes conduct within a congregation.

133. Roger W. Gehring, *House Church and Mission: The Importance of Household Structures in Early Christianity* (Peabody, MA: Hendrickson, 2004), 280, in summary of the discussion at 278–80.
134. Ibid., 279.
135. Ibid., 278–80.

There are various minor variations on the manner in which the "monepis-copate" of the Pastoral Epistles is seen to emerge and to express itself—for instance, it is suggested that just as the *episkopos* is really a *presbyteros* with particular functions, he stands apart from the presbyters solely as being a *primus inter pares*[136]—but all are predicated on the basis that individual lead-ership had emerged from corporate leadership at a congregational level. As such, they are all bound to fail.

The fourth explanation of the church order of the Pastoral Epistles is a complex set of solutions based on the idea that there has been some kind of combination (*Verschmelzung*) of systems of office within these letters, and that the current situation is the result of the combination. There are various versions of the theory of *Verschmelzung*. Either there is a graft of elders (de-rived either from the synagogue directly or from the synagogue and mediated through Pauline tradition) with preexisting *episkopoi* and *diakonoi*,[137] or there is a graft of (also Pauline) *episkopoi* and *diakonoi* onto a system of preexist-ing (synagogal) elders.[138]

Campbell's general criticism is that there is no need to reconcile the two systems, as the terms are effectively interchangeable. It is odd that Campbell should invoke the consensus of synonymy here, since his entire argument—presbyters are honored persons rather than officers—would seem to militate against it; part of the problem is his assumption that each honored person became, by virtue of honor, an officer. Campbell's overall picture, which largely fits with that sketched in the chapter above, is that churches in the first phases of the church's mission originated in homes, and that they received oversight from the householders. He actually terms these householders *episkopoi*, but I have suggested that *episkopoi* are appointed only once there is more than one householder in a house-church. However, he also suggests that these *episkopoi* might collectively be known as *presbyteroi*, a suggestion that I have found cause to support, but with the important clarification that they were not known as such within a single house. Consequently, although there is a degree of overlap in the terms, they are not identical; the failure properly to define synonymy and to define the precise nature of the relationship between the two terms is what has caused the confusion here. Nonetheless, I may agree that there is no need to combine two systems, simply because there were never two systems to combine. There are Christian communities under the leadership of *episkopoi*, but no evidence has been found of any Christian church under the leadership

136. So, e.g., von Lips, *Glaube*, 114–15.
137. E.g., Jürgen Roloff, *Der erste Brief an Timotheus*, EKKNT 15 (Zürich: Benziger; Neu-kirchen-Vluyn: Neukirchener Verlag, 1988), 175.
138. So Prast, *Presbyter und Evangelium*, 400–401.

of *presbyteroi* without any officers. I may state at this point that, although the inquiry is not yet complete, no such evidence will be found. It is a scholarly chimera conjured from the assumption of synagogal origins to the church and presbyteral leadership within synagogues.

I may, however, look at some of these solutions in more detail simply to show the manner in which the confusion over the relationship between *presbyteroi* and *episkopoi* and the assumption that *presbyteroi* were a synagogal mode of leadership have caused confusion and unclarity to multiply.

According to Quinn, the purpose of the Pastoral Epistles overall is the introduction of presbyters. With reference to Titus 1:5–6 he notes that "Paul" begins by stating that presbyters should be appointed in every town, then goes on to state that an *episkopos* must be blameless, and then proceeds with a further list of qualifications. As already noted, the shift from the plural to the singular is odd, and Quinn suggests that the term belongs with the subsequent list of qualifications, a solution that has already been accepted. However, for Quinn this qualification list is derived from a different Jewish background, namely, an Essene background (he believes that the *episkopos* here is derived from the *mebaqqer*), and has been left in place by the redactor to assure the hearers of the fundamental compatibility of the presbyters, who are now being appointed, and the *episkopos*, who is a known quantity.[139] The terms, for Quinn, are intended to be "nearly" synonymous, but he is not clear exactly what the extent of their similarity and distinction actually is. If they are synonymous, one may ask, why confuse matters by introducing a new term, or indeed introducing a new office that is almost the same as the office that is supposedly being replaced or supplemented? Similarly, Meier sees the introduction of *presbyteroi* as critical, yet similarly he equates presbyter and *episkopos*; he likewise recognizes that the qualifications at Titus 1:7–8 are traditional, and that they relate to the *episkopos*, and similarly smooths over the transition from plural presbyters to single *episkopoi* by reading the singular as generic.[140] Again, I suggest that if the terms are more or less the same, then there would be no need for the fictive Paul to introduce new terms and new offices. Moreover, it is odd that the role and existence of presbyters should be taken for granted in 1 Timothy if this institution is a new introduction, as it would appear to be in Titus, although Quinn manages to explain this by suggesting that Titus was the first letter in the collection. If that is the case, and the three letters are read as one, it might be argued that by the

139. Jerome D. Quinn, *The Letter to Titus: A New Translation with Notes and Commentary and an Introduction to Titus, I and II Timothy, the Pastoral Epistles*, AB 35 (New York: Doubleday, 1990), 88.

140. John P. Meier, "Presbyteros in the Pastoral Epistles," *CBQ* 33 (1973): 337–39.

time we meet presbyters in 1 Timothy 5, the reader is acquainted with them because they had been met in Titus 1:5. But if they are the same, effectively, as *episkopoi*, why introduce them at all? And why then give qualifications for *episkopoi* all over again in 1 Timothy? Roloff similarly speaks of the influx of presbyters (derived from the synagogue) into the (Pauline) system of overseers and *diakonoi* (Pauline, because these are specific functions observed in Phil. 1:1).[141] He suggests that "Paul's" strategy here is to encourage the elders to become *episkopoi*. This might be a possible reading of Titus 1:5–7 had the instruction been that *episkopoi* should be appointed, but it is not.

Alternatively, it might be the *episkopos* that is being introduced into a system of elders.[142] Given the attention that the *episkopos* receives in 1 Timothy, and given the apparently defensive tone in the letter regarding Timothy's youth as against the age of the presbyters, this would seem to be a *prima facie* possibility. But, as Campbell points out, instructing the appointment of elders in Titus is a strange way of introducing the episcopate.[143] If 1 Timothy is taken on its own, we may read the passing references to the presbyters as indicating that this group had acknowledged existence already, whereas the extended discussion of *episkopoi* and *diakonoi* may be read as indicating that this is a relatively new, and controversial, introduction. However, apart from the fact that no synagogal bench of presbyters has been found, no trace of this controversy is to be found in the letter. Indeed, to see passages concerning the *episkopos* as a new and difficult introduction rather strains the reading because, as in the *Didache*, the existence of *episkopoi* is not proposed; rather, qualifications for the office are being laid down.[144] Similarly, Merkel argues that the *episkopoi* and *diakonoi* are being introduced to supplement and strengthen the existing leadership structure of presbyters; this may be possible in 1 Timothy, but once again, it runs up against Titus, which appears to have these officers already, but no presbyters. Although Merkel tries to make Titus 1:5–8 mean that the *episkopos* is selected from among the presbyters,[145] this is a completely counterintuitive reading; rather, as we have seen, the presbyters are selected from the *episkopoi*.

Lohse's suggestion is typical, in that he sees the combination of systems as being a combination of (multiple) presbyters and (a single) *episkopos*, the

141. Roloff, *Timotheus*, 175–76.
142. Helmut Merkel, *Die Pastoralbriefe*, 13th ed., NTD 9/1 (Göttingen: Vandenhoeck & Ruprecht, 1991), 12–13, 90–93.
143. Campbell, *Elders*, 191, at the conclusion of an extensive critique. Nonetheless, the same criticism may be made of Campbell's own theory.
144. See Merkel, *Pastoralbriefe*, 92. Merkel suggests that the extent of the list of qualifications implies a new kind of appointment.
145. Ibid., 13.

one deriving from Jewish congregations, the other from Gentile.[146] However, in order to have his cake and eat it too, he then suggests that the *episkopos* is really just a member of the presbytery, as the office either emerges from the presbytery or is being joined to it. A single episcopate is thus in the process of emerging. I agree that the episcopate is singular, but how can a single episcopate emerge when it is the result of combining two systems? This is hard to envisage, but more to the point, it is unnecessary. It is more possible that the office is joined to a presbytery, but once again this is simply the result of a hypothesis of the juncture of two systems (one of which never existed).

At this point I may turn to a fifth group of solutions, one that is very close to that provided above: the elders of the Pastoral Epistles are honored older men, and the *episkopos* and *diakonoi* are officers. The solution proposed in this chapter is distinct solely in that it excepts from this the elders mentioned in Titus 1:5 because of the *kata polin* qualification, thus rescuing the hypothesis from the objection that elders would appear to have been appointed and cannot therefore simply be older men.

The proposal that the elders are simply older men and that the *episkopos* is an officer is found in the work of Jeremias, of Harvey, and of Young.

Young proposes that whereas only *episkopoi* and *diakonoi* are the officers of the congregation of 1 Timothy, nonetheless elder members in the community might collectively form a council that the *episkopos* might consult.[147] The office of presbyter emerges somewhat later from this council of elders. On this basis, the elders are not offices but rather persons of esteem within the church, whereas the officers are the *episkopos* and the *diakonoi*, a conclusion that Young reaches from observing Ignatius's imagery from a generation later, in which the *episkopos* is a type of the Father, and the *diakonoi* of Christ, where the *presbyteroi* are a type of the apostles. The origin of the offices of *episkopos* and *diakonos* are derived, she argues, from the household. Thus, largely in keeping with the argument in chapter 2 above, she identifies the *episkopos* as the *oikonomos* of the household. However, she then states that in an ancient household there would be many *diakonoi*. I may assume that she is thinking of domestic servants, though we have already seen that *diakonoi*, when servants, are cult officials, serving as a *leitourgia*. She then further confuses matters by suggesting that the presbytery as a council of older men is inspired by Jewish models, and finally that the *episkopos* took on aspects of the *archisynagōgos*, and the *diakonoi* aspects of the role of the *hazzan*. In each instance this is

---

146. Eduard Lohse, "Episkopos in den Pastoralbriefen," in *Kirche und Bibel: Festgabe für Bischof Eduard Schick* (Paderborn: Schöningh, 1979), 229–31.

147. Frances M. Young, "On ΕΠΙΣΚΟΠΟΣ and ΠΡΕΣΒΥΤΕΡΟΣ," *JTS* 45 (1994): 146.

entirely without rationale and thus mars the entire hypothesis, though the theory is undoubtedly derived from the supposition that the council of elders must reflect a Jewish model.[148]

Jeremias's point is that *presbyteros* fundamentally denotes age rather than office.[149] I may agree with this justification to a point, although, as we have seen, the *presbyteroi* of Hellenistic communities, while not officers, nonetheless are a clearly defined and powerful group. Harvey's point is similar to that of Jeremias: the older men are an organized group within the church, as are the younger men.[150]

Campbell points out that the major problem with this view is that it is hard to square with Titus 1:5. If elders are not officers, why are they appointed? Jeremias suggests that the presbyters who receive a double *honor* are those presbyters who hold an office—in other words, the *episkopoi*—and that Titus 1:5 refers to the appointment of these presbyters as officers.[151] Harvey similarly suggests that the text should be rendered "Appoint (to positions of responsibility) those of your elders (i.e., elder members) who have such and such a character."[152] But this is a very difficult reading of the text. If we are meant to read "appoint elders" as "appoint elders to be *episkopoi*," this would involve a high degree of understanding on the part of people who, in their fictive setting, know nothing of officers. Marshall's understanding is similar; he suggests that matters are in transition, and that the group of elders (by which he means older men), from whom officers would be drawn, are beginning to be identified specifically as officers.[153] But once again, the hearers of Titus are meant to understand that the older men are to be appointed to an office. Harvey argues that 1 *Clement* 43 provides a parallel: "They [the apostles] appointed their firstfruits . . . as *episkopoi* and *diakonoi*." But Roberts points out that the parallel does not hold, as there is nothing corresponding here to "as *episkopoi* and *diakonoi*," and there is no obvious reference to selection from the group, as there is in the passage from 1 *Clement*.[154] However, this is a problem that comes about only if one is trying to reconcile 1 Timothy and Titus 1:5. If the issue is 1 Timothy alone, the probability is that it would never occur to anyone that the elders were anybody but people of age and honor. Jeremias's solution is more or less the same as that presented here,

148. As is clear from the parallel discussion found in Young, *Pastoral Letters*, 109–10.
149. Joachim Jeremias, *Die Briefe an Timotheus und Titus; Der Brief an die Hebräer*, 11th ed., NTD 9 (Göttingen: Vandenhoeck & Ruprecht, 1975), 31, 36.
150. Harvey, "Elders."
151. Jeremias, *Timotheus und Titus*, 41–43.
152. Harvey, "Elders," 331.
153. Marshall, *Pastoral Epistles*, 170–81, in conclusion at 180–81.
154. C. H. Roberts, "Elders: A Note," *JTS* 26 (1975): 404.

though with one significant distinction, which in turn leads to a further refinement.

Principally, I suggest that to see the *kalōs proestōtes presbyteroi* in 1 Timothy 5:17 as those presbyters who had been appointed as *episkopoi* is unnecessary. If the author had meant *episkopoi*, he would simply have used the word. Jeremias's suggestion is made only because of the need to reconcile 1 Timothy and Titus, a reconciliation that, I have suggested, is no longer necessary in the light of the interpretation of the presbyters of Titus as presbyters *kata polin*. Who, then, are the *kalōs proestōtes presbyteroi*? Although the Pastoral Epistles assume a single household setting for the church, officers within the household have come about through the fusion of households, and so through the adoption of some associational practices. This is indicated both by the domestic imagery used of the *episkopos* and by the stipulation that *kalōs proestōtes presbyteroi* should receive a double *honor*. Although this is often interpreted as a payment, a payment is improbable as the function of these presbyters is, in keeping with the models of patronage, social and financial support of the church rather than receipt of support. Given that the payment of clergy is unknown for a further two hundred years, and then as a result of clergy becoming clients of a patron-bishop,[155] a more likely interpretation is that a double portion of food is given at community banquets, as a mark of honor. Such additional portions are known in Greco-Roman meal practice, and this practice is a link with the meal liturgy that the household celebrated.[156] Such is the meaning of the term: the presbyters are patrons of the communities.[157] We may compare, in reading *proestōtes* as indicating patronage, the *presbyteroi proistamenoi* who are mentioned by Hermas, and who are recognized by Maier as the patrons of the Roman house-churches.[158] There

155. See Alistair Stewart(-Sykes), "Ordination Rites and Patronage Systems in Third-Century Africa," *VC* 56 (2002): 115–30.

156. So Georg Schöllgen, "Die διπλῆ τιμή von I Tim 5,17," *ZNW* 80 (1989): 233–39. Although, as Schöllgen notes, associations had a similar practice, the origin of this lies in the household and is found in a household setting in 1 Timothy. There is evidence of double payment being given in some religious settings. In *PGM* 4.2455 the tale is told of Pachrates, whose command of magic so impressed the king that he instructed that Pachrates should be given διπλᾶ ὀψώνια; it is to be noted, however, that even here the payment is made in food. In terms of monetary payment, however, we may note *GIBM* 3.481, an extensive decree regarding the distribution of a bequest to the city of Ephesus by C. Vibius Salutaris, singling out as recipients for payment the γερουσιασταί, the θεολόγοι, and the ὑμνῳδοί. These gifts, however, would seem to be marks of honor rather than payment for services rendered.

157. Compare Hatch, *Organization*, 64n23: the elders who rule well are those who govern, as distinct from those who are simply elderly. He makes the same suggestion with regard to *Herm.* 8:3. However, Meier ("Presbyteros," 326) suggests that presiding is what elders simply do.

158. Harry O. Maier, *The Social Setting of the Ministry as Reflected in the Writings of Hermas, Clement and Ignatius* (Waterloo, ON: Wilfrid Laurier University Press, 1991), 63.

is an ambiguity in the word *proistamenos*, by which both governance and patronage might be indicated. Given the necessity for domestic Christianity to have wealthy leaders who might also give social support to the church, the *proistamenoi*, and the *proestōtes presbyteroi* likewise, are both leaders and patrons.[159] Since the presbyters here form a patronal group, I may suggest that those who *kalōs proestōtes* are those who are exceptionally generous, as Dio Chrysostom refers to those who have liturgized *kalōs*.[160] The failure to recognize the language of patronage and *honor* in the phrase *kalōs proestōtes presbyteroi*, and thus to see this as the language of office,[161] is a further critical failure in the interpretation of the Pastoral Epistles. It provides a means to reconcile 1 Timothy 5:17 with Titus 1:5, and so to explain the appointment of elders, but since both phrases have been misunderstood, the connection is unnecessary, as Titus 1:5 is referring to a different kind of presbyter altogether. This in turn leads me to suggest a further refinement to Jeremias's hypothesis: recognition as a *presbyteros* derived not only from age but also from wealth; recognition after this manner would appear to have derived in part from the ability to offer patronage. This patronal role is entirely in keeping with the practice of the associational presbyters found in the inscriptional evidence.

Elsewhere we find that the *episkopoi* are patrons; here, I suggest, the *episkopoi* are already becoming professionalized, even if the office is taken on as a *leitourgia*. In chapter 5 I note the significance of the qualifications for *episkopoi* within the Pastoral Epistles, and in particular the statement that they should be qualified to teach. Once this qualification is introduced, then wealth and the ability to offer patronage is no longer the primary qualification; it would seem that in the period of the Pastoral Epistles the *episkopos* and *diakonoi* were continuing to serve as a *leitourgia*, but that already the locus of patronage was shifting, and with it the status and role of the *episkopos*.

The solution by Jeremias seems to accord with that proposed here, but it is to be applied solely to 1 Timothy 5:1, 17, and not artificially extended to cover Titus 1:5. Moreover, the occurrence in Titus 2:2 of *presbyteroi* who can only be older men, since the following instruction is aimed at older women, would tend in turn to lend support to this reading of *presbyteroi* in 1 Timothy. The presbyters of 1 Timothy are not officers at all; they are the senior male patrons

159. On the ambiguity inherent in the term, see the brief discussion by Wayne E. Meeks, *The First Urban Christians: The Social World of the Apostle Paul* (New Haven: Yale University Press, 1983), 134, 234n75, with reference to Rom. 12:8, where the προϊστάμενος is clearly a patron, and 1 Thess. 5:12, where either or both senses of the word may be intended.
160. Dio Chrysostom, *2 Tars.* 1.4.
161. So also Prast, *Presbyter und Evangelium*, 471.

of the community, their role entirely analogous to that of the *presbyteroi* of associations and gymnasia.

In suggesting that the presbyters of 1 Timothy are identical with the city-presbyters of Titus, Wagner states that the only other possible explanation is that there was a college of presbyters in each household.[162] This is precisely what I am suggesting here. Wagner thinks that this cannot be the case because such domestic presbyters do not appear in Acts. This, however, is an argument from silence, as Acts says remarkably little about the internal organization of the individual congregations. The suggestion is made here fundamentally on the grounds of the close similarities between such a college of presbyters and the group of presbyters in city governance and gymnasia. It is true that households do not naturally give rise to a presbyteral group, and that, as already argued, an individual leader is more likely to emerge from a domestic organization, but it is entirely feasible that the congregations of 1 Timothy are leaving the household behind and taking on aspects of associational behavior. It is also possible that, as part of this associational orientation, households have combined. This might result in a patronal group rather than a single *episkopos*-patron, with the resulting need to extend recognition to those patrons and householders who themselves are not officers exercising a liturgy. Their designation as presbyters and the grant to them of a double helping of food at the meals of the community provide precisely such a recognition.

Further support for this hypothesis will be found in the appearance of similarly patronal groups of presbyters within a single congregation elsewhere. However, for the moment, consideration must be given to the officers of the congregation of 1 Timothy, the *episkopos* and the *diakonoi*.

THE *EPISKOPOS* AND *DIAKONOI* OF 1 TIMOTHY

With the nature of the presbyters in 1 Timothy now clarified, it is relatively simple to understand that of the *episkopos* and *diakonoi* as distinct.

I begin by noting the suggestion of Young, who likewise sees the presbyters as older men and maintains that the offices of *episkopos* and *diakonos* are based on the household in that the *episkopos* is the steward (*oikonomos*) of the household and the *diakonoi* are the servants.[163] The basis for this characterization is Titus 1:7, which describes the bishop as God's steward (*theou oikonomos*); again, I may broadly agree, as this is entirely in keeping with the hypothesis sketched above by which the office of *episkopos* derived from the necessity of household management in the provision of the meal that was the central ritual of the

---

162. Wagner, *Anfänge*, 165.
163. Young, "ΕΠΙΣΚΟΠΟΙ," 147–48.

Christian group. Although there is development in the period of the Pastoral
Epistles, the original structure of the *oikos* is far from left behind; rather, as
Verner points out, the *oikos* becomes a model for the church.[164] We may be less
certain that the *diakonoi* are servants as such, given that, as already noted, little
is said regarding their function, but insofar as their qualifications indicate that
they are men of standing, householders themselves,[165] we may rather see this
office as a liturgy; even if acting as servants, or ritual waiters, they are acting
out this role within the context of the church modeled on a household rather
than, literally, being the servants. The household is not left behind but rather is
used as model by the Paul of the Pastorals, even though what is being described
is something more like a state, with the presbyters holding authority and the
episkopos being more like a city *oikonomos* than an *oikonomos* of a simple
household. Since in antiquity the household was considered something of a
ministate, this is not problematic.

We should compare this characterization of the respective roles of presbyters and *episkopos* to that propounded by a number of those who claim or
imply that the terms are synonymous but seem, rather, to mean that they are
perionomynous. Fee suggests that *presbyteroi* is a generic term (which is not
the same as synonymy).[166] For Spicq, the terms *episkopos* and *presbyteros* are
"à peu près synonymes," since the overseer is an elder charged with exercising *episkopē*.[167] Similarly, Johnson suggests that an *episkopos* is a *presbyteros*
charged with a particular function.[168]

These are, to a great extent, coherent with the picture that I have painted
here. They are slightly deficient, however, in that there is a failure to observe
the patronal basis of the presbyterate; by asserting that the presbyters lead,
they are thinking of the presbyterate as an office, often stating that it is derived
from the synagogue,[169] rather than simply a status within the community that
naturally leads to governance.

I thus conclude that some domestic Christian communities had a group
within them that offered patronage and that was particularly honored. These
presbyteroi were not officers as such, but they were an identifiable group.[170] Al-

---

164. David C. Verner, *The Household of God: The Social World of the Pastoral Epistles*,
SBLDS 71 (Chico, CA: Scholars Press, 1981), 127, in summary of the preceding argument.

165. So ibid., 133, 155.

166. Gordon D. Fee, *1 and 2 Timothy, Titus*, NIBC 13 (Peabody, MA: Hendrickson, 1988), 128.

167. Ceslas Spicq, *Saint Paul: Les Épitres Pastorales*, EB (Paris: Gabalda, 1947), xlvi–xlvii.

168. Luke Timothy Johnson, *Letters to Paul's Delegates: 1 Timothy, 2 Timothy, Titus*, NTC
(Valley Forge, PA: Trinity Press International, 1996), 145–49.

169. E.g., ibid., 146.

170. Compare Wagner, *Anfänge*, 161. Wagner suggests that the presbyters, originally persons
of *honor*, are on the way to becoming officers on the basis that they have an honorarium, the
διπλῆ τιμή. However, this is, itself, an *honor*.

though I cannot be sure that the *episkopos* and *diakonoi* were recruited from within the group, the nature of the qualifications required for these officers, namely, that they themselves were householders of standing,[171] tends to imply that the presbyters are the constituency for the officeholders.[172]

However, whereas it may be that the patron-presbyters supply the candidates for office at the time of the Pastoral Epistles, it is a situation that is in flux. For it is possible that the *episkopos* and *diakonoi* need not pass the qualification of age; thus, Timothy, acting as apostolic delegate (and model *episkopos*), is advised that people should not look down on him because of his age,[173] and in a slightly later period we find an *episkopos* who is certainly not a presbyter.[174] Although a solution for this may lie in Powell's suggestion that the age that qualified one as a presbyter was not age in years but rather age in conversion,[175] the evidence that he cites is thin, being limited to Stephanas's characterization both as leader among Corinthian Christians and firstfruits[176] (it is notable that he is not termed *presbyteros*), and so it would be unwise to build too much on such slight evidence; in addition, this does not explain why, if the role of *episkopos* was open only to elders in the faith, 1 Timothy 3:6 needs to direct that the *episkopos* should not be a neophyte. Some support for Powell's view of the presbyterate more generally, as age in conversion rather than years, may be taken from the comment of Philo that the *presbyteroi* among the Therapeutae are not simply the elderly, for they might be recent converts, but those who are senior in contemplation.[177] But this does not mean that these are the constituency for the appointment of officers, for the young (*neoi*) among the Therapeutae act as *diakonoi*.[178] The associational language employed by Philo in this section of *De vita contemplativa* is also noteworthy, implying, once again, that the use of the term *presbyteroi* derives from the divisions familiar in Hellenistic associative life. Thus, not only is the qualification of age somewhat fluid in the period immediately following that of the Pastoral Epistles, but also, I may suggest, the link between patronage and episcopacy is soon to be broken. As it is,

---

171. Merkle (*Elder and Overseer*, 134) denies that they are to be householders, as this is not explicitly stated. But this is to be taken as read by virtue of the nature of the qualifications demanded.

172. As suggested by Douglas Powell, "Ordo presbyterii," *JTS* 26 (1975): 306.

173. 1 Tim. 4:12.

174. Namely, Damas at Magnesia (Ign. *Magn.* 3:1).

175. Powell, "Ordo presbyterii," 305–6. He also suggests (311) that this explains why elders need to be appointed at Titus 1:5. Again, this is a question already answered.

176. 1 Cor. 16:15–16.

177. Philo, *Contempl.* 67.

178. Philo, *Contempl.* 72.

the episcopate is both liturgy and task, but it might be a task without being a liturgy, especially since the patrons are the presbyters.

If the *episkopos* is not necessarily a *presbyteros*, we may ask what the relationship of authority between the elders and *episkopos* might be. I may indeed suggest that the *episkopos* was in some sense subject to the presbytery as their agent,[179] and as such, he need not be a presbyter. Thus I may answer the objection, raised above, to seeing the term *episkopos* as associational on the grounds that the *episkopos* is not known as the head of any association by suggesting that he is, once again, broker—here, however, for the patronage of the presbyters rather than that of God. What I may now add is that the *presbyteroi* are likewise of associational origin. This may appear to conflict with the household imagery employed throughout the Pastoral Epistles but, as already pointed out, the models are not mutually contradictory. The emphasis on household imagery in these epistles may even be an indication of development beyond the simple household, as a fictive household now substitutes for a real one.[180]

Presbyters and *Episkopoi* at Ephesus

This part of the examination of the history of church order at Ephesus, following on from the sketch in chapter 1, was intended to test the hypothesis that the *tagma* of presbyters was derived from gymnastic and civic practice.

That this is the case looks probable from the evidence provided by 1 Timothy; the fact that the congregation is Pauline, however, and thus probably fundamentally Gentile, certainly indicates that the formerly prevailing hypothesis, namely, that Christian presbyters derived from the synagogue, is rather less than likely. The very corporate nature of the presbytery as described by Paul, moreover, is an indication that they did not exercise an actual ministry but rather formed an identifiable group nonetheless, and as such, mirror closely the presbyters of the gymnasia and associations. Gehring similarly suggests that presbyters are a Christian creation, but he traces the creation of presbyters to Jerusalem.[181] I will argue below that the Jerusalem presbyters are presbyters *kata polin*, and so this derivation will not work; the evidence of gymnastic and associational presbyters, however, is an indication that this inner Christian development was not *creatio ex nihilo* but rather had derived from contemporary and local usage in the Asian *poleis*. These presbyters, therefore, are

179. This question is further discussed in chap. 5 below, under the heading "Monepiscopacy as Centralization."

180. So Georg Schöllgen, "Hausgemeinden, οἶκος-Ekklesiologie und monarchischer Episkopat," *JAC* 31 (1988): 84–86.

181. Gehring, *House Church*, 279–81.

not directly subordinate officers, which indicates in turn that the *episkopos* of 1 Timothy is a domestic *episkopos* and not the sole *monepiskopos* of Ephesus.

THE CHURCH ORDER OF 1 TIMOTHY AND OF APOSTOLIC CHURCH ORDER

Support for my reading of the situation in Ephesus at the time of the Pastoral Epistles may be gained from noting *Apostolic Church Order* (*Canones ecclesiastici apostolorum*), a church order that, I have suggested elsewhere, derives from somewhere between Ephesus and Syria, possibly in Cilicia or Cappadocia. Although *Apostolic Church Order* derives from the third century, it is a particularly revealing document for the history of the development of office in early Christianity, for in spite of its third-century date and its outline of what was by then an established threefold ministerial order of *episkopos*, *presbyteroi*, and *diakonoi*, a source that reflects conditions at about the middle of the second century, or possibly earlier, lies patent behind it. This, following Harnack, I have termed *katastasis tou klērou* (κκ).[182] I will note below that this same source was employed in the construction of *Didascalia apostolorum*.

It will be suggested that κκ shows a stage of development in church order that in many ways is comparable to that represented in the Pastoral Epistles, in that it identifies a group of patrons while designating a single officer, the *episkopos*.

This church order starts out by suggesting a situation where there might not be twelve persons in a community competent to elect a bishop from among themselves.[183] The fact that the bishop is to be taken from their number indicates that these twelve are not simply the entire male congregation, but that they are patrons within the community and, as such, are candidates and electors for the office of *episkopos* by virtue of their ability to provide patronage. That is to say, they are the honored male members of the community. As such, they are directly comparable to the presbyters of 1 Timothy.

Subsequently, we find presbyters gathering with the bishop at the distribution of gifts; this implies that they too are agents of patronage because they are distributing as patrons of the community, but also it reminds us that the locus of patronage is, as suggested above, liturgical. The distribution of "gifts of honor" takes place from the altar. I may thus suggest that these presbyters at the altar are the same people of whom mention is made at the beginning of the

---

182. In Alistair Stewart(-Sykes), *The Apostolic Church Order: The Greek Text with Introduction, Translation and Annotation*, ECS 10 (Sydney: St. Pauls, 2006), following Adolf von Harnack, *Die Lehre der zwölf Apostel: Nebst Untersuchungen zur ältesten Geschichte der Kirchenverfassung und des Kirchenrechts*, TUGAL 2/1–2 (Leipzig: Hinrichs, 1886), 213–14.

183. *Can. eccl. ap.* 16.1: ἐντὸς δεκαδύο ἀνδρῶν.

document, even though they are not identified at the beginning as presbyters, since they likewise are exercising patronage within the community and are close in their operation to the *episkopos* who had been elected from among their number. At this point, the concern is the conduct of the eucharist in the community, where it is said that the presbyters on the right of the *episkopos* distribute the gifts of honor and receive them as necessary.[184] We may thus see that the eucharist is no longer a meal but retains aspects of such a setting in that it remains a locus for charity. Food is distributed by the *presbyteroi*, but it is not being consumed at the table. As such, I may suggest that this part of the document is from the second, rather than the first, century because it reflects a time at which the eucharist has been moved from the evening to the following Sunday morning, with the consequent disappearance of the full meal.

Beyond participating in the distribution of gifts of honor, they are to keep order in the congregation. The officer of the congregation, however, is the *episkopos*. These twelve are grouped around the bishop at the distribution. We are so reminded of the manner in which the elders of the apocalypse are grouped around the throne, an image that indeed is made explicit.[185] I may thus suggest that the *episkopos* is seated among the presbyters and, with them, distributes, both as an officer of the presbytery and as a member. With this description we are very close to the situation envisaged in 1 Timothy.

There are also directions for the selection of presbyters in *Apostolic Church Order*,[186] but these are manifestly later than the directions given regarding the selection of an *episkopos*. For instance, the presbyters are expected to be celibate, whereas the *episkopos* is simply to be once-married. This reflects a yet later stage, therefore, in the community's development of office, a time at which the presbyterate has become a distinct and clericalized office rather than an appointment received by virtue of the ability to offer patronage. This is the stage at which presbyters are, I will suggest below, introduced to the community of *Didascalia apostolorum*. In *Apostolic Church Order*, however, we see that the language of 1 Timothy has been adopted even as its church setting continued to manifest the same social structures.

Thus, we may see that the office of *episkopos* in this community is appointed from and by the presbyterate for the management of the community. However, these presbyters are not alternatively known as "bishops," but there is simply one bishop, who is chief officer.[187] It is hard precisely to characterize

184. *Can. eccl. ap.* 18.3.
185. *Can. eccl. ap.* 18.1, making reference to Rev. 4:4, 8. See also chap. 4 below, pp. 293–94.
186. *Can. eccl. ap.* 18.2.
187. Note the comments in Stewart(-Sykes), *Apostolic Church Order*, 56, in response to Alexandre Faivre, "Le texte grec de la Constitution ecclésiastique des apôtres 16–20 et ses sources,"

the relationship between the presbyters, before their clericalization, and the *episkopos* with regard to whether the *episkopos*, on appointment, remains also a member of the presbytery. However, the point overall is made that as soon as diverse households are gathered together, it is necessary for the householders to find recognition, but that these presbyters do not hold office; in this community the sole office is that of the *episkopos*, and such an office was created, as already suggested, as a means of ensuring that food is available in sufficient quantities. As such, the office of *episkopos* in this community has neither grown out of the presbyterate nor come about through the combination of systems.[188]

CONCLUSION

The identification of the patronal group as presbyters is significant for our understanding of other appearances of groups of presbyters in early Christian literature. I have already argued that a group of presbyters across a city might be made up of those who held office in individual households, and that "presbyters" was their collective designation, and that in 1 Timothy we meet presbyters other than those *kata polin*, namely, presbyters within a single household; I suggested that these are the patron-householders of the church. The fact that the same institution is found independently in κκ is evidence for the correctness of that position.

These patrons appoint a single *episkopos*. One of the implications of seeing the terms *episkopos* and *presbyteros* as synonymous has been the assumption that when mention is made of *episkopoi*, this means that a Christian community might have multiple *episkopoi*. Across a town there may well be multiple *episkopoi*, as there are multiple households. But here there is only one *episkopos*, as, at this point in the argument, is only what we should expect. If the appointment of an *episkopos* is the result of combining more than one household into a single household, as was argued above, I may now go on to suggest that only one of these householders was ever designated as such, and that the other patrons designated themselves as the *presbyteroi*, as here. One of the arguments frequently met in discussions of the relationship between *episkopoi* and *presbyteroi* is the point that the term *episkopos* is normally found in the singular, while *presbyteroi* are normally plural. I may suggest, as

---

RevScRel 55 (1981): 31–42; Bernadette Lemoine, "Étude de la notice sur l'évêque dans la 'Constitution ecclésiastique des apôtres (C.E.A.),'" *QL* 80 (1999): 5–23. Both attempt to make the bishop simply one of the presbyters.

188. However, I argue elsewhere that the *diakonoi* in this community are a graft from a different church-order tradition (Alistair Stewart[-Sykes], "Deacons in the Syrian Church Order Tradition: A Search for Origins," in *Diakonia, diaconiae, diaconato: Semantica e storia nei Padri della Chiesa; XXXVIII Incontro di studiosi dell'antichità cristiana, Roma, 7–9 maggio 2009*, ed. V. Grossi et al., SEA 117 [Rome: Institutum patristicum Augustinianum, 2010], 111–20).

a working hypothesis, that κκ gives the clue to the rationale: there was only ever one *episkopos* in any given Christian house-church, but there may well have been multiple *presbyteroi*. Consequently, the term *monepiskopos*, used simply to denote a sole bishop in a community or congregation, as opposed to multiple *episkopoi*, is tautologous. Unless strict synonymy is to be maintained between *episkopos* and *presbyteros* across the first century, the idea of multiple leadership disappears, along with the Jewish presbyters from whom these multiple leaders were meant to derive.

Presbyters at Rome

In an earlier chapter I examined a number of the appearances of the term "presbyter" from the first and second centuries in a Roman context and in each instance suggested that it was a reference to a gathering of Christian leaders from across the city. There is no evidence, therefore, that within individual households there had earlier been benches of presbyters, whether superior to, subordinate to, or coequal with the *episkopos*.

By the time of the establishment of a monepiscopate, however, presbyters who are subordinate to the single *episkopos* are found. In *Traditio apostolica* an ordination prayer is found for presbyters.[189] Since the presbyter is ordained by an *episkopos*, I may suggest that this is a presbyter who is not an *episkopos* but rather a presbyter who is subordinate to an *episkopos*. This is therefore a development that is to be dated to a period after the development of monepiscopacy in Rome and the recognition of a single Roman *episkopos* by the Hippolytean community. Those who, as *episkopoi*, were recognized as presbyters retain the title of presbyter, whereas one alone is recognized as their *episkopos* and is now their superior. Following Brent, who takes the manner in which the exile and martyrdom of Pontianus and Hippolytus (designating Hippolytus as a presbyter and Pontianus as an *episkopos*) is recorded in the Liberian catalog alongside the fact that Pontianus is the first bishop in the Liberian catalog whose dates are accurately given rather than simply being dated by consular years, we may see the period of Pontianus's episcopate as the time at which monepiscopacy is established and the nature of presbyters as subordinates established.[190] It is from this time that the ordination of presbyters comes about in the Hippolytean community.[191]

189. *Trad. ap.* 7.

190. Allen Brent, *Hippolytus and the Roman Church in the Third Century: Communities in Tension before the Emergence of a Monarch-Bishop*, VCSup 31 (Leiden: Brill, 1995), 452.

191. As is argued at length in Alistair Stewart(-Sykes), *Hippolytus: On the Apostolic Tradition* (Crestwood, NY: St. Vladimir's Seminary Press, 2001); and previously in Alistair Stewart(-Sykes),

This view should be put against the alternative, perhaps widely assumed if not stated, that the ordination rites for a presbyter necessarily precede those for an *episkopos* in *Traditio apostolica*, fundamentally on the grounds that presbyters necessarily preceded *episkopoi* and that *episkopoi* are necessarily *monepiskopoi*.[192] Such a view is set forth by Hayes.[193] His argument essentially is that the ordination prayer for a presbyter in *Traditio apostolica* 7 creates a degree of common ground between the *episkopos* and the presbyters, whereas that for an *episkopos* in *Traditio apostolica* 2 elevates the *episkopos*. As such, he suggests, the episcopate emerged from a barely distinguished presbyterate/ episcopate. However, it is equally possible to read the evidence as going the other way: the (later, I would argue) prayer in *Traditio apostolica* 7 creates a common ground between the offices because at this point presbyters are becoming officers. We must note, moreover, the rubric that introduces the presbyteral ordination prayer: "When a presbyter is ordained the bishop will lay a hand upon his head, the presbyters likewise touching him, and he shall speak as we said above, as we said before concerning the bishop, praying and saying. . . ."[194] This rubric must be either contemporary with or later than the ordination prayer in *Traditio apostolica* 3 to which it refers. Thus, if the prayer in *Traditio apostolica* 7 is earlier, then it was introduced without rubric.[195] We would then have to anticipate the rubric being introduced, either with or later than the ordination prayer for an *episkopos*. This is not absolutely impossible, except that what follows is an entirely distinct prayer, which already exists, according to the hypothesis that presupposes its priority. It surely is impossible that a later redactor would supply a rubric at this point that stood in flat contradiction to the text that stood in front of him. However, it is entirely reasonable, were we to accept that *Traditio apostolica* 7 is the later prayer, for a redactor to insert a prayer that really does make a distinction between *episkopos* and presbyters (which would not otherwise have been made, were the prayer in *Traditio apostolica* 3 really used for both).

"The Integrity of the Hippolytean Ordination Rites," *Aug* 39 (1999): 97–127. My approach to *Traditio apostolica* is much debated; the debate is not extended here.

192. Thus, the sole critique aimed at my treatment of ordination rites is a throwaway comment from Bradshaw (*Search for the Origins*, 209), who finds it improbable that a presbyteral ordination prayer should be later than an episcopal.

193. Alan L. Hayes, "Christian Ministry in Three Cities of the Western Empire (160–258 CE)," in *Community Formation in the Early Church and in the Church Today*, ed. Richard N. Longe-necker, (Peabody, MA: Hendrickson, 2002), 146–48.

194. *Trad. ap.* 7.1.

195. It is impossible to suggest that the rubric has been expanded, because at its core is the single *episkopos* laying a hand.

This point is followed at length because it demonstrates, first, that *Traditio apostolica* is a composite document, providing evidence from an earlier period alongside that which derives from the time of monepiscopacy. Second, it demonstrates that the presbyters of this community were not, originally, ordained officers. Third, it demonstrates that the *episkopos* ordained in *Traditio apostolica* 3 is not a *monepiskopos*, as he had no subordinate presbyters, but is rather head of a single community.

Nonetheless, I may note at this point a peculiarity in the presbyteral ordination prayer observed by Barlea: it falls into two distinct sections.[196] In the first part there is a prayer for an individual, apparently being introduced to the presbyterate:

> God and Father of our Lord Jesus Christ, look upon your this your servant and impart the Spirit of grace and counsel of presbyterate so that he might assist and guide your people with a pure heart.[197]

What follows, however, is a prayer for all the presbyters:

> And now Lord, grant that the Spirit of your grace may be preserved unceasingly in us, filling us and making us worthy to minister to you in simplicity of heart, praising you through your child Jesus Christ.[198]

It is possible that this prayer has been constructed from preexisting material, in particular that the second part of the prayer was a freestanding unit, said by the presbyters themselves (and not by the *episkopos*). As such, the former part of the prayer is the redactional construction, the ordination prayer produced so that an *episkopos* might say it in appointing a presbyter. As such, it is even less likely that the ordination prayer for a presbyter lies at an earlier redactional layer than the preceding rubric.

In the ordination rite for an *episkopos* in *Traditio apostolica*, it is directed that the people come together with the presbytery and any bishops who are present. These bishops, I may suggest, are other *episkopoi* from Rome, not *monepiskopoi* from other locations. It is directed that one of these *episkopoi* should say the ordination prayer while the *presbyteroi* stand silent. From this I may deduce that here we have mention of a presbytery that clearly is not a gathering of *episkopoi* from within the city, as it is said that one of the

---

196. Octavian Barlea, *Die Weihe der Bischöfe, Presbyter und Diakone in vornicänischer Zeit*, APT 3 (Munich: Societas Academica Dacoromana, 1969), 114.
197. *Trad. ap.* 7.2.
198. *Trad. ap.* 7.4.

episkopoi says the ordination prayer, this *episkopos* clearly being distinguished from the presbytery. This presbytery would appear to be a group within the individual Christian community whose *episkopos* is now being appointed. The fact that they are enjoined to be silent is an indication that their role in the ordination of an *episkopos* is being deliberately diminished, as the honor is given to a visiting *episkopos*. Since we have here an "internal" presbytery, we may ask whether there were indeed benches of presbyters as well as *episkopoi* and *diakonoi* in some Roman Christian communities, or whether there has been a development between the end of the first century (a time to which we may tentatively assign the work of Hermas) and the end of the second (a time to which we may reasonably assign the first level of Hippolytean redaction of *Traditio apostolica*), or whether this is a peculiarity of this Christian group. In any event, this group of presbyters is here in some way being made subordinate to the *episkopos* (an indication that the relationship was not always one of subordination) through the manner in which silence is enjoined on them, the manner in which their handlaying is subordinated to that of a visiting *episkopos*, the manner in which their election is subordinated to the consent of the people present,[199] and in the use of Abraham as the type of the priest who is chosen rather than Aaron, since Abraham is a priest who is also a leader rather than being subject, as was Aaron, to one who was not a priest.[200] Subsequently, when the presbyters are ordained and accept their subordinate role, it is possible to generate a prayer that refers to the shared spirit of Moses and the elders, which is that found in *Traditio apostolica* 7.

In the absence of evidence I cannot assert that there were no benches of *presbyteroi* within Christian communities of Rome any more than it can be assumed that they must have existed, even though they are not mentioned. The only evidence at our disposal prior to *Traditio apostolica*—*1 Clement*, Hermas, the brief report of worship found in Justin's work, the brief references to the condemnation of Marcion, and the fragments of information in Eusebius regarding the paschal controversy (all of which were discussed in chap. 1)—indicates a single leader of worship in each community holding office by virtue of an ability to offer patronage, a single *episkopos* exercising what would appear to be an economic ministry, and a presbytery consisting of gathered Christian leaders from across the city, of whom a member was responsible for correspondence with other churches, from which figure the *monepiskopos* emerges. The community of *Traditio apostolica* provides a

---

199. These conclusions derive from observing a number of peculiarities in the rubrics attaching to this ordination, which are discussed in detail in Stewart(-Sykes), *Hippolytus*.

200. Brent, *Hippolytus*, 305.

different picture. Here there are multiple patrons[201] and an *episkopos*. Moreover, I may state of this *episkopos* that his duty is principally didactic, as may be deduced from the overall concern of *Traditio apostolica* to set the church aright (in view of how the leaders, patrons I might suggest, were ill-taught), and, moreover, given the separation of the *episkopos* from the patron-presbyters, that he himself is no longer (if ever he was) expected to be a patron.

There are grounds for seeing the presbyters of this community as found at the time of the composition of the episcopal ordination prayer in precisely the light of the civic or gymnastic presbyters discussed above, namely, as leading persons in the community who exercise influence and who hold a defined position but exercise a liturgical duty not in the modern sense of the word, but rather in its ancient sense. The grounds lie in the implied conflict between them and the *episkopos*; they in turn may be identified with those who were ignorant and who led the church into error. The tension appears elsewhere in *Traditio apostolica*; as Bobertz points out, the directions concerning the *cena dominica* in *Traditio apostolica* 28, which bid silence while the bishop speaks and which instruct that the *benedictio* be the work of the bishop, or in the bishop's absence that of a presbyter or deacon, are a direct challenge to the role of the patron in a supper, who would expect to have the honor due a host in normal Roman society.[202]

As such, they have something in common with the *presbyteroi* of 1 Timothy. A degree of conflict, moreover, between these presbyters and the *episkopos* indicates that the *episkopos*—like Damas at Magnesia, who, as is argued below, is too young to be a *presbyteros*,[203] and indeed like the Timothy of the Pastoral Epistles, who is also young—need not be a member of the presbytery. The model, we may recollect, for this kind of presbyter was derived from the cities of Asia; I may thus suggest that this model had been transplanted into Rome with the Hippolytean school, a Christian community itself of demonstrably Asian origin. The appearance of presbyters within this community, therefore, is not a development that had taken place at Rome in a general way in the century or so since Hermas, but was a peculiarity of this community. As further evidence of this I may note the manner in which the (suppressed) ordination of the *episkopos* by the presbyters of the community reflects that presupposed in 1 Timothy 4:14, in which the presbytery lays hands on Timothy.

In the next stage of development the presbyterate is clericalized, and so the later redaction of *Traditio apostolica* provides an ordination prayer for

201. Those *qui ecclesiae praesunt* (*Trad. ap.* 1.5).
202. Charles A. Bobertz, "The Role of Patron in the *cena dominica* of Hippolytus' *Apostolic Tradition*," *JTS* 44 (1995): 180–81.
203. See Ign. *Magn.* 3.

presbyters, to be said by the *episkopos*. It is in their clericalization that the subordination of presbyters is completed; prior to this, however, they are patrons.

Congregational Presbyters as Patrons in Ephesus and Rome

I have argued throughout this chapter that Christian presbyters originated as a patronal group within churches that had united more than one household, and that the civic and gymnastic presbyters of the city-states provided the model by which this might occur. However, although they provide patronage, they are not officers as such.

A further illustration of this phenomenon may be provided by *Acts of Peter*. As noted above in chapter 2, Stoops makes a persuasive case for seeing *Acts of Peter* as rejecting the model by which patrons became leaders in the church. However, he further points out that there is no clear model by which a second generation of leaders (or brokers of Christ's benefits) might come to replace Peter. "Unless the reference to a bishop in APt 27 is original—which I doubt—the only mention of a church-officer is of a presbyter."[204] It seems probable that Stoops is misled by the consensus into assuming that the *episkopos* must be a *monepiskopos*, and that as such, this is a development later than the presbyterate.

However, I may put this aside for the moment to note Stoops's suggestion that church officers are not relied on as mediators between Christ and the community, as this would threaten the equality among Christ's servants. Thus he suggests the possibility that short-term charismatic leaders might be supplied by Christ. However, he then goes on to suggest that it was precisely this lack of institutional leadership that left the community open to "manipulation by patrons."[205]

We have already seen the dangers in the possibility of manipulation by patrons, but I suggest that the author of *Acts of Peter* was well aware of this, as Stoops points out so clearly. However, I may also note that charisma is not the same as leadership; this common assumption, as I have argued elsewhere, derives from a misreading of Weber and from a confusion between charismatic leadership and the religious phenomenon of charisma.[206] Charismatic

---

204. Robert F. Stoops Jr., "Patronage in the Acts of Peter," in *The Apocryphal Acts of Apostles*, ed. Dennis R. MacDonald, Semeia 38 (Decatur, GA: Scholars Press, 1986), 99.

205. Ibid., 100.

206. Alistair Stewart(-Sykes), "Prophecy and Patronage: The Relationship between Charismatic Functionaries and Household Officers in Early Christianity," in *Trajectories through the New Testament and the Apostolic Fathers*, ed. A. F. Gregory and C. M. Tuckett, NTAF (Oxford: Oxford University Press, 2005), 165–89. See also my comments in chap. 5, under the heading "Institutionalization as an Explanation of Monepiscopacy."

individuals may provide prophecy, but this does not constitute or necessitate leadership. There is no reason, moreover, to doubt, on this or on any other basis, the originality of the reference to a bishop in *Acts of Peter* 27. This is the widow's son who is raised up and to whom Peter says that he should serve him as deacon and then as bishop. This is the succession of Peter that is being proposed by Peter. We may likewise see that Peter is proposing a diaconal-episcopal system. These, namely, *episkopoi* and *diakonoi*, are the officers, as they are in the community of the Pastoral Epistles.

If these are the officers, and if the situation is similar to that presupposed in the Pastoral Epistles, we may note in *Acts of Peter* the appearance, several times, of Narcissus the presbyter.[207] Significantly, it is at Narcissus's house that Peter stays, despite the offers of rather better-heeled patrons. Narcissus is, I may suggest, presbyter by virtue of patronage, and not an officer as such. There is thus a slightly nuanced view of patronage in *Acts of Peter*. The patronage of the wealthy is not denied altogether, but it is not grounds for leadership or authority. Leadership and authority are in the hands of the deacon and bishop, once again as brokers, whereas the presbyters may provide support but not leadership.

Further evidence, moreover, may be provided for the hypothesis that some communities had *episkopoi* and *diakonoi* as officers with presbyters as a defined patronal group not holding office by noting communities in which there were likewise groups of patrons but in which the designation "presbyter" did not occur. The fact that the designation is found in Ephesus and in a Roman community under strong Asian influence (that of Hippolytus) may indeed indicate that the term originated in that area and traveled from there. However, I may note two Syrian Christian communities that did not know the institution of presbyters but still knew the phenomenon of a group of patrons functioning as the Asian presbyters did, yet without such a title. As such, the alternative hypothesis that has been canvassed, namely, that the presbyterate originated in Jerusalem and spread out from there, is shown to be even less probable.

Patronal Groups Not Designated as Presbyters

Thus far, in seeking to understand the relationship between elders and *episkopoi*, I have found elders who act *kata polin*, but beyond that, in the church to which 1 Timothy is addressed, I have found a group of persons exercising

207. *Acts Pet.* 3; 4; 6; 13.

patronage and leadership but not exercising a particular ministry *qua* elders. As such, I suggested, they are directly comparable to the elders of the gymnasia and associations. In turn, I suggested that this designation might be something that came about in the Asian churches even though the possibility of a group of patrons in a church might well be a wider social phenomenon. In the following sections, therefore, I illustrate this point from two Syrian church orders, both of which illustrate precisely such a phenomenon: the existence of a patronal group that is not known as "elders."

The Didache

In discussing in chapter 1 the lack of synonymy between *episkopos* and *presbyteros*, I noted that the *Didache*, like Philippians, simply makes no mention of presbyters. In chapter 2 I noted that the *episkopoi* and *diakonoi* whose appointment the *Didache* proposes are patrons of the community, financially underwriting the ministry exercised by prophets and teachers.

In this chapter I have established that the presbyters in some communities were, like the *episkopoi* and *diakonoi* of the *Didache*, patrons. It is in this light that I may return to the question of the absent presbyters of this document.

Jefford notes four possible explanations for the failure to mention presbyters.[208] I do not take them, however, in the order in which he gives them, but rather take Jefford's own proposal first.

Jefford proposes, as a means of breaking what he perceives as a deadlock, that presbyters are not mentioned because presbyters, or persons aspiring to be presbyters, are the audience of the *Didache*. This would explain the failure to mention them, but in order to understand the *Didache* as addressed to this group, it is necessary to see that presbyters might exercise all the functions described in the *Didache*, from which they are receiving direction. That is to say, presbyters should be the primary agents of instruction, of baptism, of eucharist, and of the appointment of officers who would in turn exercise patronage. Jefford attempts to show that they indeed did perform all these functions, but the evidence that he presents for liturgical functions, as for charitable functions, is weak.

To make his argument, Jefford has to take evidence from without the Didachist community. That in itself is a dangerous undertaking. He cites Polycarp's instructions to presbyters as an example of presbyters performing a liturgical

---

208. C. N. Jefford, "Presbyters in the Community of the *Didache*," in *Papers Presented at the Tenth International Conference on Patristic Studies Held in Oxford 1987: Second Century, Tertullian to Nicaea in the West, Clement of Alexandria and Origen, Athanasius*, ed. E. A. Livingstone, StPatr 21 (Louvain: Peeters), 123–26.

and charitable role.[209] Certainly this passage concerns the social duties of *presbyteroi*, but I will argue below that these presbyters are actually *episkopoi*, and the reference to presbyters here is a reference to presbyters *kata polin*. Similarly, the presbyters of *1 Clement* and of the *Shepherd of Hermas*, which Jefford employs as evidence for presbyters performing functions in the community and the liturgical assembly, are, as we have already seen, *presbyteroi kata polin*.[210]

Second, it may be argued that the *presbyteroi* existed in the community but are not mentioned because they do not come within the purview of the work. This is the suggestion of Harnack, who saw presbyters in the *Didache* as those who hold seniority within the community but do not hold office as such.[211] This is a solution that may be rejected rapidly. It may be an adequate explanation of the situation of 1 Timothy, where the presbyters are identified but exercise no ministry as such, but it cannot work for the Didachist community, because those who would be honored would be honored on the basis of patronage, whereas we are already told who the patrons of the Didachist community actually are: the *episkopoi* and *diakonoi*.

Third, we may note the solution based on synonymy suggested by Lightfoot with regard to Philippians: the presbyter is functionally equivalent to the *episkopos* and therefore is included in this designation. Jefford cites various supporters of the consensus on *episkopoi* and *presbyteroi* as adherents of this solution.[212] This would assume a priori that there must have been presbyters in the community; otherwise, there would be no need to explain their absence. However, the Didachist community knew the term "presbyter" but chose on this occasion to use different terms. This is a large and unproveable set of assumptions with no external support, but it lies nonetheless behind the statement of the consensus that we have already seen to be entirely wanting.

Fourth, it is possible that this community simply had no presbyters.[213] This solution would have the virtue of simplicity and poses no problems itself. Jefford rejects it because he would anticipate that the Jewish-Christian *Didache* would be expected to know the (Jewish) institution of presbyters.[214] However, since I have shown that there was no such Jewish institution, these can cease to trouble us. If the designation "presbyters" of those who held seniority and honor within the Christian community is, however, a designation deriving from the Hellenistic

209. Pol. *Phil.* 6:1.
210. Jefford ("Presbyters," 125) points to *1 Clem.* 40 as evidence for presbyters performing liturgical duties, but presbyters are not even mentioned in that chapter.
211. Harnack, *Lehre*, 142–43.
212. Jefford, "Presbyters," 123–24.
213. So Kurt Niederwimmer, *The Didache: A Commentary*, trans. Linda M. Maloney, ed. Harold W. Attridge (Minneapolis: Fortress, 1998), 200.
214. Jefford, "Presbyters," 123.

poleis of Asia, then we may readily see why the *Didache* does not know the term, but rather terms them with the designation of *episkopoi* and *diakonoi*.

A problem may, however, be posed by the plural of *episkopoi*. I suggested above that there was only ever one *episkopos* in a household, but here we seem to meet a plurality; it might be argued that, whatever their title, these are the multiple leaders of the consensus, functionally, at least, presbyters, the term *episkopos* here being a synonym. Thus Kleist opines that the plural means "a bishop and his presbyters."[215] However, alongside the plural nouns there is a plural verb, *cheirotonēsate*, for which an implied addressee must be envisaged; I suggest that the direction, like the other plural directions, such as to baptize (*baptisate* [*Did.* 7:1]) or to be watchful (*grēgoreite* [*Did.* 16:1]), is addressed to the nations,[216] and that it is a general direction aimed not at a single community but rather to a multiplicity of communities. Thus, the deduction that the *monepiskopos* has not yet emerged,[217] if taken to mean a sole bishop in a single household, is meaningless, but if taken to mean an *episkopos* set over a number of communities, is certainly the truth, if not a statement of the obvious, given the absence of presbyters to represent the absent *episkopos*. The direction that the communities addressed by the apostles through the *Didache* should appoint *episkopoi* means that each household should appoint an *episkopos*.

The absence of the title *presbyteroi* from the *Didache*, therefore, strengthens the possibility that the term itself is derived from the civic life of Asia. Moreover, since the *Didache* probably envisages single-household churches, this also implies that the development of congregational presbyters is one that results from the growth of the church beyond a single household and the necessity to take on aspects of associational organization.

The Syrian Didascalia Apostolorum

Here I remain with the church-order literature by investigating the subject of the role of presbyters within *Didascalia apostolorum*.

215. James A. Kleist, *The Didache, the Epistle of Barnabas, the Epistles and the Martyrdom of St. Polycarp, the Fragments of Papias, the Epistle to Diognetus* (Mahwah, NJ: Newman, 1948), 164n91. Similarly Everett Ferguson ("The Ministry of the Word in the First Two Centuries," *ResQ* 1 [1957]: 23, 29n21) opines that the *Didache* assumes the same situation that he had discerned in the New Testament: "a large number of congregations under the supervision of a council of presbyter-bishops."

216. So the proem of the *Didache*. It should go without saying that this is a fictive address; it is not deniable that the *Didache* addresses specific needs within a specific community, but the fictive address is general, and so the instructions are likewise generalized.

217. Niederwimmer, *Didache*, 200.

The classic view of ministry in *Didascalia apostolorum* is put forth by
Achelis: the bishop is a *monepiskopos*, standing at the center of the congregation.[218] However, the bishop of the *Didascalia apostolorum* is the head of a
single congregation rather than of a group of congregations, as he is assumed
to be the normal minister of baptism and has personal responsibility for the
exercise of discipline within the congregation.[219] As such, therefore, he is not
monepiskopos in the sense that the term is used in this book, but simply the
only bishop at the head of the ministry and, as such, nothing remarkable. The
episkopos is assisted by *diakonoi*, particularly in the administration of charity,
as the duties of the *episkopos* are, as already noted, fundamentally economic.

However, whereas there are directions for the appointment of bishops, deacons, and widows, there are none concerning the appointment of presbyters,
and when presbyters appear, they are marginal to the concerns being discussed.
The virtual absence of presbyters from the text, and the corresponding prominence of bishops and deacons, observed first by Nau,[220] have caused great
puzzlement and some suggestions that imply a degree of desperation in the
attempt to explain the phenomenon—for instance, that of Connolly, who
explains the virtual silence concerning presbyters in *Didascalia apostolorum*
by suggesting that they existed but simply had nothing to do.[221] I may suggest,
rather, that when they appear, they are a redactional importation, and that
the community lying behind *Didascalia apostolorum* had originally known
episcopal-diaconal ministry. There may have been patrons, but they were not
designated as presbyters. Thus, when presbyters do appear in the final version of the document, deriving probably from the fourth century, they are a
redactional importation into the text, since the redaction derives from the
time when the threefold order has been established. This may be illustrated
from the book's eleventh chapter. The chapter is addressed to bishops and
deacons and discusses their respective pastoral duties. In particular, it states
that the deacons are to be the bishop's eyes and ears. It goes on to discuss the
resolution of lawsuits and disputes:

218. H. Achelis and J. Flemming, *Die ältesten Quellen des orientalischen Kirchenrechts*, vol.
2, *Die syrische Didaskalia übersetzt und erklärt*, TUGAL 10/2 (Leipzig: Hinrichs, 1904), 269–70.
219. Note, e.g., *Did. ap.* 2.26.4.
220. F. Nau, *La Didascalie, c'est-à-dire l'enseignement catholique des douze Apôtres et des
saints disciples de nôtre Sauveur* (Paris: Lethielleux, 1902), 27.
221. R. Hugh Connolly, *Didascalia apostolorum: The Syriac Version Translated and Accompanied by the Verona Latin Fragments, with an Introduction and Notes* (Oxford: Clarendon,
1929), xxxix–xl. Achelis (Achelis and Flemming, *Quellen*, 272–73) argues along similar lines.
For further literature and some discussion, see Georg Schöllgen, *Die Anfänge der Professionalisierung des Klerus und das kirchliche Amt in der Syrischen Didaskalie*, JAC 26 (Münster:
Aschendorff, 1998), 92–93.

But if they do not know the saying which was spoken by our Lord in the Gospels, when he said: "How many times should I forgive my brother when he offends me?," and grow angry with one another and become enemies, you are to teach them and you are to reprove and make peace between them, since the Lord has said: "Blessed are the peacemakers."

And be aware that it is required of the bishop and presbyters to judge with caution; as our Savior said when we asked him "How many times should I forgive a brother when he wrongs me? As many as seven times?" Our Lord, however, taught us and said to us: "I say to you, not seven times only, but seventy times seven."[222]

There has already been an allusion to this same logion concerning forgiveness, and so the citation is repetitive and otiose here. More to the point, the entire chapter so far has discussed the respective disciplinary functions of bishop and deacons. Suddenly presbyters intrude and deacons disappear when it is stated that the "bishop and presbyters" should judge with caution. This is a clear example of redactional intrusion, bringing with it presbyters who do not belong in the source.

Thus, at the very beginning of this section it is said that the bishop is head of the presbytery,[223] but from then on there is no mention of a presbyter until the ninth chapter, in a list of types, in which the presbyters appear after the deaconess![224] The community that produced the church order on which this section of *Didascalia apostolorum* is based seems indeed to have known no presbyters originally but to have been managed by *episkopoi* and *diakonoi*, and thus the mention of presbyters is at each point awkward. The description of the *episkopos* as head of the presbytery may be explained by suggesting that the introductory section on the episcopate is derived from a source; it is, moreover, possible to identify this source because, as has already been noted, the same source lies patent behind the comparable section of the *Apostolic Church Order*. By contrast to that of *Didascalia apostolorum*, the system of governance in that community was, as has already been seen, fundamentally presbyteral, in that the presbytery formed a group of patrons who appointed one of their number as *episkopos*. Thus *Didascalia apostolorum*, following the source, states that the bishop is the head of the presbytery, following which the presbyters disappear. There is a single point at which a reader appears, and a single point at which a subdeacon appears,[225] and in each instance these ministries appear in the company of presbyters; each is, I may suggest, an

222. *Did. ap.* 2.46.5–6.
223. *Did. ap.* 2.1.1.
224. *Did. ap.* 2.26.7.
225. *Did. ap.* 2.28.5 (reader); 2.34.3 (subdeacon).

interpolation. The passage concerning the subdeacon has long been suspected,[226] and in agreeing with this assessment, I may suggest that the interpolation is more extensive than previously thought. The context in which the reader appears is a free-floating and independent piece of tradition that has been inserted into the text in support of the argument that officers of the congregation had a right to support. Presbyters may have stood originally in this text, but it is not from the main source of *Didascalia apostolorum*. In other words, presbyters were not known in the church that produced the original version of the section of *Didascalia apostolorum* relating the duties of *episkopoi*; rather, that community knew only the ancient episcopal-diaconal system. Presbyters appear largely in material that is extraneous to the main source and occasionally in redactional interventions, but never with any particular centrality, nor with to any great extent in *Didascalia apostolorum* overall.

At this level of redaction, however, *Didascalia apostolorum* does know of a patronal class. In particular, we may examine the chapters regarding widows to note the insistence that charity be channeled through the officers of the congregation, the *episkopos* and his *diakonoi*. Before the main discussion of widows there is a brief direction concerning the giving of suppers to widows,[227] implying that private patronage might take place. When the subject turns to widows, they are directed not to leave their homes and, when they pray for those from whom they had received charity, not to reveal the name of the donor. Whereas this has been read as a means of putting women under male control, the significant issue may be less the control of widows than the control of those offering patronage as rivals to the *episkopos*. Mobile widows are more likely to attract attention, in particular as the source indicates that the reason they leave their homes is to seek patronage, and the revelation of the name of the donor would threaten the bishop's position as agent by giving public recognition to a donor. It is in this context that the prohibition on women teaching is found; again, I may suggest that this is bound up to the control of patronage, as a teacher might in turn attract a patron.

As has already been noted, the eucharist, while no longer a full meal, remains the locus for the collection of goods, though not distribution. "Whenever you receive the oblation of the eucharist, lay down whatever happens to be in your hands so that you may share it with strangers, for it is collected by the bishop for the support of all strangers."[228] However, there is total insistence that the *episkopos* be the agency for such distribution.

226. So Achelis (Achelis and Flemming, *Quellen*, 265).
227. *Did. ap.* 2.28.1.
228. *Did. ap.* 2.36.4.

So you now should hear what was said of old: Put aside portions and tithes and firstfruits for Christ, the high priest, and for his servants, tithes of salvation, for him whose name begins the decade. Listen then, sacred and catholic church, who escaped the ten plagues, and received the ten words, and learned the law and held to the faith, who knows the decade, and has believed in the iota at the beginning of the name, and is established at the last in his glory. There are prayers and petitions and thanksgivings where there were sacrifices, and now are there offerings that are offered through the bishops to the Lord God where there were firstfruits and tithes and portions and gifts. For they are your high priests.[229]

Therefore just as it was not allowed to a stranger, that is to anyone who was not a Levite, to go up to the altar or to make any offering without the high priest, so you likewise should do nothing without the bishop.[230]

The patronal class, as is made clear here, was the lay class. The presbyters did not exist in this community; when they come into existence, however, they are clergy and not patrons. The Ignatian refrain that nothing should be done without the *episkopos* is repeated, as the threat to episcopal power lies precisely in those who might offer an alternative locus of patronage.

Conclusion

At least one church in Ephesus knew the existence of a patronal group within itself and termed these patrons "presbyters." Such a usage seems in time to have come to Syria, was probably known elsewhere in Asia, and certainly was present in Rome, albeit in an Asian émigré community. However, we may wonder whether the congregational presbyters of 1 Timothy and other Asian communities are, as it were, the Neanderthals of church order—a species that did not survive; that would seem to be indicated by the clericalization of the presbyteral order in *Traditio apostolica*. However, it will not be until chapter 5 that this question can be answered, as first I must turn to the question of the emergence of monepiscopacy. In chapter 1 I suggested that monepiscopacy at Rome had resulted from the federation of the individual churches. I also showed that federations existed elsewhere, thus providing the conditions under which the same process might have occurred. I need to ask whether, given the conditions, this process actually occurred.

229. *Did. ap.* 2.26.1–3.
230. *Did. ap.* 2.27.1.

Presbyters and *Episkopoi* in Emerging Christian Communities

In previous chapters I have sketched out the growth of monepiscopacy at Rome and, to a lesser extent, at Ephesus, as well as noting the continued strength of household episcopacy in Syria into the third century. I have also shown that many previously prevailing assumptions are wanting, and that they have skewed reading of the ancient sources. In this chapter, therefore, I reexamine the evidence for the emergence of monepiscopacy in those Christian communities of which we have evidence, aware in particular that the idea of synonymy of *presbyteros* and *episkopos* is difficult, aware that the fundamental duties of the first *episkopoi* were economic, and mindful that the term *presbyteros* may be a term of honor attached to a senior patron in a Christian congregation or may refer to somebody holding representative office in a citywide federation but does not denote somebody holding collective responsibility for ministerial function. The communities are treated in no particular order, though all the communities discussed in the first part of this chapter at some point have been alleged, with a fair degree of unanimity, to have been under presbyteral office. The purpose of this chapter is to examine evidence for monepiscopacy or federation in such communities for which such evidence is available.

The Alexandrian Community

We turn first to Alexandria because it has classically been seen as a city in which presbyteral governance as imagined by the consensus continued into the third century and is apparently well attested. Support for this position is derived from evidence that the presbyterate at Alexandria not only elected the bishop from among their number but apparently ordained him as well, and from evidence that the introduction of the episcopate into the Egyptian *chōra* (countryside) was a relatively late development. Thus, when Ritschl suggests that the ordination of an *episkopos* by presbyters in Alexandria is a mark of the original identity of the two offices,[1] he is expressing a long-held position[2] disputed solely by Baur,[3] who explains the apparent lack of distinction between the orders in Alexandria by suggesting not that the terms are synonymous but that originally there had been no distinct order of presbyter but only, initially, *episkopoi*. We may see Ritschl as defending the consensus from the only serious attempt to dispute it, and doing so by pointing to the apparent role of presbyters at Alexandria. I intend to show that the evidence points neither to synonymy nor to the existence of collegial, presbyteral leadership as a predecessor to monepiscopacy, but that Baur was fundamentally correct, and that the references to presbyters in the early Alexandrian sources are references to those who were, in effect, *episkopoi*.

We have seen that the Alexandrian synagogue had a tight central organization, though it was less clear whether this same organization extended to local synagogues. I may, however, ask whether such an organization casts any light on the organization of Christianity at Alexandria. In my brief examination of the Jewish communities of Rome I observed that their somewhat diffuse nature was mirrored in the diffuse nature of the Christian communities of that city; I may thus inquire whether Alexandria provides the mirror image of Rome with regard to Christian community organization, as it does Jewish. It would, moreover, be reasonable to suggest that the Jewish model of citywide organization was followed by Christians if only because of the persistence of Jewish forms of Christianity; thus, both Clement and Origen have knowledge of the *Gospel of the Hebrews*.[4] Clement, according to Eu-

---

1. Albrecht Ritschl, *Die Entstehung der altkatholischen Kirche: Eine kirchen- und dogmengeschichtliche Monographie*, 2nd ed. (Bonn: Adolph Marcus, 1857), 426, following Baur's observation of the custom of presbyters joining in ordaining another presbyter laid down in the *Statuta ecclesiae antiqua* 52 (which he attributes to the fourth Council of Carthage).

2. I find it expressed in Edward Stillingfleet, *Irenicum: A Weapon-Salve for the Churches Wounds* (London: Henry Mortlock, 1662), 273–75.

3. F. C. Baur, *Das Christenthum und die christliche Kirche*, 2nd ed. (Tübingen: Fues, 1860), 269.

4. The relevant texts demonstrating their knowledge are gathered at A. F. J. Klijn and G. J. Reinink, *Patristic Evidence for Jewish-Christian Sects*, NovTSup 36 (Leiden: Brill, 1973), 110–11, 125–36.

sebius, writes against Judaizing,[5] and Origen knows of Christians who also attend the synagogue.[6] Finally, I may note the name of the second bishop given by Eusebius in his succession list of early Alexandrian bishops, Annianus,[7] whose name is a Hebrew name.[8]

Eusebius traces the origin of the Alexandrian episcopate to Mark, but although the tradition connecting Mark to Alexandria can be traced to the second century,[9] this is hardly reliable. There is, however, perhaps a toehold of history in the name of Annianus given by Eusebius as Mark's successor: "Annianus was the first after Mark the evangelist to succeed to the public office [*leitourgian*] of the diocese [*paroikias*]."[10] It is interesting that Annianus is described as the first to succeed after Mark, and subsequently simply as the first and, in the same context, his successor as second.[11] This implies that the succession list that Eusebius employed was independent of the Mark legend in its origin; it is indeed possible that Mark's name has been inserted by Eusebius into the first report. Moreover, it is noteworthy that nothing is said within the Mark legend of Mark's death, implying a certain uncertainty on Eusebius's part as to how it is that Annanius comes to be bishop.

This succession list is worthy of close attention, particularly since it seems to be a source lying behind Eusebius. Beyond stating that Annianus was the first bishop, it consistently uses the same term for the office of the Alexandrian bishop:

He [Kerdōn] was the third to succeed there after the first [*sic*] president [*proestē*] Annianus.[12]

Primus departed in the twelfth year of his presidency [*prostasias*] and was succeeded by Justus.[13]

After Keladiōn presided [*prostantos*] for fourteen years, Agrippinus received the succession.[14]

5. Eusebius, *Hist. eccl.* 6.13.3.

6. Origen, *Hom. Lev.* 5.8.

7. Eusebius, *Hist. eccl.* 2.24.

8. Roelof van den Broek ("Juden und Christen in Alexandrien," in *Juden und Christen in der Antike*, ed. J. van Amersfoort and J. van Oort, SPA 1 [Kampen: Kok, 1990], 101–15) derives the entire structure of Alexandrian Christianity from its Jewish heritage.

9. B. A. Pearson, "Earliest Christianity in Egypt: Some Observations," in *The Roots of Egyptian Christianity*, ed. B. A. Pearson and J. E. Goehring (Philadelphia: Fortress, 1986), 137–45.

10. Eusebius, *Hist. eccl.* 2.24.

11. Eusebius, *Hist. eccl.* 3.11.14: τῆς κατ' Ἀλεξάνδρειαν παροικίας ὁ πρῶτος Ἀννιανός. διαδέχεται δ' αὐτὸν δεύτερος Ἀβίλιος.

12. Eusebius, *Hist. eccl.* 3.21.

13. Eusebius, *Hist. eccl.* 4.4.

14. Eusebius, *Hist. eccl.* 4.19.

The word consistently employed here may refer to the head of a school, or it may be used of a patron. That it is the latter is indicated by the term *leitourgia*, found in this succession list,[15] an indication that the post is a public office, as in the case of the *Didache*, taken on by a person of means at his own expense.[16] Eusebius surely is employing a source when he refers to the succession of the early Alexandrian bishops, and it seems that despite Eusebius's use of the source, and whatever its provenance, it is more revealing than Eusebius recognizes. It describes a succession of patrons and mentions neither ordination nor *episkopē* until relatively late in the list.[17]

The first evidence of this to note is that of Jerome, who states, "At Alexandria, from Mark the evangelist until Heraklas and Dionysius, the bishops, the presbyters always elected one from themselves, and put him in a higher rank, and named him bishop."[18] There is no doubt that, according to Jerome, there was a bishop in Alexandria, but that this bishop was simply elected and ordained from the number of the presbyters and by the presbyters.

At about the same time, Ambrosiaster states that it had been the custom in Alexandria that if there was no bishop, a new bishop was appointed by a presbyter.[19] In this light we may read the statement of Epiphanius that there is no delay in the appointment of a new bishop in Alexandria,[20] which implies that there is a standing electoral college and field of qualified candidates and also may imply that the presence of bishops from without the city was unnecessary to ordain the bishop's successor.

Next, chronologically, we may observe a tale from the Apothegmata of Poemon the anchorite. Some Arians come to Poemon the anchorite and allege that the archbishop of Alexandria received ordination by presbyters.[21]

Next we may note the evidence of Severus of Antioch, who, in arguing that ancient customs may be overturned, states that the bishop of Alexandria was at one time appointed by presbyters.[22] Although he is a Syrian bishop, writing

15. In Eusebius, *Hist. eccl.* 6.1; 6.11.6; as well as *Hist. eccl.* 2.24, noted above.

16. Noticed also by Attila Jakab, *Ecclesia alexandrina: Évolution sociale et institutionelle du christianisme alexandrin (IIe et IIIe siècles)*, CA 1 (Bern: Peter Lang, 2001), 176–77.

17. Ibid., 177–78.

18. Jerome, *Ep.* 146.1.

19. Ambrosiaster, *Quaest.* 101.5.

20. Epiphanius, *Pan.* 69.11.

21. Poemon, *Apothegmata patrum* 78 (PG 65, 341B). C. H. Turner drew this to scholarly attention in a note appended to E. W. Brooks, "The Ordination of the Early Bishops of Alexandria," *JTS* 2 (1901): 612–13.

22. In a letter cited by Brooks (ibid.) and subsequently published in E. W. Brooks, ed., *The Sixth Book of the Select Letters of Severus, Patriarch of Antioch in the Syriac Version of Athanasius of Nisibis* (London: Williams & Norgate, 1902), 213.

two hundred years after the time he is describing, his statement that the presbyters elected clarifies the other evidence pointing to such a method of election.

Finally, there are two very late witnesses. First, we may note Severus ibn al-Mukaffa, in the tenth century, who writes, "When Abba Theonas went to his rest, the clergy of Alexandria assembled, with the people, and laid their hands on the presbyter Peter, his son and disciple, and seated him upon the episcopal throne of Alexandria, as Theonas, the holy Father, bade them."[23] Once again we see nothing of bishops from outside the city taking part in the ordination, but rather a handlaying and seating by the clergy of the city. Earlier, in his account of the election and appointment of Abilius, he states that the Orthodox people "consulted together and elected him patriarch."[24] To this may be added the (again late) witness of Eutychius:

> The evangelist Mark appointed, with the patriarch Ananias, twelve presbyters to be with the patriarch so that at a vacancy they might choose one out of the twelve on whom they might lay their hands in blessing and make him patriarch. They must then choose some eminent man and make him presbyter, in the room of the new patriarch so that there are still twelve presbyters. This institution for creating a patriarch from out of the twelve presbyters was kept up till the time of Alexander.[25]

Although the number "twelve" has a legendary ring, it does cohere with the directions of *Apostolic Church Order* (*Canones ecclesiastici apostolorum*) that there must be twelve men in a community capable of electing a bishop,[26] as with the concern of the same church order that the new bishop should appoint presbyters. Certainly the number of presbyters in Alexandria would not be large, and if presbyters are so powerful within the city, this explains why Arius, a presbyter, should come to such prominence early in the fourth century.

I may thus suggest that there are at least grounds to see the organization of the Alexandrian church as presbyteral. This is argued, in the strongest terms, by Telfer in particular.[27]

23. Severus ibn al-Mukaffa, *Hist. patr.* 1.6.
24. Severus ibn al-Mukaffa, *Hist. patr.* 1.3.
25. Eutychius, *Ann.* 332.
26. *Can. eccl. ap.* 16. See also *Rec.* 3.66 (Zacchaeus is ordained bishop alongside twelve presbyters and four deacons) and *Rec.* 6.15 (also *Hom.* 11.36) (Maro is ordained bishop alongside twelve presbyters, with deacons, and the order of widows is established). Finally, note that in *Test. Dom.* 34 twelve presbyters are to be seated in front. It is possible that this provision is related to *Apostolic Church Order*, as both make a similar use of Rev. 4 (*Test. Dom.* 40; cf. *Can. eccl. ap.* 19.1).
27. W. Telfer, "Episcopal Succession in Egypt," *JEH* 3 (1952): 1–13. Telfer is interesting because he argues strongly for presbyteral ordination due to ecclesial motivation relating to ecumenical discussions in his own day.

Telfer's arguments are little different from those of his seventeenth- and
nineteenth-century predecessors, though he introduces one novelty. He proposes, on the basis of a tale told by Liberatus, a Carthaginian deacon of the
sixth century, and on the basis of an account of Peter's martyrdom, which
contains an account of the appointment of Achillas, his successor, that the
new bishop was ordained through the laying on of the hand of the deceased
bishop.[28] Liberatus is speaking of an occasion when the succession to Alexandria is disputed, and the two parties each consecrate a bishop, each laying
a hand of the deceased bishop on the head of their candidate, each putting
on an *omophorion* from the prior bishop, and each then being seated on the
throne.[29] This coheres to an extent with the account of the enthronement of
Achillas, for the *omophorion* is likewise transferred from Peter to Achillas
while the body of Peter is seated on the throne.

This report of Liberatus is, however, the only record of a rite involving the
hand of the deceased bishop, and I may suggest that in a turbulent political
situation both parties were attempting to legitimate their own bishop with
reference to the prior patriarch.[30] Nonetheless, the evidence of being seated
on a throne and the transfer of the *omophorion* coheres with that provided
by the account of Peter's martyrdom, as well as with later evidence. The later
rite of ordination for the Alexandrian bishop has the Gospel book being held
over the head of the new bishop at the ordination prayer, and although there
is no certainty regarding the origin of this rite, it may be a relic of ordination by investiture as opposed to the laying on of hands. Thus, although the
report of the burial of Peter of Alexandria and the appointment of Achillas
enshrined in the account of Peter's martyrdom does not speak of laying the
deceased bishop's hand on the head of his successor, in describing the setting
of the body of Peter upon his throne, and the transfer of the *omophorion*
from the body of Peter to Achillas, his successor,[31] it indicates that ordination took place by investiture. It is possible that the rite of the Gospel book
preserves a relic of the time when the ordination of the bishop of Alexandria
was undertaken without the involvement of bishops from outside the city and
is a relic moreover of investiture as a means of making the bishop. This rite
might readily be carried out by presbyters.

28. Ibid., 7–10.

29. Liberatus, *Brev.* 20.

30. Everett Ferguson ("Origen and the Election of Bishops," *CH* 43 [1974]: 32) plausibly
suggests that this gesture is meant as a substitution for the choice of a successor by the outgo-
ing bishop.

31. Note the discussion of this passage by Tim Vivian, *St. Peter of Alexandria: Bishop and
Martyr*, SAC (Philadelphia: Fortress, 1988), 47–49. Vivian, though uncertain of the rite described
by Telfer, accepts that ordination largely consisted of the transfer of the *omophorion*.

All this evidence implies that the presbyters of Alexandria formed an electoral college from whose number the new bishop would be elected, and, moreover, that the electors also ordained the *episkopos* whom they had appointed.[32] Thus, if the presbyters of the Alexandrian church were so remarkably powerful, and given that there is a peculiar organization among the synagogues, it might be suggested that this group of presbyters is rooted in the Jewish origins of Christianity in the city. When Origen states that Heraklas sits in the presbytery of Alexandria,[33] it is easy to see this in terms of the seats of the elders in the Alexandrian synagogue. There is the possibility that Alexandria was of a fundamentally presbyteral orientation, as Telfer alleges.

However, I must pause at this point to observe that there is no early evidence that individually these persons were known as presbyters within their own churches. I must countenance the possibility that their presbyteral title indicated that they were *presbyteroi kata polin*. We do not know this, but it must be recognized as a possibility. The sources, though ancient, are nonetheless considerably later, and it is entirely possible that they might not realize that presbyters, collectively, might individually be *episkopoi*. When they read that "presbyters" had elected and ordained a bishop, they would assume that these were presbyters as they were known in the fourth and fifth centuries, namely, subordinate officers, and would not imagine that there might be a bishop in a single congregation. This is, of necessity, speculative, as we simply do not know what the sources were on which these later commentators based their writings,[34] but nonetheless it is a possible reading of the evidence. It would, moreover, accord with the hypothesis of a Jewish model for the organization of Alexandrian Christianity, for it would imply that federation was in place from a very early stage, and that the references to elders are references to the elders as a collective body gathered from the city. The absence, moreover, of any evidence of individual functionaries designated as presbyters also tends to strengthen this hypothesis. If this is the case, then the names in the succession list of Alexandria probably are references to the elected or otherwise recognized chief among the collected presbyters. Eusebius's succession list is a succession list of these leaders.

32. So, likewise, E. W. Kemp, "Bishops and Presbyters at Alexandria," *JEH* 6 (1955): 138–39. Kemp otherwise is highly critical of Telfer's article, particularly disputing presbyteral ordination of the bishop. Again, however, Kemp was no disinterested historian.

33. Cited by Eusebius, *Hist. eccl.* 6.19.13.

34. Telfer suggests that Jerome is indebted to Origen, but there is no passage of Origen extant that clearly asserts the mode of electing a bishop of Alexandria, as Kemp ("Bishops and Presbyters"), in response to Telfer, points out.

In time, however, one of these presbyters *kata polin*, who may be *episkopoi* in their own churches, becomes properly *monepiskopos*. Again, Eusebius's succession list gives us a clue: Julian is said to be the first to have exercised *episkopē*.[35] As such, we may see a *monepiskopos* arising from the citywide presbytery at about the same time that the same thing occurred at Rome. Of course, nothing is said of the mode of election or of ordination, though we may reasonably assume that the presbyters of the city continued to elect, and I may suggest that the references to presbyters laying on hands in Severus and in Eutychius are a misunderstanding of *cheirotonia*, which may refer to a rite of laying on hands for ordination, but may equally refer simply to election. Indeed, given that the means of ordination probably was by porrection and seating, it is more likely that the sources employed by Severus and Eutychius referred to election and that these later authors believed this to be a reference to ordination by laying on hands. Moreover, the later sources discussed here vary among themselves about the point at which the presbyters cease to ordain their bishop, Jerome stating that this was the case up to the time of "Heraklas and Dionysius," thus being rather vague, whereas Severus of Antioch and Eutychius claim that this continued until the time of Alexander. However, regardless of the mode of appointment, I may suggest that Julian was the first *monepiskopos* on the basis of the source preserved by Eusebius.

Demetrius is more often taken as the first *monepiskopos*, for instance, by Griggs.[36] The basis for such a characterization is Demetrius's treatment of Origen. However, although the dispute with Origen provides clear evidence of Demetrius acting as *monepiskopos*, this does not mean that he was the first.

If Julian is said to have been the first to exercise *episkopē* in an ancient source, I may suggest that he exercised *episkopē* over a number of churches, but not necessarily over all the Christian communities of Alexandria. For although I have suggested that Alexandrian Christians had a tight organization from the beginning, there is nothing to prevent the institution of other schools or households, or indeed of schools within household settings, beyond those already within the federation. The report that Demetrius appointed Origen, and that he subsequently appointed Heraklas to the headship of Origen's catechetical school,[37] may imply that Demetrius was extending the extent of episcopal control within the city to take over all Christian schools and

35. Eusebius, *Hist. eccl.* 5.9.
36. C. Wilfred Griggs, *Early Egyptian Christianity: From Its Origins to 451 CE* (Leiden: Brill, 1990), 61–62.
37. Eusebius, *Hist. eccl.* 6.3.3; 6.3.8.

households, turning Origen's entirely independent establishment into an arm of the centralized Alexandrian church.[38]

There are a number of indications that Origen's school was originally independent of external ecclesial control. First, Origen's course of instruction clearly went far beyond what might normally be understood as catechesis;[39] like Justin and Hippolytus at Rome in the second century, he was a teacher not only of catechumens but also of those who were already Christians, and of those who were not Christians at all.[40] Given the output of Clement of Alexandria, the same would appear to have been true of his teaching,[41] as would that of Pantaenus, who is described by Eusebius at one point as directing the "school of the faithful" and the "school of sacred writings,"[42] both of which titles indicate that the curriculum extended well beyond catechesis. Second, after the death of Leonidas, his father, Origen enjoyed the patronage of an Alexandrian woman in whose house he dwelt, together with Paul, an Antiochene. An account is given of Paul's teaching and of prayer within the house, which indicates that this was some kind of household-school, though, according to Eusebius, Origen would not join in prayer with Paul, on the grounds of Paul's heresy.[43] Thus, further evidence is provided of an independent scholastic household in Alexandria early in the third century. Third, the presence in Alexandria in the second century of Christian teachers who were seen as deviant, notably Basilides and Valentinus, is an indication that there was a diversity of Christian schools in the city.

We cannot know which household-schools within Alexandria were part of the federation and which were independent. Reports that Clement was a presbyter may indicate that his school was one of those within the federation of mutual recognition.[44] This would make sense, as he appears to have been

---

38. So Roelof van den Broek, "The Christian 'School' of Alexandria in the Second and Third Centuries," in *Centres of Learning: Learning and Location in Pre-Modern Europe and the Near East*, ed. Jan Willem Drijvers and Alasdair A. MacDonald, BSIH 61 (Leiden: Brill, 1995), 44–45. Here, however, he overestimates Origen's independence on the basis that Origen's school continues in domestic premises.

39. Eusebius, *Hist. eccl.* 6.8 refers to Origen's instruction of more advanced students.

40. A point observed by Clemens Scholten, "Die alexandrinische Katechetenschule," *JAC* 38 (1995): 19. For Scholten, this is one of the marks of Origen's academy as a philosophical school, since the presence of the uncommitted was one of the marks of the Platonic academies.

41. So John Behr, *The Way to Nicaea* (Crestwood, NY: St Vladimir's Seminary Press, 2001), 163–64.

42. Eusebius, *Hist. eccl.* 5.10.1.

43. Eusebius, *Hist. eccl.* 6.2.13–14.

44. He is described as such by Alexander of Jerusalem, cited by Eusebius, *Hist. eccl.* 6.11.6. Although Neymeyr notes that this holds good only for Palestine, he is persuaded that Clement likewise was a presbyter in Alexandria. Note the extensive and balanced discussion by Ulrich Neymeyr, *Die christlichen Lehrer im zweiten Jahrhundert: Ihre Lehrtätigkeit, ihr Selbstverständnis*

of relatively high social status, and so likely to be accepted within a social circle of patrons, even though he himself was a teacher. His status may be deduced from his name (which is that of the imperial *gens*) and the exalted audience, which may be deduced from the social directives that he gives. The fact that Clement instructs catechumens and the newly baptized, as well as giving advanced instruction,[45] similarly indicates that Clement's school was at the same time a church and was a church allied to the federation of Alexandrian churches under Julian.

It is possible, I may note, that he succeeded Pantaenus by taking over the school on Pantaenus's departure, but it should be made very clear that Origen, even if a pupil of Clement, did not succeed him; his own school was independent of the federation, at least at first.[46] Speculation regarding Pantaenus's departure from Alexandria, or that of Clement, as resulting from the rise of an *episkopos* from among the number of the presbyters, who after all elected, and possibly ordained, the *episkopos*, is fruitless.[47] Both are presbyters, and although there is conflict elsewhere between the *episkopos* and presbyters, because of the organization of the Alexandrian church such a conflict does not arise. There may be tension within the presbytery, and that may be the cause of either Clement's or Pantaenus's departure, but that is a tension between persons of equal standing.

I may thus suggest that the monepiscopate started to form about the time of Julian. It is significant that we may date Clement's activity more or less to that time, as what he tells us of Christian order may well reflect that obtaining at the time in Alexandria. Certainly, as a philosopher, he was not greatly interested in church order, but nonetheless there are two passages that bear upon the issue.

In the first instance we may note *Stromata* 6.13. Clement suggests that those who live in accordance with the commands of God might be considered

---

und ihre Geschichte, VCSup 4 (Leiden: Brill, 1989), 45–95. There is no contradiction between membership of the presbyterate and the activity of teaching, as Clement refers to teaching as a presbyteral duty in *Strom.* 6.106.2.

45. That Clement instructs catechumens and the newly baptized is patiently demonstrated by A. van den Hoek, "The 'Catechetical' School of Early Christian Alexandria and Its Philonic Heritage," *HTR* 90 (1997): 67–71.

46. Van den Broek ("Christian 'School,'" 40–41) denies any succession between the three altogether and further denies that Clement was a presbyter. It seems that there is insufficient subtlety in his position, for he seems unable to perceive of any alternative to either complete independence of the school from the church (which is, as I would agree, the position of Origen at first) and being a completely ecclesial creature. That is to say, an independent institution might be part of a network of mutually recognized schools and churches.

47. A speculation originated by Pierre Nautin, *Lettres et écrivains chrétiens des ii*[e] *et iii*[e] *siècles*, CPPC 2 (Paris: Cerf, 1961), 18, 140, followed by Joseph W. Trigg, *Origen: The Bible and Philosophy in the Third-Century Church*, 2nd ed. (London: SCM, 1985), 131.

presbyters not through ordination but through righteousness. From this one might deduce that he considers the presbyterate the fundamental order of ministry. However, he goes on to say that there are grades within the church of bishop, presbyter, and deacon. Consequently, we may see him recognizing a threefold order. Finally, he states that those who ascend will first minister (*diakonēsein*) and will then be enrolled in the presbyterate (*enkatatagēnai tō presbyteriō*). One might deduce from this that the presbyterate is synonymous with the episcopate, but were that the case, then one needs to explain why he previously distinguished the two offices. Rather, I may use this as evidence, once again, that the presbyterate was a collective term, and it included both presbyters as such and *episkopoi*. There is a degree of terminological overlap, nonetheless, which implies that the monepiscopate is a new development and is not yet fully distinguished from the episcopate that leads to presbyterate *kata polin*. Nonetheless, even this may be overemphasized, for Dionysius of Alexandria, long after monepiscopacy is clearly established, writes regarding presbyters and describes them as his fellow presbyters (*sympresbyteroi*).[48]

The other passage often adduced to argue that the terms were not distinguished is a tale told in Clement, *Quis dives salvetur* 42.[49] This speaks of John appointing bishops in the area around Ephesus. As such, we may assume that these are bishops in single households rather than *monepiskopoi*. On seeing a youth, John entrusts him to the care of a newly appointed *episkopos*. On his return to that town he asks the bishop, addressing him as an *episkopos*, for the deposit that he had entrusted to the bishop's care, the youth. The youth, it transpires, has left and become a robber. John goes out to meet the youth, bringing about his conversion.

Although the bishop is described consistently as such, there is one point at which he is described as a presbyter. Although this has been taken in a technical sense, here it is employed in a nontechnical sense to indicate an older man. The context is after the *episkopos* has agreed to adopt the youth: "the older man [*presbyteros*], taking home the youth [*neaniskon*] who had been entrusted to him." Thus the bishop is being described as "elder" in contrast to the youth of the other man. That this *episkopos* is indeed old is made clear subsequently when, after being asked by John for the deposit (that is to say, the young man), he is described as "the old man" (*ho presbytēs*). He is simply a bishop who happens to be old.[50]

Finally, we should note Clement, *Paedagogus* 3.97.2. Here there is no question of confusion; it is simply said that some instructions are for presbyters,

---

48. Eusebius, *Hist. eccl.* 7.5.6.

49. By, e.g., van den Hoek, "'Catechetical' School," 78–79.

50. It is noteworthy that when John asks to see the youth, asking the bishop for the deposit that was handed over to him, the bishop is confused and thinks that John is talking about money. This thought implies that financial matters might here too be episcopal responsibilities.

some for bishops and deacons. Although there is no confusion, it is interesting that presbyters are mentioned first, an indication that as a council they have a greater seniority than individual officers in individual churches.

The period of Clement is a time of transition from local to urban *episkopē*. Demetrius thus certainly was a *monepiskopos*, but not necessarily the first. It is also possible that it was under Demetrius that the prior federation extended its influence to all the existing schools and households, as well, as I will note below, to a wider area beyond the city. Here we may note Severus's assertion that Demetrius was illiterate.[51] This may be completely ill-informed, but we should beware nonetheless of casting every Alexandrian church into the mold of the school; it is entirely reasonable to suspect that some were simply based on households, but our view is skewed in that nothing is known of the early Alexandrian churches, while we are well aware of the prominent teachers and their activity.

Thus a case may be made that Alexandria is a major center of Christianity in which a presbyteral mode of governance obtained until the third century, and that this mode of governance was derived from a Jewish foundation within Alexandria. Against that, however, is, once again, the possibility that the individual church leaders are known only as presbyters collectively. It is to be noted that I could say nothing about the management of the individual synagogues of Alexandria, and so no model is provided beyond the model of the *politeuma*. Similarly, we do not know whether each household-school in the city was managed by an individual or by a group, but the two of which we do know—that to which Clement succeeded Pantaenus and that which Origen ran independently—were the property of individual teachers and did not exhibit presbyteral governance. The distinction between the household-school of Clement and that of Origen is that Clement's appears to have achieved wider recognition from the Alexandrian church, whereas Origen's, once monepiscopacy is established in the city, looks like an anachronism.

I may conclude that the evidence provided by the Alexandrian church does not bear out the consensus position that presbyters were the primary order in the church, even though the reports of presbyteral appointment of the bishop might at first sight appear to bear this out; rather, it seems that, as at Rome, the monepiscopate grew out of a gathering of individual heads of households and schools collectively known as elders. The difference between Alexandria and Rome is that this seems to begin to take place slightly earlier, a result perhaps of the rather tighter central organization of the church in Alexandria inherited from the Jewish model that was available.

51. Severus ibn al-Mukaffa, *Hist. part.* 1.4.

As to the cause of the growth of monepiscopacy, we can only speculate. It is not impossible that it came about due to the need to more closely define the limits of Christian belief, given the presence in the city of a number of variants of Christian practice; but this would hardly seem to require the establishment of monepiscopacy, given the strength of the gathering of presbyters. Likewise, persecution does not appear to play a role. Demetrius begins to tighten the control of the central federation after a period of persecution, and this may be linked with the perceived need for a more structured central control, but this is the extension of episcopal authority and not the beginning of monepiscopacy.

Christian Leadership in Egypt beyond Alexandria

Whereas I have been able to construct a fairly complete history of office in Alexandria leading up to the establishment of monepiscopacy, the evidence beyond Alexandria is somewhat patchier. Nonetheless, we may be assured that Christianity spread through much of Egypt at a relatively early date, as may be witnessed from the appearance of so many Gospel fragments, both canonical and extracanonical, on papyrus dating from the second and third centuries. Notably, P.Rylands 457, a fragment of the Gospel of John, may be dated not later than the middle of the second century and comes from Middle Egypt. This indicates that Christian literature is circulating here. Much the same may be said of P.Egerton 2; regardless of whether it was authored in Egypt,[52] it is a Christian papyrus of the second century found within Egypt. Finally, I may point to P.Oxy. 654, a further noncanonical Gospel fragment that may be dated to the end of the second century and, from about the same period, P.Oxy. 405, a fragment of Irenaeus *Adversus haereses*. I am not concerned to discuss the "orthodoxy" or otherwise of this Egyptian Christianity[53] but simply wish to observe that Christianity is established in Egypt within the second century. Its roots may well be earlier, given the widespread diffusion of Jews in Egypt, but to make such a claim is to go beyond the evidence.

I would likewise be going beyond the evidence were I to essay a discussion of the organization of Christian groups in Egypt beyond Alexandria. However, there is one incident in the life of Dionysius that has attracted attention and has been employed to suggest that Christianity in Egypt continued presbyteral until a relatively late period (which assumes, of course, that it was ever presbyteral).

52. For a conspectus of opinions, see Griggs, *Early Egyptian Christianity*, 27, and references.
53. For some discussion see Pearson, "Earliest Christianity," 132–34, contra Griggs and also Walter Bauer, *Orthodoxy and Heresy in Earliest Christianity*, trans. Philadelphia Seminar on Christian Origins, ed. Robert A. Kraft and Gerhard Krodel (Philadelphia: Fortress, 1971), 44–53.

This is the occasion when Dionysius goes to Arsinoe after the deposition of the bishop Nepos, who had taught a chiliastic interpretation of the book of Revelation. Dionysius convokes there a gathering of "the presbyters and the teachers who were in the villages of the brothers." The implication that is drawn from this is expressed typically by van den Broek: "In Alexandria, and later on also in the Egyptian *chōra*, lay teachers played an eminent role in the church. There are strong indications that in second-century Alexandrian Christianity the *didaskaloi* and the *presbyteroi* continued the roles of the rabbis and elders of the Jewish community."[54] Similarly, Griggs states of these churches that "no living bishop is mentioned or associated with them."[55]

We may recall that there was at least one Jewish community around Arsinoe that had an active bench of elders,[56] so some influence is not to be ruled out altogether. However, the community has a bishop nonetheless; the reason why no bishop is mentioned here is that he has been deposed, not because a bishop is unnecessary or unknown. We can be even less sure that the *didaskaloi* are Christianized rabbis. Origen mentions Christian teachers in *Contra Celsum*,[57] but these would seem to have more in common with the apostles of early Christianity, as they go from house to house evangelizing.

There are some puzzling references to the activity of early Alexandrian bishops in late sources. Severus speaks of Julian ordaining in secret outside Alexandria (which leads Griggs to suggest that some alternative form of government is being secretly imposed on these churches),[58] and Eutychius states that there were no bishops outside Alexandria before Demetrius, who ordained three.[59] Any discussion of such late sources is inevitably speculative. Griggs reads this as the imposition of monepiscopacy on an Alexandrian model on the Egyptian countryside,[60] which is possible; but it is also possible that rather than episcopacy as such, it is Alexandrian leadership that is being established, along the model of a Roman province. It is also possible that there were indeed *episkopoi*, but that they were ordained by local presbyters, and that this system is being replaced by ordination by the Alexandrian *episkopos*.[61] In fact, there is not the evidence to say precisely what is happening. It may simply be that

54. Van den Broek, "Christian 'School,'" 43.
55. Griggs, *Early Egyptian Christianity*, 91–92.
56. See the discussion of P.Monac. 3.49 in chap. 3 above, under the heading "Presbyters in the Jewish Communities of Alexandria."
57. Origen, *Cels.* 3.9.
58. Griggs, *Early Egyptian Christianity*, 91.
59. Eutychius, *Ann.* 332.
60. Griggs, *Early Egyptian Christianity*, 92.
61. We may note that *Can. Hipp.* 2, which probably is representative of an Egyptian Christian community outside Alexandria (so Heinzgard Brakmann, "Alexandreia und die Kanones des

these rural Egyptian churches were still under the leadership of individual householders. But any reconstruction is speculative. Thus we may take the statement of Athanasius that in the Mareotis there is neither *episkopos* nor *chorepiskopos*, but that each of the largest villages is under the charge of a presbyter, as implying not a persistence of presbyteral governance but rather the triumph of Alexandrian monepiscopacy to the extent that these presbyters are under the direct control of the Alexandrian *episkopos*.[62] We cannot argue back from there to state that presbyters were always in charge of the churches, for even if there were no *episkopoi*, the churches were not under the charge of colleges of *presbyteroi* but under individuals. The designation of these individuals is to an extent irrelevant; there is no evidence for collective leadership in the somewhat confusing accounts of church life in early Egypt beyond Alexandria, even as the Alexandrian accounts point not to governance by presbyters without *episkopoi* but rather to *episkopoi* holding office as presbyters *kata polin*.

Bithynia

In seeking to understand the development of church order in Bithynia, we are dependent on one passage in 1 Peter, until the middle of the second century, when we read of presbyters in federation. The passage in question is this:

> Therefore I exhort the elders among you, a fellow-presbyter [*sympresbyteros*] and a witness of the sufferings of Christ, and a sharer in the glory which is to be revealed: shepherd the flock of God among you, keeping watch over them [*episkopountes*] not as under obligation but willingly, as God would have it, not for sordid gain but eagerly, not lording it over those in your care, but being examples for the flock. And when the chief-shepherd appears you will obtain the unfading crown of glory. Likewise you younger men [*neōteroi*], be subject to those who are older [*hypotagēte presbyterois*].[63]

In chapter 1 I noted that the text was uncertain, and that the participle *episkopountes* is absent from part of the manuscript tradition.[64] The sole point made there was that the text does not necessarily demonstrate synonymy

---

Hippolyt," *JAC* 22 [1979]: 139–49), alters the text of *Traditio apostolica* (requiring episcopal ordination) to make presbyteral ordination a possibility, thus reflecting earlier practice.

62. Athanasius, *Apol. sec.* 85. See Hans Lietzmann, "Zur altchristlichen Verfassungsgeschichte," in *Kleine Schriften I*, ed. Kurt Aland, TUGAL 67 (Berlin: Akademie-Verlag, 1958), 184.

63. 1 Pet. 5:1–4a.

64. As discussed in the conclusion to chap. 1.

between *episkopos* and *presbyteros*, though that is a possible reading. In the light of the discussion of *presbyteroi* above, we may return to the text.

The uncertainty in the text may be interpreted in various ways. Ysebaert takes the omission of the participle as an indication that later scribes were uncertain about the propriety of assigning the verb to a presbyter,[65] and thus that the participle is original and was omitted by later scribes (I may agree with him that, at a later stage, the direction to watch over the flock did not sit well with the term "presbyter," but not with the conclusion that he draws from this, that the terms were used interchangeably in the first century). Nauck suggests that the term is a scribal insertion clarifying that these are the proper duties of *episkopoi* (noting that the participle disrupts the flow of the clause),[66] while Spicq similarly suggests that the participle is an intrusion, noting that the phrase adds no meaning to *poimanate*.[67]

However, Ysebaert points out that there is even more association here between *episkopoi* and presbyters. For when the presbyters are told to shepherd the flock of God that is among them, we may pick up images that had been used of Christ earlier in the letter where the author states, "You have now turned to the shepherd and supervisor [*ton poimena kai episkopon*] of your souls."[68] But all this stops short of stating that the presbyters were known as *episkopoi*; once again we may have reference to the texts cited by Schnackenberg that indicate that a duty of a shepherd was to look out for his flock and ask whether the participle is found here simply because the elders were to look out for the flock like a shepherd would.

If the presbyters are not simply *episkopoi* under another name, then there are two possible interpretations. Either they are, once again, honored older men in the community, or else they are *episkopoi* who are being collectively addressed as *presbyteroi kata polin*. Thus it is not a matter of presbyters being known as *episkopoi*, but rather of *episkopoi*, collectively, being known as *presbyteroi*.

In favor of the second possibility is, first, the manner in which these presbyters are called on to minister.[69] If they are actually *episkopoi*, this would

---

65. Joseph Ysebaert, *Die Amtsterminologie im neuen Testament und in der alten Kirche: Eine lexikographische Untersuchung* (Breda: Eureia, 1994), 67; similarly Rudolf Schnackenberg, "Episkopos und Hirtenamt: Zu Apg 20,28," in *Schriften zum Neuen Testament: Exegese in Fortschritt und Wandel* (Munich: Kösel, 1971), 247–66.

66. W. Nauck, "Probleme des frühchristlichen Amtsverstandnisses (I Ptr 5.35)," *ZNW* 48 (1957): 200–201.

67. Ceslas Spicq, *Les Épitres de Saint Pierre*, SB (Paris: Lecoffre, 1966), 164.

68. 1 Pet. 2:25.

69. The grounds on which Hans von Campenhausen (*Ecclesiastical Authority and Spiritual Power in the Church of the First Three Centuries*, trans. J. A. Baker [London: A&C Black, 1969], 83) rejects the reading of *presbyteroi* here as "older men."

make sense. In addition, we may note the fact that the letter is addressed to a number of communities. This in turn implies some degree of communication between the churches that are to circulate the letter. It may in turn be the case, therefore, that the presbyters addressed in the letter by one who claims to be a fellow presbyter (*sympresbyteros*) are all fellow presbyters; that is to say, the letter is addressed to those who collectively form a presbyterate for the scattered Christian communities of Bithynia. If this is the case, then again we may see that this presbyterate is closely allied to the transmission of a text, namely, 1 Peter itself. If the participle is included, then we might deduce that these leaders were known as *episkopoi* within their own communities, but in any event we may note that the pastoral duties that are set out are those of *episkopoi* and thus read the address to presbyters as *presbyteroi kata polin*. In the middle of the second century the anonymous anti-Montanist, active among the communities addressed by 1 Peter, speaks of the presbyters local to the Ancyrene church where he had refuted Montanism. He refers, using the same language as "Peter," to his fellow presbyter (*sympresbyteros*) Zoticus,[70] who is then said to be an *episkopos*.[71] We may see these presbyters as a group of local *episkopoi*, in federation and gathered, as Roman presbyters had gathered, for the control of the boundaries of Christian expression. Monepiscopacy has not developed, for the individual *episkopoi* are still in charge of their congregations. This may imply that the presbyters addressed in the first century are already forming a federation, and that they are already presbyters *kata polin*. Although this does not prove the point, as it is entirely possible that this is a development that has occurred in the intervening century, we must bear in mind the manner in which the paraenesis indicates that those addressed, the *presbyteroi*, exercise a ministry.

In favor of the first possibility, however, is the subsequent address to younger men (*neōteroi*). We now have a clear idea of the nature of elders in early Christian communities: they were a designated group selected on the basis of age and the ability to offer patronage to the community, along the lines of the same designated group in associations. I have also already argued from the same basis that the *neōteroi*, like the *presbyteroi*, are a defined group within the church. In particular, the *neōteroi* are not ministers;[72] the attempt to see

---

70. Eusebius, *Hist. eccl.* 5.16.5.

71. Eusebius, *Hist. eccl.* 5.16.17. See the treatment of this passage by Lietzmann, "Zur altchristlichen Verfassungsgeschichte," 181. Lietzmann takes this as evidence that the *episkopos* (he assumes a *monepiskopos*) is a member of the presbytery.

72. On such attempts, see Ceslas Spicq, "La place ou le rôle des jeunes dans certaines communautés néotestamentaires," *RB* 76 (1969), 508–27. Notable among these attempts is that of Manuel Guerra Gómez, "Diáconos helénicos y biblicos," *Burgense* 4 (1963): 86–89.

the *neōteroi* as ministerial, in particular to identify them with deacons, is motivated by the prior assumption that the presbyters must be officehold-ers *qua* presbyters. Since there are addresses to *presbyteroi* and *neōteroi*, we would appear to be facing paraenesis aimed at differing groupings within the church. Indeed, it is possible that the material should, as Boismard suggested, be joined to 1 Peter 3:7, a point at which the address to distinct groups is broken off.[73] When paraenesis is addressed to diverse groups within the com-munity, this should include directions to the older men (*presbyteroi*), as it does in Titus 2.[74] The problem that would seem to face us is that presbyters, who elsewhere had an office and not a ministry, are here appearing to minister *qua* elders. Whereas proponents of the older consensus of synonymy would be untroubled by this,[75] it cuts across the very nature of presbyterate that has manifested itself in other Christian communities and, indeed, in associations. If the participle is included, it might be read as implying that these presbyters are exercising their ministry not *qua* presbyter but *qua episkopos*. But that in turn means that the paraenesis has been rewritten, for if we take this as an address to older men, then the implication is that there was no older man who was not also an *episkopos*.

This is effectively what Boismard is arguing, as he suggests that material relating to *presbyteroi* has been brought together at 1 Peter 5:1–5. Moreover, it is not impossible. Nauck analyzes 1 Peter 5:2–3 and demonstrates that there is a great deal of traditional material here, arguing that the passage constitutes an address to those who hold office (an *Amtsverweisung*), which suggests that its roots lie in the Essene directions regarding the *mebaqqer*.[76] That a forming

73. M.-É. Boismard, "Une liturgie baptismale dans la Prima Petri II: Son influence sur l'Épitre de Jacques," *RB* 64 (1957): 177–80.

74. So also J. H. Elliott, "Ministry and Church Order in the NT: A Traditio-Historical Analysis (1 Pt 5,1–5 & plls.)," *CBQ* 32 (1970): 389, with additional argument.

75. So Franz Prast, *Presbyter und Evangelium in nachapostolischer Zeit: Die Abschiedsrede des Paulus in Milet (Apg 20,17–38) im Rahmen der lukanischen Konzeption der Evangeliumsverkün-digung*, FB 29 (Stuttgart: Katholisches Bibelwerk, 1979), 384. Prast argues that ἐπισκοποῦντες is simply a reference to the function of these presbyters rather than to a named office. This would imply that these leaders were known as presbyters in their congregations and exercised ministry as such. Similarly untroubled is Friedrich Schröger, "Die Verfassung der Gemeinde des ersten Petrusbriefes," in *Kirche im Werden: Studien zum Thema Amt und Gemeinde im Neuen Testament*, ed. Josef Hainz (Munich: Schöningh, 1976), 239–52. Schröger writes simply of "presbyteriale Verfassung." His notion is that a charismatic non-office-based church order has been replaced by this presbyteral order. Similarly, we may note Dietrich-Alex Koch, "Die Entwicklung der Ämter in frühchristlichen Gemeinden Kleinasiens," in *Neutestamentliche Ämtermodelle im Kontext*, ed. Thomas Schmeller, Martin Ebner, and Rudolf Hoppe, QD 239 (Freiburg: Herder, 2010), 182–83. Koch suggests that 1 Peter provides evidence of the emergence of presbyteral governance in *Einzelgemeinden*.

76. Nauck, "Probleme," 201–7.

tradition should be enshrined in 1 Peter is not surprising, since a great deal else of the paraenesis of the epistle has been shown to be part of a forming tradition.[77] According to this argument, a paraenesis aimed at older men in the community has been transformed in order to alter the address to those who exercise a ministry, those, in other words, who are not simply *presbyteroi* but *presbyteroi kata polin*. Having altered the paraenesis, the redactor picks up again with the tradition at 1 Peter 5:5; here the *presbyteroi* are indeed honored older men to whom the younger are to be subject, and the term is left intact, having derived from the traditional material that is here being incorporated. This in turn might explain the inclusion of the participle, a use of which the redactor is fond. The participle serves to clarify the fact that this is an address not simply to all presbyters but to those who hold office as *episkopos* in their communities, its apparent intrusion being the result of its introduction into traditional material. These presbyters are instructed to exercise their ministry not with the hope of gaining anything (*aischrokerdōs*), whether financial (through the opportunity to misappropriate funds) or social (the building of a *clientela*), and not as a means to gain social control (*katakyrieuontes*).

Though possible, this interpretation is somewhat complicated and runs into the problem that this traditional material, supposedly addressed to older men, is an address to those who hold office (Nauck's *Amtsverweisung*) and remains so even if the participle is removed. It is particularly notable that this material, in directing that the elders are to be shepherds and in stating that they are to do so without expectation of financial or social advantage, is similar to the directions given to the elders at Miletus by "Paul" in Acts 20, again indicating that traditional material has been incorporated here.[78]

Moreover, a simpler explanation lies at hand. The nature of paraenesis is essentially persuasive; is it therefore possible that the redactor, in addressing the senior men of the community, is encouraging them to take on the ministry of the *episkopos*, a ministry that they are not at present fulfilling. This interpretation would be clearer if the participle is included, but it does not depend on it. In the context of persecution, to which the letter is addressed, there are ample reasons to avoid the episcopate, and thus the writer identifies himself as one who is also a *presbyteros*, and who has witnessed the

77. Demonstrated notably by E. G. Selwyn, *The First Epistle of St. Peter: The Greek Text, with Introduction, Notes and Essays*, 2nd ed. (London: Macmillan, 1947), 365–466.

78. Note Jürgen Roloff, "Themen und Traditionen urchristlicher Amtsträgerparänese," in *Neues Testament und Ethik: Für Rudolf Schnackenberg*, ed. Helmut Merklein (Freiburg: Herder, 1989), 509. Roloff suggests that 1 Pet. 5:2a-4 is taken from an *Ordinationsvermahnung*. He demonstrates (510–19) the network of relationships between this material and, in particular, the similar warning by Paul in Acts 20.

sufferings of Christ, and who is exercising a ministry. Thus, the traditional material identified by Nauck is included as part of the expanded paraenesis, and there is no exchange of meanings between *presbyteros* in 5:1 and 5:5.[79] Rather, a traditional baptismal catechesis has been expanded to fit its epistolary purpose through the inclusion of other traditional material from a different setting.[80] These senior men in the community are being encouraged to minister, and the nature of their ministry is described in a manner that, as Elliott observes, fits the needs of the community for leadership, not the least in being "examples of the humility which was to bond and characterize the whole community."[81]

The advantage of this reading is that it depends neither on redactional reconstruction and the identification of traditions (which are always debatable) nor on an uncertain text. Moreover, it respects the proper nature of paraenesis as persuasive. However, what is decisive for its acceptance is the extent to which such a reading coheres with what is already known of the communities to which this letter is addressed. That is to say, they are divided into classes, among which that of the *presbyteroi* had prominence, but that ministry is not exercised by this group in that capacity.

The date of 1 Peter is uncertain; however, if it were conservatively dated to the last quarter of the first century, then this would take us to about the time of the birth of Marcion in Sinope.[82] Marcion's father is said by Hippolytus to have been an *episkopos*;[83] that Marcion is reported to have been a wealthy shipowner[84] does not stand in tension with this but rather indicates that Marcion's father, as a man of wealth, served as patron and thus as *episkopos*. This proves the existence of an *episkopos* in the area addressed by 1 Peter at about the same time as it is alleged that ministry was solely in the hands of *presbyteroi*.

---

79. An exchange of signification that, as Elliott ("Ministry and Church Order," 371) points out, is awkward, and that, alongside his suggestion that the *neōteroi* are the recently baptized, leads to his conclusion that in both instances presbyters as ministers is meant.

80. Elliott ("Ministry and Church Order") writes of a ministry and church order tradition while identifying the material forming 1 Peter, I believe correctly, as catechetical. But catechesis is not the place for a ministry tradition. The ministerial element must therefore, as I argue here, have been introduced into the catechesis, in a combination of traditional materials.

81. J. H. Elliott, "Elders and Leaders in I Peter and the Early Church," *HvTSt* 64 (2008): 691. Elliott comes close to the understanding proposed here; he is prevented from doing so altogether, however, by his acceptance of the twin hypotheses of synonymy and collective leadership in early Christian communities (685–89).

82. Adolf von Harnack (*Marcion: Das Evangelium vom fremden Gott*, TUGAL 45 [Leipzig: Hinrichs, 1924], 15) suggests 85 CE or later.

83. Hippolytus, quoted in Epiphanius, *Pan.* 42.

84. Tertullian (*Praescr.* 30; *Marc.* 4.4) refers to Marcion's generosity to the Roman Christian community.

From this, and from the report of the anonymous anti-Montanist, may be drawn the conclusion that the developments in this area fit with the overall narrative of a growth of individual Christian households toward federation, a ministry exercised by local *episkopoi* leading to localized federation. Even so, monepiscopacy has not fully come about in the remoter parts of this region even by the fourth century, as two persons from Bithynia, Theophanes and Eulalius, described as *chorepiskopoi*, are present at Nicaea.[85]

Smyrna

In turning to study the development of church order in Smyrna, we find a relative wealth of material; we may take into account Ignatius's letters to the Smrynaean Christians and to Polycarp, and what is said by Polycarp himself in his own letter to the Philippians. In addition, there are other scattered fragments that may have some significance. Here we meet, for the first time in this work, the controversial figure of Ignatius. The issue of Ignatius's date may be put to one side for the present,[86] though the authenticity of the correspondence with Smyrna is necessarily assumed. That it is possible to discuss the nature of the church order of Smyrna without reference to Ignatius's own episcopate, which is yet to be discussed, will transpire in the light of the discussion below.

Just as with Alexandria, so likewise it has been suggested that Smyrna was an entirely presbyteral community at the time of Polycarp. This case is presented definitively by Brent:

> Polycarp shows no understanding of the former's [Ignatius's] central point and its theological justification, that each individual Church must be governed by a single bishop with a council of presbyters and attendant deacons. In Polycarp the three-fold order is not explicit. Polycarp does not use nor claim to be the one *episkopos*, and it seems strange that he should disregard the title that Ignatius clearly gives to him in that sense. There appears to be a college of presbyters, with a number of deacons and an order of widows. . . . The letter begins: "Polycarp and his fellow-presbyters." Though these words seem to indicate Polycarp's de facto pre-eminence, they do not seem to suggest that he held an office distinct from the presbyterate that he could exercise de iure, as Ignatius claims about the bishop's office would require. There is a suggestive parallel here with the pseudonymous writer of 1 Peter v. 1 when he says: "I exhort presbyters amongst you who am your fellow presbyter and witness of the sufferings of Christ." In

---

85. Heinrich Gelzer, Heinrich Hilgenfeld, and Otto Cuntz, *Patrum Nicaenorum nomina Latine, Graece, Coptice, Syriace, Arabice, Armeniace*, BSGRT (Leipzig: Teubner, 1898), lxiv.
86. It is discussed below on pp. 239–40.

the meeting of Ignatius and Polycarp, given the literary integrity of Philippians, there are therefore two distinct, early Christian worlds.[87]

Brent is right that there is a suggestive parallel in 1 Peter 5:1, although this has been disputed.[88] Indeed, I may hypothesize at the outset that precisely the same situation is prevalent in Smyrna as in the Bithynia of 1 Peter; that is to say, there are individual householders and *episkopoi* who, collectively, may be considered presbyters, and the term *sympresbyteros* has the same significance as it does in the writing of the anonymous anti-Montanist.[89] Polycarp's preeminence, as the one writing to Ignatius, and indeed as the one who writes to the Philippians and who visits the Asian communities in Rome,[90] may indicate that he is the acknowledged leader among the presbyters, the one who in time might become the *monepiskopos*, though this has not yet occurred. He is writing, as Clement had done, on behalf of the church and so describes himself as a *sympresbyteros*. His involvement in writing to the Philippians, as to other churches at Ignatius's request,[91] and in traveling to Rome may also indicate that, like Clement, he represents the presbyters of Smyrna in relations with foreign churches, and his role in the transmission of Ignatius's correspondence[92] indicates that the circulation of literature was, as in Rome, a function of the gathering of presbyters and a responsibility of the leader among them. Elsewhere, making the same point about Polycarp's reception of Ignatius, Brent is clear that his vision of a college of presbyters is derived from the consensus of synonymy, suggesting that the same *ordo* known to Polycarp is that of the Pastoral Epistles, and while admitting that *episkopos* is used in those letters, suggesting that the term is used in a collective sense, as well as reading the references to presbyters and *episkopoi* in *1 Clement* as functionally identical.[93]

However, Ignatius addresses Polycarp as an *episkopos*[94] and, Trevett suggests, encourages him to act in a more positive manner as such.[95] If federa-

87. Allen Brent, "The Enigma of Ignatius of Antioch," *JEH* 57 (2006): 433.

88. So J. B. Bauer, *Die Polykarpbriefe*, KAV 5 (Göttingen: Vandenhoeck & Ruprecht, 1995), 33, in response to Bauer (*Orthodoxy and Heresy*, 70), who suggests that "those with him" does not imply equal status, as otherwise one would have to assume the same of the *episkopos* of Philadelphia who is greeted by Ignatius with presbyters and *diakonoi*. This is not the case, as there is made clear that there is a single *episkopos*.

89. Quoted in Eusebius, *Hist. eccl.* 5.16.5.

90. Reported by Irenaeus, as quoted in Eusebius, *Hist. eccl.* 5.24.16–17.

91. In Ign. *Pol.* 8:1 Ignatius requests that Polycarp write to other churches on his behalf.

92. Pol. *Phil.* 13:2.

93. Brent, "Enigma of Ignatius," 433.

94. Ign. *Pol.* preface.

95. Christine Trevett, *A Study of Ignatius of Antioch in Syria and Asia*, SBEC 29 (Lewiston, NY: Edwin Mellen, 1992), 101–2.

tion is a reality at Smyrna, there is no reason why he should not indeed be an *episkopos*, although his *episkopē* is exercised within a single congregation.

Whereas this may readily be seen as an arguable case, there is more evidence that may be brought to support it. Although Polycarp comes to him and is recognized by Ignatius as an *episkopos*,[96] it is clear that other households came to him, as they receive mention by name and greetings.[97] The fact that other families visit him is an indication that there are multiple households in Smyrna and loose central organization. Again this implies that Polycarp may be an *episkopos*, but not that he is the *monepiskopos*. Rather he is simply an *episkopos* among others in the Smyrnaean ecclesiastical community, and it is as a household *episkopos* that he visits Ignatius. Irenaeus, moreover, who was in a position to know, refers to him as an *episkopos*;[98] again the language is vague enough to leave open the possibility that he was an *episkopos* among others in Smyrna.

We may begin therefore to make sense of some of the contradictory evidence. In this instance, we may put aside the possibility that Ignatius is confused, as, being at Smyrna for some time, he would be informed of the situation there.

At first we must be clear that Ignatius's letter to the Smyrnaeans is concerned principally not with church order but rather with the danger presented by docetists. Indeed, what is said of church order follows on closely from statements regarding docetism; therefore, it is worth paying close attention both to the structure and to the substance of what Ignatius states here.

In his letter to the Smyrnaeans, having warned them about the wild beasts (chap. 4), he states that he wishes no congress with the docetists whatsoever (chap. 5). Judgment is indeed prepared for them, just as it is for angels and principalities, if they refuse to recognize the blood of Christ. So he goes on to say,

> Let position [*topos*] puff up nobody, for faith and love are everything, to which nothing is to be preferred. Take note of those whose opinions regarding the good gift of Jesus Christ which has come to us are false, how opposed they are to the mind of God. Love is of no interest to them [*peri agapēs ou melei autois*], nor the widow, nor the orphan, nor the suffering, nor anyone who is in chains or who has been released, nor anyone who is hungry or thirsty. They abstain from the eucharist and prayer, since they do not confess that the eucharist is the flesh of our Savior Jesus Christ.[99]

96. Ign. *Magn.* 15:1.
97. Ign. *Smyrn.* 13:1–2.
98. Irenaeus, *Haer.* 3.3.4.
99. Ign. *Smyrn.* 6:1–7:1.

The first point to note is that some of these heretics are claiming a *topos*; that is to say, they are using ecclesiastical titles for themselves. I may hazard the guess that they claim to have *episkopoi*.[100] This suggestion is made because the point of what follows is that they do not act as *episkopoi* should act; that is to say, they do not convene for meals (they have no concern *peri agapēs*), do not assist widow and orphan, and do not celebrate the eucharist. As such, they are, Ignatius is arguing, vacating any claim to any title. They should, he states, engage in the *agapē*.[101] They should, indeed, be demonstrating the concern for the poor and the weak, which is at the heart of the episcopal ministry and is brought about through convening for meals, whether eucharistic or agapic, at which charity might be shown.[102] In short, they should be exercising an economic and caritative function.

The advice is then given to shun people like this, as to flee division. It is then stated that the Smyrnaeans should follow the *episkopos* and the presbytery, and that they should respect the *diakonoi*, and in particular that nothing be done without the *episkopos*.[103] The eucharist thus should be celebrated only under episcopal oversight, either in person or through a delegate, and likewise baptisms and *agapai* should be held only under episcopal supervision. The rationale is, first, that it is through keeping to the *episkopos*, who is the agent of all true charity, that the people will be kept united in a true (and non-docetic) faith, and, second, that the *episkopos* alone should be the agent of that charity; hence, as I have suggested elsewhere,[104] baptisms and *agapai* are singled out because they are acts by which a patronage relationship might come to be constructed, and the *episkopos*, Ignatius argues, is to be the sole patron (or possibly broker) within the church. It is for the same reason that he forbids the manumission of slaves from corporate funds;[105] those freed through the agency of individual house-churches would have *fides* as clients of those individual churches and their leaders rather than the body corporate of Smyrnaean Christianity.[106] I may at

100. See Paul Trebilco, *The Early Christians in Ephesus: From Paul to Ignatius* (Grand Rapids: Eerdmans, 2007), 643. Trebilco takes this as a reference to presbyters within the ("orthodox") federation under Polycarp.

101. Ign. *Smyrn.* 7:1: συνέφερεν δὲ αὐτοῖς ἀγαπᾶν.

102. So, also reading the references to ἀγάπη here as referring to meals, William R. Schoedel, "Theological Norms and Social Perspectives in Ignatius of Antioch," in *Jewish and Christian Self-Definition*, vol. 1, *The Shaping of Christianity in the Second and Third Centuries*, ed. E. P. Sanders (Philadelphia: Fortress, 1980), 33.

103. Ign. *Smyrn.* 8:1.

104. In my *The Life of Polycarp: An Anonymous Vita from Third-Century Smyrna*, ECS 4 (Sydney: St. Pauls, 2002), 70–71.

105. Ign. *Pol.* 4:3.

106. So J. Albert Harrill, "Ignatius *Ad Polycarp* 4.3 and the Corporate Manumission of Christian Slaves," *JECS* 1 (1993): 136, 140–41.

this point suggest, as a prefatory remark to the treatment of church order in Antioch and in the other Asian communities addressed by Ignatius, that concern for the poor is fundamental to Ignatius's vision of episcopacy, that his opposition to scholastic forms of Christianity is the result of the diversion of patronage toward teachers and away from the poor (and the brokerage of the *episkopos*),[107] and that his concern for the unity of the spiritual and the fleshly[108] is not simply a theological opposition to docetism but a concern that the eucharist continue to be the locus for the feeding of those unable otherwise to find food.

This account may be both compared and contrasted to that of Bauer, who interprets the puffed up *topos*-holder as a "gnostic anti-bishop."[109] The term "gnostic" may be too general, but the point is nonetheless well made that there is an opponent claiming an episcopal title who is docetic in Christology. However, for Bauer, these are the only opponents, whereas, as Trevett points out, it is hardly likely that those who abstain from the eucharist are also celebrating separate *agapai* and baptisms.[110] The identification is unconvincing. However, Trevett's own suggestions that the individual is within the Smyrnaean federation "a presbyter, more dynamic and ambitious than Polycarp himself" or that he may have been a leader in a rival congregation,[111] fail for the same reason that Bauer's suggestion fails: the same people would not both be abstaining from the eucharist and practicing private charity. Rather, the puffed up individual is, as Bauer states, a heretic, but those celebrating without Polycarp's control, the dynamic presbyter(s) identified by Trevett, are within the federation or may even be (congregational) presbyters from within Polycarp's church. Ignatius's point is that docetism is a threat to charity, and this may best be guarded by putting all of this under a tighter episcopal control. It is in this light that we may understand his suggestion to Polycarp that he should vindicate his position.[112] In associational or governmental language, moreover, he is to do this with all diligence (*en pasē epimeleia*), both physical and spiritual.[113] It is thus that he goes on to outline the duties of an *episkopos*, duties that are, as already

---

107. On Ignatius's general conflict with scholastic expressions of Christianity, see Alistair Stewart(-Sykes), "Prophecy and Patronage: The Relationship between Charismatic Functionaries and Household Officers in Early Christianity," in *Trajectories through the New Testament and the Apostolic Fathers*, ed. A. F. Gregory and C. M. Tuckett, NTAF (Oxford: Oxford University Press, 2005), 165–89. On the diversion of patronal resources, see below on Ign. *Magn.* 7:2.

108. So, e.g., Ign. *Magn.* 13:2; Ign. *Eph.* 8:2.

109. Bauer, *Orthodoxy and Heresy*, 69.

110. Trevett, *Study of Ignatius*, 103. However, Schoedel ("Theological Norms," 33), reckoning that Ign. *Smyrn.* 8:1 continues to refer to the docetic opponents, suggests that Ignatius is exaggerating the extent to which the docetists deny sacramentality.

111. Trevett, *Study of Ignatius*, 104.

112. Ign. *Pol.* 1:2.

113. Ign. *Pol.* 1:2.

observed, economic. It is part of Ignatius's anti-docetic vision, however, to see that these economic duties have a spiritual dimension.

It is true to say that there is no monepiscopate at Smyrna, though there would seem to be some degree of federation. Thus, when Ignatius writes of the duties of an *episkopoi*, it is possible that he is simply referring to individual households with their own *episkopoi*, and that all of the Smyrnaean household leaders are *oikonomoi*.[114] However, it is also possible that Ignatius is encouraging the Smyrnaeans to move their federation onward into monepiscopacy, seeing Polycarp as the leader among the *presbyteroi kata polin* as the obvious candidate.[115] The rationale for such a move is that this would strengthen the church against docetism. However, Ignatius is not clear. His language reflects the realities of a single domestic congregation; with a single *episkopos* and gathered presbyters, his vision, as Brent reminds us, is liturgical rather than juridical,[116] and the idea that Ignatius is encouraging Polycarp to become a *monepiskopos* is predicated on the basis that collective leadership is more original than individual (the old consensus), and that reference to a sole bishop must be reference to a *monepiskopos* rather than to a domestic leader.

Clearly, Polycarp is no *monepiskopos*. Thus, the suggestion that an ambassador be sent from Smyrna to Antioch is put to the church (perhaps to the presbyters *kata polin*) and also to Polycarp. However, it is not assumed that Polycarp may simply appoint somebody; rather, he is to call a council to make the election.

Perhaps not long after Ignatius's visit, Polycarp writes to the Philippians. When he does so, he states that presbyters should perform the fundamental episcopal-diaconal duty of caring for the weak; given that these duties are, as I have now argued extensively, properly episcopal, I may suggest that Polycarp is talking of presbyters collectively, *kata polin*.[117] After his martyrdom he is indeed described as *episkopos*,[118] but still we do not know whether this refers to a domestic or a citywide position. We may suspect, however, that it is the former.

Before leaving the subject of the development of monepiscopacy in Smyrna, I should acknowledge that the argument above is entirely predicated on the basis that Smyrna knows the kind of federation that is known elsewhere,

114. Ign. *Pol.* 6:1.
115. Even though, as Trevett puts it, "Ignatius painted a picture of Polycarp as less than top-flight management material" (*Study of Ignatius*, 102).
116. E.g., Allen Brent, "The Ignatian Epistles and the Threefold Ecclesiastical Order," *JRH* 17 (1992): 24.
117. See also the discussion under the heading "Philippi" below.
118. *Mart. Pol.* 16:2. In favor of seeing him as *monepiskopos* is his identification by the Smyrnaeans as the leader of the Christians, though that may simply result from his holding a leading position among the presbyters, as would further be indicated by his responsibility for correspondence with the Philippian churches.

particularly in Ephesus and in Rome. The reason for this supposition is that the language that Polycarp employs of himself in the letter to the Philippians, which is discussed below, makes most sense should he be seen as a presbyter operating on behalf of other presbyters *kata polin*; that his activities beyond Smyrna, in the circulation of literature, the summoning of the council, and in writing to and visiting other churches, are those of the gathered presbyters in Rome; and that, again in the letter to the Philippians, he attributes properly episcopal duties to presbyters, which means that these presbyters must be a federated group. Had we Ignatius's letter alone, we might wonder whether Polycarp's congregation was the sole congregation in Smyrna, because much of the language regarding unity might equally be aimed at a single congregation with an *episkopos* and a group of elders. Ultimately, it is the coherence of Polycarp's language and activity with the system of federation that leads to the suggestion that this is the context of Smyrna. Nonetheless, however much uncertainty continues to surround the subject, I may state two conclusions with confidence.

First, central organization remains weak into the third century, as Noetus is condemned by the presbyters in Smyrna (again, I may suggest, a gathering of *episkopoi* and household heads).[119] Such a loose central organization, with the continued prominence of individual communities, may be the reason why the Hippolytean school in Rome, with its close ties to Smyrna, is so slow to recognize monepiscopacy in that city. By the time of *Vita Polycarpi*, perhaps in the middle of the third century, a monepiscopate is established, as we find the fictive Polycarp elected to that position, and yet, as he goes through the *cursus*, we read that Boukolos the bishop "recognized that he [Polycarp] would be the best of fellow counselors to him in the discussion of the church's matters and a worthy partner in the ministry of teaching."[120] The role and status of presbyters *kata polin* is continued, even though there is a monepiscopate.

The second conclusion, though perhaps obvious, should be stated, given the strength of the consensus: whatever the church order of Smyrna, it was not based on presbyters without any *episkopos*.

Philippi

In the light of the picture that has emerged of a federated group of households (and perhaps schools) in Smyrna, we may examine Polycarp's letter to the Philippians.

119. Hippolytus, *Noet.* preface.
120. *Vit. Pol.* 17.

As we have already seen, Polycarp designates himself a presbyter and addresses himself to *presbyteroi*. This might be taken to indicate governance by a group of presbyters,[121] but at this stage in the argument this conclusion can perhaps be dispensed with speedily. I have already identified the nature of Polycarp's address as that of a presbyter *kata polin*, and I intend to argue that the same identification is that of the addressees.[122] The argument is, however, less straightforward than it might seem at first glance.

The duties of these *presbyteroi* are set out by Polycarp in his letter to the Philippians.[123] These are social duties, consisting of the patronage of the poor. As such, the question is raised as to why presbyters are functioning as *episkopoi*. Various answers are possible.

A first solution might be possible in the claim that the Philippian community has no knowledge of *episkopoi*, and thus that their order is simply presbyteral.[124] This might appear to be a straightforward solution, but three problems beset it.

First, any such claim immediately confronts the problem that already *episkopoi* and *diakonoi* had been found at Philippi. Therefore, account must be taken of what had happened to the *episkopoi* and *diakonoi* of the community in the intervening period. It is insufficient simply to state that some change had taken place[125] without explaining the nature of that change or its rationale. Second, the fact that there are *diakonoi* alongside the presbyters is odd, as *diakonoi* are otherwise found solely in the company of *episkopoi*. Third, this would provide a sole example of the hypothesis of presbyteral office; this in itself is not a fatal objection, but it would seem odd that a term that indicates a rank in any other context should in this one instance indicate an office. Proponents of this solution might take comfort from the fact that the *episkopos* is not named, an indication therefore of the absence of any *episkopos*; rather, I may suggest, this indicates the absence of any *monepiskopos*.[126]

121. As it is most clearly by Patrick Burke, "The Monarchical Episcopate at the End of the First Century," *JES* 7 (1970): 511; Jochen Wagner, *Die Anfänge des Amtes in der Kirche: Presbyter und Episkopen in der frühchristlichen Literatur*, TANZ 53 (Tübingen: Francke, 2011), 273–74.
122. A solution already proposed by F. C. Baur, *Die sogenannten Pastoralbriefe des Apostels Paulus aufs neue kritisch untersucht* (Stuttgart and Tübingen: J. G. Cotta, 1835), 83.
123. Pol. *Phil.* 6:1.
124. Eric G. Jay, "From Presbyter-Bishops to Bishops and Presbyters," *SecCent* 1 (1981): 141–42; James Tunstead Burtchaell, *From Synagogue to Church: Public Services and Offices in the Earliest Christian Communities* (Cambridge: Cambridge University Press, 1992), 307.
125. So Peter Pilhofer, *Philippi*, vol. 1, *Die erste christliche Gemeinde Europas*, WUNT 87 (Tübingen: Mohr Siebeck, 1995), 226–28, followed by Peter Oakes, "Leadership and Suffering in the Letters of Paul and Polycarp to the Philippians" in *Trajectories through the New Testament and the Apostolic Fathers*, ed. A. F. Gregory and C. M. Tuckett, NTAF (Oxford: Oxford University Press, 2005), 359–61.
126. Robert M. Grant (*After the New Testament* [Philadelphia: Fortress, 1967], 53) suggests that the bishop had been Valens (on whom, see below), and so no bishop is named

A second solution might lie in claiming presbyter and *episkopoi* are simply to be taken as synonymous;[127] this is especially attractive in view of Polycarp's words that the presbyters are watching over (*episkeptomenoi*) all those who are sick. Thus one might suggest that the *presbyteroi* of which Polycarp writes were identical to the *episkopoi* (or the *episkopoi* and *diakonoi*) of the Philippian congregations to which Paul wrote; this solution, however, though attractively easy, depends on assuming a synonymy that has been found nowhere else, needs to solve the problems presented by synonymy elsewhere, and raises the question of why the designation of the congregational officers had changed since the first century. The solution adopted below, namely, that the presbyters *are* the *episkopoi*, is of course close to this; however, it results not from a simple equation but rather from a recognition that the words, though not identical in meaning, share the same semantic domain. A similar solution to that of synonymy is proposed by Rohde, who suggests that there are still multiple *episkopoi* within each congregation, so that Polycarp, for whom *episkopos* now means *monepiskopos*, addresses them by the more general title of *presbyteroi*.[128] This assumes that there was ever more than one *episkopos* in any congregation, a state of affairs that I have seen to be impossible. Rohde is right, however, in seeing the title as generic.

For a third solution, it might be argued that Polycarp is presupposing that Smyrnaean church order is to be found in Philippi without knowledge of their organization, and that, like Smyrna, there are simply *presbyteroi* and *diakonoi*. If it is the case that Polycarp has no knowledge of Philippi, then it might explain the identical language employed; however, the point has already been made that there is no evidence of presbyteral governance in Smyrna. Since Polycarp is acquainted with Paul's letter to the Philippians, we must wonder how he understood the *episkopoi* and *diakonoi* of that letter's opening address, had he no knowledge of *episkopoi*.

As a fourth solution, we may note the suggestion of Lietzmann that *presbyteroi* have taken over the role of the *episkopoi*.[129] This is predicated on the

because Valens had been separated. Why, therefore, we might ask, has no replacement been appointed?

127. So Lukas Bormann, *Philippi: Stadt und Christengemeinde zur Zeit des Paulus*, NovTSup 78 (Leiden: Brill, 1995), 210–12. Also close to this position is J. A. Fischer, *Die apostolischen Väter*, SU 1 (Darmstadt: Wissenschaftliche Buchgesellschaft, 1958), 241. Campenhausen (*Ecclesiastical Authority*, 119n304) also suggests that there are multiple *episkopoi*, and thus that Polycarp, who sees episcopate solely in monarchical terms, perceives them as presbyters.

128. Joachim Rohde, *Urchristliche und frühkatholische Ämter: Eine Untersuchung zur frühchristlichen Amtsentwicklung im Neuen Testament und bei den apostolischen Vätern*, ThA 33 (Berlin: Evangelische Verlagsanstalt, 1976), 144.

129. Lietzmann, "Zur altchristlichen Verfassungsgeschichte," 170.

basis of his theory that there was a combination of presbyteral and episcopal church order. I return to this theory overall below, though I may note here that it is not without its difficulties, as its premise is that Christian communities deriving from Jewish communities were always under presbyteral leadership following the model of the synagogue, a premise that has been found to be without foundation. Moreover, if such a combination of orders had taken place at Philippi, it leaves open the question of what had happened to the *episkopoi*, given that, according to Lietzmann's theory, one would expect presbyters to be added to the orders of *episkopos* and *diakonos* and not to replace one of them. Beyond that, once again, this solution stumbles on the difficulty that we have yet to find a Christian community headed solely by presbyters without any officer.

For a fifth solution, it might be argued that the *presbyteroi* here are simply older men. Support for such an argument may be found in the fact that the prior instruction is addressed to *neōteroi*.[130] According to this solution, the situation would be much as it is in 1 Peter: the older men of the community are being encouraged to act as *episkopoi*. The problem with this solution is that in the address to *neōteroi* the young are told to be subject to the presbyters and the deacons (*tois presbyterois kai diakonois*) as to God and Christ. That the *diakonoi* here are found alongside the presbyters implies that the presbyters are, like the *diakonoi*, officeholders. The rather Ignatian language points, moreover, to the *episkopos* rather than the Ignatian presbyters. Moreover, the paraenesis of the sixth chapter of Polycarp's letter does not seem to be encouraging presbyters to become *episkopoi* but rather to direct the nature of their duties.

This leaves the sixth solution to the puzzle: the presbyters are presbyters *kata polin* addressed from one who is likewise a presbyter *kata polin*. On this hypothesis, there is no difficulty in reading the text. The writer knows that these presbyters are, in their own congregations, *episkopoi*, but he is addressing himself to the Christians of the town, not to one congregation among them. This solution obviates the problem of the existence of *diakonoi* alongside the presbyters, explains why no *episkopos* is mentioned (there is no single *episkopos*), and explains why the presbyters are said to be watching over (*episkeptomenoi*) and exercising the functions that are otherwise known to be episcopal, apart from being in complete conformity with the situation known elsewhere.

It might be objected, however, that the term *episkopos* is not employed, and so its importation remains illegitimate. One argument, however, may be

---

130. Pol. *Phil.* 5:3. However, no commentator appears to be worried about this threat to the ministerial nature of the *presbyteroi*.

adduced to support the continuance of the title from the time of Paul into the second century: the statement that a particular evil (the statement refers back to the sentence that precedes it, which states that the love of money leads to idolatry, with the result that it is unclear which evil is intended) is not found among the Philippians "in quibus laboravit beatus Paulus, qui estis in principio epistulae eius."[131] Commentators have struggled to make sense of this statement, suggesting that a word such as "laudati" has fallen out before or after "estis."[132] However, the phrase makes sense on its own: Paul labored among them, who are (namely, who are to be found, the original Greek being *tynchanete*) at the beginning of his letter. At the beginning of Paul's letter are the *episkopoi* and *diakonoi*, those who form the gathered elders whom Polycarp is addressing, those for whom love of money (*avaritia*) is a particular issue in view of their patronal and economic duties.

The one thing that militates against this solution is the address to *neōteroi*. However, the continued existence of a *taxis* of *neōteroi* is not inconsistent with the *presbyteroi* under changed conditions. I may suggest that the rank of *presbyteroi* was always made up of those capable of providing patronage, of acting as *episkopoi*, whereas the younger men may be recognized as their own *taxis* on the basis of age alone. As the focus shifts from the household to the city and the number of congregations grows, so all those in a position to offer patronage take leadership of churches rather than being found within a single congregation.

I may test this hypothesis, moreover, by examining what is said of Valens, formerly a presbyter among the Philippians. Valens had not understood, Polycarp says, the position that he held within the Philippian church but had failed in some way connected with the love of money.[133] Whereas there have been attempts to connect this failing with some form of heresy,[134] Maier points out that the social setting, by which presbyters act as patrons of the church, provides a ready context for understanding the nature of Valens's sin: his misuse of money in some way connects to the fact that he himself is a wealthy householder acting as patron to the church. Maier's own suggestion is that Valens has maintained his prosperity through continued involvement in pagan society.[135] This may be so, or it may simply mean that Valens had failed to show

131. Pol. *Phil.* 11:3.
132. See Bauer, *Polykarpbriefe*, 66, and references.
133. Pol. *Phil.* 11:1.
134. E.g., P. N. Harrison, *Polycarp's Two Epistles to the Philippians* (Cambridge: Cambridge University Press, 1936), 166–67.
135. Harry O. Maier, "Purity and Danger in Polycarp's Epistle to the Philippians: The Sin of Valens in Social Perspective," *JECS* 1 (1993): 238.

proper generosity, or even that he had embezzled money held in common on behalf of the Christian community; we need not come to any conclusion on this particular matter to see that Maier's characterization of Valens as presbyter is entirely in conformity with a wider pattern both in the church and in contemporary society. As to the nature of Valens's office, however, I may suggest that his duties were as already set out, and that part of his sin was a failure to show proper charity. He is described as "one who was formerly a presbyter among you" (*qui presbyter factus est aliquando apud vos*), but if the term is understood as pointing, once again, to a presbyter *kata polin*, nothing here prevents his being a localized *episkopos*, a role that put him in a position to commit financial wrongdoing. Hence, the statement that he was "among you" (*apud vos*) may be understood as indicating that he was one presbyter among a gathered number, and the nature of his disconnection from the Philippian presbyters simply as a withdrawal of recognition of his household with his consequent removal from reckoning among the presbyters of the city.

I argue, therefore, for federation at Philippi on the basis that this is the best understanding of the words addressed by Polycarp to the situation, on the grounds of internal coherence and on the grounds that it conforms to church organization known elsewhere. Although this stops short of absolute proof, it is the solution with the least to be said against it. In time, monepiscopacy emerges from this federation, as it did elsewhere,[136] but it had not emerged at the time at which Polycarp wrote.

Presbyteral Church Order in Jerusalem?

Just as Alexandria has been seen as preserving a presbyteral, as opposed to monepiscopal, form of church order, so Jerusalem has been seen as the original locus of presbyteral leadership, the origin of such a "Jewish" form of organization;[137] in the light of the argument above, this clearly needs to be revisited. However, in attempting to explore the early history of Christian leadership in Jerusalem, we are faced once again by the problem of Acts as a

---

136. The date of this emergence is not certain. Roderic L. Mullen (*The Expansion of Christianity: A Gazetteer of Its First Three Centuries*, VCSup 69 [Leiden: Brill, 2004], 164) notes an inscription referring to a "new presbyter of the catholic church" at Philippi (*RIChrM* 233) that may date from the third century. That a presbyter would be thus appointed tends to indicate that he is a presbyter subject to a *monepiskopos*, but this, as well as the date, is uncertain. Otherwise, we can only refer to the presence of a bishop from Philippi at Serdica in 343. Pilhofer (*Philippi*, 226–27) denies that the later *episkopoi* have anything to do with the *episkopoi* of the first century. It is hard to see why an evolutionary line should not be drawn.

137. So, e.g., beyond references below, Karl Kertelge, *Gemeinde und Amt im neuen Testament* (Munich: Kösel, 1972), 98–103.

historical source. There is no question that the narrative is overlaid by Luke's own controlling hand, but likewise he certainly has employed sources, and such sources, on occasion, stand out strongly from the surrounding narrative. It will emerge in the discussion that the significant points derive from the apparent use of a source.

Beyond Acts, there is the evidence provided by a succession list preserved by Eusebius. Eusebius states that bishops of the circumcision gave way to Gentile bishops and provides us with two succession lists, the first of which is without chronology and is claimed as the succession of Jewish bishops, the second a succession of Gentile bishops.[138] These lists, each of fifteen, are, as O'Connor points out, simply "too neat to be historical."[139] Recent discussions agree that the arrangement of the lists in chronological order is secondary. According to Lederman, the first list consists of Christian leaders in Jerusalem from the time of Trajan,[140] whereas Bauckham argues that it demonstrates the existence of a Christian sanhedrin alongside James, suggesting that it records a sanhedrin of twelve together with James and his two successors.[141] In no event is this a succession list, but rather a group of names of early Christian leaders in Jerusalem arranged in order to construct a succession; indeed, Bauckham suggests that Eusebius has turned an ancient list of Jewish Christian leaders into a succession list in order to present a parallel with his succession list of fifteen Gentile bishops in Jerusalem, a means of effectively denying the continued existence or influence of Jewish Christians.[142]

As I begin my reconstruction based on these sources, I may note the apparent confusion of language in the book of Acts as first we hear of apostles, then of the twelve at 6:2, and then suddenly, at 11:30, we are told that the Antiochene church sends a gift to the elders at the hands of Barnabas and Saul. Subsequently, we hear of the apostles and elders several times in chapter 15, and finally of the elders along with James in 21:18.

I intend to argue that the elders are the household leaders of Jerusalem churches, distinct from the group of apostles. The argument may be presented

---

138. Eusebius, *Hist. eccl.* 4.5; 5.12.

139. Jerome Murphy-O'Connor, "The Cenacle: Topographical Setting for Acts 2:44–45," in *The Book of Acts in Its Palestinian Setting*, ed. Richard J. Bauckham, BAFS 4 (Grand Rapids: Eerdmans, 1995), 310.

140. So Y. Lederman, "Les évêques juifs de Jérusalem," *RB* 104 (1997): 211–22. Lederman's hypothesis is proposed on the basis of coded references to Christian leaders at *b. Sanh.* 43a.

141. Richard J. Bauckham, *Jude and the Relatives of Jesus in the Early Church* (Edinburgh: T&T Clark, 1990), 70–79.

142. Ibid., 71–72. Arnold Ehrhardt (*The Apostolic Succession in the First Two Centuries of the Church* [London: Lutterworth, 1953], 39–40) suggests that something of this sort had been undertaken by Narcissus, the last name to appear on the list.

fairly simply. In the first instance, I may suggest that there was more than one Christian gathering in Jerusalem. The narrative of Acts indicates this in speaking of breaking bread "by household" (*kat' oikon*)[143] and in referring to Peter's going to a different house when he leaves prison from that to which reference is made in the opening chapters,[144] the upper room where the disciples are gathered. Second, I may suggest that these individual houses were not under the direct leadership of apostles either collectively or individually, but under the leadership of individual householders, as elsewhere. Although there is no independent proof for this premise, it is entirely reasonable, as it would be unusual, to say the least, if there was any other arrangement. Whereas Karrer objects that we do not know of household churches in Jerusalem and, on these grounds, rejects any identification of the Jerusalem (or any other) elders with householders,[145] the very mention of breaking bread *kat' oikon*, alongside the references to different households, suggests that there were indeed multiple household churches within the city.[146]

This therefore means that there are two groups: the apostles and the household leaders. We have seen household leaders designated as presbyters elsewhere, and therefore I suggest that the same is true here: the presbyters are the household leaders, here comprising a group distinct from the apostles. The chief difficulty with this interpretation is that it assumes Acts at this point to be a historically reliable source. However, this is not problematic in its own right, as I suggest that what is preserved at these points is the source employed by Luke rather than any redactional material of his own construction. The terminology may conceivably be Luke's, as the situation of presbyters as a collective term reflects the manner in which I argued above that the term was employed at Acts 20, but the presence of the apostles alongside the elders would seem to indicate that Luke is not simply projecting his own church order back on to Jerusalem, and the fact that the elders of Jerusalem are invested with no theological weight, as are the apostles and the presbyters of Ephesus,[147] would indicate that they are not a Lukan creation.[148]

---

143. Acts 2:46; 5:42.

144. Acts 12:17.

145. Martin Karrer, "Das urchristliche Ältestenamt," *NovT* 32 (1990): 157.

146. For an extensive discussion of Luke's references to households in Jerusalem with an attempt to distinguish sources from Lukan redaction, see Roger W. Gehring, *House Church and Mission: The Importance of Household Structures in Early Christianity* (Peabody, MA: Hendrickson, 2004), 62–79; followed by Wagner, *Anfänge*, 40–41.

147. So Prast, *Presbyter und Evangelium*, 356–57.

148. Hans Conzelmann (*Acts of the Apostles: A Commentary on the Acts of the Apostles*, trans. James Limburg, A. Thomas Kraabel, and Donald H. Juel, ed. Eldon Jay Epp with Christopher R. Matthews [Hermeneia; Philadelphia: Fortress, 1987], 91), on Acts 11:30, similarly

I may distinguish this explanation from those previously offered.

First, I may note the suggestion of Karrer that the Jerusalem presbyters are an eschatologically representative group.[149] This hypothesis is derived from the LXX of Isaiah 24:23, which sees the elders of Jerusalem beholding the reign of God in Jerusalem. There are grounds, albeit insufficient, to see the twelve as continuing to maintain a representative eschatological role, and were the twelve and the elders to be identified, then this text might be brought into play, but on its own this is scarcely sufficient.

Second, I may abruptly dismiss the suggestion that this is a self-conscious act of organization by the Jerusalem Christian community to model itself on the synagogue,[150] simply on the grounds, argued above, that such synagogal elders did not exist, in Jerusalem or anywhere else.

Third, I may note the suggestion of Campbell that the elders are those chosen by the apostles to supplement the group of twelve apostles as the number of apostles is reduced. This is an ancient view, for Lightfoot had likewise held that the elders replace the apostles as the twelve die or depart.[151] I may also note Barlea's attempt to characterize Jerusalem Christianity as a form of Jewish Christianity mirroring the synagogue, which develops as James, with the elders, takes over from Peter among the apostles.[152] However, this assumes not only that the apostles indeed departed, which is questionable in view of their function in representing an eschatological Israel,[153] but also, moreover, that there is a degree of identity of function at least between the apostles and the elders. Thus, at Acts 11:30 Campbell is forced to suggest that the elders *are* the apostles under another name (since the presence of apostles is very much still in evidence), and that the offering would not be placed into the hands of any subordinate group.[154] It might not be placed into the hands of a subordinate group, and the term "presbyters" certainly does not carry any note of subordination, but it might be placed into a leadership group that simply was not the apostles, namely, the elders.

---

suggests that the mention of elders is derived from a source, due to the unannounced manner of their appearance.

149. Karrer, "Das urchristliche Ältestenamt," 167–68.

150. So, e.g., Campenhausen, *Ecclesiastical Authority*, 77.

151. The view is also maintained by Benjamin L. Merkle, *The Elder and Overseer: One Office in the Early Church*, SBL (Frankfurt: Peter Lang, 2003), 124.

152. Octavian Barlea, *Die Weihe der Bischöfe, Presbyter und Diakone in vornicänischer Zeit*, APT 3 (Munich: Societas Academica Dacoromana, 1969), 47–62. Here he sees two movements: the replacement of apostles by elders and the replacement of Peter by James as the "Coryphaeus" of the group. The view of Gehring (*House Church*, 96–105) is similar.

153. So R. Alastair Campbell, "The Elders of the Jerusalem Church," *JTS* 44 (1993): 512.

154. Ibid., 524.

There is a great deal in Campbell's argument with which I may readily agree, and much has been adopted from him in the argument presented, in particular his suggestion that Jerusalem Christianity consisted of a series of domestically based Christian gatherings and his further suggestion that the leaders of these gatherings were drawn from the households themselves. Thus far, I accept that Campbell gives a coherent picture of Jerusalem Christianity.[155] However, he goes on to argue that the elders are those who replace the apostles in a group of twelve as individual apostles die or depart. The elders are, more or less, the apostles themselves. Bauckham's view is quite close; he suggests that as apostles died or departed, a new body, the elders, was constituted out of the remaining apostles and other leaders; in other words, the group was reconstituted when their numbers had become rather less than twelve.[156] Bauckham assumes that the apostles were irreplaceable, whereas Campbell suggests that the contrary was the case, but in either event we have to ask whether the group of apostles, whether a self-replenishing group or a replacement group, was the only group of leaders.

The only corroborating evidence for this view is the succession list, and this is evidence only if it is interpreted as being a list of James, his two successors, and twelve coworkers with James, as Bauckham reads it. Bauckham depends on the use of six of the names in an apocryphal and pseudonymous letter of James to Quadratus the apologist, in a context that implies that the six are contemporaries.[157] However, even if they are contemporaries, they need not be contemporaries of James, as the setting in the apocryphal letter is secondary. Nodet and Taylor note that thirteen of the fifteen names appear dated in the Armenian version, all beginning in 107.[158] This may imply that there was a leader with a group of twelve, as Bauckham suggests, but that this "sanhedrin" existed not under James but under Justus, early in the second century.

The reason for Campbell's insistence that the group was self-replicating is the importance of the number "twelve." Certainly, I may admit that this number was significant, and it is indeed possible that a group of twelve continued in Jerusalem (though there is no evidence beyond the succession list),

155. Gehring (*House Church*, 100–105) likewise accepts the main substance of Campbell's argument.

156. Richard J. Bauckham, "James and the Jerusalem Church," in Bauckham, *Book of Acts*, 437–41.

157. So Roelof van den Broek, "Der *Brief des Jakobus an Quadratus* und das Problem der judenchristlichen Bischöfe von Jerusalem (Eusebius *HE* IV, 5,1–3)," in *Text and Testimony: Essays on New Testament and Apocryphal Literature in Honour of A. F. J. Klijn*, ed. T. Baarda et al. (Kampen: Kok, 1988), 56–65.

158. Étienne Nodet and Justin Taylor, *The Origins of Christianity: An Exploration* (Collegeville, MN: Liturgical Press, 1998), 252.

but there is no reason why the term "elders" should be restricted to those men who supplemented the apostles in order to sustain that number. Campbell constantly reminds us that "elders" were not officers, and that the term constitutes a vague designation, but here he is treating the elders as a defined group and thus as holding something close to office. The same applies to Bauckham's reconstruction; once again, the elders appear to be exercising some form of oversight, whereas elders, we have seen, when seen across a city as they are here, exercise collective oversight in distinct areas, but they do so not by virtue of their office as elders but by virtue of their office in individual Christian communities, "elders" here being a collective term. Thus they would constitute a group, but they would not relate to another group in terms of being replacements or supplements to that group.

If we allow that, as elsewhere, the elders are representatives and household leaders, and that the term is collective, we may explain each appearance of the term. First, they receive the gift, as it is a gift not for the apostles but rather for Christians throughout Judea; therefore, we may see that Christian leaders from a wider area, collectively designated *presbyteroi*, receive the gift.[159] Then we find them gathered with the apostles at the council of Jerusalem because they join the apostles at points at which decision is needed, particularly when determining what the limits of Christianity might be, much as do the other gathered elders in federation. Thus, the letter from the council is sent from "the apostles and the elders, your brothers" (*hoi apostoloi kai hoi presbyteroi adelphoi*).[160] Unless the *kai* is read epexegetically, to do which there is no obvious reason, then this seems to denote two distinct groups of people. This letter has particular value, we may note, because of the possibility that it reflects the incorporation into Luke's account of a source, preserving the original wording of the Jerusalem Christians' self-designation.[161] Finally, the *presbyteroi* gather with James to receive Paul, again because they are receiving a gift. As such, we may see this group of *presbyteroi* functioning much as we have seen gathered *presbyteroi* elsewhere, namely, as a group of gathered household leaders. This explanation has the particular merit that it explains the phenomenon of the Jerusalem *presbyteroi* in a manner coherent with other evidence of the use of the term and sees the Jerusalem church gathered in a manner similar to that found elsewhere. It also takes account of the mention of houses within Luke's descriptions of Christianity within Jerusalem; this

---

159. So, already, Richard Rothe, *Die Anfänge der christlichen Kirche und ihrer Verfassung: Ein geschichtlicher Versuch* (Wittenberg: Zimmermann, 1837), 186–87.

160. Acts 15:23.

161. For assessment of this as evidence, note Bauckham, "James and the Jerusalem Church," 438n73.

is a critical point in Campbell's reconstruction, as he notes the description of breaking bread *kat' oikon*, suggesting on this basis that in Jerusalem, as elsewhere, Christianity is domestically based.[162]

Thus, the elders are not a group that takes over from the apostles, nor a group (whether consisting of twelve or of any other number) by supplementation of the original apostles, but rather a group distinct from the apostles that coexists with them. Neither Bauckham nor Campbell seems to anticipate the view presented here. Bauckham, it is true, rejects the idea that there would be two groups of twelve, one denoted as apostles, the other as elders, but this would indeed be a highly unlikely scenario. It does reveal, however, the extent to which the number "twelve" has dominated thinking about the Jerusalem leadership, since both Campbell and Bauckham's reconstructions are fundamentally motivated by the idea of retaining this number. There are points in favor of such an understanding, among which we should note the symbolic value of the number as representing an eschatological Israel and the provision found elsewhere for twelve presbyters to hold office alongside an *episkopos* or, in *Apostolic Church Order*, to provide the quorum for the election of an *episkopos*[163] (although I may note that this is not a fixed number in *Apostolic Church Order* but a minimum). The succession list, however, is less compelling evidence, in particular because we do not know precisely what kind of group this is. It could be the members of the community centered on James, rather than any form of "sanhedrin." Moreover, other questions are raised if the fixing of the number as twelve is accepted. In particular, we might ask how those making up the twelve are selected from among the potential candidates, who are, presumably, the household leaders. We hear nothing of this; indeed, it is significant that after the martyrdom of James we hear nothing of anyone taking his place. Fixation on the twelve, I may suggest, is a psychological leftover from the idea that leadership must be collective, and collective in each congregation, and, moreover, that this is a particular organizational aspect of Jewish Christianity. Bauckham is forced to find a point at which the supplementation of the twelve ceases, and he fixes on 66 CE, a date that cuts across the evidence of the Armenian version of the succession list and is hard to square with Eusebius's version of the succession, which continues until the foundation of Aelia. I may suggest that the fixation of a number of twelve for the combined group is unnecessary speculation, and that it is more probable that the twelve did not form a distinctly functioning group after the very

162. R. Alastair Campbell, *The Elders: Seniority within Earliest Christianity*, SNTW (Edinburgh: T&T Clark, 1994), 151–53.

163. So also van den Broek, "*Brief des Jakobus*," 64–65.

early period. It is indeed noteworthy that the twelve named as such appear in Luke's narrative only once, at Acts 6:2, and then disappear from the narrative.

There is no doubt that the twelve had an eschatologically representative role in the ministry of Jesus; the question is when they ceased to play that role. Roloff suggests that the failure to maintain the number is indicative of a paradigm shift by which the purpose of the apostolic group moved away from immediate expectation with an emphasis on the gathering of Israel for salvation toward a matter of seeing the apostles as the legitimate successors of Jesus with a consequent intention to evangelize.[164] This is perhaps reading too much into too little evidence, in particular because of evidence that will be presented below to the effect that James at least continued to look for an eschatological formation of a renewed Israel; it is, nonetheless, perhaps true to say that the Jerusalem church became concerned with legitimating the mission that inevitably had started, and hence Peter and John go to Samaria, and Barnabas goes to Antioch. It is likewise true to say, with Roloff, that the tight definition of an apostle in Jerusalem, namely, one of the original group, is to be contrasted with the looser use of the term elsewhere to indicate someone sent from a congregation.[165]

The reconstruction offered here—the elders of Acts are, like the elders elsewhere, gathered domestic church leaders—faces a main objection: the absence of any reference to elders in Paul's report of his visit to Jerusalem at Galatians 2:1–10.[166] Such an absence might imply that the elders in Jerusalem are a Lukan creation, since it is only in Acts that they appear. However, without embarking on a full discussion of the relationship of this account to the chronology of Acts, I may note that this is a private meeting, as Paul states in Galatians 2:2, and might therefore not necessitate a wider involvement of Christian leaders in Jerusalem. The request that Paul remember the poor in Galatians 2:10 might well imply that this is a meeting between Essene leaders,[167] alongside Peter.

Gehring, while acknowledging value in Campbell's work, likewise criticizes one aspect of the argument, namely, that the household leaders, the "presbyters," were known as *episkopos* or *mebaqqer* within their own communities. Although clear that there were no synagogal elders, he nonetheless

164. Jürgen Roloff, *Die Kirche im Neuen Testament*, GNT 10 (Göttingen: Vandenhoeck & Ruprecht, 1993), 77.

165. Ibid.

166. Observed by Koch, "Entwicklung," 168–70.

167. I argue below that there was a Christianized Essene community in Jerusalem of which Barnabas was part and that there were close links between this community and the church of Antioch.

suggests that the office of elder must have come about within early Christianity, suggesting that it is an inner-Christian development. The basis of this suggestion is, first, that James is not a householder, and therefore the link between house ownership and leadership in the Jerusalem church is less clear than in the Pauline mission, and, second, that the term *episkopos/ mebaqqer* does not appear anywhere in Luke's discussion of the household leaders, but solely the plural *presbyteroi*.[168] With regard to the first argument, I may preempt at this point the argument that follows with regard to James: although he was not a householder, he was indeed a *mebaqqer*, though distinct because *mebaqqer* of an Essene community within Jerusalem. With regard to the second argument, I may refer, again, to the argument in chapter 1, in which I suggested that *presbyteroi* is a collective term and the members of this group might well be *episkopoi* within their own individual communities.

However, if the reconstruction offered here is accepted, two particular groups of questions remain: one regarding the role of James and one regarding the role and status of the seven. Both sets of questions are, however, peculiar to Jerusalem.

Was James *monepiskopos* of Jerusalem or a domestic *episkopos*? And how does he come to prominence in the community, given that at the beginning of Acts the spokesperson is Peter? What is his relationship with the elders? Later writings make him the *monepiskopos* of Jerusalem,[169] and although, obviously, these are not to be taken at face value, we may ask whether there is any basis for the growth of this tradition.[170] Bauckham is right when he states that the greatest weakness in Campbell's explanation is that no proper account is taken of the role of James.[171] Campbell sees James effectively succeeding to the role of Jesus vis-à-vis the twelve. However, James does not appear in the narrative at the beginning of Acts, whereas Peter is prominent at the beginning but seems to be supplanted by James. If James is the successor of Jesus, one would expect him to succeed at the beginning.

What was the role of the seven? Were they assistants to the apostles, or were they likewise household leaders? Traditionally, they are taken as the foundation

---

168. Gehring, *House Church*, 103–5.

169. E.g., Hegesippus, quoted in Eusebius, *Hist. eccl.* 2.23.4; Clement, quoted in Eusebius, *Hist. eccl.* 2.1.2–5; Eusebius, *Hist. eccl.* 7.19.1; Epiphanius, *Pan.* 29.3.8.

170. Compare the rhetorical and argumentative rejection of any claim to Jacobean *episkopē* or any basis for the tradition by Hans von Campenhausen, "Die Nachfolge des Jakobus," in *Aus der Frühzeit des Christentums: Studien zur Kirchengeschichte des ersten und zweiten Jahrhunderts* (Tübingen: Mohr Siebeck, 1963), 135–51.

171. Bauckham, "James and the Jerusalem Church," 431–32.

of the diaconate, but if that is the case, we would expect them to be *diakonoi* of an *episkopos*, whereas it is unclear who the *episkopos* is.[172]

In tackling the issue of James's role, I may note first that there is no link here between house ownership and leadership. The house in Jerusalem in which we find the apostles staying at the time of Jesus's arrest and death, as at Pentecost, if not in the intervening period, certainly is not owned by the apostles, or by James, or by Jesus's family. It is set in what was in the first century one of the wealthiest quarters of Jerusalem[173] and so is hardly likely to be owned by a peasant family from Galilee. Whether other elders within Jerusalem derived leadership from house ownership is less certain, though this is probable, but the point is made that there is a peculiarity about the Jerusalem leadership simply by virtue of the privileged position of the apostles and of Jesus's family. Thus, whereas it is often suggested that James had leadership of the elders comparable to that exercised by Peter among the apostles,[174] an explanation that has the virtue of explaining the shift of emphasis from Peter to James, as the presbyters become more numerous even as the circle of apostles shrinks, it is strange that the group of householders might be led by one who is unlikely to be a householder. There is the additional issue that James appears alongside Peter and John, apostles, as a group identified as the "pillars" in Galatians 2:9; if James is solely leader of the elders, and not related to the group of apostles, it is strange that here he should be gathered with two apostles.

In answering this question, I may suggest that this house, not owned by the apostles but occupied by them, was the property of an Essene sympathizer, and that the apostles formed an Essene community within it. To secure this point, I offer three arguments: first, Jesus had contacts with Essene networks; second, the manner in which the community in Jerusalem is described in Acts fits with descriptions of the Essene manner of life; and third, this is consistent

---

172. Guerra Gómez ("Diáconos," 89–98) takes them as assistants to the apostles collectively. However, his reconstruction is complex, not the least because he hypothesizes a group of Hebrew assistants besides, whom he identifies with the *neōteroi* who bury the body of Ananias (Acts 5:6). This in turn derives from his conviction that *neōteroi* represent an office, which in turn derives from the conviction that *presbyteroi* necessarily connotes an office, an office to which the *neōteroi* must in some sense correspond.

173. Murphy-O'Connor, "Cenacle," 318–21.

174. Thus Leonhard Goppelt, "Kirchenleitung in der palästinischen Urkirche und bei Paulus," in *Reformatio und Confessio: Festschrift für D. Wilhelm Maurer zum 65. Geburtstag am 7. Mai 1965*, ed. Friedrich Wilhelm Kantzenbach and Gerhard Müller (Berlin: Lutherisches Verlagshaus, 1965), 1–3; Martin Hengel, "Jakobus der Herrenbruder: Der erste 'Papst,'" in *Glaube und Eschatologie: Festschrift für Werner Georg Kümmel zum 80. Geburtstag*, ed. Erich Grässer and Otto Merk (Tübingen: Mohr Siebeck, 1985), 100–101; Rohde, *Urchristliche und frühkatholische Ämter*, 70.

with the collections for the "poor" solicited by Paul. In the first two instances I am dependent on the work of Capper.[175]

Capper argues that Bethany, near Jerusalem, was an Essene foundation. He points to the manner in which the Essenes established houses for the care of the poor, to which witness is borne not only in the *Damascus Document* but also by Philo and Josephus, and so points out that at Bethany we find the house of Simon the leper, and that Lazarus is found mortally ill in Bethany. He suggests, moreover, that the name "Bethany" simply means "house of the poor" (*bet 'any'a*). On this basis he goes on to suggest that the anointing at Bethany described at John 12:1–8 was an action taken by a patron of the Essenes, proclaiming him as the Messiah. The manner in which Jesus goes on into the city implies that there is a connection with the city, perhaps linked with the Essene connection, and that the upper room belongs to an Essene sympathizer within Jerusalem. Capper suggests that this might link with an ascetic quarter of Jerusalem, and that Jesus, having moved from an Essene house at Bethany, goes on to an Essene sympathizer within the city to keep the Passover.[176] Such a sympathizer, with a house in what has already been seen to be a wealthy area of Jerusalem, may indeed be a patron of the Essene movement, and of Jesus and his group. It is entirely coherent to see a temple-attending Essene group resident in the area around the location proposed for the upper room, adjacent to the gate of the Essenes, so able to worship in enhanced ritual purity through ready access to the temple.[177] The close location of the upper room to this Essene gate is not of itself sufficient grounds to identify

175. Capper is cited below, but I may note Capper's dependence, in turn, on the work of Bargil Pixner (note particularly the essays in his *Wege des Messias und Stätten der Urkirche: Jesus und das Judenchristentum im Licht neuer archäologischer Erkenntnisse*, ed. Rainer Riesner, SBAZ 2 [Giessen: Brunnen, 1991]) and of Rainer Riesner, *Essener und Urgemeinde in Jerusalem: Neue Funde und Quellen*, SBAZ 6 (Giessen: Brunnen, 1998). Detailed aspects of their arguments are disputed by Richard J. Bauckham ("The Early Jerusalem Church, Qumran and the Essenes," in *The Dead Sea Scrolls as Background to Postbiblical Judaism and Early Christianity: Papers from an International Conference at St. Andrews in 2001*, ed. James R. Davila, STDJ 46 [Leiden: Brill, 2003], 66–72), though he nonetheless considers as probable the overall case that there was an Essene settlement in the area of Jerusalem where the house at which the Last Supper took place is located.

176. Brian Capper, "'With the Oldest Monks . . .': Light from Essene History on the Career of the Beloved Disciple?" *JTS* 49 (1998): 1–55; idem, "The New Covenant in Southern Palestine at the Arrest of Jesus," in Davila, *Dead Sea Scrolls*, 90–116.

177. The question of Essene attitudes toward sacrifice and the temple is complex and is complicated due to the variant readings of Josephus, *A.J.* 18.19. A complete discussion of this issue would be disproportionate here; for a review of the issue, see Todd S. Beall, *Josephus' Description of the Essenes Illustrated by the Dead Sea Scrolls*, SNTSMS 58 (Cambridge: Cambridge University Press, 1988), 115–19. The report in the *Ascents of James* that James opposed the temple cult and the sacrificial system is found after the destruction of the temple, as is Ebionite polemicization against the temple.

the householder as an Essene or an Essene sympathizer, but the general weight of evidence in favor of the development of Jesus's ministry within an Essene context combined with the evidence of Acts relating to property sharing is sufficient to make this a likely hypothesis.

The second point, that a community of goods was practiced among the early Christians in Jerusalem, indicates the possibility that this group of Christians was based on an Essene foundation.[178] Similarly, Weinfeld lists a number of parallels between practices of the Qumran Essenes and early Christianity.[179] Some are not specific to Jerusalem Christianity, such as the practice of admission procedures, and some are not specific to these two groups but are common to many associations, such as the veneration of founders and the practice of a common ritual meal. Some, however, seem to point to a close relationship, as do the number of significant parallels. Thus, both practice property sharing,[180] both have a council of twelve, both have a *mebaqqer*, both use lot casting as a means of selecting. In view of the manner in which so many parallels go beyond Essene practice and Christianity, Weinfeld is loath to speak of the mutual influence of the sects, but I may suggest that there is a particular relationship between Jerusalem Christianity and Essenism, and that the basis for this relationship lay in the foundation of the group of apostles within an Essene setting. It is this circle that practices a complete community of goods, as opposed to the more common practice of contributing to charity.[181]

It is in the light of this evidence that we are to understand the nature of the collection undertaken by Paul. The collection is, as he states in Romans 15:26, for the "poor among the saints"—that is, for those among the Jerusalem Christians who might be identified as poor, namely, those who were supported by the Essene community at the heart of the city's Christian presence.[182]

178. Thus note Brian Capper, "The Palestinian Cultural Context of Earliest Christian Community of Goods," in Bauckham, *Book of Acts*, 323–56.

179. Moshe Weinfeld, *The Organizational Pattern and the Penal Code of the Qumran Sect: A Comparison with Guilds and Religious Associations of the Hellenistic-Roman Period*, NTOA 2 (Göttingen: Vandenhoeck & Ruprecht, 1986), 48–50.

180. Thus, compare 1QS VI, 24–25 and CD-A XIV, 12–17 to the story of Ananias and Sapphira (Acts 5:1–11).

181. Justin Taylor ("The Community of Goods among the First Christians and among the Essenes," in *Historical Perspectives: From the Hasmoneans to Bar Kokhba in Light of the Dead Sea Scrolls; Proceedings of the Fourth International Symposium of the Orion Center for the Study of the Dead Sea Scrolls and Associated Literature, 27–31 January, 1999*, ed. David Goodblatt, Avital Pinnick, and Daniel R. Schwartz, STDJ 37 [Leiden: Brill, 2001], 147–61) points out that the summaries in Acts give witness to the Essene practice of complete community and also indications of the practice of charity. This may be explicable through positing the existence of multiple Christian communities within Jerusalem.

182. For problems in understanding the nature of the collection otherwise, see Merrill P. Miller, "Antioch, Paul, and Jerusalem: Diaspora Myths of Origins in the Homeland," in *Redescribing*

Thus, at the center of Jerusalem Christianity is a small, Essene-type group, resident in a house belonging to an Essene sympathizer and patron. There is, however, a particular difficulty standing in the way of seeing the group of apostles as an Essene community: at least one of these apostles, Peter, is married, as Paul states that his wife traveled with him.[183] It is this fact, however, that enables me to construct a hypothesis that explains the manner in which James comes to prominence, and in turn to continue to understand the Jerusalem *presbyteroi* in line with Campbell's broad explanation as corrected above.

I may surmise that whereas the group of apostles comes to Jerusalem and is housed by an Essene sympathizer, it is not an Essene group as such. Indeed, it is unlikely that this group of disciples had any internal organization, in particular because there could have been no long-term expectation at the very beginning that the group would continue except under Jesus; the group had come to Jerusalem for Passover, had experienced the death and vindication of their leader, and had undergone a transforming spiritual experience. It is only in the light of what has happened that the group remains in Jerusalem. Because it remains, it needs to structure itself, especially as it then becomes the center of a wider movement across the city. It is this, I suggest, that leads to the sudden prominence of James in the group: the group structures itself along Essene lines. James, having joined the group of disciples, and as the group forms itself into an Essene celibate male community, is then elected as *mebaqqer* of the group, a position for which Peter would not qualify by virtue of his married status. James, however, would qualify, at least on the basis of the manner in which he is described by Hegesippus.[184] It is this Essene community that practices community of goods and, like the Essene community known from 1QS, determines decisions in council.[185] Whereas Peter retains status by virtue of having been a member of the original twelve and is an apostle, he is no longer part of this household. It is quite possible that this occurred several years into the existence of the Christian group in Jerusalem, as Peter is prominent in Paul's first visit to Jerusalem after his departure and conversion.[186]

Christian Origins, ed. Ron Cameron and Merrill P. Miller, SBLSymS 28 (Atlanta: Society of Biblical Literature, 2004), 219–25.

183. 1 Cor. 9:5. Here it is also stated that other apostles had wives, though it is not clear that members of the original twelve are intended.

184. Hegesippus, quoted in Eusebius, *Hist. eccl.* 2.23.5. Here James is described in terms of a Greco-Roman ascetic, but underneath this gloss we may discern an Essene lifestyle. For instance, the statement that James did not anoint himself may be compared to the Essene avoidance of oil reported by Josephus, *B.J.* 2.123.

185. 1QS VI–VII.

186. Gal. 1:19.

If James is *mebaqqer*, we may see how it is that the view of James as *episkopos* would subsequently emerge, given the close similarity that has already been discerned between the *mebaqqer* of Essene communities and Christian *episkopoi*.[187] If he is *mebaqqer* of this community, moreover, we may see how James may be the "leader" of Jerusalem Christians without any appointment by Jesus, or by the apostles (both of which means of appointment are found in ancient sources),[188] or by the majority of Jerusalem Christians.

If the role of James derived from this Essene root, moreover, we may account for the manner in which Peter moves sideways in the accounts in Acts. Generally, there has been an attempt to see Peter as the initial leader, and James taking his place. Bauckham subsequently suggests that James comes to prominence as Peter and John are no longer in Jerusalem;[189] Hengel similarly suggests that James, as leader of the elders (a group that Hengel does not define), takes over from the apostles, who have left Jerusalem due to the persecution under Herod Agrippa.[190] But in each instance we have to ask why Peter and John are mentioned in Galatians 2:9, when they are present in Jerusalem, with James at the head. The same is true of Luke's account of the "apostolic council": Peter has a prominent role in proceedings, but James is in charge; even if the historicity of this gathering is denied, as it is by Campenhausen, in order to deny the fact that Peter ever returned to Jerusalem and thus to explain the prominence of James by way of Peter's absence,[191] the order of the "apparent pillars" in Galatians still needs to be explained. Stauffer does so by reading Acts 12:17 as Peter's designation of James as his replacement,[192] but there is nothing whatsoever in the text to suggest such a reading. I therefore suggest that the apostles are no longer part of the gathering in the original house, in particular that Peter was not, but that their occupation was only temporary; thus, when Peter goes to prison, on his escape he goes to a different house than that in which James is resident.[193] In time Peter does become, as Bauckham suggests, a traveling missionary;[194] although this is not the reason for his effective

187. Beyond the discussion in chap. 2 above, under the heading "The *Episkopos* as *Mebaqqer*," note also the suggestion of Campbell (*Elders*, 157–58) that the use of the term in Jerusalem Christianity was the means by which the term *episkopos* came to be used.
188. The appointment of James is said to have been by Peter, James, and John (Clement, quoted in Eusebius, *Hist. eccl.* 2.1.3), by the apostles (Eusebius, *Hist. eccl.* 2.23.1), and by Jesus and the apostles (Eusebius, *Hist. eccl.* 7.19.1).
189. Bauckham, "James and the Jerusalem Church," 435–37.
190. Hengel, "Jakobus," 100–101.
191. Campenhausen, "Nachfolge des Jakobus," 139.
192. Ethelbert Stauffer, "Zum Kalifat des Jacobus," *ZRGG* 4 (1952): 202.
193. Similarly, Paul, on his visit to Jerusalem described at Acts 21, does not stay with James.
194. Bauckham, "James and the Jerusalem Church," 441–42.

detachment from the group around James, it is evidence in itself that such a detachment has occurred. Thus, I suggest that Peter was never the leader of the Jerusalem church as such, but was leader of the original apostles, the position in which he appears in Acts.[195]

This apparent replacement of Peter by James is sometimes linked to the apparent replacement of the twelve by the elders.[196] Thus, I have noted that, for Bauckham, the elders are a replacement group for the twelve, a substitution that he links to the persecution under Herod Agrippa, suggesting that this reduction in the twelve was the means by which, in Luke's narrative, the elders replace the apostles.[197] This may or may not be an explanation of Luke's narrative superior to that of Campbell, who argues that there is a shift of emphasis from the apostolate from Jerusalem to the apostolate of Paul.[198] In either event, however, this is an explanation of Luke's narrative, which should not be confused with historical reconstruction on the basis of Luke's sources.

However, if Peter was not leader of the Jerusalem Christians, and James was the de facto leader, this does not mean that we should characterize James's leadership in the later terminology of episcopacy. A further reason for the later perception of James as *monepiskopos* of Jerusalem is the manner in which he is found with the elders.[199] I may suggest, however, that this comes about because he is occupying the house that is at the center of Jerusalem, a location the memory of which is treasured and remembered by Christians in Jerusalem.[200] Moreover, as Painter points out, both Eusebius and the *Pseudo-Clementine* literature (which identifies James as a *monepiskopos* and more) are less than clear about the manner in which the succession to James is carried out;[201] however, if he were a *monepiskopos*, we would anticipate a clear and immediate succession and an election on an agreed basis.[202] This is wanting in

195. So, likewise, John Painter, "Who Was James? Footprints as a Means of Identification," in *The Brother of Jesus: James the Just and His Mission*, ed. Bruce Chilton and Jacob Neusner (Louisville: Westminster John Knox, 2001), 10–65.

196. So, notably, Barlea, *Weihe*, 47–62.

197. Bauckham, "James and the Jerusalem Church," 433–38.

198. Campbell, "Elders of the Jerusalem Church," 520–27.

199. Thus, Roloff (*Kirche*, 81–82), while not actually claiming James as *monepiskopos*, sees the elders along synagogal lines (as so often before, particularly by Stauffer, "Kalifat," 204) and suggests that James's position among them might indicate an appearance of monepiscopacy to a later commentator such as Eusebius (*Hist. eccl.* 7.19.1).

200. See Alistair Stewart(-Sykes), "*Catecheses mystagogicae 5* and the *Birkath haMazon*: A Study in Development," *Aug* 45 (2005): 309–49, and references.

201. Painter, "Who Was James?," 42–43.

202. Thus, Ernst Dassmann ("Zur Entstehung des Monepiskopats," *JAC* 17 [1974]: 81–82), while seeing James as a *monepiskopos*, also sees him as an exception, appointed due to his relationship to Jesus.

the sources; indeed, in one of Eusebius's accounts there is a gap of about eight years between the death of James and the election of Symeon as his successor.[203] James is leader of the Jerusalem Christians by virtue of his position and his personal authority; he is *episkopos/mebaqqer* of a central community and may even have prominence among the household leaders (the elders) by virtue of that role, but he is not *episkopos* of Jerusalem in the later sense of that word.[204]

I may now turn to the relationship of the seven to the elders, having secured the identity of the apostolic group as distinct from the wider net of elders and as distinct from the group around James. I may begin by noting that all of them are from Hellenophone communities within Jerusalem. As such, it would be unlikely that they of themselves constitute the group of elders, as it is improbable that the whole extent of household leadership in the city is Hellenophone. It is, however, possible that they might be numbered among the elders without actually constituting their number.[205] Although they are portrayed as assisting the apostles, and as assistants are less likely to be termed "elders,"[206] this may represent Luke's understanding of the situation rather than the reality.

The issue that leads to their appointment is a complaint by Hellenist widows regarding food distribution.[207] I may illuminate that setting by referring, once again, to the Essene parallels in the construction of the Christianity of Jerusalem, namely, by suggesting that the widows are being fed at the common meal. Finger attempts to argue here that the widows were not recipients of charity,[208] but this argument is unnecessary because, as she herself argues, there is no real distinction between charity and commensality in early Christian practice.[209] Nonetheless, it is possible to pick up another of Finger's suggestions, that the widows themselves were engaged in the common meal

203. As Painter ("Who Was James?," 59) points out, Eusebius, *Hist. eccl.* 3.11.1, states that Symeon was elected after the siege of Jerusalem whereas James was martyred in 62.

204. So seeking a mediating position between Painter ("Who Was James?"), who describes James as leader (passim) and states (45) that we should not altogether rule out the term *episkopos* on the basis of the existence of the Qumran *mebaqqer*, and Robert E. van Voorst (*The Ascents of James: History and Theology of a Jewish-Christian Community*, SBLDS 112 [Atlanta: Scholars Press, 1989], 172), who denies any form of episcopate or leadership to James whatsoever.

205. So Raymond E. Brown, "*EPISKOPĒ* and *EPISKOPOS*: The New Testament Evidence," *TS* 41 (1980): 325–28; Campbell, "Elders of the Jerusalem Church," 514 (though with less certainty).

206. Campbell, "Elders of the Jerusalem Church," 514.

207. Acts 6:1.

208. Reta Halteman Finger, *Of Widows and Meals: Communal Meals in the Book of Acts* (Grand Rapids: Eerdmans, 2007), 80–98.

209. We may be clear, however, that this charity at tables is distinct from synagogal charitable systems of carrying food to the poor, as Nikolaus Walter ("Apostelgeschichte 6,1 und die Anfänge der Urgemeinde in Jerusalem," *NTS* 29 [1983]: 370–93) hypothesizes is the case in Jerusalem, and which he sees as the setting for this dispute.

through preparing and serving food;[210] in this event, however, in what way are they being overlooked?

To canvass yet another suggestion, on the assumption that the common meal in question is an Essene common meal funded through the common fund, which is in turn funded by donations and by daily wages paid in, I might suggest that the *diakonia* of the tables to which the twelve refer need not refer to their waiting on tables, cooking, or serving food, but actually to the means by which the funds were raised, namely, the day laboring. Whereas the statement of the twelve that they will abandon this *diakonia* would not seem to support such an understanding, as it is unlikely that there would be sufficient surplus production in this community to support additional nonproductive persons, it is possible to understand the statement in this way if the twelve are stating that they are ceasing to be permanently resident in Jerusalem in order to become *Wanderprediger* (traveling missionaries), and that, as a result, replacements are needed to ensure that the meal is liturgized.

The actual situation seems irrecoverable in detail. However, statements such as that of Sim, that Luke's account regarding "the mere distribution of food" hides more significant theological agenda,[211] underestimate the importance of food as a means of generating fellowship, as a boundary marker, and indeed as central to the ritual practice of early Christians.

Finger suggests that the issue is the allocation of widows to tables, given that multiple common meals are taking place, and that in this sense the Hellenist widows are being overlooked; that is, they are not being allocated places at table. This certainly is possible, especially since, if this is the problem, then the appointment of seven to have the responsibility of allocating people to tables would indeed be the solution, and the appointment of Hellenophone Jews, moreover, would respond to the issue being raised by Hellenophone widows. If she is correct in this identification of the role of the seven, I may note in turn that they are acting as *oikonomoi* within the community. It is, given that they are not specifically assistants to the apostles, quite possible that they are to be included among the *presbyteroi*, at least *kata polin*, even if their individual identity *kat' oikon* is unknown. Indeed, Farrer suggested precisely this, in part on the basis that there was a typological link between the seven and the seventy elders of Numbers 11, but also in that he saw their financial and charitable responsibilities as precisely episcopal.[212] It may be too

210. Finger, *Widows and Meals*, 93–94.

211. David C. Sim, *The Gospel of Matthew and Christian Judaism: The History and Social Setting of the Matthean Community*, SNTW (Edinburgh: T&T Clark, 1998), 66–71.

212. A. M. Farrer, "The Ministry in the New Testament," in *The Apostolic Ministry: Essays on the History and Doctrine of Episcopacy*, ed. Kenneth E. Kirk (London: Hodder & Stoughton, 1946), 135–40.

restrictive to limit the "elders" in the "apostles and elders" simply to these Hellenists, but it is possible that they should be numbered among the elders as house-church leaders.[213] As *oikonomoi*, moreover, they might reasonably be considered *diakonoi* as the tradition has it, or indeed *episkopoi*.

I must leave the issue unresolved; it is possible that the seven are liturgizing the meal through contributions, or that they have a role in the organization of the meal, or both. There is, nonetheless, a positive result: even if the seven are in some sense *diakonoi*, they do not readily supply a point of origin for later Christian *diakonoi*, which I may continue to maintain as lying in the *diakonoi* of associational and civic sacrifice discussed above. Moreover, whatever their precise role, the strongest possibility is that they are domestic leaders within the Hellenophone communities of Jerusalem.

We thus see a complex pattern of Christian leadership within Jerusalem. There are individual leaders, as elsewhere, gathering to consider matters of significance affecting all the Christian communities within the city, as they did in other urban centers; it is also possible that among them seven have been singled out as *oikonomoi* of the gathered community. However, there is also a group modeled on Essene lines that, on the basis that its founders were members of the immediate circle around Jesus, had a particular role of prominence. There is not, however, evidence that federation in Jerusalem led to monepiscopacy, even though the presence of elders alongside the Essene group has a degree of similarity to other federations. The existence of an inner grouping, consisting of James and his community, is unique to Jerusalem, and the presence of apostles in the city is likewise unique; these unique factors may indeed be the reason that no kind of monepiscopacy developed: there was no obvious individual who might exercise such a role. Insofar as the gatherings of *presbyteroi* seem to have been convened by James, I may suggest that he was leading *episkopos*, but *monepiskopos* he was not and thus, I may suggest, could not have provided a model for episcopacy elsewhere. However, although not *monepiskopos*, the leader of the Essene community at the center of the city might attract a particular prominence among other Christian leaders.

Although earlier studies have perhaps overestimated the break with the past caused by the destruction and refounding of Jerusalem as Aelia Capitolina, given that, as I have argued elsewhere, there was a continuing presence of Jewish Christians within the city,[214] we may nonetheless reckon that Christians coming

---

213. Similarly, F. F. Bruce (*The Acts of the Apostles: The Greek Text with Introduction and Commentary*, 3rd ed. [Grand Rapids: Eerdmans, 1990], 277), for whom the elders are the successors to the seven.

214. Stewart(-Sykes), "*Catecheses mystagogicae 5.*"

to Aelia would refound the Christian community. Subsequently, it appears, contact was made with Jewish Christians within the city already, but at least at first this foundation would be independent. Where the "alien people" came from is not absolutely known, but it may well be that a large number of settlers in the new city were drawn from the garrison and from those fighting in the war following Bar Kokhba's revolt. The Legio X Fretensis was, for a long time, stationed in Syria and Palestine, and we may suspect that it recruited chiefly from the local population. We are aware of one legionary who came from Berytus.[215] Thus, Christians settling in the city may well have been Syrian; it is from this settlement, I may suggest, that monepiscopacy developed within Jerusalem, as the past becomes a memory and as the Antiochene system is imported. Certain aspects of the older settlement, again as I have argued elsewhere, do find their way into the renewed Gentile-Jewish Jerusalem Christian community, as some Christians of Jewish heritage remain around the city and the location of the upper room is remembered and cherished, but I would suggest that the peculiarities of the constitution of the Jerusalem church in the first and early second centuries are left behind.

However, it is quite possible that, before these events, the organization of Jerusalem Christianity had exercised some influence on the development of Christianity elsewhere. In particular, the possibility that households might relate to one another may have originated in Jerusalem Christianity and been carried from there, or that it had traveled via Antioch. If Capper is right about identifying the upper room with the Beloved Disciple, it is also possible that the circle of this disciple, like that within Jerusalem, was a circle modeled on Essene lines. Commentators have noted the relative absence of hierarchy in the Johannine Gospel; it could well be that this simply reflects the circle of the disciple. I will also argue below that it is possible that the Jerusalem model impacted significantly on Antioch.

I may, however, be clear that James was no sort of *monepiskopos* himself, and that the presbyters around him were not subservient presbyters. As elsewhere, the leaders of the Jerusalem churches enjoyed a relationship that might be termed a federation, but although elsewhere this may have led to monepiscopacy, it does not do so here. Thus, in attempting to trace the origins of monepiscopacy, I cannot see the origin of this institution in the Jerusalem church under James.[216] Nor, however, can I see the origin of

215. Namely, Gaius Messius, whose details are found in P.Mas. 722 ("Legionary Pay Record").
216. As does Hengel, "Jakobus," in conclusion. Hengel sees James having authority over the presbyters and suggests that the movement toward what he calls "monarchical episcopate" grew from the east, as he reads Polycarp's letter to Philippi as an indication that Philippi had

presbyters,[217] nor, indeed, given that the associations of the Hellenistic world give a better account, can I see in the seven the origin of the diaconate.

Antioch

A discussion of the development of leadership in Jerusalem leads naturally enough to Antioch. However, in tracing the development of ecclesiastical office at Antioch, I start at the end rather than the beginnings described in Acts. That is to say that, regardless of his theological position, Paul of Samosata provokes anger by styling himself as *ducenarius* (the highest rank of equestrian official in the Roman state), acting like a procurator having an exalted throne and seeking to influence surrounding *episkopoi*.[218] Moreover, like a procurator, he gathers support from bishops around Antioch. As such, he is more than simply a *monepiskopos*, but a *monepiskopos* acting like a metropolitan. Certainly, I may say that monepiscopacy is firmly established in Antioch at this point, though it may be contrasted to the single-congregation episcopacy that still seems to be recognized further east in Syria.[219] Working back to attempt to find the point at which monepiscopacy came about, I may perhaps note Serapion. Here I am not entirely reliant on Eusebius, as he quotes a letter from Alexander of Jerusalem to the "church of the Antiochenes" rejoicing that Asclepiades, Serapion's successor, has been entrusted with the *episkopē* of the Antiochene church.[220] Thus, Narcissus seems to indicate that Asclepiades was *monepiskopos*. Moreover, Jerome records a date for the ordination of Serapion: the eleventh year of Commodus.[221] Such a precision in date is an indication that he was a recognized *monepiskopos* rather than a household leader. I may also note Serapion's involvement in a controversy regarding the *Gospel of Peter* at Rhossos[222] as an indication that his episcopal responsibilities

---

no monarchical episcopate. However, apart from how, as argued above, Philippi was one of the first places in which federation is known, we would not anticipate an even movement.

217. For Lightfoot, Jerusalem was the place of origin for the Christian presbyterate, and it spread outward from there. Karrer ("Das urchristliche Ältestenamt") continues to assume this to be the case. For Prast (*Presbyter und Evangelium*, 356–57), the *Presbyterialverfassung* of Jerusalem is a simple fact, and E. Lohse ("Die Entstehung des Bischofsamtes in der frühen Christenheit," *ZNW* 71 [1980]: 61) denies James's episcopate on the grounds that leadership is presbyteral.

218. So the synodical letter recorded by Eusebius, *Hist. eccl.* 7.30.7–10.

219. Namely in the community that produced the *Didascalia apostolorum* discussed above. However, the fact that, according to the synodical letter, Paul dealt corruptly in lawsuits may also provide a point of comparison to the dicastic bishop of *Didascalia apostolorum*.

220. Eusebius, *Hist. eccl.* 6.11.5.

221. Jerome, *Vir. ill.* 41.1.

222. Eusebius, *Hist. eccl.* 6.12.3–6.

went so far beyond a household, or a collection of households, to embrace neighboring towns in his ambit of authority. Thus, I may be clear that there is a monepiscopate in Antioch around the last quarter of the second century, and that this is earlier than the Roman episcopate is established.

Prior to this, however, our information is restricted to the witness of the New Testament, a few hints in Eusebius,[223] and the rather controversial witness of Ignatius. The witness is controversial because of uncertainty about what Ignatius means when he speaks of the episcopate, and because of the uncertainly regarding the date of his activity, even if it is agreed that he is an authentic figure and not the figment of a pseudepigrapher's imagination. Nonetheless, I must grapple with the evidence that he provides.

Ignatius of Antioch

In turning to Ignatius, I may begin by stating that, as far as the extent of the Ignatian corpus is concerned, the correctness of the consensus concerning the middle recension is accepted without further addition to the literature.

I may next, with equal bluntness, reject theories of pseudonymy. In particular, I can discount the recent argument of Schmithals supporting the relatively late dating of Ignatius on the grounds that his work is a pseudepigraph from the latter part of the second century intended to give support to the establishment of a Roman monepiscopate,[224] simply on the grounds that there was no such monepiscopate in Rome at the period to which Schmithals wishes to date the "forgery," let alone a perceived need to produce pseudonymous literature in order to support the institution. According to any hypothesis of pseudonymy, however, we are meant to believe that a pseudonymous author not only creates the Ignatian letters but also interpolates the epistle of Polycarp and takes the name of an otherwise unknown martyr in order to construct an elaborate fiction with an itinerary, with the aim of furthering the cause of monepiscopacy. It simply does not make sense for an elaborate apparatus of pseudonymy far more sophisticated than anything else known in the period to be constructed in order to promote an unknown figure who, as unknown, would have little impact, in order to promote a movement (monepiscopacy) that was barely opposed. Ignatius is a real person, and it is possible from his letters to trace his journey from Syria across Asia to condemnation at Rome, pausing first in Philadelphia, subsequently for some time in Smyrna, before being shipped from Troas, being visited in the course of his journey by representatives of various Asian churches, to whom he subsequently wrote.

---

223. Eusebius, *Hist. eccl.* 3.22; 3.36.15; 4.20.1.
224. Walter Schmithals, "Zu Ignatius von Antiochen," *ZAC* 13 (2009): 181–203.

However, the question of whether Ignatius is a figure of the latter or the earlier part of the second century is a real one. It is difficult not to engage in a circular argument, as statements about church order and the episcopate largely motivate the attempts at dating Ignatius to the latter part of the second century.[225] Even arguments centering on the nature of the docetism opposed by Ignatius, who is seen as an opponent of Valentinian and Marcionite beliefs,[226] link with a view of Ignatius's episcopate in that, as is widely suggested, the development of monepiscopacy is bound up to the defense of orthodoxy against versions of Christianity that may broadly be characterized as gnostic. Thus, if Ignatius is a *monepiskopos* encouraging monepiscopacy, as he is assumed to be, then this claim is bound up to the anti-gnostic agenda. However, here I may anticipate some of the conclusions of the final chapter by suggesting that, whatever the relationship between monepiscopacy and the tightening of doctrinal limits, Ignatius's anti-docetic episcopal vision is different and distinct from that of Irenaeus. In what follows I attempt to discuss Ignatius's date entirely without reference to assumptions regarding either the nature of Ignatius's episcopate or assumptions regarding the stage of development of church order at Antioch.

I may first, in accepting an authentic Ignatius, note that a *terminus ad quem* is provided through accepting the authenticity of the correspondence with Polycarp, who died in the mid-150s. However, the acceptance of authenticity does not mean an unquestioning acceptance of the Trajanic date given by Eusebius. The debate between proponents of a Trajanic Ignatius and those who would date him far later in the second century is a false dichotomy,[227] and an authentic Ignatius might reasonably be dated to a later period than that to which he is conventionally assigned. Barnes suggests the period of Antoninus Pius;[228] I suggest that the conclusion of Hadrian's principate might provide a context.

In presenting this argument, I may note the peculiar route that Ignatius takes to Rome: by land across Asia to Smyrna, and then northward to Troas,

---

225. So, explicitly, Robert Joly, *Le dossier d'Ignace d'Antioche* (Brussels: Éditions de l'Université de Bruxelles, 1979), 75–85. J. Rius-Camps (*The Four Authentic Letters of Ignatius, the Martyr*, OCA 213 [Rome: Pontificium Institutum Orientalium Studiorum, 1980], 298–99) also claims this, though his own view of the development of church order, discussed below under the heading "'Episkopos of Syria': Ignatius as Metropolitan," is quite unique.

226. Note particularly Thomas Lechner, *Ignatius adversus Valentinianos? Chronologische und theologiegeschichtliche Studien zu den Briefen des Ignatius von Antiochien*, VCSup 47 (Leiden: Brill, 1999). A complete bibliography of the large number of recent contributions to this aspect of the Ignatian debate is offered by Brent, "Enigma of Ignatius," 430.

227. So, rightly, Timothy D. Barnes, "The Date of Ignatius," *ExpTim* 120 (2008): 122–23.

228. Ibid., 130.

before taking ship to Neapolis. This is far from a journey direct to Rome, and, moreover, it involves some lengthy stops, both of which observations might provide grounds for suspicion. I may next note Ignatius's description of his escort as "leopards,"[229] and the suggestion of Saddington that this is a reference to the Cohors I Lepidiana.[230] This cohort was stationed in Moesia in 124/5.[231] However, Knight suggests, on the basis of a grave inscription,[232] that at some point thereafter it was transferred to Asia. I may thus ask what a group of this cohort was doing in Antioch, such that Ignatius might be traveling with them. One answer is that it had been moved east as a result of the movement of troops to Palestine for the suppression of the Bar Kokhba revolt, and that the journey of these soldiers through Asia, and their embarkation at Troas, constituted their return to Moesia.[233] It is even possible that this was part of the entourage that accompanied Hadrian on his return to Rome, since a route through Asia and on to Illyricum and Pannonia was the route taken by the emperor as the revolt came to its conclusion.[234] An extended stop in Smyrna, as occurred in the Ignatian journey, would be entirely coherent with a Hadrianic journey west from Antioch, given the honors bestowed upon the city by Hadrian. If this is the case, then Ignatius's characterization of his journey in chains as a cultic procession is even more contracultural than previously recognized. Even if this latter point be considered a guess too far, a Hadrianic date solves many of the problems posed by a Trajanic date, given that Trajan was in Antioch at the beginning of 114 and did not return to Rome, necessitating a date for Ignatius's arrest in 113, in the immediate wake of Trajan's instructions to Pliny regarding the treatment of Christians.[235]

In what follows, this date is not taken as the basis for argument, partly because the argument is perhaps insufficient to judge issues regarding the development of monepiscopacy; nonetheless, the argument for a Hadrianic date may find further support in the discussion below.

229. Ign. *Rom.* 5:1.
230. D. B. Saddington, "St. Ignatius, Leopards and the Roman Army," *JTS* 38 (1987): 411–12. Saddington suggests that there is a scribal error; I am inclined to think it a pun.
231. On the basis of a Hadrianic diploma of that date, MS 2086 in the Schøyen collection. See Margaret M. Roxan and Werner Eck, "A Diploma of Moesia Inferior: 125 Iun. 1," *ZPE* 116 (1997): 193–203.
232. D. J. Knight, "The Movements of the Auxilia from Augustus to Hadrian," *ZPE* 85 (1991): 204, on the basis of *ILS* 90.
233. As Stevan L. Davies ("The Predicament of Ignatius of Antioch," *VC* 30 [1976]: 177) suggests, the task of escorting Ignatius need not have been the soldiers' principal task.
234. So Ronald Syme, "Journeys of Hadrian," *ZPE* 73 (1988): 165–66.
235. So Davies, "Predicament of Ignatius," in conclusion.

I may thus turn to the question of Ignatius's episcopate. In particular, I must pose the question of what he means by the term *episkopos*. When I come to discuss the Ignatian letters, it will be seen that uncertainty haunts the discussion of the church order of the Asian communities that he addresses due to the problem of knowing whether by *episkopos* Ignatius means a *monepiskopos* or a household *episkopos*, and whether by presbyters he intends a circle of honored patrons within a house-church or officers who hold office *kata polin* under a *monepiskopos*. In discussing the nature of Ignatius's own episcopate, I face the same problem, not the least because these same letters are the extent of the evidence.

Ignatius and the Episcopate in Antioch

Ignatius is a figure who looms large in conventional histories of church order, as he often is seen as the first figure demonstrating the existence of monepiscopacy,[236] or even as its inventor.[237] However, monepiscopacy proper is confused through the assumption that there had once been multiple *episkopoi*, a confusion that in turn comes about in part because of the confusion between *Einzelkirche* and *Ortskirche*, as I argued in chapter 1, and through the belief that there had been elders in charge of synagogues, a belief that I have shown to be without foundation. Thus, I may agree readily enough that Ignatius speaks of a sole bishop, but, as I have argued that there was never more than a single *episkopos* in any single Christian community, his statements regarding a sole bishop are neither unique nor significant. Thus, I may note Young: "Ignatius' letters . . . are generally taken as evidence that the 'monepiscopate' already existed before the time of this early bishop of Antioch, whereas they actually show that he was its first proponent."[238] It depends, however, on what is meant by "monepiscopate." Young goes on, encapsulating the confusion that the consensus has caused: "In his [Ignatius's] view, the bishop was effectively the congregational leader."[239] Does she mean that Ignatius thought that the *episkopos* was the leader of one congregation among others in Antioch, or does she mean that he thought of himself as leader of a number of Antio-

236. Thus, notably, in view of his subsequent influence, Baur, *Christenthum*, 275–78.

237. E.g., Dassmann, "Entstehung," 81–83; similarly, Burke, "Monarchical Episcopate," 517–18. As such, they are echoing the view of B. H. Streeter, *The Primitive Church: Studied with Special Reference to the Origins of the Christian Ministry* (New York: Macmillan, 1929), 168–83. See also Bauer, *Orthodoxy and Heresy*, 61–76.

238. Frances M. Young, "Ministerial Forms and Functions in the Church Communities of the Greek Fathers," in *Community Formation in the Early Church and in the Church Today*, ed. Richard N. Longenecker (Peabody, MA: Hendrickson, 2002), 161.

239. Ibid.

chene congregations? If the former is the case, then this is no different from
the position anticipated in 1 Timothy.

The situation is further confused, however, in that Ignatius never addresses
himself to his own church. We must see what can be divined from his passing
comments regarding Antioch. Thus, before considering the possibilities—
namely, that he is a *monepiskopos*, a metropolitan even (as has been claimed),
a household *episkopos*, or *episkopos* of some Antiochene churches (though
not all)—I turn to some of his comments regarding Antioch.

CHRISTIANS IN CONFLICT AT ANTIOCH, AND THE PEACE ANNOUNCED BY IGNATIUS

Given that Ignatius comments so little on his own episcopate, and given
that what he does say is not easy to interpret, I may examine other comments
regarding Antioch and the situation there in order to gain an understanding
of the church's (or churches') life in the city, so that I may pose the question
regarding Ignatius's office from a distinct perspective. In particular, I may
focus on Ignatius's statement that the Antiochene church is now "at peace"[240]
in order to determine what conflict might have been resolved and to see if this
in turn casts light on the structures of Antiochene Christianity, in the light of
which Ignatius's episcopate may come to be understood.

First, Ignatius's statement that the church in Antioch is now "at peace"
might give some clue to the nature of his leadership in the Antiochene Christian community if it might be shown that there is some connection between
Ignatius's leadership and this peace, as is often asserted.

Trevett helpfully lists the understandings of this statement presently found.[241]

First, there is the possibility that persecution has ceased. As Trevett points
out, this is unlikely because Ignatius, in *Romans* 3:3, sees that the great work of
the church is brought about in the hatred of the world. Beyond that, she points
out, peace is linked to unity and concord in Ignatius's writings rather than the
cessation of pagan hostility.[242] The same, Harrison points out, is true in the
work of other early Christian writers.[243] Thus, I may note the peace prevailing in the Roman church about the time of the Quartodeciman controversy,[244]
the peace enjoyed by the church, according to Hegesippus, before the rise of
heresy,[245] the peace that is the opposite of schism, according to the Didachist.[246]

240. Ign. *Smyrn.* 11:2.
241. Trevett, *Study of Ignatius*, 56–66.
242. Ibid., 56–57.
243. Harrison, *Polycarp's Two Epistles*, 83–85.
244. Irenaeus quoted in Eusebius, *Hist. eccl.* 5.24.13, 15.
245. Hegesippus quoted in Eusebius, *Hist. eccl.* 3.20.6.
246. *Did.* 4:3.

Peace would thus seem to be internal. Such peace, however, as is offered by the cessation of persecution might be no more than a lull in the storm rather than the harbor of safety to which Ignatius refers.[247] This does not mean that Ignatius was necessarily simply the victim of internal dissent, but may be simply a victim of external Roman persecution, as Robinson vigorously argues against the current stream, and as Lightfoot had argued prior to the suggestions of Streeter and of Harrison that the tension was internal.[248] But the news of peace does not signify the end of such persecution.

Second, there is the possibility that Ignatius is referring to the appointment of a new *episkopos* and thus to the triumph of the hierarchical or monepiscopal party in Antioch. However, Trevett points out that no prayers are asked for his successor, nor is the successor named.[249] More problematically, it needs to be shown that there was such a party, and that the hierarchy, or the episcopate, was opposed. Streeter assumes this, but no actual evidence is offered.

Finally, there is the suggestion that the situation left by Ignatius has been resolved. This is often linked to the person of Ignatius himself, in particular with the suggestion that Ignatius was arrogating claims of monepiscopacy to himself (the interpretation favored by Trevett)[250] or some kind of disputed episcopal election.[251] However, if Ignatius never was, nor ever claimed to be, a *monepiskopos*, then this interpretation necessarily fails. We have yet to see whether this is the case, but to use this phrase to build the argument would invite circularity. In any event, we will see that Ignatius was no *monepiskopos*.

However, in part building on some of Trevett's observations, which were in turn derived from Rius-Camps, I may offer a further possible reading of the cause of discord and of the cause of peace in Ignatius's Antioch.

First, I may accept the possibility argued by Trevett that, in writing to the Romans, Ignatius is echoing *1 Clement* at a number of points.[252] This hypothesis is strengthened by noting the recent studies of Brent on Ignatius and Bakke on *1 Clement*, both of them pointing out the extent to which both documents depend on a background in which *homonoia* treaties are made between cities,

---

247. Ign. *Smyrn.* 11:3.

248. Thomas A. Robinson, *Ignatius of Antioch and the Parting of the Ways: Early Jewish-Christian Relations* (Peabody, MA: Hendrickson, 2009), 163–202, in agreement with Lightfoot, *Apostolic Fathers*, 2.1:1–22. Cf. Streeter, *Primitive Church*, 169; Harrison, *Polycarp's Two Epistles*, 169.

249. Trevett, *Study of Ignatius*, 58–59 (in response to Streeter, *Primitive Church*, 181; F. W. Schlatter, "The Restoration of Peace in Ignatius' Antioch," *JTS* 35 [1984]: 465–69).

250. Trevett, *Study of Ignatius*, 59–66, a position influentially espoused by Harrison, *Polycarp's Two Epistles*, 85–88.

251. So C. P. Hammond Bammel, "Ignatian Problems," *JTS* 33 (1982): 78.

252. Trevett, *Study of Ignatius*, 62–65.

whereby ambassadors are sent and sacrifices offered.[253] I further accept the possibility that Ignatius had given himself up for arrest,[254] not only on the basis of Ignatius's welcome expectation of his own death, and statements such as *Romans* 4:1 and *Ephesians* 4:2, but also on the basis of allusion to *1 Clement* 54–55, which encourages leaders to die a ransoming death and so to bring about peace. There is indeed a nexus of allusion to *1 Clement* in Ignatius's writing, chiefly, though not exclusively, in the letter to the Romans, addressed to a community well aware of the contents of Clement's writing.

To accept this possibility, however, does not mean that Ignatius felt personally responsible for any discord in the Antiochene church. Moreover, Trevett misses the point when she emphasizes that the Roman church had no bishop, and that "in Clement's letter he had promoted peace in Corinth for a flock *with the presbyters over it*"[255] and that to use this letter as a basis for episcopal governance, the issue which Trevett sees at the fore, is to abuse the text. Clement is equally clear that the apostles appointed *episkopoi* and *diakonoi*[256] and, as seen above, is using *presbyteroi* as a collective noun. There is no principled dispute between presbyters and *episkopos*. Nonetheless, as a disciple of Paul, as of Christ, Ignatius may see his own death as in some sense atoning and the means of bringing about peace; thus, he tells the Ephesians that his spirit is an expiation (*peripsēma*) tied to the cross[257] and describes himself as a ransom (*antipsychon*).[258] It is on this basis that I countenance the possibility that Ignatius had given himself up; we may see such an action, however, not as a confession of guilt but rather as rooted in a theology of martyrdom shared by, for example, 4 Maccabees, by which his death might serve as a ransom and expiation.[259] We should also be careful in deducing too much from Ignatius's

253. Allen Brent, *Ignatius of Antioch and the Second Sophistic: A Study of an Early Christian Transformation of Pagan Culture*, STAC 36 (Tübingen: Mohr Siebeck, 2006); Odd Magne Bakke, *"Concord and Peace": A Rhetorical Analysis of the First Letter of Clement with an Emphasis on the Language of Unity and Sedition*, WUNT 2/143 (Tübingen: Mohr Siebeck, 2001).

254. So, first, Rius-Camps, *Four Authentic Letters*, 142, followed by Trevett, *Study of Ignatius*, 61.

255. Trevett, *Study of Ignatius*, 65 (italics original).

256. *1 Clem.* 42:2.

257. Ign. *Eph.* 8:1. The term *peripsēma*, meaning "what is scrubbed off," comes in Hellenistic religious vocabulary to refer to the act of scrubbing; it is likely that Ignatius's choice of the word here is linked to Paul's employment of the term alongside περικαθάρματα at 1 Cor. 4:13.

258. Ign. *Eph.* 21:1. Cf. 4 Macc. 6:9, 17.

259. Most recently on the possibility of a direct literary relationship between Ignatius and 4 Maccabees, see Raphaëlle Ziadé, *Les martyrs Maccabées: De l'histoire juive au culte chrétien; Les homélies de Grégoire de Nazianze et de Jean Chrysostome*, VCSup 80 (Leiden: Brill, 2007), 81–87; C. N. Jefford, "The Role of 4 Maccabees in the Vision of Ignatius of Antioch," in *Papers Presented at the Fourteenth International Conference on Patristic Studies Held in Oxford 2003*, ed. F. Young, M. Edwards, and P. Parvis, StPatr 40 (Louvain: Peeters, 2006), 435–40. If direct

vocabulary of unworthiness[260] and, in particular, avoid seeing in this a confession of responsibility for the discord, not the least because such vocabulary is a rhetorical convention in Christian discourse.[261]

Moreover, is it likely that a style of governance would create such discord? His absence, however, may have caused greater tension. As I have already suggested, Ignatius's own status as *episkopos* is unclear, and so, unless he really is *monepiskopos* of Antioch, it is hard to see how his absence would solve anything. Moreover, even if he were a *monepiskopos*, we should also note the possibility that Ignatius is a charismatic leader.[262] That is to say, in spite of his insistence on the office of the *episkopos*, which would imply a degree of bureacratization (to use Weberian typology), his own leadership is charismatic, deriving legitimation not simply from his office but by the force of his personality. As such, it is possible that, I may hypothesize, even if Ignatius were nothing more than an *episkopos* in a household setting in contact with other household leaders, he might exercise some personal leadership over them by the force of his personality regardless of the structures of leadership. His influence might well go beyond the communities to which he is technically linked. Care must be taken here, however, not to confuse Ignatius's charismatic authority (which may, in part, have simply derived from his status as a martyr, a status that he would not have had while *episkopos* in Antioch) and his manifestation of charismatic communicative behavior and claim to supernatural knowledge, as charismatic manifestations relate only indirectly to the conception of charismatic legitimation of authority.[263]

Moreover, I may test the hypothesis that Ignatius as charismatic leader was the cause of strife and that his removal brought about peace by suggesting that this is not the normal course of affairs when a charismatic leader is

---

literary influence cannot in the end be established, it certainly is true that the anonymous author shares a cultural world with Ignatius.

260. As does Harrison, *Polycarp's Two Epistles*, 96–100.

261. As pointed out by Mikael Isakson ("Follow Your Bishop! Rhetorical Strategies in the Letters of Ignatius of Antioch," in *The Formation of the Early Church*, ed. Jostein Ådna, WUNT 183 [Tübingen: Mohr Siebeck, 2005], 322–23), who cites as examples *Barn.* 1:8; 4:6, 9; 6:5; 1 Cor. 15:9, comparing them with Ign. *Eph*. 3:8. Robinson (*Ignatius of Antioch*, 165–77) is right to criticize this aspect of the argument, which sees the issues at Antioch originating with Ignatius.

262. So, with argument, Harry O. Maier, *The Social Setting of the Ministry as Reflected in the Writings of Hermas, Clement and Ignatius* (Waterloo, ON: Wilfrid Laurier University Press, 1991), 156–68. Less convincing is the identification of Ignatius's leadership as charismatic by Robert R. Hann ("Judaism and Jewish Christianity in Antioch: Charisma and Conflict in the First Century," *JRH* 14 [1987]: 353–54), due to his confusion of charismatic manifestations of religiosity with charismatic leadership.

263. Thus, see comments in Stewart(-Sykes), "Prophecy and Patronage," briefly revisited in chap. 5 below, under the heading "Institutionalization as an Explanation of Monepiscopacy."

suddenly removed. According to Weber, the situation results in routinization, and it may be the achievement of such routinization that has brought about peace in Antioch. However, recent studies of the loss of charismatic leaders in organizations point out that such routinization is not easily achieved; because staff members are answerable to the departed leader, they may hold loyalty to the absent leader more highly than loyalty to the organization, and there may be an absence of routine means of administration (because administration was always routed through the leader).[264] Thus, a professional manager replacing a charismatic leader may find himself unable to lead a routinized organization simply because the professional mode of leadership cuts across the former, individually tailored way of functioning within an organization.[265] Were Antioch monepiscopal, moreover, as is widely assumed, I might also surmise that, in the absence of Ignatius, there may have been disunity as a result of the individual leaders of household churches attempting to gain the position of leadership vacated by Ignatius. Thus, if Antioch were monepiscopal, and if Ignatius were indeed a charismatic leader, it would be more likely that the strife and discord would be caused by Ignatius's absence than by his claims. If, however, Ignatius were the cause, then one would expect the strife to be resolved simply by his removal, but it is some time after his removal that he reports that peace has been attained again. It is on these grounds that I must reject any notion that the strife had been caused by Ignatius's leadership or by his promotion of monepiscopacy and must be particularly suspicious of claims that he exercised charismatic authority. Whatever the cause of discord in Antioch, it was not Ignatius; and whatever the means by which such a breach was healed, it was not Ignatius's removal from the scene. Trevett suggests that the arrest of Ignatius might "bring the factions to their senses,"[266] but if the strife is internal, then his departure is more likely to cause further division and strife.

Finally, in answering suggestions that the "peace" is the healing of a rift caused by Ignatius himself that has been healed in some way by Ignatius's departure, I may note that prior to the news of peace reaching him, Ignatius, in speaking of the Antiochene church and requesting prayer, does not use language that suggests that there is a particular crisis in need of resolution;

264. So Thomas A. McLaughlin, "Charismatic Leader: Pity the Poor Replacement CEO," *The Non-Profit Times*, October 1, 2002.

265. Cynthia M. Hernandez and Donald R. Leslie ("Charismatic Authority: The Aftermath," *Nonprofit Management and Leadership* 11 [2001], 493–97) chart a situation of breakdown caused by the retirement of a charismatic leader and the appointment of a professional manager.

266. Trevett, *Study of Ignatius*, 61. Harrison (*Polycarp's Two Epistles*, 101–3) waxes positively lyrical on this theme.

his language is very general. Thus, the "peace" would seem to be a new and unexpected departure, leading to his expression of joy and the request for ambassadors to go to Antioch in imitation of embassies from Hellenistic *poleis*, to celebrate the new and unexpected peace. This may be kept in mind as I seek to answer the question of the nature of the peace.

As such, I may be clear that the news of peace tells us little of Ignatius's episcopate. Nonetheless, although the dispute is not directly related to Ignatius, it is worth propounding a new suggestion regarding the nature of the conflict, and a possible solution, not least because in taking us to the origins of Antiochene Christianity this may provide a lens through which to see the manner in which the church order of the city developed in the time prior to Ignatius and thus enable us to understand the nature of his episcopate.

In questioning the hypothesis that Ignatius was the cause of the conflict at Antioch that required healing, I have not abandoned the insight that Ignatius might have seen his impending martyrdom as the means by which peace might be brought about. That is why, with Trevett, I may detect a tone of hope and certainty once Ignatius hears the news of peace at Antioch;[267] his offering is already bearing fruit.

In asking what the cause of conflict might be, if it is not Ignatius and not the development of monepiscopacy, I may suggest that the fundamental breach in Antiochene Christianity was that which was opened up in the 40s regarding the nature of law observance in Antioch and continuing controversy regarding the status of Gentiles within the covenant. If such a rift has been healed, then that would account for Ignatius's surprise and expression of joy. This is not a petty squabble but rather a deep point of division, which is unlikely to be healed by the removal of one protagonist. Ignatius may have been brought to think that his offering of himself had served as a *homonoia* sacrifice and brought about reconciliation between the two groups; however, this would not mean that he had brought peace simply by leaving, but that he had done so by dying.

This dispute within the city over the extent to which law obedience impacted Christians and over the extent of commensality that was possible between Jewish and Gentile Christians had continued since the first century. Thus Slee notes the difficulties met by early Jewish communities that, on confession of Christ, were faced with the issue of the admission of Gentiles to the covenant and to define the circumstances under which table fellowship

---

267. Trevett, *Study of Ignatius*, 60. So he writes in Ign. *Pol.* 7:1 that God has banished his care. Schoedel ("Ignatius and the Reception of Matthew," 131; "Theological Norms," 41–42) also notes that there is less of the language of self-deprecation in the letters from Troas than in those from Smyrna.

might take place between Jew and Gentile, each of whom confessed Christ.[268] The issue was of particular significance because the central act of Christian worship is a meal.

The parameters of the later Jewish debate may be observed in the Mishnah tractate *'Abodah Zarah*, which deals with idolatry and with the extent to which Jews might relate to Gentiles. A particular concern is that Gentiles might pollute Jewish food with idolatrous practices, such as offering a part to an idol, and so food is forbidden unless it has been in continuous Jewish sight, such that no such offering might be made. "If an Israelite was eating with a gentile at a table and he put flagons on the table and flagons on the side-table and left the other there and went out, what is on the table is forbidden and what is on the side-table is permitted. If he had said to him 'mix your cup and drink,' that which is on the side-table is also forbidden. Opened jars are forbidden."[269] It is to be noted that, although set about by suspicion, the Jew and the Gentile are nonetheless at a common table. A more extreme view is represented in the Tosefta commentary on this tractate:

> R. Simeon b. Eleazar says "Israelites who live abroad are idolaters. How so? A gentile who made a banquet for his son and went out and invited all the Jews who live in his town, even though they eat and drink their own [food and drink] and their own waiter stands over them and serves them, they nonetheless serve idolatry, as it is said 'Lest you make a covenant with the inhabitants of the land and when they play the harlot after their gods and sacrifice to their gods and one invites you, you eat of his sacrifices'" (Exod. 34:15).[270]

This evidence is read by Slee as implying that Gentile table fellowship brought about impurity by its very nature, and that any table fellowship was impossible.[271] However, as Sanders points out, ritual purity was necessary for Jews only in restricted circumstances (principally for service at the temple), and thus Jews might well eat with Gentiles without regard for the resulting ritual impurity.[272] The extent to which table fellowship between Jew and Gentile might be restricted under ordinary circumstances may thus be overstated. However, regardless of the circumstances, a law-observant Jew would require

268. Michelle Slee, *The Church in Antioch in the First Century CE: Communion and Conflict*, JSNTSup 244 (London: Sheffield Academic Press, 2003), 12–23.

269. *m. 'Abod. Zar.* 5.5.

270. *t. 'Abod. Zar.* 4.6.

271. Slee, *Church in Antioch*, 17–24.

272. E. P. Sanders, "Jewish Associations with Gentiles and Galatians 2.11–14," in *The Conversation Continues: Studies in Paul and John in Honor of J. Louis Martyn*, ed. Robert T. Fortna and Beverly R. Gaventa (Nashville: Abingdon, 1990), 170–88.

that the food and drink had a minimal level of purity in not being in any way brought into contact with idolatrous practice.

The inner Jewish debate about table fellowship and the extent and nature of Gentile participation becomes acute for those Jews who accept Christ, and it becomes a particular issue in Antioch, leading to a dispute between Peter and Paul, behind which is the figure of James.[273] However, Zetterholm reads this report in Galatians distinctly, suggesting that table fellowship is not really the issue. He notes that the description of the incident at Antioch in Galatians functions as the *narratio* of the letter, setting the scene for the argumentative speech that follows. There must, therefore, be some connection between this narrative and the argument that follows. The argument in Galatians, clearly, is about circumcision. Since circumcision was the means by which the covenant was demonstrated for male Jews, those males who are uncircumcised are therefore outside the covenant of Israel. The same argument may well motivate the dispute to which Acts 15 makes reference. Zetterholm thus suggests that the argument concerned the manner in which Jews and Gentiles might be members of a single group, of which commensality might be a sign; Jews had a covenantal relationship with God that Gentiles might not enter except through becoming full proselytes, as a sign of which circumcision was considered essential. Although Gentiles might be saved, they were not saved through that same covenant. If this is James's understanding, that of Paul is different, as he sees a single covenant for Jews and Gentiles alike.[274]

Zetterholm, however, does not explore the extent to which this might impact table fellowship, disregarding suggestions that the true issue was eucharistic fellowship.[275] Consequently, he fails to notice that the very issue of covenantal theology would come to a head at the table. For him, the matter is private dinner invitations,[276] but this impinges only marginally on covenantal theology (a minimum requirement for purity, as discussed above, being the sole issue), whereas the eucharist is replete with covenantal significance.

Here we come across the differing eucharistic covenantal theologies of the participants. For Paul, the eucharistic meal was one that constructed and undergirded the covenant through the act of sharing one food; the cup is a sharing in the new covenant,[277] and the Israelites had eaten a single manna,

273. Gal. 2:11–16.

274. Magnus Zetterholm, *The Formation of Christianity in Antioch: A Social-Scientific Approach to the Separation between Judaism and Christianity* (London: Routledge, 2003), 129–66.

275. Ibid., 149–50.

276. Ibid., 155.

277. 1 Cor. 11:25. See, on the significance of the wording pointing up the significance of the act of sharing, Bruce Chilton, *A Feast of Meanings: Eucharistic Theologies from Jesus through Johannine Circles*, NovTSup 72 (Leiden: Brill, 1994), 113.

being baptized covenantally in the cloud. However, if Gentiles are not within the covenant, or if Jews and Gentiles are seen as under different covenantal dispensations, then they cannot share the food that constructs and represents the single covenant. He may see this clearly, and hence he sets out precisely that argument to Peter and reports it in Galatians. For Peter and his circle, however, the covenant of Jesus is supplemental to the covenant of Israel, not a replacement. They continue to participate in the worship of the temple, even as they break bread within households. The sole concern, when the gospel extends to Gentiles, is that a minimal level of ritual purity is extended to the foods that constitute the eucharistic meal, as it is a sacrifice of sharing, following Exodus 24, so that the central focus is not on the act of fellowship but rather on the food that constructs the fellowship.[278]

Commensality was at the heart of the conflict at Antioch because the basic ritual of Christianity was a meal, and a dispute over eating together was thus a dispute about worshiping together. This in turn brought into relief the extent to which it was possible for law-observant Jews and non-law-observant Gentiles to eat together and the extent to which this act of sharing food characterized the covenant. Zetterholm characterizes the group of Jewish Christians at Antioch as a synagogue like any other.[279] That may be so in meeting as a synagogue, but this was a group that ate together beyond their participation in synagogal activities of reading and study. Thus, Zetterholm is right in seeing that for the theologian Paul, covenantal theology is the heart of the issue, but he fails to see that this issue is made acute in the context of the eucharistic banquet, for these law-observant Jews were seated at a covenantal ceremony with those who, as is evident from their table manners, are not part of the (Jewish) covenant community.[280]

This sharing of food brought with it distinct levels of concern about purity and distinct understandings of the manner in which it related to the covenant. It was, moreover, a dispute not only about food (and thus worship) but also about the leader of worship, for if the duty of an *episkopos* was the provision of food, then the Jewish congregants would need assurance that the food was ritually clean, an assurance hard to find should the *episkopos* be a Gentile. Likewise, given that food is served from side tables by waiters, then a Jew would require assurance that the *diakonos* was likewise Jewish. This might be possible, and so Peter, say, might share the eucharistic banquet with Gentiles

278. So summarizing Chilton's treatment of the Petrine eucharist in *Feast of Meanings*, 81–92. This is not to say that I accept his characterization of the Jacobean eucharist.

279. Zetterholm, *Formation of Christianity*, 194.

280. So also Dennis E. Smith, *From Symposium to Eucharist: The Banquet in the Early Christian World* (Minneapolis: Fortress, 2003), 184–85, in summary.

on the basis that the foods are protected from Gentile interference, and thus represent a position by which there are two covenants and distinct meals in one room. If, however, one is convinced (as are Paul and James) that there is a single covenant, then there has to be a single meal.

The eucharistic meal provided a particular point of conflict and led on to a fundamental division within Antiochene Christianity. Here I may build upon the conclusions reached earlier that James's role in Jerusalem was as *mebaqqer* of the Essene Jesus group within Jerusalem by suggesting that the aboriginal Christian household in Antioch was formed from the same stock. Barnabas, who had handed over his wealth to the apostles' group in Jerusalem,[281] and thus was acting in a manner consistent with joining an Essene community, was sent to Antioch in the 30s and, I may suggest, took up a similar role to that of James in Jerusalem, this being the reason for his dispatch to Antioch.[282] As evidence for this, I may note that money is sent from Antioch to Jerusalem by the hand of Barnabas, together with Saul. If this is an Essene celibate community, moreover, this would explain the authority that is accorded to those who were sent from James.[283] The community is based on those from the seven who had left Jerusalem, who had also functioned within the Essene matrix centered on James, and thus there is ample reason to see this Antiochene Christian household as an Essene community. With this insight, there is likewise ample reason to see that it would be impossible to sustain such a community once there is a press of Gentiles. It is this Essene connection, rather than the exercise of metropolitical authority by James or a mystical connection with Jerusalem,[284] that explains the relationship between James and Barnabas and the nature of the authority that James exercises over the

281. Acts 4:36–37.

282. Acts 11:22. Nonetheless, there is widespread doubt about the historicity of this account. As Martin Hengel puts it, "This sending of Barnabas as 'inspector' to this new development in Antioch comes much too close to Luke's particular bias for us to be able to accept it without further ado" (*Earliest Christianity*, trans. John Bowden [London: SCM, 1986], 101). Thus Hengel joins others in seeing Barnabas's relocation to Antioch as a personal initiative. However, as John P. Meier (Raymond E. Brown and John P. Meier, *Antioch and Rome: New Testament Cradles of Catholic Christianity* [London: Geoffrey Chapman, 1983], 34) notes, disaffection with Jerusalem would hardly account for his subsequent siding with James and breach with Paul.

283. Gal. 2:11–14.

284. Such is the explanation of Bengt Holmberg, *Paul and Power: The Structure of Authority in the Primitive Church as Reflected in the Pauline Epistles* (Philadelphia: Fortress, 1980), 19–20, by way of explaining and suggesting a dependence of the Antiochene church on Jerusalem denoted by the Antiochene attempt to gain approval from Jerusalem for its mission. Holmberg (24) notes that Paul does not state why the community in Jerusalem is able to give binding guidance to other churches. Miller ("Antioch, Paul, and Jerusalem," 187–89) too finds Holmberg's explanation somewhat strained.

Antiochene church.[285] I might indeed add that the recognition of this Essene dimension to the relationship between the Christian communities of Jerusalem and Antioch solves this particular nest of problems.

This does not deny that there might have been other incursions of Christianity into Antioch,[286] but I suggest that this Essene center, in contact with Jerusalem, was a center of cardinal importance. This single community was forced to divide so that law-obedient Christians might maintain purity at table. The nature of such division is denied by Meier, but the very nature of his denial is what demonstrates that such division did take place. He writes, "It does not seem likely, then, that after the departure of Paul, the Antiochene church broke into two totally separate groups of Jewish Christians and gentile Christians. . . . The most likely outcome is that Gentile and Jewish Christians abided by the wishes of the James party by holding meals (and therefore probably eucharists) separately. . . . Therefore some sort of fellowship (koinōnia)—however tenuous and uneasy—could be maintained."[287] But if separate meals, separate eucharists, are taking place, then there are separate Christian communities. The issue is whether the two maintained relations at any level. They certainly would not eat together.

Insofar as there might be a dispute about leadership, it was a dispute about the religious identity of the leader, not about whether he should be termed an *episkopos* or whether there should be a single leader; such a dispute is the product of the Reformation and is consistently read back into the early evidence and confused with the real issue,[288] namely, the extent to which the law is binding on Christians, whether Jewish or Gentile.

If this is the fundamental conflict at Antioch, one is entitled to ask how it is that peace should come about in the time of Ignatius. I wish to suggest two possibilities. First, the nature of the meal had changed around the time of Ignatius with the result that purity issues are no longer so apparent; second, the Jewish Christians abandoned a demand for circumcision.

As already noted, fundamental to Essene life is the common meal, and fundamental to Christian worship is the eucharistic meal, a regular community meal that might take on a particular character when celebrated in memory of Jesus. This meal had, I suggest, been celebrated at Antioch, as elsewhere,

285. See Robert Lee Williams, *Bishop Lists: Formation of Apostolic Succession of Bishops in Ecclesiastical Crises*, GDECS 3 (Piscataway, NJ: Gorgias, 2005), 70. Williams sees Barnabas, as I do, in a position of leadership in the Antiochene church but sees James exercising authority over him from Jerusalem.

286. So pointed out by Hann, "Judaism and Jewish Christianity," 343–44.

287. Meier, in Brown and Meier, *Antioch and Rome*, 40.

288. As an example of this confusion, note Trevett (*Study of Ignatius*, 47–48), who follows the highly contentious reconstruction of Streeter, *Primitive Church*, 151–52.

on the eve of the sabbath. Thus, I have argued elsewhere that the gathering at Troas,[289] the gathering of the Bithynian Christians known to Pliny,[290] that of Roman Christians reported in *Traditio apostolica*,[291] that of Egyptian Christians reported by Socrates,[292] and those that took place at Smyrna according to *Vita Polycarpi*[293] occurred on the Saturday evening by virtue of concluding the sabbath, which had been spent in the synagogal activities of reading and learning.[294] There is no reason why Antioch should know a distinct practice.

However, I may next suggest that here, as elsewhere, the meal on the eve of the sabbath was moved to the following morning.[295] Once there is a breach with the synagogue, the logic of the time for the gathering is less obvious. There is no strong reason to retain a celebration at the conclusion of the sabbath once the group has not met first at the synagogue; moreover, under pressure of the Trajanic rescript, it would be natural to move the meal to a Sunday. Indeed, Ignatius is an apologist for that movement.[296]

However, one result of the movement of the main liturgy to dawn on a Sunday rather than at the close of the sabbath is that the nature of the meal changes. No longer is it to the same extent a *Sättigungsmahl*, as it no longer takes place in the evening but rather in the morning, and for the same reason, apart from the necessity of many congregants to work, it does not continue in sympotic manner; so the Christians interrogated by Pliny say that the meal has been abandoned. An effect of the movement of the meal from the end of the sabbath to a Sunday is that, because the nature of the meal changes, issues of commensality are rather less acute as the food is reduced to symbolic food.

289. Acts 20:7–12.
290. Pliny, *Ep.* 10.96. The day is not specified, but the sabbath evening is the only obvious occasion.
291. *Trad. ap.* 25. See Alistair Stewart(-Sykes), *Hippolytus: On the Apostolic Tradition* (Crestwood, NY: St. Vladimir's Seminary Press, 2001), 140–42.
292. Socrates, *Hist eccl.* 5.22. Sozomen, *Hist eccl.* 7.19.8, likewise records this Egyptian practice.
293. *Vit. Pol.* 22, 23, 24.
294. So Stewart(-Sykes), *Life of Polycarp*, 55–58. In presenting the argument I have followed H. Riesenfeld, "Sabbat et jour du Seigneur," in *New Testament Essays: Studies in Memory of Thomas Walter Manson, 1893–1958*, ed. A. J. B. Higgins (Manchester, UK: Manchester University Press, 1958), 210–17.
295. As suggested previously in Alistair Stewart(-Sykes), "The Domestic Origin of the Liturgy of the Word," in *Papers Presented at the Fourteenth International Conference on Patristic Studies Held in Oxford 2003*, ed. F. Young, M. Edwards, and P. Parvis, StPatr 40 (Louvain: Peeters, 2006), 115–20, a position now adopted by Paul F. Bradshaw and Maxwell E. Johnson, *The Origins of Feasts, Fasts and Seasons in Early Christianity* (London: SPCK, 2011), 6–7. Note also E. Dekkers, "L'église ancienne a-t-elle connu la messe du soir?" in *Miscellanea Liturgica in Honorem L. Cuniberti Mohlberg*, vol. 1, BEL 22 (Rome: Edizioni Liturgiche, 1948), 235.
296. Ign. *Magn.* 9:1.

This in turn means that Christians of Jewish descent, who are concerned to maintain table purity through separation from Gentile foods, are able to participate in the common meal, and the covenantal issue is not raised because there is no means by which the boundary marker of food law may be made evident through separate eating practices. Thus it is possible for peace and unity between Antiochene Christians to come about, as the fundamental root of the tension is removed, and Jewish and Gentile Christians might worship together under a common *episkopos*. They may do so because there is no disagreement about leadership. One may ask whether such an understanding is consonant with the date for Ignatius's activity proposed above. However, the evidence is not such that we are in a position to date such a development. The first we know of its occurrence is early in the second century, when Pliny reports that the evening gatherings have been abandoned, yet the first we know of the reduction of the eucharist from symposium to symbolic meal in Rome is the report of Justin, though this could have happened earlier.[297] We simply do not know at what point this move took place at Antioch, and it may simply be that the peace, if it is related to this movement at all, is prompted by Jewish Christian adoption of a practice already normal among Gentile congregations.

An alternative understanding to the manner in which the situation in Antioch might come to resolution is the abandonment of the Jewish Christian demand for circumcision. This might seem the most improbable of events, but it is possible to construct a situation in which this could come about.

First, I advert to the suggestion made above regarding dating, seeing the Ignatian letters written even as the Bar Kokhba revolt was finally being put down. If this dating is accepted, I may speculate reasonably regarding the attitude of Christians of Jewish practice and heritage to circumcision. The revolt may have been sparked by Hadrian's objection to circumcision,[298] but as

297. See L. Michael White, *The Social Origins of Christian Architecture*, vol. 1, *Building God's House in the Roman World: Architectual Adaptation among Pagans, Jews, and Christians*, HTS 42 (repr., Valley Forge, PA: Trinity Press International, 1996), 119–20; idem, "Regulating Fellowship in the Common Meal: Early Jewish and Christian Evidence," in *Meals in a Social Context: Aspects of the Communal Meal in the Hellenistic and Roman World*, ed. Inge Nielsen and Hanne Sigismund Nielsen, ASMA 1 (Aarhus: Aarhus University Press, 1998), 180–81. White suggests that this takes place at the end of the second century. He has, however, overlooked Justin's evidence. Whereas the architectural record would point to a later date, in that it is only at this time that sanctuaries fit only for a formalized eucharistic celebration are found, I may suggest that separate and non-eucharistic meals continued in churches until that time due to the lack of separation between domestic and religious premises; the architectural record cannot tell us the nature of the meals eaten in the *triclinia*.

298. *Historia Augusta, Hadrianus* 14.2. For discussion of the trustworthiness of the *Historia Augusta* at this point, see E. Mary Smallwood, *The Jews under Roman Rule: From Pompey to Diocletian; A Study in Political Relations*, 2nd ed., SJLA 20 (Leiden: Brill, 1981), 428–32.

such, it might have come to be seen as a nationalistic, rather than a religiously, covenantal trait, in such a way as to alienate Jews who had confessed Jesus, rather than Bar Kokhba, as the Messiah. Even if we may doubt the statement of Justin that adherents of Bar Kokhba had persecuted Christians,[299] the existence of such a story might serve to put further distance between Christians of Jewish heritage and Jews who had not recognized the messiahship of Christ. As such, rapprochement with Christians who are not of Jewish descent becomes a possibility. Thus, Sim suggests that the Matthaean community joined itself at this period to the Gentile Christian majority in Antioch, and that this explains the ongoing interest in exegesis of the Hebrew Bible in later Antiochene Christianity.[300]

Whether the conflict in Antioch is brought to its close as a result of the transference of the time of the Christian gathering or as a result of a new understanding of circumcision on the part of Antiochene Christians of Jewish heritage, or indeed by a combination of these factors, in that two of the clearest boundary markers between Jews and others are erased, neither the conflict nor its resolution is directly related to Ignatius's episcopate. However, I may have the fundamental division in Antiochene Christianity in mind as I seek to determine the nature of his office. I may, moreover, note here that Ignatius is an apologist for the transfer of the gathering to a Sunday morning,[301] investing with theological meaning a practice whose origins were purely practical. For him, it might be a means to put distance between his own Christian community and Judaism, whereas, equally, it might instead be a means of closing the gap.[302]

Inevitably, the argument presented here is somewhat hypothetical. However, the various aspects relating to the division and reunification of Antiochene Christianity, namely, the impact of purity laws surrounding food and the issue of whether the meal should occur on the evening of the sabbath or on the following morning, have previously been observed. Thus, Donahue also observes the impact of food laws on eucharistic fellowship, suggesting that this is what motivates Ignatius's emphasis on a single eucharist;[303] since separated eucharists were Ignatius's experience at Antioch, he sees it as possible that the

299. Justin, *1 Apol.* 31.5–6.

300. Sim, *Gospel of Matthew*, 290–91.

301. So in Ign. *Magn.* 9.

302. Here I must take issue with the comments of Robinson (*Ignatius of Antioch*, 69–70n86) that Galatians is not useful for constructing the situation of Ignatius, as the events described therein had happened long before. However, although the fundamental breach was buried in the past, its effects would be felt into the present.

303. Paul J. Donahue, "Jewish Christianity in the Letters of Ignatius of Antioch," *VC* 32 (1978): 89–90.

adoption of purity laws, even by Gentile Christians in the Asian communities, quite apart from a new "Judaizing" of those who were, in any case, of Jewish heritage, would lead to a similar situation as that already obtaining and, I suggest, newly healed, at Antioch. The sabbath/Sunday distinction is raised as a potential issue between Jewish and Gentile congregations at Antioch by Robinson,[304] but he suggests that if this were the case, then the split would have been relatively recent. However, I may see the movement to Sunday not as a cause of division, since the division was already ancient, but instead as the means of healing the division. Thus, even if this reconstruction is not accepted in all its detail, issues surrounding table fellowship as a covenantal rite certainly must be seen as the fundamental motivating factor for division between Christians of Jewish observance and non-Jewish observance at Antioch, and this division, rather than any debate about polity or Ignatius's personality, as the fundamental division within Antiochene Christianity in the period leading up to Ignatius's arrest.

How this relates to Ignatius's self-abandonment to the Roman authorities is indeed uncertain. If Zetterholm's hypothesis over the payment of the *fiscus Judaeus* is to be rejected, which it probably is, then there is no obvious motivation;[305] more to the point, to inquire into this is to distract the inquiry yet further. We do not know what brought Ignatius to present himself to the Roman authorities; possibly, as a person of some education and, perhaps, a person with a relatively high profile within Antioch,[306] his confession might draw attention away from other, lowlier Christians. This is, however, but educated guesswork, and a frank confession of ignorance is better than ill-grounded speculation.

Nonetheless, in the light of this reconstruction of the fundamental division in Antiochene Christianity, I may turn to the question of the nature of Ignatius's *episkopē*, considering in turn each possibility, aware that any solution must take account of the relationship between law-obedient and non-law-observant Christians within the city.

---

304. Robinson, *Ignatius of Antioch*, 59n58, 81.

305. Zetterholm argues that the imposition of the *fiscus Judaeus* following the Jewish war was the cause of the final breach between Jews and Gentiles in Antioch, as it obliged Gentile Christians who had previously claimed to be Jews to make a fundamental choice. For a critique, see Robinson, *Ignatius of Antioch*, 89–94.

306. H. Riesenfeld ("Reflections on the Style and Theology of Ignatius of Antioch," in *Papers Presented at the Third International Conference on Patristic Studies Held at Christ Church, Oxford 1959: Biblica, Patres Apostoloci, Historica*, ed. F. L. Cross, StPatr 4/2 [Berlin: Akademie-Verlag, 1961], 312–22) points toward the Asianist elements in Ignatius's style, the paradox and word play, the parallelism and antitheses, and he suggests (317) that in the light of Ignatius's rhetorical education, he might have been an *advocatus* or local politician.

Ignatius's Episcopate

"*Episkopos* of Syria": Ignatius as Metropolitan?

In opening the question I may begin, again, with the work of Trebilco, who gives a good representation of the consensus reading. I may follow Trebilco's line of argument in particular because he is at least clear that he thinks that Ignatius is a *monepiskopos* in the sense that the term is employed here and argues, moreover, for that position, stating that "he seems to have thought of himself as the one bishop of Antioch."[307]

In support of this claim he notes that Ignatius, in *Romans* 9:1, refers to the church of Syria that "has God for its shepherd instead of me"[308] and refers to himself as "*episkopos* of Syria" in *Romans* 2:2. However, this latter reference, given that the point is made that he has gone from the east of the empire to the west, may mean simply "*episkopos* from Syria."[309] As such, he is making the same point that is made in *Ephesians* 1:2: Syria is being contrasted with Rome as opposite ends of an empire.[310] Moreover, to call himself *episkopos* of Syria would imply a rather larger area of responsibility than churches within Antioch, something like a metropolitan responsibility. Both Grant and Stoops indeed read Ignatius as claiming precisely this extent of responsibility,[311] as does Rius-Camps, here meaning an authentic and first-century Ignatius. Rius-Camps's view, however, reflects a rather eccentric view of the development of church order by which the scattered Christian communities within provinces have an "administrator, coordinator and supervisor," a system that, though it sounds very much like archiepiscopacy, he considers more primitive than local monepiscopacy.[312] In answer to those according responsibility over the whole of Syria to Ignatius, Trebilco suggests that this cannot be so because he speaks elsewhere of the church at Antioch in Syria.[313] However, if churches in

307. Trebilco, *Early Christians in Ephesus*, 643.

308. "The church in Syria" is used elsewhere (e.g., Ign. *Eph.* 21:2; Ign. *Mag.* 14:1), but not in connection with Ignatius's relationship with it.

309. So J. B. Lightfoot, *The Apostolic Fathers*, 5 vols. (1890; repr., Peabody, MA: Hendrickson, 1989), 2.2:201: a genitive "denoting not the extent of his jurisdiction, but the place of his abode."

310. So William R. Schoedel, "Ignatius and the Reception of Matthew in Antioch," in *Social History of the Matthean Community: Cross-Disciplinary Approaches*, ed. David L. Balch (Minneapolis: Fortress, 1991), 135–36.

311. Robert M. Grant, *The Apostolic Fathers: A New Translation and Commentary*, vol. 4, *Ignatius of Antioch* (Camden, NJ: Nelson, 1966), 87–88; Robert F. Stoops Jr., "If I Suffer: Epistolary Authority in Ignatius of Antioch," *HTR* 80 (1987): 164. Note also Virginia Corwin, *St. Ignatius and Christianity in Antioch* (New Haven: Yale University Press, 1960), 44–45, on the basis of Antioch's central place in the province.

312. Rius-Camps, *Four Authentic Letters*, 130. He suggests that Polycarp held the same position vis-à-vis Asia.

313. Trebilco, *Early Christians in Ephesus*, 643n66.

urban centers federated, then it is possible that they included in their federation congregations around the city; certainly Ignatius, if he means "the bishop of Syria" or "the bishop of Antioch" in a monepiscopal sense, may be claiming authority wider than the city itself. Indeed, if he is in fact *monepiskopos*, we may envisage his monepiscopate spreading as far as that of later Antiochene *monepiskopoi*, such as Serapion.[314] However, if he is *monepiskopos*, it seems odd that a new appointment (apart from God) has not been made once he is taken from Antioch, whereas if he is a domestic *episkopos* leading a house-church, then the Christians under his care may well be without an *episkopos*, thus being overseen (*episkopēsei*) directly by God, whose broker Ignatius might see himself. As such, Ignatius would seem not to have been *monepiskopos* of Antioch, but rather an Antiochene *episkopos*. In any event, "*episkopos* from Syria" cannot be made to mean "bishop of Syria." This does not mean that Ignatius cannot have been *monepiskopos*, but the phrase at *Romans* 2:2 cannot be employed to support the assertion. In order to explore the question, distinct evidence must be brought into play. He most certainly did not exercise authority over any church beyond Antioch itself.

Ignatius as *Monepiskopos*?

Although the declaration of peace at Antioch is not directly related to Ignatius's episcopate, this fundamental division in Antiochene Christianity and the survival in Antioch of different versions of Christianity make it unlikely that Ignatius was *monepiskopos* over all Christian congregations within the city, even if we take "gnostic" Christian communities out of the equation. If Ignatius is recognized in some sense by all the Christian groups of the city, these issues must be firmly in the past; that would, however, seem unlikely.[315] In the first instance, Ignatius is concerned in several letters with the position and activity of Judaizing or Jewish Christians within the Christian communities of Asia, and in particular he is also concerned with issues caused by the interpretation of Jewish Scriptures. Here, as Trevett persuasively shows, the Judaizers are within the Christian communities.[316] It is, however, unlikely that he would be taking a different line with regard to these Christians, and their attitude toward the law, than he would have taken within Antioch. It is indeed possible that Ignatius is particularly sensitive to the issues raised by the presence of Jewish Christians and Judaizing Gentile Christians within Christian communities as a result of Antiochene experience; it is not that he is simply reflecting onto

---

314. As noted above, with reference to Eusebius, *Hist. eccl.* 6.12.3–6, Serapion becomes involved in the affairs of the nearby town of Rhossos.

315. So also Trevett, *Study of Ignatius*, 42.

316. Ibid., 169–94.

Asian communities the Antiochene issues,[317] as these are real issues for the Asian churches, but his response to the issue nonetheless reflects back on his position at Antioch,[318] making it improbable that he would be recognized as *episkopos* by law-obedient Christians. A second, related point is that Ignatius makes an appeal to Paul and is an open admirer of Paul, whereas it is likely that Paul was still a controversial figure within Antiochene Christian circles, particularly within law-observant circles.[319] I may thus suggest again that it is unlikely that he was a single *episkopos* over all Antiochene Christian communities, if only because the role of the *episkopos* at table would compromise the ritual separation of Christians of Jewish descent, heritage, and practice.

If Ignatius is purely *monepiskopos* and undisputed as such, we must also give an account of how it is, early in the second century, that such a monepiscopal system has arisen, unless we are to posit that the city had monepiscopacy from the beginning, which is difficult, given the fractured and diverse nature of Christianity within the city. Williams gives a highly speculative account, suggesting that James had exercised some form of metropolitical control over the Antiochene church, and that after the death of James the Antiochene church declared some form of independence, setting itself against the conservatism of the Jerusalem elders.[320] I have already explained James's authority in Jerusalem on quite a different basis from this form of juridical authority. Williams's evidence is, first, his speculation that the *Didache*, as Antiochene, is proposing the appointment of a *monepiskopos* (which is, as I have already argued, not the nature of the episcopal office in the *Didache* at all, as it is economic rather than gubernatorial) and, second, that the primacy accorded to Peter in Matthew represents the declaration of independent authority on the basis of Peter as against any claim on succession from James. If Matthew is Antiochene, then I may agree that the focus on Peter is possibly a reflection of an alternative strand of leadership,[321] but from within the Antiochene context, as I have reconstructed it, a focus on Petrine leadership would constitute an assertion of a distinct form of Christ-confessing Judaism rather than the Essene-influenced religion of James, or indeed the Gentile Christianity espoused by Ignatius. Equally speculative is Burke's suggestion that Ignatius had brought about monepiscopacy at Antioch by the force of his own personality (and in-

---

317. See Schoedel, "Theological Norms," 44, in summary. For Schoedel, the issue is not relations between Gentile and Jewish Christians but rather the matter of the bishop's authority.
318. Similarly Donahue ("Jewish Christianity," 82), who, while arguing that Ignatius is really writing about Antioch, suggests that the issues facing the Asian churches are similar enough.
319. So, strongly, Sim, *Gospel of Matthew*, 262–69.
320. Williams, *Bishop Lists*, 74–77.
321. For Matthew as Antiochene, see Meier in Brown and Meier, *Antioch and Rome*, 22–27.

deed that his passage through Asia brought it about there also).[322] Even if this could be imagined, we would then have to suppose that the absence of peace at Antioch was brought about through his removal, in keeping with findings noted above relating to the chaos that follows the departure of a charismatic leader, and in turn we would have to explain the manner in which peace was returned in a relatively short time.

The virtual impossibility of explaining how monepiscopacy comes to emerge within such a divided Christian community is a further argument against seeing Ignatius as undisputed *monepiskopos* of the diverse Christian communities of the city.

IGNATIUS AS *MONEPISKOPOS* OF SOME CHRISTIAN COMMUNITIES?

I thus reach the conclusion that Ignatius was not *monepiskopos*, simply on the grounds that a single *episkopos* might not be recognized by Jewish and Gentile congregations alike. However, it might be argued that even if he is not sole *monepiskopos*, he might exercise some form of monepiscopacy within communities of Pauline heritage,[323] or within Gentile communities, or indeed within those of mixed origin who nonetheless did not insist on Gentile observance of the law. This will be seen to be yet further fruitless speculation, but here I give some attention to the possibility simply because there has already been much along similar lines. Thus Robinson suggests that Ignatius represents a majority through his espousal of forming orthodoxy and may be *monepiskopos* on that basis;[324] yet, being the representative of a majority might be the position of a domestic *episkopos* in federation.

First, I note that there is no evidence of ministries at Antioch prior to Ignatius apart from the statement at Acts 13:1 that there were prophets and teachers in the Antiochene church. These ministries, I may suggest, were distinct from any economic office that may or may not have been practiced by *episkopoi* and *diakonoi*;[325] we simply do not know whether these offices were known at the time, though it is reasonable to say that, in order for the group to eat together, there must have been individuals performing these functions even for the dispute between Peter and Paul over table fellowship to have occurred. Even if there was no individual designated an *episkopos*, for the meal to take place there has to be an *oikonomos*, in other words, somebody functioning as an *episkopos* functioned, and there have to be assistants at the

322. Burke, "Monarchical Episcopate," 516–18.
323. On the extent to which Ignatius was a "Paulinist," note Trevett, *Study of Ignatius*, 19–20.
324. So Robinson, *Ignatius of Antioch*, 96–97.
325. See Gehring, *House Church*, 110. Gehring follows a long tradition by suggesting that these ministries represent "charismatic leadership."

tables, those who, whether termed as such and holding office as such or not, acted as *diakonoi*. And in order for purity to be maintained, all these would have to be Jewish. This, I have already suggested, was fundamental to the breach between Gentile and law-observant Jewish congregations at Antioch.

However, although Acts 13:1 identifies prophets and teachers, I may note Gehring's suggestion that those named—Simeon, Lucius, and Manaen—alongside Barnabas and Saul, are householders, and that they might have formed a leadership council akin to the gathering of elders in Jerusalem, for which reason their names are found together.[326] In particular, the royal connections of Manaen would indicate that he was a person of substance and therefore able to offer patronage to the church. Whereas Gehring accepts that there can be no certainty here, it seems more probable that this group is a leadership group of householders, alongside the Essene household, rather than simply representing a single house-church. It is, of course, possible that this tradition lists the major figures in the Essene household, but if this is the case then it is hard to account for Paul's toleration, even at this stage, of admitting Gentiles into the fellowship. Rather, Acts 11:26 may be taken as implying that, after a year within Barnabas's Essene community, Paul had started his own household congregation, albeit one that maintained relations with Barnabas.

Against this must be set the discussion of Zetterholm, who seems to assume that the Christian groupings were monolithic groupings in his suggestion of the Gentile congregations in Antioch as "challengers" to the polity. He argues that since they were not recognized as Jews, and therefore excluded from the Jewish *politeuma* but unable fully to participate in the life of the Hellenistic *polis*, they organize themselves as a distinct *collegium*.[327] As such, they might take on associational aspects of behavior, such as the appointment of officers. Whereas in Ephesus we meet distinct schools of Christian practice with relatively little contact, here there are offshoots from a single branch that are seeking to strengthen group identity. We might, following Zetterholm, see Jewish and law-observant Christians as similarly forming a single *collegium*. Thus, the statement in *Constitutiones apostolorum* 7.46 that Paul ordained Ignatius while Peter ordained Euodius as bishops of Antioch might be more than a "confused echo" of historical events,[328] particularly in view of the possibility

---

326. Ibid., 111–12.

327. Zetterholm, *Formation of Christianity*, 193–202. Beyond the critique offered here there are other problems with Zetterholm's narrative. First, it would seem strange for Christians to seek official recognition as a *collegium*, which in view of already hostile attitudes toward Christianity would be a somewhat foolhardy exercise. Second, any breach occurred in the wake of the incident at Antioch, and not in the 90s as Zetterholm suggests. For further critique of the specifics of Zetterholm's account, see Robinson, *Ignatius of Antioch*, 89–94.

328. So Trevett, *Study of Ignatius*, 41.

that "Euodius" is a Hellenization of an Aramaic name,[329] namely, that at some
point there were two Christian leaders within Antioch, one of Jewish descent
heading a law-observant community and one of Gentile descent.

Zetterholm argues for the characterization of Gentile Christianity at Antioch as an association on the grounds that it displays the indicators that one
would expect for a social movement: a goal (non-Jewish Christianity), evidence
of conflict (the clear distinction between this version of Christianity and Judaism), and organizational adaptation (episcopacy).[330] This associational view of
Christianity, though hypothetical as far as Antioch is concerned, certainly is
imported into the Asian context by Ignatius and may well be derived from the
self-understanding of the church derived from Antioch. Thus, he refers to the
diakonia of the *episkopos* for the commonwealth (*eis to koinon*),[331] employing
the language of civic and associational governance, and similarly he forbids
manumission from the common fund (*apo tou koinou*) in writing to Polycarp.[332]
As Ignatius characterizes the church in Smyrna as a corporation (*sōmateion*),[333]
I may again note the use of associational language. The problem with this
analysis is that it seems to see the two groups as single groups rather than as
a loose collection. In particular, we need to account for the community that
gave rise to the Gospel of Matthew, which would seem to fit into neither. For
Zetterholm, who dates the breach in the 90s, Matthew was the foundational
document of both communities and was brought into the Gentile community at
the time of the division. Thus he is not confronted with this question, though
he faces the problem of understanding why a breach in the 90s should come
about after fifty or more years of worshiping together.[334] Equally difficult is
the hypothesis of Meier that Matthew lay in the same line of development as
Ignatius,[335] as we may characterize Matthew as having a law-observant vision

329. Eusebius counts Ignatius as *episkopos* of Antioch second in succession to Peter (*Hist.
eccl.* 3.36.2), after Euodius. However, the episcopal list of Eusebius itself is far from unproblem-
atic and may well represent a degree of idealization. On this, see C. Munier, "Á propos d'Ignace
d'Antioche: Observations sur la liste épiscopale d'Antioche," *RevScRel* 55 (1981): 126–31. The
confused nature of Eusebius's succession list is taken by Bauer (*Orthodoxy and Heresy*, 63–64)
as evidence that there was no *monepiskopos* at the time of Ignatius, and that Ignatius's claims
are utterly inflated (though Ignatius never claims to be *monepiskopos*).
330. Zetterholm, *Formation of Christianity*, 203–11.
331. Ign. *Phld.* 1:1
332. Ign. *Pol.* 4:3. For this language as civic and associational, see William R. Schoedel, *Ignatius of Antioch: A Commentary on the Letters of Ignatius of Antioch*, ed. Helmut Koester,
Hermeneia (Philadelphia: Fortress, 1985), 14, 271.
333. Ign. *Smyrn.* 11:2.
334. So Robinson, *Ignatius of Antioch*, 94. Of course, I am not suggesting that these communities had worshiped together since the 40s.
335. In Brown and Meier, *Antioch and Rome*, 45–72.

of Christianity. Although Matthew has a polemical relationship to Pharisaic Judaism and to its leaders, contrasting those who are to have leadership in the Matthaean community with those of Pharisaic circles, and although it is a community inclusive of Gentiles, it is equally hostile to those who dispense with the requirements of the law.[336] Although there is tradition in common between Matthew and Ignatius, this may simply be the common ground of the Antiochene Christian tradition, especially since all of it is to be found in what is identified as the "M" material,[337] material found only in Matthew among the Synoptic Gospels. It is possible, as already suggested, that the figure of Peter represents a strand of Jewish Christianity alternative to the circle around James, which means in turn that there are not two groupings in Antioch, but three.[338] Further to this, I may note the presence of distinct forms of Christianity at Antioch in the period, noting with Bauer the presence of Menander, Saturninus, Cerdo, and Basilides at various times in the late first and second centuries.[339] The picture suddenly looks more complicated than that of two blocks of Christians, each with its own overseer.

On the basis of his view of a single breach, Zetterholm suggests that the (Gentile) Christian communities sought recognition, and they did so by virtue of claiming a status as a *collegium*. It seems unlikely that these Christian communities (or rather, this Christian community) should seek such formal recognition, but the nature of the Jewish *politeuma* from which they had departed might nonetheless inform their *self*-understanding as a single grouping. I might add that the *collegium* would be a single *collegium*

336. See the extensive argument of Anthony J. Saldarini, *Matthew's Christian-Jewish Community*, CSHJ (Chicago: University of Chicago Press, 1994), notably 84–123.

337. See Paul Foster, "The Epistles of Ignatius of Antioch and the Writings That Later Formed the New Testament," in *The Reception of the New Testament in the Apostolic Fathers*, ed. Andrew F. Gregory and C. M. Tuckett (Oxford: Oxford University Press, 2005), 173–81. Foster discusses all the alleged parallels between the Gospel of Matthew and the writings of Ignatius and reaches the tentative conclusion that Ignatius had knowledge of the written Gospel. The strongest parallel, however, as Foster admits, is Ign. *Smyrn.* 1:1 // Matt. 3:15; given the context in *Smyrnaeans*, the citation may be creedal or liturgical. Nonetheless, Foster's account is careful and gives the most adequate account of alleged parallels.

338. We may not, however, set up a conflict between these congregations and those of Ignatius on the basis of the legitimation of leadership, Ignatius being seen as a type of the charismatic, Matthew as a type of the rational-legal, as does Hann ("Judaism and Jewish Christianity," 349–54), because this is to build too much on too flimsy evidence. Thus, e.g., Matthew's comments about leadership are interpreted by Hann as sustaining leadership by tradition, whereas for David L. Bartlett (*Ministry in the New Testament* [Minneapolis: Fortress, 1993], 85–88) it is the voice of suspicion regarding the claims of leaders that speaks more loudly. Meier (in Brown and Meier, *Antioch and Rome*, 72) rightly describes Matthew's attitude as "ambivalent." Moreover, any such conflict would be entirely secondary to the more fundamental conflict over the relationship between law observance and covenantal belonging.

339. Bauer, *Orthodoxy and Heresy*, 66.

and, as such, when the office of *episkopos* is so named and appointed, has a single *episkopos*.

The problem with this picture is that it supposes a breach of Gentile Christians from a single household. Whereas the household of Barnabas might be characterized as a household of central significance in Antiochene law-observant Christianity, it was, as we have already seen, far from the only household. If, as an intentional social movement with a clear social aim, namely, corporate recognition, we might follow Zetterholm in seeing the Gentile Christian community of Antioch as a single body from the beginning, it might be led by a single *episkopos*. And then, as further households are added, each household either would come under its own leadership or would acknowledge the leadership of the original house. If this latter event had occurred, then in a later period Ignatius might be found as *monepiskopos* of Gentile Christian congregations at Antioch, and if issues over commensality subsequently break down, it might be possible for a number of Jewish Christian congregations to come into the same grouping. On this picture, when the Gentile Christians removed themselves from the Essene household of Barnabas, they set themselves up as a single community with a single *mebaqqer*, and as this community in turn subdivided, the separate households continued in close relationship with the original household as a result of their self-consciousness as a single association. Having said all this, it is equally possible that these Gentile households might simply have existed as a federation as did, it appears, the law-observant households. Moreover, the relationship between the Essene household in Jerusalem and those domestic congregations headed by the elders would provide a model for this latter arrangement, whereas otherwise we are mired in speculation without the benefit of evidence.

Whereas it is possible to argue that monepiscopacy might have originated very early in Gentile Antiochene Christianity as a result of the manner in which the original single Essene community divided, and thus to see Ignatius as some kind of *monepiskopos*, this is possible only, and far from proved. On balance, it is more likely that these Gentile households followed a model of federation, and that Ignatius is simply a domestic *episkopos* among others.

IGNATIUS AS CONGREGATIONAL *EPISKOPOS*?

We are led to consider the almost inevitable conclusion. Just as was observed in studying the Pastoral Epistles, language applying to a *monepiskopos* may readily apply simply to a congregational *episkopos*. It is thus possible that Ignatius was simply a domestic *episkopos* among others in the city. It is even possible that, although there was no established system of monepiscopacy, the other leaders deferred to him by virtue of the extent to which he appears to have exhibited charismatic leadership,[340] though this would still mean that when he speaks of *episkopoi* to the Asian churches, he is more likely to be speaking of domestic *episkopoi*. Moreover, the characterization of Ignatius's episcopate does not depend on this latter point.

When Ignatius speaks of the church at worship, with the *episkopos* at the center, surrounded by a crown of presbyters, the picture that may readily be derived is one of a single domestic Christian community, like that of *Apostolic Church Order*.

Moreover, I have already noted that when Ignatius directs Polycarp in the performance of the duties of an *episkopos*, these duties are fundamentally economic,[341] that in writing to the Smyrnaeans he lends spiritual significance to the economic activity of an *episkopos* in *agapē* as in eucharist, and further below we will see Ignatius supporting the model of domestic and economic *episkopē* in writing to the Ephesians. This provides yet further evidence that the *oikonomia* of a household was the basis of Ignatius's understanding of episcopacy, and that his office in Antioch was that of exercising precisely such *oikonomia*.

Ignatius may have a well-developed and reflective attitude toward the episcopal office; indeed, as Vogt suggests,[342] the system must be well established and already of relative antiquity by the time of Ignatius to enable him to have constructed his reflective theology of episcopacy. But if, as argued above, single-congregation episcopacy is the fundamental form of Christian leadership in the first generations, then even if we continue to date Ignatius to the first decade (rather than the fourth) of the second century, that is sufficient time for Ignatius to form a theology of (congregational) episcopacy.

All that militates against this understanding is Ignatius's interest in the peace that had been brought about within the Antiochene church. Ignatius states that the church at Antioch is at peace, and not that the church in a particular household is at peace. It is this consideration alone that might lead us to question the possibility that he is *episkopos* of a single household. And yet, even the interest in peace within the Antiochene church does not militate entirely against seeing Ignatius as purely a domestic *episkopos*, for, as noted above, it might have been possible, even after the fundamental split within Antiochene

---

340. A position distinct from that of Bauer (*Orthodoxy and Heresy*, 62–63), who, while seeing Ignatius as a domestic *episkopos*, also suggests that he is in a minority of one, whereas it is possible for a domestic *episkopos*, by virtue of recognition by a putative federation, to be a member of a majority party.

341. See chap. 2, under the heading "The Economic Function of *Episkopoi* in the Directions of Ignatius to Polycarp."

342. Hermann J. Vogt, "Ignatius von Antiochen über den Bischof und seine Gemeinde," *TQ* 158 (1978): 18–19.

Christianity between observant and non-observant Christ-confessing communities, for the communities to maintain some form of communication akin to federation. There were law-observant Christian communities in Rome at the time of Justin that appear to have received some form of recognition within the federation, and I may suggest that the same may be true at Antioch. As such, Ignatius may be a domestic *episkopos*, leader of a single Christian household, in some form of federation with other Christian households within the city.

Conclusion on the Nature of Ignatius's Episcopate

For all that Ignatius is claimed to be *monepiskopos*, the one certainty we may have regarding the nature of his episcopate is that he was not that. Had he been undisputed *monepiskopos* within all the congregations of the city, it would mean that all the multifarious issues resulting from tension between differing attitudes toward the law had been resolved.

There are, however, three other possibilities. Unfortunately, all are hypothetical, as each depends on further hypothesis to sustain it.

First, it is possible that Ignatius was simply a single *episkopos* among many. If this is the case, then it must further be hypothesized that, as a single *episkopos*, his household is in contact with other Christian communities within the city, including law-observant Christian communities, because of the manner in which he sees peace at home come about, as this peace would have to be brought about across a number of Christian communities. This in turn is not impossible, given that it is known extensively elsewhere in the Christian world, but it is likewise not proven.

The second possibility is that he was a *monepiskopos* of a group of Gentile, non-law-observant Christian congregations. Again, to sustain such a view, further hypothesization is necessary, for this group, as a group, would seem to have made peace with another group. Such is arguable due to the nature of the growth of Christian communities at Antioch from a single identifiable beginning, but is, again, without proof. Moreover, to sustain this view would mean that there was no federation of Christian leaders as there was elsewhere.

The third possibility is that he was a domestic *episkopos* among others but had a position of prominence among Gentile *episkopoi* rather as James had a position of prominence among the congregations of Jerusalem. This is possible if the Jerusalem model had been adopted in Antioch; however, although this is a possible development, we cannot state with certainty that it had taken place.

Certain conclusions thus elude us. Monepiscopacy in Antioch came about at some time between the presence of Peter and the episcopate of Serapion.

The evidence available for the intervening period is restricted to that provided by Ignatius, and this evidence is inconclusive.

Nonetheless, the period of Ignatius provides a vital turning point that, whatever the prior situation, would supply the necessary condition for monepiscopacy to come about: the healing of the fundamental breach in Antiochene Christianity. This happened not, however, through any trait, action, or belief of Ignatius, but through the simple force of historical circumstance, quite possibly resulting from events south of Antioch. How monepiscopacy developed from this point depends on what was in place before, and we simply do not know what was in place before. If a "partial" monepiscopacy already existed, such a well-established polity would enable others to enter the same monepiscopal system, and once there is unity between a group of Gentile Christians and some of Jewish heritage, it becomes possible for others to affiliate, extending the scope of the responsibilities of the *episkopos*. If, however, there is federation in place, without any, even partial, monepiscopacy, then the same centralizing forces that led to monepiscopacy at Rome and Alexandria might operate within Antioch. Finally, if one among the *episkopoi* is viewed as *primus inter pares*, like James at Jerusalem, then, once again, the relatively early development of monepiscopacy in Antioch may be explained on this basis.

The nature of Ignatius's episcopate is uncertain, and although I have argued above for a Hadrianic date, this largely depends on the identification of Ignatius's "leopards" with the Cohors I Lepidiana and on educated guesses about troop and imperial movements. However, it is at least possible that he was a domestic *episkopos* in a single congregation operating at the time of Hadrian. Such a picture certainly is preferable to the unthinkable image of a *monepiskopos* exercising metropolitan authority in the reign of Trajan.

Conclusion

At the end of a complex and wide-ranging discussion I am left confessing ignorance regarding the nature of Ignatius's episcopate. Two possibilities remain, both of which are hypothetical, and both of which require further hypothesis to sustain them. The possibilities are that Ignatius is simply a domestic *episkopos*, or that he is *episkopos* of a group of Christians within Antioch. The uncertainty over Ignatius means that it is even harder to discuss the manner in which monepiscopacy emerged in the city.

On balance, I have preferred to see Ignatius as simply the *episkopos* of a single Christian community, simply because the descriptions that Ignatius gives of worship within the Asian congregations seem to reflect the worship of a single Christian household, and because his insistence on a single meeting would seem to reflect a mindset formed in a single congregation rather than a group of congregations meeting separately by necessity.

This is, however, of all the conclusions reached in this work, the most provisional and the most partial. However, a frank confession of uncertainty surely is preferable to the past confident assertions of Ignatius's monepiscopate based solely on mistaken assumptions regarding the nature of aboriginal systems of Christian leadership. Ignatius provides no evidence for the formation of monepiscopacy in Antioch, and so suspicion about Ignatius's monepiscopate does not necessitate dating his writing to a period late in the second century. My positive conclusion is that any discussion of Ignatius, of episcopacy in Antioch, and of the liturgy any *episkopos* might oversee should take account of the relationship between Jewish and Gentile Christians in the city.

The Asian Communities Addressed by Ignatius

It is on the basis of this discussion of Ignatius's episcopate that I may proceed to see what may be gathered regarding the institutions of Christian leadership in the Asian communities to which he wrote, apart from Smyrna, which has already been discussed.

A few general points may also precede the main discussion. That I have been able to discern a distinct pattern in Smyrna indicates that Ignatius is responding to real situations in the churches of which he has knowledge, and to the real governance exercised in these churches, as do various hints of real acquaintance with the churches, albeit in some situations at second hand.[343] Interpretation of the Smyrnaean correspondence was made easier through external knowledge, and I might not have deduced that federation was in place were we solely in possession of Ignatius's letters to the church and to Polycarp, although there is nothing in them to contradict such a conclusion. If each letter is examined on its own basis, this may also reveal some insights into the relationship between the *episkopos*, the presbyters, and the *diakonoi*. However, although rejecting suggestions that Ignatius really knew only his own community and speaks in reality of Antioch when he speaks of the

---

343. So Christine Trevett, "The Other Letters to the Churches of Asia: Apocalypse and Ignatius of Antioch," *JSNT* 37 (1989): 121. I may point to the knowledge of Onesimus's silence (Ign. *Eph.* 6:1) as genuine knowledge of issues in churches that he had not visited. The methodology of taking each letter individually without seeking an overall solution to any issue posed by them, or attempting to subsume the material into an overarching picture derived from elsewhere, is employed by Jerry L. Sumney, "Those Who 'Ignorantly Deny Him': The Opponents of Ignatius of Antioch," *JECS* 1 (1993): 345–65, though focusing on the nature of Ignatius's opponents rather than the communities' church order.

Asian churches,[344] I remain aware that he had not worshiped with them in their house-churches. As such, whereas he is responding to real issues in these churches, he must imagine and construct the individual meetings in accordance with those with which he is familiar, and so his descriptions of the assemblies may reflect his Antiochene experience rather than the everyday realities of the churches that he visits. Beyond that, of course, his fundamental theological principles, in particular his view of the relationship between Judaism and Christianity and his conviction that unity under an *episkopos* is the means by which heresy is kept out of the churches, would be formed by the Antiochene experience. Thus, I must seek at each point to determine what relates to the Asian communities, and what Ignatius is bringing with him from Antioch.[345]

In doing so, I may work on the basis that he does not assume the existence of monepiscopacy. Even if he is aware of the system, a conclusion that I have shown to be debatable, we need not see him as imposing it on, or even assuming its existence in, other churches. As noted in my discussion of Smyrna, his vision is essentially that of a single house-church, and so great caution should be taken in assuming that the *episkopoi* who are mentioned are anything other than single domestic leaders, and that the presbyters are anything other than patrons like those discerned in the community of 1 Timothy. My examination is also a test of the hypotheses of Wagner and Campbell, who see monepiscopacy (as it is meant here) emerging at the time of 1 Timothy.[346] While focusing on the city as the unit in which monepiscopacy emerged (and thus improving considerably on the old consensus), they largely assume the dating of the old consensus, by which monepiscopacy emerges at the time of a Trajanic Ignatius. In the light of the new picture of Ignatius that is emerging, it is worth discussing the communities to which he wrote in order to see whether there is any evidence for monepiscopacy beyond the assumption that this is what Ignatius means when he writes of an *episkopos*.

Ephesus

In discussing the Asian churches, I turn first to Ephesus. Here there is some control to the discussion in that we are aware that there was some federation among Ephesian congregations from the end of the first century (assuming

344. E.g., Corwin (*St. Ignatius*, 57–58) suggests that the problem of Judaizing to which *Philadelphians* and *Magnesians* refer is an issue at Antioch rather than in the communities addressed.
345. A mediating view as adopted by John P. Meier, "Matthew and Ignatius: A Response to William R. Schoedel," in *Social History of the Matthean Community: Cross-Disciplinary Approaches*, ed. David L. Balch (Minneapolis: Fortress, 1991), 178–79.
346. Wagner, *Anfänge*; Campbell, *Elders*.

this to be the date of Titus). I have also noted that 1 Timothy presupposes a situation in which congregations are formed of various households that have come together, and thus that there are local groups of congregational presbyters, who are honored senior patrons, but that there is no evidence that the *episkopos* of 1 Timothy is a *monepiskopos*. The fundamental unit of the church was still the individual congregation, presbyters were leading older men within the individual Christian community, and the *episkopos* continued to exercise an economic role, either as a *leitourgia* or as an appointee of the patrons, even though there is some scholasticization within this community, which is affecting the bishop's role. I thus examine what Ignatius says of Ephesian Christianity to see whether there is any development in the direction of monepiscopacy and to see, moreover, whether the status of the presbyters has changed since the time of 1 Timothy, since monepiscopacy necessarily leads to the clericalization of the presbytery, since the presbyters, under a *monepiskopos*, hold the position formerly held by domestic *episkopoi*.

These conclusions derive from examination of the Pastoral Epistles, as Titus speaks of federation, whereas 1 Timothy addresses the individual congregation. Thus, the question posed by the Ignatian letter to Ephesus is that of whether, by the time of Ignatius, there has been any development from the situation presumed by the Pastoral Epistles, from federation toward monepiscopacy. Once again, of course, this raises the question of dating. Whereas I have prescinded from answering the question of the date of the Pastoral Epistles, I have argued above that Ignatius met martyrdom in the last year of Hadrian's principate. It is not unreasonable in this light to suggest that, whatever the date of the Pastoral Epistles, it is prior to 135/6.

In discussing this situation, I assume that Ignatius understands something of the nature of the polity of the Ephesian congregation(s) that he is addressing. For instance, it is theoretically possible that he met a domestic *episkopos* but believed him to be something akin to a *monepiskopos*, and that whereas Ephesus is still a loose federation with no *episkopos* as such, Ignatius perceived Onesimus as *monepiskopos* of the Ephesian congregations. But such suspicion is groundless, not least because, having neither experience nor knowledge of monepiscopacy, he would not assume that such a system is found elsewhere. Moreover, I may anticipate that Ignatius has some understanding of the church order in the city on the basis that he has knowledge of Onesimus, the *episkopos* who came to him, and of whom Ignatius claimed a mystical understanding.[347]

In examining the situation at Ephesus, I may note in the first instance Ignatius's view that the people are to be subject to the *episkopos* and presbytery

347. Ign. *Eph*. 1.

together.[348] Whoever the presbyters are, they are joined to the *episkopos* in terms of the authority that they exercise. Thus, even if the *episkopos* here is a *monepiskopos*, he is not totally a *monarch* bishop in that he is not empowered to act without the presbyters; however, if the presbyters are not actually officers but continue as a group of honored elders, this does not prevent them from exercising authority within the community. Although, when the Ephesian presbyters and *episkopos* are said to be in harmony,[349] this statement may be treated with a degree of suspicion that they are not entirely so, but surely such harmony, in the Ephesian polity, is at least the ideal.

However, we do not know whether the presbytery here is a presbytery within a single congregation or a reference to the gathered presbyters of Ephesus, and whether the *episkopos* is a single-household *episkopos* like the *episkopos* of 1 Timothy or an *episkopos* claiming some kind of authority over more than one church. If Onesimus is a *monepiskopos*, then these are subordinate presbyters, whereas if he is simply a single domestic *episkopos*, then the situation is the same as that prevailing earlier, and these presbyters are the patronal group within the congregation.

The possibilities are the same as already outlined in the discussion of Ignatius's Antioch.

First, a single household or congregation is addressed, and the presbyters and the *episkopos* are within that single congregation. That is to say, it is possible that Ignatius is addressing only a single household *episkopos* among others in Ephesus (so still mirroring the situation of the community addressed by 1 Timothy).

Second, the *episkopos* is a *monepiskopos*, and the presbyters are subordinate officers. Although we cannot a priori rule out the possibility that the degree of federation, which we have seen to have been relatively early and relatively strong, has reached the point where *presbyteros* is the primary designation of the leaders apart from the *episkopos*, especially given our uncertainty about the date of Ignatius's writing, if the dating proposed above is accepted, then it seems unlikely that so much progress would have been made in that direction.

Third, the presbyters are in charge of a number of churches within Ephesus that are grouped under an *episkopos*. As such, the *episkopos* is not a *monepiskopos* in the sense that he is the sole *episkopos* within Ephesus but is so in the sense that he has subordinate officers and responsibility for more than one congregation, presumably congregations of Pauline descent, and that had been born out of the original Pauline gathering.

348. With reference to Ign. *Eph.* 2:2.
349. Ign. *Eph.* 4.

The distinction between the second and third is slight but significant. The degree of authority that the *episkopos* would exercise might be seen as somewhat less, and, significantly for the argument, the number of Christians in question would be somewhat smaller.

There is also a nonpossibility: Ignatius cannot be addressing a federation of independent households in which Onesimus plays a leading role as an *episkopos* among others in the federation. This is impossible because of Ignatius's statement that the presbytery and the *episkopos* are in harmony, which indicates that these are two distinct institutions. If the *episkopos* is a functioning officer where the *presbyteroi* are a group of patrons, the situation addressed by Paul in 1 Timothy, then certainly they are to be seen as distinct. The same is true if the *episkopos* is a *monepiskopos*. If, however, the presbytery is a presbytery *kata polin*, then the *episkopos* is a presbyter among others and therefore not to be distinguished from the presbytery and given a distinct title; there is no distinction between *episkopos* and presbytery such that they may harmonize with one another. Either Onesimus is *episkopos* of more than one community, or he is an *episkopos* within a single household. Here, again, I should clarify that my assumption is that Ignatius was not confused in order to flesh out the arguments from within his letter. We can determine the nature of the address only through what Ignatius says. We test each possibility.

ONESIMUS AS *MONEPISKOPOS* AND THE *PRESBYTEROI* AS SUBORDINATE OFFICERS?

In constructing the situation met by Ignatius at Ephesus, Trebilco suggests that something like monepiscopacy (in the sense in which I use the term here) must be intended.[350] Though far from being alone in making such an assertion, he is representative of this view. But Ignatius's language would be the same if he were addressing a single church made up of several households such as that of 1 Timothy, or indeed of Corinth at the time of Paul. Although there are indications that more than one congregation is being addressed—the opening addresses the whole church, the exhortations to gather together,[351] and the indications that there are some who are separated from the church,[352] as well as the manner in which elsewhere, as here, Ignatius insists on unity through the means of the *episkopos*—this does not necessitate monepiscopacy but may instead reflect a situation in which a church drawn from a number of households might meet separately within their own houses on occasion, as well as together.

350. Trebilco, *Early Christians in Ephesus*, 643–45.
351. Ign. *Eph.* 13:1–2.
352. Ign. *Eph.* 5:2–3.

The problem with the idea that multiple congregations are being addressed lies in the exhortation that they are to gather. It is hard to imagine that the entire Christian population of Ephesus might realistically gather under a single roof. Although, in noting the evidence both for common meetings and for distinct meetings in various of Ignatius's letters, Maier suggests that some meetings might include the whole church whereas others might take place during the week within smaller groups,[353] this still does not avoid the problem of how the entire Christian population of a city is to be gathered in one place. It is true that Paul implies that this might happen in Corinth,[354] but it would be reasonable to suggest that the number of Christians in Corinth was somewhat smaller. One may, perhaps, envisage the use of a public space, recollecting Paul's use of the *scholē* of Tyrannus in the city,[355] or the possibility that rooms within houses might be enlarged;[356] we may also consider that, in the third century, *Vita Polycarpi* describes the gathering of a church from across the city of Smyrna and beyond for the election of a bishop (without specifying where such a gathering took place, beyond stating that "the Lord's house" was full).[357] However, it might be possible to argue that Ignatius is confused at this point, and that he fails to appreciate the number of Christians involved with the consequent difficulties of gathering them in one place, and that he has in mind a relatively small number of congregations. As such, although this points away from complete monepiscopacy, it is not an entirely secure argument.

However, a possible answer is provided by Robinson, who suggests that a metaphysical rather than a concrete unity is intended, and that this metaphysical unity is obtained through the single *episkopos*.[358] This is not as desperate a solution as it might sound at first; it is possible to argue that a single gathering for a single act might take place in a number of distinct households. The first point to note is that Ignatius employs extensive cultic imagery; his reference to himself as god-bearer (*theophoros*), and to the Ephesians as neighbors in the procession (*synodoi*) as god-bearers and temple-bearers (*naophoroi*),

353. Maier, *Social Setting*, 153–54.
354. At 1 Cor. 14:23.
355. Acts 19:8–10.
356. The suggestion of Georg Schöllgen, "Hausgemeinden, οἶκος-Ekklesiologie und monar-chischer Episkopat," *JAC* 31 (1988): 80. Schöllgen also deals with this issue in arguing that the Pauline communities met only in single groupings, and that there were no separate household meetings apart from the single gathering as one church. This may well be the case among the properly Pauline communities, for although the Philippian Christian community was made up of individual households that might meet separately, we have already seen that the church in this place is exceptional.
357. *Vit. Pol.* 21.
358. Robinson, *Ignatius of Antioch*, 87n153.

adorned with the commandments,[359] is intended to recall the cult practices of the festivals of Hellenistic cities.[360] I may next note that a fundamental purpose of these festivals is to manifest and reinforce the unity of the citizen body.[361] However, this need not mean that sacrifices might not be offered in smaller units. At Teos sacrifices were offered in groups, *symoriai*, at the festival of Antiochos and Laodikē, and individuals were enjoined to sacrifice within their own households on the same occasion,[362] and at the Pergamene festival of Attalos III a sacrifice described as being of the entire people (*pandēmei*) is actually offered in separate *phylai* by the individual phylarchs.[363] Against Robinson, however, I may also note that this metaphysical unity does not require a *monepiskopos*, as it is equally obtainable within a loose federation of individual domestic *episkopoi*.

A further objection to seeing Onesimus as a *monepiskopos* lies in the fact that part of the object of the letter is to ask that the *diakonos* Burrhus continue with him;[364] as Trebilco points out, this is not something that the *episkopos* alone can determine, for it is up to the addressees to decide whether Burrhus is to continue on with Ignatius.[365] And yet it hardly seems likely that this is a matter for democratic decision by the entire church, as Trebilco seems to imagine. In any event, whereas the issue of a single *diakonos* indicates that a single gathering is being addressed, it seems unlikely that this should be a gathering of the entire Ephesian church.

One argument employed in favor of seeing Onesimus as a *monepiskopos* is the suggestion that this monepiscopacy is meeting with opposition. However, this argument will not work. For if the path suggested here by which church order in Ephesus developed monepiscopacy out of federation has any merit, then the formation of a federation and the subsequent development of citywide Christianity would happen only by mutual consent. It is, however, possible that individual presbyters who thought that they should be the *episkopos* instead of the one appointed might absent themselves from gathering with the *episkopos*, but there is nothing in Ignatius's letter to suggest that this had happened. Trebilco says, once again indicating the confusion caused by the consensus, that "leadership was plural, so the emergence of one *episkopos* as the key leader would involve some change."[366] However, leadership in individual

359. Ign. *Eph.* 9:2.
360. So Brent, *Ignatius of Antioch*.
361. On the unifying function of civic sacrifice, see Dio Chrysostom, *Conc. Apam.* 29.
362. *SEG* 41, 1003, I + II.
363. *OGIS* 332.
364. Ign. *Eph.* 2:1–2.
365. Trebilco, *Early Christians in Ephesus*, 680.
366. Ibid., 669.

communities was, I suggest, never plural, and thus, for an individual Christian community as opposed to the gathered group of leaders, there was no change as monepiscopacy emerges. In the context of this discussion Trebilco suggests that opposition to the monepiscopate derived from those who valued prophetic media of communication;[367] these could have been from any of the identified groups of Christians in Ephesus, for the Johannine school, the circle of the seer, and the Pauline circle represented by the Pastoral Epistles all knew the practice of prophecy. But, as I have argued before, prophetic communication is a means of communication only, and not a mode of leadership; suggestions of tension between prophetic leadership and episcopal leadership derive from a misreading of Weber, confusing charismatic communication with charismatic leadership.[368] There is no contradiction, therefore, between episcopal governance and prophetic communication in the assembly, as the two phenomena are completely independent. Indeed, Ignatius himself spoke prophetically and made reference to other related phenomena.[369]

Thus, although the idea that Onesimus is *monepiskopos* is not altogether impossible, numerous difficulties stand in its way. In particular, further hypothesization about the nature of the gathering and the need to assign a locus for such a meeting are required for this to be sustained. More to the point, the language used of Onesimus's episcopate might equally apply to a bishop in a single congregation and so be applied without the need for further hypothesization.

ONESIMUS AS *EPISKOPOS* OF MORE THAN ONE HOUSEHOLD BUT NOT ALL

In asking whether Onesimus exercised a limited monepiscopate, I have in mind that the same suggestion was made (though rejected) with regard to Ignatius at Antioch. Nonetheless, I may observe Trebilco's germane question of whether the epistle is written to all the Christians in Ephesus or to a group among Ephesian Christians (having in mind the question of whether Johannine as well as Pauline Christians are participating in the federation that he believes Ignatius to be addressing). He rightly points out that there is no attempt by Ignatius to deny the orthodoxy of those Christians who do not gather with

367. Ibid., 670–74.
368. Stewart(-Sykes), "Prophecy and Patronage." Note also the comments in chap. 5 below, under the heading "Institutionalization as an Explanation of Monepiscopacy."
369. Ign. *Phld.* 7:1. Compare discussion of this passage in Stewart(-Sykes), "Prophecy and Patronage," with that of Christine Trevett, "Prophecy and Anti-Episcopal Activity: A Third Error Combatted by Ignatius?" *JEH* 34 (1983): 1–18. See also Vogt, "Ignatius von Antiochen," 17–18, similarly noting that Ignatius's own charismatic activity means that there can hardly be grounds for charismatic opposition.

the bishop, but they are nonetheless not offering a true eucharist.[370] Although this may well refer to the existence of Christian communities of other origin that, while coexisting with the Pauline group, were not in any sense subject to their *episkopos*, the same might be the case were we considering distinct or breakaway households from within the Pauline group. In other words, it is possible that the Pauline group had become so large that it could not readily be contained in a single house, and therefore distinct meetings were taking place, leading to officers other than the *episkopos* having responsibility, rather as Maier suggests.[371] This makes sense of Ignatius's call for them to gather; moreover, if the group is to gather, and perhaps three or four households are intended—a number of households that would accord to the number of those from Ephesus who were able to visit Ignatius[372]—then the question of numbers is less pressing. Finally, if the *diakonoi* are attached still to the *episkopos* but are themselves members of the presbytery, then the question of whether a *diakonos* might be allowed to accompany Ignatius may well be discussed in a more general setting. This is, therefore, a possible solution.

Onesimus as a Household Bishop and the Presbyters as the Leaders in the Community

As already noted, much of the language that Ignatius uses could be understood as applying to a *monepiskopos* or to a congregational bishop. However, if he is a congregational bishop, there is more than one household within his congregation. For whereas the presbytery is said to be in harmony with the *episkopos*, it is also clear that there are other gatherings occurring through the statements that some have not joined the church, the emphasis on a single eucharist,[373] and perhaps also in the statement regarding those who corrupt their households, which may be a reference to household churches and the potential that, through heresy, the households of the church might be corrupted.[374] If the households and the household leaders in question here are not allied to the presbytery (which is in harmony with the *episkopos*), then they are households that are distinct from the group that Ignatius addresses

---

370. Trebilco, *Early Christians in Ephesus*, 681.

371. Maier, *Social Setting*, 53–54.

372. Robinson (*Ignatius of Antioch*, 87) notes this number as evidence for a number of household-churches under Onesimus's control.

373. Ign. *Eph.* 20:2.

374. Ign. *Eph.* 16:1. The primary reference of "corrupting households" is to adultery, although, as P. T. Camelot (*Ignace d'Antioche, Polycarpe de Smyrne: Lettres; Martyre de Polycarpe*, 4th ed., SC 10 [Paris: Cerf, 1998], 72) points out, heresy may be taken as a form of spiritual adultery. The household is often taken as a reference to the individual Christian, particularly in the light of the immediately preceding reference at Ign. *Eph.* 15:3 to the Christians as "temples" of the Spirit.

but that might be expected to join with them. As such, this may mean that multiple households are already gathered under a single *episkopos* in some form of grouping, but it might also simply mean that households have come together to form a single, intentional congregation, as was suggested had been the case at the time of 1 Timothy.

One factor, however, that does point toward the possibility that Onesimus is an *episkopos* in a single household is his reported silence. Although a great deal has been made about the silence of Onesimus in modern scholarship, this rather implies an expectation that the bishop should speak.[375] This in turn derives from an assumption that the *episkopos* has a teaching role within the community. Although this particular issue has yet to be discussed in detail, I may preempt the conclusions of the final chapter and state here that a teaching role for the *episkopos* was a new departure. As such, Onesimus's silence is nothing remarkable. Nonetheless, the very fact that it is mentioned is odd. I may suggest here that although the expectation that the bishop teach was new, it nonetheless had taken hold in some quarters, and thus Onesimus's silence is taken as a negative quality by some in the community; it would seem that the requirement of 1 Timothy that the *episkopos* be *didaktikos* was upheld by some, but not by the *episkopos* himself. Given his silence, it is hard to characterize Onesimus's position on this, but Ignatius's statement in *Ephesians* 6:1 may be significant: "We should receive as the sender himself anyone whom the master of the house [*oikodespotēs*] sends with regard to his own household affairs [*oikonomia*]." The *episkopos* is still principally concerned with the

---

375. The extent of the literature on the silence of Ignatian bishops is perhaps reflective of the extent to which such silence defeats modern, rather than ancient, expectations. Interpretations that see this silence as somehow reflecting a gnostic view of the Godhead (e.g., Henry Chadwick, "The Silence of Bishops in Ignatius," *HTR* 43 [1950]: 169–72) are less convincing than those that suggest that this silence is grounded in a refusal to engage with heretics and their arguments (e.g., Luigi Franco Pizzolato, "Silenzio del vescovo e parola degli eretici in Ignazio d'Antiochia," *Aevum* 44 [1970]: 205–18; Werner Bieder, "Zur Deutung des kirchlichen Schweigens bei Ignatius von Antiochien," *TZ* 12 [1956]: 28–43). Note also A. L. Pettersen, "Sending Heretics to Coventry? Ignatius of Antioch on Reverencing Silent Bishops," *VC* 44 (1990): 335–50; idem, "The Rehabilitation of Bishop Onesimus," in *Papers Presented at the Eleventh International Conference on Patristic Studies Held in Oxford 1991: Liturgica, Second Century, Alexandria before Nicaea, Athanasius and the Arian Controversy*, ed. E. A. Livingstone, StPatr 26 (Louvain: Peeters, 1993), 156–66. Pettersen tends to fuse these arguments by having recourse to the idea of divine silence as a justification for the bishops' refusal to engage with heretics. Most convincing is Harry O. Maier, "The Politics of the Silent Bishop: Silence and Persuasion in Ignatius of Antioch," *JTS* 55 (2004): 503–19. Maier roots this silence in Hellenistic rhetorical theory. In view of the economic role of Onesimus, it is tempting to accept Reinhart Staats's (rejected) suggestion that this should be viewed in the light of the directions of *Did. ap.* 3.10.6–7, 10–11 that the *episkopos* should not discuss the church's finances (made, and discounted, in Staats, "Die katholische Kirche des Ignatius von Antiochen und das Problem ihrer Normativität im zweiten Jahrhundert," *ZNW* 77 [1986]: 144).

management of God's household, and is still fundamentally an *oikonomos*.[376] This indicates that he is *episkopos* of a single household, and that the separate meetings are simply gatherings occurring beyond the main assembly, presumably under the control of individual domestic presbyters. As such, Onesimus is not a *monepiskopos*, since he has no direct control over these gatherings, though there is something of the beginnings of monepiscopacy in that his "church" is something of a mini-federation.

There is, however, a danger posed by these other meetings, since there have been visitors to Ephesus with evil teaching.[377] It is in this light that Ignatius proposes tighter gatherings, but I may also suggest that it is in this light that we may view the prominent household imagery in this letter. That is to say, just as I have suggested that there is a fundamental conflict between domestic and scholasticized forms of Christianity, due to the differing legitimation of the leaders,[378] so this is a particularly dangerous conflict at Ephesus. Just as the author of 1 Timothy encouraged the scholasticization of Ephesian Christianity through the requirement that the *episkopos* be able to teach, and through the recognition of those presbyters who taught alongside acting as patrons, so Ignatius opposes such a development.[379] It is better to be silent than to speak of what is not real, for teaching is good only if the teacher acts in accordance with what is taught, and there is but one true teacher.[380]

Thus, there is no significant argument that militates against seeing Onesimus as simply a single domestic *episkopos* in Ephesus, though this explanation does require some understanding of Ignatius's emphasis on gathering for a single eucharist. We may understand this by seeing that it is possible to see a "metaphysical" unity within a federated group that might nonetheless exist and be represented across a series of domestic churches, each with its own *episkopos*, each celebrating the eucharistic mystery. We may do this by recollecting the manner in which, in the civic festivals of Teos and Pergamon, a civic unity was represented even as distinct groups celebrated their own sacrifices.

376. See Staats, "Die katholische Kirche," 144. For Staats, this is a recollection of the time at which the bishop's office had been economic. However, in common with many others, he fails to note the economic implications of the bishop's liturgical role, noting this original role but suggesting (ibid., 136–37) that it is not prominent in the Ignatian schema.

377. Ign. *Eph.* 9:1.

378. Stewart(-Sykes), "Prophecy and Patronage," developing comments made in *From Prophecy to Preaching: A Search for the Origins of the Christian Homily*, VCSup 59 (Leiden: Brill, 2001), 270–75.

379. So, here, in agreement with Staats, "Die katholische Kirche," 144, that Ignatius's defense of Onesimus's silence is a sign of opposition to scholasticization, though we differ as to the reasons for such opposition.

380. Ign. *Eph.* 15:1.

There is allusion to the federation existing within Ephesus, but monepiscopate is in no way intended, nor is it attributed to Onesimus by Ignatius. His vision of a unified church might bring about monepiscopacy were it to take place, but that in itself is an indication that it had not yet occurred.

CONCLUSION

It is hard to be certain what precisely the status of Onesimus as *episkopos* actually was. Although the possibility that Ignatius is addressing more than one congregation under a sole bishop cannot be stated as an established fact, it cannot be ruled out altogether. However, any further conclusions based on what is no more than a hypothesis are very shaky. The same is true were I to suggest that the situation has not developed since the time of the Pastoral Epistles. Because it seems improbable that monepiscopacy has emerged from federation with such completeness so early (whether Ignatius is a Trajanic or a Hadrianic figure), and because of the difficulty conceiving of a gathering of the whole Ephesian church, full monepiscopacy is less likely. But unless Ignatius is confused about the nature of Onesimus's episcopate and assumes a household *episkopos* to be a *monepiskopos*, there are also arguments, due to the nature of Ignatius's insistence on unity, that point away from seeing the situation as similar to that addressed by "Paul." A possible explanation is that some congregations have divided on practical, but not ideational, grounds from the household of Onesimus, and that while continuing to recognize him as *episkopos*, the presbyters in each congregation continue as before as honored members, offering food in the absence of the *episkopos*. This, however, is a possibility only and nothing like an assured result, and it raises the question of why they do not simply adopt the title of *episkopos*. If, however, it is the case that Onesimus is *episkopos* over more than one congregation, then it is more likely that the multiplicity of congregations had formed by process of division from a single congregation than that other congregations had joined themselves to the Pauline household and submitted to Onesimus's authority. The final possible means by which this limited monepiscopacy might emerge is the formation of something like an *Ortsgemeinde*. This need not mean that all Ephesian congregations had gathered, but that the leaders had and, in doing so, had worshiped together and shared the common meal, so of necessity causing one to act as *episkopos*. However, this is a hypothesis beset with assumptions. As noted in the discussion of 1 Timothy above, there are many reasons, one of them being concern for purity among Christian groups of Jewish heritage and law observance, that militate against this occurring.

Thus, on balance, it probably is best to assume that Onesimus is simply a domestic *episkopos* in a single congregation, and that the presbyters are, like the presbyters of 1 Timothy, senior patrons. It is possible that some of these patrons convened meetings other than that overseen by the *episkopos*, but this can only be a matter of speculation based on Ignatius's comment regarding the possibility of a single gathering of the church, a comment that is itself susceptible of a variety of interpretations.

What is most frustrating about this lack of an assured result is that it casts no light on the situation obtaining at Ephesus at the end of the second century. In chapter 1 I noted the existence of Polycrates, and I suggested that although he certainly is an *episkopos*, we could not know whether he was a domestic *episkopos* writing on behalf of the federation, *episkopos* of Johannine congregations in Ephesus, or properly speaking a *monepiskopos*. That there is no clear marker laid down after the period of the domestic *episkopos* of the Pastoral Epistles means that there is no basis on which to draw a trajectory.

However, it may be that a trajectory from the Pastoral Epistles to Polycrates would be illegitimate in any event. Polycrates certainly stood within the Johannine tradition, self-consciously claiming a familial relationship (*syngeneia*) between himself and John.[381] Whereas I have agreed with Trebilco that there was non-hostile interaction between the Pauline and the Johannine communities at Ephesus, we cannot be sure that the Pauline communities survived intact. It may thus be the case that Polycrates has emerged from a purely Johannine tradition. The evidence from Smyrna, which likewise was Quartodeciman, and thus likewise Johannine, indicates the survival of federation in Johannine circles. The continuing influence of the language, if not the practice, of federation within Johannine circles may be illustrated from that of Irenaeus, whose usage and understanding is formed in Smyrna, and who refers to the succession of *episkopoi* at Rome as a guarantee of the apostolic tradition and also to the presbyters as the successors of the apostles and as the means by which that same tradition is conveyed.[382] Whereas the synonymy of *episkopos* and *presbyteros* may be invoked to explain Irenaeus's language here, it would seem strange that the undifferentiated office imagined (as I have held) by proponents of collective leadership should continue into a period where Irenaeus is simultaneously listing a succession of *(mon)episkopoi* at Rome; rather, I may appeal to the hypothesis of federation and the evidence that presbyters may be a collective noun to explain his usage here. Thus, on the assumption that Polycrates is a *monepiskopos*, and not the correspondent with Victor

---

381. Quoted in Eusebius, *Hist. eccl.* 5.24.6.
382. Irenaeus refers to the tradition and succession of the presbyters (*Haer.* 3.2.2), and then he gives an episcopal succession list for Rome (*Haer.* 3.3.3).

on behalf of the federation, his monepiscopate was the result, once again, of federation and through the inclusion of distinct theological trajectories within the "catholic" church of Ephesus.

Magnesia

Having discussed the situation at Ephesus first, on the basis that we already have some knowledge of the situation there derived from the Pastoral Epistles, I extend the discussion of Ignatius's letters to the other Asian cities, taking the letters in their canonical order.

Thus, to turn to *Magnesians*, I may note in the first instance that the principal issue addressed here is that of continued Jewish practice rather than the nature of the episcopate. However, mention is made of the presbyterate, of the *episkopos*, and of *diakonoi*; there is indeed one extraordinarily significant statement regarding the Magnesian *episkopos*. Ignatius says that the presbyters have not taken advantage of his apparent membership of the rank of younger men (*neōterikēn taxin*).[383] In the identification of a neoteric *taxis* I may note the echo of gymnastic language, indicating that the presbytery of Magnesia, at least in its origin, was precisely such a *taxis* of older male patrons as identified in the Asian communities of the first century. The *episkopos* here is independent of the presbytery to such an extent that, by virtue of his age, he is not even qualified to be a member. The significance of the fact that the *episkopos* is not qualified as a *presbyteros* is enormous; generally, throughout his correspondence, Ignatius stresses the unity of the presbyters and the *episkopos* to the extent that it is not entirely clear whether the *episkopos* might not be seen as an extension of the presbytery. We may see here that the *episkopos* is entirely separate and distinct, as was the case in the Ephesus of the Pastoral Epistles. Although the ideal is that the *episkopos* and presbyters should work harmoniously together, there is no question that they are two distinct *taxeis*. The clear distinction here between the *episkopos* and presbyterate points to the possibility that the *episkopos* may even be an agent of the presbyters and, in effect, their subordinate. This in turn may motivate Ignatius's characterization of the presbyters as the apostles, compared to the exalted position that

383. Ign. *Magn.* 3:1. Some commentators take *taxis* to mean "appearance." Fernando Rivas Rebaque ("Los obispos en Ignacio de Antioquía: Cuadros sociales dominantes de la memoria colectiva cristiana," *EstEcl* 83 [2008]: 35) suggests that this means that Damas had recently attained orders. This would mean not only that he had only just become an *episkopos*, but also that he had only just become a member of the hierarchy on becoming an *episkopos*. This in turn would still mean that he was not a presbyter. In the light of the associational language of *taxis*, as well as of the clear statement that Damas was indeed young, it is by far the most preferable reading to see him as a member of the rank of the younger members of the church.

he gives the *episkopos* in his typology.[384] The importance of the *episkopos* derives, I suggest, from Ignatius's stress on the episcopal nature of charity, in a manner reminiscent of *Didascalia apostolorum*.

As before, I must ask whether a single congregation is intended or whether there are more than one, whether the *episkopos* is a *monepiskopos* and the presbytery a gathering of subordinate officers, or whether there is a single household.

In order to determine this issue, I may note first that there is a specific polemic against private gatherings.[385] The purpose of these private gatherings is not made clear, but since they are contrasted with the gatherings of the whole church in which there is a single prayer, hope, and love, I may surmise that the private meetings have the same purpose as the meeting of the church as a whole. Although Ignatius does not spell it out, these meetings may be seen as occasions of patronage and the grant of charity, since this would be the expression of love. The proper occasion, however, is the meal at which the *episkopos* presides. The Magnesians are not to look upon their neighbors in accordance with the flesh (*kata sarka*), but are to love each other in Jesus Christ.[386] That is to say, charity is not to be a means to obtain social advantage. It is also possible, given the extent to which the letter concerns issues relating to the keeping of Jewish law, that patronage is being extended to private teachers rather than to the needy through the *episkopos*.

I may then ask who the private patrons are. There are three possibilities that lead us in turn to determine the nature of the episcopate at Magnesia: (1) the *episkopos* is a domestic *episkopos*, and the patrons are congregational presbyters; or (2) the *episkopos* is a *monepiskopos*, and the patrons are the subordinate presbyters; or (3) the *episkopos* is a *monepiskopos*, and the patrons are those who formerly had been congregational presbyters and are now without position.

In suggesting the first possibility, I may again note Ignatius's statement that the *presbyteroi* have not taken advantage of the youth of the *episkopos*.[387] Although we may wonder whether this is simply a rhetorical technique, and that indeed they have, I may also observe that the presbyters are not directly instructed; rather, people are told to act with the "*episkopos* and presbyters."[388] It would thus seem that it is not these presbyters who are holding independent

---

384. In Ign. *Magn.* 6:1 the presbyters represent the apostles, whereas the *episkopos* represents God the Father.

385. Ign. *Magn.* 7:1.

386. Ign. *Magn.* 6:2.

387. Ign. *Magn.* 3:1.

388. Ign. *Magn.* 7:1.

meetings. Moreover, since the *episkopos* as a *neos* is clearly distinct from the presbyters, I may go on from there to suggest that these presbyters have the ability effectively to control the *episkopos*. It may indeed be the case that the *episkopos* himself is in a relationship of *clientela* to the presbyters, and that if there is tension between them, one might expect the will of the presbyters to prevail. As already suggested, it is for this reason that Ignatius rhetorically exalts the episcopal position. For the same reason, it is less likely that the patrons are the presbyters addressed here.

The same consideration, that people are told to act in concert with the *episkopos* and presbyters, also tends to make the second possibility, that the patrons are subordinate presbyters, less likely. Moreover, we should note the possibility that as congregational leaders they may, in any event, continue within their own congregations to act as patrons.

However, to turn to the third possibility, and if we were to assume for the present that the episcopate is a monepiscopate, and the presbyters are thus those who hold office at the head of individual Christian communities (having previously been *episkopoi* within their households) and continue to do so as presbyters, we may recollect the problem that has already been noted. Namely, because there were gatherings of patrons in some early Christian household communities who collectively organized themselves as a presbyterate on the model of civic society, and because the result of cooperation between independent Christian communities inevitably meant the exaltation of the status of the household *episkopos* as *episkopoi* began to gather and are recognized as *presbyteroi kata polin*, the domestic presbyters lose their status altogether. As long as the individual congregation remains effectively independent, they retain their status, but if the household itself becomes simply a subsidiary of a wider organization, then their significance necessarily becomes diminished. Is it possible that it is these (congregational) presbyters in Magnesia who are dividing the church (as Ignatius would see it) by removing their funds and their support from the church (and thus from the federation headed by the *monepiskopos*) in order to host gatherings in their own houses, to host other (Judaizing) teachers, and so to sustain their own patronal standing in the Christian community? Thus, Ignatius suggests that meetings are being held by those who call somebody *episkopos* (implying that there is but one) but then act as though he were not there.[389] This is the same concern that Ignatius shows at Smyrna, where he suggests to Polycarp that care for widows should be channeled through the *episkopos*.[390] Against this, however, is the statement

389. Ign. *Magn.* 4.
390. Ign. *Pol.* 4:1.

that the *episkopos* is not qualified as a presbyter, is of the rank of younger men. It would seem strange that all the subordinate presbyters would be presbyters (in age) except the one who is their *episkopos*. This can make sense only in the context of a single, domestic congregation like that addressed by the Paul of 1 Timothy, where senior patrons might appoint a younger *episkopos*.

Although it is not straightforward to see the domestic presbyters, who are patrons in any event, as offering alternative patronage, it does seem that this is the most likely possibility. As such, Ignatius addresses a single, domestic Christian community in Magnesia whose presbyters, as a *taxis*, have appointed an *episkopos* as *oikonomos* from among the *neōteroi* in order to promote their own interests. This would depend on taking the statement that the presbyters had not taken advantage of the bishop's youth[391] as a rhetorical device, describing an ideal rather than a reality, though this is not a fatal objection; it is more difficult, however, to see how the patron presbyters would fail to exercise their collective advantage over the *episkopos* and therefore hold distinct and separate meetings. Nonetheless, a solution is possible.

Before essaying such a solution, however, I may compare this account to that of Sim. He notes that here, as elsewhere, there are problems with law-observant Jewish Christians who do not gather with the bishop on grounds of purity. These are principled grounds for opposition to the *episkopos* on the basis that the institution of an *episkopos* is a Gentile institution.[392] There are three problems here. First, we do not know whether these are law-observant Jews or law-observant Gentiles;[393] second, the idea that there is a principled basis for opposition to episcopacy through Judaism is, as we have seen, absolutely without any evidential base; and third, purity at table is something that, while potentially an issue as it had been in Antioch, is not actually addressed in *Magnesians*. However, there may be some connection between the issue of Judaizing, in particular that of keeping the sabbath (which is the particular issue addressed here), and the issue regarding patronage and private meetings.

The major point that Ignatius has against the "Judaizers" is that they are maintaining the sabbath rather than Sunday morning. I have already argued that this shift from the second sabbath evening until the following morning brought about the significant change in the eucharist from a *Sättigungsmahl* to

391. Ign. *Magn.* 3:1.
392. Sim, *Gospel of Matthew*, 280–81. Similarly Donahue ("Jewish Christianity," 91) contrasts Gentile episcopal governance with (Jewish) governance by elders. Since Donahue believes that Ignatius is inscribing the Antiochene situation here, he would need to show governance by elders in Antioch.
393. The latter is the more probable. So Judith Lieu, *Image and Reality: The Jews in the World of the Christians in the Second Century* (Edinburgh: T&T Clark, 1996), 31.

a ritual repast. This, moreover, would mean that the opportunity for patronage through feeding would be similarly diminished, which in turn restricts the potential power of patrons. However, I may surmise that if individual patrons are seeking to maintain their position within the Christian community, they might maintain the keeping of sabbath and the conduct of a meal as a means to do so. As such, they may then point to the practice of Judaism, which previously had been that of Christianity. There is a connection between Ignatius's promotion of episcopacy and the issue of Jewish practice; it is simply not, however, that which Sim believes to be the case.

On the basis that the *episkopos* is not elected from among the presbyters but rather is an entirely independent institution, I may suggest that Ignatius has a single Magnesian congregation in mind. The identification of the different *taxeis* within the congregations is still intact. The *episkopos* is thus no *monepiskopos*, and the presbyters do not hold office in individual congregations under the *episkopos* but rather are patrons of the single church—patrons who resist the movement of the ritual meal from Saturday evening to Sunday morning in order to maintain the power of patronage through continuing to supply food, or perhaps who continue to offer a *Sättingungsmahl* on Saturday evening alongside their participation at the purely symbolic meal that the eucharist on Sunday had become.

Philadelphia

In turning to Philadelphia, we are faced once again with the same problem, namely, that of knowing whether by *episkopos* is intended a *monepiskopos* or a household *episkopos*. Since the greater part of the letter, like that to the Magnesians, is taken up with the Judaizing opponents, there is relatively little reflecting the church order of Philadelphia.

Nonetheless, it has been suggested that opposition to the *episkopos* here derives from a party who based their church order on charismatic lines.[394] I have already argued against that elsewhere and have suggested that the opposition rather comes from those who are organizing their Christian communities on synagogal lines and who are giving a significant place to teachers as interpreters of the Scriptures.[395] It is indeed possible that these teachers have formed an opposition independent of the bishop and the presbytery. Ignatius will not recognize them as Christians because he states that all who are with Christ

394. So Trevett, "Prophecy"; similarly, Paul Trebilco, "Christian Communities in Western Asia Minor into the Early Second Century: Ignatius and Others as Witnesses against Bauer," *JETS* 49 (2006): 27–30.

395. Stewart(-Sykes), "Prophecy and Patronage."

are with the *episkopos*.[396] Given the emphasis on the interpretation of the Scriptures, I may well agree with Sim that these opponents are law-obedient Jewish or Judaizing Christians opposed by Ignatius elsewhere;[397] however, I may be less certain than Sim that what prevents them from gathering with the other Christians is the problem created by purity issues. This would depend, in particular, on whether the change to Sunday has already taken place. Nonetheless, that is a possibility here; since the seer addresses a letter to the Christians of Philadelphia,[398] it is not beyond the bounds of possibility that these Christians have continued in law observance, whereas those addressed by Ignatius are of a Pauline inheritance. If it is the case that there is more than one distinct Christian community in Philadelphia, this raises the question of the nature of the relationship between them. Either there is no relationship, or else the Christian communities are in a loose federation.

There is one indication of a single Christian gathering in the city, as Ignatius urges, "Be eager to celebrate one eucharist. For there is one flesh of our Lord Jesus Christ and one cup."[399] This, however, may be read in other ways, as an indication that, for all that Ignatius encourages the celebration of a single eucharist, none took place, or as an indication that there was one Christian community that Ignatius recognized, and that law-observant communities were not in any form of communication with that with which Ignatius was communicating. We may recall at this point that the federation was not a eucharistic community, but if Ignatius is indeed addressing a federation, then his agendum would seem to be that of turning it into one. Thus, the question regarding the possibility of federation leads, once again, to the issue of what kind of *episkopos* is in view here. Given that a sole bishop is mentioned, I may deduce either that the Philadelphian community as a whole has federated and has evolved some form of monepiscopacy, or else that Ignatius is addressing a single household. One clue suggests that the former is the case: Ignatius's statement that the *episkopos* holds his office "for the commonwealth" (*eis to koinon*).[400] That is to say, the term describing a federation of city-states is employed, indicating that the Philadelphian church likewise is a federation. In this light, I may note that Ignatius states that the Philadelphians should love unity (*henōsis*)[401] rather than simply *homonoia*, which might describe relations between independent but cooperating Christian communities, and describes

396. Ign. *Phld.* 3:2.
397. Sim, *Gospel of Matthew*, 280.
398. Rev. 3:7–13.
399. Ign. *Phld.* 4:1.
400. Ign. *Phld.* 1:1.
401. Ign. *Phld.* 7:2.

himself as a man set on unity.[402] This supposes that the federation has developed from being simply a federation into some form of single community, and that the issues regarding law observance are no longer issues. This is a very large assumption. As such, I may suggest that the unity that is threatened is the unity of a single congregation, and that the language of federation takes account of the congregation being the result of the gathering of more than one household. If the call for unity is to be read as an exhortation for the members of the federation to gather in one place and to worship together, then issues regarding purity and food would need to have been solved. I may at least be clear that it would be for this reason, and not because of any principled objection to monepiscopacy, that the law-observant communities would not gather with the Gentile *episkopos*.

Equal uncertainty surrounds Ignatius's references to division that is to be healed through attention to the *episkopos*, the presbytery, and the deacons.[403] The division may be that of strained federation, but may, once again, simply refer to a divided congregation. The statement that one may hear of Christianity from a circumcised man[404] may be an indication that there are law-observant Christian communities within Philadelphia, and that there is contact between them and those that are not law-observant, but this contact need not have led beyond a very loose federation.

This in turn leads to the question of the relationship between Ignatius's opponents and the communities of the federation. It is possible that the insistence on law observance, whether aimed at the already law-observant community or at individuals within the non-law-observant community, is causing the federation to break apart. This would explain Ignatius's comment that the Lord forgives those who repent if their repentance restores them to unity and to the gathering (*synedrion*) of the *episkopos*;[405] that is, those who were withdrawing from federation, not only to follow law observance but also to break contact with those who were not so observant, should return to the federation. But, once again, it may simply be that individuals are leaving the congregation addressed by Ignatius, possibly to join the law-observant community.

We may thus see that it is possible that there had been movement from federation to a single community within Philadelphia, but that it is equally possible that there was none. We know very little.

Certain things, however, we know were not the case. We know that, whatever the issues besetting the *episkopos*, opposition from charismatic prophets was

402. Ign. *Phld.* 8:1.
403. Ign. *Phld.* 7:1–2.
404. Ign. *Phld.* 6:1.
405. Ign. *Phld.* 8:1.

not one of them. And we know that whatever issues continued to separate the community addressed by the seer from that addressed by Ignatius, the matter of episcopacy was not one of them. Brent suggests that the communities are the same on the basis that the seer and Ignatius alike employ language derived from the imperial cult within the Asian cities, and thus that the picture of worship derived from Ignatius and from Revelation is fundamentally the same. But whereas their worship might be of great similarity, the issue of law observance might well separate them. He also suggests that the fifteen or so years that separated the two documents is an indication that there had been progress in church order in the intervening period.[406] Whereas we may not be sure that the communities of Revelation had *episkopoi* alongside patron-elders, Brent persuasively suggests that this is possible. As such, there is no need to draw a line of development, nor to conflate the two communities on the grounds that each knew episcopal order, for the two communities may well continue separate, aware of each other and each with its own *episkopos*.

Tralles

If the nature of church order at Philadelphia is uncertain, that at Tralles is equally unclear. There is mention of an *episkopos*, of presbyters, and of *diakonoi*, but whether they represent a single household or a federated series of Christian communities is, again, unknowable. Trebilco picks up a hint of criticism of the attitude of presbyters in *Trallians* 12:2, which states that all Christians, but in particular the presbyters, should refresh the bishop, and suggests that Christians in Tralles are acting other than the bishop on the basis of *Trallians* 7:2, which states that those outside the sanctuary are impure.[407] However, Ignatius specifically states that they do nothing without the bishop. Thus, Trevett, in seeking to argue that what is at stake is the matter of church order, in particular episcopal order (again noting *Trall.* 12:2), identifies the problem as lying with the presbyters. Thus, "It should not be overlooked that our bishop called for loyalty from the *presbyters* in particular."[408] However, it seems to be the issue that there is none *for* the presbyters. Ignatius writes, "It is necessary, as already you do, that you do nothing without the *episkopos*, but also be subject to the presbytery,"[409] and, "Let them respect . . . the pres-

---

406. Allen Brent, *The Imperial Cult and the Development of Church Order: Concepts and Images of Authority in Paganism and Early Christianity before the Age of Cyprian*, VCSup 45 (Leiden: Brill, 1999), 210–11.

407. Trebilco, *Early Christians in Ephesus*, 642–43.

408. Trevett, *Study of Ignatius*, 88.

409. Ign. *Trall.* 2:2.

byters like the council of God and the band of the apostles. Apart from these a gathering cannot be called a church."[410] It is possible that the presbyters had contributed to this lack of respect. There is indeed muted criticism of them at *Trallians* 12:2. When the term "refresh" is used elsewhere in Ignatius's writing, it seems to refer to the supply of charity, or of goods. Thus, the *presbyteroi* are being encouraged to act as patrons to the community through the *episkopos*, a role that may well have been fundamental to them in any case. However, it is noteworthy that the *episkopos* alone attended Ignatius from Tralles, without any accompanying *presbyteroi*. If the presbyters were not adequately performing their liturgical duty, then this might well lead to loss of respect. Ignatius calls not for loyalty from the presbyters but rather for economic support.

There may be other consequences beyond a failure of respect. Ignatius urges that the Trallians use only Christian food.[411] What other food, one might ask, would they use? The answer might be that Trallian Christians are participating in cultic festivities that are not Christian, in *collegia* or in civic sacrifice. For this reason, I may suggest, the *diakonoi* are said not to be *diakonoi* of food but assistants to the church.[412] As I have constantly stressed throughout this work, the *diakonoi* were indeed servants of food, but the Christian *diakonoi* are here being contrasted with *diakonoi* of the civic or associational sacrifices. Moreover, it is for this reason, I suggest, that generosity is urged on the presbyters at *Trallians* 12:2; that is, the presbyters are to ensure that the *episkopos* has a sufficient food supply for all the Christians of the community, as a means to ensure that they do not participate in other associations or the gatherings of the *polis* in order to eat. The fact that, as Strabo reports,[413] Tralles is populated significantly by those who are well off would provide a particularly attractive alternative to the gatherings of the church. A similar, relatively relaxed, attitude toward non-Christian religious practice may lie behind the statement that no entry point (*aphormas*) to heathens should be given;[414] it is not that dissension within the Christian community might give cause for criticism from outside, but that participation in cultic activity without the church might lead in turn to participation by non-Christians in the cultic eating of the church.

That such behavior might not be expected of Christians represents an ideal, held by Ignatius as well as by Paul, rather than a reality. That the seer should charge Christians at Pergamum with idolatry is an indication that

410. Ign. *Trall.* 3:1.
411. Ign. *Trall.* 6:1.
412. Ign. *Trall.* 2:3.
413. Strabo, *Geogr.* 14.1.42.
414. Ign. *Trall.* 8:2.

some indeed are taking part in pagan sacrificial cults.[415] Some Jews certainly did so, participating in the imperial cult and making donations to Dionysiac festivals.[416] The *Didache* insists on the avoidance of food offered in sacrifice,[417] and when Justin states that Christians would rather die than worship idols or eat meat offered to idols, Trypho responds that many do indeed eat it.[418] This is also a significant issue in Alexandria, as Clement similarly advises abstention from what is offered to idols.[419] The manner in which civic life and associational life and religion were bound up to each other means that it is hard altogether to avoid the pagan gods, but as Ignatius is constructing the Christians as their own association, he sees that this brings about a demand of exclusivity. I may also observe that this is closely bound up to his rhetorical approach. Thus, Ignatius urges that no opportunity be given to the heathen to accuse Christians.[420] If the Christians are eating with pagans, then there are indeed such occasions.

There are particular issues at Tralles. What cannot be deduced from what is said, however, is the nature of the church order of the city; in particular, we cannot say whether there is a single congregation still under its *episkopos* or whether the *episkopos* is the *monepiskopos* of a series of congregations. The presbyters, whether household leaders or domestic presbyters would, in each instance, be expected to act patronally. However, the fact that the *episkopos* is to be a recipient of the presbyters' charity indicates that he may simply be their agent, which implies in turn a single, domestic-associational gathering. This is, however, far from assured; the one thing that can be said is that church order is not an issue here.

Conclusion

We have seen that we cannot be sure of the extent to which the Asian churches addressed by Ignatius may have instituted monepiscopacy. Smyrna seems to have continued to have federated households, as, probably, did Ephesus, whereas the evidence from the letters to the other cities allows nothing to be said with certainty. Although it is possible that the Magnesian and Philadelphian congregations had united under a single *episkopos*, this is difficult, and

---

415. Rev. 2:14.
416. Note the examples cited by Peder Borgen, "'Yes,' 'No,' 'How Far?' The Participation of Jews and Christians in Pagan Clubs," in *Paul in His Hellenistic Context*, ed. Troels Engberg-Pedersen, SNTW (Edinburgh: T&T Clark, 1995), 36–37.
417. *Did.* 6:2.
418. Justin, *Dial.* 34–35. Justin replies that all these are gnostics.
419. Clement, *Paed.* 2.1; *Strom.* 4.16.
420. Ign. *Trall.* 8:5; 15:2.

on balance it is more probable that Ignatius's references to *episkopoi* are to *episkopoi* in single congregations. It seems that the church at Tralles consisted of a single household, but this is likewise an uncertain conclusion. The very fact that monepiscopacy is not certainly found in the Asian churches at the time of Ignatius may indicate a Trajanic date for Ignatius's writing, though once again the danger of a circular argument beckons, since beyond seeing monepiscopacy developing in Rome and Alexandria early in the third century, we do not know the date of the development of this institution. As such, the absence of monepiscopacy does nothing to gainsay the Hadrianic date for Ignatius suggested above. Were it not for knowledge gleaned elsewhere, we would not imagine that Ignatius knew churches other than single households, and it is in this light that we struggle to see whether his exhortations to unity, and to close gatherings, refer to single churches or to federations moving toward monepiscopacy. The same uncertainty, moreover, confronts us in examining the development of monepiscopacy in Antioch.

Although this may be seen as the lack of a result, in itself this is significant. Ignatius is held up so often as the first *monepiskopos*, or as a monarch *episkopos*, or as the creator of monepiscopacy that it is significant in itself to find out that such is not necessarily the case. It is also significant to find that there is no principled opposition to monepiscopacy. Opposition to the *episkopos* there was, but such opposition (apart from the opposition of heretics without the church) came from disgruntled patrons and not out of any principled objection to episcopal governance or polity. Similarly, there were groups, at least in Ephesus, and probably in Philadelphia as well, who, while Christian, were not within, nor ever had been within, the episcopal grouping addressed by Ignatius. The most likely characterization of these groups is as Jewish law-obedient groups who could not join a single eucharist on grounds of purity and separation. But their separation had nothing to do with opposition to episcopacy on principled grounds and nothing, I may note, to do with a predilection for prophecy. Even less was there prophetic opposition to episcopal institutions.

There are also some positive results amid the uncertainty.

First, I may note that the *episkopoi*, whether *monepiskopoi* or household *episkopoi*, continue to exercise a charitable and economic ministry. At Tralles Ignatius supports the *episkopos* as an agent of the love and charity of God, and at Smyrna he charges that the heretics are wanting in such charity (by implicit contrast to those under the charge of an *episkopos*). Moreover, we may observe the people who visit Ignatius on his journey through Asia. From Ephesus comes Onesimus the *episkopos* together with a *diakonos*, Burrhus.[421]

---

421. Ign. *Eph.* 1:3; 2:1.

The Magnesians send Damas the bishop with two presbyters and a deacon.[422] Polybius, a bishop, comes to him from the Trallians.[423] The Philadelphian *episkopos* is not named, but since Ignatius seems to have personal knowledge of him, as well as having learned about him, it would seem that the *episkopos* visited him while he was in Philadelphia.[424] Is it not possible that the reason for the prominence of the *episkopoi* lay less in the representative role of the *episkopos* with regard to the community, but rather more in that the *episkopos*, as *oikonomos*, was charged with bringing the gifts of the community to the Christian in chains?[425] The principal reason that Ignatius meets *episkopoi* is that they are responsible for bringing him the charity of the church.

Second, we have gained some insight into the issue raised at the end of chapter 3: the fate and diminishing influence of the domestic presbyters. At Magnesia it seems possible that some patrons had withdrawn their support from the bishop's brokerage and had transferred to alternative teachers. At Tralles, moreover, the domestic presbyters continue to be found, but the implicit charge that they are deficient in their duty toward the *episkopos* indicates that even when the domestic presbyterate is in place, the relationship between this group and their *episkopos* is not necessarily free of tension. In the light of the tension between the patronal group and the officers, we may see that this group may ultimately be marginalized.

Third, I may note that, as a reader of Paul, Ignatius shows particular knowledge of the Letter to the Ephesians,[426] the import of which is the reconciliation of Jews and Gentiles through Christ's death. Is it possible that, as he sees himself as an imitator of Paul both in his journey to martyrdom in Rome and in his writing activity,[427] he is also an imitator of Christ, whom Paul likewise imitated in seeing his life poured out like a sacrifice, seeing the reconciliation that, I suggest, had taken place in Antioch as the result of his own impending death, sealing agreement between the Jewish and Gentile factions of Antiochene Christianity like a *synthysia* (a sacrifice jointly made by two parties in order to unite them)?[428] Like the reconciliation to which the canonical Ephesians refers,

422. Ign. *Magn.* 2:1.
423. Ign. *Trall.* 1:1.
424. Ign. *Phld.* 1:1–2.
425. Brent remarks, "All references to the bishop's functions are to liturgical functions" ("Ignatian Epistles," 24). However, as has already been more generally argued, the eucharist is the occasion at which the alms of the community are received and hospitality is practiced.
426. Thus, the thorough investigation of Heinrich Rathke, *Ignatius von Antiochien und die Paulusbriefe*, TUGAL 99 (Berlin: Akademie-Verlag, 1967), 65–66, in summary of extensive discussion.
427. Ign. *Eph.* 12:2.
428. Rathke (*Ignatius von Antiochien*, 74–75) similarly sees the manner in which Ignatius sees his death as an offering in keeping with his reading of Paul, although here it is not tied to

moreover, it is reconciliation between Jew and Gentile in Christ, not between presbyteral and episcopal forms of governance.[429] Thus, the third positive result is that we may cease to see the fundamental theological dispute underlying Ignatius's formation as being a dispute regarding ecclesiastical governance and may be brought to see instead that it something much more profound.

Before leaving Ignatius altogether, I may attempt to give some picture of the eucharistic gatherings as he knew them. I have suggested that this is a time of transition from evening keeping of sabbath to morning keeping of Sunday, as theologically encouraged by Ignatius, but in reality to avoid the notice of the authorities.[430] I have, moreover, suggested that this is the basis on which a new rapprochement might be brought about between Jewish and Gentile Christian groups in Antioch, since the removal of the eucharist from the *Sättigungsmahl* meant that issues of commensality were no longer so complex. I may, however, explain the strictly hierarchical manner of the relationship of the *diakonoi* and of the *presbyteroi* to the *episkopos*, and the call for submission by the people to *episkopos* and presbytery, by reference to the seating arrangements within the triclinium, since although the nature of the meal might have changed, the arrangement of the assembly need not change with such rapidity.

Something of a picture may be gathered from the manner in which the elders of Revelation are gathered around the throne.[431] I do not intend to argue that the elders depicted are purely and simply a reflection of the elders known in the church, for, as Satake points out, if this were the case, we would also expect to find beasts in the church as well as presbyters![432] However, not all of Satake's arguments, which are intended to deny that this vision is a reflection of the church at worship, are equally convincing. For instance, it is not sufficient to say, as Satake does, that these elders cannot reflect an earthly reality because otherwise the seer does not know of elders; this is in danger of rapidly becom-

---

the specific problematic of relations between Jews and Gentiles in Christ. On the *synthysia*, see Brent, *Ignatius of Antioch*, 230–40.

429. See Trevett, *Study of Ignatius*, 64–66.

430. Namely, the legal situation brought about through Trajan's rescript. It is also possible that laws aimed against *collegia* from the period might have come into play, for although these laws, as Ilias N. Arnaoutoglou ("Roman Law and *collegia* in Asia Minor," *RIDA* 49 [2002]: 27–44) persuasively demonstrates, were somewhat patchily applied, they might be of some use in suppressing a society that is already considered suspect.

431. So Allen Brent, "Pseudonymy and Charisma in the Ministry of the Early Church," *Aug* 27 (1987): 360–61, likewise tying together Ignatius's and John's visions of the church in worship. Note, however, that Brent (*Imperial Cult*, 201) attributes the appearance of elders to "Jewish-Christian concepts." I may suggest, rather, that they are derived from the prominence of patrons within civic festivals.

432. Akira Satake, *Die Gemeindeordnung in der Johannesapokalypse*, WMANT 21 (Neukirchen-Vluyn: Neukirchener Verlag, 1966), 149.

ing circular. Moreover, as Brent points out, the crowns of the elders need not imply that these are heavenly, rather than earthly, beings, as these crowns may reflect the use of crowns in the imperial cult.[433] More significantly, less convincing is Satake's overall thesis that the leaders of the seer's community were the prophets,[434] simply on the grounds that this is to confuse two spheres of activity: communication and leadership. Nonetheless, his suggestion that the presbyters here are a reflection of the musicians of 1 Chronicles 25:9–31 seems compelling once noticed, given that they are likewise divided into twenty-four courses. Less certain is his further suggestion that the priestly courses of 1 Chronicles 24 are likewise divided into twenty-four courses, even though these priests might be termed "elders,"[435] for we have seen enough to know how vague a term this may be. Nonetheless, even if we accept that the principal referent here is the musicians of the temple, the manner in which they are seated around the throne perhaps requires some explanation because such a position does not lie patent in the text of Chronicles, and it is possible that a vision based on the model of Chronicles has undergone some *Vergegenwärtigung* (updating), and that the elders are presented seated as they might be at the banquet of the community. Ignatius thus similarly refers to the presbyters as a crown,[436] so giving us a picture of the elders seated around; Brent reminds us several times that the manner in which Ignatius describes the presidency of the *episkopos*, with the cluster of presbyters around him and the *diakonoi* assisting, is an image of the liturgy.[437] Support for this may be found in his letter to Polycarp, where Ignatius suggests that through cooperation the corpus of clergy might be raised together as the stewards (*oikonomoi*), assessors (*paredroi*), and servants (*hypēretai*) of God.[438] We may see the term *paredroi* as indicating the seating of the presbyters alongside the presiding *episkopos* at the eucharistic table.

Similarly, *Apostolic Church Order*, here employing a source deriving from the same period, implies the presence around the table of elders with the *episkopos*,[439] and the same must be implied by the manner in which *Traditio apostolica* states that the whole presbytery joins the *episkopos* in laying hands on the offering.[440] As has already been suggested, these are in each case domestic presbyters. This in turn implies that Ignatius's principal focus is on the single, domestic assembly, and his vision of an *episkopos* is of a domestic *episkopos*.

433. Brent, *Imperial Cult*, 203–4, 215.
434. Satake, *Gemeindeordnung*, 194.
435. Ibid., 150, with reference to *m. Yoma* 1.5; *m. Tamid* 1.1.
436. E.g., Ign. *Magn.* 13:1.
437. E.g., Brent, *Ignatius of Antioch*, 26–29.
438. Ign. *Pol.* 6:1.
439. *Can. eccl. ap.* 18.3.
440. *Trad. ap.* 4.2.

As such, Ignatius is reflecting the imagery and presuppositions of civic life within the empire;[441] as van Nijf—discussing one inscription making provision for a public banquet and distribution—recognizes, "the image of the social order presented by Aba's generosity [Aba was the patron making this distribution] as a form of collective self-representation by the entire city of the Histrians."[442] I may observe the same of the arrangements for the procession at the festival of Zeus Sosipolis in Magnesia, as the procession is led by the *stephanophoros*, followed by the priest and priestess, and then the *gerousia*, the priests, the magistrates, the ephebes, the *neoi*, and the *paides*.[443] The Christian banquet likewise reflected the social order of the Christian community, presbyters as patrons taking the places, as well as the portions, of honor.

Some Fragmentary Evidence

In tracing the history of monepiscopacy, Lightfoot derives evidence of monepiscopacy at Corinth, in Athens, and in two Cretan communities from the correspondence of Dionysius of Corinth.[444] Although there is a prima facie likelihood that these communities might have developed monepiscopacy out of federation by the middle of the second century (particularly if the fictive Crete of the Letter to Titus has any historical basis), the epistolary nature of this evidence means that we cannot be sure whether the recipients of these letters, any more than their sender, are genuine *monepiskopoi* or *episkopoi* representing federations who are responsible for correspondence. It is noteworthy that one letter is addressed to Soter, who certainly was not *(mon)episkopos* of Rome but who could well have succeeded to Clement's position of responsibility with regard to correspondence without the federation. Given that these are urban centers, it is unlikely that these are simply domestic *episkopoi* outside of federations. In particular, I may point out that, as already argued, Corinth knew collectively described *presbyteroi* who must have been in federation, in part because of their collective designation and in part because Clement is able to write to the federation on behalf of the Roman Christian communities. That these had grown out of diverse households was deduced from the manner in which separate households are addressed by Paul in his Corinthian correspondence; distinct households are addressed, but there has to be some

---

441. So Brent, *Ignatius of Antioch*, passim.

442. Onno M. van Nijf, *The Civic World of Professional Associations in the Roman East*, DMAHA 17 (Amsterdam: J. C. Gieben, 1997), 160, discussing *IScM* 1.57 (from Histria).

443. *IMagn.* 98.

444. Lightfoot, *Philippians*, 216–17, with reference to Eusebius, *Hist. eccl.* 4.23.

relationship between them for the letter to be circulated. Although uncertainty extends to the writer, Dionysius, as well as to his correspondents, it is entirely feasible that by this time monepiscopacy had developed. Hegesippus, who, as will be noted below, ties orthodoxy to the presence of effective *monepiskopoi* within Christian communities, states that orthodoxy had prevailed in Corinth "until Primus was bishop,"[445] the point being that "heresy" is an *arriviste* on the Christian scene. As such, he is indicating that he recognizes Primus as a *monepiskopos*, though we can only guess whether Primus was contemporary with Hegesippus.[446] Moreover, it is possible, especially if he came from the east, as Eusebius implies,[447] that Hegesippus is imposing his monepiscopal views on a leading domestic *episkopos* among others.

In regard to Athens, however, it is possible that this correspondence records the triumph of monepiscopacy there, as Eusebius writes, "He [Dionysius] mentions Quadratus also, stating that he was appointed their bishop after the martyrdom of Publius, and testifying that through his zeal they were brought together again and their faith revived."[448] This unification of the Athenian congregations may signify their unification under a *monepiskopos*.

I may also note from this correspondence the possibility that monepiscopacy had developed in some of the communities of Pontus by now, since letters are addressed there, though Eusebius's report here is somewhat confusing. He states, "Writing to the church that is in Amastris, together with those in Pontus, he [Dionysius] refers to Bacchylides and Elpistus, as having urged him to write, and he adds explanations of passages of the divine Scriptures, and mentions their bishop Palmas by name."[449] Is Palmas bishop of Amastris, and if so, who are Bacchylides and Elpistus? The best we can hazard is that Palmas is in some sense *episkopos* of Amastris, since this is a major urban center within Pontus; it is possible that the others are either presbyters of Amastris (and in federation) or *episkopoi* of outlying rural centers.

The same consideration regarding the value of epistolary evidence was the case when I examined the role of Polycrates at Ephesus. Polycrates lists seven others who, like him, kept the Pascha on the fourteenth day of Nisan, and who were, he states, all, like him, *episkopoi* within Asia.[450] Given that Polycarp, who was, I have argued, a domestic *episkopos*, is numbered among them, alongside

445. Eusebius, *Hist. eccl.* 4.22.2.
446. H. J. Lawlor ("The *Hypomnemata* of Hegesippus," in *Eusebiana: Essays on the Ecclesiastical History of Eusebius* [Oxford: Clarendon, 1912], 69–70) thinks not.
447. Eusebius, *Hist. eccl.* 4.22.7.
448. Eusebius, *Hist. eccl.* 4.23.3.
449. Eusebius, *Hist. eccl.* 4.23.6.
450. Polycrates, quoted in Eusebius, *Hist. eccl.* 4.24.4.

John and Philip, figures certainly predating the rise of monepiscopacy in Asia, we may be cautious about counting the others, Thraseas, Sagaris, Papirius, and Melito, as *monepiskopoi*. As such, once again, we are frustrated by the restricted nature of the evidence and the ambiguous nature of the title *episkopos*.

Finally, in gathering up fragments, I may revisit the suggestion made in passing in chapter 1 that the elders who, according to Papias, gathered with John might actually be elders within a Johannine federation. There are the peculiarities in his usage in that apostles are characterized as *presbyteroi*, as well as others, though this may reflect Johannine usage; but the apostles, like the others, need not be *Wanderprediger*, but rather may be envisioned by Papias as local *episkopoi*. I may certainly agree with Körtner that fundamental to the term is the idea that the transmission of tradition is the fundamental role of these presbyters, but without denying, as he does, any connection with local presbyteries in Asia.[451] It may well be that the Asian presbyteries functioned, as did those of Rome and Smyrna, in determining the boundaries of orthodoxy, and, as is indicated by the functioning of a presbytery in (the Johannine, because Quartodeciman) Smyrna, were the agents for the transmission of Johannine tradition.[452] Papias is identified as *episkopos* of Hierapolis only by Eusebius,[453] and he may indeed have been a domestic *episkopos* and, as such, a member of a presbytery.

Conclusion

Thus far in this work I have managed to give an account of the rise of monepiscopacy in a number of Christian communities.

For Rome, I have followed Brent and Lampe in seeing monepiscopacy deriving from federation, and I have suggested that the same process took place in Smyrna, Philippi, Alexandria, Corinth, and in the Bithynian communities addressed by 1 Peter, though there are gaps in the evidence. I am aware of individual communities in federation, and subsequently of monepiscopacy, but I must draw a hypothetical trajectory between the two. It also seems possible that this process took place elsewhere in Asian cities. In Ephesus, however, it is also possible that there had already been some form of limited monepiscopacy due to the division of individual households, and it is also possible that, due to

---

451. Ulruch H. J. Körtner, *Papias von Hierapolis: Ein Beitrag zur Geschichte des frühen Christentums*, FRLANT 133 (Göttingen: Vandenhoeck & Ruprecht, 1983), 121–22.

452. Eusebius (*Hist. eccl.* 3.9.7) actually refers to his citations from Papias as τοῦ πρεσβυτέρου Ἰωάννου παραδόσεις.

453. Eusebius, *Hist. eccl.* 3.36.2.

the manner in which the Antiochene church originated in a single household founded by Jerusalem Christians, a household that in turn divided, the same had happened in Antioch, though this is far from certain. However, even if the division of households had generated some form of limited monepiscopacy in some subcommunities of Christians within these cities, this did not of itself result in the eventual emergence of monepiscopacy proper; rather, the inclusion of Christians of distinct theological heritages within the monepiscopal grouping indicates that federation was the immediate cause.

In Jerusalem it seems that the original system did not give rise to any outgrowth beyond some Essene influence on the original foundation in Antioch, though it is interesting to note, nonetheless, that Christians here had formed a federation, prefiguring what would, in time, occur elsewhere. However, the eventual development of church order in the city was an importation, possibly from Syria.

As I noted at the beginning of the work, monepiscopacy had formed within the urban centers of the empire by about the first quarter of the third century, and we may now see that it had done so from origins in individual and diverse Christian households, which had federated. The centralization of federation seems to have brought this about in some cities, whereas in others we can be less sure of the process. It is also noteworthy that although we have evidence for federation in Rome, Alexandria, Smyrna, Corinth, Philippi, and Ephesus, it is only in the first two communities that we may have any clarity about the date and nature of the eventual development of monepiscopacy, namely, the centralization of Alexandrian Christianity brought about under Demetrius in the wake of persecution (although we may recall that he was not the first Alexandrian *monepiskopos*) and, in Rome, the evidence of reconciliation between Pontianus and the Hippolytean school that provides a terminus ad quem of 235.

The transformation of episcopacy into monepiscopacy also brings about the threefold order of ministry, in which presbyters represent the *(mon)episkopos* in individual communities. As such, the presbyters there are more likely to have derived from the *presbyteroi kata polin* than from the groups of presbyters within household churches, though again this leads us to ask what happened to these congregational presbyters in the communities that knew them.

Although, admittedly, this is a very partial and hypothetical account, I must again emphasize that a rather slender narrative is preferable to a confident narrative without foundation in the evidence. In the final chapter I seek to give an account, equally provisional and uncertain, of the rationale behind such centralization.

5

The Causes of Monepiscopacy

In a final brief chapter, having traced the narrative of the emergence of monepiscopacy, I attempt to give some account of the reason for the development. Like the foregoing narrative, this is a provisional and uncertain conclusion, consisting largely of suggestions; it is possible that, should the overall thrust of the narrative be found convincing, others may build on it and suggest a rationale behind the events described better than that offered here.

The previous underlying narrative of the consensus traced the emergence of monepiscopacy from collective forms of leadership in individual Christian communities, though, as we have seen, there was much confusion about the definition of an individual Christian community. Beyond this overall narrative there have been three metanarratives that to some extent undergird the larger story. In the first instance, we may note the powerful narrative of *Verschmelzung*, by which monepiscopacy is seen as deriving from a combination of distinct systems. Second, the narrative has been linked to Weberian theories about the emergence of institutions and the manner in which forms of domination emerge as institutions form; often this is presented as a narrative describing the decline, as much as the routinization, of charisma and the replacement of an office-free pneumatic Christianity with a legalistic and office-based religion. Third, and more particularly, monepiscopacy has been linked to the process that I have termed and described elsewhere as scholasticization, the process by which Christian communities emerging from the household and distinguishing themselves from their forming-Jewish origins take on many of the aspects of the school, in communication and in reading. Thus, according to this view, monepiscopacy emerged as a defense against heresy. This may be seen as a particular form of institutionalization. Inevitably, all these explanations are confused in that they seek to explain the emergence of a single leader in local communities (*Einzelgemeinden*) that previously had been under collective governance,[1] a process that never took place; the same processes, it might be argued, would take place as a single leader emerges in cities from the collective group of individual household leaders.

Before examining these explanations, I restate the narrative with which I have sought to replace the consensus, so that the phenomenon under examination may more readily be understood, prior to any explanation being offered.

Monepiscopacy as Centralization

In essence, I have suggested that Christian communities originated in households, and that the householder took on responsibilities of leadership, functioning as such, even if not so entitled. However, as soon as the membership of the group extended beyond the immediate household, an office was necessary to regulate the meal that was at the center of Christian worship. At this point Christianity took on an associational aspect; titles that commended themselves readily through associational usage were *episkopos*, as the agent for the provision of the meal, and *diakonos*, as the assistant. In the case of the title *episkopos*, echoes of Scripture gave additional commendation to the usage. These roles often were taken on as *leitourgiai*. As part of the associational model, Asian communities organized themselves in *taxeis*, and prominent among them were the *presbyteroi*, older male patrons. In time, in the major urban centers, the associations federated, and the individual congregational leaders met as *presbyteroi kata polin*. From this grouping grew the *episkopos* of the federation, a *monepiskopos*, as the federation moved from being a loose group to a single institution and as the individual congregational leaders moved into a position of subordination to the single *episkopos*. The purposes of the federation were those of policing the boundaries of orthodoxy (as with the exclusion of Marcion at Rome, and

1. So, as emerges with brutal clarity, Kenneth A. Strand, "The Rise of the Monarchical Episcopate," *AUSS* 4 (1966): 65–88. Strand considers these rationales, in particular thinking that the need to defend against heresy is the foremost motivation, while also being clear that he is thinking of the emergence of a single leader in single congregations.

possibly the discussion within the Jerusalem church of the extent to which Gentiles should keep Jewish laws), the transmission of literature (thus, at Rome, the forwarding of Hermas's account of his visions and, at Smyrna, the transmission of Ignatius's letters), and relations with other Christian churches (thus, at Rome, the writing of *1 Clement* and, possibly, the visit of Polycarp to Rome). These functions required an agent, and we may see Clement operating in this capacity at Rome and Polycarp likewise operating at Smyrna. This agent, in time, came to be the sole *episkopos* among the gathered presbyters. In many ways, the associations were already federations, in that they united distinct households, and so the model of *episkopos* and presbyters was readily transferrable.

This narrative, while distinct from the consensus that it seeks to replace, has much in common with recent attempts to provide distinct narratives, in particular with those recently proposed by Wagner[2] and Gehring[3] because, like theirs, this narrative depends on Campbell's exegesis of Titus 1:5,[4] as well as on the now common view that early Christian communities were domestically based. Quite apart from matters of detail, it is distinct in that both Wagner and Gehring date the development of monepiscopacy a full century before my own narrative suggests that it emerged, by reckoning the *episkopos* of 1 Timothy to be a *monepiskopos*, rather as Campbell does. Thus, rather than seeing the Roman monepiscopate as a remarkably late development, as Wagner does,[5] I suggest that it emerges only slightly later than the same system emerged elsewhere. This distinction derives, I suggest, because the supposed *monepiskopos* deriving from the household federation is seen by Wagner as functioning within a household. In other words, the distinction between *Einzelgemeinde* and *Ortskirche* is confused. In his conclusion Wagner suggests that the *(mon)episkopos* operates in multiple households. This might be one means by which the problem of the relationship between the *Ortskirche* and the *Einzelgemeinde* is solved, but it raises the problem in turn of how this *episkopos* might continue to have economic oversight of the various meals happening in various communities. Gehring is not confused in this respect, but because he does not look beyond the canonical literature, he does not realize that if his view of the *episkopos* of 1 Timothy is correct, it

---

2. Jochen Wagner, *Die Anfänge des Amtes in der Kirche: Presbyter und Episkopen in der frühchristlichen Literatur*, TANZ 53 (Tübingen: Francke, 2011).

3. Roger W. Gehring, *House Church and Mission: The Importance of Household Structures in Early Christianity* (Peabody, MA: Hendrickson, 2004), 268–81, here solely with regard to the Pastoral Epistles.

4. R. Alastair Campbell, *The Elders: Seniority within Earliest Christianity*, SNTW (Edinburgh: T&T Clark, 1994), 197–98.

5. Wagner, *Anfänge*, 292.

is an exceptionally early development. Nonetheless, the extent to which this narrative conforms to those of Gehring and Wagner may well indicate that this is the direction that research is to take.

A proof of the narrative of centralization deriving from federation is provided by the legislation regarding the activity of *episkopoi* who were not *monepiskopoi* in the fourth century—that is, *episkopoi* who were the sole ministers in single congregations who did not have subordinate ministers in distinct congregations. Whereas it may seem perverse to prove the narrative by employing an example of monepiscopacy *not* developing, the point is that monepiscopacy as understood here is something that took place in urban centers. The existence of bishops in villages was noted above, where it was suggested that their survival into the fourth century derived from the fact that there was no rationale to federation; this hypothesis gains support from the further argument of this work, as we may now see the extent to which federation, which gives rise to monepiscopacy, is an urban phenomenon.[6] The argument of chapter 1, supported by further evidence provided in subsequent chapters, indicates not a move from multiple leaders to single leadership but a transition from small, independent communities through federation to centralization. However, the non-monepiscopal *episkopoi* remain in their small and independent communities and are overtaken by centralization only in the fourth century, as rural *episkopoi* are forbidden to ordain, and are subsequently replaced by presbyters, agents of the urban *episkopoi*. The urban nature of monepiscopacy is given particular prominence by the statement of the thirteenth canon of Ancyra (314) forbidding rural bishops to ordain[7] and going on to state that they should most certainly not ordain presbyters for the city; by the thirteenth canon of Neocaesarea, which forbids them from offering the oblation in any city church should the *episkopos* or presbyters of the city be present; and by the sixth canon of Sardica, which likewise forbids the appointment of an *episkopos* to a village or a small town, where a priest would suffice, lest this compromise the dignity of the episcopate.[8] Beyond these rural *episkopoi*, who are found concentrated in Asia, I may also suggest that the *episkopos* of *Didascalia apostolorum*, a document whose final redaction came in the fourth century but whose main redaction, in particular in dealing with *episkopoi*, derived from the third, also reflects the situation of a single *episkopos* in a single congregation, here in Syria, and that *Apostolic Church Order* likewise, which I have suggested may be Cappadocian or Cilician in

6. So also ibid., 300.

7. A provision also made in the tenth canon of the Council of Antioch (341).

8. The fifty-seventh canon of the Synod of Laodicea (380) forbids the appointment of rural bishops altogether.

origin,[9] similarly reflects a single *episkopos* in a single, relatively small Christian community.

In the laying out of this narrative there was a degree of uncertainty with regard to a number of Christian centers. In particular, whereas it is possible that Christianity at Antioch at the time of Ignatius was made up of federated individual communities, as elsewhere, it is also possible that a single congregation had split over issues of law observance, that the divided non-law-observant household further subdivided, meaning that there were two large groupings from the beginning, and meaning that monepiscopacy might develop early. However, even if this did take place, which is far from certain, this was a strand of development that becomes indistinguishable in the end from the major narrative. In the rural districts, however, as already noted, there was no centralization, although as the fourth century dawns, the process of centralization caught up here as well,[10] leaving only Christian communities that were not of the *Großkirche* (wider catholic church) under the management of individual *episkopoi* without subordinate presbyters.

There is one loose end in this account that may be tied up at this point, and that is the fate of the congregational presbyters, the household elders of the Asian communities, characterized above as the Neanderthals of church order.[11] The answer to the fate of the domestic presbyters is that they simply died out, as the term becomes restricted to those who hold presbyteral office under the *(mon)episkopos*. The term had been applied to the gathering of leaders from across a city, I may suggest, because of its honorific value and because the gathering mirrored those that took place within individual congregations. Once the focus shifted from the individual Christian community to the gathered communities *kata polin*, then the domestic presbyters cease to have significance; the *episkopoi* of independent communities are no longer the agents of the presbyters, but are agents of the city *episkopos*. This is bound up to appointment; I may suggest that in the Asian communities the *episkopos* of the household was appointed by the presbyters, a process depicted in 1 Timothy where hands are laid on Timothy, the representative and ideal *episkopos*, by the presbytery.[12] I may further suggest that the *episkopos* in these communities need not have been a presbyter at all. Thus we meet criticism of Onesimus in Ephesus,[13] perhaps

9. Alistair Stewart(-Sykes), *The Apostolic Church Order: The Greek Text with Introduction, Translation and Annotation*, ECS 10 (Sydney: St. Pauls, 2006).

10. It is noteworthy that in the account of the trial of Paul of Samosata Eusebius cites a letter from rural *episkopoi* around Antioch (*Hist. eccl.* 7.30.2), which implies that even at that stage they were in some kind of subordinate relationship to the urban center.

11. As discussed in the conclusion to chap. 3.

12. 1 Tim. 4:14.

13. Ign. *Eph.* 6.

from among the presbyters, and Damas, the young *episkopos* of the Magnesian Christians who, by virtue of his age, cannot be a presbyter.[14] The result of this is that conflict, such as that seen in the Asian community of the Hippolytean school in Rome, would readily develop between a professionalized *episkopos*, especially once teaching functions come to the fore, and the lay patrons. The lines of authority in such circumstances are not clear; the situation may best be understood by analogy to the relationship in English schools between the head teacher and the board of governors. The board of governors is composed of local political appointees, parents, local clergy, and other local worthies who may or may not have expertise. The head, a professional teacher, is an ex officio member. The United Kingdom Department of Education defines the respective roles by stating, "The head teacher shall be responsible for the internal organisation, management and control of the school, and the implementation of the strategic framework established by the governing body," whereas "The governing body shall exercise their functions with a view to fulfilling a largely strategic role in the running of the school."[15]

The distinction between leadership and governance is thus a fine one, and the reality is either that the governing body becomes otiose and ineffective as all matters are delegated to the headteacher, or else conflict between the two groups comes about, as is evidenced by official and quasi-official guidance given to meet this situation.[16] It is in the light of potential conflict between the (now professionalized) *episkopos* and the patron-presbyters that we are to understand the development of ordination rites in the Hippolytean community, and in particular the hieratic language employed in the ordination prayer, the enforced silence of the presbyters, and the delegation of the ordination prayer to a visiting *episkopos*. In this Asian community of Rome we see the fate of the Asian congregational presbyters, finding themselves diminished and marginalized, until monepiscopacy finally takes even their title, as the sole *presbyteros* is the *presbyteros kata polin* standing at the head of the community.

This characterization of the relationship between presbyters and *episkopos* at the time of Ignatius is more satisfactory than the characterization of the *episkopos* as "chairman of the board" of presbyters,[17] which is offered on the assumption that an *episkopos* is little more than a *presbyteros* writ large,

14. Ign. *Magn.* 3:1.
15. Education (School Government) (Terms of Reference) (England) Regulations 2000, paragraphs 4.1 and 5.1.
16. E.g., http://www.education.gov.uk/governorline/faqs/a00204359/disputes; http://www.education.gov.uk/governorline/faqs/a00204372/managingconflict (viewed on March 1, 2013).
17. So Everett Ferguson, "The Ministry of the Word in the First Two Centuries," *ResQ* 1 (1957): 26, neatly encapsulating many earlier characterizations of the *episkopos*, understood as simply a presbyter with particular responsibilities.

which is in turn based on the assumption of an originally corporate leadership of congregations. It is to be observed that Ignatius does not identify himself with the presbyters at any point, but rather with the *diakonoi*,[18] an observation that may be taken as evidence of the close relationship between the offices in an episcopal-diaconal system and the distinct nature of the congregational presbyters. It is worth noting, however, that a similar institution of patron elders, the *seniores*, is found in Africa, and that it survives as a lay rank within the church. The survival of this group, as compared to the disappearance of the presbyters of Asian congregations, may be attributed to the distinct way in which the threefold order of office forms in Africa.[19]

The narrative of centralization may best be compared to the political process of centralization of powers that formerly had been federated. Political science has yet to find a convincing theoretical model to explain the process. Although there are numerous studies of the interplay of federation and centralization in federal states such as Canada and the West Indian Federation of 1958 (a *Bundesstaat*, that is, a single state that delegates certain powers to autonomous geographical regions) and, indeed, of federations of independent states (*Staatenbund*) such as those forming CARICOM and the European Union (though arguably the latter is turning into a *Bundesstaat*), these take into account the complexities of modern politics such as the issue of fiscal flows between the (geographical and social) center and the periphery with particular regard to taxation, the benefit received or perceived by participants in a democratic society, and the role of lobby groups in the political process. Clearly, there is little relevance in such studies to the issue at hand here. Issues regarding distinct ethnicities and language groups within federations, which frequently affect the success of federations and lead either to breakup (as in the former Yugoslavia) or an abandonment of federation in favor of centralism (as in postcolonial Sudan, now broken up into two nations), are also largely irrelevant once Jews and Gentiles become part of a single, central Christian community within Antioch (with the result that, by the time of John Chrysostom's homilies *Adversus Judaeos*, there is no opportunity to leave the federation without splitting entirely from the church) and once the Hellenophone Christian community of Rome becomes a minority. However, using this political terminology, I may characterize the formation of dioceses under *monepiskopoi* as the transformation of a *Staatenbund* into a *Bundesstaat*. When this occurred in Switzerland in 1848, it was the result of a deliberate

---

18. E.g., Ign. *Eph.* 2:1; Ign. *Magn.* 2; Ign. *Smyrn* 12.

19. The formation of office in Africa and the question of the status of the *seniores* are discussed below, under the heading "*Verschmelzung* as an Explanation of Monepiscopacy."

adoption of a centralizing constitution; in the first centuries of development in the life of the Christian churches it was an organic process.

In the absence of a theoretical model produced by political scientists to explain the process of centralization, it is hardly likely that I may construct one here. My sole claim is accurately to have described and classified the process that took place in early Christian communities. Wagner, likewise, prescinds from any consideration of why such a development came about, listing a number of possibilities.

> This may have occurred on the basis of the necessity of speaking with one voice, on the basis of natural developments within collegially structured organizations, on the basis of the threat of heresy or on the basis of theological considerations. In addition, individuals might have gained a prominent position in these city groupings on the basis of their place in society or their authority as disciples of an apostle.[20]

These are possible, though given the dating (and recalling that Wagner is dating this development rather earlier than I do), the last suggestion is somewhat unlikely, whereas the second, the "natural developments within collegially structured organizations," perhaps that which is the most probable is one that requires much more in terms of theoretical underpinning. It is also to be noted that these explanations are those given for the emergence of a single leader in individual communities, though it is reasonable to employ them, as Wagner does, in speaking of a similar process, namely, the emergence of a single leader from multiple but federated communities. For this reason I will briefly discuss some here, as well as some further possibilities at the end of the chapter. But I make no claim here to a final answer; I simply have opened a new avenue of research, by giving an account of the process, so that the process in turn might be explained.

With the process now classified and understood as centralization, we may come to an understanding of the extent to which Ignatius is or is not an advocate of monepiscopacy—that is, whether we should understand his emphasis on unity as indicating centralization over and against federalism, or federation over and against congregationalism. He gives us some insight into his reasoning: "Be keen, therefore to come together more tightly [*pyknoteron*],

---

20. "Dies kann, aufgrund der Notwendigkeit, mit einer Stimme zu sprechen, geschehen sein, aufgrund natürlicher Entwicklungen innerhalb von kollegial strukturierten Organen, aufgrund der Bedrohung durch Irrlehre oder aufgrund von theologischen Gesichtspunkten. Zudem können Einzelne aufgrund ihrer gesellschaftlichen Position oder ihrer Autorität als Apostelschüler eine herausragende Stellung in diesen Stadtgremien gewonnen haben" (Wagner, *Anfänge*, 300).

for God's thanksgiving [*eis eucharistian theou*] and glory. For when you are tightly together as one the powers of Satan are destroyed and his destruction is dissolved through the harmony of your faith."[21] A tight community organization is seen as strength; such tightness must, however, be based on a harmony of mind and will.

As Brent has shown, this idea is in turn derived from Hellenistic political theory.[22] In *The Republic* Plato points out the importance of the agreement of the ruled and the rulers in forming the social contract by which governance comes about.[23] This is described as a sounding together (*symphōnia*) and agreement (*homonoia*). It is noteworthy that Ignatius is continuing to use the same language and imagery. He is not alone in using the same language in second century Asia, as Dio Chrysostom is very close to Plato in describing to the Prusans the ideal city in which the governors are wise and prudent and the populace submits readily to the just rule of the governors, in the same way that a choir with a competent conductor who is closely followed is a properly musical choir.[24] In addressing the Nicaeans after the settlement of civil strife, he puts a twist on the imagery by stating that those who live in *homonoia* are heard by the gods and by the imperial rulers, whereas when a choir is not harmonious, no one listens to it.[25] It is easy to parallel this imagery from within the Ignatian corpus. Brent further points out that in seeing the earthly liturgy of the church as mirroring the heavenly realities, Ignatius is similarly using a familiar image from political discourse, in that a city working harmoniously mirrors the order of the heavens. Thus, in spite of the realities of Roman rule, the classical conception of the *polis* is still strong, particularly in the Asian cities, and discourse continues on the importance of *homonoia* within the city, its internal accord. So Polemo is said to have brought accord to Smyrna, riven by local factions,[26] and at Pisidian Antioch, a dicast, Pythodotus, is honored for bringing about *homonoia* between individuals by his wise judgment.[27] Such a political discourse applied to churches is likewise reflected, Maier points out,

21. Ign. *Eph.* 13:1. This translation embodies the important observation of Taras Khomych, "The Notion of *puknôs* as a Distinctive Characteristic of Liturgical Celebrations in the Letters of St Ignatius of Antioch," in *Papers Presented at the Fourteenth International Conference on Patristic Studies Held in Oxford 2003*, ed. F. Young, M. Edwards, and P. Parvis, StPatr 40 (Louvain: Peeters, 2006), 441–46, regarding the translation of πυκνότερον and πυκνῶς in this passage.

22. Allen Brent, *Ignatius of Antioch and the Second Sophistic: A Study of an Early Christian Transformation of Pagan Culture*, STAC 36 (Tübingen: Mohr Siebeck, 2006), 231–40.

23. Plato, *Resp.* 431D–432A.

24. Dio Chrysostom, *In. cont.* 48.7–8.

25. Dio Chrysostom, *Nicaeen.* 39.2, 4.

26. Philostratus, *Vit. soph.* 531

27. *IMagn.* 90.

in the construction of Ignatius's letters, in particular in the manner in which the opening *laudatio* of each church reflects the conventions of the panegyric of cities in the Second Sophistic.[28]

However, the question remains as to the level at which this *homonoia* operates. For whereas such cooperation might function within an individual *polis*, it might equally be seen as characterizing the relations between cities in a *koinon*, a federation. Thus the Asian cities, hypothetically self-governing but in reality part of the Roman *imperium*, formed a *koinon* and celebrated their *homonoia*.

Ignatius's view of *homonoia* would be formed by his Antiochian experience. If I am correct that the discord was between congregations of Jewish and of Gentile descent and that peace, the constant companion of *homonoia*, had been brought about through the recognition of the possibility that these congregations might, theoretically at least, worship together, it is precisely this peace that is threatened by the activities of Judaizing teachers in the Asian churches. It certainly is this that threatens the unity of the Philadelphian Christians. But such a unity brings further questions in its wake, for although a tight federation, operating in *homonoia*, does not require monepiscopacy, if the members of the federation worship together, then the question arises of who is to be the *episkopos*. For Capper, it is the gathering of the hosts of communities with their congregations, requiring a single host, that brings about monepiscopacy, as the responsibility for presiding falls on one of the number of the gathered household heads.[29] If this is the case, then again we see the emergence of monepiscopacy bound up to centralization. However, attractive as this idea is, there is not the evidence to sustain it. We do not know of the extent to which Ignatius's advice was heeded at Ephesus, or even whether Ignatius intends, literally, a single gathering in one place; certainly, it seems that there was none at Smyrna. At Rome there is no evidence that there was ever a single gathering, even were such a thing possible, and so this is not the cause of monepiscopacy here. Whereas elsewhere there is evidence of federation and early collaboration between congregations, there is insufficient evidence to enable us to trace the process by which this led to centralization. Ignatius's idea of the single gathering, we may now see, is modeled on the idea of a civic festival, but although he may be referring to participants from different federated churches, he may simply be referring to a single congregation made up of distinct households, whose householders formed the presbytery and appointed the *episkopos*.

28. Harry O. Maier, "The Politics of the Silent Bishop: Silence and Persuasion in Ignatius of Antioch," *JTS* 55 (2004): 517–18.

29. Brian Capper, "Order and Ministry in the Social Pattern of the New Testament Church," in *Order and Ministry*, ed. Christine Hall and Brian Hannaford (Leominster, UK: Gracewing, 1996), 91–94.

Thus, Ignatius's insistence on gathering as the means by which a proper unity, harmony, and agreement may be achieved and maintained might lead to monepiscopacy, though much depends on how he is to be understood at this point. Such a monepiscopacy might defend against heresy not by virtue of being a teaching office but rather by tightening the social structure of the church so that heresy, seen as alien, might not enter in. According to Blasi, however, it is not the external threat of heresy but rather the external threat of Roman persecution that is the motivating factor behind the construction of a tight single Christian grouping.[30] There is less evidence for this in Ignatius's letters, but this represents the same view nonetheless, namely, there is an intentional focusing of the group as a means to withstand external pressure. Ignatius's fundamental concern is that the Christian group be tightly integrated; episcopal office as such is not his concern, except in that it is taken for granted.

However, although the Ignatian theory may be readily explained through this means, it does not account for the move overall. We do not know the extent of the influence of the Ignatian epistles, but there is no evidence that others appropriated the ideology of *homonoia* as part of the rationale for episcopacy. In the same way, we may observe Cyprian's idea of the single *episcopus* representing Christ by being the focus of unity[31] as a valuable theological idea but not in any way as a means to bring monepiscopacy about, not the least because, in Cyprian's case at least, it was ex post facto.

Having characterized the nature of the emergence of monepiscopacy, I may go on to compare prior explanations based on distinct narratives, in particular the almost unquestioned underlying consensus that early Christian leadership was always collective. We may, moreover, be mindful that it is a development that generally takes place at the end of the second century and not at the end of the first, as is otherwise generally assumed, and mindful also that Ignatius speaks not of monepiscopacy—that is, episcopacy *kata polin*—but rather of *episkopoi* in single congregations.

Verschmelzung as an Explanation of Monepiscopacy

In the discussion of 1 Timothy, I made reference to the idea that distinct systems of church order had combined. In that instance it was shown not to account for the church order of the epistle; in particular, I suggested that the two forms of governance that were meant to be being combined, presbyteral and episcopal,

30. Anthony J. Blasi, "Office Charisma in Early Christian Ephesus?" *SocRel* 56 (1995): 253.

31. On this, see John D. Laurance, "Eucharistic Leader according to Cyprian of Carthage: A New Study," *StLit* 15 (1982): 66–75.

did not combine because there was no presbyteral form of governance (without any other officer) that might combine with any other system. In particular, the theory is often presented on the basis that the presbyters were a Jewish institution that needed to be united with the (Gentile) system of episcopacy.[32] Clearly, this cannot be sustained, not only because of the absence of evidence for Jewish presbyters but also because *presbyteroi* themselves emerge from the same Hellenistic associational origins as *episkopoi*. Alternatively, the confluence of two streams of Jewish governance, that of synagogal elders and that of the Essenes, the *mebaqqer* once again being seen as the model for the *episkopos*, is suggested.[33] Again, this falls foul of the same fundamental objection, that there is no evidence whatsoever for Jewish presbyters in the synagogue, and there is no possibility that this synagogal system might combine with another form of office. More recently Blasi, apparently (and perhaps advantageously) without knowledge of much of the work undertaken on early Christian office, has generated a *Verschmelzungshypothese* of his own by suggesting that the Pastoral Epistles and Acts 20 serve to bolster Paul's position by creating an association between the (Jewish heritage) presbytery that, he suggests, already existed in Ephesus and the *episkopoi* of the Gentile churches, and to bolster the episcopal office by associating it directly with Paul, and so to lend Pauline charisma to the office.[34] Apart from the fact that this hypothesis assumes synonymy (though Blasi's work has the merit of at least explaining the rationale behind synonymy: it was manufactured in order to bring the combination about), it assumes the preexistence of a historically Jewish presbytery in Ephesus for which there is no evidence, and it assumes that by the time of

32. Franz Prast (*Presbyter und Evangelium in nachapostolischer Zeit: Die Abschiedsrede des Paulus in Milet [Apg 20,17–38] im Rahmen der lukanischen Konzeption der Evangeliumsverkündigung*, FB 29 [Stuttgart: Katholisches Bibelwerk, 1979], 361–69) presents the hypothesis of (collective and Jewish) presbyters and (collective and Gentile) *episkopoi* combining initially at about the time of Acts (his evidence being Acts 20, as discussed above). C. N. Jefford ("Presbyters in the Community of the *Didache*," in *Papers Presented at the Tenth International Conference on Patristic Studies Held in Oxford 1987: Second Century, Tertullian to Nicaea in the West, Clement of Alexandria and Origen, Athanasius*, ed. E. A. Livingstone, StPatr 21 [Louvain: Peeters], 122–28) similarly suggests that the instruction to appoint *episkopoi* is an attempt to reorient Jewish presbyters in a Hellenistic church. For Markus Tiwald ("Die vielfältigen Entwicklungslinien kirchlichen Amtes im Corpus paulinum und ihre Relevanz für heutige Theologie," in *Neutestamentliche Ämtermodelle im Kontext*, ed. Thomas Schmeller, Martin Ebner, and Rudolf Hoppe, QD 239 [Freiburg: Herder, 2010], 117–18), this has attained the status of a fact.

33. Raymond E. Brown, "*EPISKOPĒ* and *EPISKOPOS*: The New Testament Evidence," *TS* 41 (1980): 333–34.

34. Blasi, "Office Charisma," 248–49. Hans von Campenhausen (*Ecclesiastical Authority and Spiritual Power in the Church of the First Three Centuries*, trans. J. A. Baker [London: A&C Black, 1969], 81) also explains the apparent synonymy in the passage by suggesting that Luke is creating a literary combination of systems.

Acts and the Pastorals the essential dispute between Christians of Jewish and non-Jewish descent and practice, namely, the necessity of circumcision, is no longer an issue, which is a very dangerous assumption.

The classic statement of the hypothesis is that of Lietzmann. For him, it explains the rather confusing vocabulary of Hermas and Clement regarding presbyters and *episkopoi*—for instance, the fact that there is a dispute over *episkopē* in Corinth that has led to the deposition of presbyters. The texts that he employs in his argument are those that I employed in my suggestion above that the terms denoted officers in their own individual communities (as *episkopoi*) or viewed *kata polin* (as presbyters). Lietzmann notes the absence of presbyters from the *Didache*, and notes that, like that of the Philippians, this community knows *episkopoi* (and *diakonoi*) and no presbyters. These officers are, he suggests, derived from associational and Greek civic usage, presenting extensive evidence of the use of the terms.[35] These offices are in turn, he suggests, imported into originally presbyteral communities of Rome, whereas presbyteral order, derived from Hellenistic Jewish circles, is introduced where previously *episkopoi* and *diakonoi* hold office,[36] leading to a threefold order like that described by Ignatius. This leads to what I have termed the perionymous relationship between the terms; thus, he suggests, an *episkopos* is a *presbyteros* acting in a liturgical ministry. What is vital here is his suggestion that the offices of *episkopos* and *diakonos* are liturgical, whereas the presbyters are managerial. This distinction comes about as the result of his following Harnack's reading of *leitourgousi* in *Didache* 15:1, where the *episkopoi* are seen to be taking over the liturgical ministries of the prophets and teachers;[37] the *presbyteroi*, insofar as there is a distinction, take on the managerial and economic aspect of the episcopal office. Thus, he explains the manner in which the presbyters, in Polycarp's letter to the Philippians, are exercising what we saw above as an episcopal office and explains Valens's fall from grace as a result of his misappropriation of funds.[38]

The fundamental problems with Lietzmann's argument are, first, that it presupposes presbyteral government in some communities and, second, that it does not make the vital distinction between office at the level of an individual community and at the level of a group of communities (though perhaps this

35. Hans Lietzmann, "Zur altchristlichen Verfassungsgeschichte," in *Kleine Schriften I*, ed. Kurt Aland, TUGAL 67 (Berlin: Akademie-Verlag, 1958), 144–53.

36. Ibid., 169–75. Similarly, Campenhausen, *Ecclesiastical Authority*, 84–85.

37. Adolf von Harnack, *Die Lehre der zwölf Apostel: Nebst Untersuchungen zur ältesten Geschichte der Kirchenverfassung und des Kirchenrechts*, TUGAL 2/1–2 (Leipzig: Hinrichs, 1886), 140–41.

38. Lietzmann, "Zur altchristlichen Verfassungsgeschichte," 170.

is the one fundamental problem, which leads to the assertion of presbyteral governance). There are other issues, in particular deriving from his view of officers taking over the ministries of prophets, whereas we have seen that the Didachist means that they should offer financial support to these ministries, as well as the obvious objection that presbyteral government is not, as Lietzmann thinks and as is still so often asserted, present in Jewish communities. It is for these reasons that the hypothesis is set aside.

I may also mention the similar, yet distinct, hypothesis of Barlea, for whom the two systems, presbyteral and episcopal-diaconal, derive from the origins of Christianity. He attributes the presbyteral system to developments within Jerusalem, noting the manner in which the elders of Jerusalem appear to take over from the apostles and suggesting that this therefore mirrored the synagogue.[39] The episcopal system he identifies with the beginnings of Antiochene Christianity as distinct from that of Jerusalem. He then suggests that these streams coalesce first at Rome, employing *Traditio apostolica* and its ordination rites as principal evidence,[40] though 1 Peter is also seen as evidence of reconciliation between the systems,[41] although they continue in independent existence for some time elsewhere, until Nicaea. Thus he suggests the evidence for elders in the Egyptian churches reflects the Jerusalem system, whereas the Pastoral Epistles and the Corinth addressed by *1 Clement* represent the Antiochene system.[42] However, although this is a laudable attempt to break the deadlock of the consensus and is interesting because it employs liturgical evidence as primary, it has too many inconsistencies and problems, quite apart from its reliance on the continuing belief in synagogal presbyters, to be convincing. For instance, in suggesting that these streams of influence tended to mirror the similar varieties in local governance under Roman rule, Barlea states that there is no evidence of elders in Asia,[43] whereas we have seen that Asia is a principal source for the existence of this *ordo*. Most problematic, however, is his inability, which is frankly admitted and then put aside, firmly to tie any evidence of episcopal governance to the evidence provided by Acts for Antioch.[44]

---

39. Octavian Barlea, *Die Weihe der Bischöfe, Presbyter und Diakone in vornicänischer Zeit*, APT 3 (Munich: Societas Academica Dacoromana, 1969), 48–60.

40. Ibid., 111–17. These inconsistencies are explained, briefly above and more extensively in Alistair Stewart(-Sykes), *Hippolytus: On the Apostolic Tradition* (Crestwood, NY: St. Vladimir's Seminary Press, 2001), as the result of developments within the Hippolytean congregation at Rome resulting from the formation of Roman monepiscopate.

41. Barlea, *Weihe*, 90.

42. Ibid., 75–82.

43. Ibid., 65.

44. Ibid., 73–74.

However, although the combination of systems is not an underpinning narrative, it is mentioned not simply because it has previously, in various forms, been the principal challenge to the consensus, but because in some instances there have been elements of borrowing from other churches in the development of threefold order. I may in the first instance recall the situation of the marginal presbyters of *Didascalia apostolorum* discussed above.[45] Clearly, they are not native to this Syrian community's church order, as they are found without function. I may reasonably suggest, therefore, that the presbyteral order in this community had been imported from some other Christian community. A further example is, I have suggested elsewhere, provided by the *diakonoi* of *Apostolic Church Order*.[46] Here *diakonoi* are an importation into a Christian community that did not know such officers originally; thus, the liturgical duties performed by *diakonoi* in *Didascalia apostolorum*, namely, overseeing order at worship, particularly in the distribution of the gifts, are performed by presbyters within this order,[47] leaving the *diakonoi* as pastoral assistants without a liturgical focus.

A particularly interesting example of probable *Verschmelzung* is provided by Africa, a region of Christianity on which this study has yet to touch. It is precisely because the earliest evidence, which is from the period in which monepiscopacy is generally forming, implies that office here has taken shape as the result of a combination of systems that this part of the narrative has postponed until this point.

The first evidence of African Christianity derives from the late second century, and although we may be assured that Christians had existed in Africa for some time already, there is no evidence that enables us clearly to trace a history of the formation of office in these communities. I may affirm in the first instance that monepiscopacy is firmly established by the time of Cyprian; in the writings of a previous generation alongside reference to an *episcopus* there is also reference to an *antistes*.[48] This may simply be another word for the *episkopos*, but it seems strange that the regular word employed is a Greek loan word, unless the institution itself had been imported from a Hellenophone environment. Hence, it is possible that the term *antistes* is a relic of older usage. Either the whole system of governance in African Christianity

45. See chap. 3, under the heading "The Syrian *Didascalia Apostolorum*."
46. Alistair Stewart(-Sykes), "Deacons in the Syrian Church Order Tradition: A Search for Origins," in *Diakonia, diaconiae, diaconato: Semantica e storia nei Padri della Chiesa; XXXVIII Incontro di studiosi dell'antichità cristiana, Roma, 7–9 maggio 2009*, ed. V. Grossi et al., SEA 117 (Rome: Institutum patristicum Augustinianum, 2010), 111–20.
47. Compare *Can. eccl. ap.* 17–18 with *Did. ap.* 2.57.6.
48. Tertullian, *Cor.* 3.2.

is an importation, or African Christianity at an early stage knew the office of
antistes, which, as we step into the daylight of literate Christianity at the time
of Tertullian, has been identified with the *episcopus*. If the latter is the case,
then I may suggest that it was the result of the association with other Christian
communities, whether Asian or Roman. There are, moreover, two reasons to
prefer the latter explanation. First, the earliest Christians in Africa of whom
we have evidence are Punic, and not part of the cultured elite who might have
contact with Hellenophone culture.[49] Second, there is the existence of a rank
of *seniores* alongside the existence of presbyters. These *seniores* appear in a
vision of Saturus within the *Passio Perpetuae*, where they flank the throne of
the Lord and share in leading worship.[50] We may be sure that presbyters are
not intended, as subsequently a presbyter (the Greek word is employed) appears.[51] It is these same *seniores* of whom we hear from Tertullian, who states
that "the tried men of our elders preside over us [*praesident probati quique
seniores*], obtaining that honor not by purchase, but by established character."[52]
As I have argued elsewhere, these *seniores*, who are subsequently found active
in the fourth and fifth centuries, constitute the patronal element in the church
and are not clergy.[53] I may thus suggest that early African Christianity knew
a system much like that of the early stages of the community lying behind
the production of the *Apostolic Church Order*: there is a recognized patron
group[54] and a single leader. It is possible that these patrons are recognized still
with a double portion.[55] With the influence of other Christian communities,

49. Note that the Scillitan martyrs are native Africans; a typical African Christian of the
period may be represented by the baker's wife depicted by Apuleius, *Metam.* 2.19.

50. *Passio Perpetuae* 12.

51. *Passio Perpetuae* 13.1.

52. Tertullian, *Apol.* 39.

53. As argued in Alistair Stewart(-Sykes), "Ordination Rites and Patronage Systems in Third-
Century Africa," *VC* 56 (2002): 115–30. Note also, for the argument that these *seniores* are not
clergy, William Tabbernee, "Perpetua, Montanism and Christian Ministry in Carthage c203 CE,"
PRSt 32 (2005): 435–38.

54. I would now agree yet more firmly with Brent D. Shaw ("The Elders of Christian Africa," in
Mélanges offerts en hommage au Révérend Père Étienne Gareau [Quebec: Éditions de l'Université
d'Ottawa, 1982], 221–26) that they are a continuation of the practice of elders common in the
pagan villages of the Maghreb than I did in "Ordination Rites." The alternative view is that
they are derived from the synagogue (so W. H. C. Frend, "The *seniores laici* and the Origins of
the Church in North Africa," *JTS* 12 [1961]: 280–84; G. Quispel, "African Christianity before
Minucius Felix and Tertullian," in *Actus: Studies in Honour of H. L. W. Nelson*, ed. J. den Boeft
and A. H. M. Kessels [Utrecht: Instituut voor Klassieke Talen, 1982], 275–77). It is the absence
of evidence for synagogal elders noted above that makes the conclusion that the villages of the
Maghreb are the source of this institution most pressing.

55. Tertullian (*Jejun.* 17), referring to the "psychics," states that those *apud te praesentibus*
are given double portions, which he contrasts to the double *honor* proposed by "the apostle," the
double *honor* being given to those who are both brothers and leaders (*fratribus et praepositis*).

the *antistes* is soon identified with the *episcopus*, whereas presbyters and deacons make an entrance through borrowing. Rather than becoming clericalized, as do the patrons in the community of the *Apostolic Church Order*, or dying out, as did the *presbyteroi* of the Asian churches, *seniores* survive as a distinct lay rank. There is thus a combination of a single officer system (with presbyteral patronage) with a threefold order.[56] The officers, those in the threefold order, are the proper sacramental ministers,[57] whereas the *seniores* are the patrons, whose patronage is uneasily shared, by the time of Cyprian, with the *episcopus*.

Thus, whereas I have suggested that the fundamental means by which monepiscopacy emerged within the urban centers of Asia, in Alexandria, and in Rome was the tightening of federation, I admit that there may be elements of borrowing in other areas. This comes about, however, only once the threefold order is established in these urban centers and is able to be exported thence. *Verschmelzung* is the result of the emergence of monepiscopacy, not a cause.

Institutionalization as an Explanation of Monepiscopacy

Campbell points out that the debate over office has been dominated by two questions: the relationship of elders to bishops, and the relationship of charisma to office. The first matter, he notes, was discussed largely by English scholars, the second by German scholars.[58] Clearly, the present work has been concerned with the former question. However, some brief recognition of the second field of debate is inevitable if there is to be any attempt to explain the development set out in the preceding narrative.

The discussion will be brief indeed, not the least because I have discussed this elsewhere. According to this narrative, the development of office in the church is seen as an example of institutionalization by which the charismatic ministries of the first period of Christianity die out and are replaced by an investment in office.[59]

---

56. Compare this brief account with that of Alan L. Hayes, "Christian Ministry in Three Cities of the Western Empire (160–258 CE)," in *Community Formation in the Early Church and in the Church Today*, ed. Richard N. Longenecker (Peabody, MA: Hendrickson, 2002), 136–42. Hayes seeks to downplay the significance of the officers in Carthage at the time of Tertullian by contrast with the more charismatic leadership of the confessors.

57. Tertullian, *Bapt.* 17; *Exh. cast.* 7.

58. Campbell, *Elders*, 2.

59. Beyond literature cited below, note particularly Ernst Käsemann, "Ministry and Community in the New Testament" in *Essays on New Testament Themes*, trans. W. J. Montague (London: SCM, 1964), 63–94. Käsemann's picture of the Pauline church is one in which both none and all are officeholders, a situation overtaken by the early catholic conception set forth

As I have suggested elsewhere, this narrative is without foundation either in sociological theory or in historical occurrence.[60] The originator of the theory was Sohm, whose motives were unashamedly apologetic; a debate ensued in which Sohm's idea of an originally pure charismatic church is set against a church in which local offices coexist alongside charismatic ministries but ultimately take them over.[61] However, Sohm's theory of charismatic organization, which was for him the mark of *Urchristentum*, gained an entrée into more generalized social theory through being taken up by Weber and contributing to the Weberian theory of institutionalization.[62] According to Weber, the development of institutions comes about through the routinization of charisma; further studies have defined institutionalization but continue to see a journey from charisma to routine.

I do not concern myself with a critique of Weber because the debate is entirely couched in Weberian terms. However, as I have suggested elsewhere, the discussion starts from a false premise, namely, that leadership in early Christian communities is charismatic. The failure or replacement of this charismatic leadership then has to be explained. If studies of recent years pointing to the domestic origin of Christianity have any value, however, they indicate that there was no charismatic leadership in early Christian circles; rather, if Christian leadership was based on leadership within the household, then the form of legitimation of this form of domination may be expressed in Weberian terms as traditional. The false premise comes about partly through the historic failure to understand the significance of the household in the construction of early Christian leadership patterns; this of itself is why theories of charismatic domination giving way to routinization are groundless, for there never was a situation in which there were no leaders in the Pauline churches, but rather leadership devolved onto householders.[63] The charismatic democracy envisaged by, for instance, Käsemann, is a fantasy. However, such is the spell of the theory

---

in Acts and the Pastoral Epistles in which office becomes a permanent possession of designated officeholders, an outcome that he sees as a betrayal of the Pauline charismatic ideal.

60. Alistair Stewart(-Sykes), "Prophecy and Patronage: The Relationship between Charismatic Functionaries and Household Officers in Early Christianity," in *Trajectories through the New Testament and the Apostolic Fathers*, ed. A. F. Gregory and C. M. Tuckett, NTAF (Oxford: Oxford University Press, 2005), 165–89.

61. For a brief description of this early debate, fundamentally between Sohm and Harnack, but with other, less well-known contributions, see Enrique Nardoni, "Charism in the Early Church since Rudolph Sohm: An Ecumenical Challenge," *TS* 53 (1992): 647–55.

62. On Weber's debt to Sohm, see Peter Haley, "Rudolph Sohm on Charisma," *JR* 60 (1980): 185–97.

63. This is the basis of the critique of the theory put by Campbell, *Elders*. Noteworthy as offering this critique earlier is Leonhard Goppelt, "Kirchenleitung in der palästinischen Urkirche und bei Paulus," in *Reformatio und Confessio: Festschrift für D. Wilhelm Maurer*

of routinization that even when the phenomenon of household leadership is observed, its significance goes unnoticed. This emerges with particular clarity in the work of Holmberg, who is one of the first to recognize the significance of house leadership in the emergence of Christian leadership in Pauline circles,[64] and who presents a sophisticated discussion of institutionalization. But because he is following the model by which institutionalization is of necessity a routinization of charisma (that is to say, the charisma of Jesus), he looks for institutionalization in the structures of the Pauline churches and concludes that the power structures in these churches must involve a manifestation of charismatic authority.[65] His whole assumption is that because Christianity is a new phenomenon, its institutions must have been created from nothing. However, the household was not a new institution; rather than simply forming institutions, Christians adopted institutions, and although this gives rise to the formation of something that is new, the church, this new thing is not a creation ex nihilo but is something that grows out of what had previously existed, the household, and the legitimation of leadership is initially at least the same as that which was known in the host institution: leadership is legitimated on the basis of the ability to offer hospitality to the church within a house. This household leadership simply cannot be characterized as charismatic. The starting point for those who argue for charismatic organization in these Pauline households is the manner in which leadership and organization is barely discussed; lists of charismata such as 1 Corinthians 12:28, however, which is for Campenhausen a proof text of the charismatic organization of the Pauline church,[66] are concerned with the subordination of certain charismata under those of the communication of the word—apostleship, prophecy, teaching—and make no mention of community organization. Organization is taken for granted because it is based on the household. While noting that Stephanas volunteered for his position of leadership, as well as noting Paul's exhortation that the people should be subject to him, Campenhausen pays no attention to the problematic that Christians are being called to be subject to a wealthy householder.[67]

A yet more fundamental false premise in the debate, however, is created by the confusion between charisma as a form of leadership and charisma as

zum 65. Geburtstag am 7. Mai 1965, ed. Friedrich Wilhelm Kantzenbach and Gerhard Müller (Berlin: Lutherisches Verlagshaus, 1965), 4–7.

64. Bengt Holmberg, Paul and Power: The Structure of Authority in the Primitive Church as Reflected in the Pauline Epistles (Philadelphia: Fortress, 1980), 105.

65. Ibid., 159–60, 188–90.

66. Campenhausen, Ecclesiastical Authority, 60–61.

67. Ibid., 67, with reference to 1 Cor. 16:15–16.

a religious phenomenon, principally as a form of communication; these are entirely distinct sociological categories. This false premise derives from Sohm but has led to a misreading of Weber. There is no question that religious charisma is found in early Christian communities, but this does not mean that leadership is charismatic. Yet because "charisma" in both instances is taken as synonymous, the presence of religious charisma is taken to imply the existence of charismatic leadership. Thus, because of the presence of charismatic communication in early Christianity in the ministry of prophets, it is assumed that these prophets are leaders. Again, I have already argued extensively that this is not the case. Harnack saw the local leadership of *episkopoi* and *diakonoi* in the *Didache* as replacing that exercised by prophets and teachers due to the failure of charisma.[68] I may rejoin that not only is there no evidence of the failure of charisma, but also there is no prophetic leadership in need of replacement simply because prophets did not exercise leadership on the basis of their prophecy; Harnack was seeking to modify Sohm's view, but the premises are shared, and they led to a misreading of the vital term *leitourgousi* in *Didache* 15:1. It is to be noted that the communities of the charismatic communicators par excellence, the prophets known as Montanists, had structures of leadership.[69] Harnack's view is still alive in the work of Theissen, who interprets Diotrephes as a local leader refusing hospitality to wandering charismatics.[70] However, the leadership that is described is traditionally legitimated leadership, and if there is tension, it lies not between these local leaders and the charismatic communicators but rather, I may suggest, between teachers communicating ordered discourse on a basis of tradition and prophets whose communication is of new material.

If I were to characterize the emergence of monepiscopacy in Weberian terms, I might describe the process as the replacement of traditional forms of legitimation by bureaucratic forms. Whereas in the earliest period it was sufficient legitimation of leadership to be a householder, already by the time of the Pastoral Epistles criteria beyond that are being laid down. In particular, I may note the qualification of *didaktikos* for an *episkopos*,[71] which befits him for the duties of reading and *paraklēsis*.[72] These are new duties, and they go beyond those of being a patron and host; the qualification is a new one,

68. Harnack, *Lehre*, 140–41.

69. Note, e.g., Sozomen, *Hist. eccl.* 7.19.3 (complaining that Montanist bishops had charge of villages, the signficance of which is noted in the conclusion to chap. 1); Epiphanius, *Pan.* 49.2.3 (complaining that Montanist "presbyters and the rest" might be female).

70. Gerd Theissen, *The First Followers of Jesus: A Sociological Analysis of the Earliest Christianity*, trans. John Bowden (London: SCM, 1978), 21.

71. 1 Tim. 3:2.

72. As set out in 1 Tim. 4:13.

not appearing in corresponding qualification lists, as it is a competence, not a moral quality, and a competence specific to the duties of the *episkopos* as "Paul" would envisage the post.[73] The other qualifications laid down, like those laid down in the *Didache*, befit the holder to be an economic administrator and patron-householder and, as noted above, are similar to those laid down elsewhere for persons in authority, whereas a new element of competence is introduced by the Paul of the Pastoral Epistles. There is still an assumption that the officers are householders, but being a householder would now seem to be a necessary but not sufficient condition for Christian leadership. Contrast, however, Schillebeeckx's account of the developments at the time of the Pastoral Epistles, representing the Sohmian view: "Here the strictly hierarchical structures of the *oikos* of the time are taken over, in contrast to earlier situations in which the house communities were a free association of equals . . . on the basis of a contribution inspired by the spirit."[74] However, as already seen, the household model meant that some Christians were more equal than others and had been so from the beginning; it is clear from the Corinthian correspondence that patronage had a major role to play in the regulation of the community and that wealthy and powerful members of the congregation were using their wealth and status to the disadvantage of those who lacked either.[75] The free association of equals never existed, and the hierarchical structures had always been found within the household churches. However, these hierarchical structures are now being tempered through qualification; if *Frühkatholizismus* (early Catholicism) has any heuristic value, which is dubious, then it may positively be seen as a period in which the stranglehold of class on the churches begins to be released.

To an extent, traditional legitimation is not entirely left behind in the period under discussion; we need only think of Cyprian's rapid elevation to the episcopate, which, I may suggest, derived as much from his social status and wealth as any other quality, but traditional legitimation is not sufficient

73. B. S. Easton ("New Testament Ethical Lists," *JBL* 51 [1932]: 11) finds the list of qualities unchanged from its contemporary models. Boris A. Paschke ("The *cura morum* of the Roman Censors as Historical Background for the Bishop and Deacon Lists of the Pastoral Epistles," *ZNW* 98 [2007]: 105–19) sees the list of qualities as closer to the *cura morum* carried out by the Roman censors. He has a case, insofar as moral qualities are discussed. The *Berufspflichtenlehren* favored by Easton and others, however, contain both moral qualities and specific competencies. It is in this light that the presence of *didaktikos* as a competence stands out.

74. Edward Schillebeeckx, *The Church with a Human Face: A New and Expanded Theology of Ministry*, trans. John Bowden (London: SCM 1985), 66–67.

75. Thus Gerd Theissen, *The Social Setting of Pauline Christianity: Essays on Corinth*, trans. and ed. John H. Schütz (Philadelphia: Fortress, 1982); John K. Chow, *Patronage and Power: A Study of Social Networks at Corinth*, JSNTSup 75 (Shefffield: JSOT Press, 1992).

of itself. Whereas it is possible to align the emergence of leadership within
Christian communities with a Weberian typology of domination, this would
explain only the emergence of fixed forms of leadership and does not explain
the particular form of leadership that emerged; that is to say, it does not explain *mon*episcopacy. For Sohm, the betrayal of the charismatic ideal was not
monepiscopacy but rather the emergence of presbyters. I may disagree with
the very idea that the charismatic ideal was betrayed, while recognizing that
if the ideal was betrayed, it is not monepiscopacy that betrayed it but, indeed,
any form of leadership. I may note moreover that for those who maintain that
office replaces charisma, this is an occurrence at the time of the Pastoral Epistles
and the *Didache*. Yet neither community exhibits monepiscopacy. Similarly, if
Ignatius is taken as the first witness to something approaching monepiscopacy,
I may observe that there is no trace of "charismatic" opposition, even though
some have seen it there.[76] Ignatius is a charismatic communicator as well as a
proponent of episcopacy. The final emergence of monepiscopacy in the third
century takes place long after office is an established reality in the churches,
and yet prophecy continues within monepiscopal communities.

In spite of these fundamental flaws, the notion of opposition and tension
between charisma and office has provoked a great deal of literature. I may,
for instance, note Campenhausen's argument that the Pauline "pneumatic"
church is overtaken by the Jewish-Christian "patriarchal" system of eldership,
with its roots in the church order of Jerusalem, and is combined, moreover,
with an episcopal system.[77] Here the fundamental flaws in the *Verschmelzung*
theory and the "institutionalization" theory are combined. More interesting,
but ultimately suffering from the same misunderstanding of Weber, is Bonneau's account, given that he locates the motivation for institutionalization
in internal conflict;[78] as such, I may note that, on this understanding, the
formation of office is not of itself a cause of conflict, as so often assumed,
but rather is the means by which, through the establishment of structures of
office that represent authentic teaching, conflict is avoided. However, there is
the assumption underlying this account that office had to be formed out of a

76. Thus P. Meinhold, *Studien zu Ignatius von Antiochien*, VIEGM 97 (Wiesbaden: Steiner,
1979); Christine Trevett, "Prophecy and Anti-Episcopal Activity: A Third Error Combatted by
Ignatius?" *JEH* 34 (1983): 1–18. Compare the approaches of Harry O. Maier, *The Social Setting
of the Ministry as Reflected in the Writings of Hermas, Clement and Ignatius* (Waterloo, ON:
Wilfrid Laurier University Press, 1991), 156–68; Robert R. Hann, "Judaism and Jewish Christianity in Antioch: Charisma and Conflict in the First Century," *JRH* 14 (1987): 353–54. Both
identify Ignatius as a charismatic leader.
77. Campenhausen, *Ecclesiastical Authority*, 76–123.
78. Guy Bonneau, "'Pour y achever l'organisation' (Tite 1,5): L'institutionalisation de l'Église
au temps du Nouveau Testament," *ScEs* 52 (2000): 87–107.

situation in which there was none, and, more to the point, there is no explanation as to why the particular offices of *episkopos* and *diakonos* emerged.

Although the narrative strand of charisma and office concentrates on the Pauline and Gentile churches, it is taken up elsewhere. Thus, for the Roman churches, Jeffers has attempted to contrast the charismatic authority of Hermas the prophet with the bureaucratic legitimation of Clement.[79] This attempt is flawed in the same way as studies of Pauline communities, not only in the failure to distinguish charismatic communication from charismatic leadership but also in the failure to note that Hermas himself was a householder; as a householder, his legitimation is not due to his prophetic gifts but rather derives from his relatively exalted social status. As such, therefore, we learn nothing about the development of office in Rome and even less about the emergence of monepiscopacy, which was, as argued above, completely unknown at the time of Clement and Hermas. Also to be criticized in Jeffers's approach is the easy correlation between bureaucratic legitimation and bourgeois values made here, with the corresponding correlation between charisma and poverty.[80] In this instance Jeffers is in error in identifying Hermas with the poor, since as a literate householder Hermas is of relatively high social status, albeit not of the elite. Jeffers is led to that characterization through the assumptions of the model with which he is operating, assuming a correlation between charismatic manifestation in religion and low socioeconomic status that is not empirically grounded.[81]

Similarly, I may note the manner in which Schröger attempts to analyze what 1 Peter says regarding office in terms of the transition from charismatic ministries to church order.[82] His overall suggestion is that Pauline charismatic order, which he finds in 1 Peter 4:10–11, is replaced by the presbyteral order to which 1 Peter 5:1–5 bears witness. The rationale for this substitution, he suggests, is the persecution to which the letter bears witness, and he suggests that Pauline congregations elsewhere also adopted presbyteral order at the same time, pointing to *1 Clement* and to Paul's speech at Miletus as evidence for the Pauline adoption of presbyters. What he does not do, however, is explain why presbyteral order might strengthen the church in persecution. The thesis is interesting but ultimately unsuccessful.

79. James S. Jeffers, *Conflict at Rome: Social Order and Hierarchy in Early Christianity* (Minneapolis: Fortress, 1991).

80. So also Hann, "Judaism and Jewish Christianity," with respect to Antioch.

81. Note in particular Stephen J. Hunt, "Deprivation and Western Pentecostalism Revisited: The Case of 'Classical' Pentecostalism," *PentecoStudies* 1 (2002): 1–32, and references.

82. Friedrich Schröger, "Die Verfassung der Gemeinde des ersten Petrusbriefes," in *Kirche im Werden: Studien zum Thema Amt und Gemeinde im Neuen Testament*, ed. Josef Hainz (Munich: Schöningh, 1976), 239–52.

The early Christianity of Jerusalem is likewise not amenable to such pseudo-Weberian analysis. It might be possible to argue that James is a charismatic leader and point to the possibility that charisma is seen as an inherited trait, and thus to suggest that his recognition by the householder-elders of Jerusalem is the result of the perception of charisma inherited by virtue of his familial relationship with Jesus. But I have already argued that James was no kind of *monepiskopos*, and that, whereas the early development of church order in Jerusalem shows similarities to the development of church order elsewhere, the disruption caused by the occupation and Gentilization of the city meant that the heritage of order within Jerusalem Christianity was not passed on.

Examples may be multiplied and refuted. Again I may refer to my earlier refutation of Trevett's suggestion that charismatic prophets were opposed to the hierarchically-minded Ignatius at Philadelphia,[83] a view adopted by Trebilco, again with reference to supposed opposition to Ignatius's (supposed) program of introducing monepiscopacy;[84] as by Pieterson, who presents yet another version of the hypothesis, relating to the development of office in the Pastoral Epistles;[85] and Müller, who identifies this "charismatic" opposition with the circle of the Johannine apocalypse.[86] However, the point is made that the consensus regarding the conflict between charisma and office is as shaky as that regarding synonymy.

Ideas regarding the formation of institutions derived from Weber may be of some use in understanding the emergence of office in early Christian communities, but they do not serve to explain the emergence of monepiscopacy. There is no historical inevitability that means that leadership is necessarily concentrated in the hands of an individual holding office on a citywide or provincial basis with subordinate officers holding authority more locally.

None of this is to deny that institutionalization occurred; indeed, I may suggest that institutionalization is marked in Christian circles by the adoption of associational practices, and that this took place as soon as the church ceased to be based on single households. This meant that office inevitably developed, rather than the de facto exercise of office by a householder; but office, and episcopal office in particular, is not to be equated with monepiscopacy.

---

83. Stewart(-Sykes), "Prophecy and Patronage," with reference to Trevett, "Prophecy."

84. Paul Trebilco, *The Early Christians in Ephesus: From Paul to Ignatius* (Grand Rapids: Eerdmans, 2007), 660–75.

85. Lloyd K. Pietersen, *The Polemic of the Pastorals: A Sociological Examination of the Development of Pauline Christianity*, JSNTSup 264 (London: T&T Clark, 2004), esp. 97–106.

86. Ulrich B. Müller, "Zwischen Johannes und Ignatius: Theologischer Widerstreit in den Gemeinden der Asia," ZNW 98 (2007): 60. See chap. 4 above, pp. 290–95, in which it is suggested that John's vision of heavenly worship is formed in part from a worshiping context similar to that known by Ignatius.

Scholasticization as an Explanation of Monepiscopacy

Although institutionalization of itself may be inadequate as a means of explaining the centralization that led to monepiscopacy, there is a species of institutionalization that often has been posited as a cause of monepiscopacy, namely, scholasticization, the means by which the domestic *ekklēsia* took on the functions of a school.

As Dassmann notes, defense against heresy is often given as a rationale for the development of monepiscopacy, but he also suggests that of itself this does not explain the rapid growth of the phenomenon.[87] The problem with such claims is that they concentrate on the end of the first century and the beginning of the second, seeing monepiscopacy as something emerging at a stage between the Pastoral Epistles and Ignatius, whereas monepiscopacy proper, I have argued, is a phenomenon that fully emerges a century later. As such, attempts to explain the emergence of monepiscopacy at the end of the first century as a defense against heresy are bound to fail because monepiscopacy did not emerge in this period. It is because this is the period in which collective leadership (by presbyters) is seen as giving way to individual leadership (by an *episkopos*), and also the period in which it begins to be possible to speak of heretical and proto-orthodox Christianities, that the two phenomena are conflated,[88] even though there is no obvious reason why an individual should better be able to defend a church against heresy than a group.

Typical of those more recently claiming the growth of monepiscopacy as due to teaching is Lohse. As evidence Lohse sees the requirement of the *episkopos* of the Pastoral Epistles to teach and the manner in which he sees the *episkopoi* and *diakonoi* of the *Didache* taking over the instructing ministry of prophets and teachers.[89] In asserting that the duty of the bishop according to Ignatius is teaching and preaching, Lohse is able to adduce only one passage that is a proverbial use of the term "disciples" (*mathētai*), which tells us nothing about a bishop's responsibilities, and a much adduced passage that is often taken to refer to preaching but actually concerns conversation:[90] "Flee

---

87. Ernst Dassmann, "Hausgemeinde und Bischofsamt," in *Vivarium: Festschrift Theodor Klauser zum 90. Geburtstag*, JAC 11 (Münster: Aschendorff, 1984), 82–84.

88. As emerges with particular clarity in the work of Dietrich-Alex Koch, "Die Entwicklung der Ämter in frühchristlichen Gemeinden Kleinasiens," in Schmeller, Ebner, and Hoppe, eds., *Neutestamentliche Ämtermodelle im Kontext*, 199.

89. Eduard Lohse, "Die Entstehung des Bischofsamtes in der frühen Christenheit," *ZNW* 71 (1980): 71. He refers to *Did.* 15:1, which passage I have already shown to be seriously misunderstood since Harnack.

90. Ibid., 59.

the evil arts; rather, allow conversation regarding them."[91] That the speech here is not teaching or public proclamation but conversation I have argued at length elsewhere.[92] Anyone might speak at the dinner table of the Ignatian communities, as perhaps at that of the *Didache*, but none, not even the *episkopos*, is under obligation to speak. There may be an anticipation that teachers and prophets speak, but not bishop, deacon, or presbytery.

So it is that in Ignatius's letter to the Ephesians we meet the silent bishop Onesimus, whose silence Ignatius defends.[93] If Onesimus lacked eloquence, this would lead to the implicit defense of Onesimus's silence, but a defense would be impossible on any terms were a bishop's fundamental role to teach in the assembly. Clearly, there is some expectation that Onesimus should be refuting heresy, but this is to be undertaken in the same way that Polycarp is to refute the evil arts, namely, in discussion among the members of the household. In the event, according to Onesimus at least, this is not necessary.[94] This implies, in turn, that whatever the competence of the Ignatian bishop, his role did not extend to teaching in the assembly.[95] Nonetheless, the *episkopos* of the Pastoral Epistles *is* a teacher, even if not a *monepiskopos*, and I may suggest here that this is an innovation on the part of this community. As has already been observed, the term *didaktikos*, in the list of qualifications set out, is something of a cuckoo in the nest of the traditional virtue list.

Lohse cannot prove his case because it is based on the incorrect assumption that teaching was fundamental to the office of episcopacy from the beginning, whereas the very separation between teachers (and prophets) and *episkopoi* (and *diakonoi*) in the *Didache* is an indication that their roles were originally entirely distinct. It is true that in a later period *episkopoi* take on teaching functions, and we may see this beginning at the time of the Pastoral Epistles; Merkel argues that the fundamental purpose of these epistles is to bolster the offices of these communities and that the need to strengthen order comes

---

91. Ign. *Pol.* 5:1: τὰς κακοτεχνίας φεῦγε, μᾶλλον δὲ περὶ τούτων ὁμιλίαν ποιοῦ.

92. Alistair Stewart(-Sykes), *From Prophecy to Preaching: A Search for the Origins of the Christian Homily*, VCSup 59 (Leiden: Brill, 2001), 20–22, 77, 90–91, 276–78.

93. Ign. *Eph.* 6:1.

94. Ign. *Eph.* 6:2.

95. So Campenhausen candidly admits: "It is part of this man's duty to instruct his congregation . . . but . . . it is astonishing how little weight is put upon this side of his work" (*Ecclesiastical Authority*, 101). The only references to instruction that Campenhausen is able to quote are references to converse (Ign. *Pol.* 1:2; 5:1). Reinhart Staats ("Die katholische Kirche des Ignatius von Antiochen und das Problem ihrer Normativität im zweiten Jahrhundert," *ZNW* 77 [1986]: 144) makes the interesting suggestion that Ignatius defends Onesimus's silence on the basis that he is opposing any idea that the episcopal office should be a teaching office.

about because of the threat of heresy.[96] I may agree that presbyters appointed on the basis of the ability to offer patronage, and *episkopoi* who lead on the basis of their headship of a household, are not necessarily equipped to combat false teaching. I have already argued against Roloff's assertion that the Pastoral Epistles represent the introduction of *episkopoi*, but I may agree with him that there is a degree of redefinition of the role through the introduction of qualifications for anyone wishing to be an *episkopos* and the expectation that the *episkopos* should have a role in teaching.[97] It is also recognized that presbyters might have a teaching role, and the double *honor* is given as much to those who teach as to those who liturgize well. Thus the *episkopos* is now required to read, teach, and provide an activity of exhortation functionally equivalent to prophecy, and in this way he is distinct from the *episkopoi* of associations whose concern is solely economic. Likewise, he is distinct from his counterpart in synagogal associations, for the *rosh ha-knesset* might read, but only when nobody else is available,[98] and so it is far from being a regular function, but rather is an emergency provision, whereas here it is the principal duty of the *episkopos*. Effectively this restricts the appointment to one so qualified. I may thus explain the concentration on the *episkopos* in 1 Timothy not as the introduction of the episcopate,[99] but as the restraint of the (patronal) episcopate through the introduction of qualifications. It is interesting that in a later period the possibility of illiterate *episkopoi* is discussed,[100] indicating that even though the *episkopos* was meant to take on teaching functions, other considerations might continue to weigh more heavily. In Titus the emphasis on the teaching function of the *presbyteroi kata polin* is also extremely clear.

If what is new about the Pastoral Epistles is the demand that the bishop, unlike the *archisynagogos*, should teach, I may return briefly to the discussion of charisma by suggesting that this, rather than episcopacy, may be seen as the exercise of an anti-prophetic ministry. The "heretics" of the Pastoral Epistles may well appeal to prophecy, whereas the appeal of "Paul" is principally to Scripture and only secondarily to prophecy, which prophecy is prophecy that is already tried and tested, fundamentally on the basis of conformity to Scripture.[101]

There are others who see the emergence of a teaching office and the threat of heresy as the reason behind the emergence of office in the Pastoral Epistles.

96. Helmut Merkel, *Die Pastoralbriefe*, 13th ed., NTD 9/1 (Göttingen: Vandenhoeck & Ruprecht, 1991), 92.

97. Jürgen Roloff, *Der erste Brief an Timotheus*, EKKNT 15 (Zürich: Benziger; Neukirchen-Vluyn: Neukirchener Verlag, 1988), 170–77.

98. *t. Meg.* 4.21.

99. So Merkel, *Pastoralbriefe*, 92.

100. E.g., *Can. eccl. ap.* 16.2.

101. Stewart(-Sykes), *From Prophecy to Preaching*, 170–74.

Thus Marshall: "This [what is seen as the relatively unordered situation in Crete] may suggest that earlier organisation was informal and that the rise of heresy meant that some more formal procedure was required. There is a tendency to encourage the overseers to be active in teaching, since sound teaching is so important over against the rise of heresy."[102] I may agree that presbyters appointed on an honorific basis and *episkopoi* who lead on the basis of their headship of a household are not necessarily equipped to combat false teaching, and they may indeed encourage it. But none of this explains the introduction of monepiscopacy. Indeed, however much the church of the Pastoral Epistles is becoming a scholastic institution, it has yet to know a *monepiskopos*.

Similarly, heresy and (scholasticized) monepiscopacy as a response is seen as the means by which monepiscopacy emerges in Antioch. Meier asks, "How is one to conceive of the transition from the relatively loose structure of Matthew's church around A.D. 85 to the three-part hierarchy of Ignatius?" One answer is that we cannot and should not do so, since Matthew tells us nothing of the structure of the church and is, in any event, derived from a law-observant Christian community as opposed to Ignatius's non-law-observant community. Meier answers the question by suggesting that a situation of crisis obliged a tightening up of church structures, and that this crisis was principally theological, identifying the rise of docetic teaching and, secondarily, that persecution might pull the church together.[103] It is far from clear, however, why or how a *monepiskopos* should provide a necessary defense against false teaching or should in any way strengthen the church against persecution. In a later period at Antioch it is a teacher who is responsible for convicting the *episkopos* of heresy. The history of heretical bishops is sufficient proof that, of itself, monepiscopacy is no defense against heresy, whereas, as already noted, a strong corporate body like that formed by the *presbyteroi kata polin* is more likely to defend against the possibility of an unorthodox individual. Thus Marcion's exclusion from the Roman federation is undertaken by presbyters and teachers, and the condemnation of Noetus is the work of the presbyters of Smyrna.

As far as Ignatius is concerned, there are further arguments against seeing a relationship between Ignatius's insistence on monepiscopacy and the need to guard against heresy through teaching. In an earlier essay I argued

---

102. I. Howard Marshall, *A Critical and Exegetical Commentary on the Pastoral Epistles*, ICC (Edinburgh: T&T Clark, 1999), 181. Similarly, Campenhausen (*Ecclesiastical Authority*, 109–11) notes the central significance of teaching entrusted to the officers of the Pastoral Epistles and suggests that the rise of heresy (he actually says gnosticism) is the cause.

103. In Raymond E. Brown and John P. Meier, *Antioch and Rome: New Testament Cradles of Catholic Christianity* (London: Geoffrey Chapman, 1983), 75.

that insofar as a coherent opposition to epispocacy within Asia might be discerned, it certainly was not charismatic, but that it might be due to scholastic households,[104] in particular because the *episkopos* had inherited a duty of economic empowerment, whereas increasingly scholasticizing communities had sought teaching. Such teaching, however, was derived as often as not from Jewish background and maintained the law and the keeping of the sabbath, whereas Ignatius is from a purely Gentile background in Antioch. Although I have argued here that there is a problem in Tralles and Magnesia with private patrons and alternative meals from those of the *episkopos*, there is no contradiction. The Jewish teachers themselves may be the objects of patronage, detracting therefore from the support of the poor. If this is the case, then scholasticization, far from encouraging monepiscopacy, may have delayed the development. It is noteworthy that Smyrna, which manifests strong elements of scholasticization in its organization, continues to have a strong presbyterate even after monepiscopacy has come about.

Paul's discourse in Acts 20 is also significant as evidence of the manner in which a teaching office is given to *episkopoi* alongside their economic duties, even though, once again, monepiscopacy is not in view. So Campenhausen, on the basis of this passage, similarly suggests that it is the emergent threat of heresy that brings about the institutionalization that he so much deplores, but it is notable that the duty of preventing the church from going astray is, in his view, placed into the hands of the *presbyteroi*.[105] I may note at this point the degree of common ground between the Ephesus of the Pastoral Epistles and the Ephesus of Acts 20 as the fictive hearers of Acts 20 may well be envisaged as the *episkopoi* of the Ephesian households of 1 Timothy.[106] The same fundamental concern with heterodox teaching, moreover, is a fundamental motivation behind both sets of instructions to local leaders, as is the concern, more prominent in 1 Timothy, that nothing be done out of greed or for gain.[107] Thus, similar charges are given to the *episkopoi* in order to confront similar issues. I identified, in discussion with Lambrecht, the teachers, rather than *episkopoi*, as the potential recipients of payment, and I may note now that they likewise are likely to be the source of false teaching. The solution is for the *episkopoi* themselves, or rather, as the language of Acts 20 has it, the *presbyteroi*

104. Stewart(-Sykes), "Prophecy and Patronage."

105. Campenhausen, *Ecclesiastical Authority*, 81.

106. As pointed out in chap. 1, under the heading "Acts 20 as Evidence for Federation at Ephesus."

107. So Pius-Roman Tragan, "Les 'destinateurs' du discours de Milet: Une approche du cadre communautaire d'Ac 20,18–35," in *À cause de l'évangile: Études sur les Synoptiques et les Actes offertes au P. Jacques Dupont à l'occasion de son 70e anniversaire*, LD 123 (Paris: Cerf, 1985), 779–98.

(*kata polin*), to become, like the apostles and their delegates, teachers and agents of tradition.[108] But in doing so, they do not become *monepiskopoi*.

The ultimate scholasticization of the *episkopos* is found in the Hippolytean community; the preface to *Traditio apostolica* is concerned with buttressing the power of the *episkopos* within the community as authoritative teacher against the ill-taught,[109] whom, I have argued elsewhere, are the patrons within the Hippolytean community. However, this *episkopos* is not a *monepiskopos*, but rather is a household-school *episkopos* among others within (or perhaps disconnected from) the federation of Roman Christian communities. The real enforcement of orthodoxy is the task of the collective presbyters within Rome, as within Smyrna.[110]

In this light, I may turn again to the question as to whether scholasticization is in any way related to the emergence of monepiscopacy. The question needs to be examined afresh because of the misleading assumptions that have marked previous attempts to answer it, namely, that monepiscopacy emerges at the time of the Pastoral Epistles and that teaching was always an episcopal function.

In an earlier work I argued that scholastic activity within the church originates in the first century as a result of the separation of Christians from the synagogue with the need to perform the synagogal activities of reading and instruction within the church.[111] I may also note that the requirement for Gentile Christians to receive some instruction would bring about a degree of scholastic activity within the community. This begins to occur, I may suggest, very early in the formation of Christianity as a distinct cult. The expectation, beginning at the time of the Pastoral Epistles, that the *episkopos* should have some competence in teaching likewise precedes the emergence of monepiscopal structures. The question is whether, as prior to the emergence of monepiscopacy, the expectation that an *episkopos* should have teaching competence might also bring monepiscopacy about. The theory possibly goes back to Baur, who saw monepiscopacy (as I have termed it here) emerging as a response to gnosticism and to Montanism.[112] He saw this emerging in the Pastoral Epistles, which he dated to the latter part of the second century. Baur's theory is at least consistent, though in order to follow him I would

---

108. So also Heinz Schürmann, "Das Testament des Paulus für die Kirche," in *Traditionsgeschichtliche Untersuchungen zu den synoptischen Evangelien: Beiträge*, KBANT (Düsseldorf: Patmos, 1968), 321, 328–29.

109. *Trad. ap.* 1.

110. So Hippolytus, *Noet.* 1.6–7.

111. Stewart(-Sykes), *From Prophecy to Preaching.*

112. F. C. Baur, *Das Christenthum und die christliche Kirche*, 2nd ed. (Tübingen: Fues, 1860), 260–304.

have to accept his dating of the Pastoral Epistles. Nonetheless, I may perhaps pursue a slightly more complex hypothesis: whereas teaching gradually became a function of the domestic *episkopos*, beginning at the time of Acts and the Pastoral Epistles, the very threats to which Baur adverts, namely, gnosticism and the new prophecy, led in turn to monepiscopacy.

I thus begin to answer the question by revisiting the narrative; monepiscopacy, I have argued, emerged from presbyterate *kata polin*. We have seen that the functions of *presbyteroi kata polin* are those of defending the Christian community against heresy through policing the boundaries of the federation, through the circulation of literature, and through the maintenance of tradition.[113] Insofar as monepiscopacy grew from these federations, we may see that this growth is bound up to scholasticization because some of the functions of the presbyters, namely, the transmission of literature and the determination of doctrinal limits, are scholastic functions and are taken over by the *monepiskopos*. There is thus a relationship between monepiscopacy and scholasticization, but scholasticization does not *explain* the rise of monepiscopacy, as the collective presbyters are equally, if not more, capable of exercising these functions. In suggesting that the monepiscopate emerged from the presbyters, I have yet to explain this emergence, and perhaps I may do so by picking up on one aspect of monepiscopacy that is yet to be discussed, namely, the idea of episcopal succession.

The question of succession is raised by the speech to the Ephesian elders. Whereas there is no explicit statement that the elders are Paul's successors, this is implied by the very setting of a farewell discourse. Barrett, however, claims that this is a deliberate omission. "The omission is too striking to be accidental, and the best explanation is to be found in the stress laid, in verse 28, on the appointment of the elder-bishops by the Holy Spirit." He continues, "If this [i.e., to stress appointment by the Holy Spirit] was Luke's intention it must have been polemically conceived in a situation in which the ministry, and along with it the church, was becoming in Luke's view too institutionalized."[114] Here he sounds as if he thinks that Luke had been reading Sohm! I have already observed that the speech offers a retrospect of Paul's entire Asian activity,

---

113. It is important to note, in view of the point made in chap. 1, that the Irenaean presbyters who were the bearers of tradition might be *presbyteroi kata polin*, that this role of conveying tradition is a function of *presbyteroi kata polin* rather than of congregational presbyters. This point is stressed in view of Frances M. Young ("On ΕΠΙΣΚΟΠΟΣ and ΠΡΕΣΒΥΤΕΡΟΣ," *JTS* 45 [1994]: 148) and Hayes ("Christian Ministry"), who likewise connect the presbyters with the guardianship of tradition but who then confuse these presbyters with the congregational presbyterate.

114. C. K. Barrett, "Paul's Address to the Ephesian Elders," in *God's Christ and His People: Studies in Honour of Nils Alstrup Dahl*, ed. Jacob Jervell and Wayne A. Meeks (Oslo: Universitetsforlaget, 1977), 118.

which ends as Paul turns to the *episkopoi*, thus implying that the *episkopoi* are to take over from him.[115] Local officers take over from apostles, I suggest, not simply in their local activity but in their contact with one another. This adoption of the Pauline task by local leaders is, Roloff suggests, part of Luke's theological narrative, for these leaders accept responsibility for the apostolic task even as Paul takes over in the narrative from the other apostles.[116]

Much the same relationship, I may suggest, is envisaged between the apostolic delegates of the Pastoral Epistles and the *episkopoi* who are already there. The *episkopoi* are to continue to act as the apostolic delegates. Here the succession of teaching implicit in Acts 20 is made explicit, as Timothy is instructed to repeat what he had heard from "Paul" and to ensure that this message is in turn passed on.[117] Whereas it is not made explicit here that those who are to pass on the teaching are the local officers, the *episkopoi*, this is implied through the requirement that the *episkopos* be competent to teach.[118] Clement similarly saw the *episkopoi* of his day as successors to those appointed by the apostles,[119] though in that instance they succeeded not to teaching but to *leitourgia*. Of course, this succession is not *episcopal* succession, but the idea is formed in a climate that would foster the idea that the succession of teaching might be entrusted to the *episkopoi*.

Particularly in this regard I must note the philosophical schools, which were able to point to the succession of the heads of the school as a means by which they maintained their philosophical identities.[120] Thus, in the second and third centuries we find the same conception employed by Hegesippus, perhaps the first to do so,[121] Irenaeus, and the (possibly Hippolytean) author

115. This is seen with great clarity by Thomas L. Budesheim, "Paul's Abschiedsrede in the Acts of the Apostles," *HTR* 69 (1976): 20–23. However, his reading of the manner of the succession is vitiated by his rather eccentric understanding of the role of an *episkopos* as a missionary, a view taken over from Georgi that, as discussed in chap. 2 above, under the heading "*Diakonoi* in Other Hellenistic Contexts," has a very slight basis.

116. Jürgen Roloff, *Die Kirche im Neuen Testament*, GNT 10 (Göttingen: Vandenhoeck & Ruprecht, 1993), 216–20.

117. 2 Tim. 2:2.

118. Thus also, on the connection between succession signified by ordination and teaching, Hermann von Lips, *Glaube, Gemeinde, Amt: Zum Verständnis der Ordination in den Pastoralbriefen*, FRLANT 122 (Göttingen: Vandenhoeck & Ruprecht, 1979), 271–78.

119. *1 Clem.* 44:2.

120. So note, e.g., the succession lists provided by Diogenes Laertius, and the statement of succession in the *Academicorum philosophorum index Herculanensis*, col. M5–10.

121. Eusebius (*Hist. eccl.* 4.22.3) quotes Hegesippus as stating that he had constructed a succession list as far as Anicetus (διαδοχὴν ἐποιησάμην μέχρις Ἀνικήτου). Whereas there is much here that is obscure, the fact that he states immediately after that matters are as proclaimed by the law, the prophets, and the Lord "in each succession and in each city" (ἐν ἑκάστῃ δὲ διαδοχῇ καὶ ἐν ἑκάστῃ πόλει) implies, as H. J. Lawlor ("The *Hypomnemata* of Hegesippus," in *Eusebiana:*

of the chronicle lying behind the Liberian catalog, as authentic Christian teaching is shown to be guaranteed by the succession of *episkopoi* in various sees.[122] This is the time in which monepiscopacy is finally emerging, and the ability to point to a named individual as successor to the teaching of the overall Christian school (as opposed to the individual schools that previously might be found within the Christian federation) is a useful polemical tool, lending institutional authority to the claim of authentic succession made against the claims of succession made by teachers of divergent forms of Christianity such as Basilides and Ptolemaeus,[123] as well, perhaps, as establishing a diadochic claim to speak authoritatively that might be set against the new prophecy.[124] Thus the function of the already scholasticized domestic *episkopoi* that is exercised collectively, as it was by the presbyters *kata polin*, and had at one point been simply the property of "men of old,"[125] is concentrated into the hands of a single *episkopos* so that the bishop's chair becomes the "symbol of teaching."[126]

It is in the context of the scholastic dispute with gnostic varieties of Christianity that the doctrine of succession is grounded. As a result of conflict within Christian circles about true doctrine, and possibly as a means to control the patronage accorded to teachers, *episkopoi* were in the process of becoming teachers; to construct a *diadochē* of teaching based on the *episkopoi* is the next, natural step.

I may thus return to Wagner's suggestion that individuals might have had a particular status in the citywide gatherings (*Stadtgremien*) on the basis of

---

Essays on the Ecclesiastical History of Eusebius [Oxford: Clarendon, 1912], 70–90) argues, that his intention is to demonstrate the tradition of orthodoxy and to link this with the succession of *episkopoi*.

122. Irenaeus lays out his doctrine of succession, framed against the relatively recent rise of gnostic schools, in *Haer.* 3.2.3, returning briefly to the subject in *Haer.* 4.26 (note also Tertullian, *Praescr.* 32–38). For discussion, note Einar Molland ("Irenaeus of Lugdunum and the Apostolic Succession," *JEH* 1 [1950]: 12–28), who points out the essentially doctrinal, as opposed to sacramental, nature of Irenaeus's theory of succession; and Allen Brent ("Diogenes Laertius and the Apostolic Succession," *JEH* 44 [1993]: 367–89), who roots the idea in the schools. Note also Robert Lee Williams, *Bishop Lists: Formation of Apostolic Succession of Bishops in Ecclesiastical Crises*, GDECS 3 (Piscataway, NJ: Gorgias, 2005), 123–39.

123. Thus, Basilides is reported to claim to have received secret teaching from Matthias, who had it from Jesus (Hippolytus, *Haer.* 7.8), whereas Ptolemaeus writes of secret teaching passed through a *diadochē* of teachers (quoted in Epiphanius, *Pan.* 33.7).

124. Thus P.Oxy. 5, which, I suggest, derives from Rome in the latter part of the second century, claims a *diadochē* for the prophets as well as the *episkopos*. For Baur (*Christenthum*, 235–45), it is not the claim of prophetic speech to which monepiscopate is the "hierarchical response" as much as the rigorism of the new prophecy.

125. Such is Papias's usage as quoted in Eusebius, *Hist. eccl.* 3.39.

126. Irenaeus, *Epid.* 2.

social position or having been taught by an apostle.[127] Whereas I have suggested that this latter possibility is unlikely, it is interesting to observe in the Roman succession list that, quite apart from Callistus's succession to Zephyrinus,[128] there is a clear relationship between the two of them, and also to note Hegesippus's statement that Eleutherius was Anicetus's deacon, and that Eleutherius in time succeeds Anicetus.[129] I may suggest that the actual episcopal succession from Anicetus to Eleutherius took place within a single household church, but I may also suggest that these connections indicate that certain households may have had prominence within the gathering of leaders from across the city (Wagner's *Stadtgremium*), whether for reasons of social standing or claimed apostolic foundation, and that this in turn fed the diadochic claim that might be made for the emerging *monepiskopos*.

It cannot be said that this anti-heretical use of the scholasticized conception of succession is the cause of the emergence of monepiscopacy, for not only had the process already begun, but also a similar claim for the episcopate of apostolic succession is made by the *episkopos* of a single community within the Roman church, namely, the author of the *Elenchus*.[130] Nonetheless, it is conceivable that the need for the church to define itself over and against other versions of Christianity gave impetus to the process. If this was the efficient cause of the emergence of monepiscopacy, the material cause, however, was already present in the increasingly powerful leadership of the federations. In the context of forming orthodoxy, a forming canon of Scripture, and the gradual transformation of office within the church from economic office to teaching office the idea of a succession of authentic teachers who stand in succession to the apostles gives powerful support to what is already happening and conceivably, where the process is not yet complete, brings about the final triumph of the monepiscopal system, as the demonstration of the succession enables the Hippolytean school to join the Roman federation under a single *episkopos*. As has already been noted, transmission of teaching through officers is already suggested in 2 Timothy, apostolic appointment of officers is found in *1 Clement*, and the identification of a tradition through named individuals is made by Polycrates with reference to Quartodeciman practice;[131] thus, the ingredients for a doctrine of apostolic teaching through *episkopoi* are in place.

What is distinct in the doctrine as it emerges at the end of the second century is that officers are named individuals whose *diadochē* is traced to the apostles

127. Wagner, *Anfänge*, 300.
128. Hippolytus, *Haer.* 9.2; 9.7.
129. Hegesippus, quoted in Eusebius, *Hist. eccl.* 4.22.3.
130. Hippolytus, *Haer.* proem.
131. Polycrates, quoted in Eusebius, *Hist. eccl.* 4.24.4.

and whose function is principally scholastic. This scholastic understanding of succession is as entirely at home in Hellenized Judaism as it is in the rest of the Hellenistic world. In observing the manner in which Josephus similarly traces a *diadochē* of the high priests from Aaron onward, Mason notes that he is recalling the language and practice of the philosophical schools.[132] In other words, the manner in which Ehrhardt contrasted the succession of priests and that of teachers is artificial.[133] On the basis of Hegesippus's supposed Jewish origins, Ehrhardt traces the doctrine of succession to a Jewish source;[134] but whereas a similar succession of teachers and teaching is found in a later rabbinic work, the Babylonian Talmud tractate *'Abot*, this itself is derived from the more general Hellenistic milieu.[135]

In order to see this diadochic theory as distinct from that of Ignatius, I may note Rivas Rebaque's argument that Ignatius supports the episcopate as a means to preserve the collective memory of the church over and against the heretical threat.[136] I may respond in the first instance that outside Antioch, where federations of domestic *episkopoi* had gathered, these *presbyteroi kata polin* functioned, as we have already seen, as effective transmitters and guardians of the tradition; however, in the Ignatian schema it falls to the *episkopos* to represent the memory by incorporating the theology that he represents. Thus, Rivas Rebaque suggests that the insistence on submission to the *episkopos* is an insistence on submission, in an anti-heretical frame, to the *episkopos* as bearer of collective memory and representative of its authority, as he represents God, and as his representative role is further represented in the eucharist, over which the *episkopos* presides.[137] He further suggests that the patronal aspect of the bishop's role similarly represents his function as a receptacle of social memory.[138] Rivas Rebaque persists, in keeping with the Weberian frame described above, in seeing this as an institutionalizing tendency operating in

132. Steve Mason, "Chief Priests, Sadducees, Pharisees, and Sanhedrin in Acts," in *The Book of Acts in Its Palestinian Setting*, ed. Richard J. Bauckham, BAFS 4 (Grand Rapids: Eerdmans, 1995), 164.

133. Arnold Ehrhardt, *The Apostolic Succession in the First Two Centuries of the Church* (London: Lutterworth, 1953), 46–48.

134. Ibid., 63–66.

135. So Amram Tropper, "Tractate *Avot* and Early Christian Succession Lists," in *The Ways That Never Parted: Jews and Christians in Late Antiquity and the Early Middle Ages*, ed. Adam H. Becker and Annette Yoshiko Reed, TSAJ 95 (Tübingen: Mohr Siebeck, 2003), 159–88.

136. Fernando Rivas Rebaque, "Los obispos en Ignacio de Antioquía: Cuadros sociales dominantes de la memoria colectiva cristiana," *EstEcl* 83 (2008): 23–49. The term, with its theoretical framework, is taken from Maurice Halbwachs, *On Collective Memory*, ed. and trans. Lewis A. Coser (Chicago: University of Chicago Press, 1992).

137. Rivas Rebaque, "Los obispos," 38–40.

138. Ibid., 41–43.

opposition to charismatic and prophetic activity and considers this to be the process by which the *episkopos* had come to prominence. This is not central, however, to his thesis, which is that in his liturgical *topos* the Ignatian bishop plays a representative role and encourages group identity.[139]

Ignatius, however, shows no interest in succession, as was pointed out by Campenhausen[140] and has been recently restated by Brent.[141] The reason, we may now see, is that Ignatius does not envisage the *episkopos* in a teaching role but rather instructs through enacted drama, employing, as Brent argues, the language of the civic cults of Asia Minor.[142] As the one seated to the fore (*prokathēmenos*), the Ignatian bishop in the eucharist presents in his person the fatherhood of God, whereas the memory represented is transmitted not by the *episkopos* but by the *plēthos*. It is also interesting to note that in the Ignatian schema the apostles are represented by the presbyters rather than by the *episkopos*,[143] but since there is no interest in the transmission of teaching, as there is none in succession, this is barely relevant. It is this, moreover, that leads me to reject the idea of a later Ignatius employing monepiscopacy as a means to oppose developed forms of gnosticism, for there is no conception of *diadochē* in his view of *episkopē*.[144] Irenaeus has his own view of episcopacy and, as has already been observed, his own justification; but, as already suggested, Ignatius is not the great introducer of monepiscopacy to Asia, but rather is simply a domestic *episkopos* and has an entirely distinct logic, hieratic and liturgical rather than didactic.[145] However, the two are finally conflated as the didactic *episkopos* takes on the role of teaching within the context of the eucharist.

Scholasticization, and not the emergence of episcopal order, is, I have argued elsewhere, the cause of the disappearance of prophetic communication from within Christian communities.[146] Such is alleged on the basis that prophetic

---

139. Similarly, Allen Brent, "The Ignatian Epistles and the Threefold Ecclesiastical Order," *JRH* 17 (1992): 25.

140. Campenhausen, *Ecclesiastical Authority*, 107, 156.

141. E.g., Allen Brent, "Pseudonymy and Charisma in the Ministry of the Early Church," *Aug* 27 (1987): 348–52; idem, "The Enigma of Ignatius of Antioch," *JEH* 57 (2006): 435.

142. Brent, *Ignatius of Antioch*. Philip A. Harland ("Christ-Bearers and Fellow-Initiates: Local Cultural Life and Christian Identity in Ignatius' Letters," *JECS* 11 [2003]: 481–99) also notes the extent to which the language of Ignatius as *theophoros* parallels that of contemporary cults, though he concentrates more on associational religion.

143. As, in this context, Staats ("Die katholische Kirche," 133–34) points out.

144. So Brent, "Enigma of Ignatius," 435–37.

145. Whereas Irenaeus sees the *episkopos* in a didactic light and for this reason introduces the conception of succession. Thus, as Brent ("Diogenes Laertius," 381) makes clear, Irenaeus's succession is not a priestly succession.

146. Stewart(-Sykes), *From Prophecy to Preaching*.

communication is indicative of charismatically legitimated leadership, though we may now see that prophetic communication and episcopal leadership are not mutually exclusive because they are concerned with distinct spheres of activity. However, in time, episcopal order may have been the cause of the disappearance of the office of teacher because *episkopoi*, no longer exercising a purely economic office, and teachers come to function in the same sphere of activity, as the scholasticized *episkopos* becomes the means by which the authoritative teaching of the church is given and as independent Christian schools are brought under the aegis of the *episkopos*; thus, Origen's school becomes an agency of the Alexandrian bishop and the school of Hippolytus submits itself to the episcopate of Pontianus. The teacher might similarly be said to have triumphed in monepiscopacy, as increasingly a competence to teach becomes the quintessential qualification; the requirement of the Pastoral Epistles becomes universal, being found in the Syrian church-order literature and manifested in Alexandria, as Origen's pupil Heraklas follows Demetrius into the throne of the Alexandrian *episkopos*. However, although this interplay between teacher and *episkopos* is interesting, it explains not the emergence of the single office of *episkopos kata polin* but only the manner in which the duties of the emerging *monepiskopos* were distinct from those of the domestic *episkopos*, as the *monepiskopos* aggregated the scholastic, but not the economic, functions of the original domestic *episkopoi*.

In other words, although monepiscopacy did not eclipse the prophet, it did eclipse the (non-charismatic) teacher. Already at the time of Ignatius there is a degree of conflict between the *episkopos* and the teachers, as teachers become an alternative object of patronage; when the *episkopos* himself becomes a teacher, the conflict increases in intensity. We have seen this conflict both at Rome in the Hippolytean community and in the Asian communities addressed by Ignatius, and I may note that this is the fundamental conflict between Origen and Demetrius. This is not a return, however, to the conception of Harnack that episcopacy as an institutional local order replaces charismatic teachers and prophets. For there is a further false premise in the narrative, based on the misreading of *Didache* 15:1, namely, the inclusion of teachers among the ranks of the charismatics. Teachers appear alongside prophets at Acts 13:1 and 1 Corinthians 12:28, where apostles also appear; in the latter, teachers appear within a context of the discussion of charismata. This, together with their appearance at *Didache* 15:1 as objects of support alongside prophets—with the concomitant misunderstanding of the phrase that led to the idea that the ministry of *episkopoi* and *diakonoi* replaced that of prophets and teachers—appears to have led to their classification alongside prophets as necessarily charismatic in their activity. Thus, for instance, Stempel insists that they are charismatic officers, but the only evidence that he cites is a state-ment that the teacher might speak in the Spirit, citing *Didache* 11:7, which concerns not teachers but rather prophets.[147] In sociological terms at least, teachers are neither charismatic leaders nor charismatic communicators, as may readily be demonstrated through what is left of their activity. There is a record of early Christian teaching in the so-called Two Ways section enshrined in the *Didache*.[148] Moreover, this teaching is not isolated; it appears in other, related forms,[149] and material found within this section of the *Didache* appears in other contexts altogether, enabling us to classify these other contexts as containing remnants of catechetical instruction.[150] The sole conclusion that may be drawn from this is that the teaching is part of a forming tradition. As such, the teachers are not charismatic officers at all. Thus Greeven, who rightly points out that they are agents of tradition,[151] is clearly straining matters in his insistence that they are "no less charismatic than the prophet."[152] Harnack is right, however, in distinguishing teachers (as well as prophets) from local, economic leadership in the first generation.[153]

It is interesting, however, that the conflict between *episkopos* and teacher does not appear to have been so intense in Syria; the Antiochene *episkopos* retains a strong economic element, and independent Christian teachers are still found there. Similarly, I may note the continuing function of catechists early in the third century in the community of the *Pseudo-Clementines*,[154] although, as Faivre suggests, these teachers are in the process of becoming subordinate to the episcopally based hierarchy.[155] And further east, I may note that whereas

147. Hermann-Adolf Stempel, "Der Lehrer in der 'Lehre der zwölf Apostel,'" *VC* 34 (1980): 209–17. Note esp. 210, where he states on the basis of the text regarding prophets that teachers speak in the Spirit.

148. *Did.* 1–5.

149. See Alistair Stewart(-Sykes), *On the Two Ways: Life or Death, Light or Darkness: Foundational Texts in the Tradition* (Crestwood, NY: St. Vladimir's Seminary Press, 2011).

150. See Alistair Stewart(-Sykes), "Ἀποκύησις λόγῳ ἀληθείας: Paraenesis and Baptism in Mat-thew, James, and the *Didache*," in *Matthew, James, and Didache: Three Related Documents in Their Jewish and Christian Settings*, ed. Huub van de Sandt and Jürgen K. Zangenburg, SBLSymS 45 (Atlanta: Society of Biblical Literature), 341–59.

151. H. Greeven, "Propheten, Lehrer, Vorsteher bei Paulus: zur Frage der 'Ämter' im Urchris-tentum," *ZNW* 44 (1953): 23–24.

152. Ibid., 17.

153. Harnack, *Lehre*, 103–5.

154. As discussed by F. Stanley Jones, "The Ancient Christian Teacher in the Pseudo-Cle-mentines," in *Early Christian Voices: In Texts, Traditions, and Symbols; Essays in Honor of François Bovon*, ed. David H. Warren, Ann Graham Brock, and David W. Pao, BIS 66 (Leiden: Brill, 2003), 355–64.

155. Alexandre Faivre, "Les fonctions ecclésiales dans les écrits pseudo-Clémentins: Proposi-tion de lecture," *RevScRel* 50 (1976): 97–111.

the *episkopos* of *Didascalia apostolorum* has become a teaching *episkopos*, he continues to have a fundamentally economic role; the only friction apparent in *Didascalia apostolorum* with teachers is with specifically female teachers. It may be, however, that the class of teachers had been subsumed into the clergy within the community represented by *Didascalia apostolorum*, as in that which gave rise to the *Pseudo-Clementines*, for which reason female teachers, who are not ordained, continue to stand out as problematic, and which leads to the creation of the class of female deacons, who, among other duties, might teach women. The principal reason for this lack of tension, however, is that the economic and charitable role of the *episkopos* continued foremost.

External Pressure as a Cause of Centralization

Thus far I have looked at the process of centralization as an internal process brought about through internal dynamics, and in particular the assumption of scholastic functions within the church as a response to alternative expressions of Christianity (characterized as heresy). However, I should note that external pressure also may have played a role. I have already observed Blasi's suggestion that external persecution is a reason behind Ignatius's insistence on unity,[156] a suggestion that is uncertain, as Ignatius almost welcomes the persecution, and his discussion of unity is based entirely on internal pressures. Similarly, I have noted Meier's suggestion that persecution may lead to a tightening of central structures, though I may repeat that it is hard to account for the connection.

Nonetheless, there are some points to notice. First, the leadership of Demetrius and the manner in which previously independent schools are brought by him under the power of the *episkopos* emerge in the wake of persecution. Second, I may note again Eusebius's report of Dionysius's correspondence, and in particular his comment about the Athenian episcopate, that after the martyrdom of Publius the Athenians were gathered again and their faith revived under Quadratus.[157] Third, and less certainly, the first firm evidence of complete monepiscopacy at Rome derives from the martyrdom of Pontianus (though Rome had been moving toward monepiscopacy for some time and had weathered persecution previously without it), and Cyprian's authority, which goes beyond monepiscopacy to some kind of provincial power, emerges strengthened from persecution. The connection, however, remains hard to see, unless I were to posit that the situation of a church weakened by persecution allows the rise of a charismatic leader. Certainly, the conditions of crisis posed

156. Blasi, "Office Charisma," 253.
157. Eusebius, *Hist. eccl.* 4.23.3.

by persecution are right for the emergence of a charismatic leader,[158] though the extent to which these figures otherwise fit the charismatic category is uncertain. Centralization is not a necessary product of crisis, but given that transformational leadership might emerge in crisis conditions, and given that, in the case of the Rome of Pontianus and the Alexandria of Demetrius at least, the churches are already in federation, it is possible for the charismatic leader who emerges to accrue personal authority and for the federation to achieve a greater degree of centralization solely through the power of the leader. However, just as Hitler, the charismatic leader par excellence, rose to power through normal political channels, so these leaders are able to accrue additional authority because the existing federations provided channels by which that authority might be claimed.

Some Loose Threads

Having reached something like a conclusion, I may return to some loose threads and address some unconsidered matters. Succession in modern Western catholic understanding is bound up to ordination and not, as it was in the period in which the doctrine was formed, to a "succession of witness to tradition,"[159] and so the question of the development of ordination rites is brought to the fore, which in turn raises the issue of who undertook the appointment of *episkopoi*. To this is bound up the issue of presidency at the eucharist, as ordination in the West is seen as a guarantee of the validity of sacraments. Finally, some word should be said regarding female leadership in early Christian communities.

Episcopal Appointment and Ordination

Evidence for ordination rites in the early period is very thin. Associations appointed their officers in a number of ways: by election (so, for instance, the

158. Max Weber (*Economy and Society: An Outline of Interpretive Sociology*, ed. Guenther Roth and Claus Wittich, trans. Ephraim Fischoff et al., 2 vols. [Berkeley: University of California Press, 1978], 2:1111–12) describes the conditions of crisis under which charismatic leaders might emerge: "The 'natural' leaders in moments of distress—whether psychic, physical, economic, ethical, religious, or political—were neither appointed officeholders nor 'professionals' in the present day sense (i.e., persons performing against compensation a 'profession' based on training and special expertise), but rather the bearers of specific gifts of body and mind that were considered 'supernatural' (in the sense that not everybody could have access to them)."

159. The words of R. P. C. Hanson, "Office and Concept of Office in the Early Church," in *Studies in Christian Antiquity* (Edinburgh: T&T Clark, 1985), 125, making the theological point that succession of ordination is not in the "mind and purpose of the old fathers." Hanson suggests (128) that this idea may be traced to Cyprian.

appointment of the steward of the Iobacchoi),[160] by lot (so, for instance, the Bacchoi of Tomis),[161] by inheritance (note an association at Thera that works out the line of inheritance carefully),[162] by appointment by a designated person such as a priest (so the priest appoints the scribe in an Arcadian domestic cult association),[163] or by some combination (a *synodos* of *eranistai* at Athens both checked the moral status of their officeholders and chose them by lot).[164] I might anticipate a similar variety in Christian groupings. However, it must be stressed that I am simply gathering up some fragments here. Although they are hard to separate, I attempt to deal with appointment and ordination rites separately. For the most part, however, our sources are silent on both issues.

APPOINTMENT

In multipatron communities I might anticipate that the patrons collectively appointed the officers, and here I may point to the ordination of *episkopoi* by the *presbyteroi* in the Asian communities.[165] Although the provenance of *Apostolic Church Order* is uncertain, as is the provenance of its underlying source, here likewise, as I have argued elsewhere, it is not the entire congregation that is competent to elect the *episkopos* but rather the patrons of the community who elect an *episkopos* from among their number, those who, in Asian domestic churches, are classed as *presbyteroi*. A wider franchise is also possible, though in Asian communities this may have come in as a means to temper the power of patrons, as I may suggest is the case in the (originally Asian) Hippolytean school, where the whole community confirms the choice of the presbyters.[166] Here, as has already been argued, the complex episcopal ordination rites are constructed in order to restrict the power of the patron-presbyters, and so the recital of the ordination prayer is delegated to a visiting *episkopos* instead of the presbyters, who are bidden to stand silent.

The manner in which the church is bidden to consent to the ordination in *Traditio apostolica* might be compared to the statement of Clement that leaders are appointed "with the consent of the whole church."[167] However, given that the school of Hippolytus was an Asian émigré community, I must be chary of

160. *IG* 2² 1368, lines 146–47.
161. *IScM* 2.120.
162. *IG* 12.3 330, line 57.
163. *IG* 5.2 265.
164. *IG* 2² 1369.
165. Pierre Nautin ("L'évolution des ministères au IIe et au IIIe siècle," *RDC* 23 [1973]: 51) similarly suggests that ordination in the second century was at the hands of presbyters.
166. *Trad. ap.* 2.1.
167. *1 Clem.* 44:3: συνευδοκησάσης τῆς ἐκκλησίας πάσης. Such is the reading of Karl Müller, "Kleine Beiträge zur alten Kirchengeschichte 16," *ZNW* 28 (1929): 277–78.

making the connection with Roman practice elsewhere, and I may continue to sustain the suggestion that this secondary consent to the choice of the patrons is a secondary element in the Hippolytean rites. Clement's statement, moreover, raises the question of whether he means that these leaders who are, as argued above, domestic leaders and *presbyteroi kata polin* are being appointed within individual communities, or whether he means that recognition is being extended to domestic leaders who have already been appointed within their individual communities by the federation representing the whole church. I intend to argue at this point that the latter is the case; however, the argument goes beyond the exegesis of Clement's statement, and my understanding is set in the context of federated household leadership set out above.

The context is Clement's statement that there would be strife within the church over *episkopē*, and thus that the apostles appointed those aforementioned (*episkopoi* and *diakonoi*). "They [the apostles] subsequently added a codicil that should they die [here taken to be the successors, not the apostles themselves], then other approved [*dedokimasmenoi*] men should succeed to their *leitourgia*." Thus, Clement deduces, it is wrong to remove from ministry "those who were appointed by them [*katasathentas hyp' ekeinōn*] or by other reputable [*ellogimōn*] men, with the approval of the whole church." The question is that of who makes the appointment and who in turn approves. It might be possible to argue that the import of Clement's statement is that the successors to the apostles, namely, those who are already *episkopoi*, make the appointment of new *episkopoi* in the congregations, that these are the reputable men.[168] In this instance it would thus be the federated leaders who appoint within individual congregations, as the *episkopoi* within the congregations cannot appoint their successors because they are dead. But in a diversified church with congregations that effectively are independent, it is hard to see how a federated group might make appointments within individual congregations. They might approve and, as such, temper the power of the power bases in the congregations, and this further check would seem to be in place in the Hippolytean community as represented by the choice of a visiting *episkopos* to say the ordination prayer.

If the context is the removal of officers from within Corinthian congregations (presumably from within the congregations), then Clement is stating that, once appointed, these officers should continue to hold office, but the power of the federation would be limited to refusing recognition to those appointed

168. So, e.g., Horacio E. Lona, *Der erste Clemensbrief*, KAV 2 (Göttingen: Vandenhoeck & Ruprecht, 1998), 460–61; Hermann J. Vogt, "Frühkirche und Amt: Neu in der Diskussion," *ZAC* 8 (2003): 465–67.

in the stead of those already appointed. The reality is that the apostles' successors do not make the appointment, but rather the *ellogimoi*, those who in the Hippolytean congregation are characterized as the *presbyteroi* and who are *within* the congregations.[169] *Hyp' ekeinōn* must refer to the apostles, not to those appointed by them, but the reality is that the present generation of leaders probably has been appointed not by apostles but rather by reputable men. These reputable men may be standing in succession to the apostles, but the *episkopoi* are not, a conclusion that is derived from the historical context of the Roman church, deduced not only from *1 Clement* but also from the other pertinent literature.[170] Thus, I deduce that the appointment of *episkopoi* within the individual congregations was made by patrons (who may be characterized as *presbyteroi* and certainly were in Asian congregations like that of the Hippolytean school) and approved by the federated leaders of the individual congregations.

This procedure—recognition by the federation—would seem to have occurred in Alexandria, where federation was early and strong and monepiscopacy was late. There, the presbyters, as has been seen, appointed someone from among their own number. I may suggest that in the earliest period these teachers were effectively self-appointed, or appointed by schools independently of the federation, though by the third century the federation was strong enough to control who might be admitted to the presbyterate that formed the electoral college at Alexandria.[171]

A different method of controlling election by patrons is found in the community lying behind *Apostolic Church Order*, where, should the number be less than twelve, then three are to be brought in from another community.[172]

---

169. So Baur, *Christentum*, 264.

170. This in turn, rather than an overreading of the text making Clement himself one of those appointed by the apostles (the critique leveled by Lona, *Der erste Clemensbrief*, 458–59), undermines the claims of Gregory Dix ("The Ministry in the Early Church," in *The Apostolic Ministry: Essays on the History and Doctrine of Episcopacy*, ed. K. E. Kirk [London: Hodder & Stoughton, 1946], 256–64) and Antonio M. Javierre (*La primera "diadoché" de la patrística y los "ellógimoi" de Clemente Romano: Datos para el problema de la sucesión apostólica* [Turin: Società Editrice Internazionale, 1958]) that Clement is a witness to apostolic succession as later understood, and that Roman primacy is thereby claimed. Moreover, as Harry O. Maier ("1 Clement 40–44: Apostolic Succession or Legitimation?" in Livingstone, ed., *Papers Presented at the Tenth International Conference on Patristic Studies*, 137–41) notes, Clement is concerned not with succession as such but rather with order, of which orderly succession is part.

171. So Alistair Stewart(-Sykes), "Origen, Demetrius and the Alexandrian Presbyters," *SVTQ* 48 (2004): 415–29. Everett Ferguson ("Selection and Installation to Office in Roman, Greek, Jewish and Christian Antiquity," *TZ* 30 [1974]: 274) suggests that the federation may have installed the replacement for the vacancy from the beginning. However, at this point there would be no vacancy, as the leading *presbyteros* would still function within his own school.

172. *Can. eccl. ap.* 16.1.

Elsewhere, however, a popular election, albeit from a restricted field of candidates, is to be found. It is not clear to whom the instruction of the *Didache* to appoint *episkopoi* and *diakonoi* is addressed, but the likelihood is to all hearers within a church rather than simply to a group among them. The same is largely true in Africa in the third century, where the *episkopos* certainly is elected,[173] although the election might not altogether have met the freedom and fairness requirements of those in modern liberal democracies,[174] given the weight that would be given to *seniores* and the exercise of patronage.[175] I may also note the evidence of *Vita Polycarpi*, where, in the third century, Polycarp is depicted as being elected by the populace, though apparently not of Smyrna alone. Deacons are sent to the people to ascertain their views, and, interestingly, it is said that the "priesthood" then gave their assent to the popular election.[176] I may guess that this "priesthood" is a reference to the visiting bishops, and thus the practice of *Traditio apostolica*, in which other local bishops participate in the appointment of the Hippolytean *episkopos*.[177]

The account of *Vita Polycarpi* is of interest also because of reports of visions received by those present that indicate that Polycarp is to be the bishop.[178] Thus, I may also note that confirmation in prophecy is sought for the presbytery's choice in 1 Timothy 4:14, much as Paul and Barnabas are appointed for their missionary activity through prophecy at Acts 13:2–3.

The conclusion to be drawn from this very brief review is that there is no uniformity and no universal system for the selection of *episkopoi*. In some communities, however, the local presbyterate had a prominent role, and various strategies are found employed to temper this particular interest.

ORDINATION RITES

Similar variety is manifest in the means by which candidates, once appointed, are ordained.

The first clear and unambiguous description of ordination is found in *Traditio apostolica*, although, as has already been seen, this is the result of a complex redactional history in which handlaying by a single visiting *episkopos*

---

173. Cyprian makes repeated reference to election in *Ep.* 67, which emphasizes the extent to which validity is lent to ordinations as a result of the consent of the people and argues that this practice is derived from apostolic tradition. He further refers to his own election (*Ep.* 43.1.2) and to that of Cornelius (*Ep.* 44.3.2; 49.2.4; 55.8.4).

174. As set out in Guy Goodwin-Gill, *Free and Fair Elections*, 2nd ed. (Geneva: Inter-Parliamentary Union, 2006).

175. See discussion in Stewart(-Sykes), "Ordination Rites."

176. *Vit. Pol.* 22: συνεπινεύσαντος οὖν καὶ τοῦ ἱερατικοῦ παντός.

177. *Trad. ap.* 2.2.

178. *Vit. Pol.* 23.

appears to have replaced handlaying by the local congregational presbyters. If this redactional history is allowed, and if the Hippolytean community is recognized as an Asian ecclesial community in Rome, this may cast light on one disputed point in the interpretation in the Pastoral Epistles, namely, whether ordination was undertaken by the hands of presbyters or by the apostle singly. The question is raised because 1 Timothy 4:14 speaks of the laying of hands on Timothy by the presbytery, whereas 2 Timothy 1:6 speaks of Paul alone laying his hand on Timothy. Von Lips helpfully lists the possible solutions to this conundrum: (1) Paul had laid hands simultaneously with the elders; (2) Timothy had been appointed by Paul and was subsequently appointed by the local presbytery; (3) 1 Timothy 4:14 indicates the common practice of ordination by the local presbytery, whereas 2 Timothy is concerned to emphasize the Pauline succession of Timothy; and (4) 1 Timothy 4:14 speaks not of ordination *by* the presbytery but rather ordination *to* the presbytery.[179] The practice of the Hippolytean community indicates that the presbytery collectively laid hands upon their *episkopos*, so the first and last solutions at least may be put aside. It certainly is possible, however, that "Paul" is seeking to substitute the ordination of a successor by a teacher for the more usual appointment by a presbytery and that he is doing so in order to guarantee a succession of teaching.[180]

Further evidence that *episkopoi* were ordained by the local presbyters may be found in an interesting alteration to *Traditio apostolica* in *Canones Hippolyti*, where the provision of *Traditio apostolica* is rewritten so that rather than "one of the bishops" performing the handlaying, it is undertaken by "one of the bishops and presbyters."[181] I may suggest that a redactor familiar with presbyteral ordination of the *episkopos*, faced with a text enforcing episcopal ordination of the *episkopos*, expanded the text in order to embrace the continued involvement of the presbyterate.[182] Here I may recall the suggestion made above that the replacement of local presbyteral ordination by

179. Von Lips, *Glaube*, 240–43. He favors the third option, a version of which is essayed by Michael Wolter, *Die Pastoralbriefe als Paulustradition*, FRLANT 146 (Göttingen: Vandenhoeck & Ruprecht, 1988), 218–22.

180. So Otfried Hofius, "Die Ordination zum Amt der Kirche und die apostolische Sukzession nach der Zeugnis der Pastoralbriefe," *ZTK* 107 (2010): 261–84. The treatment is vitiated somewhat by his acceptance of the consensus, and thus by his suggestion that 1 Tim. 4:14 speaks of ordination *to* the presbytery. As such, he cannot see that "Paul" is essaying something of a departure.

181. *Can. Hipp.* 2.

182. Compare, however, the interesting reading of this text by Karl Müller, "Kleine Beiträge zur alten Kirchengeschichte 6," *ZNW* 23 (1924): 228. Müller suggests that the handlaying by the presbyter was the original reading. He asks whether a redactor in the fourth century would make the addition of a presbyter. I may respond that in an Egyptian backwater in the fourth century he might well do so.

ordination by the Alexandrian bishop was the clue to the interpretation of obscure statements in later sources regarding Alexandrian involvement in episcopal ordinations beyond the city.

Beyond the imposition of hands there are other elements found in ordination rites.

In the first instance I may note the possibility of ordination by investiture. Such is indicated in Alexandria by the account of the appointment of Achillas that is enshrined in the account of Peter's martyrdom, which describes the setting of the body of Peter upon his throne and the transfer of the *omophorion* from the body of Peter to Achillas, his successor.[183] Moreover, the later rite of ordination for the Alexandrian bishop has the Gospel book being held over the head of the new bishop; although there is no certainty regarding the origin of this rite, it is possible that this too is a relic of investiture as a means of making the bishop. It is notable that this rite is exclusively performed in the ordination of the patriarch of Alexandria. Bradshaw suggests that it is a rite of some antiquity, because of the manner in which it resisted liturgical alteration,[184] and that its origin is that it was adopted in order to avoid dispute between native presbyters and visiting *episkopoi* about who had the right of imposing hands upon the candidate.[185] But although one may surmise that such a conflict might come about where there is a strong congregational presbyterate, the only direct evidence is that of *Traditio apostolica*, in which the argument is firmly won by the visiting *episkopoi*. In a scholasticized community the handing over of a book, the manner in which the reader is appointed in *Traditio apostolica*,[186] certainly is an appropriate rite.

I may, moreover, note the role of the chair, already identified as a teacher's chair, in this rite. There are a number of references to a rite of ordination involving seating the new *episkopos*, the earliest being found in *Vita Polycarpi*,[187] a seating that takes place after the visiting bishops have laid on hands. Moreover, passing reference is made in *Canones Hippolyti*,[188] by Synesius,[189] by Eusebius, relating the election of Fabian,[190] and in *Didascalia*

183. Note the discussion of this passage by Tim Vivian, *St. Peter of Alexandria: Bishop and Martyr*, SAC (Philadelphia: Fortress, 1988), 47–49. Vivian suggests that ordination largely consisted of the transfer of the *omophorion*.
184. Paul F. Bradshaw, *Ordination Rites of the Ancient Churches of East and West* (New York: Pueblo, 1990), 41–42.
185. Ibid., 42–43.
186. *Trad. ap.* 11.
187. *Vit. Pol.* 23.
188. *Can. Hipp.* 4.
189. Synesius, *Ep.* 67.
190. Eusebius, *Hist. eccl.* 6.29.

apostolorum.[191] Twice in the *Pseudo-Clementine* literature reference is made to a rite of seating: in *Epistula Clementis* 5 the seating takes place after the laying on of hands (as it is in *Vita Polycarpi*), whereas in *Homiliae* 3.60–72 it takes place beforehand. This leads Ferguson to suggest that the two rites are independent and that they have been joined together to form the ordination rite represented in the *Pseudo-Clementines*.[192] I have suggested that the same is the case in *Vita Polycarpi*, in which, moreover, the seating is the original rite, the handlaying being added to conform the ritual to Scripture. Given the scholastic nature of a chair as the seat of a teacher, ordination by seating, although, as I have suggested, derived from Jewish practice,[193] is an entirely appropriate means for ordaining a successor in a school. I may thus posit ordination by seating as a mark of scholasticization and as representing the didactic understanding of episcopal succession.

This brief review indicates not only, once again, a variety in the means by which *episkopoi* are ordained, but also the manner in which monepiscopacy is tied up to the process of scholasticization through a doctrine of succession.

Liturgical Presidency

Standing in the liberal Protestant tradition of Sohm, though innocent of sociological analysis, Bartlett opines, "It is possible that the real slip towards Käsemann's 'early catholicism' came not so much with ordination or official structure, but with the designation of a particular officer to preside at the Eucharist."[194] The assumption that underlies the opinion is that in a Christian community without officers, no officer is designated a liturgical leader. By contrast, Greeven suggests that liturgical leadership as described in the Corinthian correspondence relates solely to prophecy.[195] In both instances, however, we are dealing with *argumenta ex silentio*. Paul does not speak of liturgical leadership to the Corinthians; the discussion of prophecy is a discussion of the communication of the word, which might take place at table, but not of presidency at the meal. However, the very fact that this presidency is not discussed simply means that it is relatively unimportant, not that there was none (for had there been none, there would have been no meal). Prophets were no more community presidents than community presidents were prophets.

---

191. *Did. ap.* 2.1.3; 2.2.3.

192. Everett Ferguson, "Jewish and Christian Ordination: Some Observations," *HTR* 56 (1963): 18; idem, "Selection and Installation," 280.

193. Alistair Stewart(-Sykes), *The Life of Polycarp: An Anonymous Vita from Third-Century Smyrna*, ECS 4 (Sydney: St. Pauls, 2002).

194. David L. Bartlett, *Ministry in the New Testament* (Minneapolis: Fortress, 1993), 56.

195. Greeven, "Propheten, Lehrer, Vorsteher," 43.

Thus far in this chapter I have argued that the *episkopos* originally had a limited role in teaching and that this role was deliberately fostered; thus, in time the roles of teaching and proclamation become episcopal roles, but this is a development.[196] The original function of the *episkopos* was as president of the meal. What that meant in practice, however, is less certain, though I may suggest that he might function as a host would function at any other meal, directing the *diakonoi*, and also that he might regulate the proceedings after the completion of the meal, in which context discussion, teaching, and prayer might be found, rather after the manner of the symposiarch.[197]

However, not even this is assured. For instance, the *Didache* says nothing about the identity of the eucharistic leader,[198] as the sole regulation concerns only the words that are to be used by those who are not prophets, and it does not regulate who is permitted to give voice to the graces that it prescribes. Thus, when the statement is made that the prophets should give thanks in whatever way they wish,[199] this does not mean that they, any more than *episkopoi*, are regular eucharistic presidents. However, on the basis of the misunderstanding of *Didache* 15:1 and the term *leitourgousi*, the presidency of the eucharist has been seen as a *leitourgia* of the prophets that was taken over by the *episkopoi*.[200] This certainly is not the case. Indeed, I may note in this respect that in Jewish custom, to which the graces of the *Didache* are acknowledged as proximate, certain graces were said individually, others by the president, and one is entitled to ask whether the *Didache* is referring to individual graces. In other words, we should see the same informality with regard to speaker in the act of thanksgiving that has been perceived in the liturgy of the word, which may largely have consisted of conversation at the table. However, Audet links the instructions regarding the appointment of *episkopoi* and *diakonoi* to the preceding instructions regarding the gathering of the community, suggesting that the link is the role of these officers

196. See, apart from the discussion above, Paul F. Bradshaw, *Liturgical Presidency in the Early Church* (Bramcote, UK: Grove, 1983), 15–21. It is interesting that in discussing the clericalization of liturgical functions he concentrates on the ministries of teaching and proclamation rather than on the properly liturgical role of eucharistic presidency.

197. On the role of symposiarch, see Plutarch, *Quaest. conv.* 1.4. I may note, in view of the Ignatian correspondence between church and *polis* noted above, the extent to which Plutarch conforms the symposiarch's role and qualifications to those of a political leader (so Philip A. Stadter, "Leading the Party, Leading the City: The Symposiarch as *politikos*," in *Symposion and Philanthropia in Plutarch*, ed. José Ribeiro Ferreira et al., HS 6 [Coimbra: Centro de Estudios Clássicos e Humanísticos da Universidade de Coimbra, 2009], 123–30).

198. So, correctly, Aaron Milavec, *The Didache: Faith, Hope, and Life of the Earliest Christian Communities, 50–70 C.E.* (New York: Newman, 2003), 404–7.

199. *Did.* 10:7.

200. By, for instance, Lietzmann, "Zur altchristlichen Verfassungsgeschichte," 143.

in the worship of the community,[201] and I may indeed note that the two sections are closely linked with the particle *oun*. Audet's view is that the link is made in order to determine the proper officers who should preside at the eucharist, which, he believes, is described in *Didache* 14. By contrast, I have argued that *Didache* 14 does not actually concern the eucharist,[202] but that nonetheless the link might not be altogether without logic. The reason for the link between the meal discussed in *Didache* 14 and the appointment of *episkopoi* and *diakonoi* is that the *episkopoi* and *diakonoi* are to supply the meal, liturgizing the prophets and teachers through the provision of food. But there is potentially more. Ignatius states that an *agapē* is an event that is not to be held without the *episkopos*,[203] and I have argued that the reason for this is that it is a means of concentrating the exercise of patronage in the hands of the *episkopos*, as a meal is an occasion on which patronage might be exercised.[204] If the concern of the Didachist is the same, then this may be a means of avoiding strife in the community through regulating the competing demands of patrons.

Although it is hard precisely to envisage the role of an *episkopos* at the early Christian eucharistic meal, he was, from the beginning, president by virtue of his economic office. I may suggest that this role transmuted into something resembling what we would understand as eucharistic presidency when the nature of the meal changed due, I have already argued, to the transferrence from the close of sabbath to the dawn of the next day. As such, there was no slip toward *Frühkatholizismus*; from the beginning there were offices, and from the beginning these offices centered on the conduct of the eucharistic meal as a means to control patronage and ensure fair distribution of the goods of the church. In the first generations this occurs within individual Christian household associations and is a function exercised by the *episkopos*; once federation has led to centralization, the presbyters naturally enough continue to exercise this fundamentally episcopal role.

Female Officeholders

It may not go unnoticed that when Paul exhorts certain persons by name in writing to the Philippians, a number of these names are female names. In

---

201. J.-P. Audet, *La Didachè: Instructions des apôtres*, EB (Paris: Gabalda, 1958), 464–67; similarly, Adolf von Harnack, *The Constitution and Law of the Church in the First Two Centuries*, trans. F. L. Pogson, ed. H. D. A. Major (London: Williams & Norgate, 1910), 79.

202. Alistair Stewart(-Sykes), "*Didache* 14: Eucharistic?" *Questions liturgiques* 93 (2012), 3–16.

203. Ign. *Smyrn.* 8:2.

204. See *Vit. Pol.* 70.

discussing the organization of the Philippian Christians, I agreed with Campbell that these were references to house-church leaders.[205] As such, it is likely that some of these were the *episkopoi* or *diakonoi* addressed in the opening of the letter. Although she does not receive a title, I may agree that Nympha was likewise a female domestic church leader.[206] I may also observe that among greetings to various Christian households sent by Ignatius are greetings to those of which women seem to have been head;[207] the question in these instances is that of whether these households are entirely independent within Smyrna (in which case, I might agree with Eisen that these women were, functionally at least, *episkopoi*),[208] or whether they were simply prominent households among those that made up Polycarp's church. Given that this church was clearly manifesting associational behavior, the latter possibility seems more probable; Eisen seems to be thinking that the church is still made up of individual and unrelated households only, whereas the discussion above has suggested that the simple equation of household and church no longer applied at that point. Even so, it would not be impossible to see these women as (congregational) presbyters within the church association over which Polycarp had oversight. Not every female domestic leader need have been the *episkopos* of that church. Nor would every female householder necessarily have been the church leader. Thus, I may observe the case of the mother of John Mark, to whose house Peter goes after his miraculous escape from prison,[209] but who is unlikely to have been the house-church leader, given the association with the house of such a prominent follower of Jesus.

Other named candidates have been proposed. Within Rome, however, I find it hard to follow Eisen in seeing Grapte as either *diakonos* or *episkopos*,[210] not because such a thing is a priori impossible, but simply because all that we hear of her is that she teaches women and orphans. If there is to be a candidate for episcopacy among the known women of Rome at the time of Hermas, it is

205. See chap. 1, under the heading "Philippians as Further Evidence of Federation (and Not Synonymy)," with reference to Campbell, *Elders*, 123–25; so also Carolyn Osiek and Margaret Y. MacDonald, *A Woman's Place: House Churches in Earliest Christianity* (Minneapolis: Fortress, 2006), 158–59.
206. Col. 4:15. On the question of the historicity of this figure and her status as leader, see Margaret Y. MacDonald, "Can Nympha Rule This House? The Rhetoric of Domesticity in Colossians," in *Rhetoric and Reality in Early Christianities*, ed. Willi Braun (Waterloo, ON: Wilfrid Laurier University Press, 2005), 101–4.
207. E.g., the household of Gavia (Ign. *Smyrn.* 13:2) and that of the wife of Epitropus (Ign. *Pol.* 8:2).
208. Ute E. Eisen, *Women Officeholders in Early Christianity: Epigraphical and Literary Studies*, trans. Linda M. Maloney (Collegeville, MN: Liturgical Press, 2000).
209. Acts 12:12–17.
210. Eisen, *Women Officeholders*, 208, with reference to *Herm.* 8:2–3.

more probably Rhoda. Moreover, with Eisen, I may also note Epiphanius's contemptuous statement that the Montanists have female *episkopoi*;[211] however, I would explain this not (as she does) as the working of the Spirit overcoming theological and social norms, but rather as the result of the same conservatism noted above, which meant that these same Montanist communities had *episkopoi* heading single, rural congregations. As such, the evidence of Epiphanius does point to the exercise of *episkopē* within congregations by women in the earliest period, an ancient practice continued in separated Montanist communities. Moreover, given that women were prominent in domestic settings in antiquity, we might anticipate that they would have prominence within the churches that met in their houses, which may in turn illuminate references in second-century literature to women offering the eucharist or participating in some way in ritual meals.[212]

Given the close connection between leadership and patronage in these earliest years, the presence of female household leaders may simply indicate that women offered patronage to the church; as such, it is hard to separate out this role from a formal episcopal role in the first generation, and although patronage need not entail presidency in a liturgical assembly, it may naturally lead to it in a single-household church. In the same way, whether Phoebe held office as *diakonos* at the church of Cenchreae in a technical sense or was simply that church's envoy, she certainly was its patron.[213] Thus, whereas the "Paul" who addresses the Ephesian community in 1 Timothy clearly did not envisage a female *episkopos*, this may well have been a deliberate attempt to prevent what otherwise might have occurred, or might even have occurred already. Women in Asian cities acted as patrons of public institutions, including public banquets,[214] as well as leading domestic associations,[215] and although prevented from holding elected office, they might hold other offices within society that bestowed *honor*. We may even observe a female gymnasiarch.[216] As such, a female *episkopos* in a Christian association should not surprise us; rather, the surprise is the relative absence of evidence.

211. Ibid., 207–8, with reference to Epiphanius, *Pan.* 49.2.2–5.

212. E.g., *Acts Phil.* 8:2; Firmilian in Cyprian, *Ep.* 75.10 (though Firmilian considers this heretical and Montanist); Hippolytus, *Haer.* 6.35 (a description of Marcosian practice, which may nonetheless mirror earlier practice in forming catholic communities).

213. So, rightly, Osiek and MacDonald, *Woman's Place*, 215–16, with reference to Rom. 16:1–2 and Paul's characterization of her as *diakonos* and *prostatis*.

214. E.g., Tata at Aphrodisias (*MAMA* 8, 492.b).

215. Such as the burial association led by Sergia Paulina at Rome (*CIL* 6.9148).

216. Namely, Menodora from Sillyon in Pamphylia (*IGRR* 3.801), who receives numerous other honors besides.

It is the very proximity of patronage and leadership, as well as the ambiguity in the title *presbyteros*, that makes it so hard to evaluate the evidence that some have taken to indicate female presbyters in a later period. Some are easy to dismiss as the fantasizing of feminist scholars; thus, the explanation offered by Torjesen of *IG* 12.3 933, "the angel of Epikto, an elder woman" (*angellos Epiktous presbytidos*), namely, that Epikto "must have been a priest," is ludicrously oversimplistic.[217] However the instruction of Canon 11 of the Council of Laodicea that "those who are called *presbytidas* or those in the first seats [*prokathēmenas*] are not to be installed [*kathistasthai*] in the first seats of the church" requires more sensitive handling. Eisen is right that the term is close to a technical term for the installation of clergy, though this does not necessarily mean, as she suggests, that they received laying on of hands.[218] It is possible that female patrons had held a role within local churches analogous to the local *presbyteroi* of 1 Timothy and that the council is either clarifying that they are not clergy or possibly preventing their activity of patronage by preventing them from receiving the *honor* of receiving seats in the church that denoted their status. There certainly is insufficient evidence to state, on the basis of this inscription, the canon of Laodicea, and one further inscription referring to a (mummified) female presbyter,[219] that these women were "presiders over their communities,"[220] not the least because this makes a large assumption about the role of the presbyter in these communities, be that presbyter male or female.

This does not mean that female roles in the church did not remain controversial, but the debate did not concern female episcopacy, or presbyterate in the later sense of a subordinate liturgical officer, but rather female ministry more generally. There is an interesting discussion of women's ministry in *Apostolic Church Order* in which the question of women's ministries is raised, and the conclusion is that it should be restricted to "supporting women in need."[221] But, as I have argued elsewhere, this is a redactional construction

217. Karen Jo Torjesen, *When Women Were Priests: Women's Leadership in the Early Church and the Scandal of Their Subordination in the Rise of Christianity* (San Francisco: HarperSanFrancisco, 1995), 10.
218. Eisen, *Women Officeholders*, 122.
219. *T.Mom.Louvre* 1115, recording Ἀρτεμιδῶρας Μικκάλου μητ[ρὸς] Πανισκιαίνης πρεσβ[υτέρας] ἐκοιήθη ἐν Κ(υρί)ῳ ("[mummy of] Artemidora, daughter of Mikkalos, her mother Paniskiainē, a presbyter"). Given that the provenance from within Egypt is unknown, and given our ignorance of development of office within early Egyptian Christianity (the inscription is of the second or third century), beyond accepting that Artemidora was a presbyter, we cannot know what that presbyterate might denote. Domestic presbyterate based on patronage is a possibility.
220. Eisen, *Women Officeholders*, 207–8.
221. *Can. eccl. ap.* 28.

from the final stages of the redaction of *Apostolic Church Order*, and thus from the third century at the earliest, and does not concern episcopal or even presbyteral office. Instead it reflects alarm regarding the role of women in other communities, possibly Montanist, possibly gnostic, but most probably those catholic communities in which widows continue to play a significant role as community (though not liturgical) leaders.[222]

I may thus conclude that beyond the first Christian generation, there is little evidence of women exercising leadership within Christian circles, except, possibly, in those settings in which the domestic basis of the church was still prominent, and in which there were single households, and that this is the rationale behind the manifestation of female leadership in Montanist communities. It thus may be that in spite of the evidence that women did participate in public life in the early empire, the adoption by Christians of associational behavior that took the church beyond the domestic sphere, ideationally if not actually physically, meant that office as it emerged was held exclusively by men. Possibly, Christians were more careful in observing the norm (albeit a norm, as has already been seen, that was not always observed) that female governance was restricted to her own household.[223] As monepiscopacy emerged over a century later, it would seem that female leadership, in urban areas at least, was no longer even a memory.

Overall Conclusion

In a narrative that has both much in common with previous narratives and much by way of distinction, I have characterized the rise of monepiscopacy as a process of centralization by which diverse and individual Christian communities formed federal relationships with other Christian communities in the locality, which federations in turn became centralized. The reason behind this process is not entirely clear, though two factors seem to have played a significant role: (1) the doctrine of succession, by which the ability to point to a named teacher within a community as successor to teaching was a tool that enabled churches to define their teaching over and against the threat of other forms of Christian belief; and (2) the impact of persecution that brought about conditions for the rise of charismatic leaders within the federation who might bring about centralization. In the process, the nature of the episcopal office changed from being principally focused

222. In *Can. eccl. ap.* 45–48.

223. Note the citation of Philo, *Spec.* 3.170 in chap. 2 above, under the heading "*Episkopoi* in Households and Associations."

on economic provision to being a teaching office, as the functions of the federated leaders in policing the boundaries of belief, passing on literature, and representing the church to other churches beyond the city pass to the emerging *monepiskopos*.

In the light of this change, I may suggest that the necessity of constructing a succession of named *episkopoi* in order to answer the claims of the gnostic schools was perhaps the more significant of these streams of influence. It is interesting that Irenaeus should stand out as representative of this doctrine, given that he is familiar with the role of presbyters collectively as representing tradition. Nonetheless, I may stress once again that whereas this would seem to be a significant factor in the emergence of monepiscopacy, the federations out of which monepiscopacy emerged may already have been tending toward centralization. Ultimately, we are in ignorance; consequently, the claim of the present work is simply to have clarified the area about which we are ignorant: the extent of centralization among federations prior to the emergence of *monepiskopoi*.

Moeover, given the diverse nature of early Christianity, the narrative is not universal; some Syrian *episkopoi* retained their economic function, *seniores* survive in Africa alongside the imported presbyters, and in rural areas monepiscopacy emerges over a century later than it had in the cities. However, insofar as there is an overarching narrative, it is one of centralization.

A Concluding
Unscientific Postscript

As a historian, I am uncomfortable drawing out theological lessons
from the history that I present, for the conclusions of a historian
must be partial and provisional, based as they are on fragmentary
evidence. The massive influence of *Traditio apostolica* on liturgical reform in
the twentieth century is sufficient as a cautionary tale for any historian tempted
to make prescriptions for the real life of a church; this document, once believed
to represent a typical early Roman liturgy and mined by Catholic churches
and Protestant denominations alike, is now a storm center of criticism. Even
those who defend its Roman provenance and fundamental integrity do not
suggest that the liturgies found therein are in any way typical of the Roman
liturgy of the third century.

A further cautionary tale, more immediately relevant to the substance of
this book, is provided once again by Wesley's justification of his presbyteral
ordination of Coke. As observed in the introduction, not only was Wesley
influenced through the work of King, but he had also read Stillingfleet, and so
he cited the precedent that he believed had been set by the ordination of the
episkopos by presbyters in ante-Nicene Alexandria.[1] This is a precedent that,
I suggested above, was as misunderstood in the twentieth century as in the

1. See Samuel Drew, *The Life of the Reverend Thomas Coke LLD* (London: [Wesleyan Meth-
odist] Conference, 1817), 64. As noted in chap. 4 above, under the heading "The Alexandrian
Community," this evidence is noticed by Edward Stillingfleet, *Irenicum: A Weapon-Salve for
the Churches Wounds* (London: Henry Mortlock, 1662), 273–75; Wesley records that he had
read Stillingfleet's work. The precedent of Alexandria is, moreover, mentioned by Coke in his
sermon at the ordination of Asbury as superintendent in 1784, in a passage concerned with the

eighteenth. Indeed, if Stillingfleet is one of the first to expound the consensus, then I may note again that he did not write as a disinterested historian but rather produced history as a means to seek reconciliation between the established (and episcopal) church and independents in the wake of the restoration.

The same discussion still continues. Indeed, in any discussion between episcopal and non-episcopal Christian communities the matter of episcopate and apostolic succession is prominent, and historians are called as witnesses. If my conclusions are correct, there is little comfort for those who maintain that the ministry of the church was originally presbyteral (with the corollary that it should therefore remain so), but likewise none for those who maintain that episcopacy as it is now recognized is fundamental to the church and had been in place from the beginning. Ministry was originally episcopal-diaconal, but the *episkopos* had charge of a single congregation and did not oversee presbyters. Insofar as a wider, and non-economic, *episkopē* existed in the earliest period, it was collective and exercised by the gathered presbyters of a defined area. Moreover, although the original ministry was episcopal-diaconal, we do not know how these *episkopoi* and *diakonoi* were appointed or ordained, beyond evidence that in Asian Christian communities this was undertaken by the local presbyters, who themselves neither were ordained nor necessarily exercised a ministry (though some might), and the (less well-evidenced) possibility that the same is true in Egyptian communities beyond Alexandria.

I may say that the doctrine of apostolic succession emerged in the latter part of the second century, but this did not mean that the *episkopoi* who were seen as representative of that succession themselves were episcopally ordained even then. Such, it would seem, is the history; church office in the first centuries is not that received in the churches today, whether those churches be episcopal or presbyteral. Both the Protestant position of presbyteral leadership of churches and the Catholic position of apostolically ordained episcopal leadership are shown, as I suggested in chapter 1 might be the case, to be dogmatic positions without foundation in history. Any confident assertion about any true biblical model of ministry,[2] or indeed any narrative of the originally collective leadership of congregations giving rise to "monarchical episcopacy" within those congregations, is to be consigned to the dustbin of exegetical history.

whole issue of apostolic succession. I find the sermon reprinted in *The Methodist Magazine and Quarterly Review* 22, no. 3 (July 1840): 242–49.

2. Such as that of David W. Miller, "The Uniqueness of New Testament Eldership," *GTJ* 16 (1985): 327: "Our Lord's church should be organized the way he has designed it in his word." According to Miller, this is a twofold ministry of elders and deacons, both collective groups. This is an extraordinary conclusion from someone who, clearly, has read no primary literature beyond the New Testament.

However, readers will differ as to what part of the narrative is to be considered normative in ecclesial communities, and in what sense. If a privileged position is to be given to the first generation of Christian practice, then the idea of a denomination, or any authorizing body recognizing independent churches beyond the immediate locality, probably should be abandoned. However, it may be that the emergence of monepiscopacy from domestic episcopacy should be seen as a development in doctrine in itself,[3] as much as a means by which doctrine might be developed in new ways, and the development of presbyteral office as such, which depends on the development of monepiscopacy, may be a legitimate political development enabling the life of the church to proceed.

In any event, it may be the case that issues regarding church order as generally understood are not the most fruitful elements in the theological discussion that the history might engender.

As to other issues that the history raises, I would point to two, which are related, involving the diaconate and the episcopate.

The original ministers within many Christian communities are *episkopoi* and *diakonoi*. As such, this raises questions regarding the decline of the diaconate in many Christian churches. To take an Anglican example of this neglect, whereas the ordinal of 1662 charges that prior to the ordination a sermon is to be preached on, among other things, "how necessary that Order is in the Church of Christ," there are dioceses in which, at any given time, this supposedly necessary order is entirely absent. The earliest sources point to *diakonoi* as agents of the *episkopos*. It may be that the transformation of the *episkopos* into a *monepiskopos* means that a recovery of the diaconate depends on a recovery of the episcopate.

When I speak of recovering the episcopate, I am referring to the role of the *episkopos* in ensuring that the poor are recognized within the eucharistic community, and also to a recognition of the eucharist as the means to model and to bring about economic and social justice, including the distribution and redistribution of goods within the Christian society as a mirror to the world, and as a means to focus the church's caritative ministry. There has been some theological reflection on the eucharist as a sign and sacrament of liberation and of social justice,[4] though none on the specific role of the bishop as the agent of

3. John Henry Newman (*Essay on the Development of Christian Doctrine* [London: Basil Montagu Pickering, 1878], 54) describes the development of episcopate (which he sees as first emerging at the time of Ignatius) as a political rather than a doctrinal development.

4. E.g., Tissa Balasuriya, *The Eucharist and Human Liberation* (London: SCM, 1977); R. Kevin Seasoltz, "Justice and the Eucharist," *Worship* 58 (1984): 507–25; Gerard Moore, *Eucharist and Justice* (Sydney: Australian Catholic Social Justice Council, 2000); Margaret Scott, *The Eucharist and Social Justice* (New York: Paulist Press, 2009).

justice within the eucharistic setting or of broker of divine gift as human gift and of food that, in Ignatian language, unites flesh and spirit in Jesus Christ, and thus none on the role of the deacon as the bishop's agent ministering both food and Christ. This perhaps has been prevented by ecumenical inability to determine who the proper eucharistic celebrant might be (again raising the question of the validity of any claim of episcopal succession) or by a suspicion of hierarchy among those whose instincts are socialist and liberationist.

Thus, I conclude my postscript by recollecting a point made in chapter 2: the only head of any congregation, of any diocese, of the universal church, is Christ; of him and of his mysteries are we stewards and servants.

Bibliography

Achelis, H., and J. Flemming. *Die ältesten Quellen des orientalischen Kirchenrechts.* Vol. 2, *Die syrische Didaskalia übersetzt und erklärt.* TUGAL 10/2. Leipzig: Hinrichs, 1904.

Ameling, Walter. "Die jüdischen Gemeinden im antiken Kleinasien." In *Jüdische Gemeinden und Organisationsformen von der Antike bis zur Gegenwart,* edited by Robert Jütte and Abraham P. Kustermann, 29–55. Aschkenas 3. Vienna: Böhlau, 1996.

Anderson, J. G. C. "An Imperial Estate in Galatia." *JRS* 27 (1931): 18–21.

Aneziri, Sophia, and Dimitris Damaskos. "Städtische Kulte im hellenistischen Gymnasion." In *Das hellenistische Gymnasion,* edited by Daniel Kah and Peter Scholz, 248–71. WGW 8. Berlin: Akademie-Verlag, 2004.

Arnaoutoglou, Ilias N. "Roman Law and *collegia* in Asia Minor." *RIDA* 49 (2002): 27–44.

Ascough, Richard S. *Paul's Macedonian Associations: The Social Context of Philippians and 1 Thessalonians.* WUNT 2/161. Tübingen: Mohr Siebeck, 2003.

———. "Translocal Relationships among Voluntary Associations and Early Christianity." *JECS* 5 (1997): 223–41.

Audet, J.-P. "Affinités littéraires at doctrinales du 'Manuel de discipline.'" *RB* 59 (1952): 219–38.

———. *La Didachè: Instructions des apôtres.* EB. Paris: Gabalda, 1958.

Bakke, Odd Magne. *"Concord and Peace": A Rhetorical Analysis of the First Letter of Clement with an Emphasis on the Language of Unity and Sedition.* WUNT 2/143. Tübingen: Mohr Siebeck, 2001.

Balasuriya, Tissa. *The Eucharist and Human Liberation.* London: SCM, 1977.

Banks, Robert. *Paul's Idea of Community: The Early House Churches in Their Cultural Setting.* Peabody, MA: Hendrickson, 1994.

Barlea, Octavian. *Die Weihe der Bischöfe, Presbyter und Diakone in vornicänischer Zeit.* APT 3. Munich: Societas Academica Dacoromana, 1969.

Barnes, Timothy D. "The Date of Ignatius." *ExpTim* 120 (2008): 119–30.

Barrett, C. K. *A Critical and Exegetical Commentary on the Acts of the Apostles.* 2 vols. ICC. Edinburgh: T&T Clark, 1994.

———. "Paul's Address to the Ephesian Elders." In *God's Christ and His People: Studies in Honour of Nils Alstrup Dahl,* edited by Jacob Jervell and Wayne A. Meeks, 107–22. Oslo: Universitetsforlaget, 1977.

Bartlett, David L. *Ministry in the New Testament.* Minneapolis: Fortress, 1993.

Barton, S. C., and G. H. R. Horsley. "A Hellenistic Cult Group and the New Testament Churches." *JAC* 24 (1981): 7–41.

Bartsch, Hans-Werner. *Die Anfänge urchristlicher Rechtsbildung.* TF 34. Hamburg: Herbert Reich, 1965.

357

Bauckham, Richard J. "The Early Jerusalem Church, Qumran and the Essenes." In *The Dead Sea Scrolls as Background to Postbiblical Judaism and Early Christianity: Papers from an International Conference at St. Andrews in 2001*, edited by James R. Davila, 63–89. STDJ 46. Leiden: Brill, 2003.

———, ed. *The Gospels for All Christians: Rethinking the Gospel Audiences.* Grand Rapids: Eerdmans, 1998.

———. "James and the Jerusalem Church." In *The Book of Acts in Its Palestinian Setting*, edited by Richard J. Bauckham, 415–80. BAFS 4. Grand Rapids: Eerdmans, 1995.

———. *Jude and the Relatives of Jesus in the Early Church.* Edinburgh: T&T Clark, 1990.

Bauer, J. B. *Die Polykarpbriefe.* KAV 5. Göttingen: Vandenhoeck & Ruprecht, 1995.

Bauer, Walter. *Orthodoxy and Heresy in Earliest Christianity.* Translated by the Philadelphia Seminar on Christian Origins. Edited by Robert A. Kraft and Gerhard Krodel. Philadelphia: Fortress, 1971.

Baur, F. C. *Das Christenthum und die christliche Kirche der drei ersten Jahrhunderte.* 2nd ed. Tübingen: Fues, 1860.

———. *Die sogenannten Pastoralbriefe des Apostels Paulus aufs neue kritisch untersucht.* Stuttgart and Tübingen: J. G. Cotta, 1835.

———. *Ueber den Ursprung des Episcopats in der christlichen Kirche: Prüfung der neuestens von Hrn. Dr. Rothe aufgestellten Ansicht.* Tübingen: Fues, 1838.

Beall, Todd S. *Josephus' Description of the Essenes Illustrated by the Dead Sea Scrolls.* SNTSMS 58. Cambridge: Cambridge University Press, 1988.

Behr, John. *The Way to Nicaea.* Crestwood, NY: St. Vladimir's Seminary Press, 2001.

Bekker-Nielsen, Tønnes. *Urban Life and Local Politics in Roman Bithynia: The Small World of Dion Chrysostomos.* BSS 7. Aarhus: Aarhus University Press, 2008.

Benoit, Pierre. "Les origines apostoliques de l'épiscopat selon le Nouveau Testament." In *L'évêque dans l'église du Christ*, edited by H. Bouëssé and A. Mandouze, 13–57. TET. Bruges: Desclée de Brouwer, 1963.

Berding, Kenneth. *Polycarp and Paul: An Analysis of Their Literary and Theological Relationship in Light of Polycarp's Use of Biblical and Extra-Biblical Literature.* VCSup 62. Leiden: Brill, 2002.

Best, Ernest. "Bishops and Deacons: Philippians 1,1." In *Studia Evangelica 4: Papers Presented at the Third International Congress on New Testament Studies Held at Christ Church, Oxford, 1965*, edited by F. L. Cross, 371–76. TUGAL 102. Berlin: Akademie-Verlag, 1968.

Beyer, H. W. "διακονέω." In *Theological Dictionary of the New Testament*, vol. 2, edited by G. Kittel and G. Friedrich, translated by G. W. Bromiley, 81–93. Grand Rapids: Eerdmans, 1964.

Bieder, Werner. "Zur Deutung des kirchlichen Schweigens bei Ignatius von Antiochia." *TZ* 12 (1956): 28–43.

Binder, Donald D. *Into the Temple Courts: The Place of the Synagogues in the Second Temple Period.* SBLDS 169. Atlanta: Society of Biblical Literature, 1999.

Black, C. C. "The Johannine Epistles and the Question of Early Catholicism." *NovT* 28 (1986): 131–58.

Blasi, Anthony J. "Office Charisma in Early Christian Ephesus?" *SocRel* 56 (1995): 245–55.

Blinkenberg, Christian. *Lindos: Fouilles et recherches, 1902–1914.* Vol. 1, *Inscriptions, Nos. 1–281.* Berlin: de Gruyter, 1941.

Bobertz, Charles A. "The Development of Episcopal Order." In *Eusebius, Christianity, and Judaism*, edited by Harold W. Attridge and Gohei Hata, 183–211. Detroit: Wayne State University Press, 1992.

———. "The Role of Patron in the *cena dominica* of Hippolytus' *Apostolic Tradition.*" *JTS* 44 (1995): 170–84.

Boismard, M.-É. "Une liturgie baptismale dans la Prima Petri II: Son influence sur l'Épitre de Jacques." *RB* 64 (1957): 161–83.

Bonneau, Guy. "'Pour y achever l'organisation' (Tite 1,5): L'institutionalisation de l'Église au temps du Nouveau Testament." *ScEs* 52 (2000): 87–107.

Borgen, Peder. "'Yes,' 'No,' 'How Far?' The Participation of Jews and Christians in Pagan Clubs." In *Paul in His Hellenistic Context*, edited by Troels Engberg-Pedersen, 30–59. SNTW. Edinburgh: T&T Clark, 1995.

Bormann, Lukas. *Philippi: Stadt und Christengemeinde zur Zeit des Paulus*. NovTSup 78. Leiden: Brill, 1995.

Bowe, Barbara E. *A Church in Crisis: Ecclesiology and Paraenesis in Clement of Rome*. Minneapolis: Fortress, 1988.

Bradley, Keith. "The Roman Family at Dinner." In *Meals in a Social Context: Aspects of the Communal Meal in the Hellenistic and Roman World*, edited by Inge Nielsen and Hanne Sigismund Nielsen, 26–55. ASMA 1. Aarhus: Aarhus University Press, 1998.

Bradshaw, Paul F. *Liturgical Presidency in the Early Church*. Bramcote, UK: Grove, 1983.

———. *Ordination Rites of the Ancient Churches of East and West*. New York: Pueblo, 1990.

———. *The Search for the Origins of Christian Worship: Sources and Methods for the Study of Early Liturgy*. 2nd ed. London: SPCK, 2002.

Bradshaw, Paul F., and Maxwell E. Johnson. *The Origins of Feasts, Fasts and Seasons in Early Christianity*. London: SPCK, 2011.

Brakmann, Heinzgard. "Alexandreia und die Kanones des Hippolyt." *JAC* 22 (1979): 139–49.

Brent, Allen. "Diogenes Laertius and the Apostolic Succession." *JEH* 44 (1993): 367–89.

———. "The Enigma of Ignatius of Antioch." *JEH* 57 (2006): 429–56.

———. *Hippolytus and the Roman Church in the Third Century: Communities in Tension before the Emergence of a Monarch-Bishop*. VCSup 31. Leiden: Brill, 1995.

———. "The Ignatian Epistles and the Threefold Ecclesiastical Order." *JRH* 17 (1992): 18–32.

———. *Ignatius of Antioch and the Second Sophistic: A Study of an Early Christian Transformation of Pagan Culture*. STAC 36. Tübingen: Mohr Siebeck, 2006.

———. *The Imperial Cult and the Development of Church Order: Concepts and Images of Authority in Paganism and Early Christianity before the Age of Cyprian*. VCSup 45. Leiden: Brill, 1999.

———. "Pseudonymy and Charisma in the Ministry of the Early Church." *Aug* 27 (1987): 347–76.

Broek, Roelof van den. "Der *Brief des Jakobus an Quadratus* und das Problem der judenchristlichen Bischöfe von Jerusalem (Eusebius *HE* IV, 5,1–3)." In *Text and Testimony: Essays on New Testament and Apocryphal Literature in Honour of A. F. J. Klijn*, edited by T. Baarda et al., 56–65. Kampen: Kok, 1988.

———. "The Christian 'School' of Alexandria in the Second and Third Centuries." In *Centres of Learning: Learning and Location in Pre-Modern Europe and the Near East*, edited by Jan Willem Drijvers and Alasdair A. MacDonald, 39–47. BSIH 61. Leiden: Brill, 1995.

———. "Juden und Christen in Alexandrien." In *Juden und Christen in der Antike*, edited by J. van Amersfoort and J. van Oort, 101–15. SPA 1. Kampen: Kok, 1990.

Brooks, E. W. "The Ordination of the Early Bishops of Alexandria." *JTS* 2 (1901): 612–13.

———, ed. *The Sixth Book of the Select Letters of Severus, Patriarch of Antioch in the Syriac Version of Athanasius of Nisibis*. London: Williams & Norgate, 1902.

Brown, Raymond E. "*EPISKOPĒ* and *EPISKOPOS*: The New Testament Evidence." *TS* 41 (1980): 322–38.

Brown, Raymond E., and John P. Meier. *Antioch and Rome: New Testament Cradles of Catholic Christianity*. London: Geoffrey Chapman, 1983.

Brox, Norbert. *Der Hirt des Hermas*. KAV 7. Göttingen: Vandenhoeck & Ruprecht, 1991.

Bruce, F. F. *The Acts of the Apostles: The Greek Text with Introduction and Commentary*. 3rd ed. Grand Rapids: Eerdmans, 1990.

Budesheim, Thomas L. "Paul's Abschiedsrede in the Acts of the Apostles." *HTR* 69 (1976): 9–30.

Burdon, Adrian. *Authority and Order: John Wesley and His Preachers*. Aldershot, UK: Ashgate, 2005.

Burke, Patrick. "The Monarchical Episcopate at the End of the First Century." *JES* 7 (1970): 499–518.

Burtchaell, James Tunstead. *From Synagogue to Church: Public Services and Offices in the Earliest Christian Communities*. Cambridge: Cambridge University Press, 1992.

Cadbury, Henry J. *The Style and Literary Method of Luke*. HTS 6. Cambridge, MA: Harvard University Press, 1920.

Calder, W. M. "Documents from Phrygia and Cyprus." *JHS* 55 (1935): 71–8.

Camelot, P. T. *Ignace d'Antioche, Polycarpe de Smyrne: Lettres; Martyre de Polycarpe*. 4th ed. SC 10. Paris: Cerf, 1998.

Campbell, R. Alastair. *The Elders: Seniority within Earliest Christianity*. SNTW. Edinburgh: T&T Clark, 1994.

———. "The Elders of the Jerusalem Church." *JTS* 44 (1993): 511–28.

Campenhausen, Hans von. *Ecclesiastical Authority and Spiritual Power in the Church of the First Three Centuries*. Translated by J. A. Baker. London: A&C Black, 1969.

———. "Die Nachfolge des Jakobus." In *Aus der Frühzeit des Christentums: Studien zur Kirchengeschichte des ersten und zweiten Jahrhunderts*, 135–51. Tübingen: Mohr Siebeck, 1963.

Capper, Brian. "The New Covenant in Southern Palestine at the Arrest of Jesus." In *The Dead Sea Scrolls as Background to Postbiblical Judaism and Early Christianity: Papers from an International Conference at St. Andrews in 2001*, edited by James R. Davila, 90–116. STDJ 46. Leiden: Brill, 2003.

———. "Order and Ministry in the Social Pattern of the New Testament Church." In *Order and Ministry*, edited by Christine Hall and Brian Hannaford, 61–103. Leominster, UK: Gracewing, 1996.

———. "The Palestinian Cultural Context of Earliest Christian Community of Goods." In *The Book of Acts in Its Palestinian Setting*, edited by Richard J. Bauckham, 323–56. BAFS 4. Grand Rapids: Eerdmans, 1995.

———. "'With the Oldest Monks . . .': Light from Essene History on the Career of the Beloved Disciple?" *JTS* 49 (1998): 1–55.

Caragounis, C. C. "From Obscurity to Prominence: The Development of the Roman Church between Romans and 1 *Clement*." In *Judaism and Christianity in First-Century Rome*, edited by K. P. Donfried and P. Richardson, 245–79. Grand Rapids: Eerdmans, 1998.

Catto, Stephen K. *Reconstructing the First-Century Synagogue: A Critical Analysis of Current Research*. LNTS 363. London: T&T Clark, 2007.

Chadwick, Henry. "The Silence of Bishops in Ignatius." *HTR* 43 (1950): 169–72.

Chilton, Bruce. *A Feast of Meanings: Eucharistic Theologies from Jesus through Johannine Circles*. NovTSup 72. Leiden: Brill, 1994

Chow, John K. *Patronage and Power: A Study of Social Networks at Corinth*. JSNTSup 75. Sheffield: JSOT Press, 1992.

Collange, Jean François. *The Epistle of Saint Paul to the Philippians*. Translated by A. W. Heathcote. London: Epworth, 1978.

Collins, John N. *Diakonia: Re-interpreting the Ancient Sources*. New York: Oxford University Press, 1990.

Connolly, R. Hugh. *Didascalia apostolorum: The Syriac Version Translated and Accompanied by the Verona Latin Fragments, with an Introduction and Notes*. Oxford: Clarendon, 1929.

Conzelmann, Hans. *Acts of the Apostles: A Commentary on the Acts of the Apostles*. Translated by James Limburg, A. Thomas Kraabel, and Donald H. Juel. Edited by Eldon Jay Epp with Christopher R. Matthews. Hermeneia. Philadelphia: Fortress, 1987.

Corwin, Virginia. *St. Ignatius and Christianity in Antioch*. New Haven: Yale University Press, 1960.

Cousineau, André. "Le sens de 'presbuteros' dans les Pastorales." *ScEs* 28 (1976): 147–62.

Cumont, Franz. "Ein neues Psephisma aus Amphipolis." *JÖAI* 1 (1898): 180–84.

D'Arms, John H. "Control, Companionship and *clientela*: Some Social Functions of the Roman Communal Meal." *EMC* 3 (1984): 327–48.

Dassmann, Ernst. "Hausgemeinde und Bischofsamt." In *Vivarium: Festschrift Theodor Klauser zum 90. Geburtstag*, 82–93. JAC 11. Münster: Aschendorff, 1984.

———. "Zur Entstehung des Monepiskopats." *JAC* 17 (1974): 74–90.

Davies, Stevan L. "The Predicament of Ignatius of Antioch." *VC* 30 (1976): 175–80.

De Halleux, A. "Ministers in the *Didache*." In *The* Didache *in Modern Research*, edited by Jonathan A. Draper, 300–320. AGJU 37. Leiden: Brill, 1996.

Dekkers, E. "L'église ancienne a-t-elle connu la messe du soir?" In *Miscellanea Liturgica in Honorem L. Cuniberti Mohlberg*, vol. 1, 233–57. BEL 22. Rome: Edizioni Liturgiche, 1948.

Delorme, Jean. *Gymnasion: Étude sur les monuments consacrés a l'éducation en Grèce (des origines à l'Empire Romain)*. BEFAR 196. Paris: de Boccard, 1960.

Dibelius, Martin. *An die Thessalonicher I, II; An die Philipper*. 3rd ed. HNT 11. Tübingen: Mohr Siebeck, 1937.

———. "The Speeches in Acts and Ancient Historiography." In *Studies in the Acts of the Apostles*, edited by Heinrich Greeven, translated by Mary Ling, 138–85. London: SCM, 1956.

Dix, Gregory. "The Ministry in the Early Church." In *The Apostolic Ministry: Essays on the History and Doctrine of Episcopacy*, edited by K. E. Kirk, 183–303. London: Hodder & Stoughton, 1946.

Dombrowski, B. W. "*HaYahad* in 1QS and τὸ κοινόν: An Instance of Early Greek and Jewish Synthesis." *HTR* 59 (1966): 293–307.

Donahue, Paul J. "Jewish Christianity in the Letters of Ignatius of Antioch." *VC* 32 (1978): 81–93.

Donfried, K. P. "Ecclesiastical Authority in 2–3 John." In *L'Évangile de Jean: Sources, rédaction, theologie*, edited by Marinus de Jonge, 325–33. BETL 44. Gembloux: Duculot, 1977.

Easton, B. S. "New Testament Ethical Lists." *JBL* 51 (1932): 1–12.

Ehrhardt, Arnold. *The Apostolic Succession in the First Two Centuries of the Church*. London: Lutterworth, 1953.

Eisen, Ute E. *Women Officeholders in Early Christianity: Epigraphical and Literary Studies*. Translated by Linda M. Maloney. Collegeville, MN: Liturgical Press, 2000.

Elliott, J. H. "Elders and Leaders in I Peter and the Early Church." *HvTSt* 64 (2008): 681–95.

———. "Elders as Honored Household Heads and Not Holders of 'Office' in Earliest Christianity." *BTB* 33 (2003): 77–82.

———. "Ministry and Church Order in the NT: A Traditio-Historical Analysis (1 Pt 5,1–5 & plls.)." *CBQ* 32 (1970): 367–91.

Estrada, Nelson P. *From Followers to Leaders: The Apostles in the Ritual of Status Transformation in Acts 1–2*. JSNTSup 255. London: T&T Clark, 2004.

Faivre, Alexandre. "Les fonctions ecclésiales dans les écrits pseudo-Clémentins: Proposition de lecture." *RevScRel* 50 (1976): 97–111.

———. "Le texte grec de la Constitution ecclésiastique des apôtres 16–20 et ses sources." *RevScRel* 55 (1981): 31–42.

Farrar, A. M. "The Ministry in the New Testament." In *The Apostolic Ministry: Essays on the History and Doctrine of Episcopacy*, edited by Kenneth E. Kirk, 113–82. London: Hodder & Stoughton, 1946.

Fee, Gordon D. *1 and 2 Timothy, Titus*. NIBC 13. Peabody, MA: Hendrickson, 1988.

Ferguson, Everett. "Jewish and Christian Ordination: Some Observations." *HTR* 56 (1963): 3–19.

———. "The Ministry of the Word in the First Two Centuries." *ResQ* 1 (1957): 21–31.

———. "Origen and the Election of Bishops." *CH* 43 (1974): 26–33.

———. "Selection and Installation to Office in Roman, Greek, Jewish and Christian Antiquity." *TZ* 30 (1974): 273–84.

Fiensy, David A. "The Composition of the Jerusalem Church." In *The Book of Acts in Its Palestinian Setting*, edited by Richard J. Bauckham, 213–36. BAFS 4. Grand Rapids: Eerdmans, 1995.

Finger, Reta Halteman. *Of Widows and Meals: Communal Meals in the Book of Acts*. Grand Rapids: Eerdmans, 2007.

Fiore, Benjamin. *The Function of Personal Example in the Socratic and Pastoral Epistles*. AnBib 105. Rome: Biblical Institute Press, 1986.

Fischer, J. A. *Die apostolischen Väter*. SU 1. Darmstadt: Wissenschaftliche Buchgesellschaft, 1958.

Foster, Paul. "The Epistles of Ignatius of Antioch and the Writings That Later Formed the New Testament." In *The Reception of the New Testament in the Apostolic Fathers*, edited by Andrew F. Gregory and C. M. Tuckett, 159–86. Oxford: Oxford University Press, 2005.

Frend, W. H. C. "The *seniores laici* and the Origins of the Church in North Africa." *JTS* 12 (1961): 280–84.

Frey, Jean Baptiste. "Les communautés juives à Rome aux premiers temps de l'église." *RSR* 20 (1930): 267–97; 21 (1931): 129–68.

———. *Corpus of Jewish Inscriptions: Jewish Inscriptions from the Third Century B.C. to the Seventh Century A.D.* New York: Ktav, 1975.

Garnsey, Peter, and Greg Woolf. "Patronage of the Rural Poor in the Roman World." In *Patronage in Ancient Society*, edited by Andrew Wallace-Hadrill, 153–70. LNSAS 1. London: Routledge, 1989.

Gehring, Roger W. *House Church and Mission: The Importance of Household Structures in Early Christianity.* Peabody, MA: Hendrickson, 2004.

Gelzer, Heinrich, Heinrich Hilgenfeld, and Otto Cuntz. *Patrum Nicaenorum nomina Latine, Graece, Coptice, Syriace, Arabice, Armeniace.* BSGRT. Leipzig: Teubner, 1898.

Georgi, Dieter. *The Opponents of Paul in Second Corinthians.* SNTW. Edinburgh: T&T Clark, 1987.

Gillmann, Franz. *Das Institut der Chorbischöfe im Orient: Historisch-kanonistische Studie.* Munich: Lentner, 1903.

Goodwin-Gill, Guy. *Free and Fair Elections*, 2nd ed. Geneva: Inter-Parliamentary Union, 2006.

Goppelt, Leonhard. "Kirchenleitung in der palästinischen Urkirche und bei Paulus." In *Reformatio und Confessio: Festschrift für D. Wilhelm Maurer zum 65. Geburtstag am 7. Mai 1965*, edited by Friedrich Wilhelm Kantzenbach and Gerhard Müller, 1–8. Berlin: Lutherisches Verlagshaus, 1965.

Grant, Robert M. *After the New Testament.* Philadelphia: Fortress, 1967.

———. *The Apostolic Fathers: A New Translation and Commentary.* Vol. 4, *Ignatius of Antioch.* Camden, NJ: Nelson, 1966.

Greeven, H. "Propheten, Lehrer, Vorsteher bei Paulus: Zur Frage der 'Ämter' im Urchristentum." *ZNW* 44 (1953): 1–43.

Griggs, C. Wilfred. *Early Egyptian Christianity: From Its Origins to 451 CE.* Leiden: Brill, 1990.

Guerra Gómez, Manuel. "Diáconos helénicos y biblicos." *Burgense* 4 (1963): 9–143.

Halbwachs, Maurice. *On Collective Memory.* Edited and translated by Lewis A. Coser. Chicago: University of Chicago Press, 1992.

Haley, Peter. "Rudolph Sohm on Charisma." *JR* 60 (1980): 185–97.

Hammond, Henry. *A Paraphrase and Annotations upon All the Books of the New Testament.* London: J. Macock and M. Flesher, for Richard Royston, 1681.

Hammond Bammel, C. P. "Ignatian Problems." *JTS* 33 (1982): 62–97.

Hann, Robert R. "Judaism and Jewish Christianity in Antioch: Charisma and Conflict in the First Century." *JRH* 14 (1987): 341–60.

Hanson, A. T. *The Pastoral Epistles.* New Cambridge Bible Commentary. London: Marshall, Morgan & Scott, 1982.

Hanson, R. P. C. "Office and Concept of Office in the Early Church." In *Studies in Christian Antiquity*, 117–43. Edinburgh: T&T Clark, 1985.

Harland, Philip A. *Associations, Synagogues, and Congregations: Claiming a Place in Ancient Mediterranean Society.* Minneapolis: Fortress, 2003.

———. "Christ-Bearers and Fellow-Initiates: Local Cultural Life and Christian Identity in Ignatius' Letters." *JECS* 11 (2003): 481–99.

Harnack, Adolf von. *The Constitution and Law of the Church in the First Two Centuries.* Translated by F. L. Pogson. Edited by H. D. A. Major. London: Williams & Norgate, 1910.

———. *Die Lehre der zwölf Apostel: Nebst Untersuchungen zur ältesten Geschichte der Kirchenverfassung und des Kirchenrechts.* TUGAL 2/1–2. Leipzig: Hinrichs, 1886.

———. *Marcion: Das Evangelium vom fremden Gott.* TUGAL 45. Leipzig: Hinrichs, 1924.

Harrill, J. Albert. "Ignatius *Ad Polycarp* 4.3 and the Corporate Manumission of Christian Slaves." *JECS* 1 (1993): 107–42.

Harrison, P. N. *Polycarp's Two Epistles to the Philippians.* Cambridge: Cambridge University Press, 1936.

Harvey, A. E. "Elders." *JTS* 25 (1974): 318–31.

Hatch, Edwin. *The Organization of the Early Christian Churches.* London: Longmans, 1881.

Hawthorne, Gerald F. *Philippians.* WBC 43. Waco: Word, 1983.

Hayes, Alan L. "Christian Ministry in Three Cities of the Western Empire (160–258 CE)." In *Community Formation in the Early Church and in the Church Today,* edited by Richard N. Longenecker, 129–56. Peabody, MA: Hendrickson, 2002.

Hengel, Martin. *Earliest Christianity.* Translated by John Bowden. London: SCM, 1986.

———. "Jakobus der Herrenbruder: Der erste 'Papst.'" In *Glaube und Eschatologie: Festschrift für Werner Georg Kümmel zum 80. Geburtstag,* edited by Erich Grässer and Otto Merk, 71–104. Tübingen: Mohr Siebeck, 1985.

Hess, Hamilton. *The Early Development of Canon Law and the Council of Serdica.* OECS. Oxford: Oxford University Press, 2002.

Hicks, E. L. "On Some Political Terms in the New Testament." *CR* 1 (1887): 4–8, 42–46.

Hoek, A. van den. "The 'Catechetical' School of Early Christian Alexandria and Its Philonic Heritage." *HTR* 90 (1997): 59–87.

Hofius, Otfried. "Die Ordination zum Amt der Kirche und die apostolische Sukzession nach dem Zeugnis der Pastoralbriefe." *ZTK* 107 (2010): 261–84.

Holmberg, Bengt. *Paul and Power: The Structure of Authority in the Primitive Church as Reflected in the Pauline Epistles.* Philadelphia: Fortress, 1980.

Holmes, Michael W. "Polycarp's *Letter to the Philippians* and the Writings That Later Formed the New Testament." In *The Reception of the New Testament in the Apostolic Fathers,* edited by Andrew F. Gregory and C. M. Tuckett, 187–227. Oxford: Oxford University Press, 2005.

Hunt, Stephen J. "Deprivation and Western Pentecostalism Revisited: The Case of 'Classical' Pentecostalism." *PentecoStudies* 1 (2002): 1–32.

Isakson, Mikael. "Follow Your Bishop! Rhetorical Strategies in the Letters of Ignatius of Antioch." In *The Formation of the Early Church,* edited by Jostein Ådna, 317–40. WUNT 183. Tübingen: Mohr Siebeck, 2005.

Jakab, Attila. *Ecclesia alexandrina: Évolution sociale et institutionelle du christianisme alexandrin (IIe et IIIe siècles).* CA 1. Bern: Peter Lang, 2001.

Javierre, Antonio M. *La primera "diadoché" de la patrística y los "ellógimoi" de Clemente Romano: Datos para el problema de la sucesión apostólica.* Turin: Società Editrice Internazionale, 1958.

Jay, Eric G. "From Presbyter-Bishops to Bishops and Presbyters." *SecCent* 1 (1981): 125–62.

Jeffers, James S. *Conflict at Rome: Social Order and Hierarchy in Early Christianity.* Minneapolis: Fortress, 1991.

Jefford, C. N. "Conflict at Antioch: Ignatius and the Didache at Odds." In *Papers Presented at the Thirteenth International Conference on Patristic Studies Held in Oxford 1999: Critica et Philogica, Nachleben, Tertullian to Arnobius, Egypt before Nicea, Athanasius and His Opponents,* edited by M. F. Wiles and E. J. Yarnold, 262–69. StPatr 36. Louvain: Peeters, 2001.

———. "Presbyters in the Community of the Didache." In *Papers Presented at the Tenth International Conference on Patristic Studies Held in Oxford 1987: Second Century, Tertullian to Nicaea in the West, Clement of Alexandria and Origen, Athanasius,* edited by E. A. Livingstone, 122–28. StPatr 21. Louvain: Peeters, 1989.

———. "The Role of 4 Maccabees in the Vision of Ignatius of Antioch." In *Papers Presented at the Fourteenth International Conference on Patristic Studies Held in Oxford 2003,* edited by F. Young, M. Edwards, and P. Parvis, 435–40. StPatr 40. Louvain: Peeters, 2006.

Jeremias, Joachim. *Die Briefe an Timotheus und Titus; Der Brief an die Hebräer.* 11th ed. NTD 9. Göttingen: Vandenhoeck & Ruprecht, 1975.

———. *Jerusalem in the Time of Jesus: An Investigation into Economic and Social Conditions during the New Testament.* Translated by F. H. Cave and C. H. Cave. 3rd ed. London: SCM, 1969.

Johnson, Luke Timothy. *Letters to Paul's Delegates: 1 Timothy, 2 Timothy, Titus.* NTC.

Valley Forge, PA: Trinity Press International, 1996.

Joly, Robert. *Le dossier d'Ignace d'Antioche*. Brussels: Éditions de l'Université de Bruxelles, 1979.

Jones, F. Stanley. "The Ancient Christian Teacher in the Pseudo-Clementines." In *Early Christian Voices: In Texts, Traditions, and Symbols; Essays in Honor of François Bovon*, edited by David H. Warren, Ann Graham Brock, and David W. Pao, 355–64. BIS 66. Leiden: Brill, 2003.

Josaitis, Norman F. *Edwin Hatch and Early Church Order*. Gembloux: Duculot, 1971.

Karrer, Martin. "Das urchristliche Ältestenamt." *NovT* 32 (1990): 152–88.

Käsemann, Ernst. "Ministry and Community in the New Testament." In *Essays on New Testament Themes*, translated by W. J. Montague, 63–94. London: SCM, 1964.

Kasher, Aryeh. *The Jews in Hellenistic and Roman Egypt: The Struggle for Equal Rights*. TSAJ 7. Tübingen: Mohr Siebeck, 1985.

Kelly, J. N. D. *A Commentary on the Pastoral Epistles: I Timothy, II Timothy, Titus*. BNTC. London: A&C Black, 1963.

Kemp, E. W. "Bishops and Presbyters at Alexandria." *JEH* 6 (1955): 125–42.

Kertelge, Karl. *Gemeinde und Amt im neuen Testament*. BH 10. Munich: Kösel, 1972.

Khomych, Taras. "The Notion of *puknôs* as a Distinctive Characteristic of Liturgical Celebrations in the Letters of St Ignatius of Antioch." In *Papers Presented at the Fourteenth International Conference on Patristic Studies Held in Oxford 2003*, edited by F. Young, M. Edwards, and P. Parvis, 441–46. StPatr 40. Louvain: Peeters, 2006.

King, Peter. *An Enquiry into the Constitution, Discipline, Unity and Worship of the Primitive Church*. London: J. Wyat and R. Robinson, 1713.

Klauck, Hans-Josef. *Hausgemeinde und Hauskirche im frühen Christentum*. SBS 103. Stuttgart: Katholisches Bibelwerk, 1981.

Kleberg, Tönnes. *Hôtels, restaurants et cabarets dans l'antiquité romaine: Études historiques et philologiques*. BE 61. Uppsala: Almqvist & Wiksell, 1957.

Kleist, James A. *The Didache, the Epistle of Barnabas, the Epistles and the Martyrdom of St. Polycarp, the Fragments of Papias, the Epistle to Diognetus*. Mahwah, NJ: Newman, 1948.

Klijn, A. F. J., and G. J. Reinink. *Patristic Evidence for Jewish-Christian Sects*. NovTSup 36. Leiden: Brill, 1973.

Kloppenborg, John S. "Collegia and *Thiasoi*: Issues in Function, Taxonomy and Membership." In *Voluntary Associations in the Graeco-Roman World*, edited by John S. Kloppenborg and Stephen G. Wilson, 16–30. London: Routledge, 1996.

———. "Edwin Hatch, Churches and Collegia." In *Origins and Method: Towards a New Understanding of Judaism and Christianity; Essays in Honour of John C. Hurd*, edited by Bradley H. McLean, 212–23. JSNTSup 86. Sheffield: JSOT Press, 1993.

Knibb, M. A. *The Qumran Community*. CCWJCW 2. Cambridge: Cambridge University Press, 1987.

Knight, D. J. "The Movements of the Auxilia from Augustus to Hadrian." *ZPE* 85 (1991): 189–208.

Knight, George W., III. *The Pastoral Epistles: A Commentary on the Greek Text*. NIGTC. Grand Rapids: Eerdmans; Carlisle: Paternoster, 1992.

Knopf, Rudolf. *Die Lehre der zwölf Apostel; Die zwei Clemensbriefe*. HNT. Tübingen: Mohr Siebeck, 1920.

Koch, Dietrich-Alex. "Die Entwicklung der Ämter in frühchristlichen Gemeinden Kleinasiens." In *Neutestamentliche Ämtermodelle im Kontext*, edited by Thomas Schmeller, Martin Ebner, and Rudolf Hoppe, 166–206. QD 239. Freiburg: Herder, 2010.

Körtner, Ulrich H. J. *Papias von Hierapolis: Ein Beitrag zur Geschichte des frühen Christentums*. FRLANT 133. Göttingen: Vandenhoeck & Ruprecht, 1983.

Kraeling, C. H. "The Jewish Community at Antioch." *JBL* 51 (1932): 130–60.

Lambrecht, J. "Paul's Farewell-Address at Miletus (Acts 20,17–38)." In *Les Actes des Apôtres: Traditions, rédaction, théologie*, edited by J. Kremer, 307–37. BETL 48. Gembloux: Ducolot, 1979.

Lampe, Peter. "The Roman Christians of Romans 16." In *The Romans Debate*, edited by K. P. Donfried, 216–30. Peabody, MA: Hendrickson, 1991.

———. *Die stadtrömischen Christen in den ersten beiden Jahrhunderten: Untersuchungen zur Sozialgeschichte.* WUNT 18/2. Tübingen: Mohr Siebeck, 1987.

Lane, William L. "Social Perspectives on Roman Christianity in the Formative Years from Nero to Nerva." In *Judaism and Christianity in First-Century Rome,* edited by K. P. Donfried and P. Richardson, 196–244. Grand Rapids: Eerdmans, 1998.

Launey, Marcel. *Recherches sur les armées Hellénistiques.* Vol. 2. BEFAR 169. Reprint, Paris: de Boccard, 1987.

Laurance, John D. "Eucharistic Leader according to Cyprian of Carthage: A New Study." *StLit* 15 (1982): 66–75

Lawlor, H. J. "The *Hypomnemata* of Hegesippus." In *Eusebiana: Essays on the Ecclesiastical History of Eusebius,* 1–107. Oxford: Clarendon, 1912.

Le Bas, P., and W. H. Waddington. *Voyage archéologique en Grèce et en Asie Mineure.* Vol. 3, *Inscriptions grecques et latines recueillies en Grèce et en Asie Mineure.* Paris: Didot, 1870.

Leaney, A. R. C. *The Rule of Qumran and Its Meaning: Introduction, Translation and Commentary.* London: SCM, 1966.

Lechner, Thomas. *Ignatius adversus Valentinianos? Chronologische und theologiegeschichtliche Studien zu den Briefen des Ignatius von Antiochien.* VCSup 47. Leiden: Brill, 1999.

Lederman, Y. "Les évêques juifs de Jérusalem." *RB* 104 (1997): 211–22.

Lemoine, Bernadette. "Étude de la notice sur l'évêque dans la 'Constitution ecclésiastique des apôtres (C.E.A.).'" *QL* 80 (1999): 5–23.

Leon, Harry J. *The Jews of Ancient Rome.* Philadelphia: Jewish Publication Society, 1960.

Levine, Lee I. *The Ancient Synagogue: The First Thousand Years.* 2nd ed. New Haven: Yale University Press, 2005.

Lietzmann, Hans. "Zur altchristlichen Verfassungsgeschichte." In *Kleine Schriften I,* edited by Kurt Aland, 141–85. TUGAL 67. Berlin: Akademie-Verlag, 1958.

Lieu, Judith. *Image and Reality: The Jews in the World of the Christians in the Second Century.* Edinburgh: T&T Clark, 1996.

Lightfoot, J. B. *The Apostolic Fathers.* 5 vols. 1890. Reprint, Peabody, MA: Hendrickson, 1989.

———. *Saint Paul's Epistle to the Philippians.* 4th ed. London: Macmillan, 1878.

Linton, Olof. *Das Problem der Urkirche in der neueren Forschung: Eine kritische Darstellung.* Uppsala: Almqvist & Wiksell, 1932.

Lips, Hermann von. *Glaube, Gemeinde, Amt: Zum Verständnis der Ordination in den Pastoralbriefen.* FRLANT 122. Göttingen: Vandenhoeck & Ruprecht, 1979.

Lohse, Eduard. "Die Entstehung des Bischofsamtes in der frühen Christenheit." *ZNW* 71 (1980): 58–73.

———. "Episkopos in den Pastoralbriefen." In *Kirche und Bibel: Festgabe für Bischof Eduard Schick,* 225–31. Paderborn: Schöningh, 1979.

Lona, Horacio E. *Der erste Clemensbrief.* KAV 2. Göttingen: Vandenhoeck & Ruprecht, 1998.

Lorencin, Igor. "Hospitality versus Patronage: An Investigation of Social Dynamics in the Third Epistle of John." *AUSS* 46 (2008): 165–74.

Lövestam, Evald. "Paul's Address at Miletus." *ST* 41 (1987): 1–10.

Lüdemann, Gerd. *Early Christianity according to the Traditions in Acts: A Commentary.* Translated by John Bowden. London: SCM, 1989.

MacDonald, Margaret Y. "Can Nympha Rule This House? The Rhetoric of Domesticity in Colossians." In *Rhetoric and Reality in Early Christianities,* edited by Willi Braun, 99–120. Waterloo, ON: Wilfrid Laurier University Press, 2005.

———. "The Ideal of the Christian Couple: Ign. *Pol.* 5.1–2 Looking Back to Paul." *NTS* 40 (1994): 105–25.

Mahaffy, John P. *The Flinders Petrie Papyri: With Transcriptions, Commentaries, and Index.* Vol. 2, *Autotypes I. to XVIII; Appendix: Autotypes I. to III.* Dublin: Academy House, 1893.

Maier, Harry O. "1 Clement 40–44: Apostolic Succession or Legitimation?" In *Papers*

Presented at the Tenth International Conference on Patristic Studies Held in Oxford 1987: Second Century, Tertullian to Nicaea in the West, Clement of Alexandria and Origen, Athanasius, edited by E. A. Livingstone, 137–41. StPatr 21. Louvain: Peeters, 1989.

———. "The Politics of the Silent Bishop: Silence and Persuasion in Ignatius of Antioch." *JTS* 55 (2004): 503–19.

———. "Purity and Danger in Polycarp's Epistle to the Philippians: The Sin of Valens in Social Perspective." *JECS* 1 (1993): 229–47.

———. *The Social Setting of the Ministry as Reflected in the Writings of Hermas, Clement and Ignatius.* Waterloo, ON: Wilfrid Laurier University Press, 1991.

Malherbe, Abraham J. "The Inhospitality of Diotrephes." In *God's Christ and His People: Studies in Honour of Nils Alstrup Dahl,* edited by Jacob Jervell and Wayne A. Meeks, 222–32. Oslo: Universitetsforlaget, 1978.

———. *Social Aspects of Early Christianity.* 2nd ed. Philadelphia: Fortress, 1983.

Mango, Elena. "Bankette im hellenistischen Gymnasion." In *Das hellenistische Gymnasion,* edited by Daniel Kah and Peter Scholz, 273–311. WGW 8. Berlin: Akademie-Verlag, 2004.

Marshall, I. Howard. *A Critical and Exegetical Commentary on the Pastoral Epistles.* ICC. Edinburgh: T&T Clark, 1999.

Martin, Dale B. *Slavery as Salvation: The Metaphor of Slavery in Pauline Christianity.* New Haven: Yale University Press, 1990.

Martin, Matthew J. "Interpreting the Theodotus Inscription: Some Reflections on a First-Century Jerusalem Synagogue Inscription and E. P. Sanders' 'Common Judaism.'" *ANES* 39 (2002): 160–81.

Mason, Steve. "Chief Priests, Sadducees, Pharisees, and Sanhedrin in Acts." In *The Book of Acts in Its Palestinian Setting,* edited by Richard J. Bauckham, 115–77. BAFS 4. Grand Rapids: Eerdmans, 1995.

McCready, Wayne O. "*Ekklēsia* and Voluntary Associations." In *Voluntary Associations in the Graeco-Roman World,* edited by John S. Kloppenborg and Stephen G. Wilson, 59–73. London: Routledge, 1996.

McGowan, Andrew B. *Ascetic Eucharists: Food and Drink in Early Christian Ritual Meals.* OECS. Oxford: Oxford University Press, 1999.

McLean, Bradley H. "The Agripinilla Inscription: Religious Associations and Early Church Formation." In *Origins and Method: Towards a New Understanding of Judaism and Christianity; Essays in Honour of John C. Hurd,* edited by Bradley H. McLean, 239–70. JSNTSup 86. Sheffield: JSOT Press, 1993.

Meeks, Wayne E. *The First Urban Christians: The Social World of the Apostle Paul.* New Haven: Yale University Press, 1983.

Meeks, Wayne E., and Robert L. Wilken. *Jews and Christians in Antioch in the First Four Centuries of the Common Era.* SBLSBS 13. Missoula, MT: Scholars Press, 1978.

Meier, John P. "Matthew and Ignatius: A Response to William R. Schoedel." In *Social History of the Matthean Community: Cross-Disciplinary Approaches,* edited by David L. Balch, 178–86. Minneapolis: Fortress, 1991.

———. "Presbyteros in the Pastoral Epistles." *CBQ* 33 (1973): 323–45.

Meinhold, Peter. *Studien zu Ignatius von Antiochien.* VIEGM 97. Wiesbaden: Steiner, 1979.

Merkel, Helmut. *Die Pastoralbriefe.* 13th ed. NTD 9/1. Göttingen: Vandenhoeck & Ruprecht, 1991.

Merkle, Benjamin L. *The Elder and Overseer: One Office in the Early Church.* SBL. Frankfurt: Peter Lang, 2003.

Merklein, Helmut. *Das kirchliche Amt nach dem Epheserbrief.* SANT 33. Munich: Kösel, 1973.

Metso, Sarianna. *The Textual Development of the Qumran Community Rule.* STDJ 21. Leiden: Brill, 1997.

Metzger, Bruce M. *A Textual Commentary on the Greek New Testament: A Companion Volume to the United Bible Societies' Greek New Testament.* London: United Bible Societies, 1971.

Metzger, Hubert. "Zur Stellung der liturgischen Beamten Ägyptens in frührömischer Zeit." *MH* 2 (1945): 54–62.

Milavec, Aaron. *The Didache: Faith, Hope, and Life of the Earliest Christian Communities, 50–70 C.E.* New York: Newman, 2003.

Milik, J. T. *Ten Years of Discovery in the Wilderness of Judaea.* Translated by J. Strugnell. London: SCM, 1959.

Miller, David W. "The Uniqueness of New Testament Eldership." *GTJ* 16 (1985): 315–327.

Miller, Merrill P. "Antioch, Paul, and Jerusalem: Diaspora Myths of Origins in the Homeland." In *Redescribing Christian Origins,* edited by Ron Cameron and Merrill P. Miller, 177–235. SBLSymS 28. Atlanta: Society of Biblical Literature, 2004.

Molland, Einar. "Irenaeus of Lugdunum and the Apostolic Succession." *JEH* 1 (1950): 12–28.

Moore, Gerard. *Eucharist and Justice.* Sydney: Australian Catholic Social Justice Council, 2000.

Mounce, William. *Pastoral Epistles.* WBC 46. Nashville: Nelson, 2000.

Moxnes, Halvor, "Patron-Client Relations and the New Community in Luke-Acts." In *The Social World of Luke-Acts: Models for Interpretation,* edited by Jerome H. Neyrey, 241–68. Peabody, MA: Hendrickson, 1991.

Mullen, Roderic L. *The Expansion of Christianity: A Gazetteer of Its First Three Centuries.* VCSup 69. Leiden: Brill, 2004.

Müller, Karl. "Kleine Beiträge zur alten Kirchengeschichte 6." *ZNW* 23 (1924): 226–31.

———. "Kleine Beiträge zur alten Kirchengeschichte 16." *ZNW* 28 (1929): 274–96.

Müller, Ulrich B. "Zwischen Johannes und Ignatius: Theologischer Widerstreit in den Gemeinden der Asia." *ZNW* 98 (2007): 49–67.

Munier, C. "Á propos d'Ignace d'Antioche: Observations sur la liste épiscopale d'Antioche." *RevScRel* 55 (1981): 126–31.

Murphy-O'Connor, Jerome. "The Cenacle: Topographical Setting for Acts 2:44–45." In *The Book of Acts in Its Palestinian Setting,* edited by Richard J. Bauckham, 303–21. BAFS 4. Grand Rapids: Eerdmans, 1995.

Nardoni, Enrique. "Charism in the Early Church since Rudolph Sohm: An Ecumenical Challenge." *TS* 53 (1992): 646–61.

Nau, F. *La Didascalie, c'est-à-dire l'enseignement catholique des douze Apôtres et des saints disciples de nôtre Sauveur.* Paris: Lethielleux, 1902.

Nauck, W. "Probleme des frühchristlichen Amtsverständnisses (I Ptr 5.35)." *ZNW* 48 (1957): 200–220.

Nautin, Pierre. *Lettres et écrivains chrétiens des iie et iiie siècles.* CPPC 2. Paris: Cerf, 1961.

———. "L'évolution des ministères au IIe et au IIIe siècle." *RDC* 23 (1973): 47–58.

Neander, August. *Geschichte der Pflanzung und Leitung der christlichen Kirche durch die Apostel.* 4th ed. Hamburg: Friedrich Berthes, 1847.

Nellessen, E. "Die Presbyter der Gemeinden in Lykaonien und Pisidien (Apg 14,23)." In *Les Actes des Apôtres: Traditions, rédaction, théologie,* edited by J. Kremer, 493–98. BETL 48. Gembloux: Ducolot, 1979.

Newman, John Henry. *Essay on the Development of Christian Doctrine.* London: Basil Montagu Pickering, 1878.

Neymeyr, Ulrich. *Die christlichen Lehrer im zweiten Jahrhundert: Ihre Lehrtätigkeit, ihr Selbstverständnis und ihre Geschichte.* VCSup 4. Leiden: Brill, 1989.

Niebergall, Alfred. "Zur Entstehungsgeschichte der christlichen Eheschliessung." In *Glaube, Geist, Geschichte: Festschrift für Ernst Benz zum 60. Geburtstag am 17. November 1967,* edited by Gerhard Müller and Winfried Zeller, 107–24. Leiden: Brill, 1967.

Niederwimmer, Kurt. *The Didache: A Commentary.* Translated by Linda M. Maloney. Edited by Harold W. Attridge. Minneapolis: Fortress, 1998.

Nijf, Onno M. van. *The Civic World of Professional Associations in the Roman East.* DMAHA 17. Amsterdam: J. C. Gieben, 1997.

Nilsson, Martin P. *Die hellenistische Schule.* Munich: Beck, 1955.

Nodet, Étienne, and Justin Taylor. *The Origins of Christianity: An Exploration.* Collegeville, MN: Liturgical Press, 1998.

Oakes, Peter. "Leadership and Suffering in the Letters of Paul and Polycarp to the Philippians." In *Trajectories through the New Testament and the Apostolic Fathers,* edited by A. F. Gregory and C. M. Tuckett, 353–73. NTAF. Oxford: Oxford University Press, 2005.

Osiek, Carolyn, and Margaret Y. MacDonald. *A Woman's Place: House Churches in*

Earliest Christianity. Minneapolis: Fortress, 2006.

Painter, John. "Who Was James? Footprints as a Means of Identification." In *The Brother of Jesus: James the Just and His Mission,* edited by Bruce Chilton and Jacob Neusner, 10–65. Louisville: Westminster John Knox, 2001.

Parisot, J. "Les chorévêques." *ROC* 6 (1901): 157–71, 419–43.

Paschke, Boris A. "The *cura morum* of the Roman Censors as Historical Background for the Bishop and Deacon Lists of the Pastoral Epistles." *ZNW* 98 (2007): 105–19.

Pearson, B. A. "Earliest Christianity in Egypt: Some Observations." In *The Roots of Egyptian Christianity,* edited by B. A. Pearson and J. E. Goehring, 132–56. Philadelphia: Fortress, 1986.

Pettersen, A. L. "The Rehabilitation of Bishop Onesimus." In *Papers Presented at the Eleventh International Conference on Patristic Studies Held in Oxford 1991: Liturgica, Second Century, Alexandria before Nicaea, Athanasius and the Arian Controversy,* edited by E. A. Livingstone, 156–66. StPatr 26. Louvain: Peeters, 1993.

———. "Sending Heretics to Coventry? Ignatius of Antioch on Reverencing Silent Bishops." *VC* 44 (1990): 335–50.

Pietersen, Lloyd K. *The Polemic of the Pastorals: A Sociological Examination of the Development of Pauline Christianity.* JSNTSup 264. London: T&T Clark, 2004.

Pilhofer, Peter. *Philippi.* Vol. 1, *Die erste christliche Gemeinde Europas.* WUNT 87. Tübingen: Mohr Siebeck, 1995.

Pixner, Bargil. *Wege des Messias und Stätten der Urkirche: Jesus und das Judenchristentum im Licht neuer archäologischer Erkenntnisse.* Edited by Rainer Riesner. SBAZ 2. Giessen: Brunnen, 1991.

Pizzolato, Luigi Franco. "Silenzio del vescovo e parola degli eretici in Ignazio d'Antiochia." *Aevum* 44 (1970): 205–18.

Poland, Franz. *Geschichte des griechischen Vereinswesens.* Leipzig: Teubner, 1909.

Powell, Douglas. "Ordo presbyterii." *JTS* 26 (1975): 290–328.

Prast, Franz. *Presbyter und Evangelium in nachapostolischer Zeit: Die Abschiedsrede des Paulus in Milet (Apg 20,17–38) im Rahmen der lukanischen Konzeption der Evangeliumsverkündigung.* FB 29. Stuttgart: Katholisches Bibelwerk, 1979.

Quass, Friedmann. *Die Honoratiorenschicht in den Städten des griechischen Ostens: Untersuchungen zur politischen und sozialen Entwicklung in hellenistischer und römischer Zeit.* Stuttgart: Franz Steiner, 1993.

Quinn, Jerome D. "The Last Volume of Luke: The Relation of Luke-Acts to the Pastoral Epistles." In *Perspectives on Luke-Acts,* edited by C. H. Talbert, 62–75. PRStSS 5. Edinburgh: T&T Clark, 1978.

———. *The Letter to Titus: A New Translation with Notes and Commentary and an Introduction to Titus, I and II Timothy, the Pastoral Epistles.* AB 35. New York: Doubleday, 1990.

Quispel, G. "African Christianity before Minucius Felix and Tertullian." In *Actus: Studies in Honour of H. L. W. Nelson,* edited by J. den Boeft and A. H. M. Kessels, 257–335. Utrecht: Instituut voor Klassieke Talen, 1982.

Rajak, Tessa, and David Noy. "*Archisynagogoi*: Office, Title and Social Status in the Greco-Jewish Synagogue." *JRS* 83 (1993): 76–93.

Rathke, Heinrich. *Ignatius von Antiochien und die Paulusbriefe.* TUGAL 99. Berlin: Akademie-Verlag, 1967.

Reinach, Théodore. "Inscriptions d'Iasos." *REG* 6 (1893): 153–203.

Reumann, John. "Church Office in Paul, Especially in Philippians." In *Origins and Method: Towards a New Understanding of Judaism and Christianity; Essays in Honour of John C. Hurd,* edited by Bradley H. McLean, 82–91. JSNTSup 86. Sheffield: JSOT, 1993.

———. "'Stewards of God': Pre-Christian Religious Application of *oikonomos* in Greek." *JBL* 77 (1958): 339–49.

Rhodes, P. J., and David M. Lewis. *The Decrees of the Greek States.* Oxford: Clarendon, 1997.

Richardson, Peter. "Building 'An Association (*synodos*) . . . and a Place of Their Own.'" In *Community Formation in the Early Church and in the Church Today,* edited by Richard N. Longenecker, 36–56. Peabody, MA: Hendrickson, 2002.

———. "Early Synagogues as Collegia in the Diaspora and Palestine." In *Voluntary Associations in the Graeco-Roman World*, edited by John S. Kloppenborg and Stephen G. Wilson, 90–109. London: Routledge, 1996.

Riesenfeld, H. "Reflections on the Style and Theology of Ignatius of Antioch." In *Papers Presented at the Third International Conference on Patristic Studies Held at Christ Church, Oxford 1959: Biblica, Patres Apostoloci, Historica*, edited by F. L. Cross, 312–22. StPatr 4/2. Berlin: Akademie-Verlag, 1961.

———. "Sabbat et jour du Seigneur." In *New Testament Essays: Studies in Memory of Thomas Walter Manson, 1893–1958*, edited by A. J. B. Higgins, 210–17. Manchester, UK: Manchester University Press, 1958.

Riesner, Rainer. *Essener und Urgemeinde in Jerusalem: Neue Funde und Quellen.* SBAZ 6. Giessen: Brunnen, 1998.

———. "Synagogues in Jerusalem." In *The Book of Acts in Its Palestinian Setting*, edited by Richard J. Bauckham, 179–211. BAFS 4. Grand Rapids: Eerdmans, 1995.

Ritschl, Albrecht. *Die Entstehung der altkatholischen Kirche: Eine kirchen- und dogmengeschichtliche Monographie.* 2nd ed. Bonn: Adolph Marcus, 1857.

Rius-Camps, J. *The Four Authentic Letters of Ignatius, the Martyr.* OCA 213. Rome: Pontificium Institutum Orientalium Studiorum, 1980.

Rivas Rebaque, Fernando. "Los obispos en Ignacio de Antioquía: Cuadros sociales dominantes de la memoria colectiva Cristiana." *EstEcl* 83 (2008): 23–49.

Rives, J. B. *Religion and Authority in Roman Carthage from Augustus to Constantine.* Oxford: Clarendon, 1995.

Roberts, C. H. "Elders: A Note." *JTS* 26 (1975): 403–5.

Roberts, C. H., T. C. Skeat, and A. D. Nock. "The Gild of Zeus Hypsistos." *HTR* 29 (1936): 39–88.

Robinson, Thomas A. *Ignatius of Antioch and the Parting of the Ways: Early Jewish-Christian Relations.* Peabody, MA: Hendrickson, 2009.

Rohde, Joachim. *Urchristliche und frühkatholische Ämter: Eine Untersuchung zur frühchristlichen Amtsentwicklung im Neuen Testament und bei den apostolischen Vätern.* ThA 33. Berlin: Evangelische Verlagsanstalt, 1976.

Roloff, Jürgen. *Der erste Brief an Timotheus.* EKKNT 15. Zürich: Benziger; Neukirchen-Vluyn: Neukirchener Verlag, 1988.

———. *Die Kirche im Neuen Testament.* GNT 10. Göttingen: Vandenhoeck & Ruprecht, 1993.

———. "Themen und Traditionen urchristlicher Amtsträgerparänese." In *Neues Testament und Ethik: Für Rudolf Schnackenberg*, edited by Helmut Merklein, 507–26. Freiburg: Herder, 1989.

Rordorf, Willy, and André Tuilier. *La doctrine des douze apôtres (Didachè).* SC 248. Paris: Cerf, 1998.

Rostovtzeff, M. *The Social and Economic History of the Hellenistic World.* Oxford: Clarendon, 1941.

Rothe, Richard. *Die Anfänge der christlichen Kirche und ihrer Verfassung: Ein geschichtlicher Versuch.* Wittenberg: Zimmermann, 1837.

Roxan, Margaret M., and Werner Eck. "A Diploma of Moesia Inferior: 125 Iun. 1." *ZPE* 116 (1997): 193–203.

Saddington, D. B. "St. Ignatius, Leopards and the Roman Army." *JTS* 38 (1987): 411–12.

Saldarini, Anthony J. *Matthew's Christian-Jewish Community.* CSHJ. Chicago: University of Chicago Press, 1994.

Saller, Richard P. *Personal Patronage under the Early Empire.* Cambridge: Cambridge University Press, 1982.

Salmasius (Claude de Saumaise). *Walonis Messalini de episcopis et presbyteris contra D. Petauium.* Leiden: Johannis Maire, 1641.

Sanders, E. P. "Jewish Associations with Gentiles and Galatians 2.11–14." In *The Conversation Continues: Studies in Paul and John in Honor of J. Louis Martyn*, edited by Robert T. Fortna and Beverly R. Gaventa, 170–88. Nashville: Abingdon, 1990.

———. *Judaism: Practice and Belief.* London: SCM, 1992.

Satake, Akira. *Die Gemeindeordnung in der Johannesapokalypse.* WMANT 21. Neukirchen-Vluyn: Neukirchener Verlag, 1966.

Schillebeeckx, Edward. *The Church with a Human Face: A New and Expanded Theology of Ministry.* Translated by John Bowden. London: SCM, 1985.

Schlatter, F. W. "The Restoration of Peace in Ignatius' Antioch." *JTS* 35 (1984): 465–69.

Schnackenberg, Rudolf. "Episkopos und Hirtenamt: Zu Apg 20,28." In *Schriften zum Neuen Testament: Exegese in Fortschritt und Wandel*, 247–66. Munich: Kösel, 1971.

Schneider, Theodor. "Das Amt in der frühen Kirche: Versuch einer Zusammenschau." In *Das kirchliche Amt in apostolischer Nachfolge.* Vol. 2, *Ursprünge und Wandlungen*, edited by Gunther Wenz, Wolfgang Beinert, and Dorothea Sattler, 11–38. DK 13. Freiburg: Herder, 2006.

———. "Ignatius and the Reception of Matthew in Antioch." In *Social History of the Matthean Community: Cross-Disciplinary Approaches*, edited by David L. Balch, 129–77. Minneapolis: Fortress, 1991.

———. *Ignatius of Antioch: A Commentary on the Letters of Ignatius of Antioch.* Edited by Helmut Koester. Hermeneia. Philadelphia: Fortress, 1985.

———. "Theological Norms and Social Perspectives in Ignatius of Antioch." In *Jewish and Christian Self-Definition.* Vol. 1, *The Shaping of Christianity in the Second and Third Centuries*, edited by E. P. Sanders, 30–56. Philadelphia: Fortress, 1980.

Schöllgen, Georg. *Die Anfänge der Professionalisierung des Klerus und das kirchliche Amt in der Syrischen Didaskalie.* JAC 26. Münster: Aschendorff, 1998.

———. "Die διπλῆ τιμή von I Tim 5,17." *ZNW* 80 (1989): 233–39.

———. "Hausgemeinden, οἶκος-Ekklesiologie und monarchischer Episkopat." *JAC* 31 (1988): 74–90.

———. "Monepiskopat und monarchischer Episkopat: Eine Bemerkung zur Terminologie." *ZNW* 77 (1986): 146–51.

Scholten, Clemens. "Die alexandrinische Katechetenschule." *JAC* 38 (1995): 16–37.

Scholz, Peter. "Elementarunterricht und intellektuelle Bildung im hellenistischen Gymnasion." In *Das hellenistische Gymnasion*, edited by Daniel Kah and Peter Scholz, 103–28. WGW 8. Berlin: Akademie-Verlag, 2004.

Schmithals, Walter. "Zu Ignatius von Antiochen." *ZAC* 13 (2009): 181–203.

Schröger, Friedrich. "Die Verfassung der Gemeinde des ersten Petrusbriefes." In *Kirche im Werden: Studien zum Thema Amt und Gemeinde im Neuen Testament*, edited by Josef Hainz, 239–52. Munich: Schöningh, 1976.

Schürmann, Heinz. "Das Testament des Paulus für die Kirche." In *Traditionsgeschichtliche Untersuchungen zu den synoptischen Evangelien: Beiträge*, 310–40. KBANT. Düsseldorf: Patmos, 1968.

Scott, Margaret. *The Eucharist and Social Justice.* New York: Paulist Press, 2009.

Seasoltz, R. Kevin. "Justice and the Eucharist." *Worship* 58 (1984): 507–25.

Selwyn, E. G. *The First Epistle of St. Peter: The Greek Text, with Introduction, Notes and Essays.* 2nd ed. London: Macmillan, 1947.

Shaw, Brent D. "The Elders of Christian Africa." In *Mélanges offerts en hommage au Révérend Père Étienne Gareau*, 207–26. Quebec: Éditions de l'Université d'Ottawa, 1982.

Sim, David C. *The Gospel of Matthew and Christian Judaism: The History and Social Setting of the Matthean Community.* SNTW. Edinburgh: T&T Clark, 1998.

Simonetti, Manlio. "Roma cristiana tra vescovi e presbiteri." *VetChr* 43 (2006): 5–17.

Skeel, Caroline A. J. *Travel in the First Century: With Special Reference to Asia Minor.* Cambridge: Cambridge University Press, 1901.

Slee, Michelle. *The Church in Antioch in the First Century CE: Communion and Conflict.* JSNTSup 244. London: Sheffield Academic Press, 2003.

Smalley, Stephen S. *1, 2, 3 John.* WBC 51. Waco: Word, 1984.

Smallwood, E. Mary. *The Jews under Roman Rule: From Pompey to Diocletian; A Study in Political Relations.* 2nd ed. SJLA 20. Leiden: Brill, 1981.

Smith, Dennis E. *From Symposium to Eucharist: The Banquet in the Early Christian World.* Minneapolis: Fortress, 2003.

Spicq, Ceslas. *Les Épitres de Saint Pierre.* SB. Paris: Lecoffre, 1966.

———. "La place ou le rôle des jeunes dans certaines communautés néotestamentaires." *RB* 76 (1969): 508–27.

———. *Saint Paul: Les Épitres pastorales.* EB. Paris: Gabalda, 1947.

Staats, Reinhart. "Die katholische Kirche des Ignatius von Antiochen und das Problem ihrer Normativität im zweiten Jahrhundert." *ZNW* 77 (1986): 126–45, 242–54.

Stadter, Philip A. "Leading the Party, Leading the City: The Symposiarch as *politikos*." In *Symposion and Philanthropia in Plutarch*, edited by José Ribeiro Ferreira et al., 123–30. HS 6. Coimbra: Centro de Estudios Clássicos e Humanísticos da Universidade de Coimbra, 2009.

Starobinski-Safran, Esther. "La communauté juive d'Alexandrie a l'époque de Philon." In *Alexandrina: Hellénisme, judaïsme et christianisme à Alexandrie; Mélanges offerts au P. Claude Mondésert*, 45–75. Patrimoines. Paris: Cerf, 1987.

Stauffer, Ethelbert. "Zum Kalifat des Jacobus." *ZRGG* 4 (1952): 193–214.

Stempel, Hermann-Ad. "Der Lehrer in der 'Lehre der zwölf Apostel.'" *VC* 34 (1980): 209–17.

Stewart(-Sykes), Alistair. "Ἀποκύησις λόγῳ ἀληθείας: Paraenesis and Baptism in Matthew, James, and the *Didache*." In *Matthew, James, and Didache: Three Related Documents in Their Jewish and Christian Settings*, edited by Huub van de Sandt and Jürgen K. Zangenburg, 341–59. SBLSymS 45. Atlanta: Society of Biblical Literature, 2008.

———. *The Apostolic Church Order: The Greek Text with Introduction, Translation and Annotation.* ECS 10. Sydney: St. Pauls, 2006.

———. "*Catecheses mystagogicae 5* and the *Birkath haMazon*: A Study in Development." *Aug* 45 (2005): 309–49.

———. "Deacons in the Syrian Church Order Tradition: A Search for Origins." In *Diakonia, diaconiae, diaconato: Semantica e storia nei Padri della Chiesa; XXXVIII Incontro di studiosi dell'antichità cristiana, Roma, 7–9 maggio 2009*, edited by V. Grossi et al., 111–20. SEA 117. Rome: Institutum patristicum Augustinianum, 2010.

———. "Didache 14: Eucharistic?" *Questions liturgiques*, 93 (2012), 3–16.

———. *The Didascalia Apostolorum: An English Version.* STT 1. Turnhout: Brepols, 2009.

———. "The Domestic Origin of the Liturgy of the Word." In *Papers Presented at the Fourteenth International Conference on Patristic Studies Held in Oxford 2003*, edited by F. Young, M. Edwards, and P. Parvis, 115–20. StPatr 40. Louvain: Peeters, 2006.

———. *From Prophecy to Preaching: A Search for the Origins of the Christian Homily.* VCSup 59. Leiden: Brill, 2001.

———. *Hippolytus: On the Apostolic Tradition.* Crestwood, NY: St. Vladimir's Seminary Press, 2001.

———. "The Integrity of the Hippolytean Ordination Rites." *Aug* 39 (1999): 97–127.

———. *The Life of Polycarp: An Anonymous Vita from Third-Century Smyrna.* ECS 4. Sydney: St. Pauls, 2002.

———. *On the Two Ways: Life or Death, Light or Darkness; Foundational Texts in the Tradition.* Crestwood, NY: St. Vladimir's Seminary Press, 2011.

———. "Ordination Rites and Patronage Systems in Third-Century Africa." *VC* 56 (2002): 115–30.

———. "Origen, Demetrius and the Alexandrian Presbyters." *SVTQ* 48 (2004): 415–29.

———. "Prophecy and Patronage: The Relationship between Charismatic Functionaries and Household Officers in Early Christianity." In *Trajectories through the New Testament and the Apostolic Fathers*, edited by A. F. Gregory and C. M. Tuckett, 165–89. NTAF. Oxford: Oxford University Press, 2005.

Stillingfleet, Edward. *Irenicum: A Weapon-Salve for the Churches Wounds.* London: Henry Mortlock, 1662.

Stoops, Robert F., Jr. "If I Suffer: Epistolary Authority in Ignatius of Antioch." *HTR* 80 (1987): 161–78.

———. "Patronage in the Acts of Peter." In *The Apocryphal Acts of Apostles*, edited by Dennis R. MacDonald, 91–100. Semeia 38. Decatur, GA: Scholars Press, 1986.

Stowers, Stanley K. "A Cult from Philadelphia: *Oikos* Religion or Cultic Association?" In *The Early Church in Its Context: Essays in Honor of Everett Ferguson*, edited by

Abraham J. Malherbe, Frederick W. Norris, and James W. Thompson, 287–301. NovT-Sup 90. Leiden: Brill, 1998.

Strack, Max L. "Die Müllerinnung in Alexandrien." *ZNW* 4 (1903): 213–34.

Strand, Kenneth A. "The Rise of the Monarchical Episcopate." *AUSS* 4 (1966): 65–88.

Streeter, B. H. *The Primitive Church: Studied with Special Reference to the Origins of the Christian Ministry.* New York: Macmillan, 1929.

Sumney, Jerry L. "Those Who 'Ignorantly Deny Him': The Opponents of Ignatius of Antioch." *JECS* 1 (1993): 345–65.

Syme, Ronald. "Journeys of Hadrian." *ZPE* 73 (1988): 159–70.

Tabbernee, William. "Perpetua, Montanism and Christian Ministry in Carthage c203 CE." *PRSt* 32 (2005): 421–41.

Taylor, Justin. "The Community of Goods among the First Christians and among the Essenes." In *Historical Perspectives: From the Hasmoneans to Bar Kokhba in Light of the Dead Sea Scrolls; Proceedings of the Fourth International Symposium of the Orion Center for the Study of the Dead Sea Scrolls and Associated Literature, 27–31 January, 1999,* edited by David Goodblatt, Avital Pinnick, and Daniel R. Schwartz, 147–61. STDJ 37. Leiden: Brill, 2001.

Telfer, W. "Episcopal Succession in Egypt." *JEH* 3 (1952): 1–13.

Theissen, Gerd. *The First Followers of Jesus: A Sociological Analysis of the Earliest Christianity.* Translated by John Bowden. London: SCM, 1978.

———. *The Social Setting of Pauline Christianity: Essays on Corinth.* Translated and edited by John H. Schütz. Philadelphia: Fortress, 1982.

Thiering, B. E. "*Mebaqqer* and *episkopos* in the Light of the Temple Scroll." *JBL* 100 (1981): 59–74.

Thompson, Michael B. "The Holy Internet: Communication between Churches in the First Christian Generation." In *The Gospels for All Christians: Rethinking the Gospel Audiences,* edited by Richard J. Bauckham, 49–70. Grand Rapids: Eerdmans, 1998.

Tiwald, Markus. "Die vielfältigen Entwicklungslinien kirchlichen Amtes im Corpus paulinum und ihre Relevanz für heutige Theologie." In *Neutestamentliche Ämtermodelle im Kontext,* edited by Thomas Schmeller, Martin Ebner, and Rudolf Hoppe, 101–28. QD 239. Freiburg: Herder, 2010.

Torjesen, Karen Jo. *When Women Were Priests: Women's Leadership in the Early Church and the Scandal of Their Subordination in the Rise of Christianity.* San Francisco: HarperSanFrancisco, 1995.

Towner, P. H. "Gnosis and Realized Eschatology in Ephesus (of the Pastoral Epistles) and the Corinthian Enthusiasm." *JSNT* 31 (1987): 95–124.

Tragan, Pius-Roman. "Les 'destinateurs' du discours de Milet: Une approche du cadre communautaire d'Ac 20,18–35." In *À cause de l'évangile: Études sur les Synoptiques et les Actes offertes au P. Jacques Dupont à l'occasion de son 70e anniversaire,* 779–98. LD 123. Paris: Cerf, 1985.

Trebilco, Paul. "Christian Communities in Western Asia Minor into the Early Second Century: Ignatius and Others as Witnesses against Bauer." *JETS* 49 (2006): 17–44.

———. *The Early Christians in Ephesus: From Paul to Ignatius.* Grand Rapids: Eerdmans, 2007.

Trevett, Christine. "The Other Letters to the Churches of Asia: Apocalypse and Ignatius of Antioch." *JSNT* 37 (1989): 117–35.

———. "Prophecy and Anti-Episcopal Activity: A Third Error Combatted by Ignatius?" *JEH* 34 (1983): 1–18.

———. *A Study of Ignatius of Antioch in Syria and Asia.* SBEC 29. Lewiston, NY: Edwin Mellen, 1992.

Trigg, Joseph W. *Origen: The Bible and Philosophy in the Third-Century Church.* 2nd ed. London: SCM, 1985.

Tropper, Amram. "Tractate *Avot* and Early Christian Succession Lists." In *The Ways That Never Parted: Jews and Christians in Late Antiquity and the Early Middle Ages,* edited by Adam H. Becker and Annette Yoshiko Reed, 159–88. TSAJ 95. Tübingen: Mohr Siebeck, 2003.

Turner, C. H. "Ancient and Modern Church Organization." In *Studies in Early Church History,* 31–70. Oxford: Clarendon, 1912.

Unnik, W. C. van. "The Authority of the Presbyters in Irenaeus' Works." In *God's Christ and His People: Studies in Honour of Nils Alstrup Dahl*, edited by Jacob Jervell and Wayne A. Meeks, 248–60. Oslo: Universitetsforlaget, 1978.

Verner, David C. *The Household of God: The Social World of the Pastoral Epistles*. SBLDS 71. Chico, CA: Scholars Press, 1981.

Vitringa, Campegius. *De synagogo vetere libri tres*. Frankeren: Johan Gyzelaar, 1696.

Vivian, Tim. *St. Peter of Alexandria: Bishop and Martyr*. SAC. Philadelphia: Fortress, 1988.

Vogt, Hermann J. "Frühkirche und Amt: Neu in der Diskussion." *ZAC* 8 (2003): 462–84.

——. "Ignatius von Antiochen über den Bischof und seine Gemeinde." *TQ* 158 (1978): 15–27.

Volp, Ulrich. "Liturgical Authority Reconsidered: Remarks on the Bishop's Role in Pre-Constantinian worship." In *Prayer and Spirituality in the Early Church*. Vol. 3, *Liturgy and Life*, edited by Bronwen Neil, Geoffrey D. Dunn, and Lawrence Cross, 189–209. Strathfield, New South Wales: St. Pauls, 2003.

Voorst, Robert E. van. *The Ascents of James: History and Theology of a Jewish-Christian Community*. SBLDS 112. Atlanta: Scholars Press, 1989.

Wagner, Jochen. *Die Anfänge des Amtes in der Kirche: Presbyter und Episkopen in der frühchristlichen Literatur*. TANZ 53. Tübingen: Francke, 2011.

Walker-Ramisch, Sandra. "Graeco-Roman Voluntary Associations and the Damascus Document: A Sociological Analysis." In *Voluntary Associations in the Graeco-Roman World*, edited by John S. Kloppenborg and Stephen G. Wilson, 128–45. London: Routledge, 1996.

Walter, Nikolaus. "Apostelgeschichte 6,1 und die Anfänge der Urgemeinde in Jerusalem." *NTS* 29 (1983): 370–93.

Waltzing, J. P. *Étude historique sur les corporations professionelles chez les Romains despuis les origines jusqu'à la chute de l'Empire d'Occident*. Vol. 4. Louvain: Peeters, 1900.

Weber, Max. *Economy and Society: An Outline of Interpretive Sociology*. Translated by Ephraim Fischoff et al. Edited by Guenther Roth and Claus Wittich. 2 vols. Berkeley: University of California Press, 1978.

Weinfeld, Moshe. *The Organizational Pattern and the Penal Code of the Qumran Sect: A Comparison with Guilds and Religious Associations of the Hellenistic-Roman Period*. NTOA 2. Göttingen: Vandenhoeck & Ruprecht, 1986.

Welles, C. Bradford. "New Texts from the Chancery of Philip V of Macedonia and the Problem of the 'Diagramma.'" *AJA* 42 (1938): 245–60.

Wescher, C. "Note sur une inscription de l'ile de Théra." *RAr* 13 (1866): 245–49.

White, L. Michael. "Regulating Fellowship in the Common Meal: Early Jewish and Christian Evidence." In *Meals in a Social Context: Aspects of the Communal Meal in the Hellenistic and Roman World*, edited by Inge Nielsen and Hanne Sigismund Nielsen, 177–205. ASMA 1. Aarhus: Aarhus University Press, 1998.

——. *The Social Origins of Christian Architecture*. Vol. 1, *Building God's House in the Roman World: Architectual Adaptation among Pagans, Jews, and Christians*. HTS 42. Reprint, Valley Forge, PA: Trinity Press International, 1996.

Williams, Margaret H. "The Structure of Roman Jewry Reconsidered: Were the Synagogues of Ancient Rome Entirely Homogeneous?" *ZPE* 104 (1994): 129–41.

Williams, Ritva H. *Stewards, Prophets, Keepers of the Word: Leadership in the Early Church*. Peabody, MA: Hendrickson, 2006.

Williams, Robert Lee. *Bishop Lists: Formation of Apostolic Succession of Bishops in Ecclesiastical Crises*. GDECS 3. Piscataway, NJ: Gorgias, 2005.

Wolter, Michael. *Die Pastoralbriefe als Paulustradition*. FRLANT 146. Göttingen: Vandenhoeck & Ruprecht, 1988.

Young, Frances M. "Ministerial Forms and Functions in the Church Communities of the Greek Fathers." In *Community Formation in the Early Church and in the Church Today*, edited by Richard N. Longenecker, 157–76. Peabody, MA: Hendrickson, 2002.

———. "On ΕΠΙΣΚΟΠΟΣ and ΠΡΕΣΒΥΤΕΡΟΣ." *JTS* 45 (1994): 142–48.

———. *The Theology of the Pastoral Letters.* NTT. Cambridge: Cambridge University Press, 1994.

Ysebaert, Joseph. *Die Amtsterminologie im neuen Testament und in der alten Kirche: Eine lexikographische Untersuchung.* Breda: Eureia, 1994.

Zahn, Theodor. *Introduction to the New Testament.* Translated by John Moore Trout et al. 3 vols. Edinburgh: T&T Clark, 1909.

Zetterholm, Magnus. *The Formation of Christianity in Antioch: A Social-Scientific Approach to the Separation between Judaism and Christianity.* London: Routledge, 2003.

Ziadé, Raphaëlle. *Les martyrs Maccabées: De l'histoire juive au culte chrétien; Les homélies de Grégoire de Nazianze et de Jean Chrysostome.* VCSup 80. Leiden: Brill, 2007.

Ancient Writings Index

Author Index

Subject Index